Praise for *The Political* _____ _____ ____
Second Edition

"Political economy readers tend to come in two flavors: excerpts of the classics or surveys of the present. The difficulty lies in combining the two, showing the reader how the reach of political economy has expanded over time. Barma and Vogel have managed just that and, in doing so, have set the benchmark for what students of political economy need to know."

Mark Blyth, *Brown University*

"From climate change to COVID-19, understanding the challenges policymakers confront in governing markets has never been more important. This valuable collection presents a wide variety of thoughtfully curated approaches to political economy, providing scholars and students alike with essential insights into persistent puzzles regarding how political institutions shape markets in ways that promote – or fail to promote – societies that thrive."

Greta R. Krippner, *University of Michigan*

"Barma and Vogel have produced an outstanding collection of core texts on political economy, including both classic texts and some of the most important recent contributions. This reader strikes a perfect balance between theory and applied topics and highlights the interdisciplinary nature of the field. The volume familiarizes the reader with the most influential theoretical approaches to political economy. It also includes important empirical studies that illustrate the relevance of the field to understanding a wide range of contemporary and historical developments. Thanks to the editors' carefully crafted introductions it is accessible to students encountering this material for the first time, but the volume is equally useful as a sophisticated guide to the field for advanced graduate students and anyone else who wants to learn more about political economy. This book is an indispensable and up-to-date guide to political economy, and it will be essential reading for students taking a wide range of classes in political science, sociology, economics, history, and management."

Magnus Feldmann, *University of Bristol*

"Vogel and Barma do a masterful job of selecting key yet divergent theoretical perspectives on political economy. The reader then turns to substantive contemporary debates, where these competing theories can be applied and evaluated against real-world examples. This text is an excellent choice for a graduate or advanced undergraduate course. The reading selections encourage a rigorous comparative analysis on some of the major political and economic challenges of our time."

Elizabeth Carter, *University of New Hampshire*

"*The Political Economy Reader* by Barma and Vogel brings together landmark texts and cutting-edge research on emerging questions in political economy. It allows readers to trace the major lineages of economic thought from Smith, Polanyi and Marx to contemporary theorists grappling with how to make sense of global financial crises, climate change and pandemic politics. The selections do justice to a broad range of perspectives and together with the authors' introductions to themes, they inspire debate about foundational assumptions of historical and contemporary political economy. The volume is an invaluable teaching tool."

Susanne Wengle, *University of Notre Dame*

Praise for the First Edition

"This is a superb collection of foundational works in political economy. Rather than obeying disciplinary boundaries, Barma and Vogel accomplish what we should all aspire to: bringing together key ideas and contributions from a range of scholars interested in important theoretical and substantive questions relevant to the field of political economy. I know of no other collection that spans the theoretical and empirical range of this volume."

David Leblang, *University of Colorado, Boulder*

"It's very difficult to select 'critical' readings in political economy because there is so much terrain to cover. But Barma and Vogel have made excellent selections that can be the foundation for a graduate-level course, or a scholarly immersion into foundational perspectives. I think their organization of the writing into alternative perspectives in tension with each other will make for great discussions."

Nicole Woolsey Biggart, *University of California, Davis*

"This is an outstanding anthology of classic and modern writings on political economy. Indeed, other than being asked to select the readings personally to suit your own exact tastes, it is hard to envision a better collection than *The Political Economy Reader*... Particularly given its inclusion of a number of classic theoretical readings, the book would sit well when paired with the more recent focus of many books used to teach globalization. The interdisciplinary nature of this volume with contributions from economics, history, political science, and sociology should also appeal to anyone teaching an Introduction to International Studies course. While everyone using this book might want to change an individual reading here or there, this reader is about as good as you could ever get for comprehensive coverage of political economy in one easy volume. It is likely to become highly popular and widely adopted over the coming years."

Scott Pegg, *Indiana University-Purdue University,*
in the **Journal of Political Science Education**

THE POLITICAL ECONOMY READER

The Political Economy Reader advocates a particular approach to the study of political economy – the "market-institutional" perspective – which emphasizes the ways in which markets are embedded in political and social institutions. This perspective offers a compelling alternative to the market-liberal view, which advocates freer markets and less government intervention in the economy, as if states and markets were naturally at odds with each other. The reader embraces a truly interdisciplinary approach to the study of political economy, with extensive coverage from sociology, economics, history, and political science. It includes some of the most important classical and contemporary theoretical perspectives on political economy. And it engages some of the most topical debates in political economy today, such as climate change, the global financial crisis, inequality, the digital platform economy, and the COVID-19 pandemic. For political economy courses at a variety of levels and from a range of disciplines, the reader is also of interest to scholars and citizens wanting perspective on the intersection of economics, politics, and society.

New to the Second Edition

- More than 20 new readings included by such notables as Elinor Ostrom, E. J. Hobsbawm, Dani Rodrik, Amartya Sen, Thomas Piketty, and Mariana Mazzucato among many others.
- Fully updated introductions to the book and each thematic chapter of readings.
- Coverage of key emerging debates including climate change, the financial crisis, inequality, the digital platform economy, and COVID-19.

Naazneen H. Barma is Director of the Doug and Mary Scrivner Institute of Public Policy, Scrivner Chair, and Associate Professor at the Josef Korbel School of International Studies at the University of Denver.

Steven K. Vogel is Chair of the Political Economy Program, the Il Han New Professor of Asian Studies, and a Professor of Political Science at the University of California, Berkeley.

THE POLITICAL ECONOMY READER

CONTENDING PERSPECTIVES AND CONTEMPORARY DEBATES

Second Edition

Edited by
Naazneen H. Barma and Steven K. Vogel

Routledge
Taylor & Francis Group

NEW YORK AND LONDON

Second edition published 2022
by Routledge
605 Third Avenue, New York, NY 10158

and by Routledge
2 Park Square, Milton Park, Abingdon, Oxon OX14 4RN

Routledge is an imprint of the Taylor & Francis Group, an informa business

First edition published by Routledge, 2008.

Library of Congress Cataloging-in-Publication Data
Names: Barma, Naazneen, editor. | Vogel, Steven Kent, editor.
Title: The political economy reader: contending perspectives and contemporary debates / edited by Naazneen H. Barma and Steven K. Vogel.
Description: Second Edition. | New York: Routledge, 2021. |
Includes bibliographical references and index. |
Identifiers: LCCN 2021001929 (print) | LCCN 2021001930 (ebook) |
ISBN 9780367497293 (hardback) | ISBN 9780367497248 (paperback) |
ISBN 9781003047162 (ebook)
Subjects: LCSH: International economic relations. | Capitalism.
Classification: LCC HF1359 .P6556 2021 (print) |
LCC HF1359 (ebook) | DDC 330–dc23
LC record available at https://lccn.loc.gov/2021001929
LC ebook record available at https://lccn.loc.gov/2021001930

ISBN: 978-0-367-49729-3 (hbk)
ISBN: 978-0-367-49724-8 (pbk)
ISBN: 978-1-003-04716-2 (ebk)

Typeset in Minion
by Newgen Publishing UK

Contents

Preface

This second edition of *The Political Economy Reader* offers an updated exploration of the interaction between politics and markets in both theory and practice. We feel that this reader fills a major gap among course readers and course texts on political economy. While there are some excellent course books on international political economy, there is much less available for comparative political economy. Moreover, most course readers in political economy are grounded in a single social science discipline, so they are unable to capture the interdisciplinary nature of the field. In this reader we have chosen to introduce work from four core disciplines: economics, sociology, political science, and history. We recognize that political economy is a broad field, and no single volume could possibly do justice to the full range of perspectives and topics. Some readers of this collection will inevitably be disappointed by particular choices we have made, but we have tried to assemble selections that will appeal to a wide range of readers.

In this volume, we present what we view as an emerging consensus across several disciplines – which we term the "market-institutional" perspective on political economy – and delineate the variations within this broad camp. We introduce core theoretical works in Part I, framing this section as a debate between the market-liberal paradigm and market-institutional perspectives from four disciplines. Then in Part II, we focus on market reforms in advanced industrial, post-communist, and developing countries, and present an updated set of readings on some of the most pressing issues of our day: climate change, the global financial crisis, inequality, the digital platform economy, and the COVID-19 pandemic. We frame these readings as a series of intellectual and real-world policy debates.

We are indebted to our students for trying out many of the selections in this reader, offering us their impressions, and teaching us about political economy while we tried to teach them. We have benefited enormously from input from the many graduate student instructors who have taught Political Science 138E over the years. Stephanie Ballenger, Noah Bender, Betsy Carter, Crystal Chang Cohen, Jordan Gans-Morse, Roselyn Hsueh, Khalid Kadir, Elsa Massoc, Lindsay Mayka, Brian Palmer-Rubin, Nathan Pippenger, Beth Rabinowitz, Tobias Schulze-Cleven, Rachel Sigman, Chloe Thurston, Chung-min Tsai, Eve Vogel, and Tuong Vu all advised us on the selection of readings. Anonymous reviewers provided critical feedback on our proposal and the choice of readings. We assume sole responsibility, of course, for the final selections.

We are especially grateful to Konrad Posch, who partnered with us on this second edition from the start, researching reading selections and brainstorming with us at length. He obtained copyright permissions and prepared the reading selections for submission to the publisher. Johnathan Guy also advised us extensively on reading selections, especially for the climate change section. Richard Ashcroft and Mark Vail offered valuable comments on some of the editors' introductions. Ting Yen Chen conducted research for the main introduction, and Jay Varellas offered useful suggestions for it. Several authors of the reading selections assisted in securing copyright permissions. Jennifer Knerr steered the project from review through publication; and Jacqueline Dorsey guided the transition into production.

Introduction

Steven K. Vogel

In this reader, we advocate a particular approach to studying political economy. We do not cover all of the schools of political economy, but rather we focus primarily on the "market-institutional" perspective that is increasingly prevalent across the social science disciplines. This perspective contends that markets should be viewed as institutions embedded in particular social and political contexts, and makes the study of these specific institutions its central mission. We contend that this perspective is not only essential to the study of real-world political economy, but that it has major ramifications for policy debates in advanced industrial countries, former planned economies, and developing countries today.

We contrast the market-institutional perspective to the market-liberal view, which spans from classical liberals such as Adam Smith and John Stuart Mill to "neoliberals" such as Friedrich Hayek and Milton Friedman. Market liberals tend to regard the market as an arena of voluntary exchange and government regulation as a constraint on that freedom. They view markets as naturally occurring rather than actively constructed, and market behavior as natural rather than learned.

The term "neoliberal" can be used to refer to everything from an ideology to a stage of capitalism to a basket of policies.[1] Some scholars identify neoliberalism as a particular strand of market-liberal thought that emerged in the 1930s and coalesced in the Mt. Pèlerin Society organized by Hayek and colleagues in 1947.[2] Public intellectuals such as Hayek and Friedman sought to revive a market-liberal tradition to counter socialism, both in the extreme form of Eastern European communism and in the more moderate form of the Western European welfare state. Like the classical liberals, they viewed the state as vulnerable to capture by interest groups and they sought to limit the role of the state and unleash the power of free markets. They advocated less government intervention and more market freedom – as if the two were necessarily associated. They moved beyond the classical liberals, however, in viewing the state as incapable of managing the economy, and in seeking to extend the reach of the market to as many domains of social life as possible. This form of neoliberalism motivated a broad array of market reforms around the world, beginning in the late 1970s. Margaret Thatcher and Ronald Reagan sought to privatize public corporations and government services, deregulate industry, curtail welfare spending, and cut taxes. Bolivia, Chile, and other Latin American countries experimented with radical economic reform programs, including currency stabilization, trade and capital liberalization, and privatization. Then in the late 1980s and early 1990s, Poland, Russia, and other Eastern

European countries launched "shock therapy" programs to transition from planned to market economies.

We contend that the market-institutional perspective provides a compelling alternative to market liberalism – and the neoliberalism inspired by Hayek and Friedman in particular – in both thought and practice.[3] Since market liberals view markets as naturally occurring and spontaneously evolving, they are ill-equipped to understand how governments, industry, and individuals create and sustain markets. Since they view free markets as a universal ideal, they are less inclined to appreciate the wide range of government regulations, business practices, and social norms that govern markets, and how this governance varies across time and space. And they tend to envision a single path toward market reform, one of removing obstacles to the free market. Yet many policy debates today are not really about choices of government versus market, but rather about how to move toward the market, how to govern markets, and whom to favor in the process.

To be fair, neoliberals acknowledge that markets require some basic rules of the game. Friedrich Hayek offers a sophisticated version of this argument in the excerpts in this volume, stressing that market competition requires a strong legal foundation plus some government regulations. Yet even Hayek has a relatively thin view of the range of market institutions required to make modern market systems work compared to the market institutionalists introduced in this reader.

With respect to policy, neoliberals favor limiting the role of the government in the economy and allowing market forces to operate as freely as possible. They situate the "free market" as an ideal, and support policies that move toward that ideal. They compare policy interventions to the free-market ideal rather than to real-world markets thoroughly sullied by fraud, collusion, and imbalances of power. They view economic inefficiency and stagnation as the product of excessive government intervention into free markets rather than insufficient government capacity to govern markets. This leads them to advocate policies designed to remove barriers from markets rather than to build market infrastructure.

The market-institutional perspective corrects for these pathologies, enabling a richer and more realistic understanding of markets. In this volume, our definition of market institutions includes both formal institutions, such as corporate laws, and informal institutions, such as customary business practices; and it spans from the global, such as the international monetary system, to the local, such as the village bazaar. The market-institutionalist view begets policy prescriptions that involve market governance more holistically: not less regulation but better governance. We present that case in this introduction and throughout the volume.

Theorists first used the term "political economy" in the eighteenth century to refer to the management of the economic affairs of the state. The classical political economists such as Smith and Mill challenged the earlier primacy of religion and tradition and embraced an empirical and pragmatic approach to studying political and social institutions.[4] For our purposes, we define political economy simply as the study of real-world market systems in their political and social context, including local, sectoral, national, and global markets. We dispense with the fiction of perfect markets, in which buyers and sellers are instantly and costlessly matched, and focus on the complex institutions that sustain, impede, and structure markets. In this spirit, this reader includes both classical works in political economy and contemporary research from several academic disciplines that address how markets are embedded in politics and society. We do not include, however, the branch in the contemporary study of political economy that uses the analytical tools of modern economics to study issues, such as politics or social behavior, that lie outside the main substantive concerns of economics.[5]

Some scholars have positioned an institutional perspective as a frontal attack on mainstream economics, arguing that most research in economics builds on unrealistic assumptions about perfect markets. We concur that these assumptions are unrealistic, but we stop short of arguing that it cannot be useful to make them. Economists often assume perfect markets for the purposes of devising a model or making an argument, and there is nothing inherently wrong with that. They have made some of their greatest theoretical breakthroughs and presented some of their most useful prescriptions by making precisely this sort of simplifying assumption. We also recognize that the field of economics has moved over the past few decades in many fruitful directions that transcend the neoclassical paradigm. The subfield of behavioral economics, for example, builds on insights from psychology to explore how individuals often act in ways that deviate from the rational maximization of utility.[6] Nonetheless, many economists are simply engaged in a different enterprise from the one we take up here: that of studying real-world market systems in their political and social contexts, and their variation across time, space, and fields (such as industrial sectors).

We can introduce the "market-institutional" perspective – and how it differs from classical liberal views, neoclassical economics, and contemporary neoliberalism – by way of Karl Polanyi's critique of the form of laissez-faire market liberalism that grew out of the work of Adam Smith and came to dominate economic thinking in the nineteenth and early twentieth centuries. Smith argues that people have a natural propensity to exchange. As people engage in voluntary exchange, this begets a powerful organizing principle: the market. The neoclassical economists who followed Smith interpreted this to mean that people individually make rational economic decisions based on their material self-interest, and the multitude of their expressed preferences is then communicated through the price mechanism.[7] In this view, the market provides a system of want satisfaction that is regulated neither by the family nor by the state, but rather by the famous "invisible hand." The market also provides a powerful incentive for innovation, because entrepreneurs seek to develop better ways of producing goods or services. Over time, the market becomes more efficient as the division of labor becomes more sophisticated and extends further across space.

In contrast, Polanyi stresses that people are not necessarily motivated by self-interest, and they do not have an inherent propensity to trade for profit. People are motivated more by social standing than material wealth, so they are only driven to maximize wealth within a social order that attaches status to wealth. In other words, Polanyi suggests that economic rationality is culturally conditioned, and market cultures may vary considerably across time and space. Polanyi makes this case by discussing primitive societies in which people do not maximize their own self-interest but engage in other types of economic relations, including what he calls "reciprocity" (mutual gift-giving), "redistribution" (pooling goods and then distributing them), and "householding" (production for the family).

Polanyi also offers a distinctive interpretation of the evolution from feudalism to market society in nineteenth-century Europe. He contends that the market system did not spontaneously arise. Instead, governments actively created national markets: they organized long-distance trade; broke down local barriers to trade; established the basic infrastructure of a market, including property rights, currency, and competition rules; and regulated the economy enough to buffer society from some of the worst ravages of an unbridled market. In Polanyi's famous phrase, "While *laissez-faire* economy was the product of deliberate state action, subsequent restrictions on *laissez-faire* started in a spontaneous way. *Laissez-faire* was planned; planning was not."[8] Polanyi stresses that markets undermine the traditional social fabric because they turn labor, land, and money – which are part of society itself – into commodities. Yet society inevitably fights back against the market via regulation. Polanyi refers to this interaction as a "double movement": the trading classes promote economic liberalism to foster a self-regulating market, but the working and landed classes push for social protection aimed at conserving man and nature.

In essence, the market-institutional perspective claims that markets are social and political constructions, which must be actively created and governed. The process of market development and market reform is therefore a positive endeavor of building market institutions rather than a negative endeavor of removing obstacles to market activity.

Market-Institutional Perspectives from Four Disciplines

An increasing number of scholars now stress the institutional side of market development, yet they vary considerably in how they approach the study of market institutions. Here we briefly review some of the reigning paradigms within economics, sociology, political science, and history that will be represented in this reader.[9]

The New Institutional Economics

The New Institutional Economics (NIE) is a relatively coherent school of thought in that practitioners share a common intellectual lineage, language, and core concepts, and identify themselves as working within a paradigm.[10] NIE scholars strive to be more theoretical in their approach than the "old" institutional economists, such as Thorstein Veblen and John Commons. They embrace the neoclassical assumption of utility maximization, yet they criticize standard economics for its failure to address economic institutions. As Douglass North puts it, the "neoclassical formulation appears to beg all the interesting questions. The world with which it is concerned is a frictionless one in which institutions do not exist and all change occurs through perfectly operating markets."[11]

The NIE theorists build on the study of transaction costs first introduced by Ronald Coase. They define transaction costs as the friction in the market system: anything that impedes the costless matching of buyers and sellers. They divide transaction costs into two basic categories: information costs, such as the cost of obtaining information about a firm or a product, and enforcement costs, such as the cost of monitoring and enforcing contracts. If information costs are high, then buyers may not find sellers, or workers may not find employers, or borrowers may not find lenders. Or consumers may not have enough information to decide about a purchase or an investment. If enforcement costs are high, then market actors may not have the confidence to make an exchange because they lack the backing of a legal system that enforces deals. A market system requires effective third-party enforcement to operate beyond the level of personal exchange. Institutional economists see systems of property rights as solutions to transaction cost problems.

Douglass North uses transaction cost economics to analyze the historical evolution of economic institutions. Throughout much of history, transaction costs were sufficiently high to prevent most transactions from taking place. As property rights developed, however, transaction costs declined and market systems became more efficient. North stresses that well-defined property rights spur innovation. In a simple economic system, entrepreneurs do not have an incentive to innovate because the private return to innovation (their own profit) is miniscule relative to the social return (the benefit to society as a whole). That is, the innovator cannot reap the rewards of their invention. A more developed system of property rights raises the private return to innovation, strengthening the incentive to innovate. North argues that people reform economic institutions due to exogenous shocks, such as technological change, that alter relative prices and thereby shift incentives. He takes a more "functionalist" line in his earlier work in that he implies that people develop better institutional solutions over time.[12] In later work, however, he depicts institutional change as a more open-ended process in which politics and ideology weigh heavily and changes may or may not constitute improvements.[13]

Coase first introduced transaction cost economics in an article in which he focused on one critical market institution: the firm. He asked: Why do we have firms? He argued that entrepreneurs create firms (corporate organizations) to reduce transaction costs. That is, they choose to perform certain services and to produce certain parts for themselves rather than to purchase them on the open market. They do so because transaction costs in the marketplace are sufficiently high that it is more efficient to keep these functions out of the market and to conduct them in-house. He used this logic to theorize about where the firm would end and where the market would begin: firms would expand to the point where returns disappear (that is, where the benefits of further expansion do not exceed the costs). Coase thus demonstrated how the concept of transaction costs could be applied to the study of market institutions.[14] Institutional economists have built on this logic to study a growing range of institutions, from types of corporate organization to forms of contracts. Oliver Williamson, for example, examines forms of contracts, corporate governance, franchise bidding, and antitrust enforcement.[15] Masahiko Aoki applies institutional economics to Japan, arguing that companies use institutions such as lifetime employment, the main bank system, and supplier networks to reduce transaction costs.[16]

The New Institutional Economics, and particularly the work of Williamson, has been influential in business schools, where it has been applied to a wide range of business strategy issues. It has also inspired some of the scholarship in the Law & Economics movement in law schools, which uses the tools of economic analysis to understand and evaluate legal regimes. The Law & Economics approach has dominated the study of political economy at many law schools but it has been challenged by neo-Marxists such as the "Class Crits" school (which focuses on economic justice), by economic sociologists in the "law and society" tradition, and most recently by a "law and political economy" (LPE) movement that argues that legal scholars should adopt a normative agenda that advocates for democracy and equality.[17]

Economic Sociology

Like institutional economics, economic sociology represents a relatively coherent school of thought.[18] Following Polanyi, economic sociologists believe that markets are governed by shared beliefs, customs, and norms. They particularly stress that markets are embedded in social relations, such as personal relationships between retailers and their customers or manufacturers and their suppliers. They tend to differentiate their perspective more sharply from standard economics than from institutional economics. They stress that their approach is more realistic, more historically informed, more oriented toward empirical research, and better equipped to analyze the diversity of markets across time, space, and sectors.[19] They eschew the methodological individualism of standard economics, identifying collective actors – such as groups or even social systems – as important units of analysis. Some sociologists, such as Powell and DiMaggio, reject the assumption of utility maximization, arguing that people are as likely to follow a logic of appropriateness in their actions as they are to adhere to a logic of utility.[20] Others, such as Mark Granovetter, prefer to expand the scope of rationality to incorporate social as well as economic goals.[21] For example, managers may not maximize a firm's profits because they are trying to enhance their status within a business network or to augment their power within a political coalition. As Victor Nee puts it, sociologists stress that rationality itself is bound by its context. What is rational in one society may be irrational in another.[22] In their empirical work, economic sociologists study everything from global agreements to local trade guilds. Many focus on the institutions of a particular industrial sector, such as the automobile market or the software market.[23]

Economic sociologists share more common ground with institutional economists than with mainstream economists, yet they maintain clear differences. We can bring these differences into relief by reference to two articles in which major figures within the two paradigms address each other directly: North's critique of Polanyi and Granovetter's critique of Williamson. North agrees with Polanyi that the nineteenth-century emergence of market systems was a unique event in history, and that mainstream economists fail to explain this shift. North even suggests that Polanyi's challenge could be taken further: How do we account for other substitutes for price-making markets, such as families, firms, guilds, manors, unions, or cooperatives? North points out that even today price-making markets do not dominate resource allocation, but share that role with households, voluntary organizations, and governments. He then critiques Polanyi, however, by suggesting that this has also been the case historically: markets existed earlier as well. He disagrees with Polanyi that early exchange and trade does not reflect economic motivation. He contends that transaction cost economics can account for the primitive transactional modes Polanyi describes. What Polanyi calls "reciprocity" and "redistribution," for example, are really just least-cost trading and allocation arrangements for an environment of high transaction costs (with no system of enforcing the terms of exchange). These institutions evolved as ways to reduce transaction costs. North concludes that institutional economics provides a better way to develop and test hypotheses, and to account for institutional change.[24]

Mark Granovetter develops his argument about the embeddedness of markets via a critique of Williamson. He argues that perfect competition would require atomized individuals, but in fact business relations are linked to personal relationships. Williamson sees order within firms (the hierarchy of the corporate structure) and disorder between firms (the anarchy of the market). Yet Granovetter contends that social relations generate some order even in markets, and this enhances trust and limits opportunism. The balance of order and disorder in markets depends not just on firms' decisions about what to produce within the firm and what to purchase on the market, but also on the specific nature of social relations in the sector or country in question. So a company will have less need for vertical integration (producing its own parts and subsystems) if it operates in a context of stable social relations in which it can rely on high levels of trust and good communications with its suppliers. Toyota needs less vertical integration than General Motors, for example, because it can rely on denser social relations throughout its supply chain. Granovetter concludes: "Williamson's perspective … may appear to have more kinship to a sociological perspective than the usual economic arguments. But the main thrust of the 'new institutional economists' is to deflect the analysis of institutions from sociological, historical, and legal argumentation and show instead that they arise as the efficient solution to economic problems. This mission and the pervasive functionalism it implies discourage the detailed analysis of social structure that I argue here is the key to understanding how existing institutions arrived at their present state."[25]

Research in economic sociology tends to provide a fuller and richer depiction of human motivation and interaction than the NIE school. Some NIE theorists adhere too rigidly to the assumption of human rationality, or adopt an overly functionalist view of institutional change by assuming that changes proceed toward more rational forms. The logic of the NIE proceeds backward in the sense that it moves from perfect markets to institutions. That is, NIE theorists ask: What is impeding perfect markets? They refer to the impediments as "transaction costs" and they see economic institutions as mechanisms to reduce these costs. Yet real-life history has proceeded in the opposite direction. Social institutions came first, and the market system evolved upon their foundation. There is something perverse about seeing the family as the response to a transaction-cost problem (or as a "substitute" for the market, in North's language). At the same time, however, we concur with North that the NIE approach tends to be more amenable to generating specific research questions and testable hypotheses.

Political Science

Political scientists have a strong research tradition in political economy, yet they do not have a core research paradigm as coherent as that of institutional economics or economic sociology. They are divided between those who use the analytical tools of economics to study politics and those who focus on substantive areas that bridge politics and economics. And even those in the latter camp adopt many different approaches, from the political analysis of economic policy to the integration of political and economic variables into causal models. In general, political scientists focus more on power relationships than economists or sociologists, and stress that markets are linked to political institutions.

Many political scientists have focused on the role of the state and its relationship to the economy. Chalmers Johnson, for example, argues that the Japanese state enjoyed relative autonomy from the demands of particular social groups plus a competent and powerful bureaucracy, and this enabled the government to formulate and implement pro-growth economic policies designed to shift the industrial structure toward higher-value-added sectors.[26] He extends this argument to other East Asian developmental states, such as South Korea and Taiwan, while also noting variations among them.[27] Likewise, experts on Latin America contend that "bureaucratic authoritarian" regimes were relatively insulated from short-term political pressures and thereby able to enact long-term economic growth strategies.[28]

Others have sought to flesh out the industry side of the government–industry relationship. Peter Katzenstein and his collaborators, for example, develop a typology that combines a spectrum from organized to less organized societies with one from strong to weak states.[29] Harold Wilensky and other scholars of "corporatism" (institutionalized linkages between state and industry) emphasize the role of intermediary associations, such as industry associations and labor unions.[30] John Zysman explicitly links the state, market institutions, and policy profiles. He focuses especially on financial systems, demonstrating a connection between strong states, credit-based financial systems, and industrial policies in France and Japan, on the one hand; and weak states, equity-based financial systems, and more market-based adjustment strategies in Britain and the United States, on the other.[31] Peter Hall incorporates an even wider range of firm-level features, including labor relations systems and product market structures.[32] Peter Evans links state strength not so much to autonomy from society but rather to the state's penetration of (or collaboration with) society.[33]

Peter Hall and David Soskice and their collaborators further integrate the study of political and market institutions in their work on "the varieties of capitalism." This literature builds on earlier traditions in comparative political economy, but gives greater attention to the level of the firm.[34] It adopts the basic logic of institutional economics, while also embracing a wider range of political and sociological factors. Hall and Soskice focus especially on the dichotomy between liberal market economies, such as the United States and Britain, and coordinated market economies, such as Germany and Japan, arguing that these constitute alternative models with distinctive logics and different comparative institutional advantages. They emphasize the complementarities between the various components of national models, and suggest that partial deviations from these two models are likely to be less stable and less successful than more internally consistent versions.[35] Critics of the Hall and Soskice approach suggest that their typology is less useful for hybrid cases such as France or Italy; that it goes too far in moving from a state-centric to an industry-centric perspective; that it overstates the complementarities among the components of the models; or that it focuses too much on national models at the expense of variations across industrial sectors and regions within countries.[36]

History

Like the political scientists, historians do not have a single paradigm that dominates the study of political economy within the discipline. As a rule, they are more interested in understanding the particularities of political–economic systems than in making generalizations across cases. They almost inevitably adopt a market-institutional perspective, as defined here, because they are interested in real-world markets and their evolution over time. They are less prone to identifying one or two core causal factors than in combining a multiplicity of factors – including politics, culture, and key events – into less parsimonious yet richer explanations.[37] Economic historians have especially stressed several core themes that have been overlooked by mainstream economics: entrepreneurship, innovation, personal leadership, and the evolution of market institutions. We cannot possibly do justice to the range of perspectives among economic historians here, but we can introduce several leading figures as illustrative examples.

Eric Hobsbawm combines a daunting array of factors into his influential account of the British Industrial Revolution. He acknowledges climate, geography, population, overseas discovery, and the Protestant Reformation as possible contributing factors. Yet he stresses the growth of domestic markets, enabled by improvements in transportation, and the availability of export markets, fueled by the expansion of the British Empire. The British government spurred industrial growth and technological innovation by building up its navy, and it decimated rival countries' industry and created a virtual monopoly on colonies. Like other economic historians, Hobsbawm challenges the classical economists by problematizing technological innovation. He contends that business people seek profits, not innovation, and in practice they often favor profits at the expense of innovation. They will only view industrial investment as profitable if the potential market is large and the risk is manageable. The growth in domestic and export markets in eighteenth-century England provided just these conditions, and this fostered the Industrial Revolution.[38]

Alexander Gerschenkron's argument about the timing of industrialization has been particularly influential in political economy research across disciplines. He contends that late-industrializing countries face fundamentally different challenges from Britain, the first country to industrialize. His approach contrasts, for example, to Walter Rostow's more evolutionary model of stages of growth. Although Rostow inserts some important qualifications, he still depicts a remarkably unilinear growth process: all countries progress through the same stages, albeit at different times and different speeds.[39] In contrast, Gerschenkron stresses that late-industrializing countries confront a huge technological gap, so they do not have the luxury of industrializing slowly. They must make massive investments to shift rapidly into heavy industry. This requires large-scale financing, an institutional mechanism for channeling the funds, and a powerful ideology to motivate the mobilization effort. Industrial banks provided the institutional mechanism in Germany, whereas the state played this role in Russia. Gerschenkron was particularly troubled by the political ramifications of late industrialization. It would require a more powerful state to mobilize resources to bridge the larger technological gap, and this might well take the form of an authoritarian state, as in the Russian case.[40]

Alfred Chandler also addresses the relationship between institutions and innovation, but focuses on firms rather than states or banks. Chandler addresses some of the same substantive questions addressed by Williamson – such as why firms vertically integrate – but he approaches them as a historian rather than as an economist. Where Williamson offers models, that is, Chandler provides detailed historical narrative. To Williamson's credit, he read Chandler's work carefully and he incorporated some of Chandler's insights into his models.[41] Like other theorists surveyed here, Chandler frames his work as a critique of Adam Smith and standard economic theory. He argues that beginning in the late nineteenth century in the United States, the "visible hand" of the modern business enterprise replaced the invisible hand of the market. The modern firm took over the market functions of coordinating the flow of goods and allocating resources to future production and distribution. It did so when the volume of economic activity reached a level that made administrative coordination more efficient than market coordination. And it did so by creating a managerial hierarchy that allowed it to internalize the activities of many business units within a single enterprise. In the process, the modern business enterprise became the dominant institution in the U.S. economy.[42]

Three Types of Market Reform

The market-institutional perspective not only represents an emerging consensus in some scholarly circles, but it also has major implications for policy debates. We can illustrate this via concrete examples of three types of market reform: (1) incremental reforms designed to enhance market competition in the advanced industrial countries, (2) the fundamental transition from a command economy to a market system in the former Communist states, and (3) the effort to create modern market institutions in developing countries (see Table 1.1 in the Vogel reading). The market-liberal and market-institutionalist perspectives offer different diagnoses of the challenges faced by each of these groups of countries, and different prescriptions for the policy solutions. Market liberals tend to view the problem as one of excessive government intervention in markets, and to recommend the removal of government constraints on markets as the solution. Market institutionalists are more likely to focus on market failures, and to advocate enhanced governance of markets.

In essence, we pose a very basic question: What does it take to make a market? And our first-cut answer is: It is not easy! If market activity were natural and separate from society and politics, then making a market should be straightforward. Market reform would simply mean removing constraints on market activity. If markets are complex institutions intertwined with politics and society, however, then market reform should be a painstaking process of building institutions. Moreover, we contend that the neoliberal worldview has fostered market reform failures in all of these world regions, with devastating real-world costs. The neoliberal market reforms in the three contexts we address are sometimes referred to as "deregulation," "privatization," and "liberalization," yet this language obscures more than it clarifies. In the latter half of this reader, we focus specifically on these different types of reforms, contrasting readings with a market-liberal view with those with a market-institutional perspective. We introduce applications of the market-liberal perspective to specific issues through the works of Deepak Lal, Anders Åslund, Arvind Panagariya, Peter Wallison, Gregory Mankiw, and Tyler Cowen. We turn to applications of the market-institutional perspective in the readings by Steven Vogel, Yuen Yuen Ang, and Naazneen Barma, among others.

Market Reform in the Advanced Industrial Countries

We can apply this logic to the advanced industrial countries by examining the "deregulation" movement. Many analysts view it as part of a global trend among industrial countries, beginning with the neoliberal reforms of the early 1980s under Margaret Thatcher in Britain and Ronald Reagan in the United States, that sought to reduce the role of the government and enhance the role of the market.[43] Policy debates about economic issues often pre-suppose a zero-sum relationship between governments and markets: that is, they assume that more government means less market and less government means more market. In fact, many commentators use the term "deregulation" in a way that reveals this assumption. They assume that deregulation refers to less government regulation and more market competition, as if the two were naturally associated. Yet government regulation and market competition are more complementary than contradictory. As stressed in the Vogel reading, the general trend has not been freer markets and fewer rules, but rather freer markets and *more* rules. And in fact there is a logical connection between the two. Freer markets require more rules of at least three varieties: a more sophisticated market infrastructure, including legal and financial systems; more regulation to sustain competition, such as antitrust policy; and more social regulation to buffer society from negative externalities, including health, safety, and environmental regulation. If the goal is to maximize competition, therefore, then policy should not simply reduce government regulation, nor simply increase it, but rather enhance regulation that creates, promotes, and sustains competition, and reduce regulation that impedes it. In sum, debates about market reform in these countries are less about liberating markets from the government than about retooling and recrafting market design.[44]

Market Transition in Eastern Europe and China

If regulatory reform in industrial countries is the most subtle of the three types of market reform, then the market transition of formerly planned economies is the most comprehensive. Market transition in these countries gives us the opportunity to view the process of creating market institutions in real time. We can see what types of institutions are necessary to create viable market systems, and how variations in reform policies shape market development. How does a country make the transition from plan to market? Is dismantling the old system enough? What new institutions are required? Given the scale of the transformation, the institution-building side of the process is less likely to be overlooked than it is with the more limited market reforms of the industrial countries. Even so, there is a lively debate in the field between those who stress the negative side of the reform process – dismantling the old institutions as quickly as possible and then allowing markets to flourish, and those who stress the positive side – the process of building new market institutions.

This debate is typically framed in terms of "shock therapy" versus "gradualism." We can grasp the logic of the positions with two common metaphors. In one view, market transition is like switching from driving on the right side of the road to driving on the left: you have to make the change as quickly and thoroughly as possible. You would not want to tell drivers that they have an interim period in which they can drive on whichever side they like. In the other view, market transition is more like building a bridge: you have to be sure that the new structure is sound before you demolish the old one, and you want to pay particular attention to sequencing the conversion.

The experts also differ on the proper political strategy for economic reform. Those who advocate shock therapy contend that the government must act quickly to seize the initial window of opportunity before opponents of reform have a chance to mobilize.[45] Those who favor a more gradual process suggest that leaders should orchestrate reforms carefully to contain political and social upheaval. The leaders who initiated the reform process in the Soviet Union and China, Mikhail Gorbachev and Deng Xiaoping, had very different philosophies about how political and economic reform interact. Gorbachev felt that he needed to promote political reform to facilitate economic reform because this would empower the advocates of reform and under-mine the opponents. Deng felt that he needed to maintain central authority and to limit democracy to implement economic reform.[46]

The actual debate among the experts is subtler than the stark juxtaposition of shock therapy versus gradualism implies. Those who advocate shock therapy tend to focus more on the mechanics of monetary stabilization, while those who favor gradualism stress the construction of market infrastructure. And most serious scholars concur that these countries need *both* short-term stabilization and longer-term institutional development. Jeffrey Sachs and Joseph Stiglitz, for example, offer sophisticated versions of the two positions. Neither can be neatly pigeonholed as a simple-minded shock therapist or gradualist, and yet there are clear differences in their diagnoses and their prescriptions. Sachs recognizes the need to cultivate market institutions yet he stresses the negative side of the process – the removal of government intervention – and he highlights the need for speed. He sees the market transition as a seamless web, a complex variety of measures that are more effective if they are implemented together.[47] Stiglitz stresses that the transition process takes time, and that the sequence of reforms is critical. The government should not privatize, for example, without first building a regulatory structure that promotes competition. Otherwise, privatization simply leads to asset stripping, whereby new owners sell off assets, rather than pre-serve the productive capacity of the company, and take their profits abroad – as many did in Russia.[48]

Both sides cite country case examples to bolster their argument, but the reality is sufficiently complex to leave plenty of room for rival interpretations. Some cite Poland as an example of successful shock therapy because the government acted swiftly, for example, while others categorize it as a case of gradualism because it built on a longer history of market institutions. Sachs emphasizes that the Soviet Union tried gradualism under Gorbachev and it failed, while Stiglitz stresses that Russia tried shock therapy under Boris Yeltsin and that did not work either. For Stiglitz, China's approach to reform offers a promising alternative to the Russian model. For Sachs, however, China is so fundamentally different from Russia that the lessons do not apply. China was primarily an agricultural economy at the onset of reform whereas Russia was already an industrial economy. This meant that China could achieve substantial growth simply by modernizing the agricultural sector. Russia, meanwhile, had to confront the much more daunting problem of industrial reform right from the beginning.

Given China's relatively successful experience with a gradualist approach to economic reform, there are fewer advocates of a shock therapy approach among those who study China. In an illuminating head-to-head debate, however, Wing Thye Woo argues that the benefits from reform come as government is supplanted by the market as a mechanism of allocating resources. Therefore Chinese slowness was not a virtue – it was just plain slow. Thomas Rawski counters that the Chinese have combined market reforms with institutional legacies from the pre-reform era in ways that have facilitated a successful transition. For example, the Chinese model has benefited from township and village enterprises, which compete in the marketplace yet build on the pre-reform institutions of common ownership and village community.[49]

Market Development in Developing Countries

The market-institutional perspective suggests that developing countries are not suffering from too much government interference in markets so much as from the government's failure to develop market institutions. Samuel Huntington argued that developing country governments do not have too much political authority, but too little. They are authoritarian, that is, precisely because they lack authority, both in terms of the legitimacy of the regime and the institutions of government.[50] We can make an analogous argument about the economy: in many countries the state is not too strong but too weak. The state lacks the capacity to develop the legal system, the financial system, and other core market infrastructure, and the ability to regulate market competition. It resorts to the direct provision of goods and services and other authoritative approaches to allocating resources precisely because it does not have the capacity to foster competition between private companies.[51] In other words, these countries suffer from underdeveloped political and market institutions, and this fosters authoritarian politics and statist economic policies.

Debates about the political economy of development are often framed as a competition between the "Washington consensus" and its opponents (see the Barma reading). Commentators coined the term "Washington consensus" to refer to what they viewed as the mainstream view at the World Bank and the International Monetary Fund, two international financial institutions based in Washington D.C.[52] These institutions often imposed conditions on loans or aid to developing countries such as balancing the government budget or liberalizing the economy. The critics of the Washington consensus stressed that rapid economic liberalization was not appropriate for these countries, and that developing countries should focus first on building up local agriculture and industry and cultivating market institutions.

As with shock therapy and gradualism, however, the actual contours of the debate are much subtler. In fact, the organizations at the heart of the consensus, such as the World Bank, have undergone a gradual evolution toward a more market-institutional perspective on market reform. In the 1980s, the Japanese government commissioned a study of the East Asian economic miracle. Japanese officials were unhappy that their own views on development were not better reflected in the Bank's policies, given that Japan was second only to the United States as a financial contributor. They felt that Bank policies should better reflect Japan's own development experience. After all, Japan was the first country to rise from developing country status to become an industrial power in the twentieth century. The Japanese advocated a stronger emphasis on building institutions – including a competent bureaucracy and a sound banking system – and less of an ideological commitment to free-market policies. The East Asian Miracle project generated an intense debate within the Bank yet resulted in a relatively bland compromise between the U.S.-trained economists and the Japanese sponsors.[53] The Bank did not abruptly change its position in response to this report, but it gradually adopted a more nuanced view of market development over time. The Bank's 1997 *World Development Report* focused on the role of the state in the economy, and its 2002 report turned to our core theme of building market institutions. The latter built on the literature in the New Institutional Economics in particular, proposing concrete measures to strengthen market institutions in developing countries.[54]

Hernando De Soto, the renowned Peruvian economist, popularized this line of argument with his thesis that the single biggest problem in developing countries is the lack of property rights. De Soto stresses property rights in the most literal sense: title to land. He contends that if poor people had title to their land, then they would have collateral with which to obtain a loan to start a venture. Without it, however, they are stuck in a poverty trap.[55] Many scholars in institutional economics and economic sociology agree on the importance of property rights, but favor a broader definition of property rights that encompasses the legal system and even social norms.[56] Some focus more on the political side, stressing that peace, national identity, state autonomy, regime legitimacy, and administrative capacity are all prerequisites to the development of market institutions.[57]

Contemporary Debates

If we take the market-institutional framework seriously, then we have to address how recent developments have reshaped market institutions and how emerging challenges will further transform them. Has globalization fundamentally altered national political–economic systems? Has the digital revolution generated new possibilities for more perfect markets? Addressing these challenges provides a useful way to rethink the approach to the study of political economy introduced here. Recent developments such as climate change, the global financial crisis, rising economic inequality, and the COVID-19 pandemic not only suggest new topics for study, but they present profound challenges to the reigning paradigms in political economy, both market-liberal and market-institutionalist.

Globalization

We are deluged with generalizations about "globalization," but too frequently these discussions lack precision about what globalization means, what is changing and what is not, and how that affects market systems. To move beyond this morass, we must unpack globalization into its component elements – such as finance, trade, and production – and specify the mechanisms of change. For example, finance has become more global as capital flows across borders have surged and financial markets have become more international. Trade has become more global as the flow of goods and services across national borders has increased. Production has become more global as companies, products, and production networks have become less tied to a single national origin. There is considerable debate over whether multinational companies are truly global, however, or whether they offer products or services that are really uniform throughout the world.[58] Likewise, regional production networks and international supply chains generally remain linked to specific national economies. The globalization of finance, trade, and production has strengthened pressure on governments to adjust their policies and to harmonize regulation across borders. Globalization also has a more political dimension, in which international institutions – from the World Trade Organization to private-sector accounting boards – develop and/or enforce common rules. The United States and other major powers use their political and economic leverage to impose their preferred rules on the international community. And globalization has a cultural element, including the diffusion of popular culture, ideas, and norms across national borders. This facet of globalization is neither altogether new nor all-powerful, but it does suggest that the study of discrete market cultures should be combined with an analysis of how market cultures diffuse across national borders, how they interact with each other, and how they blend in practice.

Some scholars have taken these various facets of globalization to suggest that we should reconsider our core unit of analysis, the nation-state. As noted above, important research in political economy shifts downward to the subnational level of localities, industrial sectors, and individual firms, but it must also shift upward to the regional and global level as well. Susan Strange contends that global markets have fundamentally shifted power away from the nation-state.[59] If markets are institutions, however, then governments themselves play a part in enhancing competition in international markets and governing these markets. To the extent that globalization is happening – one might quip, following Polanyi – then much of it has been planned. Scholars of comparative political economy tend to stress the continuing diversity of institutions despite the pressures of globalization. The countries of the world may face a common set of pressures that fall within the broad rubric of "globalization," but they retain considerable leeway to respond to these pressures in their own distinct ways. And precisely because of their differential institutional legacies, they vary considerably in how they respond.[60]

The Digital Revolution

We began this introduction with the assertion that the market-institutional perspective rejects the possibility of "free" markets. But does the digital revolution change that? Does it generate the possibility of near-perfect markets? Thomas Friedman contends that the Internet offers the closest thing to a perfectly competitive market in the world: there are no barriers to entry, no protection from failure for unprofitable firms, and everyone (consumers and producers) has easy access to information.[61] So doesn't electronic commerce dis-embed transactions from society? Our short answer is that the digital revolution reshapes market institutions but does not challenge the basic logic of the argument presented thus far. For one thing, digital markets are only practical for certain types of goods and certain types of transactions. They work best for standardized goods, with price as the dominant factor. The more multi-dimensional the qualities of the product, the less amenable it is to electronic trade. And many consumers and businesses still rely on face-to-face transactions. They con-duct business this way because they have to make many complicated judgments about product or service quality, or because they have to engage in complex negotiations with the other party.

More fundamentally, if we follow Polanyi's logic that all markets are embedded in society, then we must recognize that this is true for digital markets as well.[62] Market governance takes on new forms, but it is just as critical for the digital economy, per-haps even more so. The core commodity of the digital era – information – is itself the product of government regulation in the form of intellectual property rights. The gov-ernment can offer incentives for the production of intellectual property via patents, copyrights, and trademarks, yet it can also constrain information sharing and collab-orative modes of production via these same protections. The digital revolution also enables the fabrication of more elaborate markets, like electronic auctions or financial derivatives markets, which require even more complex market governance. In add-ition, digital platform firms like Amazon and Google now control core elements of the market infrastructure.[63] And they can influence market behavior via algorithms embedded in their platforms. That makes government antitrust policy all the more important to ensure that these platforms do not impede competition and stifle innov-ation. The digital platforms also pose a threat to privacy because they gather so much personal data, and use it to target advertisements, influence consumer behavior, and shut out competitors.[64] In sum, globalization and the digital revolution have dramatic-ally altered the nature of market institutions, but they have not rendered markets any less embedded in social and political institutions.

New Challenges

In the last section of this reader, we address the digital revolution in addition to four other major developments in contemporary political economy: the global financial crisis, climate change, economic inequality, and the COVID-19 pandemic. The global financial crisis provided a particularly powerful shock to the economics discipline because so few predicted it. Queen Elizabeth II famously asked: "Why did no one see it coming?"[65] The crisis defied prevalent economic models, such as the efficient markets thesis that the stock market accurately reflects the available information about corporations at any given time. It also challenged the neoliberal policy para-digm, which fostered many of the policy errors that led to the crisis: too much deregu-lation, too little supervision, and inattention to the subtleties of market design. In fact,

Alan Greenspan – the powerful Chairman of the Federal Reserve Bank and an avowed libertarian himself – famously conceded in testimony before Congress that his own ideology led him astray. Many observers expected that the crisis would prompt a paradigm shift in both analysis and policy. And, in fact, many scholars called for reforms in economics education, and governments enacted major stimulus packages and financial reforms. Yet neither the scholars nor the policy reformers fully dethroned the neoliberal paradigm.

Climate change poses an even more existential threat. To address it effectively, we will have to revise our conceptual models as well as policies and practices. For economists, it requires nothing less than a reconceptualization of the goals of economic policy: a shift from valorizing growth and efficiency to prioritizing resilience and sustainability. Perhaps economists should even reconsider the way they define welfare in terms of consumption. E. F. Schumacher argued that we should strive for maximum welfare with minimum consumption instead.[66] The climate change crisis also challenges reigning paradigms in political science, albeit in subtler ways. It poses a problem of extremely long duration, with a huge lag from policy decision to outcome, which cannot be captured by the standard interest-group models in the international political economy subfield. It requires capital investments on a scale that dwarfs most models of the politics of industrial policy. And it involves an existential risk – the survival of the species – that differs fundamentally from the more standard risks addressed in the literature on the welfare state. It also demands a paradigm shift in our conception of property rights, from open access to natural resources toward a commons model.[67]

In a very different way, the boom in economic inequality since 1980 has provoked a rethinking of some core axioms in political economy. Thomas Piketty's bestseller *Capital in the Twenty-First Century* recast the debate with a novel thesis backed by new data that argued that inequality has a strong propensity to increase over time as the returns from investment (r) tend to rise more quickly than overall growth (g). This means that those with capital grow richer more quickly than those without. That pattern was broken only during an extraordinary period from roughly 1910 to 1980 as two world wars destroyed wealth and high tax rates slowed the growth of inequality. The pattern then reasserted itself in the 1980s as the major industrial countries lowered tax rates under the neoliberal policy turn. The United States stands out in recent decades with an unprecedented leap in inequality in wage income, in addition to inequality in capital income.[68] As a result, the benefits of growth since the 1980s have overwhelmingly gone to the most wealthy, especially the top 1 percent of the income spectrum, while middle-class real incomes have stagnated. The market-institutional perspective provides some insights into the root causes of this surge in income inequality, demonstrating how elements of market governance – from labor market regulation to corporate governance and antitrust policy – have systematically favored the wealthy and powerful.[69] Meanwhile, economists have overturned the assumption of a tradeoff between growth and equity, identifying economic inequality as a major cause of secular stagnation during this century.[70] And some have argued that economic inequality has contributed to the rise of populism in the politics of advanced industrial countries, including right-wing movements opposed to globalization and immigration.[71]

The COVID-19 pandemic exposed the fallacies of the neoliberal paradigm in a particularly stark manner. It highlighted the fact that the government – and not the market – is the only viable solution to some of our greatest challenges. In a crisis, the government's administrative capacity becomes essential, and the pre-existing policy mix can sharply constrain the menu of feasible responses. The neoliberal policy legacy left the United States, Britain, and other liberal market economies particularly ill-prepared to contain the virus or to preserve employment. More state-led systems like China and South Korea and more corporatist systems like Germany and Denmark fared better. The private sector and market incentives could not manufacture, procure, or deliver the key supplies needed to combat the virus, including tests, ventilators, or personal protective equipment. Hospitals could not count on private distribution networks, and manufacturers could not rely on global supply chains. So the government had to take the lead. The pandemic – like other challenges, such as climate change – demands a rethinking of policy goals as well as means. Do we want to maximize the efficiency of our economy, or to build in some redundancy so that we are more resilient in times of crisis? Do we want to maximize the gains from trade and the efficiency of global supply chains, or preserve more domestic capacity to produce critical items? And what does it even mean to favor growth over resilience if outlier events like the global financial crisis or the Coronavirus pandemic destroy that growth? We believe that a market-institutional perspective not only offers a way to understand policy failures in these cases, but also provides an analytical approach that can help us to design better policies and stronger institutions for the future.[72]

Notes

1 Taylor Boas and Jordan Gans-Morse, "Neoliberalism: From New Liberal Philosophy to Anti-Liberal Slogan," *Studies in Comparative International Development* 44 (2009): 137–61; Daniel Rodgers, "The Uses and Abuses of 'Neoliberalism,'" *Dissent* (Winter 2018).

2 Scholars have subdivided neoliberalism into several schools: the Austrian School of Ludwig von Mises and Hayek; the Frieburg School of Walter Eucken, Franz Böhm, Wilhelm Röpke, Alexander Rüstow, and Ludwig Erhard; the Chicago School of Milton Friedman, Aaron Director, George Stigler, and Gary Becker; and the Virginia School of James Buchanan and Gordon Tullock: William Callison and Zachary Manfredi, eds., *Mutant Neoliberalism: Market Rule and Political Rupture* (New York: Fordham University Press, 2020), 6.

3 Some parts of this introduction build on Steven K. Vogel, *Marketcraft: How Governments Make Markets Work* (Oxford: Oxford University Press, 2018), especially chapter 5.

4 James A. Caporaso and David P. Levine, *Theories of Political Economy* (Cambridge: Cambridge University Press, 1992), 1–2, 33–46; Peter Gourevitch, "Political Economy," in Joel Krieger, ed., *The Oxford Companion to Politics of the World* (Oxford: Oxford University Press, 1993), 715–19.

5 This branch includes the social choice, public choice, and rational choice schools. For an overview, including definitions of the various schools, see Kristin Renwick Monroe, *The Economic Approach to Politics: A Critical Reassessment of the Theory of Rational Action* (New York: HarperCollins, 1991), especially 1–31. Elisabeth Gerber proposes that the subfield of political economy should be defined as "the study of political phenomena

using the tools of economic analysis" for the purposes of organizing the Political Economy Section of the American Political Science Association (APSA) in "What is Political Economy?" *The Political Economist* 11 (Fall 2003): 1, 3. We agree that this definition identifies an important subfield within American political science, but we do not concur that this subfield should usurp the term "political economy" from the likes of Andrew Shonfield or Peter Katzenstein, not to mention Adam Smith and Karl Marx.

6 Daniel Kahneman and Amos Tversky, "Prospect Theory: An Analysis of Decision Under Risk," *Econometrica* 47 (1979): 263–91; Richard H. Thaler and Sendhil Mullainathan, "Behavioral Economics," in David R. Henderson, ed., *Concise Encyclopedia of Economics*, 2nd edition (Indianapolis, IN: Library of Economics and Liberty, 2008); George A. Akerlof and Robert J. Shiller, *Phishing for Phools: The Economics of Manipulation and Deception* (Princeton, NJ: Princeton University Press, 2015).

7 Murray Milgate and Shannon C. Stimson, *After Adam Smith: A Century of Transformation in Politics and Political Economy* (Princeton, NJ: Princeton University Press, 2009).

8 Karl Polanyi, *The Great Transformation: The Political and Economic Origins of Our Time* (Boston, MA: Beacon Press, 1944), 141.

9 Our selection of academic disciplines that address political economy is by no means exhaustive. We have not included, for example, major works from geography, anthropology, business administration, or law.

10 See Douglass C. North, "The New Institutional Economics," *Journal of Institutional and Theoretical Economics* 142 (1986): 230–7; and Oliver Williamson, "The New Institutional Economics: Taking Stock, Looking Ahead," *Journal of Economic Literature* 38 (September 2000): 595–613. Anthologies of NIE scholarship include Oliver E. Williamson and Scott E. Master, *Transaction Cost Economics*, 2 volumes (Aldershot: Edward Elgar, 1995); Claude Ménard, ed., *The International Library of New Institutional Economics*, 7 volumes (Cheltenham: Edward Elgar, 2004); and Claude Ménard and Mary M. Shirley, eds., *Handbook of New Institutional Economics* (Dordrecht: Springer, 2005).

11 Douglass C. North, *Structure and Change in Economic History* (New York: W. W. Norton, 1981), 5.

12 North, *Structure and Change*.

13 Douglass C. North, *Institutions, Institutional Change and Economic Performance* (Cambridge: Cambridge University Press, 1990).

14 Ronald Coase, "The Nature of the Firm," *Economica* 4 (1937): 386–405.

15 Oliver Williamson, *The Economic Institutions of Capitalism* (New York: Free Press, 1985).

16 Masahiko Aoki, *Information, Incentives, and Bargaining in the Japanese Economy* (Cambridge: Cambridge University Press, 1988); and *Toward a Comparative Institutional Analysis* (Cambridge, MA: MIT Press, 2001).

17 Jedediah Britton-Purdy, David Singh Grewal, Amy Kapczynski, and K. Sabeel Rahman, "Building a Law-and-Political-Economy Framework: Beyond the Twentieth-Century Synthesis," Columbia Public Law Research Paper No. 14-657 (2020); Angela Harris and James J. Varellas, "Law and Political Economy in a Time of Accelerating Crises," *Journal of Law and Political Economy* 1 (2020): 1–27.

18 Anthologies presenting work in this subfield include Nicole W. Biggart, ed., *Readings in Economic Sociology* (Oxford: Blackwell, 2002); Frank Dobbin, ed., *The New Economic Sociology: A Reader* (Princeton, NJ: Princeton University Press, 2004); Neil J. Smelser and Richard Swedberg, eds., *The Handbook of Economic Sociology*, 2nd edition (Princeton, NJ: Princeton University Press, 2005): Victor Nee and Richard Swedberg, eds., *The Economic Sociology of Capitalism* (Princeton, NJ: Princeton University Press, 2005).

19 Biggart, ed., *Readings in Economic Sociology*.

20 Walter W. Powell and Paul J. DiMaggio, eds., *The New Institutionalism in Organizational Analysis* (Chicago, IL: The University of Chicago Press, 1991), 1–38.

21 Mark Granovetter, "Economic Action and Social Structure: The Problem of Embeddedness," *American Journal of Sociology* 91 (1985): 481–510.

22 Victor Nee, "The New Institutionalisms in Economics and Sociology," in Smelser and Swedberg, eds., *The Handbook of Economic Sociology*, 49–74.

23 Neil Fligstein, *The Architecture of Markets: An Economic Sociology of Twenty-First Century Capitalist Societies* (Princeton, NJ: Princeton University Press, 2001). John L. Campbell, J. Rogers Hollingsworth, and Leon N. Lindberg illustrate the broad range of market institutions with their typology of "governance mechanisms": Campbell, Hollingsworth, and Lindberg, eds., *Governance of the American Economy* (Cambridge: Cambridge University Press, 1991), 14.

24 Douglass North, "Market and Other Allocation Systems in History: The Challenge of Karl Polanyi," *Journal of European Economic History* (Winter 1977): 703–16.

25 Granovetter, "Economic Action and Social Structure," 505. Williamson counters that the embeddedness argument "is consistent with, and much of it has been anticipated by, transaction cost reasoning": *The Mechanisms of Governance* (Oxford: Oxford University Press, 1996), 230.

26 Chalmers Johnson, *MITI and the Japanese Miracle: The Growth of Industrial Policy, 1925–1975* (Stanford, CA: Stanford University Press, 1982).

27 Chalmers Johnson, "Political Institutions and Economic Performance: The Government–Business Relationship in Japan, South Korea, and Taiwan," in Frederic Deyo, ed., *The Political Economy of the New Asian Industrialism* (Ithaca, NY: Cornell University Press, 1987), 136–64.

28 Guillermo A. O'Donnell, *Modernization and Bureaucratic Authoritarianism* (Berkeley, CA: Institute of International Studies, University of California, 1973); David Collier, ed., *The New Authoritarianism in Latin America* (Princeton, NJ: Princeton University Press, 1979).

29 Peter Katzenstein, ed., *Between Power and Plenty: Foreign Economic Policies of Advanced Industrial States* (Madison, WI: University of Wisconsin Press, 1978), especially 323–4.

30 Harold Wilensky, *Rich Democracies: Political Economy, Public Policy, and Performance* (Berkeley and Los Angeles, CA: University of California Press, 2002).

31 John Zysman, *Governments, Markets and Growth: Financial Systems and the Politics of Industrial Change* (Ithaca, NY: Cornell University Press, 1983).

32 Peter Hall, *Governing the Economy: The Politics of State Intervention in Britain and France* (New York: Oxford University Press, 1986).

33 Peter Evans, *Embedded Autonomy: States and Industrial Transformation* (Princeton, NJ: Princeton University Press, 1995). Also see Atul Kohli, *State-Directed Development: Political Power and Industrialization in the Global Periphery* (Cambridge: Cambridge University Press, 2004).

34 A substantial body of work on the varieties of capitalism pre-dates the Hall and Soskice volume. For example: Andrew Shonfield, *Modern Capitalism: The Changing Balance of Public and Private Power* (New York: Oxford University Press, 1965); J. Rogers Hollingsworth, Philippe C. Schmitter, and Wolfgang Streeck, eds., *Governing Capitalist Economies: Performance and Control of Economic Sectors* (New York: Oxford University Press, 1994); Colin Crouch and Wolfgang Streeck, eds., *Political Economy of Modern Capitalism* (London: Sage, 1997).

35 Peter Hall and David Soskice, "An Introduction to the Varieties of Capitalism," in Hall and Soskice, eds., *Varieties of Capitalism: The Institutional Foundations of Comparative Advantage* (New York: Oxford University Press, 2001).

36 Jonah Levy, ed., *The State After Statism: New State Activities in the Age of Liberalization* (Cambridge, MA: Harvard University Press, 2006); Steven K. Vogel, *Japan Remodeled: How Government and Industry Are Transforming Japanese Capitalism* (Ithaca, NY: Cornell University Press, 2006), 12–13.

37 David S. Landes, "Introduction: On Technology and Growth," in Patrice Higonnet, David S. Landes, and Henry Rosovsky, eds., *Favorites of Fortune: Technology, Growth, and Economic Development Since the Industrial Revolution* (Cambridge, MA: Harvard University Press, 1991), especially 5.

38 Eric J. Hobsbawm, *Industry and Empire: An Economic History of Britain Since 1750* (London: Weidenfeld and Nicolson, 1968), 1–39.

39 W. W. Rostow, *The Stages of Economic Growth: A Non-Communist Manifesto* (Cambridge: Cambridge University Press, 1960).

40 Alexander Gerschenkron, "Economic Backwardness in Historical Perspective," in Bert Frank Hoselitz, ed., *The Progress of Underdeveloped Areas* (Chicago, IL: University of Chicago Press, 1952), 5–30.

41 William Lazonick argues that Williamson's transaction cost approach, unlike Chandler's historical approach, cannot explain key features of U.S. business history: *Business Organization and the Myth of the Market Economy* (Cambridge: Cambridge University Press, 1991), 228–61.

42 Alfred Chandler, *The Visible Hand: The Managerial Revolution in American Business* (Cambridge, MA: Belknap Press, 1977), 1–8.

43 Daniel Yergin and Joseph Stanislaw, *The Commanding Heights: The Battle Between Government and the Marketplace that is Remaking the Modern World* (New York: Simon & Schuster, 1998), especially 9–17, 92–124, 325–63.

44 See Marc K. Landy, Martin A. Levin, and Martin Shapiro, eds., *Creating Competitive Markets: The Politics of Regulatory Reform* (Washington, DC: Brookings Institution Press, 2006).

45 Jeffrey Sachs, "Poland and Eastern Europe: What is to be Done?" in Andras Koves and Paul Marer, eds., *Foreign Economic Liberalization: Transformations in Socialist and Market Economies* (Boulder, CO: Westview, 1991), 235–46.

46 See William Overholt, *The Rise of China: How Economic Reform is Creating a New Superpower* (New York: W. W. Norton, 1993), especially 118–31.

47 Jeffrey D. Sachs, *The End of Poverty: Economic Possibilities for Our Time* (New York: The Penguin Press, 2005), 114–30, 134–6, 145–7.

48 Joseph E. Stiglitz, *Globalization and Its Discontents* (New York: W. W. Norton & Company, 2002), 133–65.

49 Wing Thye Woo, "The Real Reasons for China's Growth," and Thomas Rawski, "Reforming China's Economy: What Have We Learned?," *The China Journal* 41 (January 1999): 115–56. Also see the exchange between Woo and Yu-Shan Wu: Yu-Shan Wu, "Chinese Economic Reform in a Comparative Perspective: Asia vs. Europe," *Issues and Studies* 38 (December 2002/March 2003): 93–138; Wing Thye Woo, "A United Front for the Common Objective to Understand China's Economic Growth: A Case of Nonantagonistic Contradiction, Wu vs. Woo," and Yu Shan-Wu, "Institutions and Policies Must Bear the Responsibility: Another Case of Nonantagonistic Contradiction," *Issues and Studies* 39 (June 2003): 1–40.

50 Samuel Huntington, *Political Order in Changing Societies* (New Haven, CT: Yale University Press, 1968), 1–2.

51 Kiren Chaudhry, "The Myths of the Market and the Common History of Late Developers," *Politics and Society* 21 (1993): 243–74.

52 John Williamson, ed., *Latin American Adjustment: How Much Has Happened?* (Washington, DC: Institute for International Economics, 1990).

53 World Bank, *The East Asian Miracle: Economic Growth and Public Policy* (Oxford: Oxford University Press, 1993); Robert Wade, "Japan, the World Bank, and the Art of Paradigm Maintenance: *The East Asian Miracle* in Political Perspective," *New Left Review* 217 (May–June 1996): 3–36.

54 World Bank, *World Development Report 1997: The State in a Changing World* (Oxford: Oxford University Press, 1997), and *World Development Report 2002: Building Institutions for Markets* (Oxford: Oxford University Press, 2002).

55 Hernando De Soto, *The Mystery of Capital: Why Capitalism Triumphs in the West and Fails Everywhere Else* (New York: Basic Books, 2003).

56 The *World Development Report 2002* (p. 12) stresses that formal title to land is not sufficient. Frank Upham charges that the property rights literature does not give sufficient attention to informal institutions, including broader social norms: "Mythmaking in the Rule of Law Orthodoxy," Carnegie Endowment for International Peace Working Paper (2002).

57 Peter Evans, *Embedded Autonomy: States and Industrial Transformation* (Princeton, NJ: Princeton University Press, 1995); Kohli, *State-Directed Development*.

58 Paul N. Doremus, William W. Keller, Louis W. Pauly, and Simon Reich, *The Myth of the Global Corporation* (Princeton, NJ: Princeton University Press, 1998).

59 Susan Strange, *The Retreat of the State: The Diffusion of Power in the World Economy* (Cambridge: Cambridge University Press, 1996).

60 Suzanne Berger and Ronald Dore, eds., *National Diversity and Global Capitalism* (Ithaca, NY: Cornell University Press, 1996); Steven K. Vogel, *Freer Markets, More Rules: Regulatory Reform in Advanced Industrial Countries* (Ithaca, NY: Cornell University Press, 1996); Herbert Kitschelt et al., eds., *Continuity and Change in Contemporary Capitalism* (Cambridge: Cambridge University Press, 1999); Hall and Soskice, eds., *Varieties of Capitalism*; Harold Wilensky, *American Political Economy in Global Perspective* (New York: Cambridge University Press, 2012).

61 Thomas Friedman, *The Lexus and the Olive Tree: Understanding Globalization* (New York: Anchor Books, 1999), 81.

62 John Zysman and Abraham Newman, eds., *How Revolutionary Was the Revolution? National Responses, Market Transitions, and Global Technology* (Stanford, CA: Stanford University Press, 2006).

63 Martin Kenney and John Zysman, "The Rise of the Platform Economy," *Issues in Science and Technology* 32 (March 2016): 61–9; Lina M. Khan, "Amazon's Antitrust Paradox," *Yale Law Journal* 126 (2017): 710–805; K. Sabeel Rahman and Kathleen Thelen, "The Rise of the Platform Business Model and the Transformation of Twenty-First Century Capitalism," *Politics & Society* 47 (2019): 177–204.

64 Shoshana Zuboff, *The Age of Surveillance Capitalism: The Fight for a Human Future at the New Frontier of Power* (New York: PublicAffairs, 2019).

65 Chris Giles, "The Economic Forecasters' Failing Vision," *Financial Times* (November 25, 2008).

66 E. F. Schumacher, *Small is Beautiful: Economics as if People Mattered* (New York: Harper & Row, 1973).

67 This paragraph builds on presentations by Eric Biber, Clair Brown, and Jonas Meckling at a panel discussion on Climate Change and Political Economy, University of California, Berkeley, February 6, 2020.

68 Thomas Piketty, *Capital in the Twenty-First Century* (Cambridge, MA: Belknap Press, 2017).

69 Herman Mark Schwartz, "Wealth and Secular Stagnaton: The Role of Industrial Organization and Intellectual Property Rights," *RSF: The Russell Sage Foundation Journal of the Social Sciences* (2016): 226–49; Heather Boushey, *Unbound: How Inequality Constricts Our Economy and What We Can Do About It* (Cambridge, MA: Harvard University Press, 2019); Thomas Philippon, *The Great Reversal: How America Gave Up On Free Markets* (Cambridge, MA: Belknap Press, 2019); Steven K. Vogel, "The Regulatory Roots of Inequality in America," *Journal of Law and Political Economy* 1 (2021).

70 Boushey, *Unbound*.

71 Dani Rodrik, "Populism and the Economics of Globalization," *Journal of International Business Policy* 1 (2018): 12–33.

72 Vogel, *Marketcraft*, 138–50.

Part I

Contending Perspectives

1

The Classics

Political economy is a relatively new discipline and its classic works are clearly identifiable. Distinct approaches to the study of political economy and views on the nature of markets emerged at the outset. The three classical theorists considered here, for example, differ on the relationship between politics and economics in the functioning of the market and the capitalist system, as well as on the role of the state in relation to the economy. The three perspectives are representatives of the capitalist, communist, and mercantilist approaches to political economy. Together they cover the theoretical poles of debates on political economy and provide much insight into the political–economic traditions of the modern world.

Adam Smith is considered by many to be the father of modern political economy. One of a group of scholars known as the Scottish moral philosophers, Smith explicitly examined the linkages between politics and economics. Grounded in an inductive, observational approach to understanding how economic activity was conducted, he was one of the first theorists of the capitalist system, breaking down how its component parts – such as the production process, the market system of exchange, and the international trade system – actually function. Smith is still remembered today for these insights into the working of markets. His analysis left enduring legacies for the subsequent discipline of economics and also lives on in prevailing worldviews about the nature of economic freedom.

Smith's *Inquiry into the Nature and Causes of the Wealth of Nations*, published in 1776, was one of the earliest attempts to study industry and commerce in Britain, where the Industrial Revolution began. The selection presented here includes insights that have had a lasting effect on the way we think about markets. The concept most commonly associated with Adam Smith is the "invisible hand" through which an unorganized and potentially chaotic market system creates the amount and variety of goods desired by society in the most efficient way possible. Economic liberals today continue to believe that markets are self-regulating and that failures are introduced externally rather than being inherent in markets. Equally influential is Smith's definition of the "division of labor," elaborated through his pin factory example. He details how the specialization that emerges through the division of labor increases the productivity of labor and how, in turn, society functions organically as a well-oiled machine, with pieces fitting together seamlessly to provide humans with all their needs.

In Smith's analysis, this well-functioning system of production and trade is not constructed artificially. It is the "consequence of a certain propensity in human nature … the propensity to truck, barter, and exchange." That propensity, in turn, is encouraged by self-interest, which Smith views as a natural phenomenon that consistently motivates human behavior and interaction. He argues that a system in which self-interest is allowed to function achieves the highest collective good.[1] A free market, animated by the pursuit of self-interest, through the unintended consequences of the invisible hand, begets a system of economic relations and social organization that surpasses any based on altruism in the production of both economic output and social harmony. This philosophy has had a lasting impact right up to the present day: market liberals, such as Friedrich Hayek and Milton Friedman, go even further than Smith in arguing that behavior driven by self-interest is a natural human trait and that the most effective and efficient way to maximize collective social welfare and the public interest is to allow individuals to act in their own self-interest.

Smith also mounts a defense of the functioning of free markets in international trade. Foreign policy practice and scholarship in the seventeenth and eighteenth centuries predominantly reflected a framework of ideas that came to be known as mercantilism.[2] *The Wealth of Nations* represented Smith's impassioned plea to the British Parliament to cease its counterproductive mercantilist strategy, which attempted to increase national wealth by enlarging reserves of gold and silver bullion through import restrictions. In a simple exposition of the gains from trade, Smith explained that foreign trade actually increases national wealth by exporting surplus production and importing needed goods in return. His analysis of the benefits of free trade continues to form the basis of pro-free trade arguments today.[3] One of the major inefficiencies of managed trade, according to Smith, is that the individual is the better judge than the state of the most valuable use of his own capital.

Smith argues more generally that any attempt by the state to direct economic activity, such as through trade barriers or industrial incentives, actually subverts those goals it hopes to achieve by tampering with the efficient functioning of the invisible hand. This analysis leaves the state with only three major functions: to defend national security, to establish and administer a framework for the just rule of law, and to provide public goods that would not be supplied by the market. Having acquitted itself of these "night-watchman" responsibilities, the state should conduct a laissez-faire policy with respect to markets, intervening in the capitalist system only where markets cannot regulate themselves. Although Smith himself was not a dogmatic advocate of laissez-faire in every circumstance, the prescription – along with the principles of self-interest and the invisible hand on which it was based – have been reified as the central tenets of the market liberal perspective.[4]

Karl Marx's analysis of capitalism and his communist school of thought provide the classical counterpoint to Adam Smith's liberal philosophy. Yet, even though capitalism and communism represent the polar extremes of political economy theory and practice, Smith and Marx share a number of interesting analytical similarities. Both saw markets as natural systems rather than as constructed institutions. Both present materialist views of history, in which economics – the mode of production and the division of labor associated with it – drives social change and history. Both also saw a natural unilinear dynamic in history, with society moving through different stages of production and associated social orders. Yet whereas Smith saw capitalism as an equilibrium political–economic state for society, Marx was more teleological, conceiving of capitalism as a stage through which societies must pass on their way to the inexorable endpoint of communism. Both theorists recognized the human alienation in the division of labor. Smith considered that to be a necessary cost in achieving economic efficiency and thereby greater wealth for everyone. For Marx, however, the division of labor represented the crux of his critique of capitalism: that capitalists reap the benefits of the system through the exploitation of labor, while labor is alienated by its own work. In Marxist thought, market relations embody power relationships and do not take place on the equal terms of exchange that the classical and neoliberal economists claim. In emphasizing the power and social relationships embedded in markets, Karl Polanyi and Charles Lindblom are the social democratic heirs to some of Marx's insights, accepting many of the tenets of Marxist analysis while rejecting its prescriptive direction.

Marxist thought holds that the capitalist system contains the seeds of its own destruction. In a dialectical relationship between the two classes associated with capital and labor, the social upheaval that results from the bourgeois class continuously revolutionizing the means of production in the quest for ever-greater efficiency and profit eventually leads to the proletarian revolution and the communist stage. Whereas Smith recognized that the state could be in thrall to special interests (such as the mercantilists), Marx saw the relationship as more insidious, calling the state the executive committee of the bourgeoisie or the "instrument of the ruling class." Furthermore, the bourgeoisie, according to Marx, strips away all social relations and reduces them to their economic essence, using ideology, such as religion and "liberalism," to legitimate its own rule. Marx theorized about the capitalist mode of production, including particularly the labor theory of value and his thinking on surplus value and exploitation, in his landmark work *Das Kapital* (1867).

The Communist Manifesto, written by Karl Marx and Friedrich Engels, is a famous and stirring critique of capitalism. It was published in February 1848, intended as a clear elaboration of the principles of the recently formed Communist League. Its force of expression remains striking and Marx and Engels saw it for many years as the classic expression of their views.[5] They theorized in the pamphlet the dynamics through which the proletarian revolution would occur and provided the inspiration for it by setting out the principles for how a socialist economy should be organized. Yet they left no real guidelines for how to get there, or, eventually, to true communism, defined by Marx as the abolition of private property and its conversion into common property. In theory, by exploiting the proletariat class upon which its prosperity rests, the bourgeoisie deterministically unleashes a set of economic and political forces that become too powerful for it to control. In practice, however, there was a big gap between Marxist theory and twentieth-century communist reality.[6]

Marxism had theorists but no statesman until Lenin, who finally intervened to tip the scales of history by arguing that the vanguard of the proletariat must actively create class consciousness and revolution. Marxism's legacy in praxis rested in the system of political economy that we know as socialism, which persisted from the Bolshevik Revolution in October 1917 in Russia until the fall of the Berlin Wall in 1989 and the subsequent collapse of the Soviet Union. In China, Mao Zedong also claimed to be an intellectual heir to Marx, arguing that peasants and workers could play an important role in the communist revolution, even in countries that had yet to go through the capitalist stage of production. Marxist theory remains important today, succeeded in the field of political economy by neo-Marxist theories of the state – which consider the state an agent of the capitalist classes – and dependency theory – which applies dialectical class analysis to the international political economy.

The final theorist presented in this section, **Friedrich List**, is a representative of the mercantilist school of thought, which Adam Smith so inveighed against. Born in 1789 in Germany, List had the luxury, in 1841, of confronting Smith's perspective directly. He developed much of his thought after a stay in the United States, inspired by the works of his mentor Alexander Hamilton, the first treasury secretary of the United States and a leading mercantilist thinker. Whereas Smith and Marx primarily developed theoretical perspectives on political economy, List's writings serve as the classical view most reflected in real practice, both past and current.[7]

List was concerned primarily with national power and prosperity, emphasizing that the national interest should be paramount in determining a country's political–economic system. He challenged Smith's "cosmopolitanism" as well as his individualism, charging that the classical liberals ignored the principles of nationality and national interest and thereby misguidedly emphasized free trade and wrongly conflated individual economy with national economy. In his view, the national interest and the collective welfare require state direction and cannot be achieved by individuals focusing on their own self-interest, as Smith and the liberal school claim. For List, the prosperity of a nation depends not on the degree to which it has amassed wealth but rather on how it has developed its powers of production. These productive powers, which produce wealth, are more essential to individual and collective well-being than wealth itself. Thus, the state must guide economic activity to build productive powers, even at the expense of immediate material prosperity or individual interests, to ensure future national prosperity. One of the core principles underlying List's theory of productive powers is that nations must develop all sectors of the economy – and manufacturing in particular must be emphasized rather than relying solely on comparative advantage in agriculture. In other words, List produces the rationale for protectionist trade practices to support a nation's "infant industries" as it begins to industrialize and grow powerful.

Contrary to the liberal view that emphasizes the mutual benefit possible through the positive-sum game of international trade, List saw interaction between nations as conflictual and zero-sum. In his view, the state is both justified and bound to impose regulations on economic activity that are in the interests of the nation. He outlined the basic contours of many of the protectionist arguments against free trade that have become so prevalent in contemporary international political economy, such as emphasizing the social dislocation that accompanies the freeing up of trade. List also contended that nations have different requirements and optimal strategies based on their circumstances and levels of development. For a nation to be successful economically – and hence powerful in the global system – it is not enough for a government to play the referee and focus on ensuring fair play or process; instead, the government has to actively guide a process of deliberate development. Along with Marxism-inspired dependency theory, List's writings were the precursor to later policy stances such as the import substitution industrialization strategy pursued by Latin American countries to protect their domestic infant industries from external competition and to build productive powers at home. Japan and the East Asian newly industrializing countries – particularly South Korea and Taiwan – successfully pursued the same strategy in transitioning to cheaper domestic production and then moving to an export-oriented strategy (see Naazneen Barma in this volume). Scholars of political economy have since built on List's arguments to assert that nations can and do pursue very different strategies concerning the role of government in industrialization and that the premises of liberalism are not self-evident truths but rather a set of choices to be made.

Notes

1 Smith did not think that people are solely motivated by self-interest. In his earlier *Theory of Moral Sentiments*, he also articulated a role for morals and advanced the broader ethics and philosophy on which his later works rest. Adam Smith, *The Theory of Moral Sentiments* (Cambridge: Cambridge University Press, 2002).

2 Jacob Viner, "Power versus Plenty as Objectives of Foreign Policy in the Seventeenth and Eighteenth Centuries," *World Politics* 1 (1948): 1.

3 David Ricardo, Smith's successor, is also a central figure in classical economics, particularly in the free trade camp. He is credited with the theory of comparative advantage, which holds that nations can always benefit from free trade if they specialize in producing the goods in which they have a comparative cost advantage in production. See David Ricardo, *On the Principles of Political Economy and Taxation* (London: John Murray, 1821).

4 Glory M. Liu, "Rethinking the 'Chicago Smith' Problem: Adam Smith and the Chicago School, 1929–1980," *Modern Intellectual History*, 1–28. DOI: https://doi.org/10.1017/S147924431900009X.

5 David McLellan, ed., *Karl Marx: Selected Writings* (Oxford: Oxford University Press, 2000), 245.

6 Sheri Berman observes that one of the fatal flaws of Marxism as a political–economic agenda was that orthodox Marxists were simply waiting for capitalism to self-destruct. Sheri Berman, "Marxism's Fatal Flaw," *Dissent* (May 2018).

7 James Fallows offers an insightful contrast between principles underlying the economic liberal and mercantilist schools of thought, arguing that the latter has formed the basis for every successful national development strategy with the exception of the first industrializer, Great Britain. James Fallows, "How the World Works," *The Atlantic* (December 1993).

Adam Smith,
An Inquiry into the Nature and Causes of the Wealth of Nations (1776)*

Book One: Of the Causes of Improvement in the Productive Powers of Labour, and of the Order according to which its Produce is Naturally Distributed among the Different Ranks of the People.

Chapter I: Of the Division of Labour

The greatest improvement in the productive powers of labour, and the greater part of the skill, dexterity, and judgment with which it is anywhere directed, or applied, seem to have been the effects of the division of labour.

The effects of the division of labour, in the general business of society, will be more easily understood by considering in what manner it operates in some particular manufactures. It is commonly supposed to be carried furthest in some very trifling ones; not perhaps that it really is carried further in them than in others of more importance: but in those trifling manufactures which are destined to supply the small wants of but a small number of people, the whole number of workmen must necessarily be small; and those employed in every different branch of the work can often be collected into the same workhouse, and placed at once under the view of the spectator. In those great manufactures, on the contrary, which are destined to supply the great wants of the great body of the people, every different branch of the work employs so great a number of workmen that it is impossible to collect them all into the same workhouse. We can seldom see more, at one time, than those employed in one single branch. Though in such manufactures, therefore, the work may really be divided into a much greater number of parts than in those of a more trifling nature, the division is not near so obvious, and has accordingly been much less observed.

To take an example, therefore, from a very trifling manufacture; but one in which the division of labour has been very often taken notice of, the trade of the pin-maker; a workman not educated to this business (which the division of labour has rendered a distinct trade), nor acquainted with the use of the machinery employed in it (to the invention of which the same division of labour has probably given occasion), could scarce, perhaps, with his utmost industry, make one pin in a day, and certainly could not make twenty. But in the way in which this business is now carried on, not only the whole work is a peculiar trade, but it is divided into a number of branches, of which

---

* Excerpts from: *An Inquiry into the Nature and Causes of the Wealth of Nations* (1776), Adam Smith. Material in the public domain.

the greater part are likewise peculiar trades. One man draws out the wire, another straights it, a third cuts it, a fourth points it, a fifth grinds it at the top for receiving, the head; to make the head requires two or three distinct operations; to put it on is a peculiar business, to whiten the pins is another; it is even a trade by itself to put them into the paper; and the important business of making a pin is, in this manner, divided into about eighteen distinct operations, which, in some manufactories, are all performed by distinct hands, though in others the same man will sometimes perform two or three of them. I have seen a small manufactory of this kind where ten men only were employed, and where some of them consequently performed two or three distinct operations. But though they were very poor, and therefore but indifferently accommodated with the necessary machinery, they could, when they exerted themselves, make among them about twelve pounds of pins in a day. There are in a pound upwards of four thousand pins of a middling size. Those ten persons, therefore, could make among them upwards of forty-eight thousand pins in a day. Each person, therefore, making a tenth part of forty-eight thousand pins, might be considered as making four thousand eight hundred pins in a day. But if they had all wrought separately and independently, and without any of them having been educated to this peculiar business, they certainly could not each of them have made twenty, perhaps not one pin in a day; that is, certainly, not the two hundred and fortieth, perhaps not the four thousand eight hundredth part of what they are at present capable of performing, in consequence of a proper division and combination of their different operations.

In every other art and manufacture, the effects of the division of labour are similar to what they are in this very trifling one; though, in many of them, the labour can neither be so much subdivided, nor reduced to so great a simplicity of operation. The division of labour, however, so far as it can be introduced, occasions, in every art, a proportionable increase of the productive powers of labour. The separation of different trades and employments from one another seems to have taken place in consequence of this advantage. This separation, too, is generally called furthest in those countries which enjoy the highest degree of industry and improvement; what is the work of one man in a rude state of society being generally that of several in an improved one. In every improved society, the farmer is generally nothing but a farmer; the manufacturer, nothing but a manufacturer. The labour, too, which is necessary to produce any one complete manufacture is almost always divided among a great number of hands. How many different trades are employed in each branch of the linen and woollen manufactures from the growers of the flax and the wool, to the bleachers and smoothers of the linen, or to the dyers and dressers of the cloth! The nature of agriculture, indeed, does not admit of so many subdivisions of labour, nor of so complete a separation of one business from another, as manufactures. It is impossible to separate so entirely the business of the grazier from that of the corn-farmer as the trade of the carpenter is commonly separated from that of the smith. The spinner is almost always a distinct person from the weaver; but the ploughman, the harrower, the sower of the seed, and the reaper of the corn, are often the same. The occasions for those different sorts of labour returning with the different seasons of the year, it is impossible that one man should be constantly employed in any one of them. This impossibility of making so complete and entire a separation of all the different branches of labour employed in agriculture is perhaps the reason why the improvement of the productive powers of labour in this art does not always keep pace with their improvement in manufactures. The most opulent nations, indeed, generally excel all their neighbours in agriculture as well as in manufactures; but they are commonly more distinguished by their superiority in the latter than in the former. Their lands are in general better cultivated, and having more labour and expense bestowed upon them, produce more in proportion to the extent and natural fertility of the ground. But this superiority of produce is seldom much more than in proportion to the superiority of labour and expense. In agriculture, the labour of the rich country is not always much more productive than that of the poor; or, at least, it is never so much more productive as it commonly is in manufactures. The corn of the rich country, therefore, will not always, in the same degree of goodness, come cheaper to market than that of the poor. The corn of Poland, in the same degree of goodness, is as cheap as that of France, notwithstanding the superior opulence and improvement of the latter country. The corn of France is, in the corn provinces, fully as good, and in most years nearly about the same price with the corn of England, though, in opulence and improvement, France is perhaps inferior to England. The corn-lands of England, however, are better cultivated than those of France, and the corn-lands of France are said to be much better cultivated than those of Poland. But though the poor country, notwithstanding the inferiority of its cultivation, can, in some measure, rival the rich in the cheapness and goodness of its corn, it can pretend to no such competition in its manufactures; at least if those manufactures suit the soil, climate, and situation of the rich country. The silks of France are better and cheaper than those of England, because the silk manufacture, at least under the present high duties upon the importation of raw silk, does not so well suit the climate of England as that of France. But the hardware and the coarse woollens of England are beyond all comparison superior to those of France, and much cheaper too in the same degree of goodness. In Poland there are said to be scarce any manufactures of any kind, a few of those coarser household manufactures excepted, without which no country can well subsist.

This great increase of the quantity of work which, in consequence of the division of labour, the same number of people are capable of performing, is owing to three different circumstances; first, to the increase of dexterity in every particular workman; secondly, to the saving of the time which is commonly lost in passing from one species of work to another; and lastly, to the invention of a great number of machines which facilitate and abridge labour, and enable one man to do the work of many.

First, the improvement of the dexterity of the workman necessarily increases the quantity of the work he can perform; and the division of labour, by reducing every man's business to some one simple operation, and by making this operation the sole employment of his life, necessarily increased very much dexterity of the workman. A common smith, who, though accustomed to handle the hammer, has never been used to make nails, if upon some particular occasion he is obliged to attempt it, will scarce, I am assured, be able to make above two or three hundred nails in a day, and those too very bad ones. A smith who has been accustomed to make nails, but whose sole or principal business has not been that of a nailer, can seldom with his utmost diligence make more than eight hundred or a thousand nails in a day. I have seen several boys under twenty years of age who had never exercised any other trade but that of making nails, and who, when they exerted themselves, could make, each of them, upwards of two thousand three hundred nails in a day. The making of a nail, however, is by no means one of the simplest operations. The same person blows the bellows, stirs or mends the fire as there is occasion, heats the iron, and forges every part of the nail: in forging the head too he is obliged to change his tools. The different operations into which the making of a pin, or of a metal button, is subdivided, are all of them much more simple, and the dexterity of the person, of whose life it has been the sole business to perform them, is usually much greater. The rapidity with which some of the operations of those manufacturers are performed, exceeds what the human hand could, by those who had never seen them, be supposed capable of acquiring.

Secondly, the advantage which is gained by saving the time commonly lost in passing from one sort of work to another is much greater than we should at first view be apt to imagine it. It is impossible to pass very quickly from one kind of work to another that is carried on in a different place and with quite different tools. A country weaver, who cultivates a small farm, must lose a good deal of time in passing from his loom to the field, and from the field to his loom. When the two trades can be carried on in the same workhouse, the loss of time is no doubt much less. It is even in this case, however, very considerable. A man commonly saunters a little in turning his hand from one sort of employment to another. When he first begins the new work he is seldom very keen and hearty; his mind, as they say, does not go to it, and for some time he rather trifles than applies to good purpose. The habit of sauntering and of indolent careless application, which is naturally, or rather necessarily acquired by every country workman who is obliged to change his work and his tools every half hour, and to apply his hand in twenty different ways almost every day of his life, renders him almost always slothful and lazy, and incapable of any vigorous application even on the most pressing occasions. Independent, therefore, of his deficiency in point of dexterity, this cause alone must always reduce considerably the quantity of work which he is capable of performing.

Thirdly, and lastly, everybody must be sensible how much labour is facilitated and abridged by the application of proper machinery. It is unnecessary to give any example. I shall only observe, therefore, that the invention of all those machines by which labour is so much facilitated and abridged seems to have been originally owing to the division of labour. Men are much more likely to discover easier and readier methods of attaining any object when the whole attention of their minds is directed towards that single object than when it is dissipated among a great variety of things. But in consequence of the division of labour, the whole of every man's attention comes naturally to be directed towards some one very simple object. It is naturally to be expected, therefore, that some one or other of those who are employed in each particular branch of labour should soon find out easier and readier methods of performing their own particular work, wherever the nature of it admits of such improvement. A great part of the machines made use of in those manufactures in which labour is most subdivided, were originally the inventions of common workmen, who, being each of them employed in some very simple operation, naturally turned their thoughts towards finding out easier and readier methods of performing it. Whoever has been much accustomed to visit such manufactures must frequently have been shown very pretty machines, which were the inventions of such workmen in order to facilitate and quicken their particular part of the work. In the first fire-engines, a boy was constantly employed to open and shut alternately the communication between the boiler and the cylinder, according as the piston either ascended or descended. One of those boys, who loved to play with his companions, observed that, by tying a string from the handle of the valve which opened this communication to another part of the machine, the valve would open and shut without his assistance, and leave him at liberty to divert himself with his playfellows. One of the greatest improvements that has been made upon this machine, since it was first invented, was in this manner the discovery of a boy who wanted to save his own labour.

All the improvements in machinery, however, have by no means been the inventions of those who had occasion to use the machines. Many improvements have been made by the ingenuity of the makers of the machines, when to make them became the business of a peculiar trade; and some by that of those who are called philosophers or men of speculation, whose trade it is not to do anything, but to observe everything; and who, upon that account, are often capable of combining together the powers of the most distant and dissimilar objects. In the progress of society, philosophy or speculation becomes, like every other employment, the principal or sole trade and occupation of a particular class of citizens. Like every other employment too, it is subdivided into a great number of different branches, each of which affords occupation to a peculiar tribe or class of philosophers; and this subdivision of employment in philosophy, as well as in every other business, improves dexterity, and saves time. Each individual becomes more expert in his own peculiar branch, more work is done upon the whole, and the quantity of science is considerably increased by it.

It is the great multiplication of the productions of all the different arts, in consequence of the division of labour, which occasions, in a well-governed society, that universal opulence which extends itself to the lowest ranks of the people. Every workman has a great quantity of his own work to dispose of beyond what he himself has occasion for; and every other workman being exactly in the same situation, he is enabled to exchange a great quantity of his own goods for a great quantity, or, what comes to the same thing, for the price of a great quantity of theirs. He supplies them abundantly with what they have occasion for, and they accommodate him as amply with what he has occasion for, and a general plenty diffuses itself through all the different ranks of the society.

Observe the accommodation of the most common artificer or day-labourer in a civilised and thriving country, and you will perceive that the number of people of whose industry a part, though but a small part, has been employed in procuring him this accommodation, exceeds all computation. The woollen coat, for example, which covers the day-labourer, as coarse and rough as it may appear, is the produce of the joint labour of a great multitude of workmen. The shepherd, the sorter of the wool, the wool-comber or carder, the dyer, the scribbler, the spinner, the weaver, the fuller, the dresser, with many others, must all join their different arts in order to complete even this homely production. How many merchants and carriers, besides, must have been employed in transporting the materials from some of those workmen to others who often live in a very distant part of the country! How much commerce and navigation in particular, how many ship-builders, sailors, sail-makers, rope-makers, must have been employed in order to bring together the different drugs made use of by the dyer, which often come from the remotest corners of the world! What a variety of labour, too, is necessary in order to produce the tools of the meanest of those workmen! To say nothing of such complicated machines as the ship of the sailor, the mill of the fuller, or even the loom of the weaver, let us consider only what a variety of labour is requisite in order to form that very simple machine, the shears with which the shepherd clips the wool. The miner, the builder of the furnace for smelting the ore, the seller of the timber, the burner of the charcoal to be made use of in the smelting-house, the brickmaker, the brick-layer, the workmen who attend the furnace, the mill-wright, the forger, the smith, must all of them join their different arts in order to produce them. Were we to examine, in the same manner, all the different parts of his dress and household furniture, the coarse linen shirt which he wears next to his skin, the shoes which cover his feet, the bed which he lies on, and all the different parts which compose it, the kitchen-grate at which he prepares his victuals, the coals which he makes use of for that purpose, dug from the bowels of the earth, and brought to him perhaps by a long sea and a long land carriage, all the other utensils of his kitchen, all the furniture of his table, the knives and forks, the earthen or pewter plates upon which he serves up and divides his victuals, the different hands employed in preparing his bread and his beer, the glass window which lets in the heat and the light, and keeps out the wind and the rain, with all the knowledge and art requisite for preparing that beautiful and happy invention, without which these northern parts of the world could scarce have afforded a very comfortable habitation, together with the tools of all the different workmen employed in producing those different conveniences; if we examine, I say, all these things, and consider what a variety of labour is employed about each of them, we shall be sensible that, without the assistance and co-operation of many thousands, the very meanest person in a civilised country could not be provided, even according to what we very falsely imagine the easy and simple manner in which he is commonly accommodated. Compared, indeed, with the more extravagant luxury of the great, his accommodation must no doubt appear extremely simple and easy; and yet it may be true, perhaps, that the accommodation of a European prince does not always so much exceed that of an industrious and frugal peasant as the accommodation of the latter exceeds that of many an African king, the absolute master of the lives and liberties of ten thousand naked savages.

Chapter II: Of the Principle which gives Occasion to the Division of Labour

This division of labour, from which so many advantages are derived, is not originally the effect of any human wisdom, which foresees and intends that general opulence to which it gives occasion. It is the necessary, though very slow and gradual consequence of a certain propensity in human nature which has in view no such extensive utility; the propensity to truck, barter, and exchange one thing for another.

Whether this propensity be one of those original principles in human nature of which no further account can be given; or whether, as seems more probable, it be the necessary consequence of the faculties of reason and speech, it belongs not to our present subject to inquire. It is common to all men, and to be found in no other race of animals, which seem to know neither this nor any other species of contracts. Two greyhounds, in running down the same hare, have sometimes the appearance of acting in some sort of concert. Each turns her towards his companion, or endeavours to intercept her when his companion turns her towards himself. This, however, is not the effect of any contract, but of the accidental concurrence of their passions in the same object at that particular time. Nobody ever saw a dog make a fair and deliberate exchange of one bone for another with another dog. Nobody ever saw one animal by its gestures and natural cries signify to another, this is mine, that yours; I am willing to give this for that. When an animal wants to obtain something either of a man or of another animal, it has no other means of persuasion but to gain the favour of those whose service it requires. A puppy fawns upon its dam, and a spaniel endeavours by a thousand attractions to engage the attention of its master who is at dinner, when it wants to be fed by him. Man sometimes uses the same arts with his brethren, and when he has no other means of engaging them to act according to his inclinations, endeavours by every servile and fawning attention to obtain their good will. He has not time, however, to do this upon every occasion. In civilised society he stands at all times in need of the cooperation and assistance of great multitudes, while his whole life is scarce sufficient to gain the friendship of a few persons. In almost every other race of animals each individual, when it is grown up to maturity, is entirely independent, and in its natural state has occasion for the assistance of no other living creature. But man has almost constant occasion for the help of his brethren, and it is in vain for him to expect it from their benevolence only. He will be more likely to prevail if he can interest their self-love in his favour, and show them that it is for their own advantage to do for him what he requires of them. Whoever offers to another a bargain of any kind, proposes to do this. Give me that which I want, and you shall have this which you want, is the meaning of every such offer; and it is in this manner that we obtain from one another the far greater part of those good offices which we stand in need of. It is not from the benevolence of the butcher, the brewer, or the baker that we expect our dinner, but from their regard to their own interest. We address ourselves, not to their humanity but to their self-love, and never talk to them of our own necessities but of their advantages. Nobody but a beggar chooses to depend chiefly upon the benevolence of his fellow-citizens. Even a beggar does not depend upon it entirely. The charity of well-disposed people, indeed, supplies him with the whole fund of his subsistence. But though this principle ultimately provides him with all the necessaries of life which he has occasion for, it neither does nor can provide him with them as he has occasion for them. The greater part of his occasional wants are supplied in the same manner as those of other people, by treaty, by barter, and by purchase. With the money which one man gives him he purchases food. The old clothes which another bestows upon him he exchanges for other old clothes which suit him better, or for lodging, or for food, or for money, with which he can buy either food, clothes, or lodging, as he has occasion.

As it is by treaty, by barter, and by purchase that we obtain from one another the greater part of those mutual good offices which we stand in need of, so it is this same trucking disposition which originally gives occasion to the division of labour. In a tribe of hunters or shepherds a particular person makes bows and arrows, for example, with more readiness and dexterity than any other. He frequently exchanges them for cattle or for venison with his companions; and he finds at last that he can in this manner get more cattle and venison than if he himself went to the field to catch them. From a regard to his own interest, therefore, the making of bows and arrows grows to be his chief business, and he becomes a sort of armourer. Another excels in making the frames and covers of their little huts or movable houses. He is accustomed to be of use in this way to his neighbours, who reward him in the same manner with cattle and with venison, till at last he finds it his interest to dedicate himself entirely to this employment, and to become a sort of house-carpenter. In the same manner a third becomes a smith or a brazier, a fourth a tanner or dresser of hides or skins, the principal part of the nothing of savages. And thus the certainty of being able to exchange all that surplus part of the produce of his own labour, which is over and above his own consumption, for such parts of the produce of other men's labour as he may have occasion for, encourages every man to apply himself to a particular occupation, and to cultivate and bring to perfection whatever talent or genius he may possess for that particular species of business.

The difference of natural talents in different men is, in reality, much less than we are aware of; and the very different genius which appears to distinguish men of different professions, when grown up to maturity, is not upon many occasions so much the cause as the effect of the division of labour. The difference between the most dissimilar characters, between a philosopher and a common street porter, for example, seems to arise not so much from nature as from habit, custom, and education. When they came into the world, and for the first six or eight years of their existence, they were perhaps very much alike, and neither their parents nor playfellows could perceive any remarkable difference. About that age, or soon after, they come to be employed in very different occupations. The difference of talents comes then to be taken notice of, and widens by degrees, till at last the vanity of the philosopher is willing to acknowledge scarce any resemblance. But without the disposition to truck, barter, and exchange, every man must have procured to himself every necessary and conveniency of life which he wanted. All must have had the same duties to perform, and the same work to do, and there could have been no such difference of employment as could alone give occasion to any great difference of talents.

As it is this disposition which forms that difference of talents, so remarkable among men of different professions, so it is this same disposition which renders that difference useful. Many tribes of animals acknowledged to be all of the same species derive from nature a much more remarkable distinction of genius, than what, antecedent to custom and education, appears to take place among men. By nature a philosopher is not in genius and disposition half so different from a street porter, as a mastiff is from a greyhound, or a greyhound from a spaniel, or this last from a shepherd's dog. Those different tribes of animals, however, though all of the same species, are of scarce any use to one another. The strength of the mastiff is not, in the least, supported either by the swiftness of the greyhound, or by the sagacity of the spaniel, or by the docility of the shepherd's dog. The effects of those different geniuses and talents, for want of the power or disposition to barter and exchange, cannot be brought into a common stock, and do not in the least contribute to the better accommodation and conveniency of the species. Each animal is still obliged to support and defend itself, separately and independently, and derives no sort of advantage from that variety of talents with which nature has distinguished its fellows. Among men, on the contrary, the most dissimilar geniuses are of use to one another; the different produces of their respective talents, by the general disposition to truck, barter, and exchange, being brought, as it were, into a common stock, where every man may purchase whatever part of the produce of other men's talents he has occasion for.

Book Four: Of Systems of Political Economy

Chapter II: Of Restraints upon the Importation from Foreign Countries of Such Goods as can be Produced at Home

By restraining, either by high duties or by absolute prohibitions, the importation of such goods from foreign countries as can be produced at home, the monopoly of the home market is more or less secured to the domestic industry employed in producing them. Thus the prohibition of importing either live cattle or salt provisions from foreign countries secures to the graziers of Great Britain the monopoly of the home market for butcher's meat. The high duties upon the importation of corn, which in times of moderate plenty amount to a prohibition, give a like advantage to the growers of that commodity. The prohibition of the importation of foreign woollens is equally favourable to the woollen manufacturers. The silk manufacture, though altogether employed upon foreign materials, has lately obtained the same advantage. The linen manufacture has not yet obtained it, but is making great strides towards it. Many other sorts of manufacturers have, in the same manner, obtained in Great Britain, either altogether or very nearly, a monopoly against their countrymen. The variety of goods of which the importation into Great Britain is prohibited, either absolutely, or under certain circumstances, greatly exceeds what can easily be suspected by those who are not well acquainted with the laws of the customs.

That this monopoly of the home market frequently gives great encouragement to that particular species of industry which enjoys it, and frequently turns towards that employment a greater share of both the labour and stock of the society than would otherwise have gone to it, cannot be doubted. But whether it tends either to increase the general industry of the society, or to give it the most advantageous direction, is not, perhaps, altogether so evident.

The general industry of the society never can exceed what the capital of the society can employ. As the number of workmen that can be kept in employment by any particular person must bear a certain proportion to his capital, so the number of those that can be continually employed by all the members of a great society must bear a certain proportion to the whole capital of that society, and never can exceed that proportion. No regulation of commerce can increase the quantity of industry in any society beyond what its capital can maintain. It can only divert a part of it into a direction into which it might not otherwise have gone; and it is by no means certain that this artificial direction is likely to be more advantageous to the society than that into which it would have gone of its own accord.

Every individual is continually exerting himself to find out the most advantageous employment for whatever capital he can command. It is his own advantage, indeed, and not that of the society, which he has in view. But the study of his own advantage naturally, or rather necessarily, leads him to prefer that employment which is most advantageous to the society.

First, every individual endeavours to employ his capital as near home as he can, and consequently as much as he can in the support of domestic industry; provided always that he can thereby obtain the ordinary, or not a great deal less than the ordinary profits of stock.

Thus, upon equal or nearly equal profits, every wholesale merchant naturally prefers the home trade to the foreign trade of consumption, and the foreign trade of consumption to the carrying trade. In the home trade his capital is never so long out of his sight as it frequently is in the foreign trade of consumption. He can know better the character and situation of the persons whom he trusts, and if he should happen to be deceived, he knows better the laws of the country from which he must seek redress. In the carrying trade, the capital of the merchant is, as it were, divided between two foreign countries, and no part of it is ever necessarily brought home, or placed under his own immediate view and command. The capital which an Amsterdam merchant employs in carrying corn from Konigsberg to Lisbon, and fruit and wine from Lisbon to Konigsberg, must generally be the one half of it at Konigsberg and the other half at Lisbon. No part of it need ever come to Amsterdam. The natural residence of such a merchant should either be at Konigsberg or Lisbon, and it can only be some very particular circumstances which can make him prefer the residence of Amsterdam. The uneasiness, however, which he feels at being separated so far from his capital generally determines him to bring part both of the Konigsberg goods which he destines for the market of Lisbon, and of the Lisbon goods which he destines for that of Konigsberg, to Amsterdam: and though this necessarily subjects him to a double charge of loading and unloading, as well as to the payment of some duties and customs, yet for the sake of having some part of his capital always under his own view and command, he willingly submits to this extraordinary charge; and it is in this manner that every country which has any considerable share of the carrying trade becomes always the emporium, or general market, for the goods of all the different countries whose trade it carries on. The merchant, in order to save a second loading and unloading, endeavours always to sell in the home market as much of the goods of all those different countries as he can, and thus, so far as he can, to convert his carrying trade into a foreign trade of consumption. A merchant, in the same manner, who is engaged in the foreign trade of consumption, when he collects goods for foreign markets, will always be glad, upon equal or nearly equal profits, to sell as great a part of them at home as he can. He saves himself the risk and trouble of exportation, when, so far as he can, he thus converts his foreign trade of consumption into a home trade. Home is in this manner the centre, if I may say so, round which the capitals of the inhabitants of every country are continually circulating, and towards which they are always tending, though by particular causes they may sometimes be driven off and repelled from it towards more distant employments. But a capital employed in the home trade, it has already been shown, necessarily puts into motion a greater quantity of domestic industry, and gives revenue and employment to a greater number of the inhabitants of the country, than an equal capital employed in the foreign trade of consumption: and one employed in the foreign trade of consumption has the same advantage over an equal capital employed in the carrying trade. Upon equal, or only nearly equal profits, therefore, every individual naturally inclines to employ his capital in the manner in which it is likely to afford the greatest support to domestic industry, and to give revenue and employment to the greatest number of people of his own country.

Secondly, every individual who employs his capital in the support of domestic industry, necessarily endeavours so to direct that industry that its produce may be of the greatest possible value.

The produce of industry is what it adds to the subject or materials upon which it is employed. In proportion as the value of this produce is great or small, so will likewise be the profits of the employer. But it is only for the sake of profit that any man employs a capital in the support of industry; and he will always, therefore, endeavour to employ it in the support of that industry of which the produce is likely to be of the greatest value, or to exchange for the greatest quantity either of money or of other goods.

But the annual revenue of every society is always precisely equal to the exchangeable value of the whole annual produce of its industry, or rather is precisely the same thing with that exchangeable value. As every individual, therefore, endeavours as much as he can both to employ his capital in the support of domestic industry, and so to direct that industry that its produce may be of the greatest value; every individual necessarily labours to render the annual revenue of the society as great as he can. He generally, indeed, neither intends to promote the public interest, nor knows how much he is promoting it. By preferring the support of domestic to that of foreign industry, he intends only his own security; and by directing that industry in such a manner as its produce may be of the greatest value, he intends only his own gain, and he is in this, as in many other cases, led by an invisible hand to promote an end which was no part of his intention. Nor is it always the worse for the society that it was no part of it. By pursuing his own interest he frequently promotes that of the society more effectually than when he really intends to promote it. I have never known much good done by those who affected to trade for the public good. It is an affectation, indeed, not very common among merchants, and very few words need be employed in dissuading them from it.

What is the species of domestic industry which his capital can employ, and of which the produce is likely to be of the greatest value, every individual, it is evident, can, in his local situation, judge much better than any statesman or lawgiver can do for him. The statesman who should attempt to direct private people in what manner they ought to employ their capitals would not only load himself with a most unnecessary attention, but assume an authority which could safely be trusted, not only to no single person, but to no council or senate whatever, and which would nowhere be so dangerous as in the hands of a man who had folly and presumption enough to fancy himself fit to exercise it.

To give the monopoly of the home market to the produce of domestic industry, in any particular art or manufacture, is in some measure to direct private people in what manner they ought to employ their capitals, and must, in almost all cases, be either a useless or a hurtful regulation. If the produce of domestic can be brought there as cheap as that of foreign industry, the regulation is evidently useless. If it cannot, it must generally be hurtful. It is the maxim of every prudent master of a family never to attempt to make at home what it will cost him more to make than to buy. The tailor does not attempt to make his own shoes, but buys them of the shoemaker. The shoemaker does not attempt to make his own clothes, but employs a tailor. The farmer attempts to make neither the one nor the other, but employs those different artificers. All of them find it for their interest to employ their whole industry in a way in which they have some advantage over their neighbours, and to purchase with a part of its produce, or what is the same thing, with the price of a part of it, whatever else they have occasion for.

What is prudence in the conduct of every private family can scarce be folly in that of a great kingdom. If a foreign country can supply us with a commodity cheaper than we ourselves can make it, better buy it of them with some part of the produce of our own industry employed in a way in which we have some advantage. The general industry of the country, being always in proportion to the capital which employs it, will not thereby be diminished, no more than that of the above-mentioned artificers; but only left to find out the way in which it can be employed with the greatest advantage. It is certainly not employed to the greatest advantage when it is thus directed towards an object which it can buy cheaper than it can make. The value of its annual produce is certainly more or less diminished when it is thus turned away from producing commodities evidently of more value than the commodity which it is directed to produce. According to the supposition, that commodity could be purchased from foreign countries cheaper than it can be made at home. It could, therefore, have been purchased with a part only of the commodities, or, what is the same thing, with a part only of the price of the commodities, which the industry employed by an equal capital would have produced at home, had it been left to follow its natural course. The industry of the country, therefore, is thus turned away from a more to a less advantageous employment, and the exchangeable value of its annual produce, instead of being increased, according to the intention of the lawgiver, must necessarily be diminished by every such regulation.

By means of such regulations, indeed, a particular manufacture may sometimes be acquired sooner than it could have been otherwise, and after a certain time may be made at home as cheap or cheaper than in the foreign country. But though the industry of the society may be thus carried with advantage into a particular channel sooner than it could have been otherwise, it will by no means follow that the sum total, either of its industry, or of its revenue, can ever be augmented by any such regulation. The industry of the society can augment only in proportion as its capital augments, and its capital can augment only in proportion to what can be gradually saved out of its revenue. But the immediate effect of every such regulation is to diminish its revenue, and what diminishes its revenue is certainly not very likely to augment its capital faster than it would have augmented of its own accord had both capital and industry been left to find out their natural employments.

Chapter IX: Of the Agricultural Systems, or of those Systems of Political Economy, which Represent the Produce of Land, as either the Sole or the Principal, Source of the Revenue and Wealth of Every Country

The greatest and most important branch of the commerce of every nation, it has already been observed, is that which is carried on between the inhabitants of the town and those of the country. The inhabitants of the town draw from the country the rude produce which constitutes both the materials of their work and the fund of their subsistence; and they pay for this rude produce by sending back to the country a certain portion of it manufactured and prepared for immediate use. The trade which is carried on between these two different sets of people consists ultimately in a certain quantity of rude produce exchanged for a certain quantity of manufactured produce. The dearer the latter, therefore, the cheaper the former; and whatever tends in any country to raise the price of manufactured produce tends to lower that of the rude produce of the land, and thereby to discourage agriculture. The smaller the quantity of manufactured produce which in any given quantity of rude produce, or, what comes to the same thing, which the price of any given quantity of rude produce is capable of purchasing, the smaller the exchangeable value of that given quantity of rude produce, the smaller the encouragement which either the landlord has to increase its quantity by improving or the farmer by cultivating the land. Whatever, besides, tends to diminish in any country the number of artificers and manufacturers, tends to diminish the home market, the most important of all markets for the rude produce of the land, and thereby still further to discourage agriculture.

Those systems, therefore, which, preferring agriculture to all other employments, in order to promote it, impose restraints upon manufactures and foreign trade, act contrary to the very end which they propose, and indirectly discourage that very species of industry which they mean to promote. They are so far, perhaps, more inconsistent than even the mercantile system. That system, by encouraging manufactures and foreign trade more than agriculture, turns a certain portion of the capital of the society from supporting a more advantageous, to support a less advantageous species of industry. But still it really and in the end encourages that species of industry which it means to promote. Those agricultural systems, on the contrary, really and in the end discourage their own favourite species of industry.

It is thus that every system which endeavours, either by extraordinary encouragements to draw towards a particular species of industry a greater share of the capital of the society than what would naturally go to it, or, by extraordinary restraints, force from a particular species of industry some share of the capital which would otherwise be employed in it, is in reality subversive of the great purpose which it means to promote. It retards, instead of accelerating, the progress of the society towards real wealth and greatness; and diminishes, instead of increasing, the real value of the annual produce of its land and labour.

All systems either of preference or of restraint, therefore, being thus completely taken away, the obvious and simple system of natural liberty establishes itself of its own accord. Every man, as long as he does not violate the laws of justice, is left perfectly free to pursue his own interest his own way, and to bring both his industry and capital into competition with those of any other man, or order of men. The sovereign is completely discharged from a duty, in the attempting to perform which he must always be exposed to innumerable delusions, and for the proper performance of which no human wisdom or knowledge could ever be sufficient; the duty of superintending the industry of private people, and of directing it towards the employments most suitable to the interest of the society. According to the system of natural liberty, the sovereign has only three duties to attend to; three duties of great importance, indeed, but plain and intelligible to common understandings: first, the duty of protecting the society from violence and invasion of other independent societies; secondly, the duty of protecting, as far as possible, every member of the society from the injustice or oppression of every other member of it, or the duty of establishing an exact administration of justice; and, thirdly, the duty of erecting and maintaining certain public works and certain public institutions which it can never be for the interest of any individual, or small number of individuals, to erect and maintain; because the profit could never repay the expense to any individual or small number of individuals, though it may frequently do much more than repay it to a great society.

Karl Marx and Friedrich Engels, "The Communist Manifesto" (1848)*

A spectre is haunting Europe—the spectre of communism. All the powers of old Europe have entered into a holy alliance to exorcise this spectre: Pope and Tsar, Metternich and Guizot, French Radicals and German police-spies.

Where is the party in opposition that has not been decried as communistic by its opponents in power? Where is the opposition that has not hurled back the branding reproach of communism, against the more advanced opposition parties, as well as against its reactionary adversaries?

Two things result from this fact:

I. Communism is already acknowledged by all European powers to be itself a power.
II. It is high time that Communists should openly, in the face of the whole world, publish their views, their aims, their tendencies, and meet this nursery tale of the spectre of communism with a manifesto of the party itself.

To this end, Communists of various nationalities have assembled in London and sketched the following manifesto, to be published in the English, French, German, Italian, Flemish and Danish languages.

I. Bourgeois and Proletarians

The history of all hitherto existing society is the history of class struggles.

Freeman and slave, patrician and plebian, lord and serf, guild-master and journeyman, in a word, oppressor and oppressed, stood in constant opposition to one another, carried on an uninterrupted, now hidden, now open fight, a fight that each time ended, either in a revolutionary reconstitution of society at large, or in the common ruin of the contending classes.

In the earlier epochs of history, we find almost everywhere a complicated arrangement of society into various orders, a manifold gradation of social rank. In ancient Rome we have patricians, knights, plebians, slaves; in the Middle Ages, feudal lords, vassals, guild-masters, journeymen, apprentices, serfs; in almost all of these classes, again, subordinate gradations.

The modern bourgeois society that has sprouted from the ruins of feudal society has not done away with class antagonisms. It has but established new classes, new conditions of oppression, new forms of struggle in place of the old ones.

---

* "The Communist Manifesto" (1848), Karl Marx and Friedrich Engels. Material in the public domain.

Our epoch, the epoch of the bourgeoisie, possesses, however, this distinct feature: it has simplified class antagonisms. Society as a whole is more and more splitting up into two great hostile camps, into two great classes directly facing each other—bourgeoisie and proletariat.

From the serfs of the Middle Ages sprang the chartered burghers of the earliest towns. From these burgesses the first elements of the bourgeoisie were developed.

The discovery of America, the rounding of the Cape, opened up fresh ground for the rising bourgeoisie. The East-Indian and Chinese markets, the colonisation of America, trade with the colonies, the increase in the means of exchange and in commodities generally, gave to commerce, to navigation, to industry, an impulse never before known, and thereby, to the revolutionary element in the tottering feudal society, a rapid development.

The feudal system of industry, in which industrial production was monopolized by closed guilds, now no longer suffices for the growing wants of the new markets. The manufacturing system took its place. The guild-masters were pushed aside by the manufacturing middle class; division of labor between the different corporate guilds vanished in the face of division of labor in each single workshop.

Meantime, the markets kept ever growing, the demand ever rising. Even manufacturers no longer sufficed. Thereupon, steam and machinery revolutionized industrial production. The place of manufacture was taken by the giant, Modern Industry; the place of the industrial middle class by industrial millionaires, the leaders of the whole industrial armies, the modern bourgeois.

Modern industry has established the world market, for which the discovery of America paved the way. This market has given an immense development to commerce, to navigation, to communication by land. This development has, in turn, reacted on the extension of industry; and in proportion as industry, commerce, navigation, railways extended, in the same proportion the bourgeoisie developed, increased its capital, and pushed into the background every class handed down from the Middle Ages.

We see, therefore, how the modern bourgeoisie is itself the product of a long course of development, of a series of revolutions in the modes of production and of exchange.

Each step in the development of the bourgeoisie was accompanied by a corresponding political advance in that class. An oppressed class under the sway of the feudal nobility, an armed and self-governing association of medieval commune: here independent urban republic (as in Italy and Germany); there taxable "third estate" of the monarchy (as in France); afterward, in the period of manufacturing proper, serving either the semi-feudal or the absolute monarchy as a counterpoise against the nobility, and, in fact, cornerstone of the great monarchies in general—the bourgeoisie has at last, since the establishment of Modern Industry and of the world market, conquered for itself, in the modern representative state, exclusive political sway. The executive of the modern state is but a committee for managing the common affairs of the whole bourgeoisie.

The bourgeoisie, historically, has played a most revolutionary part.

The bourgeoisie, wherever it has got the upper hand, has put an end to all feudal, patriarchal, idyllic relations. It has pitilessly torn asunder the motley feudal ties that bound man to his "natural superiors," and has left no other nexus between people than naked self-interest, than callous "cash payment." It has drowned out the most heavenly ecstacies of religious fervor, of chivalrous enthusiasm, of philistine sentimentalism, in the icy water of egotistical calculation. It has resolved personal worth into exchange value, and in place of the numberless indefeasible chartered freedoms, has set up that single, unconscionable freedom—Free Trade. In one word, for exploitation, veiled by religious and political illusions, it has substituted naked, shameless, direct, brutal exploitation.

The bourgeoisie has stripped of its halo every occupation hitherto honored and looked up to with reverent awe. It has converted the physician, the lawyer, the priest, the poet, the man of science, into its paid wage laborers.

The bourgeoisie has torn away from the family its sentimental veil, and has reduced the family relation into a mere money relation.

The bourgeoisie has disclosed how it came to pass that the brutal display of vigor in the Middle Ages, which reactionaries so much admire, found its fitting complement in the most slothful indolence. It has been the first to show what man's activity can bring about. It has accomplished wonders far surpassing Egyptian pyramids, Roman aqueducts, and Gothic cathedrals; it has conducted expeditions that put in the shade all former exoduses of nations and crusades.

The bourgeoisie cannot exist without constantly revolutionizing the instruments of production, and thereby the relations of production, and with them the whole relations of society. Conservation of the old modes of production in unaltered form, was, on the contrary, the first condition of existence for all earlier industrial classes. Constant revolutionizing of production, uninterrupted disturbance of all social conditions, everlasting uncertainty and agitation distinguish the bourgeois epoch from all earlier ones. All fixed, fast frozen relations, with their train of ancient and venerable prejudices and opinions, are swept away, all new-formed ones become anti-quated before they can ossify. All that is solid melts into air, all that is holy is profaned, and man is at last compelled to face with sober senses his real condition of life and his relations with his kind.

The need of a constantly expanding market for its products chases the bourgeoisie over the entire surface of the globe. It must nestle everywhere, settle everywhere, establish connections everywhere.

The bourgeoisie has, through its exploitation of the world market, given a cosmopol-itan character to production and consumption in every country. To the great chagrin of reactionaries, it has drawn from under the feet of industry the national ground on which it stood. All old-established national industries have been destroyed or are daily being destroyed. They are dislodged by new industries, whose introduction becomes a life and death question for all civilized nations, by industries that no longer work up indigenous raw material, but raw material drawn from the remotest zones; industries whose products are consumed, not only at home, but in every quarter of the globe. In place of the old wants, satisfied by the production of the country, we find new wants, requiring for their satisfaction the products of distant lands and climes. In place of the old local and national seclusion and self-sufficiency, we have intercourse in every dir-ection, universal inter-dependence of nations. And as in material, so also in intellectual production. The intellectual creations of individual nations become common property. National one-sidedness and narrow-mindedness become more and more impossible, and from the numerous national and local literatures, there arises a world literature.

The bourgeoisie, by the rapid improvement of all instruments of production, by the immensely facilitated means of communication, draws all, even the most barbarian, nations into civilization. The cheap prices of commodities are the heavy artillery with which it forces the barbarians' intensely obstinate hatred of foreigners to capitulate. It compels all nations, on pain of extinction, to adopt the bourgeois mode of production; it compels them to introduce what it calls civilization into their midst, i.e., to become bourgeois themselves. In one word, it creates a world after its own image.

The bourgeoisie has subjected the country to the rule of the towns. It has created enormous cities, has greatly increased the urban population as compared with the rural, and has thus rescued a considerable part of the population from the idiocy of rural life. Just as it has made the country dependent on the towns, so it has made barbarian and semi-barbarian countries dependent on the civilized ones, nations of peasants on nations of bourgeois, the East on the West.

The bourgeoisie keeps more and more doing away with the scattered state of the population, of the means of production, and of property. It has agglomerated population, centralized the means of production, and has concentrated property in a few hands. The necessary consequence of this was political centralization. Independent, or but loosely connected provinces, with separate interests, laws, governments, and systems of taxation, became lumped together into one nation, with one government, one code of laws, one national class interest, one frontier, and one customs tariff.

The bourgeoisie, during its rule of scarce one hundred years, has created more massive and more colossal productive forces than have all preceding generations together. Subjection of nature's forces to man, machinery, application of chemistry to industry and agriculture, steam navigation, railways, electric telegraphs, clearing of whole continents for cultivation, canalization or rivers, whole populations conjured out of the ground—what earlier century had even a presentiment that such productive forces slumbered in the lap of social labor?

We see then: the means of production and of exchange, on whose foundation the bourgeoisie built itself up, were generated in feudal society. At a certain stage in the development of these means of production and of exchange, the conditions under which feudal society produced and exchanged, the feudal organization of agriculture and manufacturing industry, in one word, the feudal relations of property became no longer compatible with the already developed productive forces; they became so many fetters. They had to be burst asunder; they were burst asunder.

Into their place stepped free competition, accompanied by a social and political constitution adapted in it, and the economic and political sway of the bourgeois class.

A similar movement is going on before our own eyes. Modern bourgeois society, with its relations of production, of exchange and of property, a society that has conjured up such gigantic means of production and of exchange, is like the sorcerer who is no longer able to control the powers of the nether world whom he has called up by his spells. For many a decade past, the history of industry and commerce is but the history of the revolt of modern productive forces against modern conditions of production, against the property relations that are the conditions for the existence of the bourgeois and of its rule. It is enough to mention the commercial crises that, by their periodical return, put the existence of the entire bourgeois society on its trial, each time more threateningly. In these crises, a great part not only of the existing products, but also of the previously created productive forces, are periodically destroyed. In these crises, there breaks out an epidemic that, in all earlier epochs, would have seemed an absurdity—the epidemic of over-production. Society suddenly finds itself put back into a state of momentary barbarism; it appears as if a famine, a universal war of devastation, had cut off the supply of every means of subsistence; industry and commerce seem to be destroyed. And why? Because there is too much civilization, too much means of subsistence, too much industry, too much commerce. The productive forces at the disposal of society no longer tend to further the development of the conditions of bourgeois property; on the contrary, they have become too powerful for these conditions, by which they are fettered, and so soon as they overcome these fetters, they bring disorder into the whole of bourgeois society, endanger the existence of bourgeois property. The conditions of bourgeois society are too narrow to comprise the wealth created by them. And how does the bourgeoisie get over these crises? On the one hand, by enforced destruction of a mass of productive forces; on the other, by the conquest of new markets, and by the more thorough exploitation of the old ones. That is to say, by paving the way for more extensive and more destructive crises, and by diminishing the means whereby crises are prevented.

The weapons with which the bourgeoisie felled feudalism to the ground are now turned against the bourgeoisie itself.

But not only has the bourgeoisie forged the weapons that bring death to itself; it has also called into existence the men who are to wield those weapons—the modern working class—the proletarians.

In proportion as the bourgeoisie, i.e., capital, is developed, in the same proportion is the proletariat, the modern working class, developed—a class of laborers, who live only so long as they find work, and who find work only so long as their labor increases capital. These laborers, who must sell themselves piecemeal, are a commodity, like every other article of commerce, and are consequently exposed to all the vicissitudes of competition, to all the fluctuations of the market.

Owing to the extensive use of machinery, and to the division of labor, the work of the proletarians has lost all individual character, and, consequently, all charm for the workman. He becomes an appendage of the machine, and it is only the most simple, most monotonous, and most easily acquired knack, that is required of him. Hence, the cost of production of a workman is restricted, almost entirely, to the means of subsistence that he requires for maintenance, and for the propagation of his race. But the price of a commodity, and therefore also of labor, is equal to its cost of production. In proportion, therefore, as the repulsiveness of the work increases, the wage decreases. What is more, in proportion as the use of machinery and division of labor increases, in the same proportion the burden of toil also increases, whether by prolongation of the working hours, by the increase of the work exacted in a given time, or by increased speed of machinery, etc.

Modern Industry has converted the little workshop of the patriarchal master into the great factory of the industrial capitalist. Masses of laborers, crowded into the factory, are organized like soldiers. As privates of the industrial army, they are placed under the command of a perfect hierarchy of officers and sergeants. Not only are they slaves of the bourgeois class, and of the bourgeois state; they are daily and hourly enslaved by the machine, by the overlooker, and, above all, in the individual bourgeois manufacturer himself. The more openly this despotism proclaims gain to be its end and aim, the more petty, the more hateful and the more embittering it is.

The less the skill and exertion of strength implied in manual labor, in other words, the more modern industry becomes developed, the more is the labor of men superseded by that of women. Differences of age and sex have no longer any distinctive social validity for the working class. All are instruments of labor, more or less expensive to use, according to their age and sex.

No sooner is the exploitation of the laborer by the manufacturer, so far at an end, that he receives his wages in cash, than he is set upon by the other portion of the bourgeoisie, the landlord, the shopkeeper, the pawnbroker, etc.

The lower strata of the middle class—the small tradespeople, shopkeepers, and retired tradesmen generally, the handicraftsmen and peasants—all these sink gradually into the proletariat, partly because their diminutive capital does not suffice for the scale on which Modern Industry is carried on, and is swamped in the competition with the large capitalists, partly because their specialized skill is rendered worthless by new methods of production. Thus, the proletariat is recruited from all classes of the population.

The proletariat goes through various stages of development. With its birth begins its struggle with the bourgeoisie. At first, the contest is carried on by individual laborers, then by the work of people of a factory, then by the operative of one trade, in one locality, against the individual bourgeois who directly exploits them. They direct their attacks not against the bourgeois condition of production, but against the instruments of production themselves; they destroy imported wares that compete with their labor, they smash to pieces machinery, they set factories ablaze, they seek to restore by force the vanished status of the workman of the Middle Ages.

At this stage, the laborers still form an incoherent mass scattered over the whole country, and broken up by their mutual competition. If anywhere they unite to form more compact bodies, this is not yet the consequence of their own active union, but of the union of the bourgeoisie, which class, in order to attain its own political ends, is compelled to set the whole proletariat in motion, and is moreover yet, for a time, able to do so. At this stage, therefore, the proletarians do not fight their enemies, but the enemies of their enemies, the remnants of absolute monarchy, the landowners, the non-industrial bourgeois, the petty bourgeois. Thus, the whole historical movement is concentrated in the hands of the bourgeoisie; every victory so obtained is a victory for the bourgeoisie.

But with the development of industry, the proletariat not only increases in number; it becomes concentrated in greater masses, its strength grows, and it feels that strength more. The various interests and conditions of life within the ranks of the proletariat are more and more equalized, in proportion as machinery obliterates all distinctions of labor, and nearly everywhere reduces wages to the same low level. The growing competition among the bourgeois, and the resulting commercial crises, make the wages of the workers ever more fluctuating. The increasing improvement of machinery, ever more rapidly developing, makes their livelihood more and more precarious; the collisions between individual workmen and individual bourgeois take more and more the character of collisions between two classes. Thereupon, the workers begin to form combinations (trade unions) against the bourgeois; they club together in order to keep up the rate of wages; they found permanent associations in order to make provision beforehand for these occasional revolts. Here and there, the contest breaks out into riots.

Now and then the workers are victorious, but only for a time. The real fruit of their battles lie not in the immediate result, but in the ever expanding union of the workers. This union is helped on by the improved means of communication that are created by Modern Industry, and that place the workers of different localities in contact with one another. It was just this contact that was needed to centralize the numerous local struggles, all of the same character, into one national struggle between classes. But every class struggle is a political struggle. And that union, to attain which the burghers of the Middle Ages, with their miserable highways, required centuries, the modern proletarian, thanks to railways, achieve in a few years.

This organization of the proletarians into a class, and, consequently, into a political party, is continually being upset again by the competition between the workers themselves. But it ever rises up again, stronger, firmer, mightier. It compels legislative recognition of particular interests of the workers, by taking advantage of the divisions among the bourgeoisie itself. Thus, the Ten-Hours Bill in England was carried.

Altogether, collisions between the classes of the old society further in many ways the course of development of the proletariat. The bourgeoisie finds itself involved in a constant battle. At first with the aristocracy; later on, with those portions of the bourgeoisie itself, whose interests have become antagonistic to the progress of industry; at all time with the bourgeoisie of foreign countries. In all these battles, it sees itself compelled to appeal to the proletariat, to ask for help, and thus to drag it into the political arena. The bourgeoisie itself, therefore, supplies the proletariat with its own elements of political and general education, in other words, it furnishes the proletariat with weapons for fighting the bourgeoisie.

Further, as we have already seen, entire sections of the ruling class are, by the advance of industry, precipitated into the proletariat, or are at least threatened in their conditions of existence. These also supply the proletariat with fresh elements of enlightenment and progress.

Finally, in times when the class struggle nears the decisive hour, the progress of dissolution going on within the ruling class, in fact within the whole range of old society, assumes such a violent, glaring character, that a small section of the ruling class cuts itself adrift, and joins the revolutionary class, the class that holds the future in its hands. Just as, therefore, at an earlier period, a section of the nobility went over to the bourgeoisie, so now a portion of the bourgeoisie goes over to the proletariat, and in particular, a portion of the bourgeois ideologists, who have raised themselves to the level of comprehending theoretically the historical movement as a whole.

Of all the classes that stand face to face with the bourgeoisie today, the proletariat alone is a genuinely revolutionary class. The other classes decay and finally disappear in the face of Modern Industry; the proletariat is its special and essential product.

The lower middle class, the small manufacturer, the shopkeeper, the artisan, the peasant, all these fight against the bourgeoisie, to save from extinction their existence as fractions of the middle class. They are therefore not revolutionary, but conservative. Nay, more, they are reactionary, for they try to roll back the wheel of history. If, by chance, they are revolutionary, they are only so in view of their impending transfer into the proletariat; they thus defend not their present, but their future interests; they desert their own standpoint to place themselves at that of the proletariat.

The "dangerous class," the social scum, that passively rotting mass thrown off by the lowest layers of the old society, may, here and there, be swept into the movement by a proletarian revolution; its conditions of life, however, prepare it far more for the part of a bribed tool of reactionary intrigue.

In the condition of the proletariat, those of old society at large are already virtually swamped. The proletarian is without property; his relation to his wife and children has no longer anything in common with the bourgeois family relations; modern industry labor, modern subjection to capital, the same in England as in France, in America as in Germany, has stripped him of every trace of national character. Law, morality, religion, are to him so many bourgeois prejudices, behind which lurk in ambush just as many bourgeois interests.

All the preceding classes that got the upper hand sought to fortify their already acquired status by subjecting society at large to their conditions of appropriation. The proletarians cannot become masters of the productive forces of society, except by abolishing their own previous mode of appropriation, and thereby also every other previous mode of appropriation. They have nothing of their own to secure and to fortify; their mission is to destroy all previous securities for, and insurances of, individual property.

All previous historical movements were movements of minorities, or in the interest of minorities. The proletarian movement is the self-conscious, independent movement of the immense majority, in the interest of the immense majority. The proletariat, the lowest stratum of our present society, cannot stir, cannot raise itself up, without the whole superincumbent strata of official society being sprung into the air.

Though not in substance, yet in form, the struggle of the proletariat with the bourgeoisie is at first a national struggle. The proletariat of each country must, of course, first of all settle matters with its own bourgeoisie.

In depicting the most general phases of the development of the proletariat, we traced the more or less veiled civil war, raging within existing society, up to the point where that war breaks out into open revolution, and where the violent overthrow of the bourgeoisie lays the foundation for the sway of the proletariat.

Hitherto, every form of society has been based, as we have already seen, on the antagonism of oppressing and oppressed classes. But in order to oppress a class, certain conditions must be assured to it under which it can, at least, continue its slavish existence. The serf, in the period of serfdom, raised himself to membership in the commune, just as the petty bourgeois, under the yoke of the feudal absolutism, managed to develop into a bourgeois. The modern laborer, on the contrary, instead of rising with the process of industry, sinks deeper and deeper below the conditions of existence of his own class. He becomes a pauper, and pauperism develops more rapidly than population and wealth. And here it becomes evident that the bourgeoisie is unfit any longer to be the ruling class in society, and to impose its conditions of existence upon society as an overriding law. It is unfit to rule because it is incompetent to assure an existence to its slave within his slavery, because it cannot help letting him sink into such a state, that it has to feed him, instead of being fed by him. Society can no longer live under this bourgeoisie, in other words, its existence is no longer compatible with society.

The essential conditions for the existence and for the sway of the bourgeois class is the formation and augmentation of capital; the condition for capital is wage labor. Wage labor rests exclusively on competition between the laborers. The advance of industry, whose involuntary promoter is the bourgeoisie, replaces the isolation of the laborers, due to competition, by the revolutionary combination, due to association. The development of Modern Industry, therefore, cuts from under its feet the very foundation on which the bourgeoisie produces and appropriates products. What the bourgeoisie therefore produces, above all, are its own grave-diggers. Its fall and the victory of the proletariat are equally inevitable.

II. Proletarians and Communists

In what relation do the Communists stand to the proletarians as a whole?

The Communists do not form a separate party opposed to the other working-class parties.

They have no interests separate and apart from those of the proletariat as a whole.

They do not set up any sectarian principles of their own, by which to shape and mold the proletarian movement.

The Communists are distinguished from the other working-class parties by this only: (1) In the national struggles of the proletarians of the different countries, they point out and bring to the front the common interests of the entire proletariat, independently of all nationality. (2) In the various stages of development which the struggle of the working class against the bourgeoisie has to pass through, they always and everywhere represent the interests of the movement as a whole.

The Communists, therefore, are on the one hand practically, the most advanced and resolute section of the working-class parties of every country, that section which pushes forward all others; on the other hand, theoretically, they have over the great mass of the proletariat the advantage of clearly understanding the lines of march, the conditions, and the ultimate general results of the proletarian movement.

The immediate aim of the Communists is the same as that of all other proletarian parties: Formation of the proletariat into a class, overthrow of the bourgeois supremacy, conquest of political power by the proletariat.

The theoretical conclusions of the Communists are in no way based on ideas or principles that have been invented, or discovered, by this or that would-be universal reformer.

They merely express, in general terms, actual relations springing from an existing class struggle, from a historical movement going on under our very eyes. The abolition of existing property relations is not at all a distinctive feature of communism.

All property relations in the past have continually been subject to historical change consequent upon the change in historical conditions.

The French Revolution, for example, abolished feudal property in favor of bourgeois property.

The distinguishing feature of communism is not the abolition of property generally, but the abolition of bourgeois property. But modern bourgeois private property is the final and most complete expression of the system of producing and appropriating products that is based on class antagonisms, on the exploitation of the many by the few.

In this sense, the theory of the Communists may be summed up in the single sentence: Abolition of private property.

We Communists have been reproached with the desire of abolishing the right of personally acquiring property as the fruit of a man's own labor, which property is alleged to be the groundwork of all personal freedom, activity and independence.

Hard-won, self-acquired, self-earned property! Do you mean the property of petty artisan and of the small peasant, a form of property that preceded the bourgeois form? There is no need to abolish that; the development of industry has to a great extent already destroyed it, and is still destroying it daily.

Or do you mean the modern bourgeois private property?

But does wage labor create any property for the laborer? Not a bit. It creates capital, i.e., that kind of property which exploits wage labor, and which cannot increase except upon conditions of begetting a new supply of wage labor for fresh exploitation. Property, in its present form, is based on the antagonism of capital and wage labor. Let us examine both sides of this antagonism.

To be a capitalist, is to have not only a purely personal, but a social STATUS in production. Capital is a collective product, and only by the united action of many members, nay, in the last resort, only by the united action of all members of society, can it be set in motion.

Capital is therefore not only personal; it is a social power.

When, therefore, capital is converted into common property, into the property of all members of society, personal property is not thereby transformed into social property. It is only the social character of the property that is changed. It loses its class character.

Let us now take wage labor.

The average price of wage labor is the minimum wage, i.e., that quantum of the means of subsistence which is absolutely requisite to keep the laborer in bare existence as a laborer. What, therefore, the wage laborer appropriates by means of his labor merely suffices to prolong and reproduce a bare existence. We by no means intend to abolish this personal appropriation of the products of labor, an appropriation that is made for the maintenance and reproduction of human life, and that leaves no surplus wherewith to command the labor of others. All that we want to do away with is the miserable character of this appropriation, under which the laborer lives merely to increase capital, and is allowed to live only in so far as the interest of the ruling class requires it.

In bourgeois society, living labor is but a means to increase accumulated labor. In communist society, accumulated labor is but a means to widen, to enrich, to promote the existence of the laborer.

In bourgeois society, therefore, the past dominates the present; in communist society, the present dominates the past. In bourgeois society, capital is independent and has individuality, while the living person is dependent and has no individuality.

And the abolition of this state of things is called by the bourgeois, abolition of individuality and freedom! And rightly so. The abolition of bourgeois individuality, bourgeois independence, and bourgeois freedom is undoubtedly aimed at.

By freedom is meant, under the present bourgeois conditions of production, free trade, free selling and buying.

But if selling and buying disappears, free selling and buying disappears also. This talk about free selling and buying, and all the other "brave words" of our bourgeois about freedom in general, have a meaning, if any, only in contrast with restricted selling and buying, with the fettered traders of the Middle Ages, but have no meaning when opposed to the communist abolition of buying and selling, or the bourgeois conditions of production, and of the bourgeoisie itself.

You are horrified at our intending to do away with private property. But in your existing society, private property is already done away with for nine-tenths of the population; its existence for the few is solely due to its non-existence in the hands of those nine-tenths. You reproach us, therefore, with intending to do away with a form of property, the necessary condition for whose existence is the non-existence of any property for the immense majority of society.

In one word, you reproach us with intending to do away with your property. Precisely so; that is just what we intend.

From the moment when labor can no longer be converted into capital, money, or rent, into a social power capable of being monopolized, i.e., from the moment when individual property can no longer be transformed into bourgeois property, into capital, from that moment, you say, individuality vanishes.

You must, therefore, confess that by "individual" you mean no other person than the bourgeois, than the middle-class owner of property. This person must, indeed, be swept out of the way, and made impossible.

Communism deprives no man of the power to appropriate the products of society; all that it does is to deprive him of the power to subjugate the labor of others by means of such appropriations.

It has been objected that upon the abolition of private property, all work will cease, and universal laziness will overtake us.

According to this, bourgeois society ought long ago to have gone to the dogs through sheer idleness; for those who acquire anything, do not work. The whole of this objection is but another expression of the tautology: There can no longer be any wage labor when there is no longer any capital.

All objections urged against the communistic mode of producing and appropriating material products, have, in the same way, been urged against the communistic mode of producing and appropriating intellectual products. Just as to the bourgeois, the disappearance of class property is the disappearance of production itself, so the disappearance of class culture is to him identical with the disappearance of all culture.

That culture, the loss of which he laments, is, for the enormous majority, a mere training to act as a machine.

But don't wrangle with us so long as you apply, to our intended abolition of bourgeois property, the standard of your bourgeois notions of freedom, culture, law, etc. Your very ideas are but the outgrowth of the conditions of your bourgeois production and bourgeois property, just as your jurisprudence is but the will of your class made into a law for all, a will whose essential character and direction are determined by the economical conditions of existence of your class.

The selfish misconception that induces you to transform into eternal laws of nature and of reason the social forms stringing from your present mode of production and form of property—historical relations that rise and disappear in the progress of production—this misconception you share with every ruling class that has preceded you. What you see clearly in the case of ancient property, what you admit in the case of feudal property, you are of course forbidden to admit in the case of your own bourgeois form of property.

Abolition of the family! Even the most radical flare up at this infamous proposal of the Communists.

On what foundation is the present family, the bourgeois family, based? On capital, on private gain. In its completely developed form, this family exists only among the bourgeoisie. But this state of things finds its complement in the practical absence of the family among proletarians, and in public prostitution.

The bourgeois family will vanish as a matter of course when its complement vanishes, and both will vanish with the vanishing of capital.

Do you charge us with wanting to stop the exploitation of children by their parents? To this crime we plead guilty.

But, you say, we destroy the most hallowed of relations, when we replace home education by social.

And your education! Is not that also social, and determined by the social conditions under which you educate, by the intervention direct or indirect, of society, by means of schools, etc.? The Communists have not intended the intervention of society in education; they do but seek to alter the character of that intervention, and to rescue education from the influence of the ruling class.

The bourgeois claptrap about the family and education, about the hallowed correlation of parents and child, becomes all the more disgusting, the more, by the action of Modern Industry, all the family ties among the proletarians are torn asunder, and their children transformed into simple articles of commerce and instruments of labor.

But you Communists would introduce community of women, screams the bourgeoisie in chorus.

The bourgeois sees his wife a mere instrument of production. He hears that the instruments of production are to be exploited in common, and, naturally, can come to no other conclusion that the lot of being common to all will likewise fall to the women.

He has not even a suspicion that the real point aimed at is to do away with the status of women as mere instruments of production.

For the rest, nothing is more ridiculous than the virtuous indignation of our bourgeois at the community of women which, they pretend, is to be openly and officially established by the Communists. The Communists have no need to introduce community of women; it has existed almost from time immemorial.

Our bourgeois, not content with having wives and daughters of their proletarians at their disposal, not to speak of common prostitutes, take the greatest pleasure in seducing each other's wives.

Bourgeois marriage is, in reality, a system of wives in common and thus, at the most, what the Communists might possibly be reproached with is that they desire to introduce, in substitution for a hypocritically concealed, an openly legalized system of free love. For the rest, it is self-evident that the abolition of the present system of production must bring with it the abolition of free love springing from that system, i.e., of prostitution both public and private.

The Communists are further reproached with desiring to abolish countries and nationality.

The workers have no country. We cannot take from them what they have not got. Since the proletariat must first of all acquire political supremacy, must rise to be the leading class of the nation, must constitute itself *the* nation, it is, so far, itself national, though not in the bourgeois sense of the word.

National differences and antagonism between peoples are daily more and more vanishing, owing to the development of the bourgeoisie, to freedom of commerce, to the world market, to uniformity in the mode of production and in the conditions of life corresponding thereto.

The supremacy of the proletariat will cause them to vanish still faster. United action of the leading civilized countries at least is one of the first conditions for the emancipation of the proletariat.

In proportion as the exploitation of one individual by another will also be put an end to, the exploitation of one nation by another will also be put an end to. In proportion as the antagonism between classes within the nation vanishes, the hostility of one nation to another will come to an end.

The charges against communism made from a religious, a philosophical and, generally, from an ideological standpoint, are not deserving of serious examination.

Does it require deep intuition to comprehend that man's ideas, views, and conception, in one word, man's consciousness, changes with every change in the conditions of his material existence, in his social relations and in his social life?

What else does the history of ideas prove, than that intellectual production changes its character in proportion as material production is changed? The ruling ideas of each age have ever been the ideas of its ruling class.

When people speak of the ideas that revolutionize society, they do but express that fact that within the old society the elements of a new one have been created, and that the dissolution of the old ideas keeps even pace with the dissolution of the old conditions of existence.

When the ancient world was in its last throes, the ancient religions were overcome by Christianity. When Christian ideas succumbed in the eighteenth century to rationalist ideas, feudal society fought its death battle with the then revolutionary bourgeoisie. The ideas of religious liberty and freedom of conscience merely gave expression to the sway of free competition within the domain of knowledge.

"Undoubtedly," it will be said, "religious, moral, philosophical, and juridicial ideas have been modified in the course of historical development. But religion, morality, philosophy, political science, and law, constantly survived this change."

"There are, besides, eternal truths, such as Freedom, Justice, etc., that are common to all states of society. But communism abolishes eternal truths, it abolishes all religion, and all morality, instead of constituting them on a new basis; it therefore acts in contradiction to all past historical experience."

What does this accusation reduce itself to? The history of all past society has consisted in the development of class antagonisms, antagonisms that assumed different forms at different epochs.

But whatever form they may have taken, one fact is common to all past ages, viz., the exploitation of one part of society by the other. No wonder, then, that the social consciousness of past ages, despite all the multiplicity and variety it displays, moves within certain common forms, or general ideas, which cannot completely vanish except with the total disappearance of class antagonisms.

The communist revolution is the most radical rupture with traditional relations; no wonder that its development involved the most radical rupture with traditional ideas.

But let us have done with the bourgeois objections to communism.

We have seen above that the first step in the revolution by the working class is to raise the proletariat to the position of ruling class to win the battle of democracy.

The proletariat will use its political supremacy to wrest, by degree, all capital from the bourgeoisie, to centralize all instruments of production in the hands of the state, i.e., of the proletariat organized as the ruling class; and to increase the total productive forces as rapidly as possible.

Of course, in the beginning, this cannot be effected except by means of despotic inroads on the rights of property, and on the conditions of bourgeois production; by means of measures, therefore, which appear economically insufficient and untenable, but which, in the course of the movement, outstrip themselves, necessitate further inroads upon the old social order, and are unavoidable as a means of entirely revolutionizing the mode of production.

These measures will, of course, be different in different countries.

Nevertheless, in most advanced countries, the following will be pretty generally applicable.

1. Abolition of property in land and application of all rents of land to public purposes.
2. A heavy progressive or graduated income tax.
3. Abolition of all rights of inheritance.
4. Confiscation of the property of all emigrants and rebels.
5. Centralization of credit in the banks of the state, by means of a national bank with state capital and an exclusive monopoly.
6. Centralization of the means of communication and transport in the hands of the state.
7. Extension of factories and instruments of production owned by the state; the bringing into cultivation of waste lands, and the improvement of the soil generally in accordance with a common plan.
8. Equal obligation of all to work. Establishment of industrial armies, especially for agriculture.
9. Combination of agriculture with manufacturing industries; gradual abolition of all the distinction between town and country by a more equable distribution of the populace over the country.
10. Free education for all children in public schools. Abolition of children's factory labor in its present form. Combination of education with industrial production, etc.

When, in the course of development, class distinctions have disappeared, and all production has been concentrated in the hands of a vast association of the whole nation, the public power will lose its political character. Political power, properly so called, is merely the organized power of one class for oppressing another. If the proletariat during its contest with the bourgeoisie is compelled, by the force of circumstances, to organize itself as a class; if, by means of a revolution, it makes itself the ruling class, and, as such, sweeps away by force the old conditions of production, then it will, along with these conditions, have swept away the conditions for the existence of class antagonisms and of classes generally, and will thereby have abolished its own supremacy as a class.

In place of the old bourgeois society, with its classes and class antagonisms, we shall have an association in which the free development of each is the condition for the free development of all.

III. Socialist and Communist Literature

1. Reactionary Socialism

(a) *Feudal Socialism.* Owing to their historical position, it became the vocation of the aristocracies of France and England to write pamphlets against modern bourgeois society. In the French Revolution of July 1830, and in the English reform agitation, these aristocracies again succumbed to the hateful upstart. Thenceforth, a serious political struggle was altogether out of the question. A literary battle alone remained possible. But even in the domain of literature, the old cries of the restoration period had become impossible.

In order to arouse sympathy, the aristocracy was obliged to lose sight, apparently, of its own interests, and to formulate its indictment against the bourgeoisie in the interest of the exploited working class alone. Thus, the aristocracy took their revenge by singing lampoons on their new masters and whispering in his ears sinister prophesies of coming catastrophe.

In this way arose feudal socialism: half lamentation, half lampoon; half an echo of the past, half menace of the future; at times, by its bitter, witty and incisive criticism, striking the bourgeoisie to the very heart's core, but always ludicrous in its effect, through total incapacity to comprehend the march of modern history.

The aristocracy, in order to rally the people to them, waved the proletarian almsbag in front for a banner. But the people, so often as it joined them, saw on their hindquarters the old feudal coats of arms, and deserted with loud and irreverent laughter. One section of the French Legitimists and "Young England" exhibited this spectacle:

In pointing out that their mode of exploitation was different to that of the bourgeoisie, the feudalists forget that they exploited under circumstances and conditions that were quite different and that are now antiquated. In showing that, under their rule, the modern proletariat never existed, they forget that the modern bourgeoisie is the necessary offspring of their own form of society.

For the rest, so little do they conceal the reactionary character of their criticism that their chief accusation against the bourgeois amounts to this: that under the bourgeois regime a class is being developed which is destined to cut up, root and branch, the old order of society.

What they upbraid the bourgeoisie with is not so much that it creates a proletariat as that it creates a revolutionary proletariat.

In political practice, therefore, they join in all corrective measures against the working class; and in ordinary life, despite their high falutin' phrases, they stoop to pick up the golden apples dropped from the tree of industry, and to barter truth, love, and honor, for traffic in wool, beetroot-sugar, and potato spirits.

As the parson has ever gone hand in hand with the landlord, so has clerical socialism with feudal socialism.

Nothing is easier than to give Christian asceticism a socialist tinge. Has not Christianity declaimed against private property, against marriage, against the state? Has it not preached in the place of these, charity and poverty, celibacy and mortification of the flesh, monastic life and Mother Church? Christian socialism is but the holy water with which the priest consecrates the heart-burnings of the aristocrat.

(b) *Petty-Bourgeois Socialism.* The feudal aristocracy was not the only class that was ruined by the bourgeoisie, not the only class whose conditions of existence pined and perished in the atmosphere of modern bourgeois society. The medieval burgesses and the small peasant proprietors were the precursors of the modern bourgeoisie. In those countries which are but little developed, industrially and commercially, these two classes still vegetate side by side with the rising bourgeoisie.

In countries where modern civilization has become fully developed, a new class of petty bourgeois has been formed, fluctuating between proletariat and bourgeoisie, and ever renewing itself a supplementary part of bourgeois society. The individual members of this class, however, are being constantly hurled down into the proletariat by the action of competition, and, as Modern Industry develops, they even see the moment approaching when they will completely disappear as an independent section of modern society, to be replaced in manufactures, agriculture and commerce, by overlookers, bailiffs and shopmen.

In countries like France, where the peasants constitute far more than half of the population, it was natural that writers who sided with the proletariat against the bourgeoisie should use, in their criticism of the bourgeois regime, the standard of the peasant and petty bourgeois, and from the standpoint of these intermediate classes, should take up the cudgels for the working class. Thus arose petty-bourgeois socialism. Sismondi was the head of this school, not only in France but also in England.

This school of socialism dissected with great acuteness the contradictions in the conditions of modern production. It laid bare the hypocritical apologies of economists. It proved, incontrovertibly, the disastrous effects of machinery and division of labor; the concentration of capital and land in a few hands; overproduction and crises; it pointed out the inevitable ruin of the petty bourgeois and peasant, the misery of the proletariat, the anarchy in production, the crying inequalities in the distribution of wealth, the industrial war of extermination between nations, the dissolution of old moral bonds, of the old family relations, of the old nationalities.

In its positive aims, however, this form of socialism aspires either to restoring the old means of production and of exchange, and with them the old property relations, and the old society, or to cramping the modern means of production and of exchange within the framework of the old property relations that have been, and were bound to be, exploded by those means. In either case, it is both reactionary and Utopian.

Its last words are: corporate guilds for manufacture; patriarchal relations in agriculture.

Ultimately, when stubborn historical facts had dispersed all intoxicating effects of self-deception, this form of socialism ended in a miserable hangover.

(c) *German or "True" Socialism.* The socialist and communist literature of France, a literature that originated under the pressure of a bourgeoisie in power, and that was the expressions of the struggle against this power, was introduced into Germany at a time when the bourgeoisie in that country had just begun its contest with feudal absolutism.

German philosophers, would-be philosophers, and beaux esprits (men of letters), eagerly seized on this literature, only forgetting that when these writings immigrated from France into Germany, French social conditions had not immigrated along with them. In contact with German social conditions, this French literature lost all its immediate practical significance and assumed a purely literary aspect. Thus, to the German philosophers of the eighteenth century, the demands of the first French Revolution were nothing more than the demands of "Practical Reason" in general, and the utterance of the will of the revolutionary French bourgeoisie signified, in their eyes, the laws of pure will, of will as it was bound to be, of true human will generally.

The work of the German literati consisted solely in bringing the new French ideas into harmony with their ancient philosophical conscience, or rather, in annexing the French ideas without deserting their own philosophic point of view.

This annexation took place in the same way in which a foreign language is appropriated, namely, by translation.

It is well known how the monks wrote silly lives of Catholic saints over the manuscripts on which the classical works of ancient heathendom had been written. The German literati reversed this process with the profane French literature. They wrote their philosophical nonsense beneath the French original. For instance, beneath the French criticism of the economic functions of money, they wrote "alienation of humanity," and beneath the French criticism of the bourgeois state they wrote "dethronement of the category of the general," and so forth.

The introduction of these philosophical phrases at the back of the French historical criticisms, they dubbed "Philosophy of Action," "True Socialism," "German Science of Socialism," "Philosophical Foundation of Socialism," and so on.

The French socialist and communist literature was thus completely emasculated. And, since it ceased, in the hands of the German, to express the struggle of one class with the other, he felt conscious of having overcome "French one-sidedness" and of representing, not true requirements, but the requirements of truth; not the interests of the proletariat, but the interests of human nature, of man in general, who belongs to no class, has no reality, who exists only in the misty realm of philosophical fantasy.

This German socialism, which took its schoolboy task so seriously and solemnly, and extolled its poor stock-in-trade in such a mountebank fashion, meanwhile gradually lost its pedantic innocence.

The fight of the Germans, and especially of the Prussian bourgeoisie, against feudal aristocracy and absolute monarchy, in other words, the liberal movement, became more earnest.

By this, the long-wished for opportunity was offered to "True" Socialism of confronting the political movement with the socialistic demands, of hurling the traditional anathemas against liberalism, against representative government, against bourgeois competition, bourgeois freedom of the press, bourgeois legislation, bourgeois liberty and equality, and of preaching to the masses that they had nothing to gain, and everything to lose, by this bourgeois movement. German socialism forgot, in the nick of time, that the French criticism, whose silly echo it was, presupposed the existence of modern bourgeois society, with its corresponding economic conditions of existence, and the political constitution adapted thereto, the very things whose attainment was the object of the pending struggle in Germany.

To the absolute governments, with their following of parsons, professors, country squires, and officials, it served as a welcome scarecrow against the threatening bourgeoisie.

It was a sweet finish, after the bitter pills of flogging and bullets, with which these same governments, just at that time, dosed the German working-class risings.

While this "True" Socialism thus served the government as a weapon for fighting the German bourgeoisie, it, at the same time, directly represented a reactionary interest, the interest of German philistines. In Germany, the petty-bourgeois class, a relic of the sixteenth century, and since then constantly cropping up again under the various forms, is the real social basis of the existing state of things.

To preserve this class is to preserve the existing state of things in Germany. The industrial and political supremacy of the bourgeoisie threatens it with certain destruction—on the one hand, from the concentration of capital; on the other, from the rise of a revolutionary proletariat. "True" Socialism appeared to kill these two birds with one stone. It spread like an epidemic.

The robe of speculative cobwebs, embroidered with flowers of rhetoric, steeped in the dew of sickly sentiment, this transcendental robe in which the German Socialists wrapped their sorry "eternal truths," all skin and bone, served to wonderfully increase the sale of their goods amongst such a public.

And on its part German socialism recognized, more and more, its own calling as the bombastic representative of the petty-bourgeois philistine.

It proclaimed the German nation to be the model nation, and the German petty philistine to be the typical man. To every villainous meanness of this model man, it gave a hidden, higher, socialistic interpretation, the exact contrary of its real character. It went to the extreme length of directly opposing the "brutally destructive" tendency of communism, and of proclaiming its supreme and impartial contempt of all class struggles. With very few exceptions, all the so-called socialist and communist publications that now (1847) circulate in Germany belong to the domain of this foul and enervating literature.

2. Conservative or Bourgeois Socialism

A part of the bourgeoisie is desirous of redressing social grievances in order to secure the continued existence of bourgeois society.

To this section belong economists, philanthropists, humanitarians, improvers of the condition of the working class, organizers of charity, members of societies for the prevention of cruelty to animals, temperance fanatics, hole-and-corner reformers of every imaginable kind. This form of socialism has, moreover, been worked out into complete systems.

We may cite Proudhon's *Philosophy of Poverty* as an example of this form.

The socialistic bourgeois want all the advantages of modern social conditions without the struggles and dangers necessarily resulting therefrom. They desire the existing state of society, minus its revolutionary and disintegrating elements. They wish for a bourgeoisie without a proletariat. The bourgeoisie naturally conceives the world in which it is supreme to be the best; and bourgeois socialism develops this comfortable conception into various more or less complete systems. In requiring the proletariat to carry out such a system, and thereby to march straightaway into the social New Jerusalem, it but requires in reality that the proletariat should remain within the bounds of existing society, but should cast away all its hateful ideas concerning the bourgeoisie.

A second, and more practical, but less systematic, form of this socialism sought to depreciate every revolutionary movement in the eyes of the working class by showing that no mere political reform, but only a change in the material conditions of existence, in economical relations, could be of any advantage to them. By changes in the material conditions of existence, this form of socialism, however, by no means understands abolition of the bourgeois relations of production, an abolition that can be affected only by a revolution, but administrative reforms, based on the continued existence of these relations; reforms, therefore, that in no respect affect the relations between capital and labor, but, at the best, lessen the cost, and simplify the administrative work of bourgeois government.

Bourgeois socialism attains adequate expression when, and only when, it becomes a mere figure of speech.

Free trade: for the benefit of the working class. Protective duties: for the benefit of the working class. Prison reform: for the benefit of the working class. This is the last word and the only seriously meant word of bourgeois socialism.

It is summed up in the phrase: the bourgeois is a bourgeois—for the benefit of the working class.

3. Critical-Utopian Socialism and Communism

We do not here refer to that literature which, in every great modern revolution, has always given voice to the demands of the proletariat, such as the writings of Babeuf and others.

The first direct attempts of the proletariat to attain its own ends, made in times of universal excitement, when feudal society was being overthrown, necessarily failed, owing to the then undeveloped state of the proletariat, as well as to the absence of the economic conditions for its emancipation, conditions that had yet to be produced, and could be produced by the impending bourgeois epoch alone. The revolutionary literature that accompanied these first movements of the proletariat had necessarily a reactionary character. It inculcated universal asceticism and social levelling in its crudest form.

The socialist and communist systems, properly so called, those of Saint-Simon, Fourier, Owen, and others, spring into existence in the early undeveloped period, described above, of the struggle between proletariat and bourgeoisie (see Section 1. Bourgeois and Proletarians).

The founders of these systems see, indeed, the class antagonisms, as well as the action of the decomposing elements in the prevailing form of society. But the proletariat, as yet in its infancy, offers to them the spectacle of a class without any historical initiative or any independent political movement.

Since the development of class antagonism keeps even pace with the development of industry, the economic situation, as they find it, does not as yet offer to them the material conditions for the emancipation of the proletariat. They therefore search after a new social science, after new social laws, that are to create these conditions.

Historical action is to yield to their personal inventive action; historically created conditions of emancipation to fantastic ones; and the gradual, spontaneous class organization of the proletariat to an organization of society especially contrived by these inventors. Future history resolves itself, in their eyes, into the propaganda and the practical carrying out of their social plans.

In the formation of their plans, they are conscious of caring chiefly for the interests of the working class, as being the most suffering class. Only from the point of view of being the most suffering class does the proletariat exist for them.

The undeveloped state of the class struggle, as well as their own surroundings, causes Socialists of this kind to consider themselves far superior to all class antagonisms. They want to improve the condition of every member of society, even that of the most favored. Hence, they habitually appeal to society at large, without the distinction of class; nay, by preference, to the ruling class. For how can people when once they understand their system, fail to see in it the best possible plan of the best possible state of society?

Hence, they reject all political, and especially all revolutionary action; they wish to attain their ends by peaceful means, necessarily doomed to failure, and by the force of example, to pave the way for the new social gospel.

Such fantastic pictures of future society, painted at a time when the proletariat is still in a very undeveloped state and has but a fantastic conception of its own position, correspond with the first instinctive yearnings of that class for a general reconstruction of society.

But these socialist and communist publications contain also a critical element. They attack every principle of existing society. Hence, they are full of the most valuable materials for the enlightenment of the working class. The practical measures proposed in them—such as the abolition of the distinction between town and country, of the family, of the carrying on of industries for the account of private individuals, and of the wage system, the proclamation of social harmony, the conversion of the function of the state into a more superintendence of production—all these proposals point solely to the disappearance of class antagonisms which were, at that time, only just cropping up, and which, in these publications, are recognized in their earliest indistinct and undefined forms only. These proposals, therefore, are of a purely utopian character.

The significance of critical-utopian socialism and communism bears an inverse relation to historical development. In proportion as the modern class struggle develops and takes definite shape, this fantastic standing apart from the contest, these fantastic attacks on it, lose all practical value and all theoretical justifications. Therefore, although the originators of these systems were, in many respects, revolutionary, their disciples have, in every case, formed mere reactionary sects. They hold fast by the original views of their masters, in opposition to the progressive historical development of the proletariat. They, therefore, endeavor, and that consistently, to deaden the class struggle and to reconcile the class antagonisms. They still dream of experimental realization of their social utopias, of founding isolated *phalansteres*, of establishing "Home Colonies," or setting up a "Little Icaria"—pocket editions of the New Jerusalem—and to realize all these castles in the air, they are compelled to appeal to the feelings and purses of the bourgeois. By degrees, they sink into the category of the reactionary conservative socialists depicted above, differing from these only by more systematic pedantry, and by their fanatical and superstitious belief in the miraculous effects of their social science.

They, therefore, violently oppose all political action on the part of the working class; such action, according to them, can only result from blind unbelief in the new gospel.

The Owenites in England, and the Fourierists in France, respectively, oppose the Chartists and the Reformistes.

IV. Position of the Communists in Relation to the Various Existing Opposition Parties

Section II has made clear the relations of the Communists to the existing working-class parties, such as the Chartists in England and the Agrarian Reformers in America.

The Communists fight for the attainment of the immediate aims, for the enforcement of the momentary interests of the working class; but in the movement of the present, they also represent and take care of the future of that movement. In France, the Communists ally with the Social Democrats against the conservative and radical bourgeoisie, reserving, however, the right to take up a critical position in regard to phases and illusions traditionally handed down from the Great Revolution.

In Switzerland, they support the Radicals, without losing sight of the fact that this party consists of antagonistic elements, partly of Democratic Socialists, in the French sense, partly of radical bourgeois.

In Poland, they support the party that insists on an agrarian revolution as the prime condition for national emancipation, that party which fomented the insurrection of Krakow in 1846.

In Germany, they fight with the bourgeoisie whenever it acts in a revolutionary way, against the absolute monarchy, the feudal squirearchy, and the petty-bourgeoisie.

But they never cease, for a single instant, to instill into the working class the clearest possible recognition of the hostile antagonism between bourgeoisie and proletariat, in order that the German workers may straightway use, as so many weapons against the bourgeoisie, the social and political conditions that the bourgeoisie must necessarily introduce along with its supremacy, and in order that, after the fall of the reactionary classes in Germany, the fight against the bourgeoisie itself may immediately begin.

The Communists turn their attention chiefly to Germany, because that country is on the eve of a bourgeois revolution that is bound to be carried out under more advanced conditions of European civilization and with a much more developed proletariat than that of England was in the seventeenth, and France in the eighteenth century, and because the bourgeois revolution in Germany will be but the prelude to an immediately following proletarian revolution.

In short, the Communists everywhere support every revolutionary movement against the existing social and political order of things.

In all these movements, they bring to the front, as the leading question in each, the property question, no matter what its degree of development at the time.

Finally, they labor everywhere for the union and agreement of the democratic parties of all countries.

The Communists disdain to conceal their views and aims. They openly declare that their ends can be attained only by the forcible overthrow of all existing social conditions. Let the ruling classes tremble at a communist revolution. The proletarians have nothing to lose but their chains. They have a world to win.

PROLETARIANS OF ALL COUNTRIES, UNITE!

Friedrich List,
The National System of Political Economy (1841)*

Chapter XII: The Theory of the Powers of Production and the Theory of Values

Adam Smith's celebrated work is entitled, 'The Nature and Causes of the Wealth of Nations.' The founder of the prevailing economical school has therein indicated the double point of view from which the economy of nations, like that of private separate individuals, should be regarded.

The causes of wealth are something totally different from *wealth itself*. A person may possess wealth, i.e. exchangeable value; if, however, he does not possess the power of producing objects of more value than he consumes, he will become poorer. A person may be poor; if he, however, possesses the power of producing a larger amount of valuable articles than he consumes, he becomes rich.

The power of producing wealth is therefore infinitely more important than *wealth itself*; it insures not only the possession and the increase of what has been gained, but also the replacement of what has been lost. This is still more the case with entire nations (who cannot live out of mere rentals) than with private individuals. Germany has been devastated in every century by pestilence, by famine, or by civil or foreign wars; she has, nevertheless, always retained a great portion of her powers of production, and has thus quickly re-attained some degree of prosperity; while rich and mighty but despot- and priest-ridden Spain, notwithstanding her comparative enjoyment of internal peace, has sunk deeper into poverty and misery. The same sun still shines on the Spaniards, they still possess the same area of territory, their mines are still as rich, they are still the same people as before the discovery of America, and before the introduction of the Inquisition; but that nation has gradually lost her powers of production, and has therefore become poor and miserable. The War of Independence of the United States of America cost that nation hundreds of millions, but her powers of production were immeasurably strengthened by gaining independence, and it was for this reason that in the course of a few years after the peace she obtained immeasurably greater riches than she had ever possessed before. If we compare the state of France in the year 1809 with that of the year 1839, what a difference in favour of the latter! Nevertheless, France has in the interim lost her sovereignty over a large portion of the European continent; she has suffered two devastating invasions, and had to pay milliards of money in war contributions and indemnities.

It was impossible that so clear an intellect as Adam Smith possessed could altogether ignore the difference between wealth and its causes and the overwhelming influence

---

* Excerpts from: *The National System of Political Economy* (1841), Friedrich List. Material in the public domain.

of these causes on the condition of nations. In the introduction to his work, he says in clear words in effect: 'Labour forms the fund from which every nation derives its wealth, and the increase of wealth depends first on the *productive power* of labour, namely, on the degree of skill, dexterity, and judgment with which the labour of the nation is generally applied, and secondly, on the proportion between the number of those employed productively and the number of those who are not so employed.' From this we see how clearly Smith in general perceived that the condition of nations is principally dependent on the sum of their *productive powers.*

It does not, however, appear to be the plan of nature that complete sciences should spring already perfected from the brain of individual thinkers. It is evident that Smith was too exclusively possessed by the cosmopolitical idea of the physiocrats, 'universal freedom of trade,' and by his own great discovery, 'the division of labour,' to follow up the idea of the importance to a nation of its *powers of production.* However much science may be indebted to him in respect of the remaining parts of his work, the idea 'division of labour' seemed to him his most brilliant thought. It was calculated to secure for his book a name, and for himself posthumous fame.

He had too much worldly wisdom not to perceive that whoever wishes to sell a precious jewel does not bring the treasure to market most profitably by burying it in a sack of wheat, however useful the grains of wheat may be, but better by exposing it at the forefront. He had too much experience not to know that a *debutant* (and he was this as regards political economy at the time of the publication of his work) who in the first act creates a *furore* is easily excused if in the following ones he only occasionally raises himself above mediocrity; he had every motive for making the introduction to his book, the doctrine of division of labour. Smith has not been mistaken in his calculations; his first chapter has made the fortune of his book, and founded his authority as an economist.

However, we on our part believe ourselves able to prove that just this zeal to put the important discovery *'division of labour'* in an advantageous light, has hindered Adam Smith from following up the idea *'productive power'* (which has been expressed by him in the introduction, and also frequently afterwards, although merely incidentally) and from exhibiting his doctrines in a much more perfect form. By the great value which he attached to his idea *'division of labour'* he has evidently been misled into representing labour itself as the 'fund' of all the wealth of nations, although he himself clearly perceives and also states that the productiveness of labour principally depends on the degree of skill and judgment with which the labour is performed. We ask, can it be deemed scientific reasoning if we assign as the cause of a phenomenon that which in itself is the result of a number of deeper lying causes? It cannot be doubted that all wealth is obtained by means of mental and bodily exertions (labour), but yet from that circumstance no reason is indicated from which useful conclusions may be drawn; for history teaches that whole nations have, in spite of the exertions and of the thrift of their citizens, fallen into poverty and misery. Whoever desires to know and investigate how one nation from a state of poverty and barbarism has attained to one of wealth and prosperity, and how another has fallen from a condition of wealth and well-being into one of poverty and misery, has always, after receiving the information that labour is the cause of wealth and idleness the cause of poverty (a remark which

King Solomon made long before Adam Smith), to put the further question, what are the causes of labour, and what the causes of idleness?

It would be more correct to describe the limbs of men (the head, hands, and feet) as the causes of wealth (we should thus at least approach far nearer to the truth), and the question then presents itself, what is it that induces these heads, arms, and hands to produce, and calls into activity these exertions? What else can it be than the spirit which animates the individuals, the social order which renders their energy fruitful, and the powers of nature which they are in a position to make use of? The more a man perceives that he must provide for the future, the more his intelligence and feelings incite him to secure the future of his nearest connections, and to promote their well-being; the more he has been from his youth accustomed to forethought and activity, the more his nobler feelings have been developed, and body and mind cultivated, the finer examples that he has witnessed from his youth, the more opportunities he has had for utilising his mental and bodily powers for the improvement of his condition, also the less he has been restrained in his legitimate activity, the more successful his past endeavours have been, and the more their fruits have been secured to him, the more he has been able to obtain public recognition and esteem by orderly conduct and activity, and the less his mind suffers from prejudices, superstition, false notions, and ignorance, so much the more will he exert his mind and limbs for the object of production, so much the more will he be able to accomplish, and so much the better will he make use of the fruits of his labour. However, most depends in all these respects on the conditions of the society in which the individual has been brought up, and turns upon this, whether science and arts flourish, and public institutions and laws tend to promote religious character, morality and intelligence, security for person and for property, freedom and justice; whether in the nation all the factors of material prosperity, agriculture, manufactures, and trade, have been equally and harmoniously cultivated; whether the power of the nation is strong enough to secure to its individual citizens progress in wealth and education from generation to generation, and to enable them not merely to utilise the natural powers of their own country to their fullest extent, but also, by foreign trade and the possession of colonies, to render the natural powers of foreign countries serviceable to their own.

Adam Smith has on the whole recognised the nature of these powers so little, that he does not even assign a productive character to the mental labours of those who maintain laws and order, and cultivate and promote instruction, religion, science, and art. His investigations are limited to that human activity which creates material values. With regard to this, he certainly recognises that its productiveness depends on the 'skill and judgment' with which it is exercised; but in his investigations as to the causes of this skill and judgment, he does not go farther than the division of labour, and that he illustrates solely by exchange, augmentation of material capital, and extension of markets. His doctrine at once sinks deeper and deeper into materialism, particularism, and individualism. If he had followed up the idea *'productive power'* without allowing his mind to be dominated by the idea of 'value,' 'exchangeable value,' he would have been led to perceive that an independent *theory of the 'productive power,'* must be considered by the side of a *'theory of values'* in order to explain the economical phenomena. But he thus fell into the mistake of explaining mental forces from material circumstances and conditions, and thereby laid the foundation for all the absurdities and contradictions from which his school (as we propose to prove) suffers up to the present day, and to which alone it must be attributed that the doctrines of political economy are those which are the least accessible to the most intelligent minds. That Smith's school teaches nothing else than the theory of values, is not only seen from the fact that it bases its doctrine everywhere on the conception of 'value of exchange,' but also from the definition which it gives of its doctrine. It is (says J.B. Say) that science which teaches how riches, or exchangeable values, are produced, distributed, and consumed. This is undoubtedly not the science which teaches how the *productive powers* are awakened and developed, and how they become depressed and destroyed. M'Culloch calls it explicitly *'the science of values,'* and recent English writers *'the science of exchange.'*

Examples from private economy will best illustrate the difference between the theory of productive powers and the theory of values.

Let us suppose the case of two fathers of families, both being landed proprietors, each of whom saves yearly 1,000 thalers and has five sons. The one puts out his savings at interest, and keeps his sons at common hard work, while the other employs his savings in educating two of his sons as skillful and intelligent landowners, and in enabling the other three to learn a trade after their respective tastes; the former acts according to the theory of values, the latter according to the theory of productive powers. The first at his death may prove much richer than the second in mere exchangeable value, but it is quite otherwise as respects productive powers. The estate of the latter is divided into two parts, and every part will by the aid of improved management yield as much total produce as the whole did before; while the remaining three sons have by their talents obtained abundant means of maintenance. The landed property of the former will be divided into five parts, and every part will be worked in as bad a manner as the whole was heretofore. In the latter family a mass of different mental forces and talents is awakened and cultivated, which will increase from generation to generation, every succeeding generation possessing more power of obtaining material wealth than the preceding one, while in the former family stupidity and poverty must increase with the diminution of the shares in the landed property. So the slaveholder increases by slave-breeding the sum of his values of exchange, but he ruins the productive forces of future generations. All expenditure in the instruction of youth, the promotion of justice, defence of nations, &c. is a consumption of present values for the behoof of the productive powers. The greatest portion of the consumption of a nation is used for the education of the future generation, for promotion and nourishment of the future national productive powers.

The Christian religion, monogamy, abolition of slavery and of vassalage, hereditability of the throne, invention of printing, of the press, of the postal system, of money weights and measures, of the calendar, of watches, of police, the introduction of the principle of freehold property, of means of transport, are rich sources of productive power. To be convinced of this, we need only compare the condition of the European states with that of the Asiatic ones. In order duly to estimate the influence which liberty of thought and conscience has on the productive forces of nations, we need only read the history of England and then that of Spain. The publicity of the administration of justice, trial by jury, parliamentary legislation, public control of State administration, self-administration of the commonalties and municipalities, liberty of the press, liberty of association for useful purposes, impart to the citizens of constitutional states, as also to their public functionaries, a degree of energy and power which can hardly be produced by other means. We can scarcely conceive of any law or any public legal decision which would not exercise a greater or smaller influence on the increase or decrease of the productive power of the nation.

If we consider merely bodily labour as the cause of wealth, how can we then explain why modern nations are incomparably richer, more populous, more powerful, and prosperous than the nations of ancient times? The ancient nations employed (in proportion to the whole population) infinitely more hands, the work was much harder, each individual possessed much more land, and yet the masses were much worse fed and clothed than is the case in modern nations. In order to explain these phenomena, we must refer to the progress which has been made in the course of the last thousand years in sciences and arts, domestic and public regulations, cultivation of the mind and capabilities of production. The present state of the nations is the result of the accumulation of all discoveries, inventions, improvements, perfections, and exertions of all generations which have lived before us; they form the mental capital of the present human race, and every separate nation is productive only in the proportion in which it has known how to appropriate these attainments of former generations and to increase them by its own acquirements, in which the natural capabilities of its territory, its extent and geographical position, its population and political power, have been able to develop as completely and symmetrically as possible all sources of wealth within its boundaries, and to extend its moral, intellectual, commercial, and political influence over less advanced nations and especially over the affairs of the world.

The popular school of economists would have us believe that politics and political power cannot be taken into consideration in political economy. So far as it makes only values and exchange the subjects of its investigations, this may be correct; we can define the ideas of value and capital, profit, wages, and rent; we can resolve them into their elements, and speculate on what may influence their rising or falling, &c. without thereby taking into account the political circumstances of the nation. Clearly, however, these matters appertain as much to private economy as to the economy of whole nations. We have merely to consider the history of Venice, of the Hanseatic League, of Portugal, Holland, and England, in order to perceive what reciprocal influence material wealth and political power exercise on each other.

The school also always falls into the strangest inconsistencies whenever this reciprocal influence forces itself on their consideration. Let us here only call to mind the remarkable dictum of Adam Smith on the English Navigation Laws.

The popular school, inasmuch as it does not duly consider the nature of the powers of production, and does not take into account the conditions of nations in their aggregate, disregards especially the importance of developing in an equal ratio agriculture, manufactures and commerce, political power and internal wealth, and disregards especially the value of a manufacturing power belonging specially to the nation and fully developed in all its branches. It commits the error of placing manufacturing power in the same category with agricultural power, and of speaking of labour, natural power, capital, &c. in general terms without considering the differences which exist between them. It does not perceive that between a State devoted merely to agriculture and a State possessing both agriculture and manufactures, a much greater difference exists than between a pastoral State and an agricultural one. In a condition of merely agricultural industry, caprice and slavery, superstition and ignorance, want of means of culture, of trade, and of transport, poverty and political weakness exist. In the merely agricultural State only the least portion of the mental and bodily powers existing in the nation is awakened and developed, and only the least part of the powers and resources placed by nature at its disposal can be made use of, while little or no capital can be accumulated.

Let us compare Poland with England: both nations at one time were in the same stage of culture; and now what a difference. Manufactories and manufactures are the mothers and children of municipal liberty, of intelligence, of the arts and sciences, of internal and external commerce, of navigation and improvements in transport, of civilisation and political power. They are the chief means of liberating agriculture from its chains, and of elevating it to a commercial character and to a degree of art and science, by which the rents, farming profits, and wages are increased, and greater value is given to landed property. The popular school has attributed this civilising power to foreign trade, but in that it has confounded the mere exchanger with the originator. Foreign manufactures furnish the goods for the foreign trade, which the latter conveys to us, and which occasion consumption of products and raw materials which we give in exchange for the goods in lieu of money payments.

If, however, trade in the manufactures of far distant lands exercises admittedly so beneficial an influence on our agricultural industry, how much more beneficial must the influence be of those manufactures which are bound up with us locally, commercially, and politically, which not only take from us a small portion, but the largest portion of their requirements of food and of raw materials, which are not made dearer to us by great costs of transport, our trade in which cannot be interrupted by the chance of foreign manufacturing nations learning to supply their own wants themselves, or by wars and prohibitory import duties?

We now see into what extraordinary mistakes and contradictions the popular school has fallen in making material wealth or value of exchange the sole object of its investigations, and by regarding mere bodily labour as the sole productive power.

The man who breeds pigs is, according to this school, a productive member of the community, but he who educates men is a mere non-productive. The maker of bagpipes or jews-harps for sale is a productive, while the great composers and virtuosos are non-productive simply because that which they play cannot be brought into the market. The physician who saves the lives of his patients does not belong to the productive class, but on the contrary the chemist's boy does so, although the values of exchange (viz. the pills) which he produces may exist only for a few minutes before they pass into a valueless condition. A Newton, a Watt, or a Kepler is not so productive as a donkey, a horse, or a draught-ox (a class of labourers who have been recently introduced by M'Culloch into the series of the productive members of human society).

We must not believe that J.B. Say has remedied this defect in the doctrine of Adam Smith by his fiction of 'immaterial goods' or products; he has thus merely somewhat varnished over the folly of its results, but not raised it out of its intrinsic absurdity. The mental (immaterial) producers are merely productive, according to his views, because they are remunerated with values of exchange, and because their attainments have been obtained by sacrificing values of exchange, and not because they produce productive powers. They merely seem to him an accumulated capital. M'Culloch goes still further; he says that man is as much a product of labour as the machine which he produces, and it appears to him that in all economical investigations he must be regarded from this point of view. He thinks that Smith comprehended the correctness of this principle, only he did not deduce the correct conclusion from it. Among other things he draws the conclusion that eating and drinking are productive occupations. Thomas Cooper values a clever American lawyer at 3,000 dollars, which is about three times as much as the value of a strong slave.

The errors and contradictions of the prevailing school to which we have drawn attention, can be easily corrected from the standpoint of *the theory of the productive powers*. Certainly those who fatten pigs or prepare pills are productive, but the instructors of youths and of adults, virtuosos, musicians, physicians, judges, and administrators, are productive in a much higher degree. The former *produce values of exchange,* and the latter *productive powers,* some by enabling the future generation to become producers, others by furthering the morality and religious character of the present generation, a third by ennobling and raising the powers of the human mind, a fourth by preserving the productive powers of his patients, a fifth by rendering human rights and justice secure, a sixth by constituting and protecting public security, a seventh by his art and by the enjoyment which it occasions fitting men the better to produce values of exchange. In the doctrine of mere values, these *producers of the productive powers* can of course only be taken into consideration so far as their services are rewarded by values of exchange; and this manner of regarding their services may in some instances have its practical use, as e.g. in the doctrine of public taxes, inasmuch as these have to be satisfied by values of exchange. But whenever our consideration is given to the nation (as a whole and in its international relations) it is utterly insufficient, and leads to a series of narrow-minded and false views.

The prosperity of a nation is not, as Say believes, greater in the proportion in which it has amassed more wealth (i.e. values of exchange), but in the proportion in which it has more *developed its powers of production*. Although laws and public institutions do not produce immediate values, they nevertheless produce productive powers, and Say is mistaken if he maintains that nations have been enabled to become wealthy under all forms of government, and that by means of laws no wealth can be created. The foreign trade of a nation must not be estimated in the way in which individual merchants judge it, solely and only according to the theory of values (i.e. by regarding merely the gain at any particular moment of some material advantage); the nation is bound to keep steadily in view all these conditions on which its present and future existence, prosperity, and power depend.

The nation must sacrifice and give up a measure of material property in order to gain culture, skill, and powers of united production; it must sacrifice some present advantages in order to insure to itself future ones. If, therefore, a manufacturing power developed in all its branches forms a fundamental condition of all higher advances in civilisation, material prosperity, and political power in every nation (a fact which, we think, we have proved from history); if it be true (as we believe we can prove) that in the present conditions of the world a new unprotected manufacturing power cannot possibly be raised up under free competition with a power which has long since grown in strength and is protected on its own territory; how can anyone possibly undertake to prove by arguments only based on the mere theory of values, that a nation ought to buy its goods like individual merchants, at places where they are to be had the cheapest—that we act foolishly if we manufacture anything at all which can be got cheaper from abroad—that we ought to place the industry of the nation at the mercy of the self-interest of individuals—that protective duties constitute monopolies, which are granted to the individual home manufacturers at the expense of the nation? It is true that protective duties at first increase the price of manufactured goods; but it is just as true, and moreover acknowledged by the prevailing economical school, that in the course of time, by the nation being enabled to build up a completely developed manufacturing power of its own, those goods are produced more cheaply at home than the price at which they can be imported from foreign parts. If, therefore, a sacrifice of *value* is caused by protective duties, it is made good by the gain of a *power of production,* which not only secures to the nation an infinitely greater amount of material goods, but also industrial independence in case of war. Through industrial independence and the internal prosperity derived from it the nation obtains the means for successfully carrying on foreign trade and for extending its mercantile marine; it increases its civilisation, perfects its institutions internally, and strengthens its external power. A nation capable of developing a manufacturing power, if it makes use of the system of protection, thus acts quite in the same spirit as that landed proprietor did who by the sacrifice of some material wealth allowed some of his children to learn a productive trade.

Into what mistakes the prevailing economical school has fallen by judging conditions according to the mere theory of values which ought properly to be judged according to the theory of powers of production, may be seen very clearly by the judgment which J.B. Say passes upon the bounties which foreign countries sometimes offer in order to facilitate exportation; he maintains that '*these are presents made to our nation.*' Now if we suppose that France considers a protective duty of twenty-five per cent sufficient for her not yet perfectly developed manufactures, while England were to grant a bounty on exportation of thirty per cent, what would be the consequence of the 'present' which in this manner the English would make to the French? The French consumers would obtain for a few years the manufactured articles which they needed much cheaper than hitherto, but the French manufactories would be ruined, and millions of men be reduced to beggary or obliged to emigrate, or to devote themselves to agriculture for employment. Under the most favourable circumstances, the present consumers and customers of the French agriculturists would be converted into competitors with the latter, agricultural production would be increased, and the consumption lowered. The necessary consequence would be diminution in value of the products, decline in the value of property, national poverty and national weakness in France. The English 'present' in mere value would be dearly paid for in loss of power; it would seem like the present which the Sultan is wont to make to his pashas by sending them valuable *silken cords.*

Since the time when the Trojans were 'presented' by the Greeks with a wooden horse, the acceptance of 'presents' from other nations has become for the nation which receives them a very questionable transaction. The English have given the Continent presents of immense value in the form of subsidies, but the Continental nations have paid for them dearly by the loss of power. These subsidies acted like a bounty on exportation in favour of the English, and were detrimental to the German manufactories. If England bound herself to-day to supply the Germans gratuitously for years with all they required in manufactured articles, we could not recommend them to accept such an offer. If the English are enabled through new inventions to produce linen forty per cent cheaper than the Germans can by using the old process, and if in the use of their new process they merely obtain a start of a few years over the Germans, in such a case, were it not for protective duties, one of the most important and oldest branches of Germany's industry will be ruined. It will be as if a limb of the body of the German nation had been lost. And who would be consoled for the loss of an arm by knowing that he had nevertheless bought his shirts forty per cent cheaper?

If the English very often find occasion to offer presents to foreign nations, very different are the forms in which this is done; it is not unfrequently done against their will; always does it behove foreign nations well to consider whether or not the present should be accepted. Through their position as the manufacturing and commercial monopolists of the world, their manufactories from time to time fall into the state which they call 'glut,' and which arises from what they call 'overtrading.' At such periods everybody throws his stock of goods into the steamers. After the elapse of eight days the goods are offered for sale in Hamburg, Berlin, or Frankfort, and after three weeks in New York, at fifty per cent under their real value. The English manufacturers suffer for the moment, but they are saved, and they compensate themselves later on by better prices. The German and American manufacturers receive the blows which were deserved by the English—they are ruined. The English nation merely sees the fire and hears the report of the explosion; the fragments fall down in other countries, and if their inhabitants complain of bloody heads, the intermediate merchants and dealers say, 'The crisis has done it all!' If we consider how often by such crises the whole manufacturing power, the system of credit, nay the agriculture, and generally the whole economical system of the nations who are placed in free competition with England, are shaken to their foundations, and that these nations have afterwards notwithstanding richly to recompense the English manufacturers by higher prices, ought we not then to become very sceptical as to the propriety, of the commercial conditions of nations being regulated according to the mere theory of values and according to cosmopolitical principles? The prevailing economical school has never deemed it expedient to elucidate the causes and effects of such commercial crises.

The great statesmen of all modern nations, almost without exception, have comprehended the great influence of manufactures and manufactories on the wealth, civilisation, and power of nations, and the necessity of protecting them. Edward III comprehended this like Elizabeth; Frederick the Great like Joseph II; Washington like Napoleon. Without entering into the depths of the industry theory, their foreseeing minds comprehended the nature of in its entirety, and appreciated it correctly. It was reserved for the school of physiocrats to regard this nature from another point of view in consequence of a sophistical line of reasoning. Their castle in the air has disappeared; the more modern economical school itself has destroyed it; but even the latter has also not disentangled itself from the original errors, but has merely advanced somewhat farther from them. Since it did not recognise the difference between productive power and mere values of exchange, and did not investigate the former independently of the latter, but subordinated it to the theory of values of exchange, it was impossible for that school to arrive at the perception how greatly the nature of the agricultural productive power differs from the nature of the manufacturing productive power. It does not discern that through the development of a manufacturing industry in an agricultural nation a mass of mental and bodily powers, of natural powers and natural resources, and of instrumental powers too (which latter the prevailing school terms 'capital'), is brought to bear, and brought into use, which had not previously been active, and would never have come into activity but for the formation and development of an internal manufacturing power; it imagines that by the establishment of manufacturing industry these forces must be taken away from agriculture, and transferred to manufacture, whereas the latter to a great extent is a perfectly new and additional power, which, very far indeed from increasing at the expense of the agricultural interest, is often the means of helping that interest to attain a higher degree of prosperity and development.

Chapter XIV: Private Economy and National Economy

We have proved historically that the unity of the nation forms the fundamental condition of lasting national prosperity; and we have shown that only where the interest of individuals has been subordinated to those of the nation, and where successive generations have striven for one and the same object, the nations have been brought to harmonious development of their productive powers, and how little private industry can prosper without the united efforts both of the individuals who are living at the time, and of successive generations directed to one common object. We have further tried to prove in the last chapter how the law of union of powers exhibits its beneficial operation in the individual manufactory, and how it acts with equal power on the industry of whole nations. In the present chapter we have now to demonstrate how the popular school has concealed its misunderstanding of the national interests and of the effects of national union of powers, by confounding the principles of private economy with those of national economy.

 'What is prudence in the conduct of every private family,' says Adam Smith, 'can scarce be folly in that of a great kingdom.' Every individual in pursuing his own interests necessarily promotes thereby also the interests of the community. It is evident that every individual, inasmuch as he knows his own local circumstances best and pays most attention to his occupation, is far better able to judge than the statesman or legislator how his capital can most profitably be invested. He who would venture to give advice to the people how to invest their capital would not merely take upon himself a useless task, but would also assume to himself an authority which belongs solely to the producer, and which can be entrusted to those persons least of all who consider themselves equal to so difficult a task. Adam Smith concludes from this: 'Restrictions on trade imposed on the behalf of the internal industry of a country, are mere folly; every nation, like every individual, ought to buy articles where they can be procured the cheapest; in order to attain to the highest degree of national prosperity, we have simply to follow the maxim of letting things alone (laisser faire et laisser aller).' Smith and Say compare a nation which seeks to promote its industry by protective duties, to a tailor who wants to make his own boots, and to a bootmaker who would impose a toll on those who enter his door, in order to promote his prosperity. As in all errors of the popular school, so also in this one does Thomas Cooper go to extremes in his book which is directed against the American system of protection. 'Political economy,' he alleges, 'is almost synonymous with the private economy of all individuals; *politics are no essential ingredient of political economy;* it is folly to suppose that the community is something quite different from the individuals of whom it is composed. Every individual knows best how to invest his labour and his capital. The wealth of the community is nothing else than the aggregate of the wealth of all its individual members; and if every individual can provide best for himself, that nation must be the richest in which every individual is most left to himself.' The adherents of the American system of protection had opposed themselves to this argument, which had formerly been adduced by importing merchants in favour of free trade; the American navigation laws had greatly increased the carrying trade, the foreign commerce, and fisheries of the United States; and for the mere protection of their mercantile marine millions had been annually expended on their fleet; according to his theory those laws and this expense also would be as reprehensible as protective duties. 'In any case,' exclaims Mr. Cooper, 'no commerce by sea is worth a naval war; the merchants may be left to protect themselves.'

Thus the popular school, which had begun by ignoring the principles of nationality and national interests, finally comes to the point of altogether denying their existence, and of leaving individuals to defend them as they may solely by their own individual powers.

How? Is the wisdom of private economy, also wisdom in national economy? Is it in the nature of individuals to take into consideration the wants of future centuries, as those concern the nature of the nation and the State? Let us consider only the first beginning of an American town; every individual left to himself would care merely for his own wants, or at the most for those of his nearest successors, whereas all individuals united in one community provide for the convenience and the wants of the most distant generations; they subject the present generation for this object to privations and sacrifices which no reasonable person could expect from individuals. Can the individual further take into consideration in promoting his private economy, the defence of the country, public security and the thousand other objects which can only be attained by the aid of the whole community? Does not the State require individuals to limit their private liberty according to what these objects require? Does it not even require that they should sacrifice for these some part of their earnings, of their mental and bodily labour, nay, even their own life? We must first root out, as Cooper does, the very ideas of 'State' and 'nation' before this opinion can be entertained.

No; that may be wisdom in national economy which would be folly in private economy, and vice versâ; and owing to the very simple reason, that a tailor is no nation and a nation no tailor, that one family is something very different from a community of millions of families, that one house is something very different from a large national territory. Nor does the individual merely by understanding his own interests best, and by striving to further them, if left to his own devices, always further the interests of the community. We ask those who occupy the benches of justice, whether they do not frequently have to send individuals to the tread-mill on account of their excess of inventive power, and of their all too great industry. Robbers, thieves, smugglers, and cheats know their own local and personal circumstances and conditions extremely well, and pay the most active attention to their business; but it by no means follows therefrom, that society is in the best condition where such individuals are least restrained in the exercise of their private industry.

In a thousand cases the power of the State is compelled to impose restrictions on private industry. It prevents the shipowner from taking on board slaves on the west coast of Africa, and taking them over to America. It imposes regulations as to the building of steamers and the rules of navigation at sea, in order that passengers and sailors may not be sacrificed to the avarice and caprice of the captains. In England certain rules have recently been enacted with regard to shipbuilding, because an infernal union between assurance companies and shipowners has been brought to light, whereby yearly thousands of human lives and millions in value were sacrificed to the avarice of a few persons. In North America millers are bound under a penalty to pack into each cask not less than 198 lbs. of good flour, and for all market goods market inspectors are appointed, although in no other country is individual liberty more highly prized. Everywhere does the State consider it to be its duty to guard the public against danger and loss, as in the sale of necessaries of life, so also in the sale of medicines, &c.

But the cases which we have mentioned (the school will reply) concern unlawful damages to property and to the person, not the honourable exchange of useful objects, not the harmless and useful industry of private individuals; to impose restrictions on these latter the State has no right whatever. Of course not, so long as they remain harmless and useful; that which, however, is harmless and useful in itself, in general commerce with the world, can become dangerous and injurious in national internal commerce, and vice versâ. In time of peace, and considered from a cosmopolitan point of view, privateering is an injurious profession; in time of war, Governments favour it. The deliberate killing of a human being is a crime in time of peace, in war it becomes a duty. Trading in gunpowder, lead, and arms in time of peace is allowed; but whoever provides the enemy with them in time of war, is punished as a traitor.

For similar reasons the State is not merely justified in imposing, but bound to impose, certain regulations and restrictions on commerce (which is in itself harmless) for the best interests of the nation. By prohibitions and protective duties it does not give directions to individuals how to employ their productive powers and capital (as the popular school sophistically alleges); it does not tell the one, 'You must invest your money in the building of a ship, or in the erection of a manufactory;' or the other, 'You must be a naval captain or a civil engineer;' it leaves it to the judgment of every individual how and where to invest his capital, or to what vocation he will devote himself. It merely says, 'It is to the advantage of our nation that we manufacture these or the other goods ourselves; but as by free competition with foreign countries we can never obtain possession of this advantage, we have imposed restrictions on that competition, so far as in our opinion is necessary, to give those among us who invest their capital in these new branches of industry, and those who devote their bodily and mental powers to them, the requisite guarantees that they shall not lose their capital and shall not miss their vocation in life; and further to stimulate foreigners to come over to our side with their productive powers. In this manner, it does not in the least degree restrain private industry; on the contrary, it secures to the personal, natural, and moneyed powers of the nation a greater and wider field of activity. It does not thereby do something which its individual citizens could understand better and do better than it; on the contrary it does something which the individuals, even if they understood it, would not be able to do for themselves.

The allegation of the school, that the system of protection occasions unjust and anti-economical encroachments by the power of the State against the employment of the capital and industry of private individuals, appears in the least favourable light if we consider that it is the *foreign* commercial regulations which allow such encroachments on *our* private industry to take place, and that only by the aid of the system of protection are we enabled to counteract those injurious operations of the foreign commercial policy. If the English shut out our corn from their markets, what else are they doing than compelling our agriculturists to grow so much less corn than they would have sent out to England under systems of free importation? If they put such heavy duties on our wool, our wines, or our timber, that our export trade to England wholly or in great measure ceases, what else is thereby effected than that the power of the English nation restricts proportionately our branches of production? In these cases a direction is evidently given by *foreign legislation* to *our* capital and *our* personal productive powers, which but for the regulations made by it they would scarcely have followed. It follows from this, that were we to disown giving, by means of *our* own legislation, a direction to our own national industry in accordance with our own national interests, we could not prevent foreign nations from regulating our national industry after a fashion which corresponds with their own real or presumed advantage, and which in any case operates disadvantageously to the development of our own productive powers. But can it possibly be wiser on our part, and more to the advantage of those who nationally belong to us, for us to allow our private industry to be regulated by a foreign national Legislature, in accordance with foreign national interests, rather than regulate it by means of our own Legislature and in accordance with our own interests? Does the German or American agriculturist feel himself less restricted if he has to study every year the English Acts of Parliament, in order to ascertain whether that body deems it advantageous to encourage or to impose restrictions on his production of corn or wool, than if his own Legislature imposes certain restrictions on him in respect of foreign manufactured goods, but at the same time insures him a market for all his products, of which he can never again be deprived by foreign legislation?

If the school maintains that protective duties secure to the home manufacturers a monopoly to the disadvantage of the home consumers, in so doing it makes use of a weak argument. For as every individual in the nation is free to share in the profits of the home market which is thus secured to native industry, this is in no respect a private monopoly, but a privilege, secured to all those who belong to our nation, as against those who nationally belong to foreign nations, and which is the more righteous and just inasmuch as those who nationally belong to foreign nations possess themselves the very same monopoly, and those who belong to us are merely thereby put on the same footing with them. It is neither a privilege to the exclusive advantage of the producers, nor to the exclusive disadvantage of the consumers; for if the producers at first obtain higher prices, they run great risks, and have to contend against those considerable losses and sacrifices which are always connected with all beginnings in manufacturing industry. But the consumers have ample security that these extraordinary profits shall not reach unreasonable limits, or become perpetual, by means of the competition at home which follows later on, and which, as a rule, always lowers prices further than the level at which they had steadily ranged under the free competition of the foreigner. If the agriculturists, who are the most important consumers to the manufacturers, must also pay higher prices, this disadvantage will be amply repaid to them by increased demands for agricultural products, and by increased prices obtained for the latter.

It is a further sophism, arrived at by confounding the theory of mere values with that of the powers of production, when the popular school infers from the doctrine, *'that the wealth of the nation is merely the aggregate of the wealth of all individuals in it, and that the private interest of every individual is better able than all State regulations to incite to production and accumulation of wealth,'* the conclusion that the national industry would prosper best if only every individual were left undisturbed in the occupation of accumulating wealth. That doctrine can be conceded without the conclusion resulting from it at which the school desires thus to arrive; for the point in question is not (as we have shown in a previous chapter) that of immediately increasing by commercial restrictions the amount of *the values of exchange* in the nation, but of increasing *the amount of its productive powers*. But that the aggregate of the productive powers of the nation is not synonymous with the aggregate of the productive powers of all individuals, each considered separately—that the total amount of these powers depends chiefly on social and Political conditions, but especially on the degree in which the nation has rendered effectual the division of labour and the confederation of the powers of production within itself—we believe we have sufficiently demonstrated in the preceding chapters.

This system everywhere takes into its consideration only individuals who are in free unrestrained intercourse among themselves, and who are contented if we leave everyone to pursue his own private interests according to his own private natural inclination. This is evidently not a system of national economy, but a system of the private economy of the human race, as that would constitute itself were there no interference on the part of any Government, were there no wars, no hostile foreign tariff restrictions. Nowhere do the advocates of that system care to point out by what means those nations which are now prosperous have raised themselves to that stage of power and prosperity which we see them maintain, and from what causes others have lost that degree of prosperity and power which they formerly maintained. We can only learn from it how in private industry, natural ability, labour and capital, are combined in order to bring into exchange valuable products, and in what manner these latter are distributed among the human race and consumed by it. But what means are to be adopted in order to bring the natural powers belonging to any individual nation into activity and value, to raise a poor and weak nation to prosperity and power, cannot be gathered from it, because the school totally ignoring politics, ignores the special conditions of the nation, and concerns itself merely about the prosperity of the whole human race. Wherever international commerce is in question, the native individual is throughout simply pitted against the foreign individual; examples from the private dealings of separate merchants are throughout the only ones adduced—goods are spoken of in general terms (without considering whether the question is one of raw products or of manufactured articles)—in order to prove that it is equally for the benefit of the nation whether its exports and imports consist of money, of raw materials, or of manufactured goods, and whether or not they balance one another. If we, for example, terrified at the commercial crises which prevail in the United States of North America like native epidemics, consult this theory as to the means of averting or diminishing them, it leaves us utterly without comfort or instruction; nay, it is indeed impossible for us to investigate these phenomena scientifically, because, under the penalty of being taken for muddleheads and ignoramuses, we must not even utter the term *balance of trade*, while this term is, notwithstanding, made use of in all legislative assemblies, in all bureaux of administration, on every exchange. For the sake of the welfare of humanity, the belief is inculcated on us that exports always balance themselves spontaneously by imports; notwithstanding that we read in public accounts how the Bank of England comes to the assistance of the nature of things; notwithstanding that corn laws exist, which make it somewhat difficult for the agriculturist of those countries which deal with England to pay with his own produce for the manufactured goods which he consumes.

The school recognises no distinction between nations which have attained a higher degree of economical development, and those which occupy a lower stage. Everywhere it seeks to exclude the action of the power of the State; everywhere, according to it, will the individual be so much better able to produce, the less the power of the State concerns itself for him. In fact, according to this doctrine savage nations ought to be the most productive and wealthy of the earth, for nowhere is the individual left more to himself than in the savage state, nowhere is the action of the power of the State less perceptible.

Statistics and history, however, teach, on the contrary, that the necessity for the intervention of legislative power and administration is everywhere more apparent, the further the economy of the nation is developed. As individual liberty is in general a good thing so long only as it does not run counter to the interests of society, so is it reasonable to hold that private industry can only lay claim to unrestricted action so long as the latter consists with the well-being of the nation. But whenever the enterprise and activity of individuals does not suffice for this purpose, or in any case where these might become injurious to the nation, there does private industry rightly require support from the whole power of the nation, there ought it for the sake of its own interests to submit to legal restrictions.

If the school represents the free competition of all producers as the most effectual means for promoting the prosperity of the human race, it is quite right from the point of view which it assumes. On the hypothesis of a universal union, every restriction on the honest exchange of goods between various countries seems unreasonable and injurious. But so long as other nations Subordinate the interests of the human race as a whole to their national interests, it is folly to speak of free competition among the individuals of various nations. The arguments of the school in favour of free competition are thus only applicable to the exchange between those who belong to one and the same nation. Every great nation, therefore, must endeavour to form an aggregate within itself, which will enter into commercial intercourse with other similar aggregates so far only as that intercourse is suitable to the interests of its own special community. These interests of the community are, however, infinitely different from the private interests of all the separate individuals of the nation, if each individual is to be regarded as existing for himself alone and not in the character of a member of the national community, if we regard (as Smith and Say do) individuals as mere producers and consumers, not citizens of states or members of nations; for as such, mere individuals do not concern themselves for the prosperity of future generations—they deem it foolish (as Mr. Cooper really demonstrates to us) to make certain and present sacrifices in order to endeavour to obtain a benefit which is as yet uncertain and lying in the vast field of the future (if even it possess any value at all); they care but little for the continuance of the nation—they would expose the ships of their merchants to become the prey of every bold pirate—they trouble themselves but little about the power, the honour, or the glory of the nation, at the most they can persuade themselves to make some material sacrifices for the education of their children, and to give them the opportunity of learning a trade, provided always that after the lapse of a few years the learners are placed in a position to earn their own bread.

Indeed, according to the prevailing theory, so analogous is national economy to private economy that J.B. Say, where (exceptionally) he allows that internal industry may be protected by the State, makes it a condition of so doing, that every probability must exist that after the lapse of a *few years* it will attain independence, just as a shoemaker's apprentice is allowed only a few years' time in order to perfect himself so far in his trade as to do without parental assistance.

2

The Liberal Paradigm

Modern economic liberals build on Adam Smith's concepts of the invisible hand, self-regulating markets, and the pursuit of self-interest leading efficiently to the maximum collective interest. They also echo his prescriptions for the role of government in relation to economic activity and society more broadly. The term *market liberal* is used in this reader to refer to free-market or economic liberals. In this sense, it refers to a philosophy with primarily European origins, as represented in the work of Friedrich Hayek.[1] Hayek was a leading twentieth-century theorist who built on the traditions of the Austrian School of economics, particularly on the teachings of his mentor Ludwig von Mises. Many of today's most famous market liberals are associated with "the Chicago School of economics," which originated at the University of Chicago in the 1930s. Milton Friedman is a paragon of the Chicago School – he stands out as a leading market-liberal voice in both scholarly and policy debates on markets and government in the latter part of the twentieth century.[2]

Friedrich Hayek was trained at the University of Vienna, spent the early part of his intellectual career at the London School of Economics, and moved finally to the University of Chicago's Committee on Social Thought. His interests spanned economics and political philosophy as well as psychology and cognitive science. His most renowned body of work mounts a defense of liberal democracy and capitalism against the socialist and collectivist thought that was influential in Europe in the mid-twentieth century. Hayek enjoyed a reputation as a leading economic theorist but his views were not always popular during his own time because mainstream European economic thought in the 1930s through the early 1960s was dominated by the Keynesian interventionist approach to the economy. Named after John Maynard Keynes, a British economist, the Keynesian perspective advocated, in opposition to laissez-faire economics, direct government intervention in the economy to manage macroeconomic phenomena such as unemployment, recession, and inflation. Keynesianism also supported a mixed economy, where both the state and private sectors had important, complementary roles to play in economic activity. This was a popular school of thought and practice from the Great Depression into the postwar period in both Europe and the United States.[3]

In 1974, Hayek received the Nobel Prize in Economics, which prompted a revival of interest in his economic theory and in the Austrian School. This renewed intellectual focus coincided with a global economic environment in which Keynesian government policy seemed no longer able to manage inflation and unemployment. The Reagan–Thatcher revolution in the 1980s drew heavily from the market-liberal perspective, especially in terms of its emphasis on getting government out of the economy through the pursuit of deregulation and privatization. By the time of Hayek's death in 1992, he was considered the father of neoliberalism.[4] Margaret Thatcher, the conservative British prime minister (1979–90), was a self-avowed disciple of Hayek; her economic philosophy, known as "Thatcherism," drew heavily from Hayek and his followers.[5] On the other side of the Atlantic, Hayek also exerted an influence on key economic advisors of U.S. President Ronald Reagan (1981–88), including Milton Friedman, a leading advocate of both the monetarist school of economic thought and a limited government role in the economy, two cornerstones of "Reaganomics."[6] Friedman won the Nobel Prize in Economics in 1976 and was central in building the intellectual community that came to be known as the Chicago School.

The selections presented here demonstrate how modern-day market liberals are descendants of Adam Smith, albeit more doctrinaire. Friedrich Hayek's *Road to Serfdom* (1944) is animated by the politics of the time, as he argues that all forms of collectivism – from Hitler's National Socialism to Stalin's Communism – lead inevitably to tyranny by the faulty logic of central economic planning. Yet Hayek reminds the reader that his is not a dogmatic laissez-faire standpoint. Building on Smith's self-interest principle, Hayek argues that a competitive framework, under-pinned by legal rules, in which individuals can make rational decisions, is superior to a planned system. He emphasizes one of the tenets of neoclassical economic theory in maintaining that competition spontaneously and efficiently coordinates economic activity through price signals. He argues that mixing competition and planning, the Keynesian approach in vogue in postwar Europe, is a problematic policy because it relies on contradictory principles that lead to poor results.

For Hayek, the "great liberal principle" is the rule of law, which safeguards indi-vidual equality before government by preventing government from acting in an arbi-trary manner. Government intervention in markets, even if well-intentioned – such as for purposes of equality or social justice – inherently violates the liberal principle of equal treatment before the law, curtails individual freedom, and endangers soci-eties with a slippery slope toward totalitarianism. Liberalism relies on competition to coordinate individual effort and thereby enable society to maximize collective welfare. Hayek concurs with Smith that the core role of the state must be to set up and admin-ister a legal framework that facilitates competition. Additional crucial roles for the state are to regulate basic public health and safety and to provide public goods where the contribution to social welfare is large.

Milton Friedman's liberal views are more strident than those of Smith and Hayek, holding that the government's role in economic activity should be extremely limited. He underlines the importance of the price system as a coordination mechanism, echoing Smith in arguing that it leads to collective welfare enhancement and social harmony. In his view, the government is a major source of price distortion, thwarting individuals as they attempt to play their economic roles as producers, consumers, owners, and workers; government failure is typically more of a problem than the "market failure" that it seeks to correct. Friedman states that attempts to use government intervention or political means to allocate resources instead of the market actually tear the social fabric. In his view, the market resolves almost all forms of resource allocation in the most efficient way possible: there are very few true public goods that require government provision and even monopolies should not be regulated in most cases.

Friedman elevates the primacy of the self-interest principle introduced by Smith, arguing that economic freedom is in fact a necessary condition for political freedom, that the individual is the ultimate entity and his needs are primary, and that government must exist only to serve the individual. In other work, Friedman emphasized that the sole responsibility that businesses have to society is to maximize profits, going so far as to suggest that the "doctrine" of corporate social responsibility dictated "the acceptance of the socialist view that political mechanisms, not market mechanisms, are the appropriate way to determine the allocation of scarce resources to alternative uses."[7]

The debate about the appropriate role of government in the economy continues to be one of the defining fault lines of contemporary political–economic discourse around the world. The market-liberal viewpoint is represented throughout the reader, including by Deepak Lal in the debate about market reform in advanced economies, Anders Åslund on market transition, Arvind Panagariya on market development in poor countries, and Tyler Cowen on the digital platform economy. Whereas Adam Smith and subsequent economic liberals argue that the state has a few circumscribed roles to play in the economy, the market-institutional perspective illuminated through other selections in the reader maintains that the state is and should be actively engaged in building and sustaining markets.

Notes

1 Beginning in the late nineteenth century, "liberalism" took on a different meaning in the United States, referring to advocacy for a larger state role in the economy, including social regulation and welfare services, a viewpoint covered in this reader by Charles Lindblom.

2 Some of Friedman's fellow Chicago School theorists include George Stigler, Gary Becker, and Robert Lucas.

3 Although Keynes and Hayek were intellectual rivals whose battle of ideas defined much of the post-World War Two economic debate about the correct relationship between markets and the state, they shared a warm friendship. Keynes made it possible for Hayek to work at Cambridge during the London Blitz. See Nicholas Wapshott, *Keynes–Hayek: The Clash that Defined Modern Economics* (New York: W. W. Norton, 2011).

4 Fred Block, "Introduction," in Karl Polanyi, ed., *The Great Transformation: The Political and Economic Origins of Our Time* (Boston, MA: Beacon Press, 2001), xx.

5 Shortly after becoming party leader, Thatcher wielded a copy of Hayek's *The Constitution of Liberty* to announce to other party members, "This is what we believe."

6 Monetarism, closely associated with Milton Friedman, maintains that inflation should be controlled by the government's management of the supply of money in the national economy. This is a direct rejection of Keynesian, "demand-side," fiscal management of the economy. Friedman began his career as a Keynes devotee but later reversed his views.

7 Milton Friedman, "The Social Responsibility of Business is to Increase its Profits," *The New York Times Magazine* (September 13, 1970).

Friedrich A. Hayek,
The Road to Serfdom (1944)[*]

III: Individualism and Collectivism

The socialists believe in two things which are absolutely different and perhaps even contradictory: freedom and organization.

—Élie Halévy.

Before we can progress with our main problem, an obstacle has yet to be surmounted. A confusion largely responsible for the way in which we are drifting into things which nobody wants must cleared be up. This confusion concerns nothing less than the concept of socialism itself. It may mean, and is often used to describe, merely the ideals of social justice, greater equality, and security, which are the ultimate aims of socialism. But it means also the particular method by which most socialists hope to attain these ends and which many competent people regard as the only methods by which they can be fully and quickly attained. In this sense socialism means the abolition of private enterprise, of private ownership of the means of production, and the creation of a system of "planned economy" in which the entrepreneur working for profit is replaced by a central planning body.

There are many people who call themselves socialists, although they care only about the first, who fervently believe in those ultimate aims of socialism but neither care nor understand how they can be achieved, and who are merely certain that they must be achieved, whatever the cost. But to nearly all those to whom socialism is not merely a hope but an object of practical politics, the characteristic methods of modern socialism are as essential as the ends themselves. Many people, on the other hand, who value the ultimate ends of socialism no less than the socialists refuse to support socialism because of the dangers to other values they see in the methods proposed by the socialists. The dispute about socialism has thus become largely a dispute about means and not about ends—although the question whether the different ends of socialism can be simultaneously achieved is also involved.

This would be enough to create confusion. And the confusion has been further increased by the common practice of denying that those who repudiate the means value the ends. But this is not all. The situation is still more complicated by the fact that the same means, the "economic planning" which is the prime instrument of socialist reform, can be used for many other purposes. We must centrally direct economic activity if we want to make the distribution of income conform to current ideas of social justice. "Planning," therefore, is wanted by all those who demand that

---

[*] From: *The Road to Serfdom,* Friedrich A. Hayek, Copyright © 1944 F. A. Hayek. (pp. 33–44, 50–52, 75–77) Reproduced by permission of Taylor and Francis Group, LLC, a division of Informa plc.

"production for use" be substituted for production for profit. But such planning is no less indispensable if the distribution of incomes is to be regulated in a way which to us appears to be the opposite of just. Whether we should wish that more of the good things of this world should go to some racial élite, the Nordic men, or the members of a party or an aristocracy, the methods which we shall have to employ are the same as those which could insure an equalitarian distribution.

It may, perhaps, seem unfair to use the term "socialism" to describe its methods rather than its aims, to use for a particular method a term which for many people stands for an ultimate ideal. It is probably preferable to describe the methods which can be used for a great variety of ends as collectivism and to regard socialism as a species of that genus. Yet, although to most socialists only one species of collectivism will represent true socialism, it must always be remembered that socialism is a species of collectivism and that therefore everything which is true of collectivism as such must apply also to socialism. Nearly all the points which are disputed between socialists and liberals concern the methods common to all forms of collectivism and not the particular ends for which socialists want to use them; and all the consequences with which we shall be concerned in this book follow from the methods of collectivism irrespective of the ends for which they are used. It must also not be forgotten that socialism is not only by far the most important species of collectivism or "planning" but that it is socialism which has persuaded liberal-minded people to submit once more to that regimentation of economic life which they had overthrown because, in the words of Adam Smith, it puts governments in a position where "to support themselves they are obliged to be oppressive and tyrannical."[1]

The difficulties caused by the ambiguities of the common political terms are not yet over if we agree to use the term "collectivism" so as to include all types of "planned economy," whatever the end of planning. The meaning of this term becomes somewhat more definite if we make it clear that we mean that sort of planning which is necessary to realize any given distributive ideals. But, as the idea of central economic planning owes its appeal largely to this very vagueness of its meaning, it is essential that we should agree on its precise sense before we discuss its consequences.

"Planning" owes its popularity largely to the fact that everybody desires, of course, that we should handle our common problems as rationally as possible and that, in so doing, we should use as much foresight as we can command. In this sense everybody who is not a complete fatalist is a planner, every political act is (or ought to be) an act of planning, and there can be differences only between good and bad, between wise and foresighted and foolish and shortsighted planning. An economist, whose whole task is the study of how men actually do and how they might plan their affairs, is the last person who could object to planning in this general sense. But it is not in this sense that our enthusiasts for a planned society now employ this term, nor merely in this sense that we must plan if we want the distribution of income or wealth to conform to some particular standard. According to the modern planners, and for their purposes, it is not sufficient to design the most rational permanent framework within which the various activities would be conducted by different persons according to their individual plans. This liberal plan, according to them, is no plan—and it is, indeed, not a plan designed to satisfy particular views about who should have what. What our planners demand is a central direction of all economic activity according to a single plan, laying down how the resources of society should be "consciously directed" to serve particular ends in a definite way.

The dispute between the modern planners and their opponents is, therefore, *not* a dispute on whether we ought to choose intelligently between the various possible organizations of society; it is not a dispute on whether we ought to employ foresight and systematic thinking in planning our common affairs. It is a dispute about what is the best way of so doing. The question is whether for this purpose it is better that the holder of coercive power should confine himself in general to creating conditions under which the knowledge and initiative of individuals are given the best scope so that *they* can plan most successfully; or whether a rational utilization of our resources requires *central* direction and organization of all our activities according to some consciously constructed "blueprint." The socialists of all parties have appropriated the term "planning" for planning of the latter type, and it is now generally accepted in this sense. But though this is meant to suggest that this is the only rational way of handling our affairs, it does not, of course, prove this. It remains the point on which the planners and the liberals disagree.

It is important not to confuse opposition against this kind of planning with a dogmatic laissez faire attitude. The liberal argument is in favor of making the best possible use of the forces of competition as a means of co-ordinating human efforts, not an argument for leaving things just as they are. It is based on the conviction that, where effective competition can be created, it is a better way of guiding individual efforts than any other. It does not deny, but even emphasizes, that, in order that competition should work beneficially, a carefully thought-out legal framework is required and that neither the existing nor the past legal rules are free from grave defects. Nor does it deny that, where it is impossible to create the conditions necessary to make competition effective, we must resort to other methods of guiding economic activity. Economic liberalism is opposed, however, to competition's being supplanted by inferior methods of co-ordinating individual efforts. And it regards competition as superior not only because it is in most circumstances the most efficient method known but even more because it is the only method by which our activities can be adjusted to each other without coercive or arbitrary intervention of authority. Indeed, one of the main arguments in favor of competition is that it dispenses with the need for "conscious social control" and that it gives the individuals a chance to decide whether the prospects of a particular occupation are sufficient to compensate for the disadvantages and risks connected with it.

The successful use of competition as the principle of social organization precludes certain types of coercive interference with economic life, but it admits of others which sometimes may very considerably assist its work and even requires certain kinds of government action. But there is good reason why the negative requirements, the points where coercion must not be used, have been particularly stressed. It is necessary in the first instance that the parties in the market should be free to sell and buy at any price at which they can find a partner to the transaction and that anybody should be free to produce, sell, and buy anything that may be produced or sold at all. And it is essential that the entry into the different trades should be open to all on equal terms and that the law should not tolerate any attempts by individuals or groups to restrict this entry by open or concealed force. Any attempt to control prices or quantities of particular commodities deprives competition of its power of bringing about an effective co-ordination of individual efforts, because price changes then cease to register all the relevant changes in circumstances and no longer provide a reliable guide for the individual's actions.

This is not necessarily true, however, of measures merely restricting the allowed methods of production, so long as these restrictions affect all potential producers equally and are not used as an indirect way of controlling prices and quantities. Though all such controls of the methods or production impose extra costs (i.e., make it necessary to use more resources to produce a given output), they may be well worth while. To prohibit the use of certain poisonous substances or to require special precautions in their use, to limit working hours or to require certain sanitary arrangements, is fully compatible with the preservation of competition. The only question here is whether in the particular instance the advantages gained are greater than the social costs which they impose. Nor is the preservation of competition incompatible with an extensive system of social services—so long as the organization of these services is not designed in such a way as to make competition ineffective over wide fields.

It is regrettable, though not difficult to explain, that in the past much less attention has been given to the positive requirements of a successful working of the competitive system than to these negative points. The functioning of a competition not only requires adequate organization of certain institutions like money, markets, and channels of information—some of which can never be adequately provided by private enterprise—but it depends, above all, on the existence of an appropriate legal system, a legal system designed both to preserve competition and to make it operate as beneficially as possible. It is by no means sufficient that the law should recognize the principle of private property and freedom of contract; much depends on the precise definition of the right of property as applied to different things. The systematic study of the forms of legal institutions which will make the competitive system work efficiently has been sadly neglected; and strong arguments can be advanced that serious shortcomings here, particularly with regard to the law of corporations and of patents, not only have made competition work much less effectively than it might have done but have even led to the destruction of competition in many spheres.

There are, finally, undoubted fields where no legal arrangements can create the main condition on which the usefulness of the system of competition and private property depends: namely, that the owner benefits from all the useful services rendered by his property and suffers for all the damages caused to others by its use. Where, for example, it is impracticable to make the enjoyment of certain services dependent on the payment of a price, competition will not produce the services; and the price system becomes similarly ineffective when the damage caused to others by certain uses of property cannot be effectively charged to the owner of that property. In all these instances there is a divergence between the items which enter into private calculation and those which affect social welfare; and, whenever this divergence becomes important, some method other than competition may have to be found to supply the services in question. Thus neither the provision of signposts on the roads nor, in most circumstances, that of the roads themselves can be paid for by every individual user. Nor can certain harmful effects of deforestation, of some methods of farming, or of the smoke and noise of factories be confined to the owner of the property in question or to those who are willing to submit to the damage for an agreed compensation. In such instances we must find some substitute for the regulation by the price mechanism. But the fact that we have to resort to the substitution of direct regulation by authority where the conditions for the proper working of competition cannot be created does not prove that we should suppress competition where it can be made to function.

To create conditions in which competition will be as effective as possible, to supplement it where it cannot be made effective, to provide the services which, in the words of Adam Smith, "though they may be in the highest degree advantageous to a great society, are, however, of such a nature, that the profit could never repay the expense to any individual or small number of individuals"—these tasks provide, indeed, a wide and unquestioned field for state activity. In no system that could be rationally defended would the state just do nothing. An effective competitive system needs an intelligently designed and continuously adjusted legal framework as much as any other. Even the most essential prerequisite of its proper functioning, the prevention of fraud and deception (including exploitation of ignorance), provides a great and by no means yet fully accomplished object of legislative activity.

The task of creating a suitable framework for the beneficial working of competition had, however, not yet been carried very far when states everywhere turned from it to that of supplanting competition by a different and irreconcilable principle. The question was no longer one of making competition work and of supplementing it but of displacing it altogether. It is important to be quite clear about this: the modern movement for planning is a movement against competition as such, a new flag under which all the old enemies of competition have rallied. And although all sorts of interests are now trying to reestablish under this flag privileges which the liberal era swept away, it is socialist propaganda for planning which has restored to respectability among liberal-minded people opposition to competition and which has effectively lulled the healthy suspicion which any attempt to smother competition used to arouse.[2] What in effect unites the socialists of the Left and the Right is this common hostility to competition and their common desire to replace it by a directed economy. Though the terms "capitalism" and "socialism" are still generally used to describe the past and the future forms of society, they conceal rather than elucidate the nature of the transition through which we are passing.

Yet, though all the changes we are observing tend in the direction of a comprehensive central direction of economic activity, the universal struggle against competition promises to produce in the first instance something in many respects even worse, a state of affairs which can satisfy neither planners nor liberals: a sort of syndicalist or "corporative" organization of industry, in which competition is more or less suppressed but planning is left in the hands of the independent monopolies of the separate industries. This is the inevitable first result of a situation in which the people are united in their hostility to competition but agree on little else. By destroying competition in industry after industry, this policy puts the consumer at the mercy of the joint monopolist action of capitalists and workers in the best organized industries. Yet, although this is a state of affairs which in wide fields has already existed for some time, and although much of the muddled (and most of the interested) agitation for planning aims at it, it is not a state which is likely to persist or can be rationally justified. Such independent planning by industrial monopolies would, in fact, produce effects opposite to those at which the argument for planning aims. Once this stage is reached, the only alternative to a return to competition is the control of the monopolies by the state—a control which, if it is to be made effective, must become progressively more complete and more detailed. It is this stage we are rapidly approaching. When, shortly before the war, a weekly magazine pointed out that there were many signs that British leaders, at least, were growing accustomed to thinking in terms of national development by controlled monopolies, this was probably a true estimate of the position as it then existed. Since then this process has been greatly accelerated by the war, and its grave defects and dangers will become increasingly obvious as time goes on.

The idea of complete centralization of the direction of economic activity still appalls most people, not only because of the stupendous difficulty of the task, but even more because of the horror inspired by the idea of everything being directed from a single center. If we are, nevertheless, rapidly moving toward such a state, this is largely because most people still believe that it is must be possible to find some middle way between "atomistic" competition and central direction. Nothing, indeed, seems at first more plausible, or is more likely to appeal to reasonable people, than the idea that our goal must be neither the extreme decentralization of free competition nor the complete centralization of a single plan but some judicious mixture of the two methods. Yet mere common sense proves a treacherous guide in this field. Although competition can bear some admixture of regulation, it cannot be combined with planning to any extent we like without ceasing to operate as an effective guide to production. Nor is "planning" a medicine which, taken in small doses, can produce the effects for which one might hope from its thoroughgoing application. Both competition and central direction become poor and inefficient tools if they are incomplete; they are alternative principles used to solve the same problem, and a mixture of the two means that neither will really work and that the result will be worse than if either system had been consistently relied upon. Or, to express it differently, planning and competition can be combined only by planning for competition but not by planning against competition.

It is of the utmost importance to the argument of this book for the reader to keep in mind that the planning against which all our criticism is directed is solely the planning against competition—the planning which is to be substituted for competition. This is the more important, as we cannot, within the scope of this book, enter into a discussion of the very necessary planning which is required to make competition as effective and beneficial as possible. But as in current usage "planning" has become almost synonymous with the former kind of planning, it will sometimes be inevitable for the sake of brevity to refer to it simply as planning, even though this means leaving to our opponents a very good word meriting a better fate.

IV: The "Inevitability" of Planning

[...]

The assertion that modern technological progress makes planning inevitable can also be interpreted in a different manner. It may mean that the complexity of our modern industrial civilisation creates new problems with which we cannot hope to deal effectively except by central planning. In a sense this is true—yet not in the wide sense in which it is claimed. It is, for example, a commonplace that many of the problems created by a modern town, like many other problems caused by close contiguity in space, are not adequately solved by competition. But it is not these problems, like those of the "public utilities", etc., which are uppermost in the minds of those who invoke the complexity of modern civilisation as an argument for central planning. What they generally suggest is that the increasing difficulty of obtaining a coherent picture of the complete economic process makes it indispensable that things should be co-ordinated by some central agency if social life is not to dissolve in chaos.

This argument is based on a complete misapprehension of the working of competition. Far from being appropriate only to comparatively simple conditions, it is the very complexity of the division of labour under modern conditions which makes competition the only method by which such co-ordination can be adequately brought about. There would be no difficulty about efficient control or planning were conditions so simple that a single person or board could effectively survey all the relevant facts. It is only as the factors which have to be taken into account become so numerous that it is impossible to gain a synoptic view of them, that decentralisation becomes imperative. But once decentralisation is necessary, the problem of co-ordination arises, a co-ordination which leaves the separate agencies free to adjust their activities to the facts which only they can know, and yet brings about a mutual adjustment of their respective plans. As decentralisation has become necessary because nobody can consciously balance all the considerations bearing on the decisions of so many individuals, the co-ordination can clearly not be effected by "conscious control", but only by arrangements which convey to each agent the information he must possess in order effectively to adjust his decisions to those of others. And because all the details of the changes constantly affecting the conditions of demand and supply of the different commodities can never be fully known, or quickly enough be collected and disseminated, by any one centre, what is required is some apparatus of registration which automatically records all the relevant effects of individual actions, and whose indications are at the same time the resultant of, and the guide for, all the individual decisions.

This is precisely what the price system does under competition, and which no other system even promises to accomplish. It enables entrepreneurs, by watching the movement of comparatively few prices, as an engineer watches the hands of a few dials, to adjust their activities to those of their fellows. The important point here is that the price system will fulfil this function only if competition prevails, that is, if the individual producer has to adapt himself to price changes and cannot control them. The more complicated the whole, the more dependent we become on that division of knowledge between individuals whose separate efforts are co-ordinated by the impersonal mechanism for transmitting the relevant information known by us as the price system.

It is no exaggeration to say that if we had had to rely on conscious central planning for the growth of our industrial system, it would never have reached the degree of differentiation, complexity, and flexibility it has attained. Compared with this method of solving the economic problem by means of decentralisation plus automatic co-ordination, the more obvious method of central direction is incredibly clumsy, primitive, and limited in scope. That the division of labour has reached the extent which makes modern civilisation possible we owe to the fact that it did not have to be consciously created, but that man tumbled on a method by which the division of labour could be extended far beyond the limits within which it could have been planned. Any further growth of its complexity, therefore, far from making central direction more necessary, makes it more important than ever that we should use a technique which does not depend on conscious control.

[...]

VI: Planning and the Rule of Law

Recent studies in the sociology of law once more confirm that the fundamental principle of formal law by which every case must be judged according to general rational precepts, which have as few exceptions as possible and are based on logical subsumptions, obtains only for the liberal competitive phase of capitalism.

—Karl Mannheim

Nothing distinguishes more clearly conditions in a free country from those in a country under arbitrary government than the observance in the former of the great principles known as the Rule of Law. Stripped of all technicalities, this means that government in all its actions is bound by rules fixed and announced beforehand—rules which make it possible to foresee with fair certainty how the authority will use its coercive powers in given circumstances and to plan one's individual affairs on the basis of this knowledge.[3] Though this ideal can never be perfectly achieved, since legislators as well as those to whom the administration of the law is intrusted are fallible men, the essential point, that the discretion left to the executive organs wielding coercive power should be reduced as much as possible, is clear enough. While every law restricts individual freedom to some extent by altering the means which people may use in the pursuit of their aims, under the Rule of Law the government is prevented from stultifying individual efforts by *ad hoc* action. Within the known rules of the game the individual is free to pursue his personal ends and desires, certain that the powers of government will not be used deliberately to frustrate his efforts.

The distinction we have drawn before between the creation of a permanent framework of laws within which the productive activity is guided by individual decisions and the direction of economic activity by a central authority is thus really a particular case of the more general distinction between the Rule of Law and arbitrary government. Under the first the government confines itself to fixing rules determining the conditions under which the available resources may be used, leaving to the individuals the decision for what ends they are to be used. Under the second the government directs the use of the means of production to particular ends. The first type of rules can be made in advance, in the shape of *formal rules* which do not aim at the wants and needs of particular people. They are intended to be merely instrumental in the pursuit of people's various individual ends. And they are, or ought to be, intended for such long periods that it is impossible to know whether they will assist particular people more than others. They could almost be described as a kind of instrument of production, helping people to predict the behavior of those with whom they must collaborate, rather than as efforts toward the satisfaction of particular needs.

Economic planning of the collectivist kind necessarily involves the very opposite of this. The planning authority cannot confine itself to providing opportunities for unknown people to make whatever use of them they like. It cannot tie itself down in advance to general and formal rules which prevent arbitrariness. It must provide for the actual needs of people as they arise and then choose deliberately between them. It must constantly decide questions which cannot be answered by formal principles only, and, in making these decisions, it must set up distinctions of merit between the needs of different people. When the government has to decide how many pigs are to be raised or how many busses are to be run, which coal mines are to operate, or at what prices shoes are to be sold, these decisions cannot be deduced from formal principles or settled for long periods in advance. They depend inevitably on the circumstances of the moment, and, in making such decisions, it will always be necessary to balance one against the other the interests of various persons and groups. In the end somebody's views will have to decide whose interests are more important; and these views must become part of the law of the land, a new distinction of rank which the coercive apparatus of government imposes upon the people.

Notes

1 Quoted in Dugald Stewart's *Memoir of Adam Smith* from a memorandum written by Smith in 1755.
2 Of late, it is true, some academic socialists, under the spur of criticism and animated by the same fear of the extinction of freedom in a centrally planned society, have devised a new kind of "competitive socialism" which they hope will avoid the difficulties and dangers of central planning and combine the abolition of private property with the full retention of individual freedom. Although some discussion of this new kind of socialism has taken place in learned journals, it is hardly likely to recommend itself to practical politicians. If it ever did, it would not be difficult to show (as the author has attempted elsewhere—see *Economica*, 1940) that these plans rest on a delusion and suffer from an inherent contradiction. It is impossible to assume control over all the productive resources without also deciding for whom and by whom they are to be used. Although under this so-called "competitive socialism" the planning by the central authority would take somewhat more roundabout forms, its effects would not be fundamentally different, and the element of competition would be little more than a sham.
3 According to the classical exposition by A.V. Dicey in *The Law of the Constitution* (8th ed.), p. 198, the Rule of Law "means, in the first place, the absolute supremacy or predominance of regular law as opposed to the influence of arbitrary power, and excludes the existence of arbitrariness, of prerogative, or even of wide discretionary authority on the part of government." Largely as a result of Dicey's work the term has, however, in England acquired a narrower technical meaning which does not concern us here. The wider and older meaning of the concept of the rule or reign of law, which in England had become an established tradition which was more taken for granted than discussed, has been most fully elaborated, just because it raised what were new problems there, in the early nineteenth-century discussion in Germany about the nature of the *Rechtsstaat*.

Milton Friedman,
Capitalism and Freedom (1962)[*]

Chapter II: The Role of Government in a Free Society

A common objection to totalitarian societies is that they regard the end as justifying the means. Taken literally, this objection is clearly illogical. If the end does not justify the means, what does? But this easy answer does not dispose of the objection; it simply shows that the objection is not well put. To deny that the end justifies the means is indirectly to assert that the end in question is not the ultimate end, that the ultimate end is itself the use of the proper means. Desirable or not, any end that can be attained only by the use of bad means must give way to the more basic end of the use of acceptable means.

To the liberal, the appropriate means are free discussion and voluntary co-operation, which implies that any form of coercion is inappropriate. The ideal is unanimity among responsible individuals achieved on the basis of free and full discussion. This is another way of expressing the goal of freedom emphasized in the preceding chapter.

From this standpoint, the role of the market, as already noted, is that it permits unanimity without conformity; that it is a system of effectively proportional representation. On the other hand, the characteristic feature of action through explicitly political channels is that it tends to require or to enforce substantial conformity. The typical issue must be decided "yes" or "no"; at most, provision can be made for a fairly limited number of alternatives. Even the use of proportional representation in its explicitly political form does not alter this conclusion. The number of separate groups that can in fact be represented is narrowly limited, enormously so by comparison with the proportional representation of the market. More important, the fact that the final outcome generally must be a law applicable to all groups, rather than separate legislative enactments for each "party" represented, means that proportional representation in its political version, far from permitting unanimity without conformity, tends toward ineffectiveness and fragmentation. It thereby operates to destroy any consensus on which unanimity with conformity can rest.

There are clearly some matters with respect to which effective proportional representation is impossible. I cannot get the amount of national defense I want and you, a different amount. With respect to such indivisible matters we can discuss, and argue, and vote. But having decided, we must conform. It is precisely the existence of such indivisible matters—protection of the individual and the nation from coercion are clearly the most basic—that prevents exclusive reliance on individual action through the market. If we are to use some of our resources for such indivisible items, we must employ political channels to reconcile differences.

The use of political channels, while inevitable, tends to strain the social cohesion essential for a stable society. The strain is least if agreement for joint action need be reached only on a limited range of issues on which people in any event have common views. Every extension of the range of issues for which explicit agreement is sought strains further the delicate threads that hold society together. If it goes so far as to touch an issue on which men feel deeply yet differently, it may well disrupt the society. Fundamental differences in basic values can seldom if ever be resolved at the ballot box; ultimately they can only be decided, though not resolved, by conflict. The religious and civil wars of history are a bloody testament to this judgment.

The widespread use of the market reduces the strain on the social fabric by rendering conformity unnecessary with respect to any activities it encompasses. The wider the range of activities covered by the market, the fewer are the issues on which explicitly political decisions are required and hence on which it is necessary to achieve agreement. In turn, the fewer the issues on which agreement is necessary, the greater is the likelihood of getting agreement while maintaining a free society.

Unanimity is, of course, an ideal. In practice, we can afford neither the time nor the effort that would be required to achieve complete unanimity on every issue. We must perforce accept something less. We are thus led to accept majority rule in one form or another as an expedient. That majority rule is an expedient rather than itself a basic principle is clearly shown by the fact that our willingness to resort to majority rule, and the size of the majority we require, themselves depend on the seriousness of the issue involved. If the matter is of little moment and the minority has no strong feelings about being overruled, a bare plurality will suffice. On the other hand, if the minority feels strongly about the issue involved, even a bare majority will not do. Few of us would be willing to have issues of free speech, for example, decided by a bare majority. Our legal structure is full of such distinctions among kinds of issues that require different kinds of majorities. At the extreme are those issues embodied in the Constitution. These are the principles that are so important that we are willing to make minimal concessions to expediency. Something like essential consensus was achieved initially in accepting them, and we require something like essential consensus for a change in them.

The self-denying ordinance to refrain from majority rule on certain kinds of issues that is embodied in our Constitution and in similar written or unwritten constitutions elsewhere, and the specific provisions in these constitutions or their equivalents prohibiting coercion of individuals, are themselves to be regarded as reached by free discussion and as reflecting essential unanimity about means.

I turn now to consider more specifically, though still in very broad terms, what the areas are that cannot be handled through the market at all, or can be handled only at so great a cost that the use of political channels may be preferable.

Government as Rule-Maker and Umpire

It is important to distinguish the day-to-day activities of people from the general customary and legal framework within which these take place. The day-to-day activities are like the actions of the participants in a game when they are playing it; the framework, like the rules of the game they play. And just as a good game requires acceptance by the players both of the rules and of the umpire to interpret and enforce them, so a good society requires that its members agree on the general conditions that will govern relations among them, on some means of arbitrating different interpretations of these conditions, and on some device for enforcing compliance with the generally accepted rules. As in games, so also in society, most of the general conditions are the unintended outcome of custom, accepted unthinkingly. At most, we consider explicitly only minor modifications in them, though the cumulative effect of a series of minor modifications may be a drastic alteration in the character of the game or of the society. In both games and society also, no set of rules can prevail unless most participants most of the time conform to them without external sanctions; unless that is, there is a broad underlying social consensus. But we cannot rely on custom or on this consensus alone to interpret and to enforce the rules; we need an umpire. These then are the basic roles of government in a free society: to provide a means whereby we can modify the rules, to mediate differences among us on the meaning of the rules, and to enforce compliance with the rules on the part of those few who would otherwise not play the game.

The need for government in these respects arises because absolute freedom is impossible. However attractive anarchy may be as a philosophy, it is not feasible in a world of imperfect men. Men's freedoms can conflict, and when they do, one man's freedom must be limited to preserve another's—as a Supreme Court Justice once put it, "My freedom to move my fist must be limited by the proximity of your chin."

The major problem in deciding the appropriate activities of government is how to resolve such conflicts among the freedoms of different individuals. In some cases, the answer is easy. There is little difficulty in attaining near unanimity to the proposition that one man's freedom to murder his neighbor must be sacrificed to preserve the freedom of the other man to live. In other cases, the answer is difficult. In the economic area, a major problem arises in respect of the conflict between freedom to combine and freedom to compete. What meaning is to be attributed to "free" as modifying "enterprise"? In the United States, "free" has been understood to mean that anyone is free to set up an enterprise, which means that existing enterprises are not free to keep out competitors except by selling a better product at the same price or the same product at a lower price. In the continental tradition, on the other hand, the meaning has generally been that enterprises are free to do what they want, including the fixing of prices, division of markets, and the adoption of other techniques to keep out potential competitors. Perhaps the most difficult specific problem in this area arises with respect to combinations among laborers, where the problem of freedom to combine and freedom to compete is particularly acute.

A still more basic economic area in which the answer is both difficult and important is the definition of property rights. The notion of property, as it has developed over centuries and as it is embodied in our legal codes, has become so much a part of us that we tend to take it for granted, and fail to recognize the extent to which just what constitutes property and what rights the ownership of property confers are complex social creations rather than self-evident propositions. Does my having title to land, for example, and my freedom to use my property as I wish, permit me to deny to someone else the right to fly over my land in his airplane? Or does his right to use his airplane take precedence? Or does this depend on how high he flies? Or how much noise he makes? Does voluntary exchange require that he pay me for the privilege of flying over my land? Or that I must pay him to refrain from flying over it? The mere mention of royalties, copyrights, patents; shares of stock in corporations; riparian rights, and the like, may perhaps emphasize the role of generally accepted social rules in the very definition of property. It may suggest also that, in many cases, the existence of a well specified and generally accepted definition of property is far more important than just what the definition is.

Another economic area that raises particularly difficult problems is the monetary system. Government responsibility for the monetary system has long been recognized. It is explicitly provided for in the constitutional provision which gives Congress the power "to coin money, regulate the value thereof, and of foreign coin." There is probably no other area of economic activity with respect to which government action has been so uniformly accepted. This habitual and by now almost unthinking acceptance of governmental responsibility makes thorough understanding of the grounds for such responsibility all the more necessary, since it enhances the danger that the scope of government will spread from activities that are, to those that are not, appropriate in a free society, from providing a monetary framework to determining the allocation of resources among individuals.

In summary, the organization of economic activity through voluntary exchange presumes that we have provided, through government, for the maintenance of law and order to prevent coercion of one individual by another, the enforcement of contracts voluntarily entered into, the definition of the meaning of property rights, the interpretation and enforcement of such rights, and the provision of a monetary framework.

Action through Government on Grounds of Technical Monopoly and Neighborhood Effects

The role of government just considered is to do something that the market cannot do for itself, namely, to determine, arbitrate, and enforce the rules of the game. We may also want to do through government some things that might conceivably be done through the market but that technical or similar conditions render it difficult to do in that way. These all reduce to cases in which strictly voluntary exchange is either exceedingly costly or practically impossible. There are two general classes of such cases: monopoly and similar market imperfections, and neighborhood effects.

Exchange is truly voluntary only when nearly equivalent alternatives exist. Monopoly implies the absence of alternatives and thereby inhibits effective freedom of exchange. In practice, monopoly frequently, if not generally, arises from government support or from collusive agreements among individuals. With respect to these, the problem is either to avoid governmental fostering of monopoly or to stimulate the effective enforcement of rules such as those embodied in our anti-trust laws. However, monopoly may also arise because it is technically efficient to have a single producer or enterprise. I venture to suggest that such cases are more limited than is supposed but they unquestionably do arise. A simple example is perhaps the provision of telephone services within a community. I shall refer to such cases as "technical" monopoly.

When technical conditions make a monopoly the natural outcome of competitive market forces, there are only three alternatives that seem available: private monopoly, public monopoly, or public regulation. All three are bad so we must choose among evils. Henry Simons, observing public regulation of monopoly in the United States, found the results so distasteful that he concluded public monopoly would be a lesser evil. Walter Eucken, a noted German liberal, observing public monopoly in German railroads, found the results so distasteful that he concluded public regulation would be a lesser evil. Having learned from both, I reluctantly conclude that, if tolerable, private monopoly may be the least of the evils.

If society were static so that the conditions which give rise to a technical monopoly were sure to remain, I would have little confidence in this solution. In a rapidly changing society, however, the conditions making for technical monopoly frequently change and I suspect that both public regulation and public monopoly are likely to be less responsive to such changes in conditions, to be less readily capable of elimination, than private monopoly.

Railroads in the United States are an excellent example. A large degree of monopoly in railroads was perhaps inevitable on technical grounds in the nineteenth century. This was the justification for the Interstate Commerce Commission. But conditions have changed. The emergence of road and air transport has reduced the monopoly element in railroads to negligible proportions. Yet we have not eliminated the ICC. On the contrary, the ICC, which started out as an agency to protect the public from exploitation by the railroads, has become an agency to protect railroads from competition by trucks and other means of transport, and more recently even to protect existing truck companies from competition by new entrants. Similarly, in England, when the railroads were nationalized, trucking was at first brought into the state monopoly. If railroads had never been subjected to regulation in the United States, it is nearly certain that by now transportation, including railroads, would be a highly competitive industry with little or no remaining monopoly elements.

The choice between the evils of private monopoly, public monopoly, and public regulation cannot, however, be made once and for all, independently of the factual circumstances. If the technical monopoly is of a service or commodity that is regarded as essential and if its monopoly power is sizable, even the short-run effects of private unregulated monopoly may not be tolerable, and either public regulation or ownership may be a lesser evil.

Technical monopoly may on occasion justify a *de facto* public monopoly. It cannot by itself justify a public monopoly achieved by making it illegal for anyone else to compete. For example, there is no way to justify our present public monopoly of the post office. It may be argued that the carrying of mail is a technical monopoly and that a government monopoly is the least of evils. Along these lines, one could perhaps justify a government post office but not the present law, which makes it illegal for anybody else to carry mail. If the delivery of mail is a technical monopoly, no one will be able to succeed in competition with the government. If it is not, there is no reason why the government should be engaged in it. The only way to find out is to leave other people free to enter.

The historical reason why we have a post office monopoly is because the Pony Express did such a good job of carrying the mail across the continent that, when the government introduced transcontinental service, it couldn't compete effectively and lost money. The result was a law making it illegal for anybody else to carry the mail. That is why the Adams Express Company is an investment trust today instead of an operating company. I conjecture that if entry into the mail-carrying business were open to all, there would be a large number of firms entering it and this archaic industry would become revolutionized in short order.

A second general class of cases in which strictly voluntary exchange is impossible arises when actions of individuals have effects on other individuals for which it is not feasible to charge or recompense them. This is the problem of "neighborhood effects." An obvious example is the pollution of a stream. The man who pollutes a stream is in effect forcing others to exchange good water for bad. These others might be willing to make the exchange at a price. But it is not feasible for them, acting individually, to avoid the exchange or to enforce appropriate compensation.

A less obvious example is the provision of highways. In this case, it is technically possible to identify and hence charge individuals for their use of the roads and so to have private operation. However, for general access roads, involving many points of entry and exit, the costs of collection would be extremely high if a charge were to be made for the specific services received by each individual, because of the necessity of establishing toll booths or the equivalent at all entrances. The gasoline tax is a much cheaper method of charging individuals roughly in proportion to their use of the roads. This method, however, is one in which the particular payment cannot be identified closely with the particular use. Hence, it is hardly feasible to have private enterprise provide the service and collect the charge without establishing extensive private monopoly.

These considerations do not apply to long-distance turnpikes with high density of traffic and limited access. For these, the costs of collection are small and in many cases are now being paid, and there are often numerous alternatives, so that there is no serious monopoly problem. Hence, there is every reason why these should be privately owned and operated. If so owned and operated, the enterprise running the highway should receive the gasoline taxes paid on account of travel on it.

Parks are an interesting example because they illustrate the difference between cases that can and cases that cannot be justified by neighborhood effects, and because almost everyone at first sight regards the conduct of National Parks as obviously a valid function of government. In fact, however, neighborhood effects may justify a city park; they do not justify a national park, like Yellowstone National Park or the Grand Canyon. What is the fundamental difference between the two? For the city park, it is extremely difficult to identify the people who benefit from it and to charge them for the benefits which they receive. If there is a park in the middle of the city, the houses on all sides get the benefit of the open space, and people who walk through it or by it also benefit. To maintain toll collectors at the gates or to impose annual charges per window overlooking the park would be very expensive and difficult. The entrances to a national park like Yellowstone, on the other hand, are few; most of the people who come stay for a considerable period of time and it is perfectly feasible to set up toll gates and collect admission charges. This is indeed now done, though the charges do not cover the whole costs. If the public wants this kind of an activity enough to pay for it, private enterprises will have every incentive to provide such parks. And, of course, there are many private enterprises of this nature now in existence. I cannot myself conjure up any neighborhood effects or important monopoly effects that would justify governmental activity in this area.

Considerations like those I have treated under the heading of neighborhood effects have been used to rationalize almost every conceivable intervention. In many instances, however, this rationalization is special pleading rather than a legitimate application of the concept of neighborhood effects. Neighborhood effects cut both ways. They can be a reason for limiting the activities of government as well as for expanding them. Neighborhood effects impede voluntary exchange because it is difficult to identify the effects on third parties and to measure their magnitude; but this difficulty is present in governmental activity as well. It is hard to know when neighborhood effects are sufficiently large to justify particular costs in overcoming them and even harder to distribute the costs in an appropriate fashion. Consequently, when government engages in activities to overcome neighborhood effects, it will in part introduce an additional set of neighborhood effects by failing to charge or to compensate individuals properly. Whether the original or the new neighborhood effects are the more serious can only be judged by the facts of the individual case, and even then, only very approximately. Furthermore, the use of government to overcome neighborhood effects itself has an extremely important neighborhood effect which is unrelated to the particular occasion for government action. Every act of government intervention limits the area of individual freedom directly and threatens the preservation of freedom indirectly for reasons elaborated in the first chapter.

Our principles offer no hard and fast line how far it is appropriate to use government to accomplish jointly what it is difficult or impossible for us to accomplish separately through strictly voluntary exchange. In any particular case of proposed intervention, we must make up a balance sheet, listing separately the advantages and disadvantages. Our principles tell us what items to put on the one side and what items on the other and they give us some basis for attaching importance to the different items. In particular, we shall always want to enter on the liability side of any proposed government intervention, its neighborhood effect in threatening freedom, and give this effect considerable weight. Just how much weight to give to it, as to other items, depends upon the circumstances. If, for example, existing government intervention is minor, we shall attach a smaller weight to the negative effects of additional government intervention. This is an important reason why many earlier liberals, like Henry Simons, writing at a time when government was small by today's standards, were willing to have government undertake activities that today's liberals would not accept now that government has become so overgrown.

Action through Government on Paternalistic Grounds

Freedom is a tenable objective only for responsible individuals. We do not believe in freedom for madmen or children. The necessity of drawing a line between responsible individuals and others is inescapable, yet it means that there is an essential ambiguity in our ultimate objective of freedom. Paternalism is inescapable for those whom we designate as not responsible.

The clearest case, perhaps, is that of madmen. We are willing neither to permit them freedom nor to shoot them. It would be nice if we could rely on voluntary activities of individuals to house and care for the madmen. But I think we cannot rule out the possibility that such charitable activities will be inadequate, if only because of the neighborhood effect involved in the fact that I benefit if another man contributes to the care of the insane. For this reason, we may be willing to arrange for their care through government.

Children offer a more difficult case. The ultimate operative unit in our society is the family, not the individual. Yet the acceptance of the family as the unit rests in considerable part on expediency rather than principle. We believe that parents are generally best able to protect their children and to provide for their development into responsible individuals for whom freedom is appropriate. But we do not believe in the freedom of parents to do what they will with other people. The children are responsible individuals in embryo, and a believer in freedom believes in protecting their ultimate rights.

To put this in a different and what may seem a more callous way, children are at one and the same time consumer goods and potentially responsible members of society. The freedom of individuals to use their economic resources as they want includes the freedom to use them to have children—to buy, as it were, the services of children as a particular form of consumption. But once this choice is exercised, the children have a value in and of themselves and have a freedom of their own that is not simply an extension of the freedom of the parents.

The paternalistic ground for governmental activity is in many ways the most troublesome to a liberal; for it involves the acceptance of a principle—that some shall decide for others—which he finds objectionable in most applications and which he rightly regards as a hallmark of his chief intellectual opponents, the proponents of collectivism in one or another of its guises, whether it be communism, socialism, or a welfare state. Yet there is no use pretending that problems are simpler than in fact they are. There is no avoiding the need for some measure of paternalism. As Dicey wrote in 1914 about an act for the protection of mental defectives, "The Mental Deficiency Act is the first step along a path on which no sane man can decline to enter, but which, if too far pursued, will bring statesmen across difficulties hard to meet without considerable interference with individual liberty."[1] There is no formula that can tell us where to stop. We must rely on our fallible judgment and, having reached a judgment, on our ability to persuade our fellow men that it is a correct judgment, or their ability to persuade us to modify our views. We must put our faith, here as elsewhere, in a consensus reached by imperfect and biased men through free discussion and trial and error.

Conclusion

A government which maintained law and order, defined property rights, served as a means whereby we could modify property rights and other rules of the economic game, adjudicated disputes about the interpretation of the rules, enforced contracts, promoted competition, provided a monetary framework, engaged in activities to counter technical monopolies and to overcome neighborhood effects widely regarded as sufficiently important to justify government intervention, and which supplemented private charity and the private family in protecting the irresponsible, whether madman or child—such a government would clearly have important functions to perform. The consistent liberal is not an anarchist.

Yet it is also true that such a government would have clearly limited functions and would refrain from a host of activities that are now undertaken by federal and state governments in the United States, and their counterparts in other Western countries. Succeeding chapters will deal in some detail with some of these activities, and a few have been discussed above, but it may help to give a sense of proportion about the role that a liberal would assign government simply to list, in closing this chapter, some activities currently undertaken by government in the U.S., that cannot, so far as I can see, validly be justified in terms of the principles outlined above:

1. Parity price support programs for agriculture.
2. Tariffs on imports or restrictions on exports, such as current oil import quotas, sugar quotas, etc.
3. Governmental control of output, such as through the farm program, or through prorationing of oil as is done by the Texas Railroad Commission.
4. Rent control, such as is still practiced in New York, or more general price and wage controls such as were imposed during and just after World War II.
5. Legal minimum wage rates, or legal maximum prices, such as the legal maximum of zero on the rate of interest that can be paid on demand deposits by commercial banks, or the legally fixed maximum rates that can be paid on savings and time deposits.
6. Detailed regulation of industries, such as the regulation of transportation by the Interstate Commerce Commission. This had some justification on technical monopoly grounds when initially introduced for railroads; it has none now for any means of transport. Another example is detailed regulation of banking.
7. A similar example, but one which deserves special mention because of its implicit censorship and violation of free speech, is the control of radio and television by the Federal Communications Commission.
8. Present social security programs, especially the old-age and retirement programs compelling people in effect (a) to spend a specified fraction of their income on the purchase of retirement annuity, (b) to buy the annuity from a publicly operated enterprise.
9. Licensure provisions in various cities and states which restrict particular enterprises or occupations or professions to people who have a license, where the license is more than a receipt for a tax which anyone who wishes to enter the activity may pay.
10. So-called "public-housing" and the host of other subsidy programs directed at fostering residential construction such as F.H.A. and V.A. guarantee of mortgage, and the like.
11. Conscription to man the military services in peacetime. The appropriate free market arrangement is volunteer military forces; which is to say, hiring men to serve. There is no justification for not paying whatever price is necessary to attract the required number of men. Present arrangements are inequitable and arbitrary, seriously interfere with the freedom of young men to shape their lives, and probably are even more costly than the market alternative. (Universal military training to provide a reserve for war time is a different problem and may be justified on liberal grounds.)

12. National parks, as noted above.
13. The legal prohibition on the carrying of mail for profit.
14. Publicly owned and operated toll roads, as noted above.

This list is far from comprehensive.

Note

1 A.V. Dicey, *Lectures on the Relation between Law and Public Opinion in England during the Nineteenth Century* (2d. ed.; London: Macmillan & Co., 1914), p. li.

3

Economic Sociology

The economic sociology perspective on political economy rests on twin insights that counter the foundational assumptions of the liberal perspective. First, markets are embedded in society, such that social relationships are central to the economic system, not the province of a separate sphere outside the market. Second, economic sociologists contest the notion that the market is a spontaneously occurring and self-regulating phenomenon. Many argue, on the contrary, that market systems require constant government action for them to work and even to come into existence in the first place. The intellectual and practical consequence of these two insights is that markets are institutions that are deliberately constructed and continuously reconstructed based on social and political values and goals. Economic sociology represents the market-institutionalist perspective that the functioning of the economic system rests on an evolving series of choices about how to manage capitalism to meet the preferences of society, often enacted via government intervention.

Karl Polanyi is one of the forefathers of the school of economic sociology. His work provides a direct counterpoint to the market-liberal school of thought, represented in this reader by Adam Smith, Friedrich Hayek, and Milton Friedman.[1] Polanyi first encountered and directly challenged the arguments of Ludwig von Mises and Friedrich Hayek as a student in Vienna in the 1920s. In writing his landmark work, *The Great Transformation*, as the Second World War drew to a close, Polanyi launched a searing critique of economic liberalism and its utopian myth of the self-regulating market. The foundation of his argument is the observation that only under a market economy is society subjugated to the economy and run as an adjunct to the market. This is contrary to traditional forms of human organization, where markets and the economy are an integrated part of society and economic motives are submerged in social principles such as reciprocity and redistribution. At the crux of the economic sociology paradigm are the insights that markets are inherently social phenomena embedded in sociopolitical structures and hence that economic life and social life are inherently interconnected.

Polanyi's critique of economic liberalism is that the notion of the self-regulating market is riddled with its own contradictions and is actually impossible in practice. To demonstrate this, he introduces the concept of the "fictitious commodities," wherein he argues that land, labor, and capital – the factors of production – are not true commodities because they are not produced for sale. Yet a true self-regulating market would require creating markets for these fictitious commodities, based on the notion that their price can and will be set by supply and demand, just like all other commodities. Polanyi's point is that if this were really the case, society would be entirely subordinated to the market system – which, in turn, would result in the collapse of the market system itself because it would demolish society. He points out that land, labor, and capital in real (not utopian) market societies are managed not as commodities for exchange but instead through social relations and the political process. Only under economic liberalism is society expected to be subjugated to the economy. Echoing Marx, Polanyi says that this notion of the self-regulating market contains its own paradox: if the market economy forced society into subordination, the socioeconomic order would inevitably be disrupted.

Polanyi introduces the famous "double movement" to illuminate how this paradox is resolved in practice. Economic liberalism is inevitably accompanied by the forces of social protectionism, as various classes in society react to protect themselves against the unbearable sociopolitical dislocations introduced by self-regulating markets. Thus two primary organizing principles in political economy – the laissez-faire movement and the protective countermovement – interact. Economic liberalism, in Polanyi's view, adopts a mystical readiness to accept the social consequences of economic advancement, instead of understanding that if the transformation wrought by economic change is too fast, it should be slowed down to safeguard community welfare. In reality, Polanyi argues, government responds to societal demands for protectionism, slowing down the rate of change and allowing a process of social adjustment to take place. He illustrates the double movement through the enclosures example: the enclosure movement was essential to economic improvement and the Industrial Revolution – but without the anti-enclosure movement, which did not stop enclosures but slowed down the rate of change, the pace of progress might have been ruinous rather than constructive. The market survives without destroying society and itself because the market is inherently embedded in society, which fights back against economic dislocation and shapes the market system.

Polanyi turns another element of market-liberal logic on its head by emphasizing the core insight of the market-institutional perspective: that state intervention is central in creating and maintaining markets. In the economic liberal school of thought, from Adam Smith on, markets arise naturally, whereas state intervention in the economy is misguided and reactionary and prevents the market from self-regulating to correct its own short-term failures. In his history of the social transformation accompanying the Industrial Revolution, Polanyi attacks this logic by arguing that markets and regulation grew up together. He argues that the construction and maintenance of the laissez-faire economy was not natural but the product of deliberate state action. Also, the great variety of forms the social protection countermovement took resulted not from deliberate anti-liberalism but spontaneously from the broad range of social interests affected by the destructive pressures of the market mechanism as it expanded. In other words, in his inimitable phrase, "Laissez-faire was planned; planning was not." Without society's protective countermoves, exercised through state involvement in the role of managing the fictitious commodities, the progress of an unchecked self-regulating market mechanism would have proved too destructive to society to survive.

Economic sociologists have built on Polanyi's insights, continuing to see economic principles not as universal precepts axiomatic to market societies but rather as economic conventions, traditions, and practices rooted in history and society.[2] Scholars in the field of economic sociology emphasize that capitalism is a constructed and continually reconstructed system, rather than a natural system that can be articulated only through one set of rules.[3] Market liberalism and Marxism see only two possible political–economic outcomes for societies: capitalism or communism. From Polanyi, instead, comes the insight that a range of alternatives in political economy is possible, because markets can be embedded in many different ways.[4] The varieties of political economy we see in the world today developed as a result of different social and political choices, often implemented through state intervention. Polanyi's concept of the "embeddedness" of the economy in society has thus come to be central to the economic sociology paradigm.[5] For economic sociologists, furthermore, the social relationships and networks surrounding economic activity are phenomena to be problematized and studied. This contrasts with the functionalist approach of the new institutional economics, which assumes that institutional and social relationships exist to reduce transaction costs.

Neil Fligstein provides a contemporary economic sociological analysis of markets with a "theory of fields." Sociologists use the term *fields* to refer to arenas of activity that have an identity as a coherent issue-area or locus of activity, with social structures that go along with them, for example, neoclassical economics, sports leagues, and human rights law. In Fligstein's view, a sectoral market (such as the American automobile industry) is such a field, encompassing a set of vertical institutions – that is, firms – and horizontal institutions – that is, relationships between firms, consumers, the state, and other societal actors. A distinctive feature of this analysis is that sectoral markets have social structures, which in turn affect market behavior in predictable ways. One insight that emerges from Fligstein's perspective of markets as fields is that incumbent firms try to produce a stable environment for themselves, so the ultimate motive of firms in this conception of markets is not simply profit but also stability or survival. Market activity plays out as a series of power struggles both within and among firms, where dominant actors, such as large incumbent firms, produce rules and meaning that allow them to maintain their advantage. A market, in this view, is a socio-organizational construct intended to establish stability in exchange relationships. Firms generate that stability by creating social structure in the form of status hierarchies: within a market there are dominant firms, incumbents, and challengers, and dominant firms create the social relations of the market to ensure their continued advantage. Examples of such behavior include Microsoft's successive attempts to maintain its market share in the software market and Coca-Cola's strategies for staying on top in the beverage industry.

Fligstein's framework also includes an expansive definition of the institutions relevant to an analysis of markets. Rather than viewing institutions as the functional outcomes of an efficient process, as does the new institutional economics, Fligstein argues that market institutions are cultural and historical products that are specific to each industry in a given society and have evolved through a continuous, contested process. These institutions have intersubjective meanings – they depend intricately on how social actors perceive them and are not constructs that are separable from their embeddedness in society. Following Polanyi, Fligstein emphasizes that the state plays a crucial role in creating markets as institutions. The entry of a country into capitalism pushes states to develop rules that market actors cannot create themselves. States are also the focal points for economic and social actors during crisis and so are central in enforcing market institutions and sustaining markets through change. How – and how much – they do so depends on what type of state they are and their administrative capacity. In a comparative sense, the configuration of rules and institutions within markets, along with the nature of social relationships between various economic actors, accounts for persistent differences in national political-economic systems.

Notes

1 Polanyi's insights are related in content, but not in conclusion, to those of Karl Marx, who saw the mode of production – which constitutes both production processes and social relations – as driving economic history.
2 Nicole W. Biggart, ed., *Readings in Economic Sociology* (Oxford: Blackwell, 2002), xiii.
3 Fred Block, "Rethinking Capitalism," in Nicole Biggart, ed., *Readings in Economic Sociology* (Oxford: Blackwell, 2002), 223.
4 Fred Block, "Introduction," in Karl Polanyi, ed., *The Great Transformation: The Political and Economic Origins of Our Time* (Boston, MA: Beacon Press, 2001), xxix.
5 See, in particular, Mark Granovetter, "Economic Action and Social Structure: The Problem of Embeddedness," *American Journal of Sociology* 91 (1985): 481–510. This article (discussed in brief in the introduction to this volume) reintroduced an evolved definition of the concept of the embeddedness of markets into the economic sociology paradigm.

Karl Polanyi,
The Great Transformation (1944)[*]

I. Satanic Mill

Chapter 3: *"Habitation versus Improvement"*

At the heart of the Industrial Revolution of the eighteenth century there was an almost miraculous improvement in the tools of production, which was accompanied by a catastrophic dislocation of the lives of the common people.

We will attempt to disentangle the factors that determined the forms of this dislocation, as it appeared at its worst in England about a century ago. What "satanic mill" ground men into masses? How much was caused by the new physical conditions? How much by the economic dependencies, operating under the new conditions? And what was the mechanism through which the old social tissue was destroyed and a new integration of man and nature so unsuccessfully attempted?

Nowhere has liberal philosophy failed so conspicuously as in its understanding of the problem of change. Fired by an emotional faith in spontaneity, the common-sense attitude toward change was discarded in favor of a mystical readiness to accept the social consequences of economic improvement, whatever they might be. The elementary truths of political science and statecraft were first discredited, then forgotten. It should need no elaboration that a process of undirected change, the pace of which is deemed too fast, should be slowed down, if possible, so as to safeguard the welfare of the community. Such household truths of traditional statesmanship, often merely reflecting the teachings of a social philosophy inherited from the ancients, were in the nineteenth century erased from the thoughts of the educated by the corrosive of a crude utilitarianism combined with an uncritical reliance on the alleged self-healing virtues of unconscious growth.

Economic liberalism misread the history of the Industrial Revolution because it insisted on judging social events from the economic viewpoint. For an illustration of this we shall turn to what may at first seem a remote subject: to enclosures of open fields and conversions of arable land to pasture during the earlier Tudor period in England, when fields and commons were hedged by the lords, and whole counties were threatened by depopulation. Our purpose in thus evoking the plight of the people brought about by enclosures and conversions will be on the one hand to demonstrate the parallel between the devastations caused by the ultimately beneficial enclosures and those resulting from the Industrial Revolution, and on the other hand—and more broadly—to clarify the alternatives facing a community which is in the throes of unregulated economic improvement.

Enclosures were an obvious improvement *if* no conversion to pasture took place. Enclosed land was worth double and treble the unenclosed. Where tillage was maintained, employment did not fall off, and the food supply markedly increased. The yield of the land manifestly increased, especially where the land was let.

But even conversion of arable land to sheep runs was not altogether detrimental to the neighborhood in spite of the destruction of habitations and the restriction of employment it involved. Cottage industry was spreading by the second half of the fifteenth century, and a century later it began to be a feature of the countryside. The wool produced on the sheep farm gave employment to the small tenants and landless cottagers forced out of tillage, and the new centers of the woolen industry secured an income to a number of craftsmen.

But—this is the point—only in a market economy can such compensating effects be taken for granted. In the absence of such an economy the highly profitable occupation of raising sheep and selling their wool might ruin the country. The sheep which "turned sand into gold" could well have turned the gold into sand as happened ultimately to the wealth of seventeenth century Spain whose eroded soil never recovered from the overexpansion of sheep farming.

An official document of 1607, prepared for the use of the Lords of the Realm, set out the problem of change in one powerful phrase: "The poor man shall be satisfied in his end: Habitation; and the gentleman not hindered in his desire: Improvement." This formula appears to take for granted the essence of purely economic progress, which is to achieve improvement at the price of social dislocation. But it also hints at the tragic necessity by which the poor man clings to his hovel, doomed by the rich man's desire for a public improvement which profits him privately.

Enclosures have appropriately been called a revolution of the rich against the poor. The lords and nobles were upsetting the social order, breaking down ancient law and custom, sometimes by means of violence, often by pressure and intimidation. They were literally robbing the poor of their share in the common, tearing down the houses which, by the hitherto unbreakable force of custom, the poor had long regarded as theirs and their heirs'. The fabric of society was being disrupted; desolate villages and the ruins of human dwellings testified to the fierceness with which the revolution raged, endangering the defenses of the country, wasting its towns, decimating its population, turning its overburdened soil into dust, harassing its people and turning them from decent husbandmen into a mob of beggars and thieves. Though this happened only in patches, the black spots threatened to melt into a uniform catastrophe.[1] The King and his Council, the Chancellors, and the Bishops were defending the welfare of the community and, indeed, the human and natural substance of society against this scourge. With hardly any intermittence, for a century and a half—from the 1490's, at the latest, to the 1640's—they struggled against depopulation. Lord Protector Somerset lost his life at the hands of the counterrevolution which wiped the enclosure laws from the statute book and established the dictatorship of the grazier lords, after Kett's Rebellion was defeated with several thousand peasants slaughtered in the process. Somerset was accused, and not without truth, of having given encouragement to the rebellious peasants by his staunch denunciation of enclosures.

It was almost a hundred years later when a second trial of strength came between the same opponents, but by that time the enclosers were much more frequently wealthy country gentlemen and merchants rather than lords and nobles. High politics, lay and ecclesiastical, were now involved in the Crown's deliberate use of its prerogative to prevent enclosures and in its no less deliberate use of the enclosure issue to strengthen its position against the gentry in a constitutional struggle, which brought death to Strafford and Laud at the hands of Parliament. But their policy was not only industrially but politically reactionary; furthermore, enclosures were now much more often than before intended for tillage, and not for pasture. Presently the tide of the Civil War engulfed Tudor and early Stuart public policy forever.

Nineteenth century historians were unanimous in condemning Tudor and early Stuart policy as demagogic, if not as outright reactionary. Their sympathies lay, naturally, with Parliament and that body had been on the side of the enclosers. H. de B. Gibbins, though an ardent friend of the common people, wrote: "Such protective enactments were, however, as protective enactments generally be, utterly vain."[2] Innes was even more definite: "The usual remedies of punishing vagabondage and attempting to force industry into unsuited fields and to drive capital into less lucrative investments in order to provide employment failed—as usual."[3] Gairdner had no hesitation in appealing to free trade notions as "economic law": "Economic laws were, of course, not understood," he wrote, "and attempts were made by legislation to prevent husbandmen's dwellings from being thrown down by landlords, who found it profitable to devote arable land to pasture to increase the growth of wool. The frequent repetition of these Acts only show how ineffective they were in practice."[4] Recently an economist like Heckscher emphasizes his conviction that mercantilism should, in the main, be explained by an insufficient understanding of the complexities of economic phenomena, a subject which the human mind obviously needed another few centuries to master.[5] In effect, anti-enclosure legislation never seemed to have stopped the course of the enclosure movement, nor even to have obstructed it seriously. John Hales, second to none in his fervor for the principles of the Commonwealth men, admitted that it proved impossible to collect evidence against the enclosers, who often had their servants sworn upon the juries, and such was the number "of their retainers and hangers-on that no jury could be made without them." Sometimes the simple expedient of driving a single furrow across the field would save the offending lord from a penalty.

Such an easy prevailing of private interests over justice is often regarded as a certain sign of the ineffectiveness of legislation, and the victory of the vainly obstructed trend is subsequently adduced as conclusive evidence of the alleged futility of "a reactionary interventionism." Yet such a view seems to miss the point altogether. Why should the ultimate victory of a trend be taken as a proof of the ineffectiveness of the efforts to slow down its progress? And why should the purpose of these measures not be seen precisely in that which they achieved, *i.e.*, in the slowing down of the rate of change? That which is ineffectual in stopping a line of development altogether is not, on that account, altogether ineffectual. The rate of change is often of no less importance than the direction of the change itself; but while the latter frequently does not depend upon our volition, it is the rate at which we allow change to take place which well may depend upon us.

A belief in spontaneous progress must make us blind to the role of government in economic life. This role consists often in altering the rate of change, speeding it up or slowing it down as the case may be; if we believe that rate to be unalterable—or even worse, if we deem it a sacrilege to interfere with it—then, of course, no room is left for intervention. Enclosures offer an example. In retrospect nothing could be clearer than the Western European trend of economic progress which aimed at eliminating an artificially maintained uniformity of agricultural technique, intermixed strips, and the primitive institution of the common. As to England, it is certain that the development of the woolen industry was an asset to the country, leading, as it did, to the establishment of the cotton industry—that vehicle of the Industrial Revolution. Furthermore, it is clear that the increase of domestic weaving depended upon the increase of a home supply of wool. These facts suffice to identify the change from arable land to pasture and the accompanying enclosure movement as the trend of economic progress. Yet, but for the consistently maintained policy of the Tudor and early Stuart statesmen, the rate of that progress might have been ruinous, and have turned the process itself into a degenerative instead of a constructive event. For upon this rate, mainly, depended whether the dispossessed could adjust themselves to changed conditions without fatally damaging their substance, human and economic, physical and moral; whether they would find new employment in the fields of opportunity indirectly connected with the change; and whether the effects of increased imports induced by increased exports would enable those who lost their employment through the change to find new sources of sustenance.

The answer depended in every case on the relative rates of change and adjustment. The usual "long-run" considerations of economic theory are inadmissible; they would prejudge the issue by assuming that the event took place in a market economy. However natural it may appear to us to make that assumption, it is unjustified: market economy is an institutional structure which, as we all too easily forget, has been present at no time except our own, and even then it was only partially present. Yet apart from this assumption "long-run" considerations are meaningless. If the immediate effect of a change is deleterious, then, until proof to the contrary, the final effect is deleterious. If conversion of arable land to pasture involves the destruction of a definite number of houses, the scrapping of a definite amount of employment, and the diminution of the supplies of locally available food provisions, then these effects must be regarded as final, until evidence to the contrary is produced. This does not exclude the consideration of the possible effects of increased exports on the income of the landowners; of the possible chances of employment created by an eventual increase in the local wool supply; or of the uses to which the land-owners might put their increased incomes, whether in the way of further investments or of luxury expenditure. The time-rate of change compared with the time-rate of adjustment will decide what is to be regarded as the net effect of the change. But in no case can we assume the functioning of market laws unless a self-regulating market is shown to exist. Only in the institutional setting of market economy are market laws relevant; it was not the statesmen of Tudor England who strayed from the facts, but the modern economists, whose strictures upon them implied the prior existence of a market system.

England withstood without grave damage the calamity of the enclosures only because the Tudors and the early Stuarts used the power of the Crown to slow down the process of economic improvement until it became socially bearable—employing the power of the central government to relieve the victims of the transformation, and attempting to canalize the process of change so as to make its course less devastating. Their chancelleries and courts of prerogative were anything but conservative in outlook; they represented the scientific spirit of the new statecraft, favoring the immigration of foreign craftsmen, eagerly implanting new techniques, adopting statistical methods and precise habits of reporting, flouting custom and tradition, opposing prescriptive rights, curtailing ecclesiastical prerogatives, ignoring Common Law. If innovation makes the revolutionary, they were the revolutionaries of the age. Their commitment was to the welfare of the commonalty, glorified in the power and grandeur of the sovereign; yet the future belonged to constitutionalism and Parliament. The government of the Crown gave place to government by a class—the class which led in industrial and commercial progress. The great principle of constitutionalism became wedded to the political revolution that dispossessed the Crown, which by that time had shed almost all its creative faculties, while its protective function was no longer vital to a country that had weathered the storm of transition. The financial policy of the Crown now restricted the power of the country unduly, and began to constrain its trade; in order to maintain its prerogatives the Crown abused them more and more, and thereby harmed the resources of the nation. Its brilliant administration of labor and industry, its circumspect control of the enclosure movement, remained its last achievement. But it was the more easily forgotten as the capitalists and employers of the rising middle class were the chief victims of its protective activities. Not till another two centuries had passed did England enjoy again a social administration as effective and well ordered as that which the Commonwealth destroyed. Admittedly, an administration of this paternalistic kind was now less needed. But in one respect the break wrought infinite harm, for it helped to obliterate from the memory of the nation the horrors of the enclosure period and the achievements of government in overcoming the peril of depopulation. Perhaps this helps to explain why the real nature of the crisis was not realized when, some 150 years later, a similar catastrophe in the shape of the Industrial Revolution threatened the life and well-being of the country.

This time also the event was peculiar to England; this time also sea-borne trade was the source of a movement which affected the country as a whole; and this time again it was improvement on the grandest scale which wrought unprecedented havoc with the habitation of the common people. Before the process had advanced very far, the laboring people had been crowded together in new places of desolation, the so-called industrial towns of England; the country folk had been dehumanized into slum dwellers; the family was on the road to perdition; and large parts of the country were rapidly disappearing under the slack and scrap heaps vomited forth from the "satanic mills." Writers of all views and parties, conservatives and liberals, capitalists and socialists invariably referred to social conditions under the Industrial Revolution as a veritable abyss of human degradation.

No quite satisfactory explanation of the event has yet been put forward. Contemporaries imagined they had discovered the key to damnation in the iron regularities governing wealth and poverty, which they called the law of wages and the law of population; they have been disproved. Exploitation was put forth as another explanation both of wealth and of poverty; but this was unable to account for the fact that wages in the industrial slums were higher than those in any other areas and on the whole continued to rise for another century. More often a convolute of causes was adduced, which again was hardly satisfactory.

Our own solution is anything but simple; it actually fills the better part of this book. We submit that an avalanche of social dislocation, surpassing by far that of the enclosure period, came down upon England; that this catastrophe was the accompaniment of a vast movement of economic improvement; that an entirely new institutional mechanism was starting to act on Western society; that its dangers, which cut to the quick when they first appeared, were never really overcome; and that the history of nineteenth century civilization consisted largely in attempts to protect society against the ravages of such a mechanism. The Industrial Revolution was merely the beginning of a revolution as extreme and radical as ever inflamed the minds of sectarians, but the new creed was utterly materialistic and believed that all human problems could be resolved given an unlimited amount of material commodities.

The story has been told innumerable times: how the expansion of markets, the presence of coal and iron as well as a humid climate favorable to the cotton industry, the multitude of people dispossessed by the new eighteenth century enclosures, the existence of free institutions, the invention of the machines, and other causes interacted in such a manner as to bring about the Industrial Revolution. It has been shown conclusively that no one single cause deserves to be lifted out of the chain and set apart as *the* cause of that sudden and unexpected event.

But how shall this Revolution itself be defined? What was its basic characteristic? Was it the rise of the factory towns, the emergence of slums, the long working hours of children, the low wages of certain categories of workers, the rise in the rate of population increase, or the concentration of industries? We submit that all these were merely incidental to one basic change, the establishment of market economy, and that the nature of this institution cannot be fully grasped unless the impact of the machine on a commercial society is realized. We do not intend to assert that the machine caused that which happened, but we insist that once elaborate machines and plant were used for production in a commercial society, the idea of a self-regulating market was bound to take shape.

The use of specialized machines in an agrarian and commercial society must produce typical effects. Such a society consists of agriculturalists and of merchants who buy and sell the produce of the land. Production with the help of specialized, elaborate, expensive tools and plants can be fitted into such a society only by making it incidental to buying and selling. The merchant is the only person available for the undertaking of this, and he is fitted to do so as long as this activity will not involve him in a loss. He will sell the goods in the same manner in which he would otherwise sell goods to those who demand them; but he will procure them in a different way, namely, not by buying them ready-made, but by purchasing the necessary labor and raw material. The two put together according to the merchant's instructions, plus some waiting which he might have to undertake, amount to the new product. This is not a description of domestic industry or "putting out" only, but of any kind of industrial capitalism, including that of our own time. Important consequences for the social system follow.

Since elaborate machines are expensive, they do not pay unless large amounts of goods are produced.[6] They can be worked without a loss only if the vent of the goods is reasonably assured and if production need not be interrupted for want of the primary goods necessary to feed the machines. For the merchant this means that all factors involved must be on sale, that is, they must be available in the needed quantities to anybody who is prepared to pay for them. Unless this condition is fulfilled, production with the help of specialized machines is too risky to be undertaken both from the point of view of the merchant who stakes his money and of the community as a whole which comes to depend upon continuous production for incomes, employment, and provisions.

Now, in an agricultural society such conditions would not naturally be given; they would have to be created. That they would be created gradually in no way affects the startling nature of the changes involved. The transformation implies a change in the motive of action on the part of the members of society: for the motive of subsistence that of gain must be substituted. All transactions are turned into money transactions, and these in turn require that a medium of exchange be introduced into every articulation of industrial life. All incomes must derive from the sale of something or other, and whatever the actual source of a person's income, it must be regarded as resulting from sale. No less is implied in the simple term "market system," by which we designate the institutional pattern described. But the most startling peculiarity of the system lies in the fact that, once it is established, it must be allowed to function without outside interference. Profits are not any more guaranteed, and the merchant must make his profits on the market. Prices must be allowed to regulate themselves. Such a self-regulating system of markets is what we mean by a market economy.

The transformation to this system from the earlier economy is so complete that it resembles more the metamorphosis of the caterpillar than any alteration that can be expressed in terms of continuous growth and development. Contrast, for example, the merchant-producer's selling activities with his buying activities; his sales concern only artifacts; whether he succeeds or not in finding purchasers, the fabric of society need not be affected. But what he *buys* is raw materials and labor—nature and man. Machine production in a commercial society involves, in effect, no less a transformation than that of the natural and human substance of society into commodities. The conclusion, though weird, is inevitable; nothing less will serve the purpose: obviously, the dislocation caused by such devices must disjoint man's relationships and threaten his natural habitat with annihilation.

Such a danger was, in fact, imminent. We shall perceive its true character if we examine the laws which govern the mechanism of a self-regulating market.

Chapter 4: Societies and Economic Systems

Before we can proceed to the discussion of the laws governing a market economy, such as the nineteenth century was trying to establish, we must first have a firm grip on the extraordinary assumptions underlying such a system.

Market economy implies a self-regulating system of markets; in slightly more technical terms, it is an economy directed by market prices and nothing but market prices. Such a system capable of organizing the whole of economic life without outside help or interference would certainly deserve to be called self-regulating. These rough indications should suffice to show the entirely unprecedented nature of such a venture in the history of the race.

Let us make our meaning more precise. No society could, naturally, live for any length of time unless it possessed an economy of some sort; but previously to our time no economy has ever existed that, even in principle, was controlled by markets. In spite of the chorus of academic incantations so persistent in the nineteenth century, gain and profit made on exchange never before played an important part in human economy. Though the institution of the market was fairly common since the later Stone Age, its role was no more than incidental to economic life.

We have good reason to insist on this point with all the emphasis at our command. No less a thinker than Adam Smith suggested that the division of labor in society was dependent upon the existence of markets, or, as he put it, upon man's "propensity to barter, truck and exchange one thing for another." This phrase was later to yield the concept of the Economic Man. In retrospect it can be said that no misreading of the past ever proved more prophetic of the future. For while up to Adam Smith's time that propensity had hardly shown up on a considerable scale in the life of any observed community, and had remained, at best, a subordinate feature of economic life, a hundred years later an industrial system was in full swing over the major part of the planet which, practically and theoretically, implied that the human race was swayed in all its economic activities, if not also in its political, intellectual, and spiritual pursuits, by that one particular propensity. Herbert Spencer, in the second half of the nineteenth century, could, without more than a cursory acquaintance with economics, equate the principle of the division of labor with barter and exchange, and another fifty years later, Ludwig von Mises and Walter Lippmann could repeat this same fallacy. By that time there was no need for argument. A host of writers on political economy, social history, political philosophy, and general sociology had followed in Smith's wake and established his paradigm of the bartering savage as an axiom of their respective sciences. In point of fact, Adam Smith's suggestions about the economic psychology of early man were as false as Rousseau's were on the political psychology of the savage. Division of labor, a phenomenon as old as society, springs from differences inherent in the facts of sex, geography, and individual endowment; and the alleged propensity of man to barter, truck, and exchange is almost entirely apocryphal. While history and ethnography know of various kinds of economies, most of them comprising the institution of markets, they know of no economy prior to our own, even approximately controlled and regulated by markets. This will become abundantly clear from a bird's-eye view of the history of economic systems and of markets, presented separately. The role played by markets in the internal economy of the various countries, it will appear, was insignificant up to recent times, and the change-over to an economy dominated by the market pattern will stand out all the more clearly.

To start with, we must discard some nineteenth century prejudices that underlay Adam Smith's hypothesis about primitive man's alleged predilection for gainful occupations. Since his axiom was much more relevant to the immediate future than to the dim past, it induced in his followers a strange attitude toward man's early history. On the face of it, the evidence seemed to indicate that primitive man, far from having a capitalistic psychology, had, in effect, a communistic one (later this also proved to be mistaken). Consequently, economic historians tended to confine their interest to that comparatively recent period of history in which truck and exchange were found on any considerable scale, and primitive economics was relegated to prehistory. Unconsciously, this led to a weighting of the scales in favor of a marketing psychology, for within the relatively short period of the last few centuries everything might be taken to tend towards the establishment of that which was eventually established, *i.e.*, a market system, irrespective of other tendencies which were temporarily submerged. The corrective of such a "short-run" perspective would obviously have been the linking up of economic history with social anthropology, a course which was consistently avoided.

We cannot continue today on these lines. The habit of looking at the last ten thousand years as well as at the array of early societies as a mere prelude to the true history of our civilization which started approximately with the publication of the *Wealth of Nations* in 1776, is, to say the least, out of date. It is this episode which has come to a close in our days, and in trying to gauge the alternatives of the future, we should subdue our natural proneness to follow the proclivities of our fathers. But the same bias which made Adam Smith's generation view primeval man as bent on barter and truck induced their successors to disavow all interest in early man, as he was now known *not* to have indulged in those laudable passions. The tradition of the classical economists, who attempted to base the law of the market on the alleged propensities of man in the state of nature, was replaced by an abandonment of all interest in the cultures of "uncivilized" man as irrelevant to an understanding of the problems of our age.

Such an attitude of subjectivism in regard to earlier civilizations should make no appeal to the scientific mind. The differences existing between civilized and "uncivilized" peoples have been vastly exaggerated, especially in the economic sphere. According to the historians, the forms of industrial life in agricultural Europe were, until recently, not much different from what they had been several thousand years earlier. Ever since the introduction of the plow—essentially a large hoe drawn by animals—the methods of agriculture remained substantially unaltered over the major part of Western and Central Europe until the beginning of the modern age. Indeed, the progress of civilization was, in these regions, mainly political, intellectual, and spiritual; in respect to material conditions, the Western Europe of 1100 A.D. had hardly caught up with the Roman world of a thousand years before. Even later, change flowed more easily in the channels of statecraft, literature, and the arts, but particularly in those of religion and learning, than in those of industry. In its economics, medieval Europe was largely on a level with ancient Persia, India, or China, and certainly could not rival in riches and culture the New Kingdom of Egypt, two thousand years before. Max Weber was the first among modern economic historians to protest against the brushing aside of primitive economics as irrelevant to the question of the motives and mechanisms of civilized societies. The subsequent work of social anthropology proved him emphatically right. For, if one conclusion stands out more clearly than another from the recent study of early societies it is the changelessness of man as a social being. His natural endowments reappear with a remarkable constancy in societies of all times and places; and the necessary preconditions of the survival of human society appear to be immutably the same.

The outstanding discovery of recent historical and anthropological research is that man's economy, as a rule, is submerged in his social relationships. He does not act so as to safeguard his individual interest in the possession of material goods; he acts so as to safeguard his social standing, his social claims, his social assets. He values material goods only in so far as they serve this end. Neither the process of production nor that of distribution is linked to specific economic interests attached to the possession of goods; but every single step in that process is geared to a number of social interests which eventually ensure that the required step be taken. These interests will be very different in a small hunting or fishing community from those in a vast despotic society, but in either case the economic system will be run on non-economic motives.

The explanation, in terms of survival, is simple. Take the case of a tribal society. The individual's economic interest is rarely paramount, for the community keeps all its members from starving unless it is itself borne down by catastrophe, in which case interests are again threatened collectively, not individually. The maintenance of social ties, on the other hand, is crucial. First, because by disregarding the accepted code of honor, or generosity, the individual cuts himself off from the community and becomes an outcast; second, because, in the long run, all social obligations are reciprocal, and their fulfillment serves also the individual's give-and-take interests best. Such a situation must exert a continuous pressure on the individual to eliminate economic self-interest from his consciousness to the point of making him unable, in many cases (but by no means in all), even to comprehend the implications of his own actions in terms of such an interest. This attitude is reinforced by the frequency of communal activities such as partaking of food from the common catch or sharing in the results of some far-flung and dangerous tribal expedition. The premium set on generosity is so great when measured in terms of social prestige as to make any other behavior than that of utter self-forgetfulness simply not pay. Personal character has little to do with the matter. Man can be as good or evil, as social or asocial, jealous or generous, in respect to one set of values as in respect to another. Not to allow anybody reason for jealousy is, indeed, an accepted principle of ceremonial distribution, just as publicly bestowed praise is the due of the industrious, skillful, or otherwise successful gardener (unless he be *too* successful, in which case he may deservedly be allowed to wither away under the delusion of being the victim of black magic). The human passions, good or bad, are merely directed towards noneconomic ends. Ceremonial display serves to spur emulation to the utmost and the custom of communal labor tends to screw up both quantitative and qualitative standards to the highest pitch. The performance of all acts of exchange as free gifts that are expected to be reciprocated though not necessarily by the same individuals—a procedure minutely articulated and perfectly safeguarded by elaborate methods of publicity, by magic rites, and by the establishment of "dualities" in which groups are linked in mutual obligations—should in itself explain the absence of the notion of gain or even of wealth other than that consisting of objects traditionally enhancing social prestige.

In this sketch of the general traits characteristic of a Western Melanesian community we took no account of its sexual and territorial organization, in reference to which custom, law, magic, and religion exert their influence, as we only intended to show the manner in which so-called economic motives spring from the context of social life. For it is on this one negative point that modern ethnographers agree: the absence of the motive of gain; the absence of the principle of laboring for remuneration; the absence of the principle of least effort; and, especially, the absence of any separate and distinct institution based on economic motives. But how, then, is order in production and distribution ensured?

The answer is provided in the main by two principles of behavior not primarily associated with economics: *reciprocity* and *redistribution*.[7] With the Trobriand Islanders of Western Melanesia, who serve as an illustration of this type of economy, reciprocity works mainly in regard to the sexual organization of society, that is, family and kinship; redistribution is mainly effective in respect to all those who are under a common chief and is, therefore, of a territorial character. Let us take these principles separately.

The sustenance of the family—the female and the children—is the obligation of their matrilineal relatives. The male, who provides for his sister and her family by delivering the finest specimens of his crop, will mainly earn the credit due to his good behavior, but will reap little immediate material benefit in exchange; if he is slack, it is first and foremost his reputation that will suffer. It is for the benefit of his wife and her children that the principle of reciprocity will work, and thus compensate him economically for his acts of civic virtue. Ceremonial display of food both in his own garden and before the recipient's storehouse will ensure that the high quality of his gardening be known to all. It is apparent that the economy of garden and household here forms part of the social relations connected with good husbandry and fine citizenship. The broad principle of reciprocity helps to safeguard both production and family sustenance.

The principle of redistribution is no less effective. A substantial part of all the produce of the island is delivered by the village headmen to the chief who keeps it in storage. But as all communal activity centers around the feasts, dances, and other occasions when the islanders entertain one another as well as their neighbors from other islands (at which the results of long distance trading are handed out, gifts are given and reciprocated according to the rules of etiquette, and the chief distributes the customary presents to all), the overwhelming importance of the storage system becomes apparent. Economically, it is an essential part of the existing system of division of labor, of foreign trading, of taxation for public purposes, of defense provisions. But these functions of an economic system proper are completely absorbed by the intensely vivid experiences which offer superabundant noneconomic motivation for every act performed in the frame of the social system as a whole.

However, principles of behavior such as these cannot become effective unless existing institutional patterns lend themselves to their application. Reciprocity and redistribution are able to ensure the working of an economic system without the help of written records and elaborate administration only because the organization of the societies in question meets the requirements of such a solution with the help of patterns such as *symmetry* and *centricity*.

Reciprocity is enormously facilitated by the institutional pattern of symmetry, a frequent feature of social organization among nonliterate peoples. The striking "duality" which we find in tribal subdivisions lends itself to the pairing out of individual relations and thereby assists the give-and-take of goods and services in the absence of permanent records. The moieties of savage society which tend to create a "pendant" to each subdivision, turned out to result from, as well as help to perform, the acts of reciprocity on which the system rests. Little is known of the origin of "duality"; but each coastal village on the Trobriand Islands appears to have its counterpart in an inland village, so that the important exchange of breadfruits and fish, though disguised as a reciprocal distribution of gifts, and actually disjoint in time, can be organized smoothly. In the Kula trade, too, each individual has his partner on another isle, thus personalizing to a remarkable extent the relationship of reciprocity. But for the frequency of the symmetrical pattern in the subdivisions of the tribe, in the location of settlements, as well as in intertribal relations, a broad reciprocity relying on the long-run working of separated acts of give-and-take would be impracticable.

The institutional pattern of centricity, again, which is present to some extent in all human groups, provides a track for the collection, storage, and redistribution of goods and services. The members of a hunting tribe usually deliver the game to the headman for redistribution. It is in the nature of hunting that the output of game is irregular, besides being the result of a collective input. Under conditions such as these no other method of sharing is practicable if the group is not to break up after every hunt. Yet in all economies of kind a similar need exists, be the group ever so numerous. And the larger the territory and the more varied the produce, the more will redistribution result in an effective division of labor, since it must help to link up geographically differentiated groups of producers.

Symmetry and centricity will meet halfway the needs of reciprocity and redistribution; institutional patterns and principles of behavior are mutually adjusted. As long as social organization runs in its ruts, no individual economic motives need come into play; no shirking of personal effort need be feared; division of labor will automatically be ensured; economic obligations will be duly discharged; and, above all, the material means for an exuberant display of abundance at all public festivals will be provided. In such a community the idea of profit is barred; higgling and haggling is decried; giving freely is acclaimed as a virtue; the supposed propensity to barter, truck, and exchange does not appear. The economic system is, in effect, a mere function of social organization.

It should by no means be inferred that socioeconomic principles of this type are restricted to primitive procedures or small communities; that a gainless and marketless economy must necessarily be simple. The Kula ring, in western Melanesia, based on the principle of reciprocity, is one of the most elaborate trading transactions known to man; and redistribution was present on a gigantic scale in the civilization of the pyramids.

The Trobriand Islands belong to an archipelago forming roughly a circle, and an important part of the population of this archipelago spends a considerable proportion of its time in activities of the Kula trade. We describe it as trade though no profit is involved, either in money or in kind; no goods are hoarded or even possessed permanently; the goods received are enjoyed by giving them away; no higgling and haggling, no truck, barter, or exchange enters; and the whole proceedings are entirely regulated by etiquette and magic. Still, it is trade, and large expeditions are undertaken periodically by natives of this approximately ring-shaped archipelago in order to carry one kind of valuable object to peoples living on distant islands situated clockwise, while other expeditions are arranged carrying another kind of valuable object to the islands of the archipelago lying counterclockwise. In the long run, both sets of objects—white-shell armbands and red-shell necklaces of traditional make—will move round the archipelago, a traject which may take them up to ten years to complete. Moreover, there are, as a rule, individual partners in Kula who reciprocate one another's Kula gift with equally valuable armbands and necklaces, preferably such that have previously belonged to distinguished persons. Now, a systematic and organized give-and-take of valuable objects transported over long distances is justly described as trade. Yet this complex whole is exclusively run on the lines of reciprocity. An intricate time-space-person system covering hundreds of miles and several decades, linking many hundreds of people in respect to thousands of strictly individual objects, is being handled here without any records or administration, but also without any motive of gain or truck. Not the propensity to barter, but reciprocity in social behavior dominates. Nevertheless, the result is a stupendous organizational achievement in the economic field. Indeed, it would be interesting to consider whether even the most advanced modern market organization, based on exact accountancy, would be able to cope with such a task, should it care to undertake it. It is to be feared that the unfortunate dealers, faced with innumerable monopolists buying and selling individual objects with extravagant restrictions attached to each transaction, would fail to make a standard profit and might prefer to go out of business.

Redistribution also has its long and variegated history which leads up almost to modern times. The Bergdama returning from his hunting excursion, the woman coming back from her search for roots, fruit, or leaves are expected to offer the greater part of their spoil for the benefit of the community. In practice, this means that the produce of their activity is shared with the other persons who happen to be living with them. Up to this point the idea of reciprocity prevails: today's giving will be recompensed by tomorrow's taking. Among some tribes, however, there is an intermediary in the person of the headman or other prominent member of the group; it is he who receives and distributes the supplies, especially if they need to be stored. This is redistribution proper. Obviously, the social consequences of such a method of distribution may be far reaching, since not all societies are as democratic as the primitive hunters. Whether the redistributing is performed by an influential family or an outstanding individual, a ruling aristocracy or a group of bureaucrats, they will often attempt to increase their political power by the manner in which they redistribute the goods. In the *potlatch* of the Kwakiutl it is a point of honor with the chief to display his wealth of hides and to distribute them; but he does this also in order to place the recipients under an obligation, to make them his debtors, and ultimately, his retainers.

All large-scale economies in kind were run with the help of the principle of redistribution. The kingdom of Hammurabi in Babylonia and, in particular, the New Kingdom of Egypt were centralized despotisms of a bureaucratic type founded on such an economy. The household of the patriarchal family was reproduced here on an enormously enlarged scale, while its "communistic" distribution was graded, involving sharply differentiated rations. A vast number of storehouses was ready to receive the produce of the peasant's activity, whether he was cattle breeder, hunter, baker, brewer, potter, weaver, or whatever else. The produce was minutely registered and, in so far as it was not consumed locally, transferred from smaller to larger storehouses until it reached the central administration situated at the court of the Pharaoh. There were separate treasure houses for cloth, works of art, ornamental objects, cosmetics, silverware, the royal wardrobe; there were huge grain stores, arsenals, and wine cellars.

But redistribution on the scale practiced by the pyramid builders was not restricted to economies which knew not money. Indeed, all archaic kingdoms made use of metal currencies for the payment of taxes and salaries, but relied for the rest on payments in kind from granaries and warehouses of every description, from which they distributed the most varied goods for use and consumption mainly to the nonproducing part of the population, that is, to the officials, the military, and the leisure class. This was the system practiced in ancient China, in the empire of the Incas, in the kingdoms of India, and also in Babylonia. In these, and many other civilizations of vast economic achievement, an elaborate division of labor was worked by the mechanism of redistribution.

Under feudal conditions also this principle held. In the ethnically stratified societies of Africa it sometimes happens that the superior strata consist of herdsmen settled among agriculturalists who are still using the digging stick or the hoe. The gifts collected by the herdsmen are mainly agricultural—such as cereals and beer—while the gifts distributed by them may be animals, especially sheep or goats. In these cases there is division of labor, though usually an unequal one, between the various strata of society: distribution may often cover up a measure of exploitation, while at the same time the symbiosis benefits the standards of both strata owing to the advantages of an improved division of labor. Politically, such societies live under a regime of feudalism, whether cattle or land be the privileged value. There are "regular cattle fiefs in East Africa." Thurnwald, whom we follow closely on the subject of redistribution, could therefore say that feudalism implied everywhere a system of redistribution. Only under very advanced conditions and exceptional circumstances does this system become predominantly political as happened in Western Europe, where the change arose out of the vassal's need for protection, and gifts were converted into feudal tributes.

These instances show that redistribution also tends to enmesh the economic system proper in social relationships. We find, as a rule, the process of redistribution forming part of the prevailing political regime, whether it be that of tribe, city-state, despotism, or feudalism of cattle or land. The production and distribution of goods is organized in the main through collection, storage, and redistribution, the pattern being focused on the chief, the temple, the despot, or the lord. Since the relations of the leading group to the led are different according to the foundation on which political power rests, the principle of redistribution will involve individual motives as different as the voluntary sharing of the game by hunters and the dread of punishment which urges the *fellaheen* to deliver his taxes in kind.

We deliberately disregarded in this presentation the vital distinction between homogeneous and stratified societies, *i.e.*, societies which are on the whole socially unified, and such as are split into rulers and ruled. Though the relative status of slaves and masters may be worlds apart from that of the free and equal members of some hunting tribes, and, consequently, motives in the two societies will differ widely, the organization of the economic system may still be based on the same principles, though accompanied by very different culture traits, according to the very different human relations with which the economic system is intertwined.

The third principle, which was destined to play a big role in history and which we will call the principle of *householding,* consists in production for one's own use. The Greeks called it *oeconomia,* the etymon of the word "economy." As far as ethnographical records are concerned, we should not assume that production for a person's or group's own sake is more ancient than reciprocity or redistribution. On the contrary, orthodox tradition as well as some more recent theories on the subject have been emphatically disproved. The individualistic savage collecting food and hunting on his own or for his family has never existed. Indeed, the practice of catering for the needs of one's household becomes a feature of economic life only on a more advanced level of agriculture; however, even then it has nothing in common either with the motive of gain or with the institution of markets. Its pattern is the closed group. Whether the very different entities of the family or the settlement or the manor formed the self-sufficient unit, the principle was invariably the same, namely, that of producing and storing for the satisfaction of the wants of the members of the group. The principle is as broad in its application as either reciprocity or redistribution. The nature of the institutional nucleus is indifferent: it may be sex as with the patriarchal family, locality as with the village settlement, or political power as with the seigneurial manor. Nor does the internal organization of the group matter. It may be as despotic as the Roman *familia* or as democratic as the South Slav *zadruga;* as large as the great domains of the Carolingian magnates or as small as the average peasant holding of Western Europe. The need for trade or markets is no greater than in the case of reciprocity or redistribution.

It is such a condition of affairs which Aristotle tried to establish as a norm more than two thousand years ago. Looking back from the rapidly declining heights of a worldwide market economy we must concede that his famous distinction of householding proper and money-making, in the introductory chapter of his *Politics,* was probably the most prophetic pointer ever made in the realm of the social sciences; it is certainly still the best analysis of the subject we possess. Aristotle insists on production for use as against production for gain as the essence of householding proper; yet accessory production for the market need not, he argues, destroy the self-sufficiency of the household as long as the cash crop would also otherwise be raised on the farm for sustenance, as cattle or grain; the sale of the surpluses need not destroy the basis of householding. Only a genius of common sense could have maintained, as he did, that gain was a motive peculiar to production for the market, and that the money factor introduced a new element into the situation, yet nevertheless, as long as markets and money were mere accessories to an otherwise self-sufficient household, the principle of production for use could operate. Undoubtedly, in this he was right, though he failed to see how impracticable it was to ignore the existence of markets at a time when Greek economy had made itself dependent upon wholesale trading and loaned capital. For this was the century when Delos and Rhodes were developing into emporia of freight insurance, sea-loans, and giro-banking, compared with which the Western Europe of a thousand years later was the very picture of primitivity. Yet Jowett, Master of Balliol, was grievously mistaken when he took it for granted that his Victorian England had a fairer grasp than Aristotle of the nature of the difference between householding and money-making. He excused Aristotle by conceding that the "subjects of knowledge that are concerned with man run into one another; and in the age of Aristotle were not easily distinguished." Aristotle, it is true, did not recognize clearly the implications of the division of labor and its connection with markets and money; nor did he realize the uses of money as credit and capital. So far Jowett's strictures were justified. But it was the Master of Balliol, not Aristotle, who was impervious to the human implications of money-making. He failed to see that the distinction between the principle of use and that of gain was the key to the utterly different civilization the outlines of which Aristotle accurately forecast two thousand years before its advent out of the bare rudiments of a market economy available to him, while Jowett, with the full-blown specimen before him, overlooked its existence. In denouncing the principle of production for gain "as not natural to man," as boundless and limitless, Aristotle was, in effect, aiming at the crucial point, namely the divorcedness of a separate economic motive from the social relations in which these limitations inhered.

Broadly, the proposition holds that all economic systems known to us up to the end of feudalism in Western Europe were organized either on the principles of reciprocity or redistribution, or householding, or some combination of the three. These principles were institutionalized with the help of a social organization which, *inter alia*, made use of the patterns of symmetry, centricity, and autarchy. In this framework, the orderly production and distribution of goods was secured through a great variety of individual motives disciplined by general principles of behavior. Among these motives gain was not prominent. Custom and law, magic and religion co-operated in inducing the individual to comply with rules of behavior which, eventually, ensured his functioning in the economic system.

The Greco-Roman period, in spite of its highly developed trade, represented no break in this respect; it was characterized by the grand scale on which redistribution of grain was practiced by the Roman administration in an otherwise householding economy, and it formed no exception to the rule that up to the end of the Middle Ages, markets played no important part in the economic system; other institutional patterns prevailed.

From the sixteenth century onwards markets were both numerous and important. Under the mercantile system they became, in effect, a main concern of government; yet there was still no sign of the coming control of markets over human society. On the contrary. Regulation and regimentation were stricter than ever; the very idea of a self-regulating market was absent. To comprehend the sudden change-over to an utterly new type of economy in the nineteenth century, we must now turn to the history of the market, an institution we were able practically to neglect in our review of the economic systems of the past.

Chapter 5: Evolution of the Market Pattern

The dominating part played by markets in capitalist economy together with the basic significance of the principle of barter or exchange in this economy calls for a careful inquiry into the nature and origin of markets, if the economic superstitions of the nineteenth century are to be discarded.[8]

Barter, truck, and exchange is a principle of economic behavior dependent for its effectiveness upon the market pattern. A market is a meeting place for the purpose of barter or buying and selling. Unless such a pattern is present, at least in patches, the propensity to barter will find but insufficient scope: it cannot produce prices.[9] For just as reciprocity is aided by a symmetrical pattern of organization, as redistribution is made easier by some measure of centralization, and householding must be based on autarchy, so also the principle of barter depends for its effectiveness on the market pattern. But in the same manner in which either reciprocity, redistribution, or householding may occur in a society without being prevalent in it, the principle of barter also may take a subordinate place in a society in which other principles are in the ascendant.

However, in some other respects the principle of barter is not on a strict parity with the three other principles. The market pattern, with which it is associated, is more specific than either symmetry, centricity, or autarchy—which, in contrast to the market pattern, are mere "traits," and do not create institutions designed for one function only. Symmetry is no more than a sociological arrangement, which gives rise to no separate institutions, but merely patterns out existing ones (whether a tribe or a village is symmetrically patterned or not involves no distinctive institution). Centricity, though frequently creating distinctive institutions, implies no motive that would single out the resulting institution for a single specific function (the headman of a village or another central official might assume, for instance, a variety of political, military, religious, or economic functions, indiscriminately). Economic autarchy, finally, is only an accessory trait of an existing closed group.

The market pattern, on the other hand, being related to a peculiar motive of its own, the motive of truck or barter, is capable of creating a specific institution, namely, the market. Ultimately, that is why the control of the economic system by the market is of overwhelming consequence to the whole organization of society: it means no less than the running of society as an adjunct to the market. Instead of economy being embedded in social relations, social relations are embedded in the economic system. The vital importance of the economic factor to the existence of society precludes any other result. For once the economic system is organized in separate institutions, based on specific motives and conferring a special status, society must be shaped in such a manner as to allow that system to function according to its own laws. This is the meaning of the familiar assertion that a market economy can function only in a market society.

The step which makes isolated markets into a market economy, regulated markets into a self-regulating market, is indeed crucial. The nineteenth century—whether hailing the fact as the apex of civilization or deploring it as a cancerous growth— naïvely imagined that such a development was the natural outcome of the spreading of markets. It was not realized that the gearing of markets into a self-regulating system of tremendous power was not the result of any inherent tendency of markets towards excrescence, but rather the effect of highly artificial stimulants administered to the body social in order to meet a situation which was created by the no less artificial phenomenon of the machine. The limited and unexpansive nature of the market pattern, as such, was not recognized; and yet it is this fact which emerges with convincing clarity from modern research.

"Markets are not found everywhere; their absence, while indicating a certain isolation and a tendency to seclusion, is not associated with any particular development any more than can be inferred from their presence." This colorless sentence from Thurnwald's *Economics in Primitive Communities* sums up the significant results of modern research on the subject. Another author repeats in respect to money what Thurnwald says of markets: "The mere fact, that a tribe used money differentiated it very little economically from other tribes on the same cultural level, who did not." We need hardly do more than point to some of the more startling implications of these statements.

The presence or absence of markets or money does not necessarily affect the economic system of a primitive society—this refutes the nineteenth century myth that money was an invention the appearance of which inevitably transformed a society by creating markets, forcing the pace of the division of labor, and releasing man's natural propensity to barter, truck, and exchange. Orthodox economic history, in effect, was based on an immensely exaggerated view of the significance of markets as such. A "certain isolation," or, perhaps, a "tendency to seclusion" is the only economic trait that can be correctly inferred from their absence; in respect to the internal organization of an economy, their presence or absence need make no difference.

The reasons are simple. Markets are not institutions functioning mainly within an economy, but without. They are meeting places of long-distance trade. Local markets proper are of little consequence. Moreover, neither long-distance nor local markets are essentially competitive, and consequently there is, in either case, but little pressure to create territorial trade, a so-called internal or national market. Every one of these assertions strikes at some axiomatically held assumption of the classical economists, yet they follow closely from the facts as they appear in the light of modern research.

The logic of the case is, indeed, almost the opposite of that underlying the classical doctrine. The orthodox teaching started from the individual's propensity to barter; deduced from it the necessity of local markets, as well as of division of labor; and inferred, finally, the necessity of trade, eventually of foreign trade, including even long-distance trade. In the light of our present knowledge we should almost reverse the sequence of the argument: the true starting point is long distance trade, a result of the geographical location of goods, and of the "division of labor" given by location. Long-distance trade often engenders markets, an institution which involves acts of barter, and, if money is used, of buying and selling, thus, eventually, but by no means necessarily, offering to some individuals an occasion to indulge in their alleged propensity for bargaining and haggling.

The dominating feature of this doctrine is the origin of trade in an external sphere unrelated to the internal organization of economy: "The application of the principles observed in hunting to the obtaining of goods found *outside the limits of the district,* led to certain forms of exchange which appear to us later as trade."[10] In looking for the origins of trade, our starting point should be the obtaining of goods from a distance, as in a hunt. "The Central Australian Dieri every year, in July or August, make an expedition to the south to obtain the red ochre used by them for painting their bodies. ... Their neighbors, the Yantruwunta, organize similar enterprises for fetching red ochre and sandstone slabs, for crushing grass seed, from the Flinders Hills, 800 kilometers distant. In both cases it might be necessary to fight for the articles wanted, if the local people offer resistance to their removal." This kind of requisitioning or treasure hunting is clearly as much akin to robbery and piracy as to what we are used to regard as trade; basically, it is a one-sided affair. It becomes two-sided, *i.e.*, "a certain form of exchange" often only through blackmail practiced by the powers on the site; or through reciprocity arrangements, as in the Kula ring, as with visiting parties of the Pengwe of West Africa, or with the Kpelle, where the chief monopolizes foreign trade by insisting on entertaining all the guests. True, such visits are not accidental, but—in our terms, not theirs—genuine trading journeys; the exchange of goods, however, is always conducted under the guise of reciprocal presents and usually by way of return visits.

We reach the conclusion that while human communities never seem to have foregone external trade entirely, such trade did not necessarily involve markets. External trade is, originally, more in the nature of adventure, exploration, hunting, piracy and war than of barter. It may as little imply peace as two-sidedness, and even when it implies both it is usually organized on the principle of reciprocity, not on that of barter.

The transition to peaceful barter can be traced in two directions, *viz.*, in that of barter and in that of peace. A tribal expedition may have to comply, as indicated above, with the conditions set by the powers on the spot, who may exact some kind of counterpart from the strangers; this type of relationship, though not entirely peaceful, may give rise to barter—one-sided carrying will be transformed into two-sided carrying. The other line of development is that of "silent trading" as in the African bush, where the risk of combat is avoided through an organized truce, and the element of peace, trust, and confidence is, with due circumspection, introduced into trade.

At a later stage, as we all know, markets become predominant in the organization of external trade. But from the economic point of view external markets are an entirely different matter from either local markets or internal markets. They differ not only in size; they are institutions of different function and origin. External trade is carrying; the point is the absence of some types of goods in that region; the exchange of English woolens against Portuguese wine was an instance. Local trade is limited to the goods of that region, which do *not* bear carrying because they are too heavy, bulky, or perishable. Thus both external trade and local trade are relative to geographical distance, the one being confined to the goods which cannot overcome it, the other to such only as can. Trade of this type is rightly described as complementary. Local exchange between town and countryside, foreign trade between different climatic zones are based on this principle. Such trade need not imply competition, and if competition would tend to disorganize trade, there is no contradiction in eliminating it. In contrast to both external and local trade, internal trade, on the other hand essentially competitive; apart from complementary exchanges it includes a very much larger number of exchanges in which similar goods from different sources are offered in competition with one another. Accordingly, only with the emergence of internal or national trade does competition tend to be accepted as a general principle of trading.

These three types of trade which differ sharply in their economic function are also distinct in their origin. We have dealt with the beginnings of external trade. Markets developed naturally out of it where the carriers had to halt as at fords, seaports, riverheads, or where the routes of two land expeditions met. "Ports" developed at the places of transshipment.[11] The short flowering of the famous fairs of Europe was another instance where long-distance trade produced a definite type of market; England's staples were another example. But while fairs and staples disappeared again with an abruptness disconcerting to the dogmatic evolutionist, the *portus* was destined to play an enormous role in the settling of Western Europe with towns. Yet even where the towns were founded on the sites of external markets, the local markets often remained separate in respect not only to function but also to organization. Neither the port, nor the fair, nor the staple was the parent of internal or national markets. Where, then, should we seek for their origin?

It might seem natural to assume that, given individual acts of barter, these would in the course of time lead to the development of local markets, and that such markets, once in existence, would just as naturally lead to the establishment of internal or national markets. However, neither the one nor the other is the case. Individual acts of barter for exchange—this is the bare fact—do not, as a rule, lead to the establishment of markets in societies where other principles of economic behavior prevail. Such acts are common in almost all types of primitive society, but they are considered as incidental since they do not provide for the necessaries of life. In the vast ancient systems of redistribution, acts of barter as well as local markets were a usual, but no more than a subordinate trait. The same is true where reciprocity rules: acts of barter are here usually embedded in long-range relations implying trust and confidence, a situation which tends to obliterate the bilateral character of the transaction. The limiting factors arise from all points of the sociological compass: custom and law, religion and magic equally contribute to the result, which is to restrict acts of exchange in respect to persons and objects, time and occasion. As a rule, he who barters merely enters into a ready-made type of transaction in which both the objects and their equivalent amounts are given. *Utu* in the language of the Tikopia[12] denotes such a traditional equivalent as part of reciprocal exchange. That which appeared as the essential feature of exchange to eighteenth century thought, the voluntaristic element of bargain, and the higgling so expressive of the assumed motive of truck, finds but little scope in the actual transaction; in so far as this motive underlies the procedure, it is seldom allowed to rise to the surface.

The customary way to behave is, rather, to give vent to the opposite motivation. The giver may simply drop the object on the ground and the receiver will pretend to pick it up accidentally, or even leave it to one of his hangers-on to do so for him. Nothing could be more contrary to accepted behavior than to have a good look at the counterpart received. As we have every reason to believe that this sophisticated attitude is not the outcome of a genuine lack of interest in the material side of the transaction, we might describe the etiquette of barter as a counteracting development designed to limit the scope of the trait.

Indeed, on the evidence available it would be rash to assert that local markets ever developed from individual acts of barter. Obscure as the beginnings of local markets are, this much can be asserted: that from the start this institution was surrounded by a number of safeguards designed to protect the prevailing economic organization of society from interference on the part of market practices. The peace of the market was secured at the price of rituals and ceremonies which restricted its scope while ensuring its ability to function within the given narrow limits. The most significant result of markets—the birth of towns and urban civilization—was, in effect, the outcome of a paradoxical development. Because the towns, the offspring of the markets, were not only their protectors, but also the means of preventing them from expanding into the countryside and thus encroaching on the prevailing economic organization of society. The two meanings of the word "contain" express perhaps best this double function of the towns, in respect to the markets which they both enveloped and prevented from developing.

If barter was surrounded by taboos devised to keep this type of human relationship from abusing the functions of the economic organization proper, the discipline of the market was even stricter. Here is an example from the Chaga country: "The market must be regularly visited on market days. If any occurrence should prevent the holding of the market on one or more days, business cannot be resumed until the market-place has been purified. ... Every injury occurring on the market-place and involving the shedding of blood necessitated immediate expiation. From that moment no woman was allowed to leave the market-place and no goods might be touched; they had to be cleansed before they could be carried away and used for food. At the very least a goat had to be sacrificed at once. A more expensive and more serious expiation was necessary if a woman bore a child or had a miscarriage on the market-place. In that case a milch animal was necessary. In addition to this, the homestead of the chief had to be purified by means of sacrificial blood of a milch-cow. All the women in the country were thus sprinkled, district by district."[13] Rules such as these would not make the spreading of markets easier.

The typical local market at which housewives procure some of their daily needs, and growers of grain or vegetables as well as local craftsmen offer their wares for sale, shows an amazing indifference to time and place. Gatherings of this kind are not only fairly general in primitive societies, but remain almost unchanged right up to the middle of the eighteenth century in the most advanced countries of Western Europe. They are an adjunct of local existence and differ but little whether they form part of Central African tribal life, or a *cité* of Merovingian France, or a Scottish village of Adam Smith's time. But what is true of the village is also true of the town. Local markets are, essentially, neighborhood markets, and, though important to the life of the community, they nowhere showed any sign of reducing the prevailing economic system to their pattern. They were not starting points of internal or national trade.

Internal trade in Western Europe was actually created by the intervention of the state. Right up to the time of the Commercial Revolution what may appear to us as national trade was not national, but municipal. The Hanse were not German merchants; they were a corporation of trading oligarchs, hailing from a number of North Sea and Baltic towns. Far from "nationalizing" German economic life, the Hanse deliberately cut off the hinterland from trade. The trade of Antwerp or Hamburg, Venice or Lyons, was in no way Dutch or German, Italian or French. London was no exception: it was as little "English" as Luebeck was "German." The trade map of Europe in this period should rightly show only towns, and leave blank the countryside—it might as well have not existed as far as organized trade was concerned. So-called nations were merely political units, and very loose ones at that, consisting economically of innumerable smaller and bigger self-sufficing households and insignificant local markets in the villages. Trade was limited to organized townships which carried it on either locally as neighborhood trade or as long-distance trade—the two were strictly separated, and neither was allowed to infiltrate the countryside indiscriminately.

Such a permanent severance of local trade and long-distance trade within the organization of the town must come as another shock to the evolutionist, with whom things always seem so easily to grow into one another. And yet this peculiar fact forms the key to the social history of urban life in Western Europe. It strongly tends to support our assertion in respect to the origin of markets which we inferred from conditions in primitive economies. The sharp distinction drawn between local and long-distance trade might have seemed too rigid, especially as it led us to the somewhat surprising conclusion that neither long-distance trade nor local trade was the parent of the internal trade of modern times—thus apparently leaving no alternative but to turn for an explanation to the *deus ex machina* of state intervention. We will see presently that in this respect also recent investigations bear out our conclusions. But let us first give a bare outline of the history of urban civilization as it was shaped by the peculiar severance of local and long-distance trade within the confines of the medieval town.

This severance was, indeed, at the heart of the institution of medieval urban centers.[14] The town was an organization of the burgesses. They alone had right of citizenship and on the distinction between the burgess and the non-burgess the system rested. Neither the peasants of the countryside nor the merchants from other towns were, naturally, burgesses. But while the military and political influence of the town made it possible to deal with the peasants of the surroundings, in respect to the foreign merchant such authority could not be exerted. Consequently, the burgesses found themselves in an entirely different position in respect to local trade and long-distance trade.

As to food supplies, regulation involved the application of such methods as enforced publicity of transactions and exclusion of middlemen, in order to control trade and provide against high prices. But such regulation was effective only in respect to trade carried on between the town and its immediate surroundings. In respect to long-distance trade the position was entirely different. Spices, salted fish, or wine had to be transported from a long distance and were thus the domain of the foreign merchant and his capitalistic wholesale trade methods. This type of trade escaped local regulation and all that could be done was to exclude it as far as possible from the local market. The complete prohibition of retail sale by foreign merchants was designed to achieve this end. The more the volume of capitalistic wholesale trade grew, the more strictly was its exclusion from the local markets enforced as far as imports were concerned.

In respect to industrial wares, the separation of local and long-distance trade cut even deeper, as in this case the whole organization of production for export was affected. The reason for this lay in the very nature of craft gilds, in which industrial production was organized. On the local market, production was regulated according to the needs of the producers, thus restricting production to a remunerative level. This principle would naturally not apply to exports, where the interests of the producers set no limits to production. Consequently, while local trade was strictly regulated, production for export was only formally controlled by corporations of crafts. The dominating export industry of the age, the cloth trade, was actually organized on the capitalistic basis of wage labor.

An increasingly strict separation of local trade from export trade was the reaction of urban life to the threat of mobile capital to disintegrate the institutions of the town.

The typical medieval town did not try to avoid the danger by bridging the gap between the controllable local market and the vagaries of an uncontrollable long-distance trade, but, on the contrary, met the peril squarely by enforcing with the utmost rigor that policy of exclusion and protection which was the *rationale* of its existence.

In practice this meant that the towns raised every possible obstacle to the formation of that national or internal market for which the capitalist wholesaler was pressing. By maintaining the principle of a non-competitive local trade and an equally noncompetitive long-distance trade carried on from town to town, the burgesses hampered by all means at their disposal the inclusion of the countryside into the compass of trade and the opening up of indiscriminate trade between the towns of the country. It was this development which forced the territorial state to the fore as the instrument of the "nationalization" of the market and the creator of internal commerce.

Deliberate action of the state in the fifteenth and sixteenth centuries foisted the mercantile system on the fiercely protectionist towns and principalities. Mercantilism destroyed the outworn particularism of local and intermunicipal trading by breaking down the barriers separating these two types of noncompetitive commerce and thus clearing the way for a national market which increasingly ignored the distinction between town and countryside as well as that between the various towns and provinces.

The mercantile system was, in effect, a response to many challenges. Politically, the centralized state was a new creation called forth by the Commercial Revolution which had shifted the center of gravity of the Western world from the Mediterranean to the Atlantic seaboard and thus compelled the backward peoples of larger agrarian countries to organize for commerce and trade. In external politics, the setting up of sovereign power was the need of the day; accordingly, mercantilist statecraft involved the marshaling of the resources of the whole national territory to the purposes of power in foreign affairs. In internal politics, unification of the countries fragmented by feudal and municipal particularism was the necessary by-product of such an endeavor. Economically, the instrument of unification was capital, *i.e.*, private resources available in form of money hoards and thus peculiarly suitable for the development of commerce. Finally the administrative technique underlying the economic policy of the central government was supplied by the extension of the traditional municipal system to the larger territory of the state. In France, where the craft gilds tended to become state organs, the gild system was simply extended over the whole territory of the country; in England, where the decay of the walled towns had weakened that system fatally, the countryside was industrialized without the supervision of the gilds, while in both countries trade and commerce spread over the whole territory of the nation and became the dominating form of economic activity. In this situation lie the origins of the internal trade policy of mercantilism.

State intervention, which had freed trade from the confines of the privileged town, was now called to deal with two closely connected dangers which the town had successfully met, namely, monopoly and competition. That competition must ultimately lead to monopoly was a truth well understood at the time, while monopoly was feared even more than later as it often concerned the necessaries of life and thus easily waxed into a peril to the community. All-round regulation of economic life, only this time on a national, no more on a merely municipal, scale was the given remedy. What to the modern mind may easily appear as a shortsighted exclusion of competition was in reality the means of safeguarding the functioning of markets under the given conditions. For any temporary intrusion of buyers or sellers in the market must destroy the balance and disappoint regular buyers or sellers, with the result that the market will cease to function. The former purveyors will cease to offer their goods as they cannot be sure that their goods will fetch a price, and the market left without sufficient supply will become a prey to the monopolist. To a lesser degree, the same dangers were present on the demand side, where a rapid falling off might be followed by a monopoly of demand. With every step that the state took to rid the market of particularist restrictions, of tolls and prohibitions, it imperiled the organized system of production and distribution which was now threatened by unregulated competition and the intrusion of the interloper who "scooped" the market but offered no guarantee of permanency. Thus it came that although the new national markets were, inevitably, to some degree competitive, it was the traditional feature of regulation, not the new element of competition, which prevailed.[15] The self-sufficing household of the peasant laboring for his subsistence remained the broad basis of the economic system, which was being integrated into large national units through the formation of the internal market. This national market now took its place alongside, and partly overlapping, the local and foreign markets. Agriculture was now being supplemented by internal commerce—a system of relatively isolated markets, which was entirely compatible with the principle of householding still dominant in the countryside.

This concludes our synopsis of the history of the market up to the time of the Industrial Revolution. The next stage in mankind's history brought, as we know, an attempt to set up one big self-regulating market. There was nothing in mercantilism, this distinctive policy of the Western nation-state, to presage such a unique development. The "freeing" of trade performed by mercantilism merely liberated trade from particularism, but at the same time extended the scope of regulation. The economic system was submerged in general social relations; markets were merely an accessory feature of an institutional setting controlled and regulated more than ever by social authority.

Chapter 6: The Self-Regulating Market and the Fictitious Commodities: Labor, Land, and Money

This cursory outline of the economic system and markets, taken separately, shows that never before our own time were markets more than accessories of economic life. As a rule, the economic system was absorbed in the social system, and whatever principle of behavior predominated in the economy, the presence of the market pattern was found to be compatible with it. The principle of barter or exchange, which underlies this pattern, revealed no tendency to expand at the expense of the rest. Where markets were most highly developed, as under the mercantile system, they throve under the control of a centralized administration which fostered autarchy both in the households of the peasantry and in respect to national life. Regulation and markets, in effect, grew up together. The self-regulating market was unknown; indeed the emergence of the idea of self-regulation was a complete reversal of the trend of development. It is in the light of these facts that the extraordinary assumptions underlying a market economy can alone be fully comprehended.

A market economy is an economic system controlled, regulated, and directed by markets alone; order in the production and distribution of goods is entrusted to this self-regulating mechanism. An economy of this kind derives from the expectation that human beings behave in such a way as to achieve maximum money gains. It assumes markets in which the supply of goods (including services) available at a definite price will equal the demand at that price. It assumes the presence of money, which functions as purchasing power in the hands of its owners. Production will then be controlled by prices, for the profits of those who direct production will depend upon them; the distribution of the goods also will depend upon prices, for prices form incomes, and it is with the help of these incomes that the goods produced are distributed amongst the members of society. Under these assumptions order in the production and distribution of goods is ensured by prices alone.

Self-regulation implies that all production is for sale on the market and that all incomes derive from such sales. Accordingly, there are markets for all elements of industry, not only for goods (always including services) but also for labor, land, and money their prices being called respectively commodity prices, wages, rent, and interest. The very terms indicate that prices form incomes: interest is the price for the use of money and forms the income of those who are in the position to provide it; rent is the price for the use of land and forms the income of those who supply it; wages are the price for the use of labor power, and form the income of those who sell it; commodity prices, finally, contribute to the incomes of those who sell their entrepreneurial services, the income called profit being actually the difference between two sets of prices, the price of the goods produced and their costs, *i.e.,* the price of the goods necessary to produce them. If these conditions are fulfilled, all incomes will derive from sales on the market, and incomes will be just sufficient to buy all the goods produced.

A further group of assumptions follows in respect to the state and its policy. Nothing must be allowed to inhibit the formation of markets, nor must incomes be permitted to be formed otherwise than through sales. Neither must there be any interference with the adjustment of prices to changed market conditions—whether the prices are those of goods, labor, land, or money. Hence there must not only be markets for all elements of industry,[16] but no measure or policy must be countenanced that would influence the action of these markets. Neither price, nor supply, nor demand must be fixed or regulated; only such policies and measures are in order which help to ensure the self-regulation of the market by creating conditions which make the market the only organizing power in the economic sphere.

To realize fully what this means, let us return for a moment to the mercantile system and the national markets which it did so much to develop. Under feudalism and the gild system land and labor formed part of the social organization itself (money had yet hardly developed into a major element of industry). Land, the pivotal element in the feudal order, was the basis of the military, judicial, administrative, and political system; its status and function were determined by legal and customary rules. Whether its possession was transferable or not, and if so, to whom and under what restrictions; what the rights of property entailed; to what uses some types of land might be put—all these questions were removed from the organization of buying and selling, and subjected to an entirely different set of institutional regulations.

The same was true of the organization of labor. Under the gild system, as under every other economic system in previous history, the motives and circumstances of productive activities were embedded in the general organization of society. The relations of master, journeyman, and apprentice; the terms of the craft; the number of apprentices; the wages of the workers were all regulated by the custom and rule of the gild and the town. What the mercantile system did was merely to unify these conditions either through statute as in England, or through the "nationalization" of the gilds as in France. As to land, its feudal status was abolished only in so far as it was linked with provincial privileges; for the rest, land remained *extra commercium*, in England as in France. Up to the time of the Great Revolution of 1789, landed estate remained the source of social privilege in France, and even after that time in England Common Law on land was essentially medieval. Mercantilism, with all its tendency towards commercialization, never attacked the safeguards which protected these two basic elements of production—labor and land—from becoming the objects of commerce. In England the "nationalization" of labor legislation through the Statute of Artificers (1563) and the Poor Law (1601), removed labor from the danger zone, and the anti-enclosure policy of the Tudors and early Stuarts was one consistent protest against the principle of the gainful use of landed property.

That mercantilism, however emphatically it insisted on commercialization as a national policy, thought of markets in a way exactly contrary to market economy, is best shown by its vast extension of state intervention in industry. On this point there was no difference between mercantilists and feudalists, between crowned planners and vested interests, between centralizing bureaucrats and conservative particularists. They disagreed only on the methods of regulation: gilds, towns, and provinces appealed to the force of custom and tradition, while the new state authority favored statute and ordinance. But they were all equally averse to the idea of commercializing labor and land—the precondition of market economy. Craft gilds and feudal privileges were abolished in France only in 1790; in England the Statute of Artificers was repealed only in 1813–14, the Elizabethan Poor Law in 1834. Not before the last decade of the eighteenth century was, in either country, the establishment of a free labor market even discussed; and the idea of the self-regulation of economic life was utterly beyond the horizon of the age. The mercantilist was concerned with, the development of the resources of the country, including full employment, through trade and commerce; the traditional organization of land and labor he took for granted. He was in this respect as far removed from modern concepts as he was in the realm of politics, where his belief in the absolute powers of an enlightened despot was tempered by no intimations of democracy. And just as the transition to a democratic system and representative politics involved a complete reversal of the trend of the age, the change from regulated to self-regulating markets at the end of the eighteenth century represented a complete transformation in the structure of society.

A self-regulating market demands nothing less than the institutional separation of society into an economic and political sphere. Such a dichotomy is, in effect, merely the restatement, from the point of view of society as a whole, of the existence of a self-regulating market. It might be argued that the separateness of the two spheres obtains in every type of society at all times. Such an inference, however, would be based on a fallacy. True, no society can exist without a system of some kind which ensures order in the production and distribution of goods. But that does not imply the existence of separate economic institutions; normally, the economic order is merely a function of the social, in which it is contained. Neither under tribal, nor feudal, nor mercantile conditions was there, as we have shown, a separate economic system in society. Nineteenth century society, in which economic activity was isolated and imputed to a distinctive economic motive, was, indeed, a singular departure.

Such an institutional pattern could not function unless society was somehow subordinated to its requirements. A market economy can exist only in a market society. We reached this conclusion on general grounds in our analysis of the market pattern. We can now specify the reasons for this assertion. A market economy must comprise all elements of industry, including labor, land, and money. (In a market economy the last also is an essential element of industrial life and its inclusion in the market mechanism has, as we will see, far-reaching institutional consequences.) But labor and land are no other than the human beings themselves of which every society consists and the natural surroundings in which it exists. To include them in the market mechanism means to subordinate the substance of society itself to the laws of the market.

We are now in the position to develop in a more concrete form the institutional nature of a market economy, and the perils to society which it involves. We will, first, describe the methods by which the market mechanism is enabled to control and direct the actual elements of industrial life; second, we will try to gauge the nature of the effects of such a mechanism on the society which is subjected to its action.

It is with the help of the commodity concept that the mechanism of the market is geared to the various elements of industrial life. Commodities are here empirically defined as objects produced for sale on the market; markets, again, are empirically defined as actual contacts between buyers and sellers. Accordingly, every element of industry is regarded as having been produced for sale, as then and then only will it be subject to the supply-and-demand mechanism interacting with price. In practice this means that there must be markets for every element of industry; that in these markets each of these elements is organized into a supply and a demand group; and that each element has a price which interacts with demand and supply. These markets—and they are numberless—are interconnected and form One Big Market.[17]

The crucial point is this: labor, land, and money are essential elements of industry; they also must be organized in markets; in fact, these markets form an absolutely vital part of the economic system. But labor, land, and money are obviously *not* commodities; the postulate that anything that is bought and sold must have been produced for sale is emphatically untrue in regard to them. In other words, according to the empirical definition of a commodity they are not commodities. Labor is only another name for a human activity which goes with life itself, which in its turn is not produced for sale but for entirely different reasons, nor can that activity be detached from the rest of life, be stored or mobilized; land is only another name for nature, which is not produced by man; actual money, finally, is merely a token of purchasing power which, as a rule, is not produced at all, but comes into being through the mechanism of

banking or state finance. None of them is produced for sale. The commodity description of labor, land, and money is entirely fictitious.

Nevertheless, it is with the help of this fiction that the actual markets for labor, land,
and money are organized;[18] they are being actually bought and sold on the market;
their demand and supply are real magnitudes; and any measures or policies that would
inhibit the formation of such markets would *ipso facto* endanger the self-regulation
of the system. The commodity fiction, therefore, supplies a vital organizing principle
in regard to the whole of society affecting almost all its institutions in the most varied
way, namely, the principle according to which no arrangement or behavior should be
allowed to exist that might prevent the actual functioning of the market mechanism
on the lines of the commodity fiction.

Now, in regard to labor, land, and money such a postulate cannot be upheld. To allow
the market mechanism to be sole director of the fate of human beings and their natural
environment, indeed, even of the amount and use of purchasing power, would result in
the demolition of society. For the alleged commodity "labor power" cannot be shoved
about, used indiscriminately, or even left unused, without affecting also the human individual who happens to be the bearer of this peculiar commodity. In disposing of a man's
labor power the system would, incidentally, dispose of the physical, psychological, and
moral entity "man" attached to that tag. Robbed of the protective covering of cultural
institutions, human beings would perish from the effects of social exposure; they would
die as the victims of acute social dislocation through vice, perversion, crime, and starvation. Nature would be reduced to its elements, neighborhoods and landscapes defiled,
rivers polluted, military safety jeopardized, the power to produce food and raw materials
destroyed. Finally, the market administration of purchasing power would periodically
liquidate business enterprise, for shortages and surfeits of money would prove as disastrous to business as floods and droughts in primitive society. Undoubtedly, labor, land,
and money markets *are* essential to a market economy. But no society could stand the
effects of such a system of crude fictions even for the shortest stretch of time unless its
human and natural substance as well as its business organization was protected against
the ravages of this satanic mill.

The extreme artificiality of market economy is rooted in the fact that the process of
production itself is here organized in the form of buying and selling.[19] No other way of
organizing production for the market is possible in a commercial society. During the
late Middle Ages industrial production for export was organized by wealthy burgesses,
and carried on under their direct supervision in the home town. Later, in the mercantile society, production was organized by merchants and was not restricted any more
to the towns; this was the age of "putting out" when domestic industry was provided
with raw materials by the merchant capitalist, who controlled the process of production as a purely commercial enterprise. It was then that industrial production was
definitely and on a large scale put under the organizing leadership of the merchant.
He knew the market, the volume as well as the quality of the demand; and he could
vouch also for the supplies which, incidentally, consisted merely of wool, woad, and,
sometimes, the looms or the knitting frames used by the cottage industry. If supplies
failed it was the cottager who was worst hit, for his employment was gone for the
time; but no expensive plant was involved and the merchant incurred no serious risk
in shouldering the responsibility for production. For centuries this system grew in

power and scope until in a country like England the wool industry, the national staple, covered large sectors of the country where production was organized by the clothier. He who bought and sold, incidentally, provided for production—no separate motive was required. The creation of goods involved neither the reciprocating attitudes of mutual aid; nor the concern of the householder for those whose needs are left to his care; nor the craftsman's pride in the exercise of his trade; nor the satisfaction of public praise—nothing but the plain motive of gain so familiar to the man whose profession is buying and selling. Up to the end of the eighteenth century, industrial production in Western Europe was a mere accessory to commerce.

As long as the machine was an inexpensive and unspecific tool there was no change in this position. The mere fact that the cottager could produce larger amounts than before within the same time might induce him to use machines to increase earnings, but this fact in itself did not necessarily affect the organization of production. Whether the cheap machinery was owned by the worker or by the merchant made some difference in the social position of the parties and almost certainly made a difference in the earnings of the worker, who was better off as long as he owned his tools; but it did not force the merchant to become an industrial capitalist, or to restrict himself to lending his money to such persons as were. The vent of goods rarely gave out; the greater difficulty continued to be on the side of supply of raw materials, which was sometimes unavoidably interrupted. But, even in such cases, the loss to the merchant who owned the machines was not substantial. It was not the coming of the machine as such but the invention of elaborate and therefore specific machinery and plant which completely changed the relationship of the merchant to production. Although the new productive organization was introduced by the merchant—a fact which determined the whole course of the transformation—the use of elaborate machinery and plant involved the development of the factory system and therewith a decisive shift in the relative importance of commerce and industry in favor of the latter. Industrial production ceased to be an accessory of commerce organized by the merchant as a buying and selling proposition; it now involved long-term investment with corresponding risks. Unless the continuance of production was reasonably assured, such a risk was not bearable.

But the more complicated industrial production became, the more numerous were the elements of industry the supply of which had to be safeguarded. Three of these, of course, were of outstanding importance: labor, land, and money. In a commercial society their supply could be organized in one way only: by being made available for purchase. Hence, they would have to be organized for sale on the market—in other words, as commodities. The extension of the market mechanism to the elements of industry—labor, land, and money—was the inevitable consequence of the introduction of the factory system in a commercial society. The elements of industry had to be on sale.

This was synonymous with the demand for a market system. We know that profits are ensured under such a system only if self-regulation is safeguarded through interdependent competitive markets. As the development of the factory system had been organized as part of a process of buying and selling, therefore labor, land, and money had to be transformed into commodities in order to keep production going. They could, of course, not be really transformed into commodities, as actually they were not produced for sale on the market. But the fiction of their being so produced became the organizing principle of society. Of the three, one stands out: labor is the technical term used for human beings, in so far as they are not employers but employed; it follows that henceforth the organization of labor would change concurrently with the organization of the market system. But as the organization of labor is only another word for the forms of life of the common people, this means that the development of the market system would be accompanied by a change in the organization of society itself. All along the line, human society had become an accessory of the economic system.

We recall our parallel between the ravages of the enclosures in English history and the social catastrophe which followed the Industrial Revolution. Improvements, we said, are, as a rule, bought at the price of social dislocation. If the rate of dislocation is too great, the community must succumb in the process. The Tudors and early Stuarts saved England from the fate of Spain by regulating the course of change so that it became bearable and its effects could be canalized into less destructive avenues. But nothing saved the common people of England from the impact of the Industrial Revolution. A blind faith in spontaneous progress had taken hold of people's minds, and with the fanaticism of sectarians the most enlightened pressed forward for boundless and unregulated change in society. The effects on the lives of the people were awful beyond description. Indeed, human society would have been annihilated but for protective, countermoves which blunted the action of this self-destructive mechanism.

Social history in the nineteenth century was thus the result of a double movement: the extension of the market organization in respect to genuine commodities was accompanied by its restriction in respect to fictitious ones. While on the one hand markets spread all over the face of the globe and the amount of goods involved grew to unbelievable proportions, on the other hand a network of measures and policies was integrated into powerful institutions designed to check the action of the market relative to labor land, and money. While the organization of world commodity markets, world capital markets, and world currency markets under the aegis of the gold standard gave an unparalleled momentum to the mechanism of markets, a deep-seated movement sprang into being to resist the pernicious effects of a market controlled economy. Society protected itself against the perils inherent in a self-regulating market system—this was the one comprehensive feature in the history of the age.

Notes

1. Tawney, R.H., *The Agrarian Problem in the 16th Century,* 1912.
2. Gibbins, H. de B., *The Industrial History of England,* 1895.
3. Innes, A.D., *England under the Tudors,* 1932.
4. Gairdner, J., "Henry VIII," *Cambridge Modern History,* Vol. II, 1918.
5. Heckscher, E.F., *Mercantilism,* 1935, p. 104.
6. Clapham, J.H., *Economic History of Modern Britain,* Vol. III.
7. See Karl Polanyi, *The Great Transformation,* Beacon Press, 2001 ed.: pp. 276–280, "Notes on Sources: 6. Selected References to "Societies and Economic Systems."
8. See Karl Polanyi, *The Great Transformation,* Beacon Press, 2001 ed.: pp. 280–285, "Notes on Sources: 7. Selected References to "Evolution of the Market Pattern."

9. Hawtrey, G.R., *The Economic Problem*, 1925, p. 13. "The practical application of the principle of individualism is entirely dependent on the practice of exchange." Hawtrey, however, was mistaken in assuming that the existence of markets simply followed from the practice of exchange.

10. Thurnwald, R.C, *Economics in Primitive Communities*, 1932, p. 147.

11. Pirenne, H., *Medieval Cities*, 1925, p. 148 (footnote 12).

12. Firth, R., *Primitive Polynesian Economics*, 1939, p. 347.

13. Thurnwald, R.C., *op. cit.*, p. 162–164.

14. Our presentation follows H. Pirenne's well-known works.

15. Montesquieu, *L'Esprit del lois*, 1748. "The English constrain the merchant, but it is in favor of commerce."

16. Henderson, H.D., *Supply and Demand*, 1922. The practice of the market is twofold: the apportionment of factors between different uses, and the organizing of the forces influencing aggregate supplies of factors.

17. Hawtrey, G.R., *op. cit.* Its function is seen by Hawtrey in making "the relative market values of all commodities mutually consistent."

18. Marx's assertion of the fetish character of the value of commodities refers to the exchange value of genuine commodities and has nothing in common with the fictitious commodities mentioned in the text.

19. Cunningham, W., "Economic Change," *Cambridge Modern History*, Vol. I.

Neil Fligstein,
The Architecture of Markets (2001)*

2: Markets as Institutions

The modern nation-state is linked to the development of market society in myriad ways. The historical problem of producing stable capital, labor, and product markets eventually required governments and the representatives of capital and labor to produce general institutional arrangements (both laws and informal rules) around property rights, governance structures, and rules of exchange for all markets in capitalist societies. Within markets, cultural and historically specific rules and practices came to govern the relations among suppliers, customers, and workers (what I call conceptions of control).

Why do rules matter? Complex patterns of interaction that are stable require actors who share cognitive assumptions and expectations. To get such stability, people need either long experiences with one another, such that they settle into habitual patterns, or more formal rules to govern novel interactions. Rules based on experience or tradition or formally agreed to through negotiation then frequently become habitual in interaction (what in "institutional theory" is called "taken for grantedness" [DiMaggio and Powell 1991, chap. 1]). It is the instability produced by interactions in which actors do not share meanings that pushes actors to seek out more stable social conditions under which to interact (for example, see Haveman and Rao 1997; Dobbin and Sutton 1998).

There are two kinds of situations in which to study rules. In normal times rules are well known and taken for granted, and interactions are predictable as a result. There is conflict and contention between actors, but those conflicts are fought out under established rules, meanings, and practices. Analysts can identify who the players are, whether they are dominant or challengers, what their interests are, and what their actions mean.

In moments of the formation or transformation of political or market fields, actors become self-aware and engage in new forms of interaction to produce new arrangements. Because they try to forge new understandings, their interests and identities are in flux. They try to figure out what they want, how to get it, and how to get along with others who might want other things. The source of rules for new fields is often understandings brought from other fields. Actors modify these understandings in the practice of interacting with other groups and create new practices. But these new practices are often laid down along lines set by existing understandings.

Why the state? As the possibility for complex patterns of interaction in the sphere of economic exchange has expanded, actors have proven incapable of providing rules for themselves. Actors have two sorts of problems. First, in the case of markets, actors

---

* From: *The Architecture of Markets: An Economic Sociology of Twenty-First-Century Capitalist Societies* Neil Fligstein, Copyright. © 2001 Princeton University Press. (pp. 27–44) Reprinted by permission of Princeton University Press.

have to worry about keeping their firms alive. It is difficult to devote resources to making rules and simultaneously to do business. Second, in the face of uncertainty and difficult competition, firms find it impossible to solve their collective problems of competition. Sometimes firms find a way to eliminate or co-opt their principal competitors. But often this does not happen. These conditions cause firms to seek out help by approaching the government to legislate to promote "fair" competition.[1]

What about power? Rules are not created innocently or without taking into account "interests." If the largest firms are able to work under a set of rules that allows them to dominate the main markets of a society and keep workers disorganized, those rules enforce a system of power. In order to get analytic leverage on real systems of rules and power, it is necessary to think systematically about how government capacity and the relative power of government officials, capitalists, and workers figure into the construction of new market rules to define the forms of economic activity that exist in a given society.

The political-cultural perspective can provide generic analytic tools to understand what a particular set of market arrangements implies about the power structure of a society. Once these arrangements are understood, it is possible to predict how existing institutions will be used by powerful actors to frame subsequent crises. This gives leverage on understanding many of the most important political-economic dynamics within societies.

There are three parts to my exposition. First, it is necessary to define markets and the institutions necessary for them to function. The key insight is that markets are a kind of field, one that depends not just on the power of incumbents, but on more general rules in society in order to stabilize the power of incumbents. Then, it is important to consider how governments in modern capitalist societies have been constructed to deal with problems of market regulation. I argue that governments develop different kinds of capacities to intervene in their economies that are characterized by three dimensions: their ability to intervene, the form of intervention, and whose interests dominate the intervention. I then generate some general propositions about how rules produced by firms and governments produce stability in market economies.

Market Institutions: Basic Definitions

One of the core ideas that differentiates modern society from the societies that preceded it is the idea that social organization is a human product. This implies that people can make choices and attempt to construct social-organizational vehicles to attain their ends. This does not mean that people are all successful or have the same opportunities to be actors. It does mean that the entire apparatus of modern economies is, at least partially, an outcome of these social technologies of organization. These have been invented and, upon reflection by the actors who use them, intentionally refined.

The organizations and institutions that existed before modernity were obviously social constructions as well. But they were not generally conceived that way. They established who was an actor and what actors could do. As people have become more self-aware in the past 350 years, they have examined existing social organizations, learned what seems to be successful, and used this knowledge to create new social arrangements. Over time, people have found ways to systematically produce new social technologies to attain ends (for example, legal incorporation to organize firms).

Modern governments, social movements, democratic politics, firms, and markets were invented by people collectively attempting to find ways to attain their ends (Fligstein 1997a). Often these "inventions" were accidental or reflected compromises between groups. The relations between the people who produced these social-organizational vehicles was, and continues to be, murky. But once these inventions were in place, other persons became aware of the various ways to organize and self-consciously built on them. The theory of fields is a generic theory of social organization in modernity. Our ability to recover that theory is itself an act of historical self-awareness. By abstracting away from the common experiences of social actors vying for control over their social arenas, social analysts have begun to appreciate that generic social processes underlie the construction of fields across states, markets, and the private nonprofit sector.

The theory of fields assumes that actors try to produce a "local" stable world where the dominant actors produce meanings that allow them to reproduce their advantage. These actors create status hierarchies that define the positions of incumbents and challengers. Actors face two related problems when constructing these fields: attaining a stable system of power and, once it is in place, maintaining it. The social organization of fields broadly refers to three features: the set of principles that organize thought and are used by actors to make sense of their situations (what might be called cognitive frames or worldviews), the routines or practices that actors perform in their day-to-day social relations, and the social relations that constitute fields that may or may not be consciously understood by actors (Bourdieu 1977).

The cognitive maps individuals possess offer them conceptual tools to understand or interpret the moves of others (White 1992; Emirbayer and Goodwin 1994). They also provide actors with tools to create new fields. Typically, the cognitive models that actors use are not included in conceptualizations of social organization. This is because human agency is typically undertheorized. Sociologists usually think that a person's position in a social structure dictates what the person does, while rational choice theories use interests as the main explanatory variable. Actors' common understandings are not assumed to be consequential to explaining their actions. But in the theory of fields, the skill of actors in interpreting their situations, constructing courses of action, and innovating on existing routines helps construct fields and maintain them once in place (Bourdieu and Wacquant 1992). While one can separate cognitive elements from social relations, social organization depends on both (Giddens 1981).

Social organization is the totality of what produces stable conditions for the privileged and not-so-privileged groups in society. It constitutes them as groups, defines their relations to one another, and maintains a certain order in existing fields. This discussion of the basic building blocks of fields is necessarily abstract. These building blocks contain no substance or, more precisely, "culture" (i.e., practices and local knowledge) (Geertz 1983). They do not tell us much about how a given field is going to be constructed and reproduced in reality because they do not specify what kind of field is being built (state, market, organization) nor the precise principles that structure the relations between the "players."

To apply the theory of fields to market society, it is necessary to define what kind of fields markets are, and what types of social organization are necessary for stable "markets as fields" to exist. Economic exchange ranges from infrequent and unstructured to frequent and structured. Markets are social arenas that exist for the production and sale of some good or service, and they are characterized by structured exchange. Structured exchange implies that actors expect repeated exchanges for their products and that, therefore, they need rules and social structures to guide and organize exchange. While the identities of their customers and suppliers may change over time, producers expect that they will continue to seek out customers and will need suppliers.

Actors in unstructured or haphazard exchange have little invested in the exchange, and participants may or may not interact again (either as buyers or sellers). While they may benefit from the exchange, the sellers' organizational survival does not depend on haphazard exchange. It is when the agents in exchange begin to view their own stability (i.e., reproduction) as contingent on stabilizing trade, that they turn to social-organizational vehicles. Exchange throughout human history has often been unstructured, but markets in the sense I use the term here preexisted modern capitalism. Markets (and this includes almost all modern production markets) are mainly structured by sellers looking for buyers.[2] A given market becomes a "stable market" (i.e., a field) when the product being exchanged has legitimacy with customers, and the suppliers of the good or service are able to produce a status hierarchy in which the largest suppliers dominate the market and are able to reproduce themselves on a period-to-period basis.

These actors produce organizations to make the good and create social relations between competitors to govern competition. Stable markets can be described as "self reproducing role structures" in which incumbent and challenger firms reproduce their positions on a period-of-period basis (White 1981).[3] The sellers generally produce the social structure in the market because their firms' existence is at stake if a stable market does not appear.[4] The particular problems of finding a stable market are the same for all sellers: they are looking to secure suppliers and customers and thereby find a way to reproduce themselves. The social relations between sellers in a stable market are such that one set of firms produces the dominant cultural meanings for the market and the other firms fall in line. This does not imply that the partners to any given exchange between buyers and sellers have to be the same actors. Sellers vie for customers, and customers may switch suppliers. The stability of the sellers, in the sense of their organizational survival, is what is important to the stability of the market. My operational definition of a market is the situation in which the status hierarchy and, by implication, the existence of the leading sellers are reproduced on a period-by-period basis.

For example, the steel industry in the United States, for much of the twentieth century, was a stable market in which firms had persistent identities and defined products. The largest firms reproduced themselves by being vertically integrated and focused on stabilizing prices even as demand shifted radically (Fligstein 1990). Since the mid-1960s, the identities of the suppliers of steel products have been transformed. Many of the largest producers disappeared, and new firms began to dominate the market. The market itself became differentiated between products that were basic commodities and higher-end, higher-value-added products. The newer firms were able to take advantage of these changes to form a new market. The field that once existed has disappeared, and two new market fields have taken its place (Hogan 1984).

I do not mean to obliterate the distinction between a market and an industry. A market is a social arena where sellers and buyers meet. But for sellers and buyers to exist, a product has to exist and someone has to produce it. A market depends on the buyers continuing to "show up" in a particular social space to purchase the product. But the sellers' firms and their status relations define what stability means in the market. They define what the market is about, and their relations define the local culture by which money is to be made and stability produced. While there is obviously an interdependency between buyers and sellers, the sellers' stake in the arena is one of survival.

In spite of elaborate social mechanisms and rules to guide market interaction, markets are inherently unstable from the point of view of sellers. One of the deep insights of economics is that market society makes it very profitable to create new markets. At the beginning of markets, first movers can often reap huge rewards. But as other economic actors realize the opportunity, they enter into the market and prices drop. Moreover, as markets slow down in growth (as they inevitably do), firms have incentives to go after more market share and to cut prices. These forces intensify competition. Products can be delegitimated, most often by being superseded by other products. It is these opportunities and problems that create unstable conditions for producers.

Even where seller relations have been stabilized, they can be upset. The "game" for the incumbent firms is to find a way to produce a market as a stable field. These stable markets contain social structures that characterize the relations between dominant and challenger seller firms. The social relations are oriented toward maintaining the advantaged positions of the largest seller firms in the face of their challengers. They define how the market works and how competition is structured. For example, two main firms dominate the soft drink industry in the United States: Pepsi-Cola and Coca-Cola. These firms compete over market share and use advertising, diversification of products, and price discounts to do so. Although the firms compete, they have produced an equilibrium whereby both survive by following the accepted tactics of competition.

As forms of social organization, market structures involve both cognitive understandings and concrete social relations. The cognitive understandings are of two sorts: general societal understandings about how to organize firms and markets and find stable ways to compete, and specific understandings about the way a particular market works. These specific understandings structure the interactions between competitors but also allow actors to make sense of their competitors' actions. The concrete social relations in a given market reflect its unique history and its dependency on other markets. The links to suppliers and customers play a role in creating stable markets. The constitution of these relations determines which firms are dominant and why, and their relations to challenger firms. The ultimate success of firms in producing stable fields (i.e., social structures to stabilize their relationships with one another) is dependent on the general principles of making markets in their society, and the ability to find a way to do this within a particular market.

The first problem for a sociology of markets is to propose theoretically what kinds of rules and understandings are necessary to make structured exchange (i.e., markets as fields) possible in the first place. There are four types of rules relevant to producing social structures in markets—what can be called property rights, governance structures, rules of exchange, and conceptions of control. These categories are necessarily abstract. They refer to general types of rules that can appear as laws, understandings, or practices. They define issues about which actors who want to generate markets must create general understandings in order for stable markets to emerge. They need these rules whether they are aware of them or not. Failure, for example, to have property rights makes it difficult to have markets. If we do not know who owns what and who has the right to dispose of it, we are in the world of illegal trade and not the world of stable markets.

These four types of social structures have emerged historically as firms and governments have recognized certain generic problems in making markets work and then reflected on general solutions. Through understandings around these institutions actors produce social structures to organize themselves, to compete and cooperate, and to exchange with one another in a regular and reproducible fashion. Each of these types of social structure is directed at different problems of instability. Some are related to the general problem of creating a market in the first place, and others have to do with ensuring the stability of firms in a particular market.

Property rights are rules that define who has claims on the profits of firms (akin to what agency theorists call "residual claims" on the free cash flow of firms (Jensen and Meckling 1976; Fama 1980)). This general statement leaves open the issues of the different legal forms of property rights (e.g., corporations vs. partnerships); the relationship between shareholders and employees, local communities, suppliers, and customers; and the role of the state in directing investment, owning firms, and preventing owners from harming workers. The holders of property rights are entitled to dispose of property or earn income from it. Patents and credentials are forms of property rights that entitle their holder to earn profits. The constitution of property rights is a continuous and contestable political process, not the outcome of an efficient process (for a similar argument, see Roe 1994). Organized groups from business, labor, government agencies, and political parties try to affect the constitution of property rights.

The division of property rights is at the core of market society. Property rights define who is in control of the capitalist enterprise and who has rights to claim the surplus. Property rights do not always favor the privileged groups in society. If, for instance, governments own firms and control investment decisions, their decisions can take into account different divisions of profits. Cooperative businesses or partnerships can allow for equal distribution of profits. Workers can receive part of their pay in profit-sharing schemes.

Property rights are necessary to markets because they define the social relationships between owners and everyone else in society. This stabilizes markets by making it clear who is risking what and who gets the reward in a particular market situation. A given firm's suppliers know who is the responsible entity. Property rights thus function to produce two forms of stability: defining the power relationships between constituencies in and around firms, and signaling to other firms who firms are.[5]

Governance structures refer to the general rules in a society that define relations of competition and cooperation and define how firms should be organized.[6] These rules define the legal and illegal forms of controlling competition. They take two forms: (1) laws and (2) informal institutional practices. Laws, called antitrust, competition, or anticartel laws, exist in most advanced industrial societies. The passage, enforcement, and judicial interpretation of these laws is contested (Fligstein 1990), and the content of such laws varies widely across societies. Some societies allow extensive cooperation between competitors, particularly when foreign trade is involved, while others try to reduce the effects of barriers to entry and promote competition. Competition is not just regulated within societies, but across societies. Countries have tariffs and trade barriers to help national industry to compete with foreign competitors. These laws often benefit particular sectors of the economy.

Firms' internal organization is also a response to legal and illegal forms of competition. Firms that vertically integrate often do so to ensure themselves supplies and deny those supplies to competitors. Firms also may horizontally integrate by buying up market share in order to produce stable order in a market. Firms may diversify products in order to protect themselves from the vagaries of particular products. They may also form long-term relationships with suppliers, customers, or financial organizations in order to respond to competition.

Market societies develop more informal institutional practices that are embedded in existing organizations as routines and are available to actors in other organizations. Mechanisms of transmission include professional associations, management consultants, and the exchange of professional managers (DiMaggio and Powell 1983; Meyer and Rowan 1977). Among these informal practices are how to arrange a work organization (such as the multidivisional form), how to write labor and management contracts, and where to draw the boundaries of the firm. So, for instance, firms can compete on price, but if they infringe on one another's patents or trade secrets, they are likely to run afoul of the law. They also include current views of what behavior of firms is legal or illegal. Governance structures help define the legal and normative rules by which firms structure themselves and their relations to competitors. In this way, they generally function to stabilize those relations.

Rules of exchange define who can transact with whom and the conditions under which transactions are carried out. Rules must be established regarding weights, common standards, shipping, billing, insurance, the exchange of money (i.e., banks), and the enforcement of contracts. Rules of exchange regulate health and safety standards of products and the standardization of products more generally. For example, many pharmaceutical products undergo extensive testing procedures. Health and safety standards help both buyers and sellers and facilitate exchange between parties who may have only fleeting interactions.

Product standardization has become increasingly important in the context of rules of exchange, particularly in the telecommunications and computer industries. National and international bodies meet to agree on standards for products across many industries. Standard setting produces shared rules that guarantee that products will be compatible. This process facilitates exchange by making it more certain that products will work the way they are intended.

Rules of exchange help stabilize markets by ensuring that exchanges occur under conditions that apply to everyone. If firms that ship their goods across a particular society do not have rules of exchange, such exchanges will be haphazard at best. Making these rules has become even more important for trade across societies. Many of the newest international trade agreements, including the European Union's Single Market Program and the last round of GATT (General Agreement on Tariffs and Trade), focus on producing and harmonizing practices around rules of exchange.

Conceptions of control reflect market-specific agreements between actors in firms on principles of internal organization (i.e., forms of hierarchy), tactics for competition or cooperation (i.e., strategies), and the hierarchy or status ordering of firms in a given market. A conception of control is a form of "local knowledge" (Geertz 1983).[7] Conceptions of control are historical and cultural products. They are historically specific to a certain industry in a certain society. They are cultural in that they form a set of understandings and practices about how things work in a particular market setting. A stable market is a social field in which a conception of control defines the social relations between incumbent and challenger seller firms such that the incumbent firms reproduce those relations on a period-to-period basis.

The purpose of action in a given market is to create and maintain stable worlds within and across firms that allow dominant seller firms to survive. Conceptions of control are social organizational vehicles for particular markets that refer to the cognitive understandings that structure perceptions of how a particular market works, as well as a description of the real social relations of domination that exist in a particular market. A conception of control is simultaneously a worldview that allows actors to interpret the actions of others and a reflection of how the market is structured.

State Building and Market Building

Creating a general set of rules whereby stable markets can be produced helps to structure exchange in particular product fields in a particular society. To move from unstructured to structured exchange in a market implies that actors became aware of systematic problems they had in stabilizing exchange. Their awareness stimulated them to search for social-organizational solutions to their problems. But this awareness did not come quickly or all at once. The emergence of the general social technologies that help actors to produce and maintain modern markets depended on discovering the problems presented by property rights (i.e., who owned what), governance structures (i.e., ways to organize, including fair and unfair forms of competition), rules of exchange (i.e., making exchanges), and conceptions of control (i.e., producing local status hierarchies within markets to stabilize the situation of dominant players).

Proposition 2.1. The entry of countries into capitalism pushes states to develop rules about property rights, governance structures, rules of exchange, and conceptions of control in order to stabilize markets.

The timing of entry of countries into capitalism has had huge effects on societal trajectories (Westney 1987; Chandler 1990; Fligstein 1990; Dobbin 1994). The alliances made at this historical moment between workers, state officials, and capitalists structure the way in which states build policy domains and the policy styles that develop in those domains. Once such styles are established, subsequent political and economic crises are interpreted from these perspectives.

This does not mean that societies are forever locked into a set of institutions. But it does mean that any new crisis is interpreted from the current dominant perspective. This works in two ways. First, a system of rules is also a system of power. Incumbent actors try to use the current rules for their benefit. But the current set of institutions also provides actors with a way to figure out how to apply the old rules to new situations. For these reasons, we tend to observe incremental change, barring massive societal failure due to war or depression. Then, crisis open up the possibility for new political alliances and new rules.

For countries just establishing modern capitalist markets, creating stable conceptions of control is more difficult precisely because property rights, governance structures, and rules of exchange are not well specified. Firms are exposed to cutthroat competition and often demand that the state establish rules about property rights, governance structures, and rules of exchange. Creating these new institutions requires the interaction of firms, political parties, states, and newly invented (or borrowed) conceptions of regulation.[8]

People did not realize historically that they had to resolve these issues to make structured exchange possible (see North 1990, chap. 1, on this point). Indeed, many practices evolved in informal ways and stayed informal. Actors in markets found ways of making themselves stable for relatively long periods of time in the absence of formal institutions. But, as time went on, social technologies to solve problems emerged in industrial societies. Large-scale social disruptions such as wars, depressions, or social movements caused political actors to craft general tools with which to respond.

Once actors became aware of more general solutions, the solutions were used in new circumstances. But novel situations often forced the modification of organizing technology. So, for example, the modern American conception of the corporation (a limited-liability joint stock corporation) started out as a state-directed conception that emphasized limits on the exercise of property rights. This gave state legislators a tool to use in development projects whereby they could delegate transportation and communications projects to private firms and still maintain control over the firm. People began to recognize two advantages to the corporate form: it allowed the bringing together of more capital, and it restricted the liability of parties to the agreement to the assets they had invested in the corporation. These advantages pushed entrepreneurs to demand more and more acts of incorporation. Finally, this led to a broad conception of incorporation that made the form widely available (Friedman 1973; Roy 1997).

One way to partially understand governments is to view them as organized entities that produce and enforce market (and other) rules. However, this rule is not a historical necessity. It is theoretically possible for firms to routinize exchange with one another without the benefit of rules or governments. After all, most trade before the eighteenth century was done in the absence of strong states and legal systems (Greif 1989; Spruyt 1994). Before modernity, the problems posed by unstable exchange were solved by private parties to those exchanges.

There was a very practical reason for developing more general rules for markets. North and Thomas (1973) noted long ago that social institutions have made entrepreneurs richer, their firms bigger and more stable. For that reason, they argued, self-interested actors had an interest in producing rules. However, though we know rules encouraged markets as fields, entrepreneurs, managers, and governments did not comprehend that creating governmental capacity to make rules would help create wealth. So, for example, Carruthers (1996) shows that the first modern capital market in England was very much organized along political party lines. People would only trade with those with whom they agreed on politics. One of the purposes of the markets was to reward people in the party, by giving them access to friendly pools of capital.

North, in his later work (1990), realized that modern economic history cannot be read as the gradual reduction of transaction costs for markets by the production of rules that facilitate trade. He saw that entrepreneurs and government officials were unaware that their actions produced positive consequences. Their actions were not framed in these terms; indeed, their actions were often framed to benefit the friends of the rulers and cut out their enemies. Moreover, the rulers of premodern European states had time horizons far too short to understand what produced long-term economic growth. Most market institutions were the outcome of political struggles whereby one group of capitalists captured government and created rules to favor themselves over their political opponents. North's central insight is at the basis of the theory of market governance theory presented here.

The general rules that did eventually emerge reflected years of interactions with various forms of structured exchange and increasing awareness of the difficulty of managing large, complex production without rules. As one problem was solved and one set of markets stabilized, another set of problems emerged. The increasing scale of production, the growth of markets, and the growing awareness of entrepreneurs and managers of their common problems pushed the search for new common understandings.

It is still possible, of course, for structured exchange to occur without shared market institutions. But we now exist in a world where those institutions are ubiquitous and social actors are aware of them. It is this increasing self-awareness that leads modern actors in governments and firms to seek out general rules and forms of enforcement from the outset. As social organizational vehicles become more sophisticated and ways of managing sources of instability become better known, entrepreneurs and managers realize that common understandings over property rights, governance structures, rules of exchange, and conceptions of control are useful for dominant firms.

There were two historical problems that militated against entrepreneurs and managers producing common rules to stabilize exchanges. If governments were formed by a small number of capitalists to intervene in market processes, the group was likely to make rules to favor themselves and cut out others, thereby capturing the state for their narrow interests. This, of course, frequently happened. But such rent seeking was met by open political conflict.

Capitalists often faced collective action problems when it came to making market rules. How could entrepreneurs who focused on existing conceptions of control in a given market simultaneously develop more general rules about competition, cooperation, property rights, and rules of exchange with actors in other markets? The basic problem is that owners have to worry about organizational survival in the context of scarce organizational resources. Why would they want to produce general rules for all firms in a society?

Systemic economic crises produced economic depressions as a result of unstable systems of exchange. These became more severe and involved more and more people in societies across Europe and North America in the nineteenth century. Those with the largest investments in plants and other facilities found themselves in difficult situations. Managers and entrepreneurs responded to these crises caused by over competition by trying to control their main competitors. They used cartels or attempted to form monopolies. Firms also faced workers' organizations that resisted their attempt to lower wages and control labor markets. Class struggle led to bitter disputes between the large groups of workers who were located in the largest factories and the owners and managers (Edwards 1979). But frequently, firms and workers could not construct stable solutions, and they certainly could not construct "general" solutions. This conflict led both sides to go to governments to get them to produce stable outcomes (Fligstein 1990; Chandler 1990).

The organizations, groups, and institutions that comprise the fields of the state in modern capitalist society claim sovereignty, that is, the right to make and enforce the rules governing all interactions in a given geographic area (Krasner 1988).[9] Firms and workers' organizations came into conflict and turmoil, and they both tried to use governments to solve their problems of instability (Fligstein 1990). While most modern discussions of state building have focused on welfare and warfare, modern capitalist states have been constructed in interaction with the development of their economies, and the governance of their economies is part of the core of state building (Fligstein 1990; Hooks 1990; Campbell, Hollingsworth, and Lindberg 1991; Dobbin 1994; Evans 1995).[10]

As was stated in chapter 1, I conceive of the modern state as a set of fields that can be defined as policy domains. Policy domains are arenas of political action where bureaucratic agencies and representatives of firms and workers meet to form and implement policy.[11] The purpose of this policymaking is to make rules and governance mechanisms to produce stable patterns of interaction in nonstate fields. Modern states also typically develop legal systems with courts that adjudicate and interpret current laws and understandings. These legal fields are domains as well that contain judges, courts, lawyers, and law schools. One way to understand the legal system is to realize that legal systems are alternative ways for challenger groups to engage in political action. By using laws against incumbents, challengers can contest the rights and privileges of dominant groups (Shapiro 1980; Stone Sweet 2000).

The building of these domains, what others have called "state capacity" (Evans, Skocpol, and Rueschmeyer 1985), occurs under a set of interactions governed by rules that were usually put into place by a revolutionary social movement or a series of such movements or were imposed by outside invaders (or a succession of such forces). Once a government is formed in capitalist societies, the political processes in a society are about dominant groups building government capacity to ensure their dominant position and challenger groups trying to reorient existing domains or creating new ones to include them. The purpose of this confrontation within domains is to provide stabilizing rules that tend to benefit the most powerful groups.

State building can be defined as the development of domains set up by and for state officials, firms, and workers. The domains, once constructed, reflect the relative power of workers, capitalists, politicians, and state bureaucrats, inscribed in the law and the forms of regulation or intervention at the time they are formed. Domains are often focused on particular industries (for example, bank regulation) but can also be concerned with more general issues that apply across industries (for example, antitrust law or patents that define property rights). The way in which states are capable of intervening in their economies is inscribed by the power relations as constituted in particular domains when they are founded.

Proposition 2.2. Initial formation of policy domains and the rules they create affecting property rights, governance structures, and rules of exchange shape the development of new markets because they produce cultural templates that determine how to organize in a given society. The initial configuration of institutions and the balance of power between government officials, capitalists, and workers at that moment account for the persistence of, and differences between, national capitalisms.

The shape of initial regulatory institutions has a profound effect on subsequent capitalist development. They define the current state of rules and what is permissible. They also provide guidelines for how states can be subsequently organized to intervene in economies as new issues arise. Indeed, any new markets that come into existence do so under a given set of institutions. This is one of the most remarkable features of institutions: they enable newly organized actors to act. They do not just support the status quo, but allow entrepreneurs to come into existence without having to invent new ways to organize.

One can observe that, as countries industrialize, the demand for laws or enforceable understandings is high, and that once such understandings are produced, demand decreases. As new industries emerge or old ones are transformed, new rules are made in the context of the old rules. Dobbin (1994) has argued that societies create "regulatory styles." These styles are embedded in regulatory organizations and in the statutes that support them. States are often the focus of market crises, but actors continue to use an existing set of laws and practices to resolve crises. These general tactics are used to construct arguments about why and how governments should directly intervene in or mediate disputes between firms and workers and intervene in or regulate markets. Property rights, governance structures, conceptions of control, and rules of exchange are institutional issues about which modern states establish rules for economic actors. There can be specific state agencies oriented toward producing and enforcing institutions, such as patent offices for the registration of property rights. More common, however, are multiple domains where institutional issues enter in different ways.

A good example is modern states' extensive policy domains organized around the problems of agriculture. Most advanced industrial societies have programs oriented toward solving problems of competition (for instance, price support programs and subsidized foreign trade) and rules of exchange (for instance, health and safety standards and standard weights and measures). In many advanced industrial societies, these policies are buttressed with concerns for the property rights of "family" farmers. In the United States, special tax laws make it easier for family farmers to pass on their farms to their children.

Proposition 2.3. State actors are constantly attending to one market crisis or another. This is so because markets are always being organized or destabilized, and firms and workers are lobbying for state intervention.

In normal times, change in markets is incremental and dependent upon the construction of interests of actors in and around the state.[12] Having stable rules is often more important than the content of the rules. However, rules do embody the interests of dominant groups, and state actors do not intentionally transform rules unless dominant, groups are in crisis. Because of their central place in the creation and enforcement of market institutions, states become the focus of crisis in any important market. Given the turmoil inherent in markets, the state is constantly attending to some form of market crisis.

Pressure on states can come from two sources: other states (and by implication, their firms) and existing markets that can be constructed either locally (within the geography of the state) or globally (across states). As economic interdependence across societies has increased, there has been an explosion of cross-state agreements, particularly about rules of exchange. States provide stable and reliable conditions under which firms organize, compete, cooperate, and exchange. They also privilege some firms over others and often national large firms over small firms and firms from foreign countries. The enforcement of these rules affects what conceptions of control can produce stable markets. There are political contests over the content of laws, their applicability to given firms and markets, and the extent and direction of state intervention in the economy.

Power in Policy Domains and Market Institutions

States are important to the formation and ongoing stability of markets. How they are important and to what degree is a matter of historical process (Evans 1995; Ziegler 1997). Some states have greater capacities for intervention than others, and the likelihood of intervention depends on the nature of the crisis and the institutional history of the state (Dobbin 1994; Evans, Skocpol, and Rueschmeyer 1985; Ziegler 1997; Laumann and Knoke 1987).[13] Current organized interests use current rules to try to reproduce their positions. This explains why there appear to be so many forms of market arrangements across and within developed and developing societies (Evans 1995; Fligstein and Freeland 1995).

Proposition 2.4. Policy domains contain governmental organizations and representatives of firms, workers, and other organized groups. They are structured in two ways: (1) around the state's capacity to intervene, regulate, and mediate, and (2) around the relative power of societal groups to dictate the terms of intervention.

There are two important ways in which to characterize the political structure of policy domains of the state that focus on the relations between government officials, their organizations, capitalist firms, and workers. One important dimension is captured by the distinctions among direct intervention, regulation, and mediation. Domains are interventionist to the degree that government officials can directly make substantive decisions for markets. Governments may own firms, control the financial sector, direct investment, and heavily regulate firms' entries, exits, and competition in markets. Government officials have strong control over firms and workers in these domains. An example of an interventionist state is France, where historically officials in ministries were able to direct investment and control firms by virtue of government ownership.

In contrast, states dominated by regulatory regimes create agencies to enforce general rules in markets but do not decide who can own what or make what investment. Regulatory states put organizations in place in policy domains to play "traffic cop." Theoretically, regulatory bodies do not reflect the interest of any one group but use rules impartially to police the interactions of firms and workers who are represented in the domain. Often, regulatory bodies become captured by the dominant firms in an industry. Examples of regulatory agencies are the Securities and Exchange Commission in the United States and the Monopolies Board in the United Kingdom.

Both regulatory and interventionist states occasionally use mediation in policy arenas to help make policy or settle disputes. Interactions between industry representatives and state officials around an issue of common concern may result in the formation of a policy for a sector of the economy. If there is conflict between the organizations of firms or between firms and workers, state officials can act as mediators. It is clear that the Ministry of International Trade and Industry (MITI) played this role in Japanese development (Johnson 1982; Evans 1995).[14]

The second dimension that structures domains concerns whether or not they have undergone "capture." Economists argue that one problem of government intervention in markets is the temptation by government officials to "rent-seek" (Buchanan, Tellison, and Tulloch 1980). Rent seeking implies that government officials seek out payments from either firms or workers in a sector that involve bribes or taxes. In this case, the sector can be captured by the state. Evans (1995) has described as predatory states in some parts of the Third World that have this capacity.

Capture can occur as well if either a set of firms or an organized group of workers gets control over a policy domain (this is in fact the point of Buchanan, Tellison, and Tulloch's book [1980]). Regulatory agencies or even interventionist parts of ministries often rely on industry guidance for information and personnel. If workers or firms capture domains, they can attempt to use the domain to narrowly defend their privilege against other claims. To the degree that the industry is organized, it is possible for a set of firms to capture the regulatory agency and get government officials to accept their view of the industry and what should be done.

Workers can capture domains as well. Groups of workers may, for example, win the right to certify new workers, which, in essence, gives them the right to decide who has a "property right," that is, who owns a certificate that entitles them to make a profit from their skill. The government may directly intervene in this process or allow certification boards to be selected from members of workers' communities. Professions, such as physicians in the United States, have used this tactic successfully for long periods of time to control the supply of doctors (Starr 1982).

I would like to reconceptualize the language of rent seeking to capture in a more neutral way who, among government officials or representatives of capitalist or worker interests, has the upper hand in making policy in a given domain. Rent seeking occurs in the sense that all groups are oriented toward using their power in policy domains for their own ends. But rent seeking can be more or less venal. When individual firms or government officials use their positions to advantage themselves and disadvantage of others in their fields, extreme predatory behavior can result.

Usually, rent seeking only occurs where there is little countervailing power. If a set of capitalist firms is not opposed by government officials or workers, the firms are more likely to set in place governance structures that allow collusion and rules of exchange that prevent other firms from competing. But it is also the case that the interests of a small set of firms and organized workers may produce the same effect. By such means textile manufacturers in the United States have been able to protect their markets by allying themselves with workers under the guise of saving jobs.

Notes

1 Incumbent firms that capture markets will try to obtain regulatory capture of states to buttress their position in markets. In societies with more interventionist traditions, governments can try to organize the market and control competition from the outset.

2 The idea of a market as a field does not assume that all market actors are in physical proximity, only social proximity. In modern society, trade shows, stock exchanges, commodity exchanges, shopping malls, shops in general are locales for physical markets. But markets do not have to be located in physical space. Many sales are made directly between buyer and seller, often through salespeople. But in these situations, buyers often compare prices of sellers by talking to multiple suppliers.

3 This model, with a little modification, can also be applied to labor markets, where some workers are organized and others are not.

4 Sellers can greatly affect the stability of market structures. If sellers stop buying a certain good, then the social organization of the market will do the producers no good. If markets are totally dependent on a single seller, then that seller can dictate market structure as well. But generally, even in these situations, sellers will frame their actions vis-à-vis one another in order to promote the survival of their firm (White 1981).

5 Institutional economics has recognized the importance of property rights for market stability (Jensen and Meckling 1976; Fama and Jensen 1983a, 1983b; Williamson 1985; North 1990). The division of property rights makes the firm possible in the first place, allows investment to occur, and constrains and enables managers and workers. In places where firm property rights do not exist, investment is haphazard and the economy is operated at the point of the barrel of a gun.

6 The term "governance" structure has been used to refer to both property rights questions (Jensen and Meckling 1976) and issues about how to draw the boundaries of firms (Williamson 1985). I have chosen to separate the question of who owns firms from the question of how markets and firms are actually organized in terms of how firms compete, how they are to be internally organized, and if competitors can cooperate to control competition. Legitimate and illegitimate ways to compete and organize are not considered governance in economics.

7 I discuss the dynamics of particular markets and the formation of conceptions of control in chapter 14.

8   Late developers have the advantage of being able to borrow institutions from other soci-
    eties. Japan, for example, self-consciously examined organizational practices of many soci-
    eties to aid its late development project (Westney 1987).

9   My purpose is not to propose a theory of the state. Instead, I want to focus on how the
    theory of fields helps make sense of the organization of modern states and consider the
    links between the markets as fields and the states as fields.

10 Much of this discussion is inspired by the recent literature in political science that defines
    itself as historical institutionalism (March and Olsen 1989; Hall 1989; Steinmo, Thelen, and
    Longstreth 1992).

11 I am using *domain* in a very abstract fashion. I want to include pluralist, corporatist, and
    even totalitarian regimes under this rubric. I have in mind the general idea that govern-
    mental capacity includes relations that organize people who run governments, firms, and
    workers. But these relations can be hierarchical, voluntary, or democratic. They can be
    inscribed in constitutions or can evolve from preexisting social institutions.

12 The purpose here is not to develop a theory of the forms of states, but only to note their
    potential influence on market formation through their power to make the rules that govern
    all forms of social activity in a given geographic area.

13 This perspective does not imply that the state is pivotal for every economic process. Even
    in societies where states have a history of intervention, state involvement is variable and its
    effects are variable as well. The state's role depends on which market is being discussed and
    the current conditions in that or related markets.

14 In practice, the distinction between intervention and mediation may be difficult to make.
    Johnson described MITI's actions more as direct interventions into markets, while Evans
    stresses the mediator role. As the Japanese economy has become more developed, firms
    have developed their own capacity for having policy preferences. This makes MITI more a
    shaper of consensus.

References

Bourdieu, P. 1977. *Outline of a Theory of Practice*. Cambridge: Cambridge University Press.

Bourdieu, P., and L. Wacquant. 1992. *An Invitation to Reflexive Sociology*. Chicago: University
    of Chicago Press.

Buchanan, J., R. Tellison, and G. Tulloch. 1980. *Toward a Theory of the Rent-Seeking Society*.
    College Station: Texas A&M Press.

Campbell, J., J. R. Hollingsworth, and L. Lindberg. 1991. *Governance of the American Economy*.
    Cambridge: Cambridge University Press.

Carruthers, B. 1996. *City of Capital: Politics and Markets in the English Financial Revolution*.
    Princeton, N.J.: Princeton University Press.

Chandler, A. 1990. *Scale and Scope: The Dynamics of Industrial Capitalism*. Cambridge: Belknap
    Press of Harvard University Press.

DiMaggio, P. and W. Powell. 1983. "The Iron Cage Revisited: Institutional Isomorphism
    and Collective Rationality in Organizational Fields." *American Sociological Review*
    48(2): 147–60.

———, eds. 1991. *The New Institutionalism in Organizational Analysis*. Chicago: University of
    Chicago Press.

Dobbin, F. 1994. *Forging Industrial Policy: The U.S., Britain, and France in the Railway Age*.
    New York: Cambridge University Press.

Dobbin, F. and J. Sutton. 1998. "The Strength of a Weak State: The Rights Revolution and the Rise of Human Resource Management Divisions." *American Journal of Sociology* 104(2): 441–76.

Edwards, R. 1979. *Contested Terrain: The Transformation of the Workplace in the Twentieth Century*. New York: Basic Books.

Emirbayer, M., and J. Goodwin. 1994. "Network Analysis, Culture and the Problem of Agency." *American Journal of Sociology* 103: 271–307.

Evans, P. 1995. *Embedded Autonomy: States and Industrial Transformation*. Princeton, N.J.: Princeton University Press.

Evans, P., T. Skocpol, and D. Rueschemeyer. 1985. "On the Road toward a More Adequate Understanding of the State." In P. Evans, T. Skocpol, and D. Ruechemeyer, eds., *Bringing the State Back In*. New York: Cambridge University Press.

Fama, E. 1980. "Agency Problems and the Theory of the Firm." *Journal of Political Economy* 88(2):288–307.

Fama, E., and M. Jensen. 1983a. "Separation of Ownership and Control." *Journal of Law and Economics* 26(2):301–25.

———. 1983b. "Agency Problems and Residual Claims." *Journal of Law and Economics* 26(2): 327–49.

Fligstein, N. 1990. *The Transformation of Corporate Control*. Cambridge: Harvard University Press.

———. 1997. "Fields, Power, and Social Skill: A Critical Analysis of the 'New Institutionalisms.'" Working paper, Center for Culture, Organizations, and Politics, University of California, Berkeley.

Fligstein, N, and R. Freeland. 1995. "Theoretical and Comparative Perspectives on Corporate Organization." *Annual Review of Sociology* 21:21–43.

Friedman, L. 1973. *A History of American Law*. New York: Simon and Schuster.

Geertz, C. 1983. *Local Knowledge: Further Essays in Interpretive Sociology*. New York: Basic Books.

Giddens, A. 1981. *A Contemporary Critique of Historical Materialism*. London: Macmillan.

Greif, A. 1989. "Reputations and Coalitions in Medieval Trade: Evidence on the Magrebhi Traders." *Journal of Economic History* 49: 857–82.

Hall, P., ed. 1989. *The Political Power of Economic Ideas: Keynesianism across Nations*. Princeton, N.J.: Princeton University Press.

Haveman, H., and H. Rao. 1997. "Structuring a Theory of Moral Sentiments: Institutional and Organizational Coevolution in the Early Thrift Industry." *American Journal of Sociology* 102(6): 1606–51.

Hogan, W. T. 1984. *Steel in the United States: Restructuring to Compete*. Lexington, Mass.: Lexington.

Hooks, G. 1990. "The Rise of the Pentagon and the U.S. State Building: The Defense Program as Industrial Policy." *American Journal of Sociology* 96(2): 358–404.

Jensen, M. and W. Meckling. 1976. "Theory of the Firm: Managerial Behavior, Agency Costs, and Ownership Structure." *Journal of Financial Economics* 3(4):305–60.

Johnson, C. 1982. *MITI and the Japanese Miracle: The Growth of Industrial Policy*. Stanford, Calif.: Stanford University Press.

Krasner, S. 1988. "Sovereignty: An Institutional Perspective." *Comparative Political Studies* 21(1): 66–94.

Laumann, E., and D. Knoke. 1987. *The Organizational State: Social Change in National Policy Domains*. Madison: University of Wisconsin Press.

March, J., and J. Olsen. 1989. *Rediscovering Institutions: The Organizational Basis of Politics*. New York: Free Press.

Meyer, J., and B. Rowan. 1977. "Institutionalized Organizations: Formal Structure as Myth and Ceremony." *American Journal of Sociology* 82(2):340–63.

North, D. 1990. *Institutions, Institutional Change, and Economic Performance*. Cambridge: Cambridge University Press.

North, D., and R. Thomas. 1973. *The Rise of the Western World: A New Economic History*. Cambridge: Cambridge University Press.

Roe, M. 1994. *Strong Managers, Weak Owners: The Political Roots of American Corporate Finance*. Princeton: Princeton University Press.

Roy, W. 1997. *Socializing Capital*. Princeton: Princeton University Press.

Shapiro, M. 1980. *Courts: A Comparative and Political Analysis*. Chicago: University of Chicago Press.

Spruyt, H. 1994. *The Sovereign State and Its Competitors: An Analysis of Systems Change*. Princeton, N.J.: Princeton University Press.

Starr, P. 1982. *The Social Transformation of American Medicine*. New York: Basic Books.

Steinmo, S., K. Thelen, and F. Longstreth. 1992. *Structuring Politics: Historical Institutionalism in Comparative Analysis*. Cambridge: Cambridge University Press.

Stone Sweet, A. 2000. *Governing with Judges: Constitutional Politics in Europe*. Oxford: Oxford University Press.

Westney, E. 1987. *Imitation and Innovation: The Transfer of Western Organizational Patterns to Meiji Japan*. Cambridge: Harvard University Press.

White, H. 1981. "Where Do Markets Come From?" *American Journal of Sociology* 87(3):517–47.

———. 1992. *Identity and Control: A Structural Theory of Social Action*. Princeton, N.J.: Princeton University Press.

Williamson, O. 1985. *The Economic Institutions of Capitalism: Firms, Markets, Relational Contracting*. New York: Free Press.

Ziegler, N. 1997. *Governing Ideas: Strategies for Innovation in France and Germany*. Ithaca, N.Y.: Cornell University Press.

4

The New Institutional Economics

The New Institutional Economics (NIE) paradigm evolves directly from neoclassical economics, sharing its foundational assumption that human beings are rational, self-interested, utility maximizers. Yet NIE theorists criticize neoclassical economics for ignoring the role of institutions and transaction costs in political economy. NIE analyses focus on market institutions, such as property rights regimes, and their role in facilitating economic activity, and they are also interested in explaining processes of institutional change. Some NIE theorists, such as Douglass North, explicitly focus on the role of the state in creating laws and enforcing the contracts necessary to reduce transaction costs. Like Adam Smith, they see the state as indispensable in providing the basic infrastructure in which markets function, but move closer to the market-institutional perspective advocated in this reader by focusing analytical attention on other core institutions that facilitate economic interaction.

NIE builds on the Nobel Prize-winning work of Ronald Coase, who introduced a theory of transaction cost economics. In a landmark 1937 article entitled "The Nature of the Firm" that sought to explain why we have firms instead of just a series of people contracting with one another, Coase observed that there are a multitude of transaction costs involved in market exchange.[1] These transaction costs – particularly information and enforcement costs – add to the price of procuring something from the market. Coase concluded that firms arise to reduce these transaction costs by producing internally and expanding to the point where the returns from production disappear; at that point, the market takes over.[2] In a later article, "The Problem of Social Cost," Coase also explored how to address negative externalities associated with the market, such as businesses polluting the community around them.[3] He proposed that to address such externalities efficiently, *how* property rights are allocated does not matter – so long as they are well defined (everyone knows what they are), divisible (can be divided and/or sold to others), and defendable (can be monitored and enforced). This central insight later became known as the Coase Theorem, much to the chagrin of Coase himself, who believed that the logic was often taken to mean the opposite of what he intended. While Coase's analysis reflected the market-institutional perspective that sometimes transaction costs are so high that government regulation is necessary to make markets work efficiently, market-liberal economists (such as George Stigler, the Chicago School economist who coined the Coase Theorem label) used the Coase Theorem to advocate for achieving zero transaction costs as a policy goal.[4]

New institutional economists have since used these and other building blocks to examine other economic institutions. **Douglass North** has been a central scholar in the paradigm, both in terms of theory development and its application to empirical economic and institutional phenomena. His broad concern was to develop an analytical framework that explains the relationships between institutions, institutional change, and economic history and performance. North's definition of institutions has come to be a standard in the field and reveals the broad scope of NIE concerns and research. In his view, institutions are the rules of the game in society, the humanly devised constraints that shape human interaction and structure incentives in political, social, and economic exchange.[5] Institutions can be formal – that is, laws and regulations – or informal – such as codes of conduct and implicit understandings informed by culture. In the piece presented here, he describes the phenomenon of market exchange, pointing out that even the simplest market transaction is underpinned by a complex legal structure of property rights and their enforcement to reduce the information and monitoring costs associated with the transaction. He also reviews Coase's and other theorists' explanations for the existence of hierarchical organizations such as the firm.

North develops a general transaction cost framework to explain all sorts of economic organization or systems of exchange. Compliance costs in any form of economic activity consist of measurement (information) and monitoring (enforcement) costs – and organizations develop to minimize those transaction costs. A transaction cost is essentially anything that impedes seamless exchange, or the perfect functioning of markets, and property rights are the solution to this problem since they reduce transaction costs. A system of perfectly specified and costlessly enforced property rights would drive transaction costs to zero. These conditions do not obtain in reality but lowering transaction costs through property rights leads to a more efficient economy. In North's view, the state is an essential coercive third party to exchange that can monitor and enforce property rights; and the property rights regime that the state develops is crucial to sustain and bolster markets.

A central tenet of the NIE, mentioned briefly in the North piece, is the view – often criticized as overly functionalist – that more efficient organizational forms and institutions continually replace less efficient ones, in a rational process. North is less insistent on this point in his later work, where he focuses more on institutional change and allows that institutional outcomes may not always be efficient. But the functionalist logic is common to the NIE, as it generally assumes that institutions develop as needed in efficient forms. This does not mean that only one set of institutional solutions is appropriate to facilitate market exchange. On the contrary, different societies approach institutional design in different ways. NIE theorists believe that a focus on institutions can help to explain divergence across national political–economic systems. For example, the "varieties of capitalism" framework (Peter Hall and David Soskice, this volume), builds on the functionalist logic in specifying two different sets of political–economic institutions that fit together in efficient, transaction cost-reducing ways.

Elinor Ostrom also situates her work in the rationalism and realism of NIE, presuming that while individuals try to solve collective action problems as efficiently as they can, there are frictions within the market that prevent it from operating perfectly. In 2009, Ostrom became the first woman and second political scientist to win the Nobel Prize in Economics for her work on how common pool resources are governed. Grazing animals on collectively owned pastureland gives us a simple example of the externality problem that the private costs of rational economic behavior are not often the same as the social cost. Each individual has an incentive to overgraze with more animals, the logic goes, and this overuse of common pool resources is what is known as the tragedy of the commons.[6] In *Governing the Commons*, Ostrom dispels the notion that common pool resources are inevitably overused with empirical case studies of local communities that are able to sustainably manage shared natural resources using hybrid market *and* state institutions.

In the selection here, Ostrom presents lucidly the market-institutional insights that a range of institutional solutions exist to cope with different economic problems, that "public and private institutions frequently are intermeshed and depend on one another," and that arriving at an efficient, desirable outcome is a difficult process that sometimes provokes conflict and always takes time. From both the decision trees that Ostrom uses to develop her theory, as well as her empirical illustrations, we see that local actors devise mechanisms to regulate their own economic activity. They do so by using detailed and accurate information from their own experience to reduce transaction costs, which proves more efficient than external monitoring and enforcement. The case studies also demonstrate the efficacy and legitimacy of informal monitoring and enforcement institutions that have evolved through context-based custom and practice. She critiques both "privatizers" and "centralizers" for advocating policy prescriptions that are metaphors – idealized and oversimplified solutions that offer few practical guidelines for the real world and can result in unintended and welfare-reducing consequences.

Notes

1 R. H. Coase, "The Nature of the Firm," *Economica* 4 (1937): 386–405.

2 Oliver Williamson further examined Coase's question about the boundary between firms and market. He considered a full spectrum of other possibilities between firms and markets, such as long-term relational contracting and modes of private enforcement. Oliver E. Williamson, *The Economic Institutions of Capitalism* (New York: Free Press, 1985).

3 R. H. Coase, "The Problem of Social Cost," *The Journal of Law & Economics* III (1960): 1–44.

4 John Cassidy, "Ronald Coase and the Misuse of Economics," *The New Yorker* (September 3, 2013); and Timothy B. Lee, "The Coase Theorem is Widely Cited in Economics. Ronald Coase Hated It," *The Washington Post* (September 4, 2013).

5 Douglass C. North, *Institutions, Institutional Change and Economic Performance* (Cambridge: Cambridge University Press, 1990).

6 See Garrett Hardin, "The Tragedy of the Commons," *Science* 162 (1968): 1243–8.

Douglass C. North,
Structure and Change in Economic History (1981)[*]

Chapter 4: A Framework for Analyzing Economic Organization in History

I

Throughout history economic activity has occurred by means of an immense variety of organizational forms. From the so-called re-distributive societies of the Egyptian dynasties, to the patron-client relationship in Republican Rome, to the feudal manor, these organizational forms have been the subject of historical investigation; but most of the research has been devoid of analytical content.[1] Much the same criticism can be made of economists' work dealing with modern-day economic organization. In fact, as recently as 1968, the *International Encyclopedia of the Social Sciences* included no essay on the market, the most fundamental institution of modern Western economies and central to the performance of economies of the past, as well.

To account analytically for economic organization we must use a theory of transaction costs together with a theory of the state. A theory of transaction costs is necessary because under the ubiquitous condition of scarcity and therefore competition, more efficient forms of economic organization will replace less efficient forms under *ceteris paribus* conditions. The state, however—as I have argued in the previous chapter—will encourage and specify efficient property rights only to the extent that they are consistent with the wealth-maximizing objectives of those who run the state. Hence the need for a model that incorporates both. I shall begin here by developing a transaction-cost approach to economic organization and then I shall combine it with the analysis of the state developed in the previous chapter.

Any form of economic organization must have provisions for the specifying and enforcing of the terms of exchange. Abstracting from the role of the state, the choice of organizational form will be dictated by the relative amount of resources required for a given amount of output. A market-price system is costly because it is costly first to measure the dimensions of the good or service transacted and then to enforce the terms of exchange. And there is really a third cost involved as well: that associated with the external effects that arise because measurement was imperfect. In contrast, hierarchical forms of organization substitute the directives of a central authority: a contractual arrangement restricts the options of the parties to exchange wherein one party gives up control of decisions to the other party.[2] The costs of this organizational form are the costs of measuring the performance of agents; the inefficiencies associated with imperfect measurement; and the costs of enforcement. Because the

---

resource costs of compliance are different from those involved in the market-price system, they lead to different results. Let me illustrate market exchange, then explore the reasons for the existence of the firm (or other hierarchical organization), and then attempt to explain economic organization in history.

II

I begin by simply describing a transaction I make every week in my local public market. It is the purchase of a quantity of oranges (fourteen oranges for one dollar in 1980). I purchase oranges for orange juice and therefore I want the oranges to contain a great deal of juice (rather than pulp) and to have a tart flavor. What I really would like to specify in the exchange is a certain quantity of orange juice with a combination of organic ingredients that produces the flavor I want. Why aren't oranges sold in a way that I can get precisely what I want? In part, they are. Valencia oranges are juice oranges and are sold separately from Navel or other eating oranges. But the amount of juice and the flavor that I will get from the oranges cannot be specified at low cost. If the measurement of these ingredients were possible at no or little cost, then I could obtain the precise combination I want. Instead, purchases are made by number, weight, volume, length; and resources are devoted to seeing that these objective measurement characteristics are met.

The seller of the oranges bought them from a wholesaler; within the crates he received were some oranges not in good condition. He stands to lose money on those oranges, since if he tries to give them to me for my dollar I will go to another stall at the public market to buy my oranges. In short, the competition of a large number of sellers constrains his behavior. Does he slip a few of the rotten oranges in the bottom of the sack where I won't notice them until I get home? He might if he never expects to see me again since it is the only way he can get rid of the oranges that otherwise would be a loss to him. But that is why I go to the same dealer, Morris, each week. He knows I will not return if he slips such oranges into my sack. I am valuable as a repeat customer; opportunism, then, is constrained by repetitive dealings. Morris, on his part, accepts my check for one dollar without inquiring whether I have sufficient funds in the bank to cover the check, or whether the dollar he gets when he cashes my check will be accepted unquestionably by his wholesaler or by anyone else from whom he wishes to purchase goods or services.

It should be readily apparent not only that this simple exercise was really complex in terms of its fundamental characteristics, but also that we have examined only its superficial manifestations. Underlying the transaction—making it possible—was a complex structure of law and its enforcement. Both Morris and I accept that we each have property rights over the oranges and the dollar—and that these rights are enforceable in a court of law. Morris accepts a piece of paper as a legitimate surrogate for a command over a certain amount of other resources and knows that he can use it for that purpose. In brief, uncertainty is reduced or completely eliminated by an accepted structure of property rights and their enforcement.

Let me summarize the implications of the foregoing illustration. One must be able to measure the quantity of a good in order for it to be exclusive property and to have value in exchange. Where measurement costs are very high, the good will be a common property resource. The technology of measurement and the history of weights and measures is a crucial part of economic history since as measurement costs were reduced the cost of transacting was reduced. The fourteen oranges in the illustration above are an imperfect surrogate for the quantity desired, which is a given quantity of juice with a certain flavor. The separation of oranges by type or the grading of oranges is a step in the right direction; but so long as *some* characteristic of a good that has economic value is not measured, then there is divergence between private and social cost.[3]

Information costs are reduced by the existence of large numbers of buyers and sellers. Under these conditions, prices embody the same information that would require large search costs by individual buyers and sellers in the absence of an organized market.[4]

Opportunism is constrained by the competition of large numbers (and by personalized exchange). We can think loosely of opportunism, at this point, as the ability of one party to an exchange to benefit at the expense of the other party by violating the agreement in his or her post-contractual behavior.

The transfer of property rights amongst individual owners through contracting in the market place requires that the rights be exclusive.[5] Not only must the rights be measurable; they must also be enforceable. Note that there are two stages to the transfer process. The first stage involves the costs of defining and policing exclusivity in the absence of exchange; the second, the costs associated with negotiating and enforcing the contracts for the exchange and transfer of rights.

A third party, the state, can lower the costs of transacting through the development of an impersonal body of law and enforcement. Since the development of law is a public good there are important scale economies associated with it. If a body of law exists, negotiation and enforcement costs are substantially reduced since the basic rules of exchange are already spelled out.

Finally before leaving this illustration, let me note one additional point. Even if Morris had known he would never see me again, he probably would not have slipped some rotten oranges in the bottom of the sack; and I know, on my part, that while Morris's back was turned, filling up the sack, I would not have slipped a couple of oranges into my pocket even though there was no chance of being detected. The reason is that both of us viewed the exchange as fair or legitimate, and we were constrained in our behavior by that conviction.

III

Why does the firm replace the market? That was the question Ronald Coase asked in his essay "The Nature of the Firm" (1937). He characterized the firm as that range of exchanges over which the market system was suppressed and resource allocation was accomplished instead by authority and direction. Alchian and Demsetz, confronting the same question (1972), emphasized the importance of monitoring the inputs where the gains of joint team production (resulting from specialization and division of labor) make it difficult to measure inputs; Jensen and Meckling (1976) extended the monitoring argument to the effort of principals (owners of a set of property rights) to control the behavior of agents (persons engaged by the principals to perform services on their behalf) so that they will act in the principal's interests. The difference between Coase and Alchian and Demsetz requires some elaboration.

According to Coase, the advantage of the firm over transacting in the market is a gain as a result of a reduction in transaction costs. (In effect, a firm has reduced one set of transactions—those in the product market—and increased another set—those in the factor market. Therefore, the efficient size of the firm is determined as that at which the gains and costs at the margin are equal.) Alchian and Demsetz stress the productivity gains from team production, which Coase ignores; but they then empha- size that a byproduct of team production will be shirking or cheating and that there- fore a monitor is needed to reduce these transaction costs.[6]

Both Williamson (1975) and Klein, Crawford, and Alchian (1978) stress the role of opportunism in inducing the vertical integration of economic activity. Where there are appropriable quasi rents (defined as the excess of an asset's value over its next best use) as assets become more specific, the costs of contracting will increase more than the costs of vertical integration; we will observe vertical integration to prevent a firm's being held up by another contracting party in the position of being able to cause the firm large losses by altering the terms of the agreement at a strategic moment.

Alchian and Demsetz (and Jensen and Meckling) emphasize that the firm is simply a legal fiction and a nexus of contracting relationships, whereas Coase emphasizes that the firm is governed by authority. Coase's position is in some respects close to that of New Left critics such as Marglin, who has argued (1974) that the productivity gains from the celebrated Smithian specialization and division of labor do not require the hierarchical organization of the firm, and that the reason for the existence of the firm is that it is an exploitative vehicle by which bosses exploit workers. The difference is that Coase emphasizes the real transaction cost gains from the firm (presumably at least partly in consequence of the authority), whereas Marglin and other New Left critics argue that there are no savings in real cost as a consequence of the hierarchy imposed by the firm. Marglin's argument, however, will not survive critical scrutiny. If there were no real costs savings from the disciplined hierarchical firm structure, then we surely would observe non-authoritative organizational forms effectively competing with firms. Since there have been literally thousands of utopian, coopera- tive, and other experimental organizational forms in American economic history, we would expect that many should survive in competition with the traditional firm. They haven't; and even a casual examination of the sources of their failure suggests that there were fundamental transaction cost problems impeding the survival of such non-authoritarian forms of organization. If that evidence were not sufficient, we could equally turn to look at the many experiments in socialist countries. Clearly there are both production-cost (from economies of scale) and transaction cost advantages to hierarchical organization.[7]

IV

Let us see if we can fit the pieces from the two previous sections into a general transac- tion cost framework of economic organization, before adding the state to the analysis.[8]

The resource costs devoted to compliance differ with alternative forms of organized economic activity. These compliance costs consist of the costs of measurement in alternative organizational forms and the costs of enforcing an agreement. Clearly, measurement costs in markets contrast to those of hierarchical organizations.

Markets dominate the sale of goods to consumers, and there will be both a subjective measurement element (such as the freshness of produce or the flavor of the orange juice) and the less costly but less accurate objective measurement costs (such as the weight, number, color, or grade of the good—the observable surrogates used by consumers). When we shift from orange juice to more complex goods or services such as a television set, the quality of repair work on an automobile or the quality of a physician's service, the costs of measurement are increased immensely and we tend to rely on various surrogates such as brand names, trade marks, warranties, reputation; but the key element is the degree of competition which constrains the principals.

When we turn to intermediate goods and services, such as a machine tool which is used in making an automobile, the exchange may be a market exchange or one internalized inside a firm, but the measurement costs will be different. When the exchange consists of purchases in the market, competition constrains the seller to meet the measurement specifications of the contract or lose out to a competitor. The pecuniary income of the seller therefore is directly tied to performance. When machine tool making is consolidated inside a firm, measurement is still necessary to see that the machine tool meets quality specifications and that the firm uses a variety of monitoring devices, such as quality-control inspectors and accounting methods, to measure performance. However, the income of the worker, now a part of team production in making the machine tool (and an agent rather than a principal), is no longer directly tied to his or her productive activity. The market no longer serves as a direct constraint on performance. If it were costless to measure the output (quantity and quality) of the individual worker, then the market would indeed be an equally effective constraint, the worker's income would be tied directly to performance, and the worker would be paid by his or her output (piece rate) rather than by input (hourly rate). But because it is costly to measure individual performance (and perfect measurement is frequently impossible), shirking, cheating, and so forth are common, workers are paid by input, and various costly but imperfect monitoring devices are employed to reduce shirking.

There are also costs in enforcing a contract: those of measuring the damages or injury to a party to the contract, of enacting penalties, and of compensating the injured party.

In order to measure damages one must first be able to measure performance; contracts therefore include detailed specifications, designed to spell out the characteristics of the exchange that indicate performance.

The enactment of penalties and compensation for damages not only entails a body of law, judicial process, and enforcement, but is heavily influenced by moral and ethical codes of behavior (that is, by the perceived legitimacy of the law and the contractual relationship). Personalized exchange in simple, unspecialized societies depends for enforcement upon such behavioral codes, and the perceived legitimacy of the contractual relationship significantly influences judges and juries. If measurement were perfect and the judicial process precisely awarded the "correct" amount of damages to injured parties in a contract violation, then opportunism would not play the part that it does in influencing economic organization. But the judicial process is implemented by rulers' agents who cannot themselves be perfectly constrained and who are guided by their own interests as well as their subjective evaluation of the justice of the contract.

Therefore enforcement is imperfect, particularly concerning such agreements as long lived contracts where future prices and risks cannot be specified.[9] It is equally imperfect where specialized physical or human capital, which can make hold-up or opportunism profitable, is employed.

With home production there are no transaction costs: therefore no proxy for subjective measurement is required, since individuals tailor their home production to their own utility function. There is complete vertical integration, but at the cost of specialization.

The greater the specialization and division of labor, the more steps in the production process from initial producer to final consumer and the greater the total costs of measurement (since measurement must occur at each step). The choice of organizational form will be influenced by the characteristics of the good or service and by the technology of measurement of the attributes.

Hierarchical organization replaces the market first of all because economies of scale arise from team production; but the scale economies come at the price of higher measurement costs of the performance of individual members of the team (agents). "A firm internalizes external effects [that is, realizes scale economies] by making an individual's productive activity external or independent of his pecuniary income from production" (McManus, 1975: 346). Hence the firm hires monitors to constrain the behavior of agents and reduce shirking and cheating.

Hierarchical organization will also replace market transactions where specialized human or physical capital investment makes the principals vulnerable to post-contractual opportunism because of imperfect enforcement. Vertical integration can reduce the likelihood of hold-up where substantial quasi-rents are appropriable; there will, however, be the same monitoring costs as above.

All of the modern neoclassical literature discusses the firm as a substitute for the market. For the economic historian this perspective is useful; its usefulness is limited, however, because it ignores a crucial fact of history: hierarchical organization forms and contractual arrangements in exchange predate the price-making market (like that for oranges). The first known price-making market was in the Athenian agora in the sixth century B.C., but exchange had been going on for millennia before that. We now possess the clue to account for such early forms of organization.

In order to do so we must clarify a confusion that has been propagated by Karl Polanyi and many subsequent writers.[10] Polanyi made a *market* synonymous with a *price-making market*. It should be readily apparent, however, that any form of voluntary contractual exchange involves a market and that its form will be dictated by the considerations advanced above. Polanyi made a basic error in thinking that any deviation from the Agora-type market implied non-economizing behavior: even the era which, in *The Great Transformation* (1957), he regarded as the epitome of the market mentality was characterized by an enormous variety of contractual arrangements that were not price-making markets.[11] Two considerations militated against the existence of price-making markets before the 6th century B.C. One was the transaction costs considerations that have been the subject of this chapter; the second was the wealth-maximizing objectives of the rulers of the state.

Price-making markets require well-defined and enforced property rights. It must be possible to measure the dimensions of a good or service; moreover, the consequent rights must be exclusive and there must be an enforcement mechanism to police the exchange of goods. Small numbers involved in exchange, the possibility of opportunism, and uncertainty as a result of a lack of well-defined property rights or an inability to forecast changes in conditions over the life of an exchange agreement all result in alternative contractual arrangements designed to reduce the attendant transactions or production costs.

V

The foregoing analysis has assumed that under the ubiquitous conditions of scarcity and competition, more efficient organizational forms will replace less efficient and that it would be possible to predict the forms that would exist. Even in the presence of a state that operated in the way that a contract theory would imply, modifications of the organizational forms would result since any form of taxation would alter the relevant measurement costs and the consequent organization; but the theory of the state elaborated in the preceding chapter implies much greater modification.

The state will specify rules to maximize the income of the ruler and his group and then, subject to that constraint, will devise rules that would lower transaction costs. Nonvoluntary forms of organization will exist if profitable to the ruler (nonvoluntary slavery, for example); relatively inefficient forms of organization will survive if more efficient forms threaten the survival of the ruler from within or without (the collective farm in the Soviet Union today, or the organization of the Athenian grain trade in the classical world, for example);[12] and forms of organization that have low measurement costs to the rulers for tax collecting will persist even though they are relatively inefficient (monopoly grants as in Colbert's France, for example).

Given this initial constraint, however, the ruler will provide the public good of a set of rules and their enforcement designed to lower transaction costs. Included will be the specification of uniform weights and measures,[13] a set of property rights to encourage production and trade, a judicial system to settle differences, and enforcement procedures to enforce contracts.

VI

The foregoing neoclassical approach to economic organization is deficient in at least two respects.

First, the more diffuse the distribution of political control as a result of the ability of groups of constituents to capture an interest in the state, the more difficult it becomes to predict or explain the ensuing forms of property rights which will develop. It is not too difficult to account for economic organization of the redistributive societies of the ancient dynasties in Egypt; it is much more difficult to explain the complex economic organization in modern democratic societies where many interests compete with each other in controlling the state and modifying property rights and, hence, economic organizations.[14]

A more serious problem is that the theory is incomplete, as even a casual inspection of the literature on industrial organization will attest. This literature is full of references to simple self-interest versus self-interest with guile (in opportunistic behavior); sometimes individuals will take advantage of each other and sometimes they won't; sometimes individuals are hard working and sometimes not. Honesty, integrity, and gentlemen's agreements are important in contractual arrangements; equally important are the ubiquitous loafing on the job, cheating, white collar crime, and sabotage.

To put it succinctly, the measurement costs of constraining behavior are so high that in the absence of ideological convictions to constrain individual maximizing, the viability of economic organization is threatened. Investment in legitimacy is as much a cost of economic organization as are the measurement and enforcement costs detailed in the preceding sections of this chapter. Indeed, as briefly discussed above, a major issue in enforcement is the perceived legitimacy of the contractual relations.

Notes

1. An exception is the work of Karl Polanyi. For a review of his contribution see North (1977).
2. In this context, authority is simply a contract in which this delegation of decision making is implied and a structure of decision making specified. In the absence of coercion by the state, which can impose nonvoluntaristic forms of organization, the neoclassical definition will serve. However, I examine the issue further in examining the literature on the firm and in considering ideology.
3. See Barzel (1974) and Cheung (1974).
4. The original contributions were those of Hayek (1937 and 1945). See also Stigler (1961).
5. The rights that are transferred must be exclusive, but we should note that the sale of a good or service does not imply unrestricted rights. When I sell my house the new owner is as constrained by zoning laws in his use of the house as I was. What I am transferring is a specific bundle of rights.
6. However, as McManus (1975) points out, Alchian and Demsetz are incorrect in asserting that team production per se is the cause of the problem. It is the costliness of measuring inputs and outputs that generates monitoring costs.
7. For psychological experiments demonstrating and measuring shirking in groups as compared to individual performance, see Latane, Silliams, and Harkinds (1979).
8. For an elaboration of the argument presented here see McManus (1975) and Barzel (unpublished 1980).
9. Goldberg (1976) has termed such contractual relations "relational exchange."
10. While Polanyi has had little influence on economists, he has had a much larger impact on the other social sciences and amongst historians.
11. See North (1977).
12. See the account of the Athenian grain trade in Polanyi (1977).
13. However, it should be noted that the way weights and measures will be devised will be with the objective of maximizing the ruler's income. The history of weights and measures makes sense only if we recognize the priority of the ruler's interest.
14. The burgeoning literature in such specialized journals as the *Bell Journal* and the *Journal of Law and Economics* provides ample evidence of this difficulty.

References

Alchian, A. and Demsetz, H. 1972. "Production, Information Costs and Economic Organization." *American Economic Review* (December).

Barzel, Y. 1974. "A Theory of Rationing by Waiting." *Journal of Law and Economics* (April).

Barzel, Y. 1980. "Measurement Cost and the Organization of Markets." Unpublished Manuscript.

Cheung, S. N. S. 1974. "A Theory of Price Control." *Journal of Law and Economics* (April).

Coase, Ronald 1937. "The Nature of the Firm." *Economica* (November).

Goldberg, Victor 1976. "Regulation and Administered Contracts." *The Bell Journal* (Autumn).

Hayek, F. A. 1937. "Economics and Knowledge." *Economica* (February).

Hayek, F. A. 1945. "The Use of Knowledge in Society." *American Economic Review* (September).

Jensen, M. and Meckling, W. 1976. "Theory of the Firm: Managerial Behavior, Agency Costs and Ownership Structure." *Journal of Financial Economics* (October).

Klein, B. Crawford, R. C., and Alchian, A. 1978. "Vertical Integration, Appropriable Rents, and the Competitive Contracting Process." *Journal of Law and Economics* (October).

Latane, Bibb; Sialliams, Kipling; and Harkinds, Stephen 1979. "Social Loafing." *Psychology Today* (October).

Marglin, Stephen 1974. "What Do Bosses Do?" *Review of Radical Political Economy* (Summer).

McManus, John 1975. "The Costs of Alternative Economic Organization." *Canadian Journal of Economics* (August).

North, Douglass C. 1977. "Non-Market Forms of Economic Organization: The Challenge of Karl Polanyi." *Journal of European Economic History* (Fall).

Polanyi, Karl 1957. *The Great Transformation*. New York: Rinehold.

Polanyi, Karl 1977. *The Livelyhood of Man*. New York: Academic Press.

Stigler, George 1961, "The Economics of Information." *Journal of Political Economy* (June).

Williamson, Oliver 1975. *Markets and Hierarchy*. New York: Free Press.

Elinor Ostrom,
Governing the Commons (1990)[*]

Chapter 1: Reflections on the commons

Hardly a week goes by without a major news story about the threatened destruction of a valuable natural resource. In June of 1989, for example, a *New York Times* article focused on the problem of overfishing in the Georges Bank about 150 miles off the New England coast. Catches of cod, flounder, and haddock are now only a quarter of what they were during the 1960s. Everyone knows that the basic problem is overfishing; however, those concerned cannot agree how to solve the problem. Congressional representatives recommend new national legislation, even though the legislation already on the books has been enforced only erratically. Representatives of the fishers argue that the fishing grounds would not be in such bad shape if the federal government had refrained from its sporadic attempts to regulate the fishery in the past. The issue in this case – and many others – is how best to limit the use of natural resources so as to ensure their long-term economic viability. Advocates of central regulation, of privatization, and of regulation by those involved have pressed their policy prescriptions in a variety of different arenas.

Similar situations occur on diverse scales ranging from small neighborhoods to the entire planet. The issues of how best to govern natural resources used by many individuals in common are no more settled in academia than in the world of politics. Some scholarly articles about the "tragedy of the commons" recommend that "the state" control most natural resources to prevent their destruction; others recommend that privatizing those resources will resolve the problem. What one can observe in the world, however, is that neither the state nor the market is uniformly successful in enabling individuals to sustain long-term, productive use of natural resource systems. Further, communities of individuals have relied on institutions resembling neither the state nor the market to govern some resource systems with reasonable degrees of success over long periods of time.

We do not yet have the necessary intellectual tools or models to understand the array of problems that are associated with governing and managing natural resource systems and the reasons why some institutions seem to work in some settings and not others. This book is an effort to (1) critique the foundations of policy analysis as applied to many natural resources, (2) present empirical examples of successful and unsuccessful efforts to govern and manage such resources, and (3) begin the effort to develop better intellectual tools to understand the capabilities and limitations of self-governing institutions for regulating many types of resources. To do this, I first describe

[*] From: *Governing the Commons: The Evolution of Institutions for Collective Action*, Elinor Ostrom, Copyright © Cambridge University Press 1990. (pp. 1–28) Reproduced with permission of Cambridge, University Press through PLSclear.

the three models most frequently used to provide a foundation for recommending state or market solutions. I then pose theoretical and empirical alternatives to these models to begin to illustrate the diversity of solutions that go beyond states and markets. Using an institutional mode of analysis, I then attempt to explain how communities of individuals fashion different ways of governing the commons.

Three Influential Models

The tragedy of the commons

Since Garrett Hardin's challenging article in *Science* (1968), the expression "the tragedy of the commons" has come to symbolize the degradation of the environment to be expected whenever many individuals use a scarce resource in common. To illustrate the logical structure of his model, Hardin asks the reader to envision a pasture "open to all." He then examines the structure of this situation from the perspective of a rational herder. Each herder receives a direct benefit from his own animals and suffers delayed costs from the deterioration of the commons when his and others' cattle overgraze. Each herder is motivated to add more and more animals because he receives the direct benefit of his own animals and bears only a share of the costs resulting from overgrazing. Hardin concludes:

> Therein is the tragedy. Each man is locked into a system that compels him to increase his herd without limit – in a world that is limited. Ruin is the destination toward which all men rush, each pursuing his own best interest in a society that believes in the freedom of the commons.
>
> (Hardin 1968, p. 1,244)

Hardin was not the first to notice the tragedy of the commons. Aristotle long ago observed that "what is common to the greatest number has the least care bestowed upon it. Everyone thinks chiefly of his own, hardly at all of the common interest" (*Politics*, Book II, ch. 3). Hobbes's parable of man in a state of nature is a prototype of the tragedy of the commons: Men seek their own good and end up fighting one another. In 1833, William Forster Lloyd (1977) sketched a theory of the commons that predicted improvident use for property owned in common. More than a decade before Hardin's article, H. Scott Gordon (1954) clearly expounded similar logic in another classic: "The Economic Theory of a Common-Property Research: The Fishery." Gordon described the same dynamic as Hardin:

> There appears then, to be some truth in the conservative dictum that everybody's property is nobody's property. Wealth that is free for all is valued by no one because he who is foolhardy enough to wait for its proper time of use will only find that it has been taken by another. ... The fish in the sea are valueless to the fisherman because there is no assurance that they will be there for him tomorrow if they are left behind today.
>
> (Gordon 1954, p. 124)

John H. Dales (1968, p. 62) noted at the same time the perplexing problems related to resources "owned in common because there is no alternative!" Standard analyses in modern resource economics conclude that where a number of users have access to a common-pool resource, the total of resource units withdrawn from the resource will be greater than the optimal economic level of withdrawal (Clark 1976, 1980; Dasgupta and Heal 1979).

If the only "commons" of importance were a few grazing areas or fisheries, the tragedy of the commons would be of little general interest. That is not the case. Hardin himself used the grazing commons as a metaphor for the general problem of over-population. The "tragedy of the commons" has been used to describe such diverse problems as the Sahelian famine of the 1970s (Picardi and Seifert 1977), firewood crises throughout the Third World (Norman 1984; Thomson 1977), the problem of acid rain (R. Wilson 1985), the organization of the Mormon Church (Bullock and Baden 1977), the inability of the U.S. Congress to limit its capacity to overspend (Shepsle and Weingast 1984), urban crime (Neher 1978), public-sector/private-sector relationships in modern economies (Scharpf 1985, 1987, 1988), the problems of international cooperation (Snidal 1985), and communal conflict in Cyprus (Lumsden 1973). Much of the world is dependent on resources that are subject to the possibility of a tragedy of the commons.

The prisoner's dilemma game

Hardin's model has often been formalized as a prisoner's dilemma (PD) game (Dawes 1973, 1975).[1] Suppose we think of the players in a game as being herders using a common grazing meadow. For this meadow, there is an upper limit to the number of animals that can graze on the meadow for a season and be well fed at the end of the season. We call that number L. For a two-person game, the "cooperate" strategy can be thought of as grazing $L/2$ animals for each herder. The "defect" strategy is for each herder to graze as many animals as he thinks he can sell at a profit (given his private costs), assuming that this number is greater than $L/2$. If both herders limit their grazing to $L/2$, they will obtain 10 units of profit, whereas if they both choose the defect strategy they will obtain zero profit. If one of them limits his number of animals to $L/2$, while the other grazes as many as he wants, the "defector" obtains 11 units of profit, and the "sucker" obtains –1. If each chooses independently without the capacity to engage in a binding contract, each chooses his dominant strategy, which is to defect. When they both defect, they obtain zero profit. Call this the Hardin herder game, or Game 1. It has the structure of a prisoner's dilemma game.[2]

The prisoner's dilemma game is conceptualized as a noncooperative game in which all players possess complete information. In noncooperative games, communication among the players is forbidden or impossible or simply irrelevant as long as it is not explicitly modeled as part of the game. If communication is possible, verbal agreements among players are presumed to be nonbinding unless the possibility of binding agreements is explicitly incorporated in the game structure (Harsanyi and Selten 1988, p. 3). "Complete information" implies that all players know the full structure of the game tree and the payoffs attached to outcomes. Players either know or do not know the current moves of other players depending on whether or not they are observable.

In a prisoner's dilemma game, each player has a dominant strategy in the sense that the player is always better off choosing this strategy – to defect – no matter what

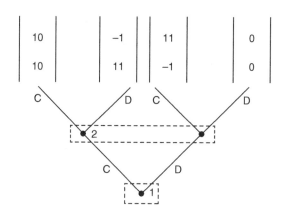

FIGURE 1.1 Game 1: The Hardin herder game.

the other player chooses. When both players choose their dominant strategy, given these assumptions, they produce an equilibrium that is the third-best result for both. Neither has an incentive to change that is independent of the strategy choice of the other. The equilibrium resulting from each player selecting his or her "best" individual strategy is, however, not a Pareto-optimal outcome. A Pareto-optimal outcome occurs when there is no other outcome strictly preferred by at least one player that is at least as good for the others. In the two-person prisoner's dilemma game both players prefer the (cooperate, cooperate) outcome to the (defect, defect) outcome. Thus, the equilibrium outcome is Pareto-inferior.

The prisoner's dilemma game fascinates scholars. The paradox that individually rational strategies lead to collectively irrational outcomes seems to challenge a fundamental faith that rational human beings can achieve rational results. In the introduction to a recently published book, *Paradoxes of Rationality and Cooperation*, Richmond Campbell explains the "deep attraction" of the dilemma:

> Quite simply, these paradoxes cast in doubt our understanding of rationality and, in the case of the Prisoner's Dilemma suggest that it is impossible for rational creatures to cooperate. Thus, they bear directly on fundamental issues in ethics and political philosophy and threaten the foundations of the social sciences. It is the scope of these consequences that explains why these paradoxes have drawn so much attention and why they command a central place in philosophical discussion.
>
> (Campbell 1985, p. 3)

The deep attraction of the dilemma is further illustrated by the number of articles written about it. At one count, 15 years ago, more than 2,000 papers had been devoted to the prisoner's dilemma game (Grofman and Pool 1975).

The logic of collective action

A closely related view of the difficulty of getting individuals to pursue their joint welfare, as contrasted to individual welfare, was developed by Mancur Olson (1965) in *The Logic of Collective Action*. Olson specifically set out to challenge the grand optimism expressed in group theory: that individuals with common interests would voluntarily act so as to try to further those interests (Bentley 1949; Truman 1958). On the first page of his book, Olson summarized that accepted view:

> The idea that groups tend to act in support of their group interests is supposed to follow logically from this widely accepted premise of rational, self-interested behavior. In other words, if the members of some group have a common interest or object, and if they would all be better off if that objective were achieved, it has been thought to follow logically that the individuals in that group would, if they were rational and self-interested, act to achieve that objective.
>
> (Olson 1965, p. l)

Olson challenged the presumption that the possibility of a benefit for a group would be sufficient to generate collective action to achieve that benefit. In the most frequently quoted passage of his book, Olson argued that

> unless the number of individuals is quite small, or unless there is coercion or some other special device to make individuals act in their common interest, *rational, self-interested individuals will not act to achieve their common or group interests.*
>
> (Olson 1965, p. 2; emphasis in original)

Olson's argument rests largely on the premise that one who cannot be excluded from obtaining the benefits of a collective good once the good is produced has little incentive to contribute voluntarily to the provision of that good. His book is less pessimistic than it is asserted to be by many who cite this famous passage. Olson considers it an open question whether intermediate-size groups will or will not voluntarily provide collective benefits. His definition of an intermediate-size group depends not on the number of actors involved but on how noticeable each person's actions are.

The tragedy of the commons, the prisoner's dilemma, and the logic of collective action are closely related concepts in the models that have defined the accepted way of viewing many problems that individuals face when attempting to achieve collective benefits. At the heart of each of these models is the free-rider problem. Whenever one person cannot be excluded from the benefits that others provide, each person is motivated not to contribute to the joint effort, but to free-ride on the efforts of others. If all participants choose to free-ride, the collective benefit will not be produced. The temptation to free-ride, however, may dominate the decision process, and thus all will end up where no one wanted to be. Alternatively, some may provide while others free-ride, leading to less than the optimal level of provision of the collective benefit. These models are thus extremely useful for explaining how perfectly rational individuals can produce, under some circumstances, outcomes that are not "rational" when viewed from the perspective of all those involved.

What makes these models so interesting and so powerful is that they capture important aspects of many different problems that occur in diverse settings in all parts of the world. What makes these models so dangerous – when they are used metaphorically as the foundation for policy – is that the constraints that are assumed to be fixed for the purpose of analysis are taken on faith as being fixed in empirical settings, unless external authorities change them.[3] The prisoners in the famous dilemma cannot change the constraints imposed on them by the district attorney;

they are in jail. Not all users of natural resources are similarly incapable of changing their constraints. As long as individuals are viewed as prisoners, policy prescriptions will address this metaphor. I would rather address the question of how to enhance the capabilities of those involved to change the constraining rules of the game to lead to outcomes other than remorseless tragedies.

The Metaphorical Use of Models

These three models and their many variants are diverse representations of a broader and still-evolving theory of collective action. Much more work will be needed to develop the theory of collective action into a reliable and useful foundation for policy analysis. Considerable progress has been made during the past three decades by theorists and empirically oriented social scientists. The sweeping conclusions of the first variants of this theory have given way to a more qualified body of knowledge involving many more variables and explicit base conditions.

As an evolving, rather than completed, theory, it provokes disagreement regarding the importance or insignificance of some variables and how best to specify key relationships.[4] The results from more recent work, particularly work focusing on the dynamic aspects of relevant empirical settings, have begun to generate more optimistic predictions than did earlier models; see, in particular, the work of Axelrod (1981, 1984) and Kreps and Wilson (1982). This is one of the most exciting areas in the social sciences, for although considerable cumulation has already occurred, some deep questions remain unanswered. Some of these puzzles are key to understanding how individuals jointly using a common-pool resource might be able to achieve an effective form of governing and managing their own commons. These puzzles are examined in Chapter 2.

Much that has been written about common-pool resources, however, has uncritically accepted the earlier models and the presumption of a remorseless tragedy (Nebel 1987). Scholars have gone so far as to recommend that "Hardin's 'Tragedy of the Commons' should be required reading for all students ... and, if I had my way, for all human beings."[5] Policy prescriptions have relied to a large extent on one of the three original models, but those attempting to use these models as the basis for policy prescription frequently have achieved little more than a metaphorical use of the models.

When models are used as meraphors, an author usually points to the similarity between one or two variables in a natural setting and one or two variables in a model. If calling attention to similarities is all that is intended by the metaphor, it serves the usual purpose of rapidly conveying information in graphic form. These three models have frequently been used metaphorically, however, for another purpose. The similarity between the many individuals jointly using a resource in a natural setting and the many individuals jointly producing a suboptimal result in the model has been used to convey a sense that further similarities are present. By referring to natural settings as "tragedies of the commons," "collective-action problems," "prisoner's dilemmas," "open-access resources," or even "common-property resources," the observer frequently wishes to invoke an image of helpless individuals caught in an inexorable process of destroying their own resources. An article in the December 10, 1988, issue of *The Economist* goes so far as to assert that fisheries can be managed successfully only if it is recognized that "left to their own devices, fisherman will overexploit stocks," and "to avoid disaster, managers must have effective hegemony over them."

Public officials sometimes do no more than evoke grim images by briefly alluding to the popularized versions of the models, presuming, as self-evident, that the same processes occur in all natural settings. The Canadian minister of fisheries and oceans, for example, captured the color of the models in a 1980 speech:

> If you let loose that kind of eonomic self-interest in fisheries, with everybody fishing as he wants, taking from a resource that belongs to no individual, you end up destroying your neighbour and yourself. In free fisheries, good times create bad times, attracting more and more boats to chase fewer and fewer fish, producing less and less money to divide among more and more people.
>
> (Romeo LeBlanc, speaking at the 50th anniversary meeting of the
> United Maritime Fishermen, March 19, 1980; quoted by
> Matthews and Phyne 1988)

The implication, of course, was that Canadian fisheries universally met that description – an empirically incorrect inference.[6] But many observers have come to assume that most resources are like those specified in the three models. As such, it has been assumed that the individuals have been caught in a grim trap. The resulting policy recommendations have had an equally grim character.

Current Policy Prescriptions

Leviathan as the "only" way

Ophuls (1973, p. 228) argued, for example, that "because of the tragedy of the commons, environmental problems cannot be solved through cooperation ... and the rationale for government with major coercive powers is overwhelming." Ophuls concluded that "even if we avoid the tragedy of the commons, it will *only* be by recourse to the tragic necessity of Leviathan" (1973, p. 229; emphasis added).[7] Garrett Hardin argued a decade after his earlier article that we are enveloped in a "cloud of ignorance" about "the true nature of the fundamental political systems and the effect of each on the preservation of the environment" (1978, p. 310). The "cloud of ignorance" did not, however, prevent him from presuming that the only alternatives to the commons dilemma were what he called "a private enterprise system," on the one hand, or "socialism," on the other (1978, p. 314). With the assurance of one convinced that "the alternative of the commons is too horrifying to contemplate" (1968, p. 1,247), Hardin indicated that change would have to be instituted with "whatever force may be required to make the change stick" (1978, p. 314). In other words, "if ruin is to be avoided in a crowded world, people must be responsive to a coercive force outside their individual psyches, a 'Leviathan,' to use Hobbes's term" (Hardin 1978, p. 314).

The presumption that an external Leviathan is necessary to avoid tragedies of the commons leads to recommendations that central governments control most natural resource systems. Heilbroner (1974) opined that "iron governments," perhaps military governments, would be necessary to achieve control over ecological problems. In a less draconian view, Ehrenfeld (1972, p. 322) suggested that if "private interests

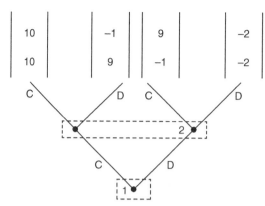

FIGURE 1.2 Game 2: The central-authority game with complete information.

cannot be expected to protect the public domain then external regulation by public agencies, governments, or international authorities is needed." In an analysis of the problems involved in water resource management in developing countries, Carruthers and Stoner (1981, p. 29) argued that without public control, "overgrazing and soil erosion of communal pastures, or less fish at higher average cost," would result. They concluded that "common property resources *require* public control if economic efficiency is to result from their development" (1981, p. 29; emphasis added).[8] The policy advice to centralize the control and regulation of natural resources, such as grazing lands, forests, and fisheries, has been followed extensively, particularly in Third World countries.

One way to illustrate these proponents' image of centralized control is to modify the Hardin herder game using the assumptions that underlie this policy advice. The proponents of centralized control want an external government agency to decide the specific herding strategy that the central authority considers best for the situation: The central authority will decide who can use the meadow, when they can use it, and how many animals can be grazed. Let us assume that the central authority decides to impose a penalty of 2 profit units on anyone who is considered by that authority to be using a defect strategy. Assuming that the central agency knows the sustainable yield of the meadow (L) and can unfailingly discover and penalize any herder using the defect strategy, the newly restructured game imposed by the central authority is represented in Game 2. Now, the solution to Game 2 is (cooperate, cooperate). Both players receive 10 profit units each, rather than the zero units they would have received in Game 1. If an external authority accurately determines the capacity of a common-pool resource, unambiguously assigns this capacity, monitors actions, and unfailingly sanctions noncompliance, then a centralized agency can transform the Hardin herder game to generate an optimally efficient equilibrium for the herders. Little consideration is given to the cost of creating and maintaining such an agency. This is seen as exogenous to the problem and is not included as a parameter of Game 2.[9]

The optimal equilibrium achieved by following the advice to centralize control, however, is based on assumptions concerning the accuracy of information, monitoring capabilities, sanctioning reliability, and zero costs of administration. Without valid and

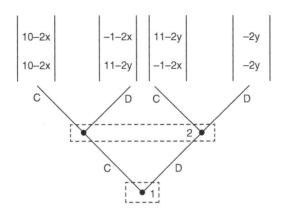

FIGURE 1.3 Game 3: The central-authority game with incomplete information.

reliable information, a central agency could make several errors, including setting the carrying capacity or the fine too high or too low, sanctioning herders who cooperate, or not sanctioning defectors. The implications of all forms of incomplete information are interesting. However, as an example, I shall focus entirely on the implications arising from a central agency's incomplete information about the herders' strategies. The implicit assumption of Game 2 is that the central agency monitors all actions of the herders costlessly and imposes sanctions correctly.

In Game 3, we assume that the central agency has complete information about the carrying capacity of the meadow, but incomplete information about the particular actions of the herders. The central agency consequently makes errors in imposing punishments. Let us assume that the central agency punishes defections (the correct response) with probability y and fails to punish defections with probability $1 - y$ (the erroneous response). Let us also assume that the central agency punishes cooperative actions (the erroneous response) with probability x and does not punish cooperative actions (the correct response) with probability $1 - x$. The payoff parameters are illustrated in Figure 1.3.

A central agency with complete information would make no errors in its punishment level; in that case, $x = 0$ and $y = 1$. Game 2 would then be a special case of Game 3 in which $x = 0$ and $y = 1$. However, if the central agency does not have complete information about the actions of the herders, it imposes both types of sanctions correctly with a probability of 0.7 ($x = 0.3$, $y = 0.7$). An example of the specific payoffs for this game is shown as Game 4 in Figure 1.4. Given this payoff structure, the herders again face a prisoner's dilemma game. They will defect (overgraze) rather than cooperate (graze within the carrying capacity). In Game 4, as in the original Game 1, the equilibrium outcomes for the herders were (0, 0). In a game in which a central agency sanctions correctly with a probability of 0.7, the equilibrium outcomes are (−1.4, −1.4). The equilibrium of the regulated game has a lower value than that of the unregulated game. Given the carrying capacity and profit possibilities of Game 1, the central agency must have sufficient information so that it can correctly impose sanctions with a probability greater than 0.75 to avoid pushing the herders to the (D, D) equilibrium.[10]

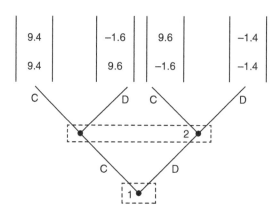

FIGURE 1.4 Game 4: An example of the central-authority game with incomplete information.

Privatization as the "only" way

Other policy analysts, influenced by the same models, have used equally strong terms in calling for the imposition of private property rights whenever resources are owned in common (Demsetz 1967; O. Johnson 1972). "Both the economic analysis of common property resources and Hardin's treatment of the tragedy of the commons" led Robert J. Smith (1981, p. 467) to suggest that "the *only* way to avoid the tragedy of the commons in natural resources and wildlife is to end the common-property system by creating a system of private property rights" (emphasis added); see also the work of Sinn (1984). Smith stressed that it is "by treating a resource as a common property that we become locked in its inexorable destruction" (1981, p. 465). Welch advocated the creation of full private rights to a commons when he asserted that "the establishment of full property rights is necessary to avoid the inefficiency of overgrazing" (1983, p. 171). He asserted that privatization of the commons was the optimal solution for all common-pool problems. His major concern was how to impose private ownership when those currently using a commons were unwilling to change to a set of private rights to the commons.

Those recommending the imposition of privatization on the herders would divide the meadow in half and assign half of the meadow to one herder and the other half to the second herder. Now each herder will be playing a *game against nature* in a smaller terrain, rather than a game against another player in a larger terrain. The herders now will need to invest in fences and their maintenance, as well as in monitoring and sanctioning activities to enforce their division of the grazing area (B. Field 1984, 1985b). It is presumed that each herder will now choose $X/2$ animals to graze as a result of his own profit incentive.[11] This assumes that the meadow is perfectly homogeneous over time in its distribution of available fodder. If rainfall occurs erratically, one part of the grazing area may be lush with growth one year, whereas another part of the area may be unable to support $X/2$ animals. The rain may fall somewhere else the next year. In any given year, one of the herders may make no profit, and the other may enjoy a considerable return. If the location of lush growth changes dramatically from year to year, dividing the commons may impoverish both herders and lead to overgrazing in those parts where forage is temporarily inadequate. Of course, it will be possible for the herder who has extra fodder in one year to sell it to the other herder. Alternatively, it will be possible for the herders to set up an insurance scheme to share the risk of an uncertain environment. However, the setup costs for a new market or a new insurance scheme would be substantial and will not be needed so long as the herders share fodder and risk by jointly sharing a larger grazing area.

It is difficult to know exactly what analysts mean when they refer to the necessity of developing private rights to some common-pool resources (CPRs). It is clear that when they refer to land, they mean to divide the land into separate parcels and assign individual rights to hold, use, and transfer these parcels as individual owners desire (subject to the general regulations of a jurisdiction regarding the use and transfer of land). In regard to nonstationary resources, such as water and fisheries, it is unclear what the establishment of private rights means. As Colin Clark has pointed out, the "'tragedy of the commons' has proved particularly difficult to counteract in the case of marine fishery resources where, the establishment of individual property rights is virtually out of the question" (1980, p. 117). In regard to a fugitive resource, a diversity of rights may be established giving individuals rights to use particular types of equipment, to use the resource system at a particular time and place, or to withdraw a particular quantity of resource units (if they can be found). But even when particular rights are unitized, quantified, and salable, the resource *system* is still likely to be owned in common rather than individually.[12] Again, referring to fisheries, Clark has argued that "common ownership is the fundamental fact affecting almost every regime of fishery management" (1980, p. 117).

The "only" way?

Analysts who find an empirical situation with a structure presumed to be a commons dilemma often call for the imposition of a solution by an external actor: The "only way" to solve a commons dilemma is by doing X. Underlying such a claim is the belief that X is necessary and sufficient to solve the commons dilemma. But the content of X could hardly be more variable. One set of advocates presumes that a central authority must assume continuing responsibility to make unitary decisions for a particular resource. The other presumes that a central authority should parcel out ownership rights to the resource and then allow individuals to pursue their own self-interests within a set of well-defined property rights. Both centralization advocates and privatization advocates accept as a central tenet that institutional change must come from outside and be imposed on the individuals affected. Despite sharing a faith in the necessity and efficacy of "the state" to change institutions so as to increase efficiency, the institutional changes they recommend could hardly be further apart.

If one recommendation is correct, the other cannot be. Contradictory positions cannot both be right. I do not argue for either of these positions. Rather, I argue that both are too sweeping in their claims. Instead of there being a single solution to a single problem, I argue that many solutions exist to cope with many different problems. Instead of presuming that optimal institutional solutions can be designed easily and imposed at low cost by external authorities, I argue that "getting the institutions right" is a difficult, time-consuming, conflict-invoking process. It is a process that requires reliable information about time and place variables as well as a broad repertoire of culturally acceptable rules. New institutional arrangements do not work in the field as they do in abstract models unless the models are well specified and empirically valid and the participants in a field setting understand how to make the new rules work.

Instead of presuming that the individuals sharing a commons are inevitably caught in a trap from which they cannot escape, I argue that the capacity of individuals to extricate themselves from various types of dilemma situations *varies* from situation to situation. The cases to be discussed in this book illustrate both successful and unsuccessful efforts to escape tragic outcomes. Instead of basing policy on the presumption that the individuals involved are helpless, I wish to learn more from the experience of individuals in field settings. Why have some efforts to solve commons problems failed, while others have succeeded? What can we learn from experience that will help stimulate the development and use of a better theory of collective action – one that will identify the key variables that can enhance or detract from the capabilities of individuals to solve problems?

Institutions are rarely either private or public – "the market" or "the state." Many successful CPR institutions are rich mixtures of "private-like" and "public-like" institutions defying classification in a sterile dichotomy. By "successful," I mean institutions that enable individuals to achieve productive outcomes in situations where temptations to free-ride and shirk are ever present. A competitive market – the epitome of private institutions – is itself a public good. Once a competitive market is provided, individuals can enter and exit freely whether or not they contribute to the cost of providing and maintaining the market. No market can exist for long without underlying public institutions to support it. In field settings, public and private institutions frequently are intermeshed and depend on one another, rather than existing in isolated worlds.

An alternative solution

To open up the discussion of institutional options for solving commons dilemmas, I want now to present a fifth game in which the herders themselves can make a binding contract to commit themselves to a cooperative strategy that they themselves will work out. To represent this arrangement within a noncooperative framework, additional moves must be overtly included in the game structure. A binding contract is interpreted within noncooperative game theory as one that is unfailingly enforced by an external actor – just as we interpreted the penalty posited earlier as being unfailingly enforced by the central authority.

A simple way to represent this is to add one parameter to the payoffs and a strategy to both herders' strategy sets.[13] The parameter is the cost of enforcing an agreement and will be denoted by e. The herders in Game 5 must now negotiate prior to placing animals on the meadow. During negotiations, they discuss various strategies for sharing the carrying capacity of the meadow and the costs of enforcing their agreement. Contracts are not enforceable, however, unless agreed to unanimously by the herders. Any proposal made by one herder that did not involve an equal sharing of the carrying capacity and of enforcement costs would be vetoed by the other herder in their negotiations. Consequently, the only feasible agreement – and the equilibrium of the resulting game – is for both herders to share equally the sustainable yield levels

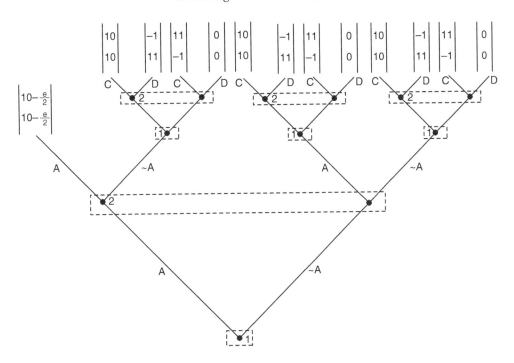

FIGURE 1.5 Game 5: Self-financed contract-enforcement game.

of the meadow and the costs of enforcing their agreement so long as each herder's share of the cost of enforcement is less than 10.[14]

Further, in Game 5, players can *always* guarantee that the worst they will do is the (defect, defect) outcome of Game 1. They are not dependent on the accuracy of the information obtained by a distant government official regarding their strategies. If one player suggests a contract based on incomplete or biased information, the other player can indicate an unwillingness to agree. They determine their own contract and ask the enforcer to enforce only that on which they have agreed. If the enforcer should decide to charge too much for its services [any number equal to or greater than $P_i (C, C) - P_i (D, D)$, $i = 1, 2$], neither player would agree to such a contract.

The "solution" of a commons-dilemma game through instrumentalities similar to Game 5 is not presented as the "only way" to solve a commons dilemma. It is merely one way. But this way has been almost totally ignored in both the policy-analysis literature and the formal-theory literature. Contemplating such an option raises numerous questions. First, might it be possible for the herders to hire a private agent to take on the role of enforcer? This is not as farfetched as it might seem at first. Many long-term business exchanges have the structure of a prisoner's dilemma.[15] Businesses are hesitant to accept promises of future performance rather than enforceable contracts, especially when beginning new business relationships. To reduce enforcement costs, however, a frequent practice is to use a private arbitrator rather than a civil court as the mechanism to achieve enforcement.[16] In *N*-person settings, all professional athletic leagues face problems similar to those illustrated here. During the play of a professional game, the temptation to cheat and break the rules is ever present. Further, accidents do happen, and rules get broken, even by players who were intending to follow the rules. Athletic leagues typically employ private monitors to enforce their rules.[17]

As soon as we allow the possibility of a private party to take on the role of an external enforcer, the nature of the "solution" offered by Game 5 to the commons dilemma begins to generate a rich set of alternative applications. A self-financed contract-enforcement game allows the participants in the situation to exercise greater control over decisions about who will be allowed to graze and what limits will be placed on the number of animals, as compared with either Game 2 or Game 3. If the parties use a private arbitrator, they do not let the arbitrator impose an agreement on them. The arbitrator simply helps the parties find methods to resolve disputes that arise within the set of working rules to which the parties themselves have agreed. Arbitrators, courts, and other arrangements for enforcement and dispute resolution make it possible for individuals to initiate long-term arrangements that they could not otherwise undertake.[18] Further, as soon as one thinks about a "solution" like Game 5, it is a small step to thinking about the possibility of several arbitrators offering enforcement services at varying charges during the negotiation stage. The payoff-dominant equilibrium is to agree on that arbitrator who will enforce the contract at the lowest e.

The key difference between Game 5 and Games 2 and 3 is that the participants themselves design their own contracts in Game 5 in light of the information they have at hand. The herders, who use the same meadow year after year, have detailed and relatively accurate information about carrying capacity. They observe the behavior of other herders and have an incentive to report contractual infractions. Arbitrators may not need to hire monitors to observe the activities of the contracting parties. The self-interest of those who negotiated the contract will lead them to monitor each other and to report observed infractions so that the contract is enforced. A regulatory agency, on the other hand, always needs to hire its own monitors. The regulatory agency then faces the principal–agent problem of how to ensure that its monitors do their own job.

The proponents of the central-authority "solution" presume that such agencies have accurate information and are able to change incentives to produce something like Game 2. It is difficult for a central authority to have sufficient time-and-place information to estimate accurately both the carrying capacity of a CPR and the appropriate fines to induce cooperative behavior. I believe that situations like that in Game 3, in which incomplete information leads to sanctioning errors, occur more frequently than has been presumed in the policy literature. The need for external monitors and enforcers is particularly acute when what is being enforced is a decision by an external agent who may impose excess costs on participants.

A further problem for consideration is that games in which enforcers have been arranged for by mutual agreement may be mistaken by analysts and public officials for games in which there have been *no* agreements about how to cooperate and enforce agreements. In other words, some examples of a "Game 5" may be mistaken for a "Game 1."[19] These situations may be construed to be "informal," carrying a presumption that they are not lawful. This goes to fundamental presumptions about the nature of governments as external authorities governing over societies.

As will be seen in the later discussion of empirical cases, users of CPRs have developed a wide diversity in their own agreements, which are enforced by many mechanisms. Some of the enforcement mechanisms are external governmental agencies. Some enforcement mechanisms involve members of the users' community who have been employed as monitors and enforcers. Some enforcement mechanisms involve the users themselves as their own monitors. When the enforcement mechanism is not an external governmental agency, some analysts presume that there is no enforcement. That is why Game 5 is mistaken for Game 1.

A self-financed contract-enforcement game is no panacea. Such institutional arrangements have many weaknesses in many settings. The herders can overestimate or underestimate the carrying capacity of the meadow. Their own monitoring system may break down. The external enforcer may not be able to enforce ex post, after promising to do so ex ante. A myriad of problems can occur in natural settings, as is also the case with the idealized central-regulation or private-property institutions.

The structure of the institutional arrangements that one finds in natural settings is, of course, far more complicated than the structure of any of the extremely simple games presented here for discussion. What I attempt to do with these simple games is to generate different ways of thinking about the mechanisms that individuals may use to extricate themselves from commons dilemmas – ways different from what one finds in much of the policy literature. To challenge this mind-set, one needs only simple mechanisms that illustrate alternatives to those that normally are presented as the dominant solutions.

An empirical alternative

Game 5 illustrated a theoretical alternative to centralization or privatization as ways to solve CPR problems. Let us now briefly consider a solution devised by participants in a field setting – Alanya, Turkey – that cannot be characterized as either central regulation or privatization. The inshore fishery at Alanya, as described by Fikret Berkes (1986b), is a relatively small operation. Many of the approximately 100 local fishers operate in two- or three-person boats using various types of nets. Half of the fishers belong to a local producers' cooperative. According to Berkes, the early 1970s were the "dark ages" for Alanya. The economic viability of the fishery was threatened by two factors: First, unrestrained use of the fishery had led to hostility and, at times, violent conflict among the users. Second, competition among fishers for the better fishing spots had increased production costs, as well as the level of uncertainty regarding the harvest potential of any particular boat.

Early in the 1970s, members of the local cooperative began experimenting with an ingenious system for allotting fishing sites to local fishers. After more than a decade of trial-and-error efforts, the rules used by the Alanya inshore fishers are as follows:

- Each September, a list of eligible fishers is prepared, consisting of all licensed fishers in Alanya, regardless of co-op membership.
- Within the area normally used by Alanya fishers, all usable fishing locations are named and listed. These sites are spaced so that the nets set in one site will not block the fish that should be available at the adjacent sites.
- These named fishing locations and their assignments are in effect from September to May.

- In September, the eligible fishers draw lots and are assigned to the named fishing locations.
- From September to January, each day each fisher moves east to the next location. After January, the fishers move west. This gives the fishers equal opportunities at the stocks that migrate from east to west between September and January and reverse their migration through the area from January to May (Berkes 1986b, pp. 73–4).

The system has the effect of spacing the fishers far enough apart on the fishing grounds that the production capabilities at each site are optimized. All fishing boats also have equal chances to fish at the best spots. Resources are not wasted searching for or fighting over a site.[20] No signs of overcapitalization are apparent.

The list of fishing locations is endorsed by each fisher and deposited with the mayor and local gendarme once a year at the time of the lottery. The process of monitoring and enforcing the system is, however, accomplished by the fishers themselves as a by-product of the incentive created by the rotation system. On a day when a given fisher is assigned one of the more productive spots, that fisher will exercise that option with certainty (leaving aside last-minute breakdowns in equipment). All other fishers can expect that the assigned fisher will be at the spot bright and early. Consequently, an effort to cheat on the system by traveling to a good spot on a day when one is assigned to a poor spot has little chance of remaining undetected. Cheating on the system will be observed by the very fishers who have rights to be in the best spots and will be willing to defend their rights using physical means if necessary. Their rights will be supported by everyone else in the system. The others will want to ensure that their own rights will not be usurped on the days when they are assigned good sites. The few infractions that have occurred have been handled easily by the fishers at the local coffeehouse (Berkes 1986b, p. 74).

Although this is not a private-property system, rights to use fishing sites and duties to respect these rights are well defined. And though it is not a centralized system, national legislation that has given such cooperatives jurisdiction over "local arrangements" has been used by cooperative officials to legitimize their role in helping to devise a workable set of rules. That local officials accept the signed agreement each year also enhances legitimacy. The actual monitoring and enforcing of the rules, however, are left to the fishers.

Central-government officials could not have crafted such a set of rules without assigning a full-time staff to work (actually fish) in the area for an extended period. Fishing sites of varying economic value are commonly associated with inshore fisheries (Christy 1982; Forman 1967), but they are almost impossible to map without extensive on-site experience. Mapping this set of fishing sites, such that one boat's fishing activities would not reduce the migration of fish to other locations, would have been a daunting challenge had it not been for the extensive time-and-place information provided by the fishers and their willingness to experiment for a decade with various maps and systems. Alanya provides an example of a self-governed common-property arrangement in which the rules have been devised and modified by the participants themselves and also are monitored and enforced by them.

The case of the Alanya inshore fishery is only one empirical example of the many institutional arrangements that have been devised, modified, monitored, and sustained by the users of renewable CPRs to constrain individual behavior that would, if unconstrained, reduce joint returns to the community of users. In addition to the case studies discussed in Chapters 3, 4, and 5, productive CPR institutional arrangements have been well documented for many farmer-managed irrigation systems, communal forests, inshore fisheries, and grazing and hunting territories.[21]

Game 5 and empirical cases of successfully governed CPRs provide theoretical and empirical alternatives to the assertion that those involved cannot extricate themselves from the problems faced when multiple individuals use a given resource. The key to my argument is that some individuals have broken out of the trap inherent in the commons dilemma, whereas others continue remorsefully trapped into destroying their own resources.[22] This leads me to ask what differences exist between those who have broken the shackles of a commons dilemma and those who have not. The differences may have to do with factors *internal* to a given group. The participants may simply have no capacity to communicate with one another, no way to develop trust, and no sense that they must share a common future. Alternatively, powerful individuals who stand to gain from the current situation, while others lose, may block efforts by the less powerful to change the rules of the game. Such groups may need some form of external assistance to break out of the perverse logic of their situation.

The differences between those who have and those who have not extricated themselves from commons dilemmas may also have to do with factors *outside* the domain of those affected. Some participants do not have the autonomy to change their own institutional structures and are prevented from making constructive changes by external authorities who are indifferent to the perversities of the commons dilemma, or may even stand to gain from it. Also, there is the possibility that external changes may sweep rapidly over a group, giving them insufficient time to adjust their internal structures to avoid the suboptimal outcomes. Some groups suffer from perverse incentive systems that are themselves the results of policies pursued by central authorities. Many potential answers spring to mind regarding the question why some individuals do not achieve collective benefits for themselves, whereas others do. However, as long as analysts presume that individuals cannot change such situations themselves, they do not ask what internal or external variables can enhance or impede the efforts of communities of individuals to deal creatively and constructively with perverse problems such as the tragedy of the commons.

Policy prescriptions as metaphors

Policy analysts who would recommend a single prescription for commons problems have paid little attention to how diverse institutional arrangements operate in practice. The centrists presume that unified authorities will operate in the field as they have been designed to do in the textbooks – determining the policies to be adopted for a resource based on valid scientific theories and adequate information. Implementation of these policies without error is assumed. Monitoring and sanctioning activities are viewed as routine and nonproblematic.

Those advocating the private-property approach presume that the most efficient use patterns for CPRs will actually result from dividing the rights to access and control such resources. Systematic empirical studies have shown that private organization of firms dealing in goods such as electricity, transport, and medical services tends to be more efficient than governmental organization of such firms; for a review of this literature, see De Alessi (1980). Whether private or public forms are more efficient in industries in which certain potential beneficiaries cannot be excluded is, however, a different question. We are concerned with the types of institutions that will be most efficient for governing and managing diverse CPRs for which at least some potential beneficiaries cannot be excluded. Privatizing the ownership of CPRs need not have the same positive results as privatizing the ownership of an airline. Further, privatizing may not mean "dividing up" at all. Privatization can also mean assigning the exclusive right to harvest from a resource system to a single individual or firm.

Many policy prescriptions are themselves no more than metaphors. Both the centralizers and the privatizers frequently advocate oversimplified, idealized institutions – paradoxically, almost "institution-free" institutions. An assertion that central regulation is necessary tells us nothing about the way a central agency should be constituted, what authority it should have, how the limits on its authority should be maintained, how it will obtain information, or how its agents should be selected, motivated to do their work, and have their performances monitored and rewarded or sanctioned. An assertion that the imposition of private property rights is necessary tells us nothing about how that bundle of rights is to be defined, how the various attributes of the goods involved will be measured, who will pay for the costs of excluding nonowners from access, how conflicts over rights will be adjudicated, or how the residual interests of the right-holders in the resource system itself will be organized.

An important lesson that one learns by carefully studying the growing number of systematic studies by scholars associated with "the new institutionalism" is that these "institutional details" are important.[23] Whether or not any equilibria are possible and whether or not an equilibrium would be an improvement for the individuals involved (or for others who are in turn affected by these individuals) will depend on the particular structures of the institutions. In the most general sense. all institutional arrangements can be thought of as games in extensive form. As such, the particular options available, the sequencing of those options, the information provided, and the relative rewards and punishments aligned to different sequences of moves can all change the pattern of outcomes achieved. Further, the particular structure of the physical environment involved also will have a major impact on the structure of the game and its results. Thus, a set of rules used in one physical environment may have vastly different consequences if used in a different physical environment.

Policies based on metaphors can be harmful

Relying on metaphors as the foundation for policy advice lead to results substantially different from those presumed to be likely. Nationalizing the ownership of forests in Third World countries, for example, has been advocated on the grounds that local villagers cannot manage forests so as to sustain their productivity and their value in reducing soil erosion. In countries where small villages had owned and regulated their local communal forests for generations, nationalization meant expropriation. In such localities, villagers had earlier exercised considerable restraint over the rate and manner of harvesting forest products. In some of these countries, national agencies issued elaborate regulations concerning the use of forests, but were unable to employ sufficient numbers of foresters to enforce those regulations. The foresters who were employed were paid such low salaries that accepting bribes became a common means of supplementing their income. The consequence was that nationalization created *open-access resources* where limited-access *common-property resources* had previously existed. The disastrous effects of nationalizing formerly communal forests have been well documented for Thailand (Feeny 1988a), Niger (Thomson 1977; Thomson, Feeny, and Oakerson 1986), Nepal (Arnold and Campbell 1986; Messerschmidt 1986), and India (Gadgil and Iyer 1989). Similar problems occurred in regard to inshore fisheries when national agencies presumed that they had exclusive jurisdiction over all coastal waters (Cordell and McKean 1986; W. Cruz 1986; Dasgupta 1982; Panayoutou 1982; Pinkerton 1989a).

A Challenge

An important challenge facing policy scientists is to develop theories of human organization based on realistic assessment of human capabilities and limitations in dealing with a variety of situations that initially share some or all aspects of a tragedy of the commons. Empirically validated theories of human organization will be essential ingredients of a policy science that can inform decisions about the likely consequences of a multitude of ways of organizing human activities. Theoretical inquiry involves a search for regularities. It involves abstraction from the complexity of a field setting, followed by the positing of theoretical variables that underlie observed complexities. Specific models of a theory involve further abstraction and simplification for the purpose of still finer analysis of the logical relationships among variables in a closed system. As a theorist, and at times a modeler, I see these efforts at the core of a policy science.

One can, however, get trapped in one's own intellectual web. When years have been spent in the development of a theory with considerable power and elegance, analysts obviously will want to apply this tool to as many situations as possible. The power of a theory is exactly proportional to the diversity of situations it can explain. All theories, however, have limits. Models of a theory are limited still further because many parameters must be fixed in a model, rather than allowed to vary. Confusing a model – such as that of a perfectly competitive market – with the theory of which it is one representation can limit applicability still further.

Scientific knowledge is as much an understanding of the diversity of situations for which a theory or its models are relevant as an understanding of its limits. The conviction that all physical structures could be described in terms of a set of perfect forms – circles, squares, and triangles – limited the development of astronomy until Johannes Kepler broke the bonds of classical thought and discovered that the orbit of Mars was elliptical – a finding that Kepler himself initially considered to be no more than a pile of dung (Koestler 1959). Godwin and Shepard (1979) pointed out a decade ago that policy scientists were doing the equivalent of "Forcing Squares, Triangles and Ellipses into a Circular Paradigm" by using the commons-dilemma model without serious attention to whether or not the variables in the empirical world conformed to the theoretical model. Many theoretical and empirical findings have been reported since Godwin and Shepard's article that should have made policy scientists even more skeptical about relying on a limited set of models to analyze the diversity of situations broadly referred to as CPR problems. Unfortunately, many analysts – in academia, special-interest groups, governments, and the press – still presume that common-pool problems are all dilemmas in which the participants themselves cannot avoid producing suboptimal results, and in some cases disastrous results.

What is missing from the policy analyst's tool kit – and from the set of accepted, well-developed theories of human organization – is an adequately, specified theory of collective action whereby a group of principals can organize themselves voluntarily to retain the residuals of their own efforts. Examples of self-organized enterprises abound. Most law firms are obvious examples: A group of lawyers will pool their assets to purchase a library and pay for joint secretarial and research assistance. They will develop their own internal governance mechanisms and formulas for allocating costs and benefits to the partners. Most cooperatives are also examples. The cases of self-organized and self-governed CPRs that we consider in Chapter 3 are also examples. But until a theoretical explanation – based on human choice – for self-organized and self-governed enterprises is fully developed and accepted, major policy decisions will continue to be undertaken with a presumption that individuals cannot organize themselves and always need to be organized by external authorities.

Further, all organizational arrangements are subject to stress, weakness, and failure. Without an adequate theory of self-organized collective action, one cannot predict or explain when individuals will be unable to solve a common problem through self-organization alone, nor can one begin to ascertain which of many intervention strategies might be effective in helping to solve particular problems. As discussed earlier, there is a considerable difference between the presumption that a regulatory agency should be established and the presumption that a reliable court system is needed to monitor and enforce self-negotiated contracts. If the theories being used in a policy science do not include the possibility of self-organized collective action, then the importance of a court system that can be used by self-organizing groups to monitor and enforce contracts will not be recognized.[24]

I hope this inquiry will contribute to the development of an empirically supported theory of self-organizing and self-governing forms of collective action. What I attempt to do in this volume is to combine the strategy used by many scholars associated with the "new institutionalism" with the strategy used by biologists for conducting empirical work related to the development of a better theoretical understanding of the biological world.

As an institutionalist studying empirical phenomena, I presume that individuals try to solve problems as effectively as they can. That assumption imposes a discipline on me. Instead of presuming that some individuals are incompetent, evil, or irrational, and others are omniscient, I presume that individuals have very similar limited capabilities to reason and figure out the structure of complex environments. It is my responsibility as a scientist to ascertain what problems individuals are trying to solve and what factors help or hinder them in these efforts. When the problems that I observe involve lack of predictability, information, and trust, as well as high levels of complexity and transactional difficulties, then my efforts to explain must take these problems overtly into account rather than assuming them away. In developing an explanation for observed behavior, I draw on a rich literature written by other scholars interested in institutions and their effects on individual incentives and behaviors in field settings.

Biologists also face the problem of studying complex processes that are poorly understood. Their scientific strategy frequently has involved identifying for empirical observation the simplest possible organism in which a process occurs in a clarified, or even exaggerated, form. The organism is not chosen because it is representative of all organisms. Rather, the organism is chosen because particular processes can be studied more effectively using this organism than using another.

My "organism" is a type of human situation. I call this situation a CPR situation and define exactly what I mean by this and other key terms in Chapter 2. In this volume, I do not include all potential CPR situations within the frame of reference. I focus entirely on small-scale CPRs, where the CPR is itself located within one country and the number of individuals affected varies from 50 to 15,000 persons who are heavily dependent on the CPR for economic returns. These CPRs are primarily inshore fisheries, smaller grazing areas, groundwater basins, irrigation systems, and communal forests. Because these are relatively small-scale situations, serious study is more likely to penetrate the surface complexity to identify underlying similarities and processes. Because the individuals involved gain a major part of their economic return from the CPRs, they are strongly motivated to try to solve common problems to enhance their own productivity over time. The effort to self-organize in these situations may be somewhat exaggerated, but that is exactly why I want to study this process in these settings. Further, when self-organization fails, I know that it is not because the collective benefits that could have been obtained were unimportant to the participants.

There are limits on the types of CPRs studied here: (1) renewable rather than non-renewable resources, (2) situations where substantial scarcity exists, rather than abundance, and (3) situations in which the users can substantially harm one another, but not situations in which participants can produce major external harm for others. Thus, all asymmetrical pollution problems are excluded, as is any situation in which a group can form a cartel and control a sufficient part of the market to affect market price.

In the empirical studies, I present a synopsis of important CPR cases that have aided my understanding of the processes of self-organization and self-governance. These cases are in no sense a "random" sample of cases. Rather, these are cases that provide clear information about the processes involved in (1) governing long-enduring CPRs, (2) transforming existing institutional arrangements, and (3) failing to overcome continued CPR problems. These cases can thus be viewed as a collection of the most salient raw materials with which I have worked in my effort to understand how individuals organize and govern themselves to obtain collective benefits in situations where the temptations to free-ride and to break commitments are substantial.

From an examination and analysis of these cases, I attempt to develop a series of reasoned conjectures about how it is possible that some individuals organize themselves to govern and manage CPRs and others do not. I try to identify the underlying design principles of the institutions used by those who have successfully managed their own CPRs over extended periods of time and why these may affect the incentives for participants to continue investing time and effort in the governance and management of their own CPRs. I compare the institutions used in successful and unsuccessful cases, and I try to identify the internal and external factors that can impede or enhance the capabilities of individuals to use and govern CPRs.

I hope these conjectures contribute to the development of an empirically valid theory of self-organization and self-governance for at least one well-defined universe of problematical situations. That universe contains a substantial proportion of renewable resources heavily utilized by human beings in different parts of the world. It is estimated, for example, that 90% of the world's fishermen and over half of the fish consumed each year are captured in the small-scale, inshore fisheries included within the frame of this study (Panayoutou 1982, p. 49). Further, my choice of the CPR environment for intensive study was based on a presumption that I could learn about the processes of self-organization and self-governance of relevance to a somewhat broader set of environments.

Given the similarity between many CPR problems and the problems of providing small-scale collective goods, the findings from this volume should contribute to an understanding of the factors that can enhance or detract from the capabilities of individuals to organize collective action related to providing local public goods. All efforts to organize collective action, whether by an external ruler, an entrepreneur, or a set of principals who wish to gain collective benefits, must address a common set of problems. These have to do with coping with free-riding, solving commitment problems, arranging for the supply of new institutions, and monitoring individual compliance with sets of rules. A study that focuses on how individuals avoid free-riding, achieve high levels of commitment, arrange for new institutions, and monitor conformity to a set of rules in CPR environments should contribute to an understanding of how individuals address these crucial problems in some other settings as well.

Notes

1 Attributed to Merrill M. Flood and Melvin Dresher and formalized by Albert W. Tucker (R. Campbell 1985, p. 3), the game is described (Luce and Raiffa 1957, p. 95) as follows: "Two suspects are taken into custody and separated. The district attorney is certain that they are guilty of a specific crime, but he does not have adequate evidence to convict them at a trial. He points out to each prisoner that each has two alternatives: to confess to the crime the police are sure they have done, or not to confess. If they both do not confess, then the district attorney states he will book them on some very minor trumped-up charge such as petty larceny and illegal possession of a weapon, and they will both receive minor punishment; if they both confess they will be prosecuted, but he will recommend less than the most severe sentence; but if one confesses and the other does not, then the confessor will receive lenient treatment for turning state's evidence whereas the latter will get 'the book'

slapped at him. In terms of years in a penitentiary, the strategic problem might be reduced"
to the following:

	Prisoner 2	
Prisoner 1	**Not confess**	**Confess**
Not confess	1 year each	10 years for prisoner 1
		3 months for prisoner 2
Confess	3 months for prisoner 1	8 years each
	10 years for prisoner 2	

R. Kenneth Godwin and W. Bruce Shepard (1979), Richard Kimber (1981), Michael Taylor
(1987), and others have shown that commons dilemmas are not always prisoner's dilemma
(PD) games. Dawes (1973, 1975) was one of the first scholars to show the similarity of
structure.

2 Hardin's model easily translates into the prisoner's dilemma structure. Many problems
related to the use of common-pool resources (CPRs) do *not* easily translate. Simple games
such as "chicken" and "assurance" games are better representations of some situations (M.
Taylor 1987). More complex games involving several moves and lacking dominant strategies for the players are better able to capture many of the problems involved in managing CPRs.

3 Hardin recommends "mutual coercion, mutually agreed upon" as a solution to the problem,
but what "mutual agreement" means is ambiguous given his emphasis on the role of central
regulators; see Orr and Hill (1979) for a critique.

4 A howling debate raged for some time, for example, regarding whether the number of
participants involved was positively, negatively, or not at all related to the quantity of the
good provided (Buchanan 1968; Chamberlin 1974; Frohlich and Oppenheimer 1970;
McGuire 1974). Russell Hardin (1982) resolved the controversy to a large extent by pointing
out that the effect of the number of contributors was largely dependent on the type of collective benefits being provided – whether or not each unit of the good was subtractable.
Thus, the initial debate did not lead to clarification until implicit assumptions about the
type of good involved had been made explicit.

5 J. A. Moore (1985, p. 483), reporting on the education project for the American Society of
Zoologists.

6 See, for example, Berkes (1987), Berkes and Kislalioglu (1989), Berkes and Pocock (1981),
A. Davis (1984), K. Martin (1979), Matthews and Phyne (1988). For strong critiques of
Canadian policy, see Pinkerton (1989a,b) and Matthews (1988).

7 Michael Taylor (1987) analyzes the structure of Hobbes's theory to show that Hobbes
proposed the creation of a Leviathan in order to avoid the equilibrium of situations
structured like prisoner's dilemmas. See also Sugden (1986).

8 Stillman (1975, p. 13) points out that those who see "a strong central government or a
strong ruler" as a solution implicitly assume that "the ruler will be a wise and ecologically
aware altruist," even though these same theorists presume that the users of CPRs will be
myopic, self-interested, and ecologically unaware hedonists.

9 The form of regulation used in Game 2 would be referred to in the resource economics
literature as a "pure quota scheme." Alternative regulatory instruments that are frequently
proposed are a "pure licensing scheme" and a "pure tax scheme." As Dasgupta and Heal
(1979) point out, however, it is "the" government in each of these schemes that takes control of the resource and sets up the regulatory scheme. "The idea, in each case, is for the
government to take charge of the common property resource and to introduce regulations

aimed at the attainment of allocative efficiency" (Dasgupta and Heal 1979, p. 66). All of the models of these various schemes assume that the costs of sustaining these systems are nil (as in Game 2). Dasgupta and Heal repeatedly stress that these costs are *not* nil in field settings and may affect whether or not any of them actually will solve a commons problem or the relative efficiency of one scheme versus another. But Dasgupta and Heal's careful warnings about the importance of the relative costs of various constitutional arrangements are rarely heeded in the policy literature.

10 More accurately, the sum of the two types of errors must be less than 0.50, given the fixed parameters of this game, for the restructured game to have a (*C, C*) equilibrium. I am grateful to Franz Weissing, who suggested this particular analysis for illustrating the problem of incomplete information on the part of a central agency.

The last two decades of work in social-choice theory also have revealed other problems that may be involved in any system where a collective choice about policy must be reached through mechanisms of collective choice. Even if complete information is available about the resources, problems associated with cycling and/or agenda control can also occur (McKelvey 1976, 1979; Riker 1980; Shepsle 1979a).

11 This overlooks the fact that in a dynamic setting the decision whether to manage the meadow at a sustainable level or to "mine" it rapidly will depend delicately on the discount rate used by the private owner. If the discount rate is high, the private owner will "overuse" a commons just as much as will a series of unorganized co-owners. See Clark (1977) for a clear statement of how overexploitation can occur under private property.

12 And it should be pointed out that the private-rights system is itself a *public* institution and is dependent on public instrumentalities for its very existence (Binger and Hoffman 1989).

13 My thanks again to Franz Weissing, who suggested this symmetric version of the contract-enforcement game. I had originally modeled Game 5 giving one herder the right to offer a contract, and the second herder only the right to agree or not agree to it.

14 See the interesting paper by Okada and Kleimt (1990), in which they model a three-player contract-enforcement game using the rule that any two (or three) persons who agree can set up their own contract to be enforced by an external agent. They conclude that three persons will not make use of a costless enforcement process, whereas two may. The article helps to illustrate how very subtle changes in conditions make important differences in results.

15 Williamson (1983) argues, however, that the numbers of actual unresolved PD situations in long-term business relationships have been exaggerated because economists have overlooked the contracts that businesses negotiate to change the structure of incentives related to long-term contracts.

16 Much of the literature in the new institutional economics tradition has stressed the importance of private orderings in the governance of long-term private contracts (Galanter 1981; Williamson 1979, 1985).

17 When considerable competition exists among arbitrators for the job of monitoring and enforcing, one can assume that arbiters are strongly motivated to make fair decisions. If there is no competition, then one faces the same problem in presuming fair decisions as one does in relation to a public bureau with monopoly status.

18 Simply iterating the PD game is not a guaranteed way out of the dilemma. The famous "folk theorem" that cooperation is a possible perfect equilibrium outcome is sometimes misrepresented as asserting that cooperation is the only equilibrium in repeated games. In addition to the "all cooperate at every iteration" equilibrium, many other equilibria are also possible. Simple repetition without enforceable agreements does not produce a clear result (Güth, Leininger, and Stephan 1990).

19 Private orderings frequently are mistaken for *no* order, given the absence of an official formal legislative or court decision. See Galanter (1981) for a review of the extensive literature on private orderings.

20 The formal game-theoretical structures and outcomes of this and three other sets of rules for allocating fishing sites are analyzed by Gardner and E. Ostrom (1990).

21 See, for example, the cases contained in National Research Council (1986), McCay and Acheson (1987), Fortmann and Bruce (1988), Berkes (1989), Pinkerton (1989a), Ruddle and Akimichi (1984), Coward (1980), and Uphoff (1986c). In addition to these collections, see citations in F. Martin (1989) for the extensive literature contained in books, monographs, articles, and research reports. There are also common-property institutions that break down when challenged by very rapid population growth or changes in the market value of the products harvested from the CPR. As discussed in Chapter 5, however, fragility of common-property systems is much more likely when these systems are not recognized by the formal political regimes of which they are a part.

22 That the "remorseless logic" was built into Hardin's assumptions, rather than being an empirical result, was pointed out by Stillman (1975, p. 14): "But the search for a solution cannot be found within the parameters of the problem. Rather, the resolution can only be found by changing one or more of the parameters of the problem, by cutting the Gordian knot rather than untying it."

23 See Shepsle (1979a, 1989a), Shepsle and Weingast (1987), Williamson (1979, 1985), North and Weingast (1989), and North (1981).

24 One can search the development literature long and hard, for example, without finding much discussion of the importance of court systems in helping individuals to organize themselves for development. The first time that I mentioned to a group of AID officials the importance of having an effective court system as an intervention strategy to achieve development, there was stunned silence in the room. One official noted that in two decades of development work she had never heard of such a recommendation being made.

References

Arnold, J. E. M., and J. G. Campbell. 1986. Collective Management of Hill Forests in Nepal: The Community Forestry Development Project. In *Proceedings of the Conference on Common Property Resource Management*, National Research Council, pp. 425–54. Washington, D.C.: National Academy Press.

Axelrod, R. 1981. The Emergence of Cooperation Among Egoists. *American Political Science Review* 75:306–18.

Axelrod, R. 1984. *The Evolution of Cooperation*. New York: Basic Books.

Bentley, A. 1949. *The Process of Government*. Evanston, Ill.: Principia Press.

Berkes, F. 1986b. Marine Inshore Fishery Management in Turkey. In *Proceedings of the Conference on Common Property Resource Management*, National Research Council, pp. 63–83. Washington, D.C.: National Academy Press.

Berkes, F. 1987. Common Property Resource Management and Cree Indian Fisheries in Subarctic Canada. In *The Question of the Commons*, eds. B. McCay and J. Acheson, pp. 66–91. Tucson: University of Arizona Press.

Berkes, F., ed. 1989. *Common Property Resources. Ecology and Community-Based Sustainable Development*. London: Belhaven Press.

Berkes, F., and M. Kislalioglu. 1989. A Comparative Study of Yield, Investment and Energy Use in Small-Scale Fisheries: Some Considerations for Resource Planning. *Fisheries Research* 7:207–24.

Berkes, F., and D. Pocock. 1981. Self-Regulation of Commercial Fisheries of the Outer Long Point Bay, Lake Erie. *Journal of Great Lakes Research* 7:111–16.

Binger, B. R., and E. Hoffman. 1989. Institutional Persistence and Change: The Question of Efficiency. *Journal of Institutional and Theoretical Economics* 145:67–84.

Buchanan, J. M. 1968. *The Demand and Supply of Public Goods.* Chicago: Rand McNally.

Bullock, K., and J. Baden. 1977. Communes and the Logic of the Commons. In *Managing the Commons,* eds. G. Hardin and J. Baden, pp. 182–99. San Francisco: Freeman.

Campbell, R. 1985. Background for the Uninitiated. In *Paradoxes of Rationality and Cooperation,* eds. R. Campbell and L. Sowden, pp. 3–41. Vancouver: University of British Columbia Press.

Carruthers, I., and R. Stoner. 1981. Economic Aspects and Policy Issues in Groundwater Development. World Bank staff working paper No. 496, Washington, D.C.

Chamberlin, J. 1974. Provision of Collective Goods as a Function of Group Size. *American Political Science Review* 68:707–16.

Christy, F. T., Jr. 1982. Territorial Use Rights in Marine Fisheries: Definitions and Conditions. FAO technical paper No. 227, Food and Agricultural Organization of the United Nations, Rome.

Clark, C. W. 1976. *Mathematical Bioeconomics.* New York: Wiley.

Clark, C. W. 1977. The Economics of Over-exploitation. In *Managing the Commons,* eds. G. Hardin and J. Baden, pp. 82–95. San Francisco: Freeman.

Clark, C. W. 1980. Restricted Access to Common-Property Fishery Resources: A Game-Theoretic Analysis. In *Dynamic Optimization and Mathematical Economics,* ed. P. T. Liu, pp. 117–32. New York: Plenum Press.

Cordell, J. C., and M. A. McKean. 1986. Sea Tenure in Bahia, Brazil. In *Proceedings of the Conference on Common Property Resource Management,* National Research Council, pp. 85–113. Washington, D.C.: National Academy Press.

Coward, E. W., Jr. 1980. *Irrigation and Agricultural Development in Asia: Perspectives from Social Sciences.* Ithaca, N.Y.: Cornell University Press.

Cruz, W. 1986. Overfishing and Conflict in a Traditional Fishery: San Miguel Bay, Philippines. In *Proceedings of the Conference on Common Property Resource Management,* National Research Council, pp. 115–35. Washington, D.C.: National Academy Press.

Dales, J. H. 1968. *Pollution, Property, and Prices: An Essay in Policy-making and Economics.* University of Toronto Press.

Dasgupta, P. S. 1982. *The Control of Resources.* Oxford: Blackwell.

Dasgupta, P. S., and G. M. Heal. 1979. *Economic Theory and Exhaustible Resources.* Cambridge University Press.

Davis, A. 1984. Property Rights and Access Management in the Small-Boat Fishery: A Case Study from Southwest Nova Scotia. In *Atlantic Fisheries and Coastal Communities: Fisheries Decision-Making Case Studies,* eds. C. Lamson and A. J. Hanson, pp. 133–64. Halifax: Dalhousie Ocean Studies Programme.

Dawes, R. M. 1973. The Commons Dilemma Game: An *N*-Person Mixed-Motive Game with a Dominating Strategy for Defection. *ORI Research Bulletin* 13:112.

Dawes, R. M. 1975. Formal Models of Dilemmas in Social Decision Making. In *Human Judgment and Decision Processes: Formal and Mathematical Approaches,* eds. M. F. Kaplan and S. Schwartz, pp. 87–108. New York: Academic Press.

De Alessi, L. 1980. The Economics of Property Rights: A Review of the Evidence. *Research in Law and Economics* 2:1–47.

Demsetz, H. 1967. Toward a Theory of Property Rights. *American Economic Review* 62:347–59.

Ehrenfield, D. W. 1972. *Conserving Life on Earth.* Oxford University Press.

Feeny, D. H. 1988a. Agricultural Expansion and Forest Depletion in Thailand, 1900–1975. In *World Deforestation in the Twentieth Century*, eds. J. F. Richards and R. P. Tucker, pp. 112–43. Durham, N.C.: Duke University Press.

Field, B. C. 1984. The Evolution of Individual Property Rights in Massachusetts Agriculture, 17th–19th Centuries. *Northeastern Journal of Agricultural and Resource Economics* 14:97–109.

Field, B. C 1985b. The Optimal Commons. *American Journal of Agricultural Economics* 67:364–7.

Forman, S. O. 1967. Cognition and the Catch: The Location of Fishing Spots in a Brazilian Coastal Village. *Ethnology* 6:405–26.

Fortmann, L., and J. W. Bruce, eds. 1988. *Whose Trees? Proprietary Dimensions of Forestry.* Boulder: Westview Press.

Frohlich, N., and J. A. Oppenheimer. 1970. I Get By with a Little Help from My Friends. *World Politics* 23:104–20.

Gadgil, M., and P. Iyer. 1989. On the Diversification of Common-Property Resource Use by Indian Society. In *Common Property Resources,* ed. F. Berkes, pp. 240–72. London: Belhaven Press.

Galanter, M. 1981. Justice in Many Rooms: Courts, Private Ordering, and Indigenous Law. *Journal of Legal Pluralism* 19:1–47.

Gardner, R., and E. Ostrom. 1990. Rules and Games. *Public Choice.*

Godwin, R. K., and W. B. Shepard. 1979. Forcing Squares, Triangles and Ellipses into a Circular Paradigm: The Use of the Commons Dilemma in Examining the Allocation of Common Resources. *Western Political Quarterly* 32:265–77.

Gordon, H. S. 1954. The Economic Theory of a Common-Property Resource: The Fishery. *Journal of Political Economy* 62:124–42.

Grofman, B., and J. Pool. 1975. Bayesian Models for Iterated Prisoner's Dilemma Games. *General Systems* 20:185–94.

Güth, W., W. Leininger, and G. Stephan. 1990. On Supergames and Folk Theorems: A Conceptual Discussion. In *Game Equilibrium Models, Vol. 2: Methods, Morals, and Markets,* ed. R Selten. Berlin: Springer-Verlag.

Hardin, G. 1968. The Tragedy of the Commons. *Science* 162:1243–8.

Hardin, G. 1978. Political Requirements for Preserving our Common Heritage. In *Wildlife and America,* ed. H. P. Bokaw, pp. 310–17. Washington, D.C.: Council on Environmental Quality.

Hardin, R. 1982. *Collective Action.* Baltimore: Johns Hopkins University Press.

Harsanyi, J., and R. Selten. 1988. *A General Theory of Equilibrium Selection in Games.* Cambridge, Mass.: MIT Press.

Heilbroner, R. L. 1974. *An Inquiry Into the Human Prospect.* New York: Norton.

Johnson, O. E. G. 1972. Economic Analysis, the Legal Framework and Land Tenure Systems. *Journal of Law and Economics* 15:259–76.

Kimber, R. 1981. Collective Action and the Fallacy of the Liberal Fallacy. *World Politics* 33:178–96.

Koestler, A. R. 1959. *The Sleepwalkers.* New York: Macmillan.

Kreps, D. M., and R. Wilson. 1982. Reputation and Imperfect Information. *Journal of Economic Theory* 27:253–79.

Lloyd, W. F. 1977. On the Checks to Population. In *Managing the Commons,* eds. G. Hardin and J. Baden, pp. 8–15. San Francisco: Freeman.

Luce, D. R., and H. Raiffa. 1957. *Games and Decisions: Introduction and Critical Survey.* New York: Wiley.

Lumsden, M. 1973. The Cyprus Conflict as a Prisoner's Dilemma. *Journal of Conflict Resolution* 17: 7–32.

McCay, B. J., and J. M. Acheson. 1987. *The Question of the Commons: The Culture and Ecology of Communal Resources.* Tucson: University of Arizona Press.

McGuire, M. 1974. Group Segregation and Optimal Jurisdictions. *Journal of Political Economy* 82:112–32.

McKelvey, R. D. 1976. Intransitivities in Multidimensional Voting Models and Some Implications for Agenda Control. *Journal of Economic Theory* 2:472–82.

McKelvey, R. D. 1979. General Conditions for Global intransitivities in Formal Voting Models. *Econometrics* 47:1085–111.

Martin, F. 1989. *Common Pool Resources and Collective Action: A Bibliography.* Bloomington: Indiana University, Workshop in Political Theory and Policy Analysis.

Martin, K. O. 1979. Play by the Rules or Don't Play at All: Space Division and Resource Allocation in a Rural Newfoundland Fishing Community. In *North Atlantic Maritime Cultures: Anthropological Essays on Changing Adaptations,* eds. R. Andersen and C. Wadel, pp. 277–98. The Hague: Mouton.

Matthews, R. 1988. Federal Licensing Policies for the Atlantic Inshore Fishery and Their Implementation in Newfoundland, 1973–1981. *Acadiensis: Journal of the History of the Atlantic Region* 17:83–108.

Matthews, R., and J. Phyne. 1988. Regulating the Newfoundland Inshore Fishery: Traditional Values versus State Control in the Regulation of a Common Property Resource. *Journal of Canadian Studies* 23:158–76.

Messerschmidt, D. A. 1986. Collective Management of Hill Forests in Nepal: The Community Forestry Development Project. In *Proceedings of the Conference on Common Property Resource Management,* National Research Council, pp. 455–80. Washington, D.C.: National Academy Press.

Moore, J. A. 1985. Science as a Way of Knowing-Human Ecology. *American Zoologist* 25:483–637.

National Research Council. 1986. *Proceedings of the Conference on Common Property Resource Management.* Washington, D.C.: National Academy Press.

Nebel, B. J. 1987. *Environmental Science,* 2nd ed. Englewood Cliffs, N.J.: Prentice-Hall.

Neher, P. A. 1978. The Pure Theory of the Muggery. *American Economic Review* 68:437–45.

Norman, C. 1984. No Panacea for the Firewood Crisis. *Science* 226:676.

North, D. C. 1981. *Structure and Change in Economic History.* New York: Norton.

North, D. C., and B. R. Weingast. 1989. Constitutions and Commitment: The Evolution of Institutions Governing Public Choice in 17th Century England. St. Louis: Washington University, Center in Political Economy.

Okada, A., and H. Kleimt. 1990. Anarchy and Agreement – A Game Theoretical Analysis of Some Aspects of Contractarianism. In *Game Equilibrium Models. Vol. II: Methods, Morals, and Markets,* ed. R. Selten. Berlin: Springer-Verlag.

Olson, M. 1965. *The Logic of Collective Action. Public Goods and the Theory of Groups.* Cambridge, Mass.: Harvard University Press.

Ophuls, W. 1973. Leviathan or Oblivion. In *Toward a Steady State Economy,* ed. H. E. Daly, pp. 215–30. San Francisco: Freeman.

Orr, D. S., and S. Hill. 1979. Leviathan, the Open Society, and the Crisis of Ecology. In *The Global Predicament. Ecological Perspectives on World Order,* eds. D. W. Orr and M. S. Soros, pp. 457–69. Chapel Hill: University of North Carolina Press.

Panayoutou, T. 1982. Management Concepts for Small-Scale Fisheries: Economic and Social Aspects. FAO Fisheries Technical Paper No. 228, Rome.

Picardi, A. C., and W. W. Seifert. 1977. A Tragedy of the Commons in the Sahel. *Ekistics* 43:297–304.

Pinkerton, E., ed. 1989a. *Co-operative Management of Local Fisheries. New Directions for Improved Management and Community Development.* Vancouver: University of British Columbia Press.

Pinkerton, E. 1989b. Competition Among B.C. Fish Processing Firms. In *Uncommon Property: The Fishing and Fish Processing Industries in British Columbia,* eds. P. Marshak, N. Guppy, and J. McMullan, pp. 66–91. Toronto: Methuen.

Riker, W. H. 1980. Implications for the Disequilibrium of Majority Rule for the Study of Institutions. *American Political Science Review* 74:432–47.

Ruddle, K., and T. Akimichi, eds. 1984. *Maritime Institutions in the Western Pacific.* Osaka: National Museum of Ethnology.

Scharpf, F. W. 1985. Ideological Conflict on the Public–Private Frontier: Some Exploratory Notes. Working paper, Wissenschftszentrum, Berlin.

Scharpf, F. W. 1987. A Game-Theoretical Explanation of Inflation and Unemployment in Western Europe. *Journal of Public Policy* 7:227–58.

Scharpf, F. W. 1988. The Joint Decision Trap: Lessons from German Federalism and European Integration. *Public Administration* 66:239–78.

Shepsle, K. A. 1979a. Institutional Arrangements and Equilibrium in Multidimensional Voting Models. *American Journal of Political Science* 23:27–60.

Shepsle, K. A. 1989a. Discretion, Institutions, and the Problem of Government Commitment. Working paper, Cambridge, Mass.: Harvard University, Department of Government.

Shepsle, K. A., and B. R. Weingast. 1984. Legislative Politics and Budget Outcomes. In *Federal Budget Policy in the 1980's,* eds. G. Mills and J. Palmer, pp. 343–67. Washington, D.C.: Urban Institute Press.

Shepsle, K. A., and B. R. Weingast. 1987. The Institutional Foundations of Committee Power. *American Political Science* 81:85–104.

Sinn, H. W. 1984. Common Property Resources, Storage Facilities and Ownership Structures: A Cournot Model of the Oil Market. *Economica* 51:235–52.

Smith, R. J. 1981. Resolving the Tragedy of the Commons by Creating Private Property Rights in Wildlife. *CATO Journal* 1:439–68.

Snidal, D. 1985. Coordination Versus Prisoner's Dilemma: Implications for International Cooperation and Regimes. *American Political Science Review* 79:923–47.

Stillman, P. G. 1975. The Tragedy of the Commons: A Re-Analysis. *Alternatives* 4:12–45.

Sugden, R. 1986. *The Economics of Rights, Co-operation, and Welfare.* Oxford: Blackwell.

Taylor, M. 1987. *The Possibility of Cooperation.* Cambridge University Press.

Thomson, J. T. 1977. Ecological Deterioration: Local-Level Rule Making and Enforcement Problems in Niger. In *Desertification: Environmental Degradation in and around Arid Lands,* ed. M. H. Glantz, pp. 57–79. Boulder: Westview Press.

Thomson, J. T., D. Feeny, and R. J. Oakerson. 1986. Institutional Dynamics: The Evolution and Dissolution of Common Property Resource Management. In *Proceedings of the Conference on Common Property Resource Management,* National Research Council, pp. 391–424. Washington, D.C.: National Academy Press.

Truman, D. B. 1958. *The Governmental Process.* New York: Knopf.

Uphoff, N. T. 1986c. *Getting the Process Right: Improving Irrigation Water Management with Farmer Participation.* Boulder: Westview Press.

Welch, W. P. 1983. The Political Feasibility of Full Ownership Property Rights: The Cases of Pollution and Fisheries. *Policy Sciences* 16:165–80.

Williamson, O. E. 1979. Transaction Cost Economics: The Governance of Contractual Relations. *Journal of Law and Economics* 22:233–61.

Williamson, O. E. 1983. Credible Commitments: Using Hostages to Support Exchange. *American Economic Review* 83:519–40.

Williamson, O. E. 1985. *The Economic Institutions of Capitalism: Firms, Markets, Relational Contracting.* New York: Free Press.

Wilson, R. K. 1985. Constraints on Social Dilemmas: An Institutional Approach. *Annals of Operations Research* 2:183–200.

5

Historical Perspectives

Historians tend to reject monocausal accounts and their explanations of events and outcomes are usually more richly descriptive than economic, sociological, or political science approaches. They also look further back in time for contributing patterns and events to explain how different phenomena arise. Historical perspectives on industrialization thus richly interweave elements that other paradigms focus on in narratives that build over time. The trade-offs to this approach are that historical explanations can seem eclectic and some may seem too particular to one specific instance of a more generalizable phenomenon.

Economic historians often examine advanced country industrialization to generate theories of economic development. We have already encountered a major economic historian in Karl Marx, who used his analysis of the history of British industrialization to lay out a sequence of stages that all political economies would pass through, driven by the economic mode of production as the engine of change. The British Industrial Revolution was a phenomenon of economic, technological, and social transformation that took place through a capitalist political–economic system. It occurred gradually from about 1760 to 1830, over a longer period of time in comparison to later industrializers, and built on two centuries of preceding economic development. It was rooted in light industries, such as textiles and rural crafts. Capital accumulation for industrial investment came from Britain's extensive trade ties, a benefit of its extractive colonial empire and also of its standing as the premier trading nation of the era. As the nation that industrialized first with no blueprint or technology to copy from another nation and no technology gap to overcome, Britain is the only pure case of early industrialization. Industrial development in later industrializers, unlike Britain, relied on advanced technology, focused on heavy industry, and was more rapid and eruptive in nature.

The British economic historian **Eric Hobsbawm** was a lifelong Marxist. Like Marx, Hobsbawm's work focused on the Industrial Revolution and was rooted in the perspective that economic and technological forces structurally shape human progress.

Yet voluntarist political forces also play a central role in Hobsbawm's history of the British Industrial Revolution because that enormous economic transformation was intimately connected to British imperialism. The history of British industrialization, Hobsbawm reminds us, is the first instance of what became the more general pattern of industrialization under capitalism – although he is clear that it does not serve as a model for later economic development.

In the selection presented here, Hobsbawm asks why Britain became the first industrializer and what explains the timing of this transformation at the end of the eighteenth century. Echoing Adam Smith's depiction of the same period, Hobsbawm argues that three elements were essential for Britain to industrialize: intertwined economic and social conditions were in place, early industrialization was simple enough in form not to require dramatic investments, and the British economy was relatively advanced. Given that these doorstep conditions were in place, what ignited the Industrial Revolution? Echoing Smith and Marx, Hobsbawm argues that specific domestic and international market features at the time were essential to encourage entrepreneurs to innovate in the search for profits instead of favoring profits at the expense of innovation. And, like Polanyi, Hobsbawm notes that the state was also crucial, emphasizing the importance of public investments in national transport infrastructure. Government was essential, too, because the British Crown was willing to wage war and colonize large parts of the world for the benefit of British manufacturers. In turn, the British Navy generated demand for technological innovation and heavy industrialization. Hobsbawm's analysis of the underpinnings and timing of the British Industrial Revolution ultimately reflects Vladimir Lenin's thesis that colonialism and capitalist industrialization evolved hand in hand.[1]

While Hobsbawm focused on the first industrializer, **Alexander Gerschenkron**'s historical analysis of industrialization is a comparative explanation of differences in the experiences of late industrializers. He delivers a direct counterpoint to the linear logic of industrialization posited by Marx and post-World War Two modernization theorists, who established the generalization that the history of advanced industrial countries maps out the trajectory for less-developed countries.[2] Gerschenkron's core insight is that the development of a "backward" country can, because of its very backwardness, differ fundamentally from that of a more advanced country. He demonstrates that countries experience different paths of growth depending on timing and environment, thereby building a framework that can account for key differences among political–economic systems today.

Gerschenkron emphasizes that the process of capital accumulation is central in overcoming the technological gap necessary for industrialization. In turn, how and when capital is mobilized and accumulated in different countries sets out varied paths to industrialization. Thus, although industrialization broadly looks the same everywhere, its institutional characteristics vary across countries, a central tenet of the market-institutional perspective. Gerschenkron provides a historical analysis of industrialization in the original group of late industrializers – France, Germany, and Russia – as well as a manual for future industrializers. Captured in his famous phrase "the magnitude of the challenge changes the *quality* of the response" is the idea that countries accumulate the capital necessary for industrialization through different sets of institutional and ideological solutions with varying degrees of state involvement. In turn, the nature of industrialization changes, becoming faster and more burst-like in the later industrializers.

Gerschenkron's argument is institutionalist at its core: institutions emerge to mobilize the capital necessary for industrialization. While he does not unpack the politics of why these institutional solutions come about, Gerschenkron provides well-defined conceptions of the role of institutions and government in industrialization. Countries are able to imitate earlier industrializers to accumulate capital and furthermore improve on the necessary institutional innovation given their own circumstances. Late industrializers can self-consciously emulate or innovate on institutional design in order to pass through the capital accumulation phase necessary for industrial development and enter into industrialization through more technologically advanced and capital-intensive sectors. From this viewpoint, economic backwardness is actually an unexpected advantage that offers leapfrogging potential. Although capital accumulation in Britain had been gradual and rested in the hands of merchants and private firms, the *crédit mobilier* or industrial bank system evolved in France to mobilize capital. German universal banks then adapted the best of French industrial banks and British commercial banks for the purpose of capital accumulation. Finally, in Russia, even stronger institutional innovation was necessary to overcome the more extreme scarcity of capital, so the state played a role in accumulating capital through a militarized state and centralized bureaucracy.[3]

Furthermore, these initial institutional substitutions were not neutral but persisted through time with path-dependent consequences. From Gerschenkron we learn the market-institutional lesson that differences in the history of industrialization shape political–economic trajectories and have a lasting subsequent impact on the varieties of political–economic systems in the world today. In the German case, for example, the universal banks established long-term and interdependent relationships with industrial enterprises, exerting corporate leverage beyond just financial control. The German political economy today continues to exhibit this close interdependence between the financial system and private firms, although it is now a more coequal relationship (see Peter Hall and David Soskice, this volume).

Gerschenkron views institutional substitution and the social ideologies of industrialization as interlinked in the pursuit of economic development. He points out that socialist ideas cloaked decidedly capitalist practices in France, and he mentions the nationalist sentiment of Friedrich List as central to the ideology of industrialization in Germany. Finally, the extreme backwardness of Russia required the powerful ideology of orthodox Marxism, which portrayed capitalist industrialization as an inexorable stage of history along the path to communism. Contemporary political–economic ideology continues to vary across states, providing a range of rationales for the institutional responses necessary to overcome economic backwardness. Gerschenkron anticipated that his historical analysis could be used to justify countries' varying institutional and ideological approaches to industrialization, replacing dogmatic notions of right and wrong practice when it comes to markets or industrialization. This is an insight that today's developing countries have since used in making the case for straying from the path of neoliberal economic orthodoxy, particularly in terms of justifying state intervention in the economy.

Notes

1 Vladimir I. Lenin, *Imperialism: The Highest State of Capitalism* (1917).
2 While they rejected the Marxist warning that the capitalist mode of production inexorably contained the seeds of its own destruction, modernization theorists followed Marx's unilinear and teleological logic in applying the Western European and American advanced country model of modernization and economic development as a template to all newly modernizing countries. See, for example, Seymour Martin Lipset, *Political Man: The Social Bases of Politics* (New York: Doubleday, 1959); and Walt Whitman Rostow, *The Stages of Economic Growth: A Non-Communist Manifesto* (Cambridge: Cambridge University Press, 1960).
3 The Russian case illustrates the potentially troubling message, since revisited by even later developers such as the East Asian newly industrializing countries, that rapid industrial transformation may be made more possible by imposing limits on democracy. See Chalmers Johnson, "Political Institutions and Economic Performance: The Government–Business Relationship in Japan, South Korea, and Taiwan," in Frederic C. Deyo, ed., *The Political Economy of the New Asian Industrialism* (Ithaca, NY: Cornell University Press, 1987), 136–47.

E.J. Hobsbawm,
Industry and Empire (1968)[*]

2. Origin of the Industrial Revolution[1]

The problem of the origin of the Industrial Revolution is not an easy one, but it is made even more difficult if we fail to clarify it. So it is as well to begin with a little clarification.

First, the Industrial Revolution is not merely an acceleration of economic growth, but an acceleration of growth because of, and through, economic and social transformation. The early observers, who concentrated their attention on the qualitatively new ways of producing – the machines, the factory system and the rest – had the right instinct, though they sometimes followed it too uncritically. It was not Birmingham, a city which produced a great deal more in 1850 than in 1750, but essentially in the old way, which made contemporaries speak of an industrial revolution, but Manchester, a city which produced more in a more obviously revolutionary manner. In the late eighteenth century this economic and social transformation took place in and through a capitalist economy. As we know from the twentieth century, this is not the only form industrial revolution can take, though it was the earliest and probably, in the eighteenth century, the only practicable one. Capitalist industrialization requires in some ways a rather different analysis from non-capitalist, because we must explain why the pursuit of private profit led to technological transformation, and it is by no means obvious that it automatically does so. In other ways, doubtless, capitalist industrialization can be treated as a special case of a more general phenomenon, but it is not clear to what extent this is helpful to the historian of the British Industrial Revolution.

Second, the British revolution was the first in history. This does not mean that it started from zero, or that earlier phases of rapid industrial and technological development cannot be found. Nevertheless, none of these initiated the characteristic modern phase of history, self-sustained economic growth by means of perpetual technological revolution and social transformation. Being the first, it is therefore also in crucial respects unlike all subsequent industrial revolutions. It cannot be explained primarily, or to any extent, in terms of outside factors such as – for instance – the imitation of more advanced techniques, the import of capital, the impact of an already industrialized world economy. Subsequent revolutions could use the British experience, example and resources. Britain could use those of other countries only to a very limited and minor extent. At the same time, as we have seen, the British revolution was preceded by at least two hundred years of fairly continuous economic development which laid its foundations. Unlike, say, nineteenth- or twentieth- century Russia, Britain entered industrialization prepared and not virtually unprepared.

However, the Industrial Revolution cannot be explained in purely British terms, for this country formed part of a wider economy, which we may call the 'European economy' or the 'world economy of the European maritime states'. It was part of a larger network of economic relationships, which included several 'advanced' areas, some of which were also areas of potential or aspiring industrialization, and areas of 'dependent economy', as well as the margins of foreign economies not yet substantially involved with Europe. These dependent economies consisted partly of formal colonies (as in the Americas) or points of trade and domination (as in the Orient), partly of region which were to some extent economically specialized in response to the demands of the 'advanced' areas (as in some parts of eastern Europe). The 'advanced' world was linked to the dependent world by a certain division of economic activity: a relatively urbanized area on one hand, zones producing and largely exporting agricultural products or raw materials on the other. These relations may be described as a system of economic flows – of trade, of international payments, of capital transfers, of migration, etc. The 'European economy' had shown marked signs of expansion and dynamic development for several centuries, though it had also experienced major economic setbacks or shifts, notably in the fourteenth to fifteenth and seventeenth centuries.

Nevertheless it is important to observe that it also tended to be divided, at least from the sixteenth century, into independent and competing politico-economic units (territorial 'states') like Britain and France, each with its own economic and social structure, and containing within itself advanced and backward or dependent sectors and regions. By the sixteenth century it was fairly obvious that, if industrial revolution occurred anywhere in the world, it would be somewhere within the European economy. Why this was so cannot be discussed here, for the question belongs to an earlier era of history than the one with which this book is concerned. However it was not clear which of the competing units would turn out to be the first to industrialize. The problem of the origins of the Industrial Revolution which concerns us here is essentially, why it was Britain which became the first 'workshop of the world'. A second and connected question is why this breakthrough occurred towards the end of the eighteenth century and not before or after.

Before setting about the answer (which remains a matter of debate and uncertainty), it may be useful to eliminate a number of explanations or pseudo-explanations which have long been current, and are still sometimes maintained. Most of them leave more unexplained than they elucidate.

This is true of theories which attempt to account for the Industrial Revolution in terms of climate, geography, biological change in the population or other exogenous factors. If (as has been held) the stimulus for the revolution came from, say, the unusually long period of good harvests in the earlier eighteenth century, then we have to explain why similar periods before this date (and they have occurred from time to time throughout history) had not similar consequences. If Britain's ample reserves of coal explain her priority, then we may well wonder why her comparatively scant natural supplies of most other industrial raw materials (e.g. iron ore) did not hamper her just as much or alternatively why the great Silesian coalfields did not produce an equally early industrial start. If the moist climate of Lancashire is to explain the concentration of the cotton industry there, then we ought to ask why the many other equally damp regions of the British isles did not also attract or hold it. And so on. Climatic factors, geography, the distribution of natural resources operate not on their own, but only within a given economic, social and institutional framework. This is true even of the strongest of such factors, ease of access to the sea or to good rivers, i.e. to the cheapest and most practicable – indeed for bulk goods the only economic form of transport in the pre-industrial age. It is almost inconceivable that a totally landlocked region should have pioneered the modern Industrial Revolution; though such regions are rarer than one thinks. Nevertheless, even here non-geographic factors must not be neglected: the Hebrides have more access to the sea than most of Yorkshire.

The problem of population is somewhat different, for its movements may be explained by exogenous factors, by the changes in human society, or by a combination of both. We shall consider it further below. At present we need note merely that purely exogenous explanations are not at present widely held by historians, and are not accepted in this book.

Explanations of the Industrial Revolution by 'historic accidents' ought also to be rejected. The mere fact of overseas discovery in the fifteenth and sixteenth centuries does not account for industrialization, and neither does the 'scientific revolution' of the seventeenth.[*] Neither can explain why the Industrial Revolution occurred at the end of the eighteenth century and not, let us say, at the end of the seventeenth, when both the European knowledge of the outer world and scientific technology were potentially quite adequate for the sort of industrialization which developed eventually. Nor can the Protestant Reformation be made responsible for it, either directly or via some special 'capitalist spirit' or other change of economic attitude induced by Protestantism; not even for why it occurred in Britain and not in France. The Reformation occurred more than two centuries before the Industrial Revolution. By no means all areas which converted to Protestantism became pioneers of industrial revolution, and – to take an obvious example – the parts of the Netherlands which remained Catholic (Belgium) industrialized before the part which became Protestant (Holland).[†]

Lastly, purely political factors must also be rejected. In the second half of the eighteenth century practically all governments in Europe wanted to industrialize, but only the British succeeded. Conversely, British governments from 1660 on were firmly committed to policies favouring the pursuit of profit above other aims, but the Industrial Revolution did not occur until more than a century later.

To reject such factors as simple, exclusive, or even primary explanations is not, of course, to deny them *any* importance. That would be foolish. It is merely to establish relative scales of importance, and incidentally to clarify some of the problems of countries setting about their industrialization today, in so far as they are comparable.

The main preconditions for industrialization were already present in eighteenth-century Britain, or could be easily brought into being. By the standards generally applied to 'underdeveloped' countries today, England was not underdeveloped,

---

[*] It is irrelevant for our purposes, whether these things were purely fortuitous or (as is much more likely) the outcome of earlier European economic and social developments.

[†] Moreover, the theory that French economic development in the eighteenth century was crippled by the expulsion of the Protestants at the end of the seventeenth, is not now widely accepted, or is, at the very least, highly debatable.

though parts of Scotland and Wales were, and Ireland certainly was. The economic, social and ideological links which immobilize most pre-industrial people in traditional situations and occupations were already weak, and could be easily severed. To take the most obvious example, by 1750 it is as we have seen already doubtful whether we can any longer speak of a landholding peasantry in large parts of England, and it is certain that we can no longer speak of subsistence agriculture.* Hence there were no major obstacles to the transfer of men from non-industrial to industrial pursuits. The country had accumulated and was accumulating a surplus of sufficient size to permit investment in the necessary, but before the railways not very costly, equipment for economic transformation. Enough of it was concentrated in the hands of men willing to invest in economic progress, while relatively little was in the hands of men likely to divert resources to alternative (and economically less desirable) uses, such as mere display. There was neither a relative nor an absolute shortage of capital. The country was not merely a market economy – i.e. one in which the bulk of goods and services outside the family are bought and sold – but in many respects it formed a single national market. And it possessed an extensive and fairly highly developed manufacturing sector and an even more highly developed commerical apparatus.

What is more, problems which are acute in modern underdeveloped countries setting about their industrialization were mild in eighteenth-century Britain. As we have seen, transport and communications were comparatively easy and cheap, since no part of Britain is further than seventy miles from the sea, and even less from some navigable waterway. The technological problems of the early Industrial Revolution were fairly simple. They required no class of men with specialized scientific qualifications, but merely a sufficiency of men with ordinary literacy, familiarity with simple mechanical devices and the working of metals, practical experience and initiative. The centuries since 1500 had certainty provided such a supply. Most of the new technical inventions and productive establishments could be started economically on a small scale, and expanded piecemeal by successive addition. That is to say, they required little initial investment, and their expansion could be financed out of accumulated profits. Industrial development was within the capacities of a multiplicity of small entrepreneurs and skilled traditional artisans. No twentieth-century country setting about industrialization has, or can have, anything like these advantages.

This does not mean that there were no obstacles in the path of British industrialization, but only that they were easy to overcome because the fundamental social and economic conditions for it already existed, because the eighteenth-century type of industrialization was comparatively cheap and simple, and because the country was sufficiently wealthy and flourishing to be untroubled by inefficiencies which might have crippled less fortunate economies. Perhaps only so lucky an industrial power as this could have ever afforded that distrust of logic and planning (even private planning), that faith in the capacity to muddle through, which became so characteristic of Britain in the nineteenth century. We shall see below how some of the difficulties of growth were overcome. The important thing to note at the outset is that they were never crucial.

---

* When early nineteenth-century writers talked of 'the peasantry', they tended to mean 'the farm-labourers'.

The question about the origin of the Industrial Revolution which concerns us here is not, therefore, how the material for the economic explosion was accumulated, but how it was ignited; and we may add, what stopped the first explosion from fizzling out after an impressive initial bang. But was a special mechanism necessary at all? Was it not inevitable that a sufficiently long period of accumulating explosive material would, sooner or later, somehow, somewhere, produce spontaneous combustion? Perhaps so. Nevertheless it is the 'somehow' and 'somewhere' which must be explained; all the more so as the way in which an economy of private enterprise brings about industrial revolution raises a number of puzzles. We know that in fact it did so in some parts of the world; but we also know that it failed to do so in other parts, and took a rather long time doing so even in western Europe.

The puzzle lies in the relationship between making profit and technological innovation. It is often assumed that an economy of private enterprise has an automatic bias towards innovation, but this is not so. It has a bias only towards profit. It will revolutionize manufactures only if greater profits are to be made in this way than otherwise. But in pre-industrial societies this is hardly ever the case. The available and prospective market – and it is the market which determines what a businessman produces – consists of the rich, who require luxury goods in small quantities, but with a high profit margin per sale, and the poor, who – if they are in the market economy at all, and do not produce their own consumer goods domestically or locally – have little money, are unaccustomed to novelties and suspicious of them, unwilling to consume standardized products and may not even be concentrated in cities or accessible to national manufacturers. What is more, the mass market is not likely to grow very much more rapidly than the relatively slow rate of population increase. It will make more sense to dress princesses in *haute couture* models than to speculate on the chances of capturing peasants' daughters for artificial silk stockings. The sound businessman, if he has any choice, will produce very expensive jewelled timepieces for aristocrats rather than cheap wrist-watches, and the more expensive the process of launching revolutionary cheap goods, the more he will hesitate to risk his money in it. A French millionaire in the mid-nineteenth century, operating in a country in which the conditions for modern industrialism were relatively poor, expressed this admirably. 'There are three ways of losing your money,' said the great Rothschild, 'women, gambling and engineers. The first two are pleasanter, but the last is much the most certain.'[2] Nobody could accuse a Rothschild of not knowing the best way to the biggest profits. In a non-industrialized country it was not through industry.

Industrialization changes all this, by enabling production – within certain limits – to expand its own markets, if not actually to create them. When Henry Ford produced his model-T, he also produced what had not existed before, namely a vast number of customers for a cheap, standardized and simple automobile. Of course his enterprise was no longer as wildly speculative as it seemed. A century of industrialization had already demonstrated that mass-production of cheap goods can multiply their markets, accustomed men to buy better goods than their fathers had bought and to discover needs which their fathers had not dreamed of. The point is that *before* the Industrial Revolution, or in countries not yet transformed by it, Henry Ford would not have been an economic pioneer, but a crank, inviting bankruptcy.

How then did conditions come about in eighteenth-century Britain which led businessmen nevertheless to revolutionize production? How did entrepreneurs come to see before them, not the modest if solid expansion of demand which could be filled in the traditional manner, or by a little extension and improvement of the old ways, but the rapid and limitless expansion which required revolution? A small, simple and cheap revolution by our standards, but nevertheless a revolution, a leap into the dark. There are two schools of thought about this question. One emphasizes chiefly the *domestic* market, which was clearly by far the largest outlet for the country's products; the other stresses the foreign or *export* market, which was equally clearly, far more dynamic and expandable. The right answer is probably that both were essential in different ways, as was a third, and often neglected factor: *government*.

The domestic market, large and expanding as it was, could grow in only four important ways, three of which were not likely to be exceptionally rapid. There could be growth of population, which creates more consumers (and, of course, producers); a transfer of people from non-monetary to monetary incomes, which creates more customers; an increase of income per head, which creates better customers; and a substitution of industrially produced goods for older forms of manufacture or imports.

The question of *population* is so important, and has in recent years been the subject of so large and flourishing a concentration of research, that it must be briefly discussed here. It raises three questions of which only the third is directly relevant to the problem of market expansion, but all of which are important for the more general problem of British economic and social development. They are: (1) What happened to British population and why? (2) What effect did these population changes have on the economy? (3) What effect did they have on the structure of the British people?

Reliable measures of the British population hardly exist before about 1840, when the public registration of births and deaths was introduced, but its general movement is not in much dispute. Between the end of the seventeenth century when there were perhaps five and a quarter million inhabitants of England and Wales, and the middle of the eighteenth century, it rose only very slightly, and may at times have been static or even falling. After the 1740s it rose substantially and from the 1770s very rapidly indeed by contemporary, though not by our standards.* It doubled in fifty to sixty years after 1780, and again in the sixty years from 1841 to 1901, though in fact both birth and death rates began to drop rapidly from the 1870s. However, these global figures conceal very substantial variations, both chronological and regional. Thus for instance, while in the first half of the eighteenth century, and even up to 1780, the London area would have been depopulated but for massive immigration from the countryside, the future centre of industrialization, the Northwest, and the East Midlands were already increasing quite rapidly. After the real start of the Industrial Revolution, rates of natural increase of the major regions (though not of migration) tended to become similar, except for the murderous environment of London.

These movements were clearly not much affected, before the nineteenth century, by international migration, not even of the Irish. Were they due to variations in the rate of births or in mortality, and what were the causes of these? Quite apart from the

---

* In 1965 the population of the fastest-growing continent, Latin America, was increasing at something not far short of double this rate.

deficiency of our information, these questions, though of great interest, are immensely complicated.* They concern us here only in so far as they throw light on the question, how far the rise in population was a cause, how far a consequence of economic factors, e.g. how far people married or conceived children earlier, because of better chances of getting a piece of land to cultivate or a job or – as has been argued – because of the demand for child labour, how far their mortality declined because they were fed better or more regularly or because of environmental improvements. (Since one of the few facts we know with any certainty is that most of the fall in death-rates was due to fewer infants, children and perhaps young adults dying, rather than to any real prolongation of life beyond the biblical span of three score years and ten,† such falls might entail a rise in the birth-rate. For instance, if fewer women die before say, thirty, more of them are likely to have the children they might be expected to have between thirty and the menopause.)

As usual, we cannot answer such questions with any certainty. It seems clear that people were much more responsive to economic factors in marrying and/or having children than has sometimes been supposed, and that some social changes (for instance, the decline in the practice of workers 'living in' with their employers) must have encouraged, or even required earlier and perhaps larger families. It is also clear that a family economy which can only be balanced by the labour of all its members, and forms of production which used child labour would also encourage population. Contemporaries certainly thought of population as something which responded to changes in the demand for labour, and the birth-rate probably went up between the 1740s and the 1780s, though it may not have risen significantly after that. As for mortality, medical improvements almost certainly played no important part in its reduction (except maybe for smallpox inoculation) until after the middle of the nineteenth century, so its changes must have been largely due to economic, social or other environmental changes. But until quite late in the nineteenth century it does not seem to have declined dramatically. At present we cannot go much beyond such generalities without entering a scholarly battlefield which remains obscured by the fog of learned dispute.

What were the economic effects of these changes? More people means more labour and cheaper labour, and it has often been supposed that this is in itself a stimulus to economic growth, at any rate under capitalism. As we can see in many underdeveloped countries today, it is not. It may produce merely distress and stagnation, perhaps catastrophe, as in Ireland and the Scottish Highlands in the early nineteenth century (see p. 258 below). Cheap labour may actually retard industrialization. If in eighteenth-century England a growing labour force assisted development, as it undoubtedly did, it was because the economy was already dynamic not because some extraneous demographic injection made it so. In any case population grew rapidly all over northern Europe, but industrialization did not occur everywhere. On the other hand more pople certainly means more consumers, and it has been argued with more

---

* For a guide to these problems, see D.V. Glass and E. Grebenik, 'World Population 1800–1950', in *Cambridge Economic History of Europe* VI, i, pp. 60–138.

† This is still so. More people survive to live out their span, but old people do not on the whole die at a greater age than in the past.

force that this certainly provides a stimulus both for agriculture (for they must be fed) and for manufactures.

But as we have seen, the national population grew only very gradually in the century before 1750, and its rapid rise coincided with the Industrial Revolution but did not (except here and there) precede it. If Britain had been a less developed economy, there might have been more room for sudden and large transfers of people from say, subsistence to a cash-economy, or from domestic and artisan manufacture to industry. But, as we have seen, England was already a market economy with a large and growing manufacturing sector. The average English income probably increased substantially in the first half of the eighteenth century, thanks if anything to a stagnant population and labour shortage, so that this period is rightly described in the Vicar of Bray's song as 'pudding time'. People were better off and could buy more; what is more, they probably at this time included a smaller percentage of children (who divert the expenditure of poor parents sharply towards the purchase of necessities) and a larger proportion of young small-family adults (who have income to spare). It is quite likely that in this period many Englishmen learned to 'cultivate new wants and establish new levels of expectation',[3] and there is some evidence that around 1750 they began to prefer to take out their extra productivity in more consumer goods rather than in more leisure. Still, this increase also resembled the movement of a respectable river rather than the exhilarating leaps of a waterfall. It explains why so many English towns were rebuilt (without any technological revolution) in the rural elegance of classical architecture, but not in itself why there was an industrial revolution.

Except perhaps in three special cases: transport, food and capital goods, particularly coal.

Very substantial and expensive improvements in inland transport – by river, canal and even road – were undertaken from the early eighteenth century, in order to diminish the prohibitive cost of moving goods overland: in the middle of the century twenty miles land transport might double the cost of a ton of goods. How important these were for the development of industrialism is uncertain, but there is no doubt that the impetus for them came from the home market, and more especially from the growing demand of the cities for food and fuel. The landlocked manufacturers of household goods in the west Midlands (potters in Staffordshire, makers of various metal goods in the Birmingham region) also pressed for cheaper transport. The difference in transport costs was so dramatic that major investments were patently worth while. Canals cut the cost per ton between Liverpool and Manchester or Birmingham by eighty per cent.

Food industries compete with textiles as the pace-setters of private enterprise industrialization, because a vast market for both exists visibly and (at least in the cities) at all times, merely awaiting exploitation. The least imaginative businessman can realize that everybody, however poor, eats, drinks and wears clothes. The demand for manufactured food and drink is admittedly more limited than that for textiles, except for such products as flour and alcoholic drinks, which are domestically manufactured only in rather primitive economies, but on the other hand food products are much more immune to foreign competition than textiles. Their industrialization therefore tends to play a rather more important part in undeveloped than in advanced countries. Still, flour-milling and beer-brewing were important pioneers of technological revolution even in Britain, though they attract less attention than textiles, because they do not so much transform the surrounding economy as appear, like giant monuments of modernity, within it, as the Guinness brewery did in Dublin and the celebrated Albion steam mills (which so impressed the poet William Blake) in London. The larger the city (and London was by far the greatest in western Europe), and the more rapid the urbanization, the greater the scope for such developments. Was not the invention of the beer-handle, known to every drinker in Britain, one of the first triumphs of Henry Maudslay, one of the great pioneers of engineering?

The home market also provided a major outlet for what later became capital goods. *Coal* grew almost entirely with the number of urban – and especially metropolitan – fire-places; iron – to a much smaller extent – reflected the demand for domestic pots, pans, nails, stoves and the like. Since the quantities of coal burned in British homes were very much greater than their needs of iron (thanks in part to the unusual inefficiency of the British fireplace compared to the continental stove), the pre-industrial base of the coal industry was much sounder than that of the iron industry. Even before the Industrial Revolution its output could already be measured in millions of tons, the first commodity to which such astronomic criteria were applicable. And steam-engines were the product of the mines: in 1769 a hundred 'atmospheric engines' had already been erected round Newcastle-on-Tyne, and fifty-seven were actually at work. (However, the more modern engines of James Watt's type, which were really the foundation of industrial technology, only made their way slowly in the mines.)

On the other hand the total British consumption of iron in 1720 was less than 50,000 tons, and even in 1788, after the Industrial Revolution was well under way, it cannot have been much more than 100,000 tons. The demand for steel was negligible at the then price of this metal. The greatest civilian market for iron was probably still agricultural – ploughs and other implements, horse-shoes, wheel-rims, etc. – which increased substantially, but was hardly large enough yet to start an industrial transformation. In fact, as we shall see, the real Industrial Revolution in iron and coal had to wait until the era of the railway provided a mass market not only for consumer goods but for capital goods. The pre-industrial domestic market, and even the first phase of industrialization, did not yet do so on a sufficient scale.

The main advantage of the pre-industrial home market was therefore its great size and steadiness. It may not have promoted much in the way of industrial revolution, but it undoubtedly promoted economic growth, and what is more, it was always available to cushion the more dynamic export industries against the sudden fluctuations and collapses which were the price they paid for their superior dynamism. It came to their rescue in the 1780s, when war and the American Revolution disrupted them, and probably again after the Napoleonic Wars. But more than this, it provided the broad foundations for a *generalised* industrial economy. If England thought tomorrow what Manchester thought today, it was because the rest of the country was prepared to take its lead from Lancashire. Unlike Shanghai in pre-communist China, or Ahmedabad in colonial India, Manchester did not remain a modern enclave in the general backwardness, but became the model for the rest of the country. The domestic market may not have provided the spark, but it provided fuel and sufficient draught to keep it burning.

Export industries worked in very different, and potentially much more revolutionary conditions. They fluctuated wildly – up to fifty per cent in a single year – so that the manufacturer who could leap in fast enough to catch the expansions could make a killing. In the long run they also expanded much more, and more rapidly, than home markets. Between 1700 and 1750 home industries increased their output by seven per cent, export industries by seventy-six per cent; between 1750 and 1770 (which we may regard as the runway for the industrial 'take-off') by another seven per cent and eighty per cent respectively. Home demand increased – but foreign demand multiplied. If a spark was needed, this is where it came from. Cotton manufacture, the first to be industrialized, was essentially tied to overseas trade. Every ounce of its raw material had to be imported from the sub-tropics or tropics, and as we shall see, its products were to be overwhelmingly sold abroad. From the end of the eighteenth century it was already an industry which exported the greater part of its total output – perhaps two thirds by 1805.

The reason for this extraordinary potential of expansion was that export industries did not depend on the modest 'natural' rate of growth of any country's internal demand. They could create the illusion of rapid growth by two major means: capturing a series of other countries' export markets, and destroying domestic competition within particular countries, i.e. by the political or semi-political means of war and colonization. The country which succeeded in concentrating other people's export markets, or even in monopolizing the export markets of a large part of the world in a sufficiently brief period of time, could expand its export industries at a rate which made industrial revolution not only practicable for its entrepreneurs, but sometimes virtually compulsory. And this is what Britain succeeded in doing in the eighteenth century.*

Yet conquering markets by war and colonization required not merely an economy capable of exploiting those markets, but also a government willing to wage war and colonize for the benefit of British manufacturers. This brings us to the third factor in the genesis of the Industrial Revolution, *government*. Here the advantage of Britain over her potential competitors is quite evident. Unlike some of them (such as France) she was prepared to subordinate *all* foreign policy to economic ends. Her war aims were commercial and (what amounted to much the same thing) naval. The great Chatham gave five reasons in his memorandum advocating the conquest of Canada: the first four were purely economic. Unlike others (such as the Dutch), her economic aims were not completely dominated by commercial and financial interests, but shaped also, and increasingly, by the pressure group of manufacturers; originally the fiscally important woollen industry, later the rest. This tussle between industry and commerce (represented most dramatically by the East India Company) was decided in the home market by 1700, when British producers won protection against Indian textile imports; it was not won in the foreign market until 1813, when the East India Company was deprived of its monopoly in India, and that sub-continent opened to deindustrialization and the massive import of Lancashire cottons. Lastly, unlike all its other rivals,

---

* It follows that if one country did this, others would be unlikely to develop the basis for industrial revolution. In other words, under pre-industrial conditions there was probably room only for one pioneer national industrialization (as it turned out the British), but not the simultaneous industrialization of several 'advanced economies'. Consequently also – at least for some time – for only one 'workshop of the world'.

British policy in the eighteenth century was one of systematic aggressiveness – most obviously against the chief rival, France. Of the five great wars of the period, Britain was clearly on the defensive only in one.* The result of this century of intermittent warfare was the greatest triumph ever achieved by any state: the virtual monopoly among European powers of overseas colonies, and the virtual monopoly of world-wide naval power. Moreover, war itself – by crippling Britain's major competitors in Europe – tended to boost exports; peace, if anything, tended to slow them up.

Furthermore, war – and especially that very commercially-minded and middle-class organization, the British navy – contributed even more directly to technological innovation and industrialization. Its demands were not negligible: the tonnage of the navy multiplied from about 100,000 in 1685 to about 325,000 in 1760, and its demand for guns grew substantially, though in a less dramatic manner. War was pretty certainly the greatest consumer of iron, and firms like Wilkinson, the Walkers, and the Carron Works, owed the size of their undertakings partly to government contracts for cannon, while the South Wales iron industry depended on battle. More generally, government contracts, or those of vast quasi-government bodies like the East India Company, came in large blocks and had to be filled on time. It was worth a businessman's while to introduce revolutionary methods to supply them. Time and again we find some inventor or entrepreneur stimulated by so lucrative a prospect. Henry Cort, who revolutionized iron manufacture, began in the 1760s as a navy agent, anxious to improve the quality of the British product 'in connexion with the supply of iron to the navy'.[4] Henry Maudslay, the pioneer of machine-tools, began his career in the Woolwich Arsenal and his fortunes (like those of the great engineer Marc Isambard Brunei, formerly of the French navy) remained closely bound up with naval contracts.†

If we are to sum up the role of the three main sectors of demand in the genesis of industrialism, we can therefore do so as follows. Exports, backed by the systematic and aggressive help of government provided the spark, and – with cotton textiles – the 'leading sector' of industry. They also provided major improvements in sea transport. The home market provided the broad base for a generalized industrial economy and (through the process of urbanization) the incentive for major improvements in inland transport, a powerful base for the coal industry and for certain important technological innovations. Government provided systematic support for merchant and manufacturer, and some by no means negligible incentives for technical innovation and the development of capital goods industries.

If we finally return to our original questions – why Britain and not another country? why at the end of the eighteenth century and not before or after? – the answer cannot be so simple. By 1750, indeed, there was not much doubt that if any state was to win the race to be the first industrial power, it would be Britain. The Dutch had retired to that comfortable role of old-established business, the exploitation of their vast commercial

---

* The Spanish Succession (1702–13), the Austrian Succession (1739–48), the Seven Years' War (1756–63), the war of American Independence (1776–83) and the Revolutionary and Napoleonic Wars (1793–1815).

† The pioneering role of the government's own establishments must not be forgotten. During the Napoleonic Wars they anticipated, among other things, conveyor belts and the canning industry.

and financial apparatus, and their colonies, the French, though expanding about as fast as the British (when the British did not prevent them by war), could not regain the ground they had lost in the great era of economic depression, the seventeenth century. In absolute figures they might look – until the Industrial Revolution – like a power of equivalent size, but *per capita* their trade and manufactures were even then far behind the British.

On the other hand this does not explain why the industrial breakthrough came when it actually did – in the last third or quarter of the eighteenth century. The precise answer to this question is still uncertain, but it is clear that we can only find it by turning back to the general European or 'world' economy of which Britain was a part,* i.e. to the 'advanced' areas of (mainly) western Europe and their relations with the colonial and semi-colonial dependent economies, the marginal trading partners, and the regions not as yet substantially involved in the European system of economic flows.

The traditional pattern of European expansion – Mediterranean, and based on Italian merchants and their associates, Spanish and Portuguese conquerors – or Baltic, and based on German city states – had perished in the great economic depression of the seventeenth century. The new centres of expansion were the maritime states bordering the North Sea and North Atlantic. The shift was not merely geographical, but structural. The new kind of relationship between the 'advanced' areas and the rest of the world, unlike the old, tended constantly to intensify and widen the flows of commerce. The powerful, growing and accelerating current of overseas trade which swept the infant industries of Europe with it – which, in fact, sometimes actually *created* them – was hardly conceivable without this change. It rested on three things: in Europe, the rise of a market for overseas products for everyday use, whose market could be expanded as they became available in larger quantities and more cheaply; and overseas the creation of economic systems for producing such goods (such as, for instance, slave-operated plantations) and the conquest of colonies designed to serve the economic advantage of their European owners.

To illustrate the first fact: around 1650 one third of the value of East India goods sold in Amsterdam consisted of pepper – the typical commodity in which profits are made by 'cornering' a small supply and selling it at monopoly prices – by 1780 this proportion had fallen to eleven per cent. Conversely, by 1780 fifty-six per cent of such sales consisted of textiles, tea and coffee, whereas in 1650 they had only amounted to 17.5 per cent. Sugar, tea, coffee, tobacco and similar products rather than gold and spices were now the characteristic imports from the tropics, as wheat, linen, iron, hemp and timber were those from the east of Europe, and not furs. The second fact can be illustrated by the expansion of that most inhuman traffic, the slave trade. In the sixteenth century less than a million Negroes were transferred from Africa to the Americas; in the seventeenth perhaps three millions – mainly in the second half, or if earlier, to the Brazilian plantations which anticipated the later colonial pattern; in the eighteenth century perhaps seven millions.† The third fact hardly requires illustration. In 1650 neither Britain nor France had much in the way of empires, and much

---

* The word must be understood to mean only that the European economy was the centre of a world-wide network, but *not* that all parts of the world were involved in this network.

† Even if, as is almost certain, these figures are exaggerated, the relative orders of magnitude are realistic.

of the old Spanish and Portuguese empires lay in ruins, or consisted of mere outlines on a world map. The eighteenth century saw not merely a revival of the older empires (e.g. in Brazil and Mexico), but the expansion and exploitation of new ones – British, French, not to mention now forgotten essays by Danes, Swedes and others. What is more, the sheer size of these empires as economies increased vastly. In 1701 the future USA had less than 300,000 inhabitants, in 1790 almost four millions, and even Canada grew from 14,000 in 1695 to almost half a million in 1800.

And as the network of international trade grew tighter, so did the role of such overseas trade in the commerce of Europe. In 1680 the East India trade amounted to perhaps eight per cent of the total foreign commerce of the Dutch, but in the second half of the eighteenth century to something like one quarter, and the evolution of French trade was similar. The British relied on colonial trade earlier. Around 1700 it amounted already to fifteen per cent of our commerce – but by 1775 to as much as a third. The general expansion of trading in the eighteenth century was impressive enough, in almost all countries, but the expansion of trade connected with the colonial system was stupendous. To take a single example: after the war of the Spanish Succession between two and three thousand tons of British ships cleared from England every year for Africa, mainly as slavers; after the Seven Years' War between fifteen and nineteen thousand; after the American War of Independence (1787) twenty-two thousand.

This vast and growing circulation of goods not merely brought to Europe new needs, and the stimulus to manufacture foreign imports at home. 'If Saxony and other countries of Europe make up fine China', wrote the Abbé Raynal in 1777,[5] 'if Valencia manufactures Pekins superior to those of China; if Switzerland imitates the muslins and worked calicoes of Bengal; if England and France print linens with great elegance; if so many stuffs, formerly unknown in our climates, now employ our best artists, are we not indebted to India for all these advantages?'* More than this, it provided a limitless horizon of sales and profit for merchant and manufacturer. And it was the British who – by their policy and force as much as by their enterprise and inventive skill – captured these markets.

Behind our Industrial Revolution there lies this concentration on the colonial and 'underdeveloped' markets overseas, the successful battle to deny them to anyone else. We defeated them in the East: in 1766 we already outsold even the Dutch in the China trade. We defeated them in the West: by the early 1780s more than half of all slaves exported from Africa (and almost twice as many as those carried by the French) made profits for British slavers. And we did so for the benefit of *British* goods. For some three decades after the war of the Spanish Succession British ships bound for Africa still carried mainly foreign (including Indian) goods; from shortly after the War of the Austrian Succession they carried overwhelmingly British ones. Our industrial economy grew out of our commerce, and especially our commerce with the underdeveloped world. And throughout the nineteenth century it was to retain this peculiar historical pattern: commerce and shipping maintained our balance of payments, and the exchange of overseas primary products for British manufactures was to be the foundation of our international economy.

---

* Within a few years he would not have failed to mention the most successful imitator of the Indians, Manchester.

While the stream of international exchanges swelled, sometime in the second third of the eighteenth century a general quickening of the domestic economies became noticeable. This was not a specifically British phenomenon, but one which occurred very generally, and is registered in the movements of prices (which began a long period of slow inflation, after a century of fluctuating and indeterminate movement), in what little we know about population, production and in other ways. The Industrial Revolution was generated in these decades – after the 1740s, when this massive but slow growth in the domestic economies combined with the rapid – after 1750 extremely rapid – expansion of the international economy; and it occurred in the country which seized its international opportunities to corner a major share of the overseas markets.

Notes

1 Modern discussion of industrial revolution and economic development starts with Karl Marx, *Capital,* Vol. I, parts 3, 4, chapters 23. For more recent marxist views, see M.H. Dobb, *Studies in Economics Development* (1946) and **Some Aspects of Economic Development* (Delhi 1951), and the immensely stimulating **K. Polanyi, Origins, of Our Time* (1945). **D.S. Landes, *Cambridge Economic History of Europe,* Vol. VI (1965), is a fine introduction to modern academic treatment of the subject; see also Phyllis Deane, *The First Industrial Revolution* (1965) (B). For Anglo-American and Anglo-French comparison **H.J. Habbakuk, *American and British Technology in the 19th Century* (1962), P. Bairoch, *Revolution industrielle et sous-development* (1963).

  For a survey of academic theories on economic development in general, several textbooks among which B. Higgins, *Economic Development* (1959). For more sociological approaches, Bert Hoselitz, *Sociological Aspects of Economic Growth* (1960), Wilbert Moore, *Industrialization and Labour* (1951), Everett Hagen, *On the Theory of Social Change* (1964) (B). See also figures 1–3, 14, 23, 26, 28, 37.

  On Britain in the eighteenth-century world economy, F. Mauro, *L'expansion européenne 1600–1870* (La Nouvelle Clio 1964), Ralph Davis, 'English Foreign Trade 1700–1774' (*Econ. Hist. Rev.* 1962).

2 C. P. Kindleberger, *Economic Growth in France and Britain* (1964), p. 158.

3 From an unpublished paper, 'Population and Labour Supply', by H. C. Pentland.

4 Samuel Smiles, *Industrial Biography*, p. 114.

5 Abbé Raynal, *The Philosophical and Political History of the Settlements and Trade of the Europeans in the East and West Indies* (1776), Vol. II, p. 288.

Alexander Gerschenkron, "Economic Backwardness in Historical Perspective" (1951)*

I: Economic Backwardness in Historical Perspective

A historical approach to current problems calls perhaps for a word of explanation. Unlike so many of their predecessors, modern historians no longer announce to the world what inevitably will, or at least what ideally should, happen. We have grown modest. The prophetic fervor was bound to vanish together with the childlike faith in a perfectly comprehensible past whose flow was determined by some exceedingly simple and general historical law. Between Seneca's assertion of the absolute certainty of our knowledge of the past and Goethe's description of history as a book eternally kept under seven seals, between the *omnia certa sunt* of the one and the *ignorabimus* of the other, modern historical relativism moves gingerly. Modern historians realize full well that comprehension of the past—and that perforce means the past itself—changes perpetually with the historian's emphasis, interest, and point of view. The search is no longer for a determination of the course of human events as ubiquitous and invariant as that of the course of the planets. The iron necessity of historical processes has been discarded. But along with what John Stuart Mill once called "the slavery of antecedent circumstances" have been demolished the great bridges between the past and the future upon which the nineteenth-century mind used to travel so safely and so confidently.

Does this mean that history cannot contribute anything to the understanding of current problems? Historical research consists essentially in application to empirical material of various sets of empirically derived hypothetical generalizations and in testing the closeness of the resulting fit, in the hope that in this way certain uniformities, certain typical situations, and certain typical relationships among individual factors in these situations can be ascertained. None of these lends itself to easy extrapolations. All that can be achieved is an extraction from the vast storehouse of the past of sets of intelligent questions that may be addressed to current materials. The importance of this contribution should not be exaggerated. But it should not be underrated either. For the quality of our understanding of current problems depends largely on the broadness of our frame of reference. Insularity is a limitation on comprehension. But insularity in thinking is not peculiar to any special geographic area. Furthermore, it is not only a spatial but also a temporal problem. All decisions in the field of economic policies are essentially decisions with regard to combinations of a

---

number of relevant factors. And the historian's contribution consists in pointing at *potentially* relevant factors and at *potentially* significant combinations among them which could not be easily perceived within a more limited sphere of experience. These are the questions. The answers themselves, however, are a different matter. No past experience, however rich, and no historical research, however thorough, can save the living generation the creative task of finding their own answers and shaping their own future. The following remarks, therefore, purport to do no more than to point at some relationships which existed in the past and the consideration of which in current discussions might prove useful.

The Elements of Backwardness

A good deal of our thinking about industrialization of backward countries is dominated—consciously or unconsciously—by the grand Marxian generalization according to which it is the history of advanced or established industrial countries which traces out the road of development for the more backward countries. "The industrially more developed country presents to the less developed country a picture of the latter's future."[1] There is little doubt that in some broad sense this generalization has validity. It is meaningful to say that Germany, between the middle and the end of the last century, followed the road which England began to tread at an earlier time. But one should beware of accepting such a generalization too whole-heartedly. For the half-truth that it contains is likely to conceal the existence of the other half—that is to say, in several very important respects the development of a backward country may, by the very virtue of its backwardness, tend to differ fundamentally from that of an advanced country.

It is the main proposition of this essay that in a number of important historical instances industrialization processes, when launched at length in a backward country, showed considerable differences, as compared with more advanced countries, not only with regard to the speed of the development (the rate of industrial growth) but also with regard to the productive and organizational structures of industry which emerged from those processes. Furthermore, these differences in the speed and character of industrial development were to a considerable extent the result of application of institutional instruments for which there was little or no counterpart in an established industrial country. In addition, the intellectual climate within which industrialization proceeded, its "spirit" or "ideology," differed considerably among advanced and backward countries. Finally, the extent to which these attributes of backwardness occurred in individual instances appears to have varied directly with the degree of backwardness and the natural industrial potentialities of the countries concerned.

Let us first describe in general terms a few basic elements in the industrialization processes of backward countries as synthesized from the available historical information on economic development of European countries[2] in the nineteenth century and up until the beginning of the First World War. Thereupon, on the basis of concrete examples, more will be said on the effects of what may be called "relative backwardness" upon the course of industrial development in individual countries.

The typical situation in a backward country prior to the initiation of considerable industrialization processes may be described as characterized by the tension between the actual state of economic activities in the country and the existing obstacles to industrial development, on the one hand, and the great promise inherent in such a development, on the other. The extent of opportunities that industrialization presents varied, of course, with the individual country's endowment of natural resources. Furthermore, no industrialization seemed possible, and hence no "tension" existed, as long as certain formidable institutional obstacles (such as the serfdom of the peasantry or the far-reaching absence of political unification) remained. Assuming an adequate endowment of usable resources, and assuming that the great blocks to industrialization had been removed, the opportunities inherent in industrialization may be said to vary directly with the backwardness of the country. Industrialization always seemed the more promising the greater the backlog of technological innovations which the backward country could take over from the more advanced country. Borrowed technology, so much and so rightly stressed by Veblen, was one of the primary factors assuring a high speed of development in a backward country entering the stage of industrialization. There always has been the inevitable tendency to deride the backward country because of its lack of originality. German mining engineers of the sixteenth century accused the English of being but slavish imitators of German methods, and the English fully reciprocated these charges in the fifties and sixties of the past century. In our own day, Soviet Russia has been said to have been altogether imitative in its industrial development, and the Russians have retorted by making extraordinary and extravagant claims. But all these superficialities tend to blur the basic fact that the contingency of large imports of foreign machinery and of foreign know-how, and the concomitant opportunities for rapid industrialization with the passage of time, increasingly widened the gulf between economic potentialities and economic actualities in backward countries.

The industrialization prospects of an underdeveloped country are frequently judged, and judged adversely, in terms of cheapness of labor as against capital goods and of the resulting difficulty in substituting scarce capital for abundant labor. Sometimes, on the contrary, the cheapness of labor in a backward country is said to aid greatly in the processes of industrialization. The actual situation, however, is more complex than would appear on the basis of simple models. In reality, conditions will vary from industry to industry and from country to country. But the overriding fact to consider is that industrial labor, in the sense of a stable, reliable, and disciplined group that has cut the umbilical cord connecting it with the land and has become suitable for utilization in factories, is not abundant but extremely scarce in a backward country. Creation of an industrial labor force that really deserves its name is a most difficult and protracted process. The history of Russian industry provides some striking illustrations in this respect. Many a German industrial laborer of the nineteenth century had been raised in the strict discipline of a Junker estate which presumably made him more amenable to accept the rigors of factory rules. And yet the difficulties were great, and one may recall the admiring and envious glances which, toward the very end of the century, German writers like Schulze-Gaevernitz kept casting across the Channel at the English industrial worker, "the man of the future … born and educated for the machine … [who] does not find his equal in the past." In our time, reports from industries in India repeat in a still more exaggerated form the past predicaments of European industrializations in the field of labor supply.

Under these conditions the statement may be hazarded that, to the extent that industrialization took place, it was largely by application of the most modern and efficient techniques that backward countries could hope to achieve success, particularly if their industrialization proceeded in the face of competition from the advanced country. The advantages inherent in the use of technologically superior equipment were not counteracted but reinforced by its labor-saving effect. This seems to explain the tendency on the part of backward countries to concentrate at a relatively early point of their industrialization on promotion of those branches of industrial activities in which recent technological progress had been particularly rapid; while the more advanced countries, either from inertia or from unwillingness to require or impose sacrifices implicit in a large investment program, were more hesitant to carry out continual modernizations of their plant. Clearly, there are limits to such a policy, one of them being the inability of a backward country to extend it to lines of output where very special technological skills are required. Backward countries (although not the United States) were slow to assimilate production of modern machine tools. But a branch like iron and steel production does provide a good example of the tendency to introduce most modern innovations, and it is instructive to see, for example, how German blast furnaces so very soon become superior to the English ones, while in the early years of this century blast furnaces in still more backward southern Russia were in the process of outstripping in equipment their German counterparts. Conversely, in the nineteenth century, England's superiority in cotton textile output was challenged neither by Germany nor by any other country.

To a considerable extent (as in the case of blast furnaces just cited), utilization of modern techniques required, in nineteenth-century conditions, increases in the average size of plant. Stress on bigness in this sense can be found in the history of most countries on the European continent. But industrialization of backward countries in Europe reveals a tendency toward bigness in another sense. The use of the term "industrial revolution" has been exposed to a good many justifiable strictures. But, if industrial revolution is conceived as denoting no more than cases of sudden considerable increases in the rate of industrial growth, there is little doubt that in several important instances industrial development began in such a sudden, eruptive, that is, "revolutionary," way.

The discontinuity was not accidental. As likely as not the period of stagnation (in the "physiocratic" sense of a period of low rate of growth) can be terminated and industrialization processes begun only if the industrialization movement can proceed, as it were, along a broad front, starting simultaneously along many lines of economic activities. This is partly the result of the existence of complementarity and indivisibilities in economic processes. Railroads cannot be built unless coal mines are opened up at the same time; building half a railroad will not do if an inland center is to be connected with a port city. Fruits of industrial progress in certain lines are received as external economies by other branches of industry whose progress in turn accords benefits to the former. In viewing the economic history of Europe in the nineteenth century, the impression is very strong that only when industrial development could commence on a large scale did the tension between the preindustrialization conditions and the benefits expected from industrialization become sufficiently strong to overcome the existing obstacles and to liberate the forces that made for industrial progress.

This aspect of the development may be conceived in terms of Toynbee's relation between challenge and response. His general observation that very frequently small challenges do not produce any responses and that the volume of response begins to grow very rapidly (at least up to a point) as the volume of the challenge increases seems to be quite applicable here. The challenge, that is to say, the "tension," must be considerable before a response in terms of industrial development will materialize.

The foregoing sketch purported to list a number of basic factors which historically were peculiar to economic situations in backward countries and made for higher speed of growth and different productive structure of industries. The effect of these basic factors was, however, greatly reinforced by the use in backward countries of certain institutional instruments and the acceptance of specific industrialization ideologies. Some of these specific factors and their mode of operation on various levels of backwardness are discussed in the following sections.

The Banks

The history of the Second Empire in France provides rather striking illustrations of these processes. The advent of Napoleon III terminated a long period of relative economic stagnation which had begun with the restoration of the Bourbons and which in some sense and to some extent was the result of the industrial policies pursued by Napoleon I. Through a policy of reduction of tariff duties and elimination of import prohibitions, culminating in the Cobden-Chevalier treaty of 1860, the French government destroyed the hothouse in which French industry had been kept for decades and exposed it to the stimulating atmosphere of international competition. By abolishing monopoly profits in the stagnating coal and iron production, French industry at length received profitable access to basic industrial raw materials.

To a not inconsiderable extent, the industrial development of France under Napoleon III must be attributed to that determined effort to untie the strait jacket in which weak governments and strong vested interests had inclosed the French economy. But along with these essentially, though not exclusively, negative policies of the government, French industry received a powerful positive impetus from a different quarter. The reference is to the development of industrial banking under Napoleon III.

The importance of that development has seldom been fully appreciated. Nor has it been properly understood as emanating from the specific conditions of a relatively backward economy. In particular, the story of the Crédit Mobilier of the brothers Pereire is often regarded as a dramatic but, on the whole, rather insignificant episode. All too often, as, for instance, in the powerful novels of Émile Zola, the actual significance of the developments is almost completely submerged in the description of speculative fever, corruption, and immorality which accompanied them. It seems to be much better in accord with the facts to speak of a truly momentous role of investment banking of the period for the economic history of France and of large portions of the Continent.

In saying that, one has in mind, of course, the immediate effects of creating financial organizations designed to build thousands of miles of railroads, drill mines, erect factories, pierce canals, construct ports, and modernize cities. The ventures of the

Pereires and of a few others did all that in France and beyond the boundaries of France over vast areas stretching from Spain to Russia. This tremendous change in economic scenery took place only a few years after a great statesman and a great historian of the July monarchy assured the country that there was no need to reduce the duties on iron because the sheltered French iron production was quite able to cope with the iron needs of the railroads on the basis of his estimate of a prospective annual increase in construction by some fifteen to twenty miles.

But no less important than the actual economic accomplishments of a few men of great entrepreneurial vigor was their effect on their environment. The Crédit Mobilier was from the beginning engaged in a most violent conflict with the representatives of "old wealth" in French banking, most notably with the Rothschilds. It was this conflict that had sapped the force of the institution and was primarily responsible for its eventual collapse in 1867. But what is so seldom realized is that in the course of this conflict the "new wealth" succeeded in forcing the old wealth to adopt the policies of its opponents. The limitation of old wealth in banking policies to flotations of government loans and foreign-exchange transactions could not be maintained in the face of the new competition. When the Rothschilds prevented the Pereires from establishing the Austrian Credit-Anstalt, they succeeded only because they became willing to establish the bank themselves and to conduct it not as an old-fashioned banking enterprise but as a crédit mobilier, that is, as a bank devoted to railroadization and industrialization of the country.

This conversion of the old wealth to the creed of the new wealth points out the direction of the most far-reaching effects of the Crédit Mobilier. Occasional ventures of that sort had been in existence in Belgium, Germany, and France herself. But it was the great eruptive effect of the Pereires that profoundly influenced the history of Continental banking in Europe from the second half of the past century onward. The number of banks in various countries shaped upon the image of the Pereire bank was considerable. But more important than their slavish imitations was the creative adaptation of the basic idea of the Pereires and its incorporation in the new type of bank, the universal bank, which in Germany, along with most other countries on the Continent, became the dominant form of banking. The difference between banks of the crédit-mobilier type and commercial banks in the advanced industrial country of the time (England) was absolute. Between the English bank essentially designed to serve as a source of short-term capital and a bank designed to finance the long-run investment needs of the economy there was a complete gulf. The German banks, which may be taken as a paragon of the type of the universal bank, successfully combined the basic idea of the crédit mobilier with the short-term activities of commercial banks.

They were as a result infinitely sounder financial institutions than the Crédit Mobilier, with its enormously swollen industrial portfolio, which greatly exceeded its capital, and its dependence on favorable developments on the stock exchange for continuation of its activities. But the German banks, and with them the Austrian and Italian banks, established the closest possible relations with industrial enterprises. A German bank, as the saying went, accompanied an industrial enterprise from the cradle to the grave, from establishment to liquidation throughout all the vicissitudes of its existence. Through the device of formally short-term but in reality long-term current account credits and through development of the institution of the supervisory boards to the position of most powerful organs within corporate organizations, the banks acquired a formidable degree of ascendancy over industrial enterprises, which extended far beyond the sphere of financial control into that of entrepreneurial and managerial decisions.

It cannot be the purpose of this presentation to go into the details of this development. All that is necessary is to relate its origins and effects to the subject under discussion. The industrialization of England had proceeded without any substantial utilization of banking for long-term investment purposes. The more gradual character of the industrialization process and the more considerable accumulation of capital, first from earnings in trade and modernized agriculture and later from industry itself, obviated the pressure for developing any special institutional devices for provision of long-term capital to industry. By contrast, in a relatively backward country capital is scarce and diffused, the distrust of industrial activities is considerable, and, finally, there is greater pressure for bigness because of the scope of the industrialization movement, the larger average size of plant, and the concentration of industrialization processes on branches of relatively high ratios of capital to output. To these should be added the scarcity of entrepreneurial talent in the backward country.

It is the pressure of these circumstances which essentially gave rise to the divergent development in banking over large portions of the Continent as against England. The continental practices in the field of industrial investment banking must be conceived as specific instruments of industrialization in a backward country. It is here essentially that lies the historical and geographic locus of theories of economic development that assign a central role to processes of forced saving by the money-creating activities of banks. As will be shown presently, however, use of such instruments must be regarded as specific, not to backward countries in general, but rather to countries whose backwardness does not exceed certain limits. And even within the latter for a rather long time it was mere collection and distribution of available funds in which the banks were primarily engaged. This circumstance, of course, did not detract from the paramount importance of such activities on the part of the banks during the earlier industrialization periods with their desperate shortages of capital for industrial ventures.

The effects of these policies were far-reaching. All the basic tendencies inherent in industrial development in backward countries were greatly emphasized and magnified by deliberate attitudes on the part of the banks. From the outset of this evolution the banks were primarily attracted to certain lines of production to the neglect, if not virtual exclusion, of others. To consider Germany until the outbreak of World War I, it was essentially coal mining, iron- and steelmaking, electrical and general engineering, and heavy chemical output which became the primary sphere of activities of German banks. The textile industry, the leather industry, and the foodstuff-producing industries remained on the fringes of the banks' interest. To use modern terminology, it was heavy rather than light industry to which the attention was devoted.

Furthermore, the effects were not confined to the productive structure of industry. They extended to its organizational structure. The last three decades of the nineteenth century were marked by a rapid concentration movement in banking. This process indeed went on in very much the same way on the other side of the English Channel. But in Britain, because of the different nature of relations between banks and industry, the process was not paralleled by a similar development in industry.

It was different in Germany. The momentum shown by the cartelization movement of German industry cannot be fully explained, except as the natural result of the amalgamation of German banks. It was the mergers in the field of banking that kept placing banks in the positions of controlling competing enterprises. The banks refused to tolerate fratricidal struggles among their children. From the vantage point of centralized control, they were at all times quick to perceive profitable opportunities of cartelization and amalgamation of industrial enterprises. In the process, the average size of plant kept growing, and at the same time the interests of the banks and their assistance were even more than before devoted to those branches of industry where cartelization opportunities were rife.

Germany thus had derived full advantages from being a relatively late arrival in the field of industrial development, that is to say, from having been preceded by England. But, as a result, German industrial economy, because of specific methods used in the catching-up process, developed along lines not insignificantly different from those in England.

The State

The German experience can be generalized. Similar developments took place in Austria, or rather in the western sections of the Austrian-Hungarian Empire, in Italy, in Switzerland, in France, in Belgium, and in other countries, even though there were differences among the individual countries. But it certainly cannot be generalized for the European continent as a whole, and this for two reasons: (1) because of the existence of certain backward countries where no comparable features of industrial development can be discovered and (2) because of the existence of countries where the basic elements of backwardness appear in such an accentuated form as to lead to the use of essentially different institutional instruments of industrialization.

Little need be said with reference to the first type of country. The industrial development of Denmark may serve as an appropriate illustration. Surely, that country was still very backward as the nineteenth century entered upon its second half. Yet no comparable sudden spurts of industrialization and no peculiar emphasis on heavy industries could be observed. The reasons must be sought, on the one hand, in the paucity of the country's natural resources and, on the other hand, in the great opportunities for agricultural improvement that were inherent in the proximity of the English market. The peculiar response did not materialize because of the absence of the challenge.

Russia may be considered as the clearest instance of the second type of country. The characteristic feature of economic conditions in Russia was not only that the great spurt of modern industrialization came in the middle of the 1880s, that is to say, more than three decades after the beginning of rapid industrialization in Germany; even more important was the fact that at the starting point the level of economic development in Russia had been incomparably lower than that of countries such as Germany and Austria.

The main reason for the abysmal economic backwardness of Russia was the preservation of serfdom until the emancipation of 1861. In a certain sense, this very fact may be attributed to the play of a curious mechanism of economic backwardness, and a few words of explanation may be in order. In the course of its process of terri-torial expansion, which over a few centuries transferred the small duchy of Moscow into the huge land mass of modern Russia, the country became increasingly involved in military conflicts with the West. This involvement revealed a curious internal conflict between the tasks of the Russian government that were "modern" in the contemporaneous sense of the word and the hopelessly backward economy of the country on which the military policies had to be based. As a result, the economic development in Russia at several important junctures assumed the form of a pecu-liar series of sequences: (1) Basic was the fact that the state, moved by its military interest, assumed the role of the primary agent propelling the economic progress in the country. (2) The fact that economic development thus became a function of mili-tary exigencies imparted a peculiarly jerky character to the course of that develop-ment; it proceeded fast whenever military necessities were pressing and subsided as the military pressures relaxed. (3) This mode of economic progress by fits and starts implied that, whenever a considerable upsurge of economic activities was required, a very formidable burden was placed on the shoulders of the generations whose lifespan happened to coincide with the period of intensified development. (4) In order to exact effectively the great sacrifices it required, the government had to subject the reluctant population to a number of severe measures of oppression lest the burdens imposed be evaded by escape to the frontier regions in the southeast and east. (5) Precisely because of the magnitude of the governmental exactions, a period of rapid devel-opment was very likely to give way to prolonged stagnation, because the great effort had been pushed beyond the limits of physical endurance of the population and long periods of economic stagnation were the inevitable consequences. The sequences just mentioned present in a schematic way a pattern of Russian economic development in past centuries which fits best the period of the reforms under Peter the Great, but its applicability is by no means confined to that period.

What must strike the observer of this development is its curiously paradoxical course. While trying, as Russia did under Peter the Great, to adopt Western techniques, to raise output and the skills of the population to levels more closely approaching those of the West, Russia by virtue of this very effort was in some other respects thrown fur-ther away from the West. Broadly speaking, placing the trammels of serfdom upon the Russian peasantry must be understood as the obverse side of the processes of Westernization. Peter the Great did not institute serfdom in Russia, but perhaps more than anyone else he did succeed in making it effective. When in subsequent periods, partly because of point 2 and partly because of point 5 above, the state withdrew from active promotion of economic development and the nobility emancipated itself from its service obligations to the government, peasant serfdom was divested of its connection with economic development. What once was an indirect obligation to the state became a pure obligation toward the nobility and as such became by far the most important retarding factor in Russia's economic development.

Readers of Toynbee's may wish to regard this process, ending as it did with the emancipation of the peasantry, as an expression of the "withdrawal and return" sequence. Alternatively they may justifiably prefer to place it under the heading of "arrested civilizations." At any rate, the challenge-response mechanism is certainly useful in thinking about sequences of that nature. It should be noted, however, that the problem is not simply one of quantitative relationship between the volume of the challenge and that of the response. The crucial point is that the magnitude of the challenge changes the *quality* of the response and, by so doing, not only injects powerful retarding factors into the economic process but also more likely leads to a number of undesirable noneconomic consequences. To this aspect, which is most relevant to the current problem of industrialization of backward countries, we shall advert again in the concluding remarks of this essay.

To return to Russian industrialization in the eighties and the nineties of the past century, it may be said that in one sense it can be viewed as a recurrence of a previous pattern of economic development in the country. The role of the state distinguishes rather clearly the type of Russian industrialization from its German or Austrian counterpart.

Emancipation of the peasants, despite its manifold deficiencies, was an absolute prerequisite for industrialization. As such it was a negative action of the state designed to remove obstacles that had been earlier created by the state itself and in this sense was fully comparable to acts such as the agrarian reforms in Germany or the policies of Napoleon III which have been mentioned earlier. Similarly, the great judicial and administrative reforms of the sixties were in the nature of creating a suitable framework for industrial development rather than promoting it directly.

The main point of interest here that, unlike the case of Western Europe, actions of this sort did not per se lead to an upsurge of individual activities in the country; and for almost a quarter of a century after the emancipation the rate of industrial growth remained relatively low. The great industrial upswing came when, from the middle of the eighties on, the railroad building of the state assumed unprecedented proportions and became the main lever of a rapid industrialization policy. Through multifarious devices such as preferential orders to domestic producers of railroad materials, high prices, subsidies, credits, and profit guaranties to new industrial enterprises, the government succeeded in maintaining a high and, in fact, increasing rate of growth until the end of the century. Concomitantly, the Russian taxation system was reorganized, and the financing of industrialization policies was thus provided for, while the stabilization of the ruble and the introduction of the gold standard assured foreign participation in the development of Russian industry.

The basic elements of a backward economy were, on the whole, the same in Russia of the nineties and in Germany of the fifties. But quantitatively the differences were formidable. The scarcity of capital in Russia was such that no banking system could conceivably succeed in attracting sufficient funds to finance a large-scale industrialization; the standards of honesty in business were so disastrously low, the general distrust of the public so great, that no bank could have hoped to attract even such small capital funds as were available, and no bank could have successfully engaged in long-term credit policies in an economy where fraudulent bankruptcy had been almost elevated to the rank of a general business practice. Supply of capital for the needs of industrialization required the compulsory machinery of the government, which, through its taxation policies, succeeded in directing incomes from consumption to investment. There is no doubt that the government as an *agens movens* of industrialization discharged its role in a far less than perfectly efficient manner. Incompetence and corruption of bureaucracy were great. The amount of waste that accompanied the process was formidable. But, when all is said and done, the great success of the policies pursued under Vyshnegradski and Witte is undeniable. Not only in their origins but also in their effects, the policies pursued by the Russian government in the nineties resembled closely those of the banks in Central Europe. The Russian state did not evince any interest in "light industry." Its whole attention was centered on output of basic industrial materials and on machinery production; like the banks in Germany, the Russian bureaucracy was primarily interested in large-scale enterprises and in amalgamations and coordinated policies among the industrial enterprises which it favored or had helped to create. Clearly, a good deal of the government's interest in industrialization was predicated upon its military policies. But these policies only reinforced and accentuated the basic tendencies of industrialization in conditions of economic backwardness.

Perhaps nothing serves to emphasize more these basic uniformities in the situation and the dependence of actual institutional instruments used on the degree of backwardness of the country than a comparison of policies pursued within the two halves of the Austrian-Hungarian monarchy, that is to say, within one and the same political body. The Austrian part of the monarchy was backward in relation to, say, Germany, but it was at all times much more advanced than its Hungarian counterpart. Accordingly, in Austria proper the banks could successfully devote themselves to the promotion of industrial activities. But across the Leitha Mountains, in Hungary, the activities of the banks proved altogether inadequate, and around the turn of the century the Hungarian government embarked upon vigorous policies of industrialization. Originally, the government showed a considerable interest in developing the textile industry of the region. And it is instructive to watch how, under the pressure of what the French like to call the "logic of things," the basic uniformities asserted themselves and how the generous government subsidies were more and more deflected from textile industries to promotion of heavy industries.

The Gradations of Backwardness

To return to the basic German-Russian paradigm: what has been said in the foregoing does not exhaust the pattern of parallels. The question remains as to the effects of successful industrializations, that is to say, of the gradual diminution of backwardness.

At the turn of the century, if not somewhat earlier, changes became apparent in the relationship between German banks and German industry. As the former industrial infants had grown to strong manhood, the original undisputed ascendancy of the banks over industrial enterprises could no longer be maintained. This process of liberation of industry from the decades of tutelage expressed itself in a variety of ways. Increasingly, industrial enterprises transformed connection with a single bank into cooperation with several banks. As the former industrial protectorates became economically sovereign, they embarked upon the policy of changing alliances with regard to the banks. Many an industrial giant, such as the electrical engineering industry, which could not have developed without the aid and entrepreneurial daring of the banks, began to establish its own banks. The conditions of capital scarcity to which the German banks owed their historical position were no longer present. Germany had become a developed industrial country. But the specific features engendered by a process of industrialization in conditions of backwardness were to remain, and so was the close relation between banks and industry, even though the master-servant relation gave way to cooperation among equals and sometimes was even reversed.

In Russia the magnificent period of industrial development of the nineties was cut short by the 1900 depression and the following years of war and civil strife. But, when Russia emerged from the revolutionary years 1905–1906 and again achieved a high rate of industrial growth in the years 1907–1914, the character of the industrialization processes had changed greatly. Railroad construction by the government continued but on a much smaller scale both absolutely and even more so relatively to the increased industrial output. Certain increases in military expenditures that took place could not begin to compensate for the reduced significance of railroad-building. The conclusion is inescapable that, in that last period of industrialization under a prerevolutionary government, the significance of the state was very greatly reduced.

At the same time, the traditional pattern of Russian economic development happily failed to work itself out. The retrenchment of government activities led not to stagnation but to a continuation of industrial growth. Russian industry had reached a stage where it could throw away the crutches of government support and begin to walk independently—and, yet, very much less independently than industry in contemporaneous Germany, for at least to some extent the role of the retreating government was taken over by the banks.

A great transformation had taken place with regard to the banks during the fifty years that had elapsed since the emancipation. Commercial banks had been founded. Since it was the government that had fulfilled the function of industrial banks, the Russian banks, precisely because of the backwardness of the country, were organized as "deposit banks," thus resembling very much the type of banking in England. But, as industrial development proceeded apace and as capital accumulation increased, the standards of business behavior were growingly Westernized. The paralyzing atmosphere of distrust began to vanish, and the foundation was laid for the emergence of a different type of bank. Gradually, the Moscow deposit banks were overshadowed by the development of the St. Petersburg banks that were conducted upon principles that were characteristic not of English but of German banking. In short, after the economic backwardness of Russia had been reduced by state-sponsored industrialization processes, use of a different instrument of industrialization, suitable to the new "stage of backwardness," became applicable.

Ideologies of Delayed Industrializations

Before drawing some general conclusions, a last differential aspect of industrialization in circumstances of economic backwardness should be mentioned. So far, important differences with regard to the character of industrial developments and its institutional vehicles were related to conditions and degrees of backwardness. A few words remain to be said on the ideological climate within which such industrialization proceeded.

Again we may revert to the instructive story of French industrialization under Napoleon III. A large proportion of the men who reached positions of economic and financial influence upon Napoleon's advent to power were not isolated individuals.

They belonged to a rather well-defined group. They were not Bonapartists but Saint-Simonian socialists. The fact that a man like Isaac Pereire, who contributed so much, perhaps more than any other single person, to the spread of the modern capitalist system in France should have been—and should have remained to the end of his days—an ardent admirer of Saint-Simonian doctrines is on the face of it surprising. It becomes much less so if a few pertinent relationships are considered.

It could be argued that Saint-Simon was in reality far removed from being a socialist; that in his vision of an industrial society he hardly distinguished between laborers and employers; and that he considered the appropriate political form for his society of the future some kind of corporate state in which the "leaders of industry" would exercise major political functions. Yet arguments of that sort would hardly explain much. Saint-Simon had a profound interest in what he used to call the "most numerous and most suffering classes"; more importantly, Saint-Simonian doctrines, as expanded and redefined by the followers of the master (particularly by Bazard), incorporated into the system a good many socialist ideas, including abolition of inheritance and establishment of a system of planned economy designed to direct and to develop the economy of the country. And it was this interpretation of the doctrines which the Pereires accepted.

It is more relevant to point to the stress laid by Saint-Simon and his followers upon industrialization and the great task they had assigned to banks as an instrument of organization and development of the economy. This, no doubt, greatly appealed to the creators of the Crédit Mobilier, who liked to think of their institution as of a "bank to a higher power" and of themselves as "missionaries" rather than bankers. That Saint-Simon's stress upon the role to be played by the banks in economic development revealed a truly amazing—and altogether "unutopian"—insight into the problems of that development is as true as the fact that Saint-Simonian ideas most decisively influenced the course of economic events inside and outside France. But the question remains: why was the socialist garment draped around an essentially capitalist idea? And why was it the socialist form that was so readily accepted by the greatest capitalist entrepreneurs France ever possessed?

It would seem that the answer must again be given in terms of basic conditions of backwardness. Saint-Simon, the friend of J.B. Say, was never averse to ideas of laissez-faire policies. Chevalier, the coauthor of the Franco-English treaty of commerce of 1860 that ushered in the great period of European free trade, had been an ardent Saint-Simonian. And yet under French conditions a laissez-faire ideology was altogether inadequate as a spiritual vehicle of an industrialization program.

To break through the barriers of stagnation in a backward country, to ignite the imaginations of men, and to place their energies in the service of economic development, a stronger medicine is needed than the promise of better allocation of resources or even of the lower price of bread. Under such conditions even the businessman, even the classical daring and innovating entrepreneur, needs a more powerful stimulus than the prospect of high profits. What is needed to remove the mountains of routine and prejudice is faith—faith, in the words of Saint-Simon, that the golden age lies not behind but ahead of mankind. It was not for nothing that Saint-Simon devoted his last years to the formulation of a new creed, the New Christianity, and suffered Auguste Comte to break with him over this "betrayal of true science." What sufficed in England did not suffice in France.

Shortly before his death, Saint-Simon urged Rouget de Lisle, the aged author of the "Marseillaise," to compose a new anthem, an "Industrial Marseillaise." Rouget de Lisle complied. In the new hymn the man who once had called upon "enfants de la patrie" to wage ruthless war upon the tyrants and their mercenary cohorts addresses himself to "enfants de l'industrie"—the "true nobles"—who would assure the "happiness of all" by spreading industrial arts and by submitting the world to the peaceful "laws of industry."

Ricardo is not known to have inspired anyone to change "God Save the King" into "God Save Industry." No one would want to detract from the force of John Bright's passionate eloquence, but in an advanced country rational arguments in favor of industrialization policies need not be supplemented by a quasi-religious fervor. Buckle was not far wrong when in a famous passage of his *History* he presented the conversion of public opinion in England to free trade as achieved by the force of incontrovertible logic. In a backward country the great and sudden industrialization effort calls for a New Deal in emotions. Those carrying out the great transformation as well as those on whom it imposes burdens must feel, in the words of Matthew Arnold, that

> ... Clearing a stage
> Scattering the past about
> Comes the new age.

Capitalist industrialization under the auspices of socialist ideologies may be, after all, less surprising a phenomenon than would appear at first sight.

Similarly, Friedrich List's industrialization theories may be largely conceived as an attempt, by a man whose personal ties to Saint-Simonians had been very strong, to translate the inspirational message of Saint-Simonism into a language that would be accepted in the German environment, where the lack of both a preceding political revolution and an early national unification rendered nationalist sentiment a much more suitable ideology of industrialization.

After what has been just said it will perhaps not seem astonishing that, in the Russian industrialization of the 1890s, orthodox Marxism can be said to have performed a very similar function. Nothing reconciled the Russian intelligentsia more to the advent of capitalism in the country and to the destruction of its old faith in the mir and the artel than a system of ideas which presented the capitalist industrialization of the country as the result of an iron law of historical development. It is this connection which largely explains the power wielded by Marxist thought in Russia when it extended to men like Struve and in some sense even Milyukov, whose Weltanschauung was altogether alien to the ideas of Marxian socialism. In conditions of Russian "absolute" backwardness, again, a much more powerful ideology was required to grease the intellectual and emotional wheels of industrialization than either in France or in Germany. The institutional gradations of backwardness seem to find their counterpart in men's thinking about backwardness and the way in which it can be abolished.

Conclusions

The story of European industrialization in the nineteenth century would seem to yield a few points of view which may be helpful for appreciation of present-day problems.

1. If the spurtlike character of the past century's industrialization on the European continent is conceived of as the result of the specific preindustrial situations in backward countries and if it is understood that pressures for high-speed industrializations are inherent in those situations, it should become easier to appreciate the oft-expressed desires in this direction by the governments of those countries. Slogans like "Factories quick!" which played such a large part in the discussions of the pertinent portions of the International Trade Organization charter, may then appear less unreasonable.

2. Similarly, the tendencies in backward countries to concentrate much of their efforts on introduction of the most modern and expensive technology, their stress on large-scale plant, and their interest in developing investment-goods industries need not necessarily be regarded as flowing mainly from a quest for prestige and from economic megalomania.

3. What makes it so difficult for an advanced country to appraise properly the industrialization policies of its less fortunate brethren is the fact that, in every instance of industrialization, imitation of the evolution in advanced countries appears in combination with different, indigenously determined elements. If it is not always easy for advanced countries to accept the former, it is even more difficult for them to acquiesce in the latter. This is particularly true of the institutional instruments used in carrying out industrial developments and even more so of ideologies which accompany it. What can be derived from a historical review is a strong sense for the significance of the native elements in the industrialization of backward countries.

A journey through the last century may, by destroying what Bertrand Russell once called the "dogmatism of the untravelled," help in formulating a broader and more enlightened view of the pertinent problems and in replacing the absolute notions of what is "right" and what is "wrong" by a more flexible and relativistic approach.

It is, of course, not suggested here that current policies vis-à-vis backward areas should be formulated on the basis of the general experience of the past century without taking into account, in each individual instance, the degree of endowment with natural resources, the climatic disabilities, the strength of institutional obstacles to industrialization, the pattern of foreign trade, and other pertinent factors. But what is even more important is the fact that, useful as the "lessons" of the nineteenth century may be, they cannot properly be applied without understanding the climate of the present century, which in so many ways has added new and momentous aspects to the problems concerned.

Since the present problem of industrialization of backward areas largely concerns non-European countries, there is the question of the effects of their specific preindustrial cultural development upon their industrialization potentialities. Anthropological research of such cultural patterns has tended to come to rather pessimistic conclusions in this respect. But perhaps such conclusions are unduly lacking in dynamic perspective. At any rate, they do not deal with the individual factors involved in terms of their specific changeabilities. At the same time, past Russian experience does show how quickly in the last decades of the past century a pattern of life that had been so strongly opposed to industrial values, that tended to consider any nonagricultural economic activity as unnatural and sinful, began to give way to very different attitudes. In particular, the rapid emergence of native entrepreneurs with peasant-serf backgrounds should give pause to those who stress so greatly the disabling lack of entrepreneurial qualities in backward civilizations. Yet there are other problems.

In certain extensive backward areas the very fact that industrial development has been so long delayed has created, along with unprecedented opportunities for technological progress, great obstacles to industrialization. Industrial progress is arduous and expensive; medical progress is cheaper and easier of accomplishment. To the extent that the latter has preceded the former by a considerable span of time and has resulted in formidable overpopulation, industrial revolutions may be defeated by Malthusian counterrevolutions.

Closely related to the preceding but enormously more momentous in its effects is the fact that great delays in industrialization tend to allow time for social tensions to develop and to assume sinister proportions. As a mild example, the case of Mexico may be cited, where the established banks have been reluctant to cooperate in industrialization activities that are sponsored by a government whose radical hue they distrust. But the real case in point overshadowing everything else in scope and importance is, of course, that of Soviet Russia.

If what has been said in the preceding pages has validity, Soviet industrialization undoubtedly contains all the basic elements that were common to the industrializations of backward countries in the nineteenth century. The stress on heavy industry and oversized plant is, as such, by no means peculiar to Soviet Russia. But what is true is that in Soviet Russia those common features of industrialization processes have been magnified and distorted out of all proportion.

The problem is as much a political as it is an economic one. The Soviet government can be properly described as a product of the country's economic backwardness. Had serfdom been abolished by Catherine the Great or at the time of the Decembrist uprising in 1825, the peasant discontent, the driving force and the earnest of success of the Russian Revolution, would never have assumed disastrous proportions, while the economic development of the country would have proceeded in a much more gradual fashion. If anything is a "grounded historical assumption," this would seem to be one: the delayed industrial revolution was responsible for a political revolution in the course of which the power fell into the hands of a dictatorial government to which in the long run the vast majority of the population was opposed. It is one thing for such a government to gain power in a moment of great crisis; it is another to maintain this power for a long period. Whatever the strength of the army and the ubiquitousness of the secret police which such a government may have at its disposal, it would be naive to believe that those instruments of physical oppression can suffice. Such a government can maintain itself in power only if it succeeds in making people believe that it performs an important social function which could not be discharged in its absence.

Industrialization provided such a function for the Soviet government. All the basic factors in the situation of the country pressed in that direction. By reverting to a pattern of economic development that should have remained confined to a long-bygone age, by substituting collectivization for serfdom, and by pushing up the rate of investment to the maximum point within the limits of endurance of the population, the Soviet government did what no government relying on the consent of the governed could have done. That these policies, after having led through a period of violent struggles, have resulted in permanent day-to-day friction between the government and the population is undeniable. But, paradoxical as it may sound, these policies at the same time have secured some broad acquiescence on the part of the people. If all the forces of the population can be kept engaged in the processes of industrialization and if this industrialization can be justified by the promise of happiness and abundance for future generations and—much more importantly—by the menace of military aggression from beyond the borders, the dictatorial government will find its power broadly unchallenged. And the vindication of a threatening war is easily produced, as is shown by the history of the cold-war years. Economic backwardness, rapid industrialization, ruthless exercise of dictatorial power, and the danger of war have become inextricably intertwined in Soviet Russia.

This is not the place to elaborate this point further with regard to Soviet Russia. The problem at hand is not Soviet Russia but the problem of attitudes toward industrialization of backward countries. If the Soviet experience teaches anything, it is that it demonstrates *ad oculos* the formidable dangers inherent in our time in the existence of economic backwardness. There are no four-lane highways through the parks of industrial progress. The road may lead from backwardness to dictatorship and from dictatorship to war. In conditions of a "bipolar world" this sinister sequence is modified and aggrandized by deliberate imitation of Soviet policies by other backward countries and by their voluntary or involuntary incorporation in the Soviet orbit.

Thus, conclusions can be drawn from the historical experience of both centuries. The paramount lesson of the twentieth century is that the problems of backward nations are not exclusively their own. They are just as much problems of the advanced countries. It is not only Russia but the whole world that pays the price for the failure to emancipate the Russian peasants and to embark upon industrialization policies at an early time. Advanced countries cannot afford to ignore economic backwardness. But the lesson of the nineteenth century is that the policies toward the backward countries are unlikely to be successful if they ignore the basic peculiarities of economic backwardness. Only by frankly recognizing their existence and strength, and by attempting to develop fully rather than to stifle what Keynes once called the "possibilities of things," can the experience of the nineteenth century be used to avert the threat presented by its successor.

Notes

1 Karl Marx, *Das Kapital* (1st ed.), preface.
2 It would have been extremely desirable to transcend the European experience at least by including some references to the industrialization of Japan. Unfortunately, the writer's ignorance of Japanese economic history has effectively barred him from thus broadening the scope of his observations. The reader must be referred, however, to the excellent study by Henry Rosovsky, *Capital Formation in Japan, 1868–1940* (Glencoe, 1961), in which the validity of this writer's approach for Japanese industrial history is explicitly discussed.

6

Political Science and Political Economy

The lenses employed by political scientists in the study of political economy range from the state level, encompassing national political systems and their relationships to the global economy, to the firm level, focusing on how innovation on the factory shop-floor is intertwined with broader political–economic processes.[1] As a group, however, political scientists are interested in relationships of power among economic actors, society, and government, and devote significant analytical attention to the role of the state and other political–economic institutions in examining how those relationships come to be embedded in markets. Political science is similar to the discipline of history and different from economic sociology or the New Institutional Economics in that it does not have a dominant paradigm for a political economy subfield so that one can trace an intellectual thread such as that from Coase to Williamson or from Polanyi to Fligstein. As noted in the volume introduction, we cannot possibly do justice to the range of works on political economy in political science, but we introduce two highly influential works here. They are both works of comparative political economy in that they examine the politics of markets as institutions in different countries.

Charles Lindblom moves away from a simplistic dichotomy of governments versus markets in his classic work on *Politics and Markets*. He builds on theories we have already examined, taking from Smith and the market liberals the notion that markets are efficient coordination mechanisms and from Marx a critique of capitalism and the class capture of the state. Lindblom wrote the book in the 1970s, when the world was divided into two major types of economic systems – market economies and planned economies – so he was particularly focused on exploring the differences between the two groups. He begins with a simple typology of three systems of control: authority, exchange, and persuasion. He then applies these as building blocks to describe cross-national variations. He stresses that all market systems rely on some systems of authority, such as government services or corporate hierarchies, and all planned economies rely on some mechanisms of exchange, such as purchasing goods or paying wages. So the difference between a market economy and a planned economy is not that one is purely a system of exchange and the other is purely a system of authority – but that they combine these mechanisms of control in different ways. He contends that a key difference is that the flow of supplies from subcontracting firms to assembly firms is determined by exchange in one and by plan in the other. In addition, the two types of systems deploy persuasion in different ways, with commercial advertising playing a major role in market economies and political indoctrination more prominent in planned economies.

Lindblom also introduces the concept of "circularity" in markets and politics in contrast to linear models of economics and politics that emphasize the power of individual choices over outcomes. For example, a standard economic model assumes consumer sovereignty: companies try to produce what consumers want. But the notion of circularity suggests a two-way causality: consumers influence producer behavior *and* producers influence consumer behavior. Producers not only react to consumer demands but they seek to shape those demands through marketing and advertising. Lindblom also introduces the concept of "corporate discretion," stressing that market signals leave corporations with considerable leeway over many decisions, such as whether to hire more workers or to invest in research and development. And these decisions within the realm of discretion have major implications for public welfare. So Lindblom concludes that it would be perfectly appropriate for the government to design policy to nudge corporations in any direction it desires – such as toward economic growth or environmental protection – within that range of discretion. Likewise, standard political science models such as David Easton's input–output model assume popular sovereignty.[2] To be fair, these models do not imply that people's demands automatically determine policy. Rather, the demands are filtered through the political system. And much of political science scholarship focuses on this filtering process: for example, how electoral systems or political parties or congressional committees or advisory bodies mediate between demands (inputs) and policies (outputs), privileging some interests more than others. But Lindblom's notion of circularity in politics turns the direction of influence the other way, demonstrating how elites shape citizens' demands in the first place, via political indoctrination, agenda setting, or ideological hegemony.

Lindblom is best known for the chapter of the book excerpted here, where he argues that business occupies a privileged position in democratic market economies. Lindblom actually calls these systems "polyarchies" (rule by many) rather than democracies (rule by the people) precisely because business enjoys such a privileged position. He argues that business power is structural, defined by its position in the economy, rather than simply instrumental, based on resources (money and organization) and lobbying effort. Government relies heavily on business for good economic performance: it counts on corporations to use their discretion to hire workers and to invest in technology to help the economy grow. So that means that governments will seek to implement policies that favor business – that encourage business to hire and invest – whether or not businesses actively lobby for those policies. David Vogel counters with a five-point critique of this position. He contends that: (1) Lindblom exaggerates the importance of business investment in economic performance. (2) Business often does not get what it wants. (3) The government has leeway in how it responds to business demands. (4) Business is not unique as a powerful group; there are many other privileged groups such as the military and doctors. (5) Business strength can be understood within a pluralist paradigm.[3] On this final point, Vogel is essentially arguing that business power is primarily instrumental, and not structural. In recent years, political scientists have returned to Lindblom's insights, producing a new literature on the structural power of business in different national contexts.[4] Lindblom's argument seems particularly prophetic in the current era when many governments are fixated on GDP growth and stock market performance to retain power.

Peter Hall and **David Soskice** state that their objective is to elaborate a new approach to understanding the variation in the political economies of developed countries. The selection presented here is the introductory chapter of a volume that attempts to make more explicit a framework that had been evolving in the study of comparative political economy. They trace their intellectual lineage to three major approaches to comparative capitalism that fall within the rubric of political economy: (1) a perspective oriented around the strategic use of "national champions" in core industrial sectors[5] and state capacity to leverage key institutional structures such as economic plans and the financial system;[6] (2) neo-corporatist analyses that focus on the interaction of trade unions, employers, and the state;[7] and (3) a series of broader viewpoints that engage sociology in studying "social systems of production," such as collective institutions at the sectoral level,[8] national systems of innovation, and flexible production regimes on the factory shop-floor.[9]

Hall and Soskice recognize that market-institutional structures are dependent on national regulatory regimes, yet their framework centers on firms and their relationships. They concentrate on four spheres of market institutions in which firms develop relationships to carry out economic activities: industrial relations between companies and employees; vocational training and education; corporate governance relations between firms and investors; and inter-firm relations. In examining the importance of institutions in a market system, they emphasize the manner and extent to which those institutions condition strategic interaction among firms and other political–economic actors. They build on the New Institutional Economics tradition, which emphasizes the development of contractual relationships to overcome transaction costs in economic collaboration. They also recognize the political factors at play and build on the economic sociology approach by recognizing that the firm is embedded in a web of interdependent social relationships and shared cultural meanings.

The centerpiece of the varieties of capitalism framework is the dichotomy of liberal market economies (LMEs) and coordinated market economies (CMEs) and the comparison of their characteristics in terms of both relationships and outcomes. In broad strokes, firms in these two types of capitalist economies coordinate their relationships and production activities through different sets of solutions. In LMEs – such as the United States and the United Kingdom – firms primarily coordinate internally through hierarchical arrangements and externally through competitive market relationships. In CMEs – such as Germany and Japan – firms are more reliant on long-term relationships such as relational contracting and collaborative networking. Even though LMEs function through the price signals and formal contracts emphasized by neoclassical economics and the New Institutional Economics, and CMEs seem to be more embedded in the social relations emphasized by economic sociology, both systems are embedded in society and politics. The varieties of capitalism approach prevents us from falling into the analytical trap of assuming that one type of system is the default, and the other the deviation to be explained.

Hall and Soskice stress that the variation in corporate practices between LMEs and CMEs reflects their different market institutions. Moreover, these two ideal-type systems are reinforced by "institutional complementarities." That means that the different elements of the systems – such as labor market, vocational training, finance, and inter-firm network systems – work together. For example, a more competitive financial system will work better with a more competitive labor system, and a more coordinated financial system will work better with a more coordinated labor system. In this sense, the LME and CME models represent two equilibria. Hall and Soskice do not claim that all countries will perfectly fit one model or the other, but they do suggest that countries with strong institutional complementarities will perform better than countries with mismatched institutions. Hall and Soskice also introduce the related concept of "comparative institutional advantage," the notion that the LME and CME models bestow distinct competitive advantages for the firms functioning within them. For example, LME firms will have the advantage in cost-based competition because they can reallocate labor and capital more rapidly, whereas CME firms will excel in quality-based competition in manufacturing because they can leverage the collaboration between management and labor and between assembly firms and subcontractors to implement incremental improvements in production processes.

There is no dominant trend in the field of comparative political economy in the twenty-first century, but plenty of creative research points in promising new directions. Hall and Soskice have inspired research that has critiqued their approach, reformulated it, or extended it to other regions of the world.[10] Some fruitful new research streams have taken political scientists from high politics further into the micro-institutions of capitalism. For example, political scientists have shown a much stronger interest in debates about corporate governance. Peter A. Gourevitch and James Shinn present an elegant model of the politics of corporate governance reforms, which focuses on two-against-one coalitions among three key groups: owners, managers, and workers.[11] And Pepper Culpepper depicts corporate governance as a realm of low-salience "quiet politics" that tends to favor business interests.[12] Other scholars have connected politics to property rights in novel ways. Regine A. Spector, for example, shows how owners of bazaars in Kyrgyzstan secure their property via political power and social networks in the absence of strong legal protection.[13] And Jordan Gans-Morse demonstrates how businesses have gradually shifted away from reliance on violence and corruption to demand the legal protection of property in post-Soviet Russia.[14] Nonetheless, we suspect that the real-world disruptions outlined at the end of the introduction to this volume – climate change, the financial crisis, inequality, the digital platform economy, and the COVID-19 crisis – will ultimately drive the most profound changes in the study of political economy in the years to come. Each of these challenges, in its own way, calls into question prevalent schools of thought and suggests new analytical models, as we shall see in Part II of this reader.

Notes

1 See, for example, Michael Piore and Charles Sabel, *The Second Industrial Divide* (New York: Basic Books, 1984).

2 David Easton, "An Approach to the Analysis of Political Systems," *World Politics* 9 (1957): 383–400.

3 David Vogel, "Political Science and the Study of Corporate Power: A Dissent from the New Conventional Wisdom," *British Journal of Political Science* 17 (1987): 385–408.

4 Pepper D. Culpepper, "Structural Power and Political Science in the Post-Crisis Era," *Business and Politics* 17 (2015): 391–409.

5 Andrew Shonfield, *Modern Capitalism: The Changing Balance of Public and Private Power* (New York: Oxford University Press, 1965).

6 See, for example, Chalmers Johnson, *MITI and the Japanese Miracle: The Growth of Industrial Policy, 1925-1975* (Stanford, CA: Stanford University Press, 1982); John Zysman, *Governments, Markets and Growth: Financial Systems and the Politics of Industrial Change* (Ithaca, NY: Cornell University Press, 1983); and Peter J. Katzenstein, ed., *Between Power and Plenty: Foreign Economic Policies of Advanced Industrial States* (Madison, WI: University of Wisconsin Press, 1978).

7 See, for example, Philippe Schmitter and Gerhard Lehmbruch, eds., *Trends Toward Corporatist Intermediation* (Beverly Hills, CA: Sage, 1979); Suzanne Berger, ed., *Organizing Interests in Western Europe: Pluralism, Corporatism, and the Transformation of Politics* (Cambridge: Cambridge University Press, 1981); and Peter J. Katzenstein, *Corporatism and Change* (Ithaca, NY: Cornell University Press, 1985).

8 Gary Herrigel, *Industrial Constructions: The Sources of German Industrial Power* (Cambridge: Cambridge University Press, 1996).

9 Piore and Sabel, *The Second Industrial Divide*.

10 See the volume introduction regarding critiques. Applications of the framework to other regions include Ben Ross Schneider, "Contrasting Capitalisms: Latin America in Comparative Perspective," in Javier Santiso and Jeff Dayton-Johnson, eds., *The Oxford Handbook of Latin American Political Economy* (Oxford: Oxford University Press, 2012), 381–402; and Dorothee Bohle and Béla Greskovits, "The State, Internationalization, and Capitalist Diversity in Eastern Europe," *Competition and Change* 2 (2007): 89–115.

11 Peter A. Gourevitch and James Shinn, *Political Power & Corporate Control: The New Global Politics of Corporate Governance* (Princeton, NJ: Princeton University Press, 2005).

12 Pepper D. Culpepper, *Quiet Politics and Business Power: Corporate Control in Europe and Japan* (Cambridge: Cambridge University Press, 2011).

13 Regine A. Spector, *Order at the Bazaar: Power and Trade in Central Asia* (Ithaca, NY: Cornell University Press, 2017).

14 Jordan Gans-Morse, *Property Rights in Post-Soviet Russia: Violence, Corruption, and the Demand for Law* (Cambridge: Cambridge University Press, 2017).

Charles E. Lindblom,
Politics and Markets (1977)[*]

13 The Privileged Position of Business

One might have expected that central planning of production, whatever its merits, would have been attempted under democratic pressure in at least a few polyarchies. The universal hostility to it, however, opens our eyes to the possibility that genuinely popular control in the polyarchies is even weaker than described in earlier chapters. We shall examine that possibility not only to explain the hostility of polyarchy to central planning and its universal dependence on markets but because we have now raised a major question about polyarchy: Is polyarchy not very democratic at all? Are the polyarchies controlled by business and property?

We begin the analysis by exploring in this chapter the political role of businessmen in all private enterprise market-oriented societies. This role is different from what it is usually perceived to be. It is not, we shall see, merely an interest-group role.

The Business Executive as Public Official in the Market System

If we can imagine a politico-economic system without money and markets, decisions on the distribution of income would obviously be political or governmental decisions. Lacking markets and wages, income shares would have to be administered by some kind of public authority, perhaps through rationing. Decisions on what is to be produced in the system would also have to be made by political or governmental authority. So also decisions on the allocation of resources to different lines of production, on the allocation of the labor force to different occupations and workplaces, on plant location, the technologies to be used in production, the quality of goods and services, innovation of new products—in short, on every major aspect of production and distribution. All these decisions would be recognized as public policy decisions.

In all societies, these matters have to be decided. They are of momentous consequences for the welfare of any society. But in a private enterprise market system, they are in larger part decided not by government officials but by businessmen. The delegation of these decisions to the businessman does not diminish their importance or, considering their consequences, their public aspect. In communist and socialist systems, heads of enterprises are government officials; it is taken for granted that their functions are governmental. In private enterprise systems, whether polyarchal or not, their functions are no less of public consequence. On all these matters, moreover, not

---

[*] From: *Politics and Markets: The World's Political-Economic Systems*, Charles E. Lindblom, Copyright © 1977 Charles E. Lindblom. (pp.170–188) Reprinted by permission of Eric Lindblom, Susan Friedman, and Steven Lindblom.

only do business executives make consequential decisions; but, as we have seen in Chapter 11, corporate executives exercise broad discretion in making them.

For example, for a twelve-year period, while European steel companies held outputs and employment relatively stable by permitting prices of steel to fluctuate, American steel companies held prices steady with the result that output and employment fluctuated. It was a discretionary choice full of consequences for jobs, economic growth, prices, and the balance of payments.[1] But it was steel industry executives, not governmental officials, who made the decision.

We hardly need, however, further illustration of the public consequences of discretionary corporate decisions in the market. The major decisions that rest in corporate hands have been outlined in Chapter 11. Corporate executives in all private enterprise systems, polyarchic or not, decide a nation's industrial technology, the pattern of work organization, location of industry, market structure, resource allocation, and, of course, executive compensation and status. They also are the immediate or proximate and discretionary decision makers, though subject to significant consumer control, on what is to be produced and in what quantities.

In short, in any private enterprise system, a large category of major decisions is turned over to businessmen, both small and larger. They are taken off the agenda of government. Businessmen thus become a kind of public official and exercise what, on a broad view of their role, are public functions. The significant logical consequence of this for polyarchy is that a broad area of public decision making is removed from polyarchal control. Polyarchal decision making may of course ratify such an arrangement or amend it through governmental regulation of business decision making. In all real-world polyarchies, a substantial category of decisions is removed from polyarchal control.

The Businessman as Public Official in Government and Politics

What we have just said, however, only begins to describe the public role of businessmen in all private enterprise market-oriented societies. As a result of the "public" responsibilities of businessmen in the market, a great deal more is implied. Businessmen generally and corporate executives in particular take on a privileged role in government that is, it seems reasonable to say, unmatched by any leadership group other than government officials themselves.[*] Let us see, step by step, how this comes about. Every step in the analysis will refer to a familiar aspect of these systems, the implications of which, taken together, have been overlooked by most of us.

Because public functions in the market system rest in the hands of businessmen, it follows that jobs, prices, production, growth, the standard of living, and the economic security of everyone all rest in their hands. Consequently, government officials cannot be indifferent to how well business performs its functions. Depression, inflation, or

---

[*] In contemporary thought, especially democratic thought, "privilege" often connotes something improper. That is not my intention in using the term. Webster says privilege is "a right or immunity granted as a peculiar benefit, advantage, or favor; *esp.*: one attached specif. to a position or an office," and something that is privileged is "not subject to the usual rules and penalties because of some special circumstance" *(Webster's Seventh New Collegiate Dictionary* [Springfield, Mass.: G. & C. Merriam]).

other economic distress can bring down a government. A major function of government, therefore, is to see to it that businessmen perform their tasks.

Every day about us we see abundant evidence of governmental concern with business performance. In the polyarchies, government responsibility for avoiding inflation and unemployment is a common issue in elections. In all market-oriented systems, a major concern of tax and monetary policy is their effects on business activity. In subsidies and other help to water, rail, highway, and air transport; in patent protection; in fair trade regulation; in tariff policy; in overseas trade promotion through foreign ministries; in subsidized research and development (recently conspicuous, the Concorde in the United Kingdom and France, the aerospace industry in the United States)—in countless ways governments in these systems recognize that businessmen need to be encouraged to perform.

But take particular note of another familiar feature of these systems. Constitutional rules—especially the law of private property—specify that, although governments can forbid certain kinds of activity, they cannot command business to perform. They must induce rather than command.* They must therefore offer benefits to businessmen in order to stimulate the required performance. The examples above are all examples of benefits offered, not of commands issued.

One of the great misconceptions of conventional economic theory is that businessmen are induced to perform their functions by purchases of their goods and services, as though the vast productive tasks performed in market-oriented systems could be motivated solely by exchange relations between buyers and sellers. On so slender a foundation no great productive system can be established. What is required in addition is a set of governmentally provided inducements in the form of market and political benefits. And because market demands themselves do not spontaneously spring up, they too have to be nurtured by government. Governments in market-oriented systems have always been busy with these necessary activities. In the eighteenth century, for example, England established almost a thousand local road improvement authorities. When railroads became feasible, special legislation—more than 600 parliamentary acts between 1844 and 1847—granted attractive benefits to railway companies. In late eighteenth and early nineteenth century England, Parliament passed almost 4,000 enclosure acts, both creating a commercial agriculture to replace subsistence farming and driving a labor force off the land into industrial employment.

In the United States, Alexander Hamilton's *Report on Manufactures* put government in an active supportive role for business. So also did early federal policy on banks, canals, and roads; governmental profligacy in indulgences to western railroads; the judicial interpretation of antimonopoly legislation to restrict unions rather than business enterprises; the deployment of Marines to protect American enterprise in Latin America; the use of public utility regulation to protect business earnings; and the diversion of fair trade laws from their ostensible public purposes to the protection of monopolistic privilege.[2]

---

* But private property is not the key to the process being described. For any market system, whether private or public enterprise is the rule, enterprises must have autonomy or "rights" to respond to market cues rather than be obliged to obey governmental commands. See chapter 22.

In the United States, as in all other market systems, the modern corporation could develop only with the assistance of new corporate law in the mid-nineteenth century that limited stockholders liability and in other ways conferred new authority on organizers of large enterprises. In the United States the courts transformed the Fourteenth Amendment, ostensibly written to safeguard the rights of former slaves, into an instrument for the protection of the corporation in its new role as a legal person.

Even more so than in England and America, continental European governments explicitly accepted a responsibility for the development of private enterprise, Germany most conspicuously. Perhaps learning from Europe, Japan went even further with loans, subsidies, and legal privileges for business enterprise.

What, then, is the list of necessary inducements? They are whatever businessmen need as a condition for performing the tasks that fall to them in a market system: income and wealth, deference, prestige, influence, power, and authority, among others. Every government in these systems accepts a responsibility to do what is necessary to assure profits high enough to maintain as a minimum employment and growth. If businessmen say, as they do, that they need tax offsets to induce investment, governments in all these systems seriously weigh the request, acknowledging that the tax concessions may indeed be necessary. In these systems such concessions are in fact granted. If corporation executives say that the chemical industries need help for research and development, governments will again acknowledge the probability that indeed they do and will commonly provide it. If corporate executives want to consult with government officials, including president or prime minister, they will be accommodated. Given the responsibilities of businessmen in these societies, it would be a foolish chief executive who would deny them consultation. If corporate executives ask, as they frequently do, for veto power over government appointments to regulatory positions, it will again be acknowledged that such a concession may be necessary to induce business performance. All this is familiar. And we shall see below that governments sometimes offer to share their formal authority with corporate officials as a benefit offered to induce business performance.

In the eyes of government officials, therefore, businessmen do not appear simply as the representatives of a special interest, as representatives of interest groups do. They appear as functionaries performing functions that government officials regard as indispensable. When a government official asks himself whether business needs a tax reduction, he knows he is asking a question about the welfare of the whole society and not simply about a favor to a segment of the population, which is what is typically at stake when he asks himself whether he should respond to an interest group.

Any government official who understands the requirements of his position and the responsibilities that market-oriented systems throw on businessmen will therefore grant them a privileged position. He does not have to be bribed, duped, or pressured to do so. Nor does he have to be an uncritical admirer of businessmen to do so. He simply understands, as is plain to see, that public affairs in market-oriented systems are in the hands of two groups of leaders, government and business, who must collaborate and that to make the system work government leadership must often defer to business leadership. Collaboration and deference between the two are at the heart of politics in such systems. Businessmen cannot be left knocking at the doors of the political systems, they must be invited in.

A leader of a West German business association comments on the world of politics, "This is not an alien world to the entrepreneur; it is his own. At stake for him is the leadership of the state."[3] Drawing on his experience in Du Pont, an American writes, "the strength of the position of business and the weakness of the position of government is that government needs a strong economy just as much as business does, and the people need it and demand it even more."[4] The duality of leadership is reminiscent of the medieval dualism between church and state, and the relations between business and government are no less intricate than in the medieval duality.

Thus politics in market-oriented systems takes a peculiar turn, one largely ignored in conventional political science. To understand the peculiar character of politics in market-oriented systems requires, however, no conspiracy theory of politics, no theory of common social origins uniting government and business officials, no crude allegation of a power elite established by clandestine forces. Business simply needs inducements, hence a privileged position in government and politics, if it is to do its job.

Other Privileged Positions?

How might the thesis that businessmen occupy a privileged position—that they constitute a second set of major leaders in government and politics—be challenged? It can hardly be denied that business performance is required in market-oriented systems. Nor that it has to be induced rather than commanded. Nor that, consequently, government officials have to be solicitous in finding and offering appropriate inducements. Perhaps, however, other groups enjoy similar privilege for similar reason? It seems reasonable to suggest that labor leaders, who might be thought the most likely occupants of a similar privileged position, do not occupy one. They and their unions do not provide, we have already noted, essential services. Their function is instead to advance the segmental interests of workers. But workers themselves provide essential services, it might be replied. If they do not work, the whole productive system halts.

The plain fact, however, is that workers do work—without special inducement from government. Their livelihoods depend on it. Their position is quite different from that of the businessman, who has a dimension of choice. He will not risk capital, reputation, or the solvency of an enterprise in order to undertake an entrepreneurial venture unless the conditions are favorable. The test of the difference is an obvious one. All over the world men work at ordinary jobs because they have no choice but to do so. But in many parts of the world the conditions that call forth entrepreneurial energy and venturesomeness are still lacking, and the energy and venturesomeness are therefore not forthcoming. The particular roles that businessmen are required to play in market-oriented systems they play well only when sufficiently indulged.

But a sufficient degree of union organization and ambition, it would seem, could at least in some circumstances put workers or their union leaders in a privileged position in government. It could happen if unions could successfully stop production, not simply in one firm or industry, but broadly as in a general strike. Ordinarily, however, a general strike—except as a demonstration for a few days—is impossible because it provokes the government, even in the polyarchies, to break the strike, as in the aborted British general strike of 1926. In short, the rules of market-oriented systems, while granting a privileged position to business, so far appear to prohibit the organizational moves that would win a comparable position for labor. Hence a privileged position for union leaders and their unions is approximated only in special circumstances. A noteworthy example is the use of the strike threat among municipal employees in New York City. Their privileged position in New York City government seems unquestionable.

From time to time other groups achieve a limited privileged position. Physicians in the United States enjoy privileges in policy making on health because government officials fear that their performance will be adversely affected if they do not. In many of the developing nations, the internal security forces hold a privileged position because higher government officials know that if unsatisfied these forces can turn on their ostensible masters. Farmers are another case. Many of them are businessmen and share in the privileged position of business. But many very small farm operators have no more choice about performing than do ordinary workers.

Changing Privileges

The level and character of privilege that businessmen require as a condition of their satisfactory performance vary from time to time and place to place. All about us is conspicuous evidence that some older privileges have been withdrawn, even to the point of nationalizing some firms and industries. In many of the market-oriented systems, business enterprise is more heavily taxed than before. It is also subjected to increasing regulation on some scores—for example, regulation of industrial relations, monopoly, and now environmental pollution. Clearly businessmen have commonly demanded of government more indulgences than are actually necessary to motivate their required performances. As some of these indulgences have been taken away, their performance has not faltered.[5]

On the other hand, the removal of some privileges appears to require the institution of offsetting new ones—for example, tax credits. Forty percent of net investments in manufacturing equipment in the United States in 1963 was estimated to be attributable to the investment tax credit of 1962.[6] In the market-oriented systems, governments underwrite much of the cost of research and development for business. They also provide security to business enterprises through a variety of protections for monopoly, like fair trade legislation. In some industries, government shares or bears the risk of new plant construction by renting facilities to firms that do not want to construct their own. Half of the plant facilities of U.S. defense plants are provided by government. Governments also bail out failing enterprises with loans. And in much of recent capital planning in Western Europe, businessmen are brought into a new intimacy of consultation with government officials.

Many of the new privileges, which offset some taken away, are not widely recognized to be such. Urban renewal, for example, comes to the aid of retailers, banks, theaters, public utilities, brokers, and builders. Highway development promotes a long list of industries including cement, automobiles, construction, petroleum, construction equipment, and trucking.[7] But the ostensible purpose of urban renewal and highway development is not aid to business.

Conflicts among *Businessmen*

On some demands—those pertaining to enterprise autonomy, private property, limited business taxation, and tax incentives, for example—business volitions are relatively homogeneous. On other demands, some businessmen want one kind of benefit; others want another. That businessmen disagree on such demands is not usually a barrier to their occupying a privileged position, for to give one kind of business a benefit is not necessarily to deprive another. On some issues, of course, privilege granted to one segment of the business community represents the withdrawal of a privilege from another. Large meat packers, for example, may press for inspection laws that, by raising the costs of small packers, give the large ones a competitive advantage. But it is possible for government officials to find an offsetting benefit to the small packers to compensate for the injury, if officials understand that redress is necessary.

Mutual Adjustment between the Two Groups

So far we have stressed controls by businessmen over government. But of course controls go in both directions. In briefest outline the reciprocal controls look like the following:

> Government exercises broad authority over business activities.
> But the exercise of that authority is curbed and shaped by the concern of government officials for its possible adverse effects of business, since adverse effects can cause unemployment and other consequences that government officials are unwilling to accept.
> In other areas of public policy, the authority of government is again curbed and shaped by concern for possible adverse effects on business.
> Hence even the unspoken possibility of adversity for business operates as an all-pervasive constraint on government authority.
> Mindful of government concern for business performance, businessmen, especially corporate executives, actively voice and negotiate demands on government, with both implicit threat of poor performance if their demands are not met.
> For all these reasons, business officials are privileged not only with respect to the care with which government satisfies business needs in general but also in privileged roles as participants in policy deliberations in government.
> At least hypothetically, government always has the option, if dissatisfied with business performance, of refusing further privilege and simply terminating private enterprise in a firm, industry or the entire system. Short of taking that course, however, government has to meet business needs as a condition of inducing business performance.

Market and private enterprise thus introduce an extreme degree of mutual adjustment and political pluralism, even in the absence of polyarchy. The mutual adjustment is not always explicit through meetings and actual negotiation. Nor does government usually enter into an explicit exchange with businessmen. Mutual adjustment is often impersonal and distant. It operates through an unspoken deference of administrations, legislatures, and courts to the needs of business. And it relies on a multitude of common tacit understandings shared by the two groups of leaders, business and governmental, with respect to the conditions under which enterprises can or cannot profitably operate.

In addition, business executives come to be admitted to circles of explicit negotiation, bargaining, and reciprocal persuasion, from which ordinary citizens are excluded. Other leaders are admitted—union and farm leaders and other interest-group representatives. In these consultations, however, corporate executives occupy a privileged position, since they and not the interest-group leaders are there mainly in their capacity as "public" officials.

It follows that evidence, which is abundant, of conflict between business and government—and of business defeats—is not evidence of lack of privilege. Knowing that they must have some privileges and knowing that government officials fully understand that simple fact, businessmen ask for great deal. They also routinely protest any proposal to reduce any of their privileges. They are not highly motivated to try to understand their own needs. It might weaken them in governmental negotiations to do so. Hence they often predict dire consequences when a new regulation is imposed on them, yet thereafter quickly find ways to perform under it.

It appears that disputes between government and business are intense because of—not in spite of—their sharing the major leadership roles in the politico-economic order. Inevitably two separate yet cooperating groups of leaders will show hostility to each other. They will also invest some of their energies in outwitting each other, each trying to gain the upper hand. Conflict will always lie, however, within a range of dispute constrained by their understanding that they together constitute the necessary leadership for the system. They do not wish to destroy or seriously undermine the function of each other.

They therefore do not dispute the fundamentals of their symbiotic relationship—private enterprise itself, private property in productive assets, and a large measure of enterprise autonomy, for example. They dispute over an ever-shifting category of secondary issues—such as tax rates and particulars of regulation and promotion of business. Imagine a continuum of possible combinations of business and governmental control over politico-economic life, ranging at far left from extraordinary autonomy for the business enterprise—some extreme form of laissez-faire—to a terminus at the extreme right at which the autonomous business enterprise vanishes in favor of production in the hands of government agencies. Extreme positions on such a continuum are not disputed by government and businessmen. Some narrow range of disagreement is, however, constantly disputed.

It appears also that the range slowly shifts, decade by decade, in the direction of less privilege for business and more authority for government. But at any time there is, even allowing for businessmen gradually learning to perform in a less privileged position in government, some minimum of privilege short of which inducements will fail to motivate business performance. An illustration is the demand for privilege that giant multinational corporations can impose on small nations. Either the demands are met, or the corporation goes elsewhere.

Dimensions of the Privileged Position

Everything we have now outlined on the privileged position of business and on the duality of leadership in all private enterprise systems rests on familiar observable aspects of these systems. Some further brief detail, however will illuminate the phenomena.

Government officials, we have seen, routinely and explicitly acknowledge the necessity of adapting public policy to the needs of business whenever, say, they talk about using tax or monetary policy to stimulate business. The explicitness and precision of their acknowledgement, however, often goes further and clarifies the full dimensions of the privileged position of business. For example, in a suit brought against the Richardson-Merrell pharmaceutical company because its product MER/29 produced a variety of symptoms including cataracts, it was established to the judge's satisfaction that over a ten-year testing period the company had repeatedly suppressed evidence of the drug's dangers, filing falsified reports to the Food and Drug Administration. Yet the judge refused to award punitive damages, fearing that if he did,

> A sufficient egregious error as to one product can end the business life of a concern that has wrought much good in the past.[8]

It is an elegantly simple example of acknowledged need to accommodate public policy to the needs of business, if business is to do its tasks.

For another example, Peter Peterson, then the chairman of the President's Council on International Economic Policy, declared: "The government has to foster in a planned and targeted way" those industries—he was speaking of American enterprise abroad—that are most promising.[9] Or, commenting on a $250 million loan to save Lockheed, U.S. Secretary of Commerce John Connally said: "We feel that the impact that the demise of this company would have would be of such proportions that it ought not to be permitted in the interest of the economic revival of the nation."[10] An Italian civil servant says: "The bureaucrat then is in a very weak position if he seeks to oppose Confindustria, particularly when the latter says, 'you must do the following regarding this industrial sector or you will cause crisis, bankruptcy, and unemployment.'"[11]

Businessmen sometimes acknowledge their privileged position in both word and deed. In the United Kingdom, for example, the Federation of British Industries (now merged in the Confederation of British Industry) routinely maintained both formal and day-to-day informal communication with the Treasury, Board of Trade, Home Office, and the ministries of Housing, Education, Local Government, Power, Transport, and Aviation, in addition to frequent communication with other ministries and offices. In so constant and broad an exercise of influence, the Federation "acted as if it were the industrial counterpart of the Civil Service, and avoided as far as possible actions which made it look like a pressure group." "It looked and acted like a government department."[12]

In Japanese politics an intimacy of connection between businessmen, civil service, and legislators goes beyond that of the United States or the Western European polyarchies. It is a connection that government officials do not establish with labor or any other groups. It is achieved by devices including family connection, old-school ties, and movement of personnel from government to business. "Business becomes the major concern of government," business and the bureaucracy achieve a "symbiosis." A prime minister describes the big business community as the "compass" of the ship of state.[13]

A former public relations officer in an American corporation advises businessmen: "Let it be publicly known that business climate is a very important factor in determining the selection of states and communities in which to locate new plants. The importance of this is that it places on the defensive the people who are beating upon, overtaxing, and harassing business."[14] He is speaking of a commonplace phenomenon that most people take for granted: extracting privileges from state and local government. Many other responses to business demands are also routinized without controversy.

But if government accommodation of business demands is often routine and familiar, it sometimes takes a twist that refreshes our understanding of the strength of corporation executives in their privileged portion. For example:

> Unless the British government agreed to provide massive aid for Chrysler's troubled British subsidiary, Riccardo [chairman of Chrysler] said, the company would be forced to shut down its five major plants in Britain and cashier its 25,000 employees there.... Wilson denounced the Riccardo ultimatum, angrily protesting that Chrysler had left the government "with a pistol at its head." But last week in a startling, if characteristically Wilsonian, about-face, the Prime Minister agreed to help out Chrysler after all.[15]

Governmental responsiveness to business demands shows up in other unexpected ways. An oddity in American law, for example, permits corporations whose officials have been convicted of crimes to continue to use their services while they are on probation or after their sentences have expired, while union officials are prohibited from returning to office for five years after conviction.[16] For another example, a subcommittee of the Senate Armed Services Committee found that stockpiling of materials ostensibly needed for national defense was actually undertaken without respect to national security needs, the "primary purpose" being the subsidization of mining companies.[17] A French businessman says of French planning:

> I would disagree ... that the primary purpose of the plan is "to bring economic power under political control." It is rather to help the businessman to expand his economic activity.[18]

And from a study of French planning:

> ... there is no doubt that the activity of planning, as it is practised in France, has reinforced the systematic influence exerted by large-scale business on economic policy. Sometimes this influence is open and apparent, as when the Fourth Plan's investment policy for steel was modified in 1963 in deference to the wishes of the steel industry, despite the barely concealed objections of certain government officials. Subsequently, when the industry was offered a sufficient financial inducement by the Government—in the form of a reduction in the tariffs on imported US coking coal and a rebate on their social security payments—they agreed to an increase in the steel manufacturing capacity to be laid down in the Fifth Plan.[19]

French planning is thus in some part even an explicit exchange of favors: industry offers performance—expansion, relocation, technological innovation, and the like—in exchange for governmental favors like tax rebates, subsidies, or credit advantages. Similarly in the National Economic Development Council in the United Kingdom "each party offers something which is conditional on certain actions by others."[20]

In Germany earlier corporate decentralization measures left business unwilling to undertake the vast tasks of postwar reconstruction. The measures had to be abandoned. Demands from business accomplished the same erosion of controls on business size in postwar Japan.[21] In Italy the Institute for Industrial Reconstruction is a focal point for business demands and governmental responses necessary to induce business to mobilize the large amounts of capital needed for modern industry.[22]

Obviously in no system do businessmen get all they ask for. The task of government is to find responses to the demands of businessmen sufficient to motivate them to perform the tasks delegated to them, but without simply turning policy making over to them lock, stock, and barrel. It is a task that requires great skill if it is to be done well enough to maintain both economic stability and growth. French planning has in recent years been applauded as a demonstration of skill in the design of indulgences to business, and sluggishness in the American economy held up as an example of its absence.

Sometimes governments fail to respond to business demands even though the penalties, which come in the form of slowed growth and unemployment, are severe. In the less developed parts of the world, the growth of markets and enterprise is repeatedly hindered by the failure of governments to provide necessary infrastructure and other supports. In India a principled hostility to private enterprise has for more than a decade constrained the Indian government not to provide the supports that business wants. The result has been retarded industrial and commercial development. The possibility arises also in the developed nations. After World War II, French business was under heavy attack for its collaborationist tendencies during the war. It was consequently not disposed to invest. Some businessmen prepared to emigrate, so great was hostility to them. The government of France had to find new inducements for French business in order to induce it to take up its responsibilities again.[23] *

Yet ordinarily as new conditions or problems arise—for example, public demands for restriction on air pollution—businessmen know that government officials will

---

* When in his inaugural address in 1953 President Eisenhower declared that "we need markets in the world for the surpluses of our farms and our factories," he was acknowledging that businessmen make demands on government in foreign policy as well as domestic policy, just as the chairman of the President's Council on International Economic Policy, we saw, understands that government has to foster business activity overseas. We would go astray if we tried to incorporate into the analysis the complexities of business in international markets and politics, but it is essential to note that the duality of leadership in market-oriented systems extends to foreign policy.

Whether business demands on government in market-oriented systems drive governments inevitably into a new form of imperialism is a somewhat different question, again beyond our inquiry. The smaller market-oriented systems are not imperialist, and France and the United Kingdom appear to be retiring from earlier imperialist roles. The charge of imperialism is an interesting allegation only when brought against the United States as a superpower—and against the U.S.S.R. as another. Yet unquestionably the superior resources and capacity to mobilize authority and other power in international relations give all the industrialized market-oriented systems, large and small, great advantages in international

understand their wishes—in this case their unwillingness or incapacity to bear without help the costs of stopping industrial discharges into the air. Businessmen will find the government official ready to acknowledge their special competence and interest, eager to welcome them into negotiation, anxious about the possible adverse effects of costly antipollution measures on prices and production. Thus, as environmental concerns mounted, President Nixon established in 1970 the National Industrial Pollution Control Council to allow businessmen communication with the president "to help chart the route by [sic] which our cooperative ventures will follow." Similarly, out of concern that widespread new consumer offices in various federal agencies might be damaging to business, he established in 1971 the National Business Council for Consumer Affairs, again to allow businessmen to communicate regularly with him.[24]

Businessmen only rarely threaten any collective action such as a concerted restriction of function. Ordinarily, they need only point to the costs of doing business, the state of the economy, the dependence of the economy's stability and growth on their profits or sales prospect—and simply predict, not threaten, that adverse consequences will follow on a refusal of their demands.

Ostensibly businessmen do nothing more than persuade. They simply acquaint government officials with the facts. But prophecies of some kinds tend to be self-fulfilling. If spokesmen for businessmen predict that new investment will lag without tax relief, it is only one short step to corporate decisions that put off investment until tax relief is granted.

Business Authority in Government

The far edge of the privileged position of business is represented by actual grants of government authority to businessmen. Decades ago in the United States the right of eminent domain was granted to private utility corporations, conferring on them

---

negotiation and commercial dealings with the less developed countries, which they typically use to their own perceived advantage. See Benjamin J. Cohen, *The Question of Imperialism* (New York: Basic Books, 1973).

It is also alleged that business demands on government drive market-oriented systems into heavy defense expenditure and into war, and indeed that these systems cannot grow without heavy defense expenditure. Again, the exploration of the many facets of these allegations is beyond us. But some points are quickly established. Military expenditure is not correlated with type of politico-economic system. The big spenders are both the United States and the Soviet Union. Most industrialized market-oriented systems spend less than the communist nations of Eastern Europe. As for whether defense spending helps the economy, among market-oriented systems those with the largest defense spending are the slowest growers. Heavy defense spending is possibly an obstacle to growth and may help explain slow American growth in recent decades, just as its absence helps explain high Japanese and Mexican growth. For a summary of evidence, see Harold J. Wilensky, *The Welfare State and Equality* (Berkeley: University of California Press, 1975), pp. 82–84.

Similarly, the military-industrial complex, called to the nation's attention by President Eisenhower at the end of his term, is, again, largely an American and Soviet phenomenon, hence presumably attributable, at least in part, to their superpower roles. In amount of military spending, intimacy and frequency of association between defense corporations and government officials, and development of a special sector of the American politico-economy, a distinctive phenomenon has developed, to which Eisenhower's term is appropriately applied. But not in the market-oriented systems as a category.

compulsory authority to acquire land for their operations. In this and other ways governments respond to demands with a formal or informal grant of authority to businessmen, cementing their privileged position in government.

Business groups that become established as clients of specific U.S. government agencies often win grants of informal authority. Examples are the civil contractors dealing with the Army Corps of Engineers, the Rural Electrification Administration, and the Small Business Administration, respectively. Their collaborations have been characterized as "joint government by public and private bodies."[25]

Some of these grants are relatively explicit. The president of the United States grants authority to executives of regulated industries to veto appointments to regulatory agencies.[26] Some are formal. Since 1933, the president, Cabinet members, and other high officials have met with the Business Council, composed of leading corporate executives.[27] The federal government has also established between 1,000 and 2,000 business councils to consult with agencies on common policies—this in addition to about 4,000 particular to the Department of Agriculture.[28] In addition, it invites corporation executives, while still active in and salaried by their own corporations, to serve as unpaid government officials.

In 1953, that practice was given a more permanent peacetime basis when the Business and Defense Services Administration was established. Of it, a congressional committee said:

> In operation, the organization arrangements of BDSA have effected a virtual abdication of administrative responsibility on the part of the Government officials in charge of the Department of Commerce in that their actions in many instances are but the automatic approval of decisions already made outside the Government in business and industry.[29]

For less formal grants, the line between granting a rule of obedience, thus establishing an acceptance of authority, and yielding to the offers or threats of exchange is often a thin one. This point is made by a report on consultations on New York city and state finance:

> One stumbling block to the [absorption of] $3 billion of New York City's short-term debt was resolved yesterday.... The one agreement reached ... was on a demand from the investment community that the city sales tax be converted to a state sales tax.[30]

In France business committees are also commonplace.[31] An industry and its associated ministry commonly develop a sharing of authority in making and implementing policy for the industry. It is intended that authority be shifted to the industry, and the shift is made even more definitive by moving much of the work of the ministry to the industry, whose cooperating staff often greatly outnumbers that of the ministry. The result is that decisions reached by the industry are ordinarily given ministerial approval.[32] In French planning, ostensibly a cooperation among government officials and business and union representatives, authority denied the latter is granted to the former: businessmen but not labor leaders can chair the *commissions*.[33]

In the United Kingdom hundreds of business advisory committees confer authority on corporate executives. In addition are special departmental committees and royal commissions, in which what begins as an advisory role for businessmen and other participants "becomes active participation in administration, as if the administrators were no longer able to bear alone the burden of the administrative State and had to pass it along to private individuals."[34]

In West Germany, representatives of national industry associations confer on new legislation with civil servants who refuse similar rights of participation to members of parliament.[35] And government agrees to membership on a special body on cartel legislation "even though to do so had the rather unorthodox effect of putting the BDI (Federation of German Industry) on an equal level with itself in the formulation of policy."[36] In Japan, the *genkyoku* offices, each responsible for certain industries, are paralleled by industry associations, and for each industry the two organizations negotiate and collaborate on policy for the industry.[37]

Under these circumstances, the "For years I thought what was good for our country was good for General Motors, and vice versa," spoken by a president of GM is easy to understand. However partisan they may be in fact, however uncritical about the coincidence of their own interests with broader public interests, businessmen do understand that they carry a public responsibility for discharging necessary public functions that other nongovernmental leaders do not carry. If they are, on the one hand, capable of gross abuse of that responsibility, they are, on the other hand, at least dimly aware of their special role as one of two groups that constitute a dual leadership in the market-oriented systems.

In a passage that could be taken as a summary comment on the line of analysis so far, Woodrow Wilson once wrote:

> The government of the United States at present is a foster-child of the special interests. It is not allowed to have a will of its own. It is told at every move: "Don't do that; you will interfere with our prosperity."[38]

In these comments, Wilson is angry. He sees these characteristics of government as inexcusable. On that, opinions will differ. My point has been only to explain the fundamental mechanism by which a great degree of business control, unmatched by similar control exercised by any other group of citizens, comes to be exercised over government and to indicate why this is inevitable in all private enterprise systems if they are to be viable.*

Again; businessmen do not get everything they want. But they get a great deal. And when they do not get enough, recession or stagnation is a consequence.

We have not wholly specified the policies or objectives that corporation executives use their privileged position to pursue. Some of their pursuits have been made

---

* The proposition does not deny that persons who have scientific, technical, and other specialized information grow in influence in a society that is increasingly dependent on that information. They do not demand influence; they simply achieve it by reason of what they know. See Daniel Bell, *The Coming of Post-Industrial Society* (New York: Basic Books, 1973), pp. 358–67, and R. E. Lane, "The Decline of Politics and Ideology in a Knowledgeable Society," *American Sociological Review* 31 (October 1966). However pervasive their influence, it is ordinarily indirect, affecting outcomes through its impact on government officials, businessmen, and others who employ the producers of knowledge.

clear: among many others, autonomy for the enterprise, tax favors and subsidies, restrictions on unions, a great variety of monopolistic privileges (tariffs, patents, retail price maintenance, weak antitrust enforcement, encouragement of mergers, fair trade restrictions on competition, occupational licensing, permissive regulation of public utilities, among others). All represent pursuits on which business prevails, though never without limit and with even occasional sharp defeat. We have also seen that the entire industrial structure is largely the result of business decisions on the whole sanctioned and sometimes implemented by responsive government officials. These decisions determine the size of plants and firms, the location of industry, the organization of markets and transport—hence the configuration of cities, on one hand, and the bureaucratization of the workplace, on the other.

It might therefore be argued that some of the most fundamental and pervasive features of industrial society are what they are because of the privileged position of business in government and politics. The possibility also has to be entertained that a remarkable historical stability in the distribution of wealth and income—despite all the policies of the welfare state, and even in egalitarian Scandinavia—owes much to the privileged position of business. So also the survival of the private enterprise system itself. All these possibilities will be explored further in later chapters. We begin by examining now the particular relations between business privilege and polyarchy.

Notes

1 U.S. Congress, Senate, Subcommittee on Antitrust and Monopoly of the Committee on the Judiciary: Hearings, Egon Sohmen testimony in *Economic Concentration,* 90th Congress, 2d session, 1968, p. 3446.

2 For a long list of U.S. business subsidies, see Clair Wilcox, *Public Policy toward Business,* 4th ed. (Homewood, III.: Irwin, 1971), chapter 33. On the variety of promotions, see Murray Weidenbaum, *The Modern Public Sector* (New York: Basic Books, 1969), esp. the table on p. 137.

3 Quoted in Heinz Hartmann, *Authority and Organization in German Management* (Princeton, N.J.: Princeton University Press, 1959), p. 229.

4 Harold Brayman, *Corporate Management in a World of Politics* (New York: McGraw-Hill, 1967), p. 57.

5 On the adjustment of protesting businessmen to the reduction of their privileges, see Robert E. Lane, *The Regulation of Businessmen* (New Haven, Conn.: Yale University Press, 1954).

6 On tax policy support, see Robert E. Hall and Dale W. Jorgenson, "Tax Policy and Investment Behavior," *American Economic Review* 57 (June 1967): 410.

7 For detail, see James O'Connor, "The Private Welfare State," in Milton Mankoff, ed., *The Poverty of Progress* (New York: Holt, Rinehart, and Winston, 1972), pp. 96–101.

8 Christopher D. Stone, *Where the Law Ends* (New York: Harper & Row, 1975), pp. 54–56.

9 Mark Green and Peter Petkas, "Nixon's Industrial State," *New Republic* 167 (16 September 1972): 20.

10 Ibid., p. 19.

11 Joseph LaPalombara, *Interest Groups in Italian Politics* (Princeton, N.J.: Princeton University Press, 1964), p. 278.

12 Stephen Blank, *Industry and Government in Britain* (Lexington, Mass.: D. C. Heath, 1973), pp. 67–70, 211.

13 Chitoshi Yanaga, *Big Business in Japanese Politics* (New Haven, Conn.: Yale University Press, 1968), pp. 3, 34, 95–96, 308. See also Hugh Patrick, "An Introduction to the Japanese Economy," mimeographed (October 1973); Ryutaro Komiya, "Economic Planning in Japan," in *Economic Planning, East and West,* ed. Morris Bernstein (Cambridge, Mass.: Ballinger, 1975); and T. F. M. Adams and N. Kobayashi, *The World of Japanese Business* (Tokyo: Kodansha International, 1969).

14 Brayman, *Corporate Management,* p. 110.

15 *Time,* 29 December 1975, p. 61.

16 Stone, *Where the Law Ends,* pp. 192–93.

17 U.S. Congress, Senate, Committee on Armed Services, draft report of the National Stockpile and Naval Petroleum Reserves Subcommittee, *Inquiry into the Strategic and Critical Material Stockpiles of the United States,* 88th Congress, 1st session, 1963, pp. 4–5, 36–46.

18 Gilbert M. Sauvage, "The French Businessman in His Milieu," in *The Business Establishment,* ed. Earl F. Cheit (New York: John Wiley & Sons, 1964), p. 236.

19 Andrew Shonfield, *Modern Capitalism* (London: Oxford University Press, 1965), p. 139.

20 Ibid., p. 164.

21 Ibid., p. 241; and Chitoshi Yanaga, *Big Business in Japanese Politics,* pp. 35–36.

22 Shonfield, *Modern Capitalism,* p. 188.

23 Henry W. Ehrmann, *Organized Business in France* (Princeton, N.J.: Princeton University Press, 1957), pp. 103ff.

24 Green and Petkas, "Nixon's Industrial State," p. 19.

25 Shonfield, *Modern Capitalism,* p. 335.

26 Louis A. Kohlmeier, *The Regulators* (New York: Harper & Row, 1969), p 49,

27 Brayman, *Corporate Management,* pp. 68–69.

28 U.S. Congress, House, hearings before a subcommittee of the Committee on Government Operations, *Amendment to the Administrative Expense Act of 1946,* 85th Congress, 1st session, 1957, pp. 2, 23.

29 Grant McConnell, *Private Power and American Democracy* (New York: Knopf, 1967), p. 271.

30 New York *Times,* 8 June 1975, p. 1.

31 Henry W. Ehrmann, *Politics in France* (Boston: Little, Brown, 1971), p. 178; Ehrmann, *Organized Business,* pp. 259ff.

32 For details on a case, see Ehrmann, *Organized Business,* p. 262.

33 Shonfield, *Modern Capitalism,* pp. 128 and 232n.

34 J. Blondel, *Voters, Parties, and Leaders* (Harmondsworth, Middlesex, England, 1966), pp. 223, 222–31.

35 Shonfield, *Modern Capitalism,* p. 243n.

36 Gerard Braunthal, *The Federation of German Industry in Politics* (Ithaca, N.Y.: Cornell University Press, 1965), p. 239.

37 Ryutaro Komiya, "Economic Planning in Japan," in *Economic Planning, East and West,* ed. Morris Bornstein (Cambridge, Mass.: Ballinger, 1975).

38 Woodrow Wilson, *The New Freedom* (New York: Doubleday, Page, 1913), p. 58.

Peter A. Hall and David Soskice,
Varieties of Capitalism (2001)[*]

1: An Introduction to Varieties of Capitalism

1.1 Introduction

Political economists have always been interested in the differences in economic and political institutions that occur across countries. Some regard these differences as deviations from 'best practice' that will dissolve as nations catch up to a technological or organizational leader. Others see them as the distillation of more durable historical choices for a specific kind of society, since economic institutions condition levels of social protection, the distribution of income, and the availability of collective goods—features of the social solidarity of a nation. In each case, comparative political economy revolves around the conceptual frameworks used to understand institutional variation across nations.

On such frameworks depend the answers to a range of important questions. Some are policy-related. What kind of economic policies will improve the performance of the economy? What will governments do in the face of economic challenges? What defines a state's capacities to meet such challenges? Other questions are firm-related. Do companies located in different nations display systematic differences in their structure and strategies? If so, what inspires such differences? How can national differences in the pace or character of innovation be explained? Some are issues about economic performance. Do some sets of institutions provide lower rates of inflation and unemployment or higher rates of growth than others? What are the trade-offs in terms of economic performance to developing one type of political economy rather than another? Finally, second-order questions about institutional change and stability are of special significance today. Can we expect technological progress and the competitive pressures of globalization to inspire institutional convergence? What factors condition the adjustment paths a political economy takes in the face of such challenges?

The object of this book is to elaborate a new framework for understanding the institutional similarities and differences among the developed economies, one that offers a new and intriguing set of answers to such questions.[1] We outline the basic approach in this Introduction. Subsequent chapters extend and apply it to a wide range of issues. In many respects, this approach is still a work-in-progress. We see it as a set of contentions that open up new research agendas rather than settled wisdom to be accepted uncritically, but, as the contributions to this volume indicate, it provides new perspectives on an unusually broad set of topics, ranging from issues in innovation,

[*] From: "An Introduction to Varieties of Capitalism" in *Varieties of Capitalism: The Institutions of Comparative Advantage*, Peter A. Hall and David Soskice, eds., Oxford, New York: Oxford University Press, 2001. (pp. 1–41) By permission of Oxford University Press.

vocational training, and corporate strategy to those associated with legal systems, the development of social policy, and the stance nations take in international negotiations.

As any work on this topic must be, ours is deeply indebted to prior scholarship in the field. The 'varieties of capitalism' approach developed here can be seen as an effort to go beyond three perspectives on institutional variation that have dominated the study of comparative capitalism in the preceding thirty years.[2] In important respects, like ours, each of these perspectives was a response to the economic problems of its time.

The first of these perspectives offers a *modernization approach* to comparative capitalism nicely elucidated in Shonfield's magisterial treatise of 1965. Devised in the post-war decades, this approach saw the principal challenge confronting the developed economies as one of modernizing industries still dominated by pre-war practices in order to secure high rates of national growth. Analysts tried to identify a set of actors with the strategic capacity to devise plans for industry and to impress them on specific sectors. Occasionally, this capacity was said to reside in the banks but more often in public officials. Accordingly, those taking this approach focused on the institutional structures that gave states leverage over the private sector, such as planning systems and public influence over the flows of funds in the financial system (Cohen 1977; Estrin and Holmes 1983; Zysman 1983; Cox 1986). Countries were often categorized, according to the structure of their state, into those with 'strong' and 'weak' states (Katzenstein 1978b; Sacks 1980; Nordlinger 1981; Skocpol and Amenta 1985). France and Japan emerged from this perspective as models of economic success, while Britain was generally seen as a laggard (Shonfield 1965; Johnson 1982).

During the 1970s, when inflation became the preeminent problem facing the developed economies, a number of analysts developed a second approach to comparative capitalism based on the concept of *neo-corporatism* (Schmitter and Lehmbruch 1979; Berger 1981; Goldthorpe 1984; Alvarez et al. 1991). Although defined in various ways, neo-corporatism was generally associated with the capacity of a state to negotiate durable bargains with employers and the trade union movement regarding wages, working conditions, and social or economic policy.[3] Accordingly, a nation's capacity for neo-corporatism was generally said to depend on the centralization or concentration of the trade union movement, following an Olsonian logic of collective action which specifies that more encompassing unions can better internalize the economic effects of their wage settlements (Olson 1965; Cameron 1984; Calmfors and Driffill 1988; Golden 1993). Those who saw neo-corporatist bargains as a 'political exchange' emphasized the ability of states to offer inducements as well as the capacity of unions to discipline their members (Pizzorno 1978; Regini 1984; Scharpf 1987, 1991; cf. Przeworski and Wallerstein 1982). Those working from this perspective categorized countries largely by reference to the organization of their trade union movement; and the success stories of this literature were the small, open economies of northern Europe.

During the 1980s and 1990s, a new approach to comparative capitalism that we will term a *social systems of production* approach gained currency. Under this rubric, we group analyses of sectoral governance, national innovation systems, and flexible production regimes that are diverse in some respects but united by several key analytic features. Responding to the reorganization of production in response to technological change, these works devote more attention to the behavior of firms. Influenced by the French regulation school, they emphasize the movement of firms away from mass production toward new production regimes that depend on collective institutions at the regional, sectoral, or national level (Piore and Sabel 1984; Dore 1986; Streeck and Schmitter 1986; Dosi et al. 1988; Boyer 1990; Lazonick 1991; Campbell et al. 1991; Nelson 1993; Hollingsworth et al. 1994; Herrigel 1996; Hollingsworth and Boyer 1997; Edquist 1997; Whitley 1999). These works bring a wider range of institutions into the analysis and adopt a more sociological approach to their operation, stressing the ways in which institutions generate trust or enhance learning within economic communities. As a result, some of these works resist national categories in favor of an emphasis on regional success of the sort found in Baden-Württemberg and the Third Italy.

Each of these bodies of work explains important aspects of the economic world. However, we seek to go beyond them in several respects. Although those who wrote within it characterized national differences in the early post-war era well, for instance, some versions of the modernization approach tend to overstate what governments can accomplish, especially in contexts of economic openness where adjustment is firm-led. We will argue that features of states once seen as attributes of strength actually make the implementation of many economic policies more difficult; and we seek a basis for comparison more deeply rooted in the organization of the private sector.

Neo-corporatist analysis directs our attention to the organization of society, but its emphasis on the trade union movement underplays the role that firms and employer organizations play in the coordination of the economy (cf. Soskice 1990a; Swenson 1991). We want to bring firms back into the center of the analysis of comparative capitalism and, without neglecting trade unions, highlight the role that business associations and other types of relationships among firms play in the political economy.

The literature on social systems of production accords firms a central role and links the organization of production to the support provided by external institutions at many levels of the political economy. However, without denying that regional or sectoral institutions matter to firm behavior, we focus on variation among national political economies. Our premiss is that many of the most important institutional structures—notably systems of labor market regulation, of education and training, and of corporate governance—depend on the presence of regulatory regimes that are the preserve of the nation-state. Accordingly, we look for national-level differences and terms in which to characterize them that are more general or parsimonious than this literature has generated.[4]

Where we break most fundamentally from these approaches, however, is in our conception of how behavior is affected by the institutions of the political economy. Three frameworks for understanding this relationship dominate the analysis of comparative capitalism. One sees institutions as *socializing agencies* that instill a particular set of norms or attitudes in those who operate within them. French civil servants, for instance, are said to acquire a particular concern for the public interest by virtue of their training or the ethos of their agencies. A second suggests that the effects of an institution follow from the *power* it confers on particular actors through the formal sanctions that hierarchy supplies or the resources an institution provides for mobilization. Industrial policy-makers and trade union leaders are often said to have such forms of power. A third framework construes the institutions of the political economy as a *matrix of sanctions and incentives* to which the relevant actors respond such that behavior can be predicted more or less automatically from the presence of specific institutions, as, for instance, when individuals refuse to provide public goods in the absence of selective incentives. This kind of logic is often cited to explain the willingness of encompassing trade unions to moderate wages in order to reduce inflation.

Each of these formulations captures important ways in which the institutions of the political economy affect economic behavior and we make use of them. However, we think these approaches tend to miss or model too incompletely the *strategic interactions* central to the behavior of economic actors. The importance of strategic interaction is increasingly appreciated by economists but still neglected in studies of comparative capitalism.[5] If interaction of this sort is central to economic and political outcomes, the most important institutions distinguishing one political economy from another will be those conditioning such interaction, and it is these that we seek to capture in this analysis. For this purpose, we construe the key relationships in the political economy in game-theoretic terms and focus on the kinds of institutions that alter the outcomes of strategic interaction. This approach generates an analysis that focuses on some of the same institutions others have identified as important but construes the impact of those institutions differently as well as one that highlights other institutions not yet given enough attention in studies of comparative capitalism.

By locating the firm at the center of the analysis, we hope to build bridges between business studies and comparative political economy, two disciplines that are all too often disconnected. By integrating game-theoretical perspectives on the firm of the sort that are now central to microeconomics into an analysis of the macroeconomy, we attempt to connect the new microeconomics to important issues in macroeconomics. Ours is a framework that should be of interest to economists, scholars of business, and political scientists alike. We turn now to an elucidation of its basic elements.

1.2 The Basic Elements of the Approach

This *varieties of capitalism* approach to the political economy is actor-centered, which is to say we see the political economy as a terrain populated by multiple actors, each of whom seeks to advance his interests in a rational way in strategic interaction with others (Scharpf 1997a). The relevant actors may be individuals, firms, producer groups, or governments. However, this is a firm-centered political economy that regards companies as the crucial actors in a capitalist economy. They are the key agents of adjustment in the face of technological change or international competition whose activities aggregate into overall levels of economic performance.

1.2.1   A Relational View of the Firm

Our conception of the firm is relational. Following recent work in economics, we see firms as actors seeking to develop and exploit *core competencies* or *dynamic capabilities* understood as capacities for developing, producing, and distributing goods and services profitably (Teece and Pisano 1998). We take the view that critical to these is the quality of the relationships the firm is able to establish, both internally, with its own employees, and externally, with a range of other actors that include suppliers, clients, collaborators, stakeholders, trade unions, business associations, and governments. As the work on transactions costs and principal-agent relationships in the economics of organization has underlined, these are problematic relationships (Milgrom and Roberts 1992). Even where hierarchies can be used to secure the cooperation of actors, firms encounter problems of moral hazard, adverse selection, and shirking. In many cases, effective operation even within a hierarchical environment may entail the formation of implicit contracts among the actors; and many of a firm's relationships with outside actors involve incomplete contracting (cf. Williamson 1985). In short, because its capabilities are ultimately relational, a firm encounters many coordination problems. Its success depends substantially on its ability to coordinate effectively with a wide range of actors.

For the purposes of this inquiry, we focus on five spheres in which firms must develop relationships to resolve coordination problems central to their core competencies. The first is the sphere of *industrial relations* where the problem facing companies is how to coordinate bargaining over wages and working conditions with their labor force, the organizations that represent labor, and other employers. At stake here are wage and productivity levels that condition the success of the firm and rates of unemployment or inflation in the economy as a whole. In the sphere of *vocational training and education,* firms face the problem of securing a workforce with suitable skills, while workers face the problem of deciding how much to invest in what skills. On the outcomes of this coordination problem turn not only the fortunes of individual companies and workers but the skill levels and competitiveness of the overall economy.

Issues of coordination also arise in the sphere of *corporate governance,* to which firms turn for access to finance and in which investors seek assurances of returns on their investments. The solutions devised to these problems affect both the availability of finance for particular types of projects and the terms on which firms can secure funds. The fourth sphere in which coordination problems crucial to the core competencies of an enterprise appear is the broad one of *inter-firm relations,* a term we use to cover the relationships a company forms with other enterprises, and notably its suppliers or clients, with a view to securing a stable demand for its products, appropriate supplies of inputs, and access to technology. These are endeavors that may entail standard-setting, technology transfer, and collaborative research and development. Here, coordination problems stem from the sharing of proprietary information and the risk of exploitation in joint ventures. On the development of appropriate relationships in this sphere, however, depend the capacities of firms to remain competitive and technological progress in the economy as a whole.

Finally, firms face a set of coordination problems vis-à-vis their own *employees*. Their central problem is to ensure that employees have the requisite competencies and cooperate well with others to advance the objectives of the firm. In this context, familiar problems of adverse selection and moral hazard arise, and issues of information-sharing become important (see Milgrom and Roberts 1992). Workers develop reservoirs of specialized information about the firm's operations that can be of value to management, but they also have the capacity to withhold information or effort. The relationships firms develop to resolve these problems condition their own competencies and the character of an economy's production regimes.

1.2.2 Liberal Market Economies and Coordinated Market Economies

From this perspective, it follows that national political economies can be compared by reference to the way in which firms resolve the coordination problems they face in these five spheres. The core distinction we draw is between two types of political economies, liberal market economies and coordinated market economies, which constitute ideal types at the poles of a spectrum along which many nations can be arrayed.[6]

In *liberal market economies,* firms coordinate their activities primarily via hierarchies and competitive market arrangements. These forms of coordination are well described by a classic literature (Williamson 1985). Market relationships are characterized by the arm's-length exchange of goods or services in a context of competition and formal contracting. In response to the price signals generated by such markets, the actors adjust their willingness to supply and demand goods or services, often on the basis of the marginal calculations stressed by neoclassical economics.[7] In many respects, market institutions provide a highly effective means for coordinating the endeavors of economic actors.

In *coordinated market economies,* firms depend more heavily on non-market relationships to coordinate their endeavors with other actors and to construct their core competencies. These non-market modes of coordination generally entail more extensive relational or incomplete contracting, network monitoring based on the exchange of private information inside networks, and more reliance on collaborative, as opposed to competitive, relationships to build the competencies of the firm. In contrast to liberal market economies (LMEs), where the equilibrium outcomes of firm behavior are usually given by demand and supply conditions in competitive markets, the equilibria on which firms coordinate in coordinated market economies (CMEs) are more often the result of strategic interaction among firms and other actors.

Market relations and hierarchies are important to firms in all capitalist economies, of course, and, even in liberal market economies, firms enter into some relationships that are not fully mediated by market forces.[8] But this typology is based on the contention that the incidence of different types of firm relationships varies systematically across nations. In some nations, for instance, firms rely primarily on formal contracts and highly competitive markets to organize relationships with their employees and suppliers of finance, while, in others, firms coordinate these endeavors differently. In any national economy, firms will gravitate toward the mode of coordination for which there is institutional support.

1.2.3 The Role of Institutions and Organizations

Institutions, organizations, and culture enter this analysis because of the support they provide for the relationships firms develop to resolve coordination problems. Following North (1990: 3), we define institutions as a set of rules, formal or informal, that actors generally follow, whether for normative, cognitive, or material reasons, and organizations as durable entities with formally recognized members, whose rules also contribute to the institutions of the political economy.[9]

From this perspective, markets are institutions that support relationships of particular types, marked by arm's-length relations and high levels of competition. Their concomitant is a legal system that supports formal contracting and encourages relatively complete contracts, as the chapters by Teubner and Casper indicate. All capitalist economies also contain the hierarchies that firms construct to resolve the problems that cannot be addressed by markets (Williamson 1985). In liberal market economies, these are the principal institutions on which firms rely to coordinate their endeavors.

Although markets and hierarchies are also important elements of coordinated market economies, firms in this type of economy draw on a further set of organizations and institutions for support in coordinating their endeavors. What types of organizations and institutions support the distinctive strategies of economic actors in such economies? Because the latter rely more heavily on forms of coordination secured through strategic interaction to resolve the problems they face, the relevant institutions will be those that allow them to coordinate on equilibrium strategies that offer higher returns to all concerned. In general, these will be institutions that reduce the uncertainty actors have about the behavior of others and allow them to make credible commitments to each other. A standard literature suggests that these are institutions providing capacities for (i) the *exchange of information* among the actors, (ii) the *monitoring* of behavior, and (iii) the *sanctioning* of defection from cooperative endeavor (see Ostrom 1990). Typically, these institutions include powerful business or employer associations, strong trade unions, extensive networks of cross-shareholding, and legal or regulatory systems designed to facilitate information-sharing and collaboration. Where these are present, firms can coordinate on strategies to which they would not have been led by market relations alone.

The problem of operating collaborative vocational training schemes provides a classic example. Here, the willingness of firms to participate depends on the security of their beliefs that workers will learn useful skills and that firms not investing in training will not poach extensively from those who do, while the participation of workers depends on assurances that training will lead to remunerative employment. As Culpepper's chapter in this volume indicates, it is easier for actors to secure these assurances where there are institutions providing reliable flows of information about appropriate skill levels, the incidence of training, and the employment prospects of apprentices (Finegold and Soskice 1988; Culpepper and Finegold 1999).

Similarly, the terms on which finance is provided to firms will depend on the monitoring capacities present in the economy. Where potential investors have little access to inside information about the progress of the firms they fund, access to capital is likely to depend on highly public criteria about the assets of a firm of the sort commonly found on balance sheets. Where investors are linked to the firms they fund through networks that allow for the development of reputations based on extensive access to information about the internal operations of the firm, however, investors will be more willing to supply capital to firms on terms that do not depend entirely on their balance sheets. The presence of institutions providing network reputational monitoring can have substantial effects on the terms on which firms can secure finance.

In short, this approach to comparative capitalism emphasizes the presence of institutions providing capacities for the exchange of information, monitoring, and the sanctioning of defections relevant to cooperative behavior among firms and other actors; and it is for the presence of such institutions that we look when comparing nations.

In addition, examination of coordinated market economies leads us to emphasize the importance of another kind of institution that is not normally on the list of those crucial to the formation of credible commitments, namely institutions that provide actors potentially able to cooperate with one another with a capacity for *deliberation*. By this, we simply mean institutions that encourage the relevant actors to engage in collective discussion and to reach agreements with each other.[10] Deliberative institutions are important for several reasons.

Deliberative proceedings in which the participants engage in extensive sharing of information about their interests and beliefs can improve the confidence of each in the strategies likely to be taken by the others. Many game-theoretic analyses assume a level of common knowledge that is relatively thin, barely stretching past a shared language and familiarity with the relevant payoffs. When multiple equilibria are available, however, coordination on one (especially one that exchanges higher payoffs for higher risks) can be greatly facilitated by the presence of a thicker common knowledge, one that extends beyond the basic situation to a knowledge of the other players sufficiently intimate to provide confidence that each will coordinate on a specific equilibrium (Eichengreen 1997). Deliberation can substantially thicken the common knowledge of the group.

As Scharpf (1987: ch. 4) has pointed out, although many think only of a 'prisoner's dilemma' game when they consider problems of cooperation, in the political economy many such problems take quite different forms, including 'battle of the sexes' games in which joint gains are available from more than one strategy but are distributed differently depending on the equilibrium chosen. Distributive dilemmas of this sort are endemic to political economies, and agreement on the distribution of the relevant gains is often the prerequisite to effective cooperation (Knight 1992). In some cases, such as those of collaborative research and development, the problem is not simply to distribute the gains but also the risks attendant on the enterprise. Deliberation provides the actors with an opportunity to establish the risks and gains attendant on cooperation and to resolve the distributive issues associated with them. In some cases, the actors may simply be negotiating from positions of relative power, but extensive deliberation over time may build up specific conceptions of distributive justice that can be used to facilitate agreement in subsequent exchanges.

Finally, deliberative institutions can enhance the capacity of actors in the political economy for strategic action when faced with new or unfamiliar challenges. This is far from irrelevant since economies are frequently subject to exogenous shocks that force the actors within them to respond to situations to which they are unaccustomed. The history of wage negotiations in Europe is replete with examples. In such instances, developments may outrun common knowledge, and deliberation can be instrumental to devising an effective and coordinated response, allowing the actors to develop a common diagnosis of the situation and an agreed response.

In short, deliberative institutions can provide the actors in a political economy with strategic capacities they would not otherwise enjoy; and we think cross-national comparison should be attentive to the presence of facilities for deliberation as well as institutions that provide for the exchange of information in other forms, monitoring, and the enforcement of agreements.

1.2.4   The Role of Culture, Informal Rules, and History

Our approach departs from previous works on comparative capitalism in another respect.[11] Many analyses take the view that the relevant outcomes in economic performance or policy follow more or less directly from differences in the formal organization of the political economy. Particular types of wage settlements or rates of inflation and unemployment are often said to follow, for instance, from the organizational structure of the union movement. Because we believe such outcomes are the products of efforts to coordinate in contexts of strategic interaction, however, we reject the contention that they follow from the presence of a particular set of institutions alone, at least if the latter are defined entirely in terms of formal rules or organizations.

As we have noted, the presence of a set of formal institutions is often a necessary precondition for attaining the relevant equilibrium in contexts of coordination. But formal institutions are rarely sufficient to guarantee that equilibrium. In multi-player games with multiple iterations of the sort that characterize most of the cases in which we are interested, it is well known that there exist multiple equilibria, any one of which could be chosen by the actors even in the presence of institutions conducive to the formation of credible commitments (Fudenberg and Maskin 1986). Something else is needed to lead the actors to coordinate on a specific equilibrium and, notably, on equilibria offering high returns in a non-cooperative context.[12] In many instances, what leads the actors to a specific equilibrium is a set of shared understandings about what other actors are likely to do, often rooted in a sense of what it is appropriate to do in such circumstances (March and Olsen 1989).

Accordingly, taking a step beyond many accounts, we emphasize the importance of informal rules and understandings to securing the equilibria in the many strategic interactions of the political economy. These shared understandings are important elements of the 'common knowledge' that lead participants to coordinate on one outcome, rather than another, when both are feasible in the presence of a specific set of formal institutions. By considering them a component of the institutions making up the political economy, we expand the concept of institutions beyond the purely formal connotations given to it in some analyses.

This is an entry point in the analysis for history and culture. Many actors learn to follow a set of informal rules by virtue of experience with a familiar set of actors and the shared understandings that accumulate from this experience constitute something like a common culture. This concept of culture as a set of shared understandings or available 'strategies for action' developed from experience of operating in a particular environment is analogous to those developed in the 'cognitive turn' taken by sociology (Swidler 1986; DiMaggio and Powell 1991). Our view of the role that culture can play in the strategic interactions of the political economy is similar to the one Kreps (1990) accords it in organizations faced with problems of incomplete contracting.

The implication is that the institutions of a nation's political economy are inextricably bound up with its history in two respects. On the one hand, they are created by actions, statutory or otherwise, that establish formal institutions and their operating procedures. On the other, repeated historical experience builds up a set of common expectations that allows the actors to coordinate effectively with each other. Among other things, this implies that the institutions central to the operation of the political economy should not be seen as entities that are created at one point in time and can then be assumed to operate effectively afterwards. To remain viable, the shared understandings associated with them must be reaffirmed periodically by appropriate historical experience. As Thelen emphasizes in this volume, the operative force of many institutions cannot be taken for granted but must be reinforced by the active endeavors of the participants.

1.2.5   Institutional Infrastructure and Corporate Strategy

This varieties of capitalism approach draws its basic conceptions of how institutions operate from the new economics of organization. We apply a set of concepts commonly used to explain behavior at the micro level of the economy to problems of understanding the macroeconomy (Milgrom and Roberts 1992). One of the advantages is an analysis with robust and consistent postulates about what kind of institutions matter and how they affect behavior. Another is the capacity of the approach to integrate analysis of firm behavior with analysis of the political economy as a whole.

However, there are at least two respects in which our account deviates from mainstream views in the new economics of organization. First, although we make use of the influential dichotomy between 'markets' and 'hierarchies' that Williamson (1975) has impressed on the field, we do not think this exhausts the relevant variation. Markets and hierarchies are features of LMEs and CMEs but we stress the systematic variation found in the character of corporate structure (or hierarchies) across different types of economies and the presence of coordination problems even within hierarchical settings (Milgrom and Roberts 1992). Even more important, we do not see these two institutional forms as the only ones firms can employ to resolve the challenges they confront. In coordinated market economies in particular, many firms develop relationships with other firms, outside actors, and their employees that are not well described as either market-based or hierarchical relations but better seen as efforts to secure cooperative outcomes among the actors using a range of institutional devices that underpin credible commitments. Variation in the incidence and character of this 'third' type of relationship is central to the distinctions we draw between various types of political economies.[13]

Second, it is conventional in much of the new economics of organization to assume that the core institutional structures of the economy, whether markets, hierarchies, or networks, are erected by firms seeking the most efficient institutions for performing certain tasks. The postulate is that (institutional) structure follows (firm) strategy (cf. Chandler 1974; Williamson 1975, 1985; Chandler and Daems 1980). In a restricted sense, this is certainly true: firms can choose whether to contract out an endeavor or perform it in-house, for instance, and they enjoy some control over their own corporate form.

However, we think it unrealistic to regard the overarching institutional structures of the political economy, and especially those coordinating the endeavors of many actors (such as markets, institutional networks, and the organizations supporting collaborative endeavor), as constructs created or controlled by a particular firm. Because they are collective institutions, a single firm cannot create them; and, because they have multifarious effects, it may be difficult for a group of firms to agree on them.[14] Instead, as Calvert (1995) observes, the construction of coordinating institutions should be seen as a second-order coordination problem of considerable magnitude. Even when firms can agree, the project may entail regulatory action by the government and the formation of coalitions among political parties and labor organizations motivated by considerations going well beyond efficiency (Swenson 1991, 1997).

As a result, the firms located within any political economy face a set of coordinating institutions whose character is not fully under their control. These institutions offer firms a particular set of opportunities; and companies can be expected to gravitate toward strategies that take advantage of these opportunities. In short, there are important respects in which strategy follows structure. For this reason, our approach predicts systematic differences in corporate strategy across nations, and differences that parallel the overarching institutional structures of the political economy. This is one of the most important implications of the analysis.

Let us stress that we refer here to broad differences. Of course, there will be additional variation in corporate strategies inside all economies in keeping with differences in the resource endowments and market settings of individual firms. The capabilities of management also matter, since firms are actors with considerable autonomy. Our point is that (institutional) structure conditions (corporate) strategy, not that it fully determines it. We also agree that differences in corporate strategy can be conditioned by the institutional support available to firms at the regional or sectoral levels (Campbell et al. 1991; Hollingsworth et al. 1994; Herrigel 1996). Many of the works making this point are congruent with our own in that they stress the importance of the institutional environment to firm strategy, even though there has been fruitful disagreement about which features of that environment matter most (cf. Streeck 1992b).[15]

However, we emphasize variations in corporate strategy evident at the national level. We think this justified by the fact that so many of the institutional factors conditioning the behavior of firms remain nation-specific. There are good reasons why that should be the case. Some of the relevant institutions were deeply conditioned by nationally specific processes of development, as are most trade unions and employers' associations. In others, the relevant institutions depend heavily on statutes or regulations promulgated by national states, as do many institutions in the financial arena and labor market, not to mention the sphere of contract law.

In sum, we contend that differences in the institutional framework of the political economy generate systematic differences in corporate strategy across LMEs and CMEs. There is already some evidence for this. For instance, the data that Knetter (1989) has gathered are especially interesting. He finds that the firms of Britain, a typical LME, and those of Germany, a CME, respond very differently to a similar shock, in this case an appreciation of the exchange rate that renders the nation's goods more expensive in foreign markets. British firms tend to pass the price increase along to customers in order to maintain their profitability, while German firms maintain their prices and accept lower returns in order to preserve market share.

Our approach predicts differences of precisely this sort. We would argue that British firms must sustain their profitability because the structure of financial markets in a liberal market economy links the firm's access to capital and ability to resist take-over to its current profitability; and they can sustain the loss of market share because fluid labor markets allow them to lay off workers readily. By contrast, German firms can sustain a decline in returns because the financial system of a coordinated market economy provides firms with access to capital independent of current profitability; and they attempt to retain market share because the labor institutions in such an economy militate in favor of long-term employment strategies and render layoffs difficult.

These are only some of the ways in which the institutional arrangements of a nation's political economy tend to push its firms toward particular kinds of corporate strategies. We explore more of these below with special emphasis on innovation.

To put the point in the most general terms, however, firms and other actors in coordinated market economies should be more willing to invest in *specific* and *co-specific assets* (i.e. assets that cannot readily be turned to another purpose and assets whose returns depend heavily on the active cooperation of others), while those in liberal market economies should invest more extensively in *switchable assets* (i.e. assets whose value can be realized if diverted to other purposes). This follows from the fact that CMEs provide more institutional support for the strategic interactions required to realize the value of co-specific assets, whether in the form of industry-specific training, collaborative research and development, or the like, while the more fluid markets of LMEs provide economic actors with greater opportunities to move their resources around in search of higher returns, encouraging them to acquire switchable assets, such as general skills or multi-purpose technologies.[16]

1.2.6 Institutional Complementarities

The presence of *institutional complementarities* reinforces the differences between liberal and coordinated market economies. The concept of 'complementary goods' is a familiar one: two goods, such as bread and butter, are described as complementary if an increase in the price of one depresses demand for the other. However, complementarities may also exist among the operations of a firm: marketing arrangements that offer customized products, for instance, may offer higher returns when coupled to the use of flexible machine tools on the shop floor (Jaikumar 1986; Milgrom and Roberts 1990, 1995).

Following Aoki (1994), we extend this line of reasoning to the institutions of the political economy. Here, two institutions can be said to be complementary if the presence (or efficiency) of one increases the returns from (or efficiency of) the other.[17] The returns from a stock market trading in corporate securities, for instance, may be increased by regulations mandating a fuller exchange of information about companies.

Of particular interest are complementarities between institutions located in different spheres of the political economy. Aoki (1994) has argued that long-term employment is more feasible where the financial system provides capital on terms that are not sensitive to current profitability. Conversely, fluid labor markets may be more effective at sustaining employment in the presence of financial markets that transfer resources readily among endeavors thereby maintaining a demand for labor (cf. Caballero and Hamour 1998; Fehn 1998). Casper explores complementarities between national systems of contract law and modes of inter-firm collaboration, and we identify others in the sections that follow.

This point about institutional complementarities has special relevance for the study of comparative capitalism. It suggests that nations with a particular type of coordination in one sphere of the economy should tend to develop complementary practices in other spheres as well.[18] Several logics may be operative here. In some cases, the institutions sustaining coordination in one sphere can be used to support analogous forms of coordination in others. Where dense networks of business associations support collaborative systems of vocational training, for instance, those same networks may be used to operate collective standard-setting. Similarly, firms may pressure governments to foster the development of institutions complementary to those already present in the economy in order to secure the efficiency gains they provide.

If this is correct, institutional practices of various types should not be distributed randomly across nations. Instead, we should see some clustering along the dimensions that divide liberal from coordinated market economies, as nations converge on complementary practices across different spheres. Figure 6.3.1 presents some support for these propositions. It locates OECD nations on two axes that provide indicators for the character of institutions in the spheres of corporate finance and labor markets respectively. A highly developed stock market indicates greater reliance on market

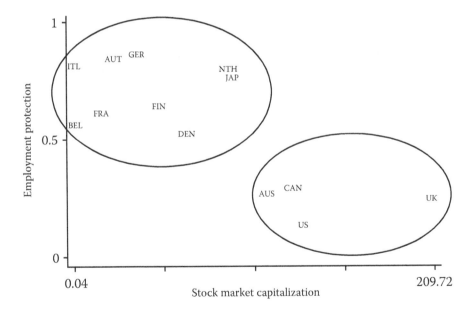

FIGURE 1.1 Institutions across sub-spheres of the political economy.
Note: Employment protection refers to the index of employment protection developed by Estevez-Abe, Iversen, and Soskice in this volume. Stock market capitalization is the market value of listed domestic companies as a percentage of GDP.
Source: International Federation of Stock Exchanges, *Annual Report.*

modes of coordination in the financial sphere, and high levels of employment protection tend to reflect higher levels of non-market coordination in the sphere of industrial relations.[19] Although there is some variation within each group, a pronounced clustering is evident. Nations with liberal market economies tend to rely on markets to coordinate endeavors in both the financial and industrial relations systems, while those with coordinated market economies have institutions in both spheres that reflect higher levels of non-market coordination.

Among the large OECD nations, six can be classified as liberal market economies (the USA, Britain, Australia, Canada, New Zealand, Ireland) and another ten as coordinated market economies (Germany, Japan, Switzerland, the Netherlands, Belgium, Sweden, Norway, Denmark, Finland, and Austria) leaving six in more ambiguous positions (France, Italy, Spain, Portugal, Greece, and Turkey).[20] However, the latter show some signs of institutional clustering as well, indicating that they may constitute another type of capitalism, sometimes described as 'Mediterranean', marked by a large agrarian sector and recent histories of extensive state intervention that have left them with specific kinds of capacities for non-market coordination in the sphere of corporate finance but more liberal arrangements in the sphere of labor relations (see Rhodes 1997).

Although each type of capitalism has its partisans, we are not arguing here that one is superior to another. Despite some variation over specific periods, both liberal and coordinated market economies seem capable of providing satisfactory levels of long-run economic performance, as the major indicators of national well-being displayed in Table 6.3.1 indicate. Where there is systematic variation between these types of political economies, it is on other dimensions of performance. We argue below that the two types of economies have quite different capacities for innovation. In addition, they tend to distribute income and employment differently. As Figure 6.3.2 indicates, in liberal market economies, the adult population tends to be engaged more extensively in paid employment and levels of income inequality are high.[21] In coordinated market economies, working hours tend to be shorter for more of the population and incomes more equal. With regard to the distribution of well-being, of course, these differences are important.

To make this analytical framework more concrete, we now look more closely at coordination in the principal spheres of firm endeavor in coordinated and liberal market economies, drawing on the cases of Germany and the United States for examples and emphasizing the institutional complementarities present in each political economy.

1.3 Coordinated Market Economies: The German Case

As we have noted, we regard capitalist economies as systems in which companies and individuals invest, not only in machines and material technologies, but in competencies based on relations with others that entail coordination problems. In coordinated market economies, firms resolve many of these problems through strategic interaction. The resulting equilibria depend, in part, on the presence of supportive institutions. Here, we use the case of Germany to illustrate how non-market coordination is achieved in each of the principal spheres of firm endeavor. Of course,

TABLE 1.1 The Economic Performance of Liberal and Coordinated Market Economies

Liberal Market Economies

	Growth Rate of GDP			GDP per Capita		Unemployment Rate		
	61–73	**74–84**	**85–98**	**74–84**	**85–97**	**60–73**	**74–84**	**85–98**
Australia	5.2	2.8	3.3	7932	16701	1.9	6.2	8.5
Canada	5.3	3.0	2.3	9160	18835	5.1	8.4	9.5
Ireland	4.4	3.9	6.5	4751	12830	5.0	9.1	14.1
New Zealand	4.0	1.8	1.7	7378	14172	0.2	2.2	6.9
UK	3.1	1.3	2.4	7359	15942	2.0	6.7	8.7
United States	4.0	2.2	2.9	11055	22862	4.9	7.5	6.0
LME average	4.3	2.5	3.2	7939	16890	3.2	6.7	8.9

Coordinated Market Economies

	Growth Rate of GDP			GDP per Capita		Unemployment Rate		
	61–73	**74–84**	**85–98**	**74–84**	**85–97**	**60–73**	**74–84**	**85–98**
Austria[a]	4.9	2.3	2.5	7852	17414	1.6	2.2	5.3
Belgium	4.9	2.0	2.2	8007	17576	2.2	8.2	11.3
Denmark	4.4	1.8	2.2	8354	18618	1.4	7.1	9.3
Finland	5.0	2.7	2.2	7219	15619	2.0	4.8	9.4
Iceland	5.7	4.1	2.7	8319	18285	0.6	0.6	2.5
Germany	4.3	1.8	2.2	7542	16933	0.8	4.6	8.5
Japan	9.7	3.3	2.6	7437	18475	1.3	2.1	2.8
Netherlands[b]	4.9	1.9	2.8	7872	16579	1.5	5.6	6.8
Norway	4.3	4.0	2.9	8181	19325	1.6	2.1	4.3
Sweden	4.2	1.8	1.5	8450	16710	1.9	2.3	4.8
Switzerland	4.4	.58	1.3	10680	21398	.01	0.4	2.5
CME average	5.1	2.4	2.3	8174	17902	1.3	3.6	6.1

Notes: Growth rate of GDP: average annual growth in GDP, averaged for the time-periods indicated. GDP per capita: per capita GDP at purchasing power parity, averaged for the time-periods indicated. Unemployment rate: annual unemployment rate.

[a] Unemployment series begins in 1964.

[b] Unemployment series begins in 1969.

Sources: Growth rate of GDP: World Bank, *World Development Indicators CD-ROM* (2000); except for Germany, for which data were taken from OECD, *Historical Statistics* (1997), for 1960–91, and *WDI* for years thereafter. GDP per capita: OECD, *OECD Statistical Compendium CD-ROM* (2000). Unemployment rate: OECD, *OECD Statistical Compendium CD-ROM* (2000).

the institutions used to secure coordination in other CMEs may differ to some extent from those of Germany.

(i) The *financial system* or *market for corporate governance* in coordinated market economies typically provides companies with access to finance that is not entirely dependent on publicly available financial data or current returns. Access to this kind of 'patient capital' makes it possible for firms to retain a skilled workforce through economic downturns and to invest in projects generating returns only in the long run. The core problem here is that, if finance is not to be dependent on balance-sheet criteria, investors must have other ways of monitoring the performance of companies in order to ensure the value of their investments. In general, that means they must have

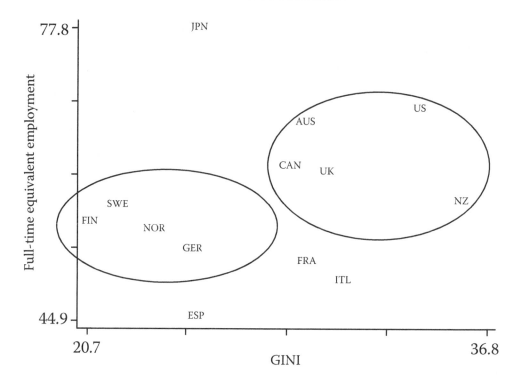

FIGURE 1.2 Distributional outcomes across political economies.
Note: Full-time equivalent employment is defined as the total number of hours worked per year divided by full-time equivalent hours per year per person times working age population. GINI refers to the gini coefficient measuring post-tax, post-transfer income inequality.
Sources: For full-time equivalent unemployment: OECD (1996*a*). For GINI index: Spain, Japan, New Zealand are from Deiniger and Squire (1996); the remaining countries are from OECD (1996*a*).

access to what would normally be considered 'private' or 'inside' information about the operation of the company.

This problem is generally resolved in CMEs by the presence of dense networks linking the managers and technical personnel inside a company to their counterparts in other firms on terms that provide for the sharing of reliable information about the progress of the firm. Reliability is secured in a number of ways. Firms may share information with third parties in a position to monitor the firm and sanction it for misleading them, such as business associations whose officials have an intimate knowledge of the industry. Reputation is also a key factor: where membership in a network is of continuing value, the participants will be deterred from providing false information lest their reputation in the network and access to it suffer. CMEs usually have extensive systems for what might be termed 'network reputational monitoring' (Vitols et al. 1997).

In Germany, information about the reputation and operation of a company is available to investors by virtue of (*a*) the close relationships that companies cultivate with major suppliers and clients, (*b*) the knowledge secured from extensive networks of cross-shareholding, and (*c*) joint membership in active industry associations that gather information about companies in the course of coordinating standard-setting, technology transfer, and vocational training. Other companies are not only represented on the supervisory boards of firms but typically engaged closely with them in joint research, product development, and the like. In short, firms sit inside dense business networks from which potential hinders can gain a considerable amount of inside information about the track record and projects of a firm.[22]

The overall structure of the market for corporate governance is equally important. Since firms often fund their activities from retained earnings, they are not always sensitive to the terms on which external finance is supplied. But they can be forced to focus on profitability and shareholder value if faced with the prospect of hostile takeover by others claiming to be able to extract more value from the company. Thus, the corporate strategies found in many CMEs also depend on tax provisions, securities regulations, and networks of cross-shareholding that discourage hostile mergers and acquisitions, which were very rare until recently, for instance, in Germany.

(ii) The *internal structure* of the firm reinforces these systems of network monitoring in many CMEs. Unlike their counterparts in LMEs, for instance, top managers in Germany rarely have a capacity for unilateral action. Instead, they must secure agreement for major decisions from supervisory boards, which include employee representatives as well as major shareholders, and from other managers with entrenched positions as well as major suppliers and customers. This structural bias toward consensus decision-making encourages the sharing of information and the development of reputations for providing reliable information, thereby facilitating network monitoring.

In the perspective we present, the incentives facing individuals, whether managers or workers, are as important as those facing firms. In CMEs, managerial incentives tend to reinforce the operation of business networks. Long-term employment contracts and the premium that firm-structure places on a manager's ability to secure consensus for his projects lead managers to focus heavily on the maintenance of their reputations, while the smaller weight given to stock-option schemes in managerial compensation in CMEs relative to LMEs inclines them to focus less on profitability than their counterparts in LMEs. The incentives for managers are broadly aligned with those of firms.

(iii) Many firms in coordinated market economies employ production strategies that rely on a highly skilled labor force given substantial work autonomy and encouraged to share the information it acquires in order to generate continuous improvements in product lines and production processes (Sorge and Warner 1986; Dore 1986). However, companies that adopt such strategies are vulnerable to 'hold up' by their employees and the 'poaching' of skilled workers by other firms, while employees who share the information they gain at work with management are open to exploitation.[23] Thus, CMEs need *industrial relations* institutions capable of resolving such problems.

The German industrial relations system addresses these problems by setting wages through industry-level bargains between trade unions and employer associations that generally follow a leading settlement, normally reached in engineering where the union is powerful enough to assure the labor movement that it has received a good deal. Although union density is only moderately high, encompassing employers' associations bind their members to these agreements. By equalizing wages at equivalent skill levels across an industry, this system makes it difficult for firms to poach workers and assures the latter that they are receiving the highest feasible rates of pay in return for the deep commitments they are making to firms. By coordinating bargaining across the economy, these arrangements also limit the inflationary effects of wage settlements (Streeck 1994; Hall and Franzese 1998).

The complement to these institutions at the company level is a system of works councils composed of elected employee representatives endowed with considerable authority over layoffs and working conditions. By providing employees with security against arbitrary layoffs or changes to their working conditions, these works councils encourage employees to invest in company-specific skills and extra effort. Their effectiveness is underpinned by the capacity of either side to appeal a disputed decision to the trade unions and employers' associations, who act as external guarantors that the councils function as intended (Thelen 1991).

(iv) Because coordinated market economies typically make extensive use of labor with high industry-specific or firm-specific skills, they depend on *education and training systems* capable of providing workers with such skills.[24] As Culpepper notes in his chapter, the coordination problems here are acute, as workers must be assured that an apprenticeship will result in lucrative employment, while firms investing in training need to know that their workers will acquire usable skills and will not be poached by companies that do not make equivalent investments in training. CMEs resolve these problems in a variety of ways.

Germany relies on industry-wide employer associations and trade unions to supervise a publicly subsidized training system. By pressuring major firms to take on apprentices and monitoring their participation in such schemes, these associations limit free-riding on the training efforts of others; and, by negotiating industry-wide skill categories and training protocols with the firms in each sector, they ensure both that the training fits the firms' needs and that there will be an external demand for any graduates not employed by the firms at which they apprenticed. Because German employer associations are encompassing organizations that provide many benefits to their members and to which most firms in a sector belong, they are well placed to supply the monitoring and suasion that the operation of such a system demands as well as the deliberative forums in which skill categories, training quotas, and protocols can be negotiated. Workers emerge from their training with both company-specific skills and the skills to secure employment elsewhere.

(v) Since many firms in coordinated market economies make extensive use of long-term labor contracts, they cannot rely as heavily on the movement of scientific or engineering personnel across companies, to effect technology transfer, as liberal market economies do. Instead, they tend to cultivate *inter-company relations* of the sort that facilitate the diffusion of technology across the economy. In Germany, these relationships are supported by a number of institutions. Business associations promote the diffusion of new technologies by working with public officials to determine where firm competencies can be improved and orchestrating publicly subsidized programs to do so. The access to private information about the sector that these associations enjoy helps them ensure that the design of the programs is effective for these purposes. A considerable amount of research is also financed jointly by companies, often in collaboration with quasi-public research institutes. The common technical standards fostered by industry associations help to diffuse new technologies, and they contribute to a common knowledge-base that facilitates collaboration among personnel from multiple firms, as do the industry-specific skills fostered by German training schemes (Lütz 1993; Soskice 1997b; Ziegler 1997).

Casper's chapter in this volume shows that Germany has also developed a system of contract law complementary to the presence of strong industry associations that encourages relational contracting among companies and promotes this sort of technology transfer. Because of the many contingencies that can arise in close inter-firm relationships involving joint research or product development, tightly written, formal contracts are often inadequate to sustain such relationships. However, the German courts permit unusually open-ended clauses in inter-firm contracts on the explicit condition that these be grounded in the prevailing standards of the relevant industry association. Thus, the presence of strong industry associations capable of promulgating standards and resolving disputes among firms is the precondition for a system of contract law that encourages relational contracting (cf. Casper 1997; Teubner in this volume).

In these respects, German institutions support forms of relational contracting and technology transfer that are more difficult to achieve in liberal market economies. One of the effects is to encourage corporate strategies that focus on product differentiation and niche production, rather than direct product competition with other firms in the industry, since close inter-firm collaboration is harder to sustain in the presence of the intense product competition that tends to characterize LMEs. The chapter by Estevez-Abe, Iversen, and Soskice examines the linkages between these product market strategies, skill systems, and social-policy regimes.

The complementarities present in the German political economy should be apparent from this account. Many firms pursue production strategies that depend on workers with specific skills and high levels of corporate commitment that are secured by offering them long employment tenures, industry-based wages, and protective works councils. But these practices are feasible only because a corporate governance system replete with mechanisms for network monitoring provides firms with access to capital on terms that are relatively independent of fluctuations in profitability. Effective vocational training schemes, supported by an industrial-relations system that discourages poaching, provide high levels of industry-specific skills. In turn, this encourages collective standard-setting and inter-firm collaboration of the sort that promotes technology transfer. The arrows in Figure 6.3.3 summarize some of these complementarities. Since many of these institutional practices enhance the effectiveness with which others operate, the economic returns to the system as a whole are greater than its component parts alone would generate.

1.4 Liberal Market Economies: The American Case

Liberal market economies can secure levels of overall economic performance as high as those of coordinated market economies, but they do so quite differently. In LMEs, firms rely more heavily on market relations to resolve the coordination problems that firms in CMEs address more often via forms of non-market coordination that entail collaboration and strategic interaction. In each of the major spheres of firm endeavor,

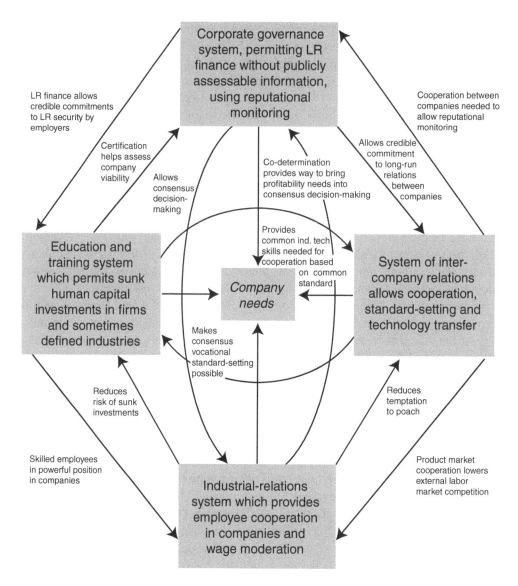

FIGURE 1.3 Complementarities across subsystems in the German coordinated market economy

competitive markets are more robust and there is less institutional support for non-market forms of coordination.

(i) Several features of the *financial systems* or *markets for corporate governance* of liberal market economies encourage firms to be attentive to current earnings and the price of their shares on equity markets. Regulatory regimes are tolerant of mergers and acquisitions, including the hostile takeovers that become a prospect when the market valuation of a firm declines. The terms on which large firms can secure finance are heavily dependent on their valuation in equity markets, where dispersed investors depend on publicly available information to value the company. This applies to both bonds, share issues, and bank lending.[25] Compensation systems that reward top management for increases in net earnings or share price are common in such economies. Liberal market economies usually lack the close-knit corporate networks capable of providing investors with inside information about the progress of companies that allows them to supply finance less dependent on quarterly balance sheets and publicly available information. The relevant contrast is with CMEs, where firms need not be as attentive to share price or current profitability in order to ensure access to finance or deter hostile takeovers.

Of course, there are some qualifications to these generalizations. Companies with readily assessable assets associated with forward income streams, such as pharmaceutical firms with a 'pipeline' of drugs, consumer-goods companies with strong reputations for successful product development, and firms well positioned in high-growth markets, need not be as concerned about current profitability. New firms in high-technology fields can often secure funds from venture-capital companies that develop the resources and technical expertise to monitor their performance directly and trade ownership stakes in these firms for the high risks they take.[26] On the whole, however, the markets for corporate governance in LMEs encourage firms to focus on the publicly assessable dimensions of their performance that affect share price, such as current profitability.

(ii) In the *industrial relations arena,* firms in liberal market economies generally rely heavily on the market relationship between individual worker and employer to organize relations with their labor force. Top management normally has unilateral control over the firm, including substantial freedom to hire and fire.[27] Firms are under no obligation to establish representative bodies for employees such as works councils; and trade unions are generally less powerful than in CMEs, although they may have significant strength in some sectors. Because trade unions and employer associations in LMEs are less cohesive and encompassing, economy-wide wage coordination is generally difficult to secure. Therefore, these economies depend more heavily on macroeconomic policy and market competition to control wages and inflation (see Franzese in this volume; Hall and Franzese 1998).

The presence of highly fluid labor markets influences the strategies pursued by both firms and individuals in liberal market economies. These markets make it relatively easy for firms to release or hire labor in order to take advantage of new opportunities but less attractive for them to pursue production strategies based on promises of long-term employment. They encourage individuals to invest in general skills, transferable across firms, rather than company-specific skills and in career trajectories that include a substantial amount of movement among firms.

(iii) The *education and training systems* of liberal market economies are generally complementary to these highly fluid labor markets. Vocational training is normally provided by institutions offering formal education that focuses on general skills because companies are loath to invest in apprenticeship schemes imparting industry-specific skills where they have no guarantees that other firms will not simply poach their apprentices without investing in training themselves. From the perspective of workers facing short job tenures and fluid labor markets, career success also depends on acquiring the general skills that can be used in many different firms; and most educational programs from secondary through university levels, even in business and engineering, stress 'certification' in general skills rather than the acquisition of more specialized competencies.

High levels of general education, however, lower the cost of additional training. Therefore, the companies in these economies do a substantial amount of in-house training, although rarely in the form of the intensive apprenticeships used to develop company-specific or industry-specific skills in CMEs. More often, they provide further training in the marketable skills that employees have incentives to learn. The result is a labor force well equipped with general skills, especially suited to job growth in the service sector where such skills assume importance, but one that leaves some firms short of employees with highly specialized or company-specific skills.

(iv) *Inter-company relations* in liberal market economies are based, for the most part, on standard market relationships and enforceable formal contracts. In the United States, these relations are also mediated by rigorous antitrust regulations designed to prevent companies from colluding to control prices or markets and doctrines of contract laws that rely heavily on the strict interpretation of written contracts, nicely summarized by MacNeil's dictum: 'sharp in by clear agreement, sharp out by clear performance' (Williamson 1985). Therefore, companies wishing to engage in relational contracts with other firms get little assistance from the American legal system, as Casper observes.

In some fields of endeavor, such as after-sales service, companies can engage successfully in incomplete contracting by building up reputations on which other parties rely. But extensive reputation-building is more difficult in economies lacking the dense business networks or associations that circulate reputations for reliability or sharp practice quickly and widely. Because the market for corporate governance renders firms sensitive to fluctuations in current profitability, it is also more difficult for them to make credible commitments to relational contracts that extend over substantial periods of time.

How then does technology transfer take place in liberal market economies? In large measure, it is secured through the movement of scientists and engineers from one company to another (or from research institutions to the private sector) that fluid labor markets facilitate. These scientific personnel bring their technical knowledge with them. LMEs also rely heavily on the licensing or sale of innovations to effect technology transfer, techniques that are most feasible in sectors of the economy where effective patenting is possible, such as biotechnology, micro-electronics, and semiconductors. In the United States, the character of standard-setting reinforces the importance of licensing. Since few sectors have business associations capable of securing consensus on new standards, collective standard-setting is rarely feasible. Instead, standards are often set by market races, whose winners then profit by licensing their technology to many users (see also Tate in this volume). The prominence of this practice helps to explain the presence of venture-capital firms in liberal market economies: one success at standard-setting can pay for many failed investments (Borrus and Zysman 1997).

In LMEs, research consortia and inter-firm collaboration, therefore, play less important roles in the process of technology transfer than in CMEs where the institutional environment is more conducive to them. Until the National Cooperative

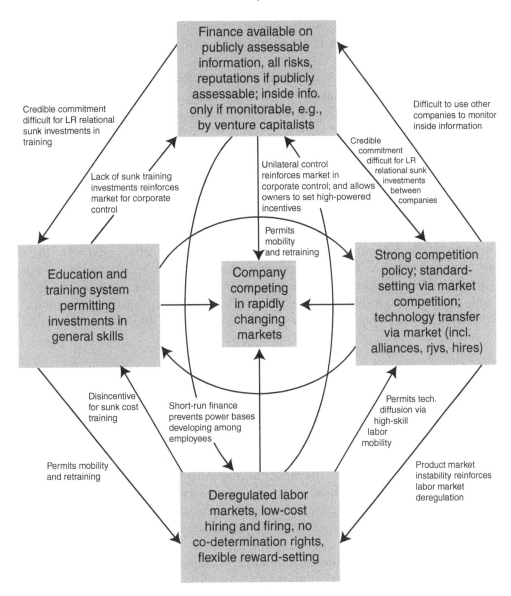

FIGURE 1.4 Complementarities across subsystems in the American liberal market economy

Research Act of 1984, American firms engaging in close collaboration with other firms actually ran the risk of being sued for triple damages under antitrust law; and it is still estimated that barely 1 to 7 per cent of the funds spent on research and development in the American private sector are devoted to collaborative research.

It should be apparent that there are many institutional complementarities across the sub-spheres of a liberal market economy (see Figure 6.3.4). Labor market arrangements that allow companies to cut costs in a downturn by shedding labor are complementary to financial markets that render a firm's access to funds dependent on current profitability. Educational arrangements that privilege general, rather than firm-specific, skills are complementary to highly fluid labor markets; and the latter render forms of technology transfer that rely on labor mobility more feasible. In the context of a legal system that militates against relational contracting, licensing agreements are also more effective than inter-firm collaboration on research and development for effecting technology transfer.

Special note should be taken of the complementarities between the internal structure of firms and their external institutional environment in liberal and coordinated market economies. In LMEs, corporate structures that concentrate authority in top management make it easier for firms to release labor when facing pressure from financial markets and to impose a new strategy on the firm to take advantage of the shifting market opportunities that often present themselves in economies characterized by highly mobile assets. By contrast, in CMEs, where access to finance and technology often depends on a firm's attractiveness as a collaborator and hence on its reputation, corporate structures that impose more consensual forms of decision-making allow firms to develop reputations that are not entirely dependent on those of its top management. By reducing the capacity of top management to act arbitrarily, these structures also enhance the firm's capacity to enter credibly into relational contracts with employees and others in economies where a firm's access to many kinds of assets, ranging from technology to skills, may depend on its capacity for relational contracting. Lehrer's chapter explores some of these linkages between corporate structure and the external environment in more detail.

1.5 Comparing Coordination

Although many of the developed nations can be classified as liberal or coordinated market economies, the point of this analysis is not simply to identify these two types but to outline an approach that can be used to compare many kinds of economies. In particular, we are suggesting that it can be fruitful to consider how firms coordinate their endeavors and to analyze the institutions of the political economy from a perspective that asks what kind of support they provide for different kinds of coordination, even when the political economies at hand do not correspond to the ideal types we have just outlined.

It is important to note that, even within these two types, significant variations can be found. Broadly speaking, liberal market economies are distinguishable from coordinated market economies by the extent to which firms rely on market mechanisms to coordinate their endeavors as opposed to forms of strategic interaction supported by non-market institutions. Because market institutions are better known, we will not explore the differences among liberal market economies here. But a few words about variation in coordinated market economies may be appropriate, if only to show that variation in the institutional structures under-pinning strategic coordination can have significant effects on corporate strategy and economic outcomes.

One important axis of difference among CMEs runs between those that rely primarily on *industry-based coordination,* as do many of the northern European nations, and those with institutional structures that foster *group-based coordination* of the sort found in Japan and South Korea. As we have seen, in Germany, coordination depends on business associations and trade unions that are organized primarily along sectoral lines, giving rise to vocational training schemes that cultivate industry-specific skills, a system of wage coordination that negotiates wages by sector, and corporate collaboration that is often industry-specific. By contrast, the business networks of most importance in Japan are built on *keiretsu,* families of companies with dense interconnections cutting across sectors, the most important of which is nowadays the *vertical keiretsu* with one major company at its center.

These differences in the character of business networks have major implications. In Germany, companies within the same sector often cooperate in the sensitive areas of training and technology transfer. But the structure of the Japanese economy encourages sharp competition between companies in the same industry. Cooperation on sensitive matters is more likely to take place within the *keiretsu,* i.e. among firms operating in different sectors but within one 'family' of companies. The sectoral cooperation that takes place usually concerns less sensitive matters, including recession cartels, licensing requirements, and entry barriers as well as the annual wage round (Soskice 1990*a*). Partly for this reason, the attempts of MITI to develop cooperative research projects within sectors have had very limited success; serious research and development remains the preserve of the laboratories of the major companies.

This pattern of *keiretsu*-led coordination also has significant implications for patterns of skill acquisition and technology transfer. Serious training, technology transfer and a good deal of standard-setting take place primarily within the vertical *keiretsu.* Workers are encouraged to acquire firm- or group-specific skills, and notably strong relational skills appropriate for use within the family of companies within which they have been trained. In order to persuade workers to invest in skills of this specificity, the large firms have customarily offered many of them life-time employment. And, in order to sustain such commitments, many Japanese firms have cultivated the capacity to move rapidly into new products and product areas in response to changes in world markets and technologies. This kind of corporate strategy takes advantage of the high levels of workforce cooperation that lifetime employment encourages. To reinforce it, Japanese firms have also developed company unions providing the workforce with a voice in the affairs of the firm.

Japanese firms tend to lack the capacities for radical innovation that American firms enjoy by virtue of fluid market settings or for sector-centered technology transfer of the sort found in Germany. Instead, the group-based organization of the Japanese political economy has encouraged firms there to develop distinctive corporate strategies that take advantage of the capacities for cross-sector technology transfer and rapid organizational redeployment provided by the *keiretsu* system. These translate into comparative institutional advantages in the large-scale production of consumer goods, machinery, and electronics that exploit existing technologies and capacities for organizational change. Although Japan is clearly a coordinated market economy, the institutional structures that support group-based coordination there have been conducive to corporate strategies and comparative advantages somewhat different from those in economies with industry-based systems of coordination.

The varieties of capitalism approach can also be useful for understanding political economies that do not correspond to the ideal type of a liberal or coordinated market economy. From our perspective, each economy displays specific capacities for coordination that will condition what its firms and government do.

France is a case in point, and the chapters in this volume by Lehrer, Culpepper, and Hancké explore some of the implications of this approach for it. Collaboration across French companies is based on career patterns that led many of the managers of leading firms through a few elite schools and the public service before taking up their positions in the private sector. Lehrer observes that the top managers of many French firms, therefore, have close ties to the state and weak ties to the rest of the enterprise. As a result, he argues, they are less likely to pursue the corporate strategies found in Britain or Germany and more likely to look to the state for assistance than their counterparts in other nations. Using the case of vocational training, however, Culpepper shows that there are clear limits to what states can do in the absence of strong business associations capable of monitoring their members. Hancké examines how large French firms are adapting to these limits, suggesting that many are taking industrial reorganization upon themselves, sometimes devising new networks to coordinate their activities.

In sum, although the contrast between coordinated and liberal market economies is important, we are not suggesting that all economies conform to these two types. Our object is to advance comparative analysis of the political economy more generally by drawing attention to the ways in which firms coordinate their endeavors, elucidating the connections between firm strategies and the institutional support available for them, and linking these factors to patterns of policy and performance. These are matters relevant to any kind of political economy.

1.6 Comparative Institutional Advantage

We turn now to some of the issues to which this perspective can be applied, beginning with a question central to international economics, namely, how to construe comparative economic advantage. The theory of comparative economic advantage is important because it implies that freer trade will not impoverish nations by driving their production abroad but enrich them by allowing each to specialize in the goods it produces most efficiently and exchange them for even more goods from other nations. It can be used to explain both the expansion of world trade and the patterns of product specialization found across nations. The most influential version of the theory focuses on the relative endowment of basic factors (such as land, labor, and capital) found in a nation and sug-gests that trade will lead a nation to specialize in the production of goods that use its most abundant factors most intensively (Stolper and Samuelson 1941).

However, recent developments have dealt a serious blow to this account of comparative economic advantage. The most important of these include the expansion of intra-industry trade and increases in the international mobility of capital. If the theory is correct, nations should not import and export high volumes of goods from the same sector; and there is a real possibility that international movements of capital will even out national factor endowments. As a result, some economists have become skeptical about whether comparative advantages really exist, and many have begun to seek other explanations for the expansion of trade and the geographic distribution of production.

Some explain the growth of trade, and intra-industry trade in particular, as the result of efforts to concentrate production in order to secure returns to scale (Helpman 1984). Others explain the concentration of particular kinds of production in some nations as the result of firms' efforts to secure the positive externalities generated by a group of firms engaged in related endeavors at the same site, whether in the form of appropriate labor pools, the availability of relevant intermediate products, or technological spillovers. This approach predicts that companies making similar products will cluster together, whether in Silicon Valley or Baden-Württemberg (Krugman 1991).

Both of these theories are valuable as far as they go, and nothing in our own is inconsistent with them, but we think they do not go far enough. Both explain why the production of some kinds of goods might be concentrated in a nation, but they say little about why production of *that* type should be concentrated in *that* particular nation, while other nations specialize in other kinds of production. Agglomeration theory explains why firms engaged in similar endeavors cluster in places like Silicon Valley or Baden-Württemberg, but it cannot explain why firms engaged in activities that entail high risks, intense competition, and high rates of labor turnover cluster in Silicon Valley, while firms engaged in very different activities that entail lower risks, close inter-firm collaboration, and low rates of labor turnover locate in Baden-Württemberg. We still need a theory that explains why particular nations tend to specialize in specific types of production or products.

We think that such a theory can be found in the concept of *comparative institutional advantage*. The basic idea is that the institutional structure of a particular political economy provides firms with advantages for engaging in specific types of activities there. Firms can perform some types of activities, which allow them to produce some kinds of goods, more efficiently than others because of the institutional support they receive for those activities in the political economy, and the institutions relevant to these activities are not distributed evenly across nations.

The contention that institutions matter to the efficiency with which goods can be produced receives considerable support from the growing body of work on endogenous growth. Many economists have observed that national rates of growth cannot be explained fully by incremental additions to the stock of capital and labor and fixed rates of technical change. Endogenous growth theorists have suggested that the institutional setting for production also seems to matter to national rates of growth; and various efforts have been made to specify what features of that setting might be important, generating suggestions that include: economies of scale available from oligopoly positions, economies of scope arising from experience in related endeavors, network externalities generated by firms engaged in similar activities, and the nature of property rights regimes (Romer 1986, 1994; Grossman and Helpmann 1992; Aghion and Howitt 1998).[28] There is now widespread recognition that the institutional context can condition rates of growth and technological progress.

To date, however, most efforts to specify these institutions have concentrated on market relationships and the legal framework for them, neglecting the non-market relations that may be equally important to such outcomes. The latter receive more emphasis in the literature on national innovation systems and some analyses of competitive advantage (Dosi et al. 1988; Porter 1990; Barro and Sala-i-Martin 1995; Edquist 1997). Most of this literature, however, looks for the ingredients of *absolute* advantage, i.e. it identifies factors more of which will improve the performance of any economy. We seek institutional features that might confer *comparative* advantage and, thus, be better suited to explaining cross-national patterns of product or process specialization (Zysman 1994).

The basic logic of our approach should be apparent. We have argued that, in some political economies, firms make more extensive use of non-market modes of coordination to organize their endeavors, while in others firms rely mainly on markets to coordinate those endeavors. Broadly speaking, these differences correspond to the level of institutional support available for market, as opposed to non-market, coordination in each political economy. Using a distinction between liberal and coordinated market economies, we have identified many of the institutional features of the political economy relevant to these differences and suggest that these correspond to cross-national differences in corporate strategy.

The important point to be added here is that the availability of these different modes of coordination conditions the efficiency with which firms can perform certain activities, thereby affecting the efficiency with which they can produce certain kinds of goods and services. In short, the national institutional frameworks examined in this volume provide nations with comparative advantages in particular activities and products. In the presence of trade, these advantages should give rise to cross-national patterns of specialization.

Although there may be types of comparative advantage that these institutional frameworks confer that we have not yet explored, we focus here on their impact on *innovation* since a firm's capacity to innovate is crucial to its long-run success. The key distinction we draw is between *radical* innovation, which entails substantial shifts in product lines, the development of entirely new goods, or major changes to the production process, and *incremental* innovation, marked by continuous but small-scale improvements to existing product lines and production processes. Over the medium to long term, efficiency in the production of some kinds of goods requires a capacity for radical innovation, while, in other kinds of goods, it requires a capacity for incremental innovation.

Radical innovation is especially important in fast-moving technology sectors, which call for innovative design and rapid product development based on research, as in biotechnology, semiconductors, and software development. It is also important to success in the provision of complex system-based products, such as telecommunications or defense systems, and their service-sector analogs: airlines, advertising, corporate finance, and entertainment. In the latter, competitiveness demands a capacity for taking risks on new product strategies and for the rapid implementation of such strategies within large, tightly coupled organizations that employ a diverse personnel.

Incremental innovation tends to be more important for maintaining competitiveness in the production of capital goods, such as machine tools and factory equipment, consumer durables, engines, and specialized transport equipment. Here, the problem is to maintain the high quality of an established product line, to devise incremental improvements to it that attract consumer loyalty, and to secure continuous improvements in the production process in order to improve quality control and hold down costs.

Coordinated market economies should be better at supporting incremental innovation. This follows from the emphasis we have put on the relational requirements of company endeavors. It will be easier to secure incremental innovation where the workforce (extending all the way down to the shop floor) is skilled enough to come up with such innovations, secure enough to risk suggesting changes to products or process that might alter their job situation, and endowed with enough work autonomy to see these kinds of improvements as a dimension of their job. Thus, incremental innovation should be most feasible where corporate organization provides workers with secure employment, autonomy from close monitoring, and opportunities to influence the decisions of the firm, where the skill system provides workers with more than task-specific skills and, ideally, high levels of industry-specific technical skills, and where close inter-firm collaboration encourages clients and suppliers to suggest incremental improvements to products or production processes.

The institutions of coordinated market economies normally provide high levels of support for these relational requirements. Highly coordinated *industrial-relations systems* and *corporate structures* characterized by works councils and consensus decision-making provide employees with the guarantees that elicit their cooperation. The *training systems* of CMEs typically provide high skill levels and the requisite mix of company-specific and more general technical skills. Appropriate *contract laws* and *dense networks of inter-corporate linkages* allow firms to form relational contracts with other firms; and *systems of corporate governance* that insulate firms against hostile takeovers and reduce their sensitivity to current profits encourage long employment tenures and the development of the inter-firm and employee relations that foster incremental innovation. By encouraging corporate strategies based on product differentiation rather than intense product competition, these inter-corporate networks also tend to promote incremental, rather than radical, innovation. A reputation for risk-taking or cut-throat competition is rarely an asset in such networks.

By contrast, although some can occur there, the institutional features of liberal market economies tend to limit firms' capacities for incremental innovation. Financial market arrangements that emphasize current profitability and corporate structures that concentrate unilateral control at the top deprive the workforce of the security conducive to their full cooperation in innovation. Fluid labor markets and short job tenures make it rational for employees to concentrate more heavily on their personal career than the firm's success and on the development of general skills rather than the industry- or company-specific skills conducive to incremental innovation. The complexion of contract law and antitrust laws discourages inter-firm collaboration in incremental product development.

However, the institutional framework of liberal market economies is highly supportive of radical innovation. *Labor markets* with few restrictions on layoffs and high rates of labor mobility mean that companies interested in developing an entirely new product line can hire in personnel with the requisite expertise, knowing they can release them if the project proves unprofitable. Extensive *equity markets* with dispersed shareholders and few restrictions on mergers or acquisitions allow firms seeking access to new or radically different technologies to do so by acquiring other companies with relative ease, and the presence of venture capital allows scientists and engineers to bring their own ideas to market. As Lehrer's study of the airline industry shows, the concentration of power at the top typical of *corporate organization* in an LME makes it easier for senior management to implement entirely new business strategies throughout a multi-layered organization delivering complex system goods or services. Such firms can also acquire or divest subsidiaries quickly. *Inter-firm relations* based primarily on markets enhance the capacities of firms to buy other companies, to poach their personnel, and to license new products—all means of acquiring new technologies quickly.

By contrast, in CMEs, although dense inter-corporate networks facilitate the gradual diffusion of technology, they make it more difficult for firms to access radically new technologies by taking over other companies. Corporate structures characterized by strong worker representation and consensus decision-making make radical reorganization of a firm more difficult, as each of the affected actors contemplates the consequences for his relationship to the company. The long employment tenures that such institutions encourage make it less feasible for firms to secure access to new technologies by hiring in large numbers of new personnel.

In short, the institutional frameworks of liberal market economies provide companies with better capacities for radical innovation, while those of coordinated market economies provide superior capacities for incremental innovation. Therefore, to the extent allowed by transport costs and the efficiency of international markets, there should be national patterns of specialization in activities and products; and these should reflect rational responses to the institutional frameworks identified here rather than random geographic agglomeration.

Notes

1 We concentrate here on economies at relatively high levels of development because we know them best and think the framework applies well to many problems there. However, the basic approach should also have relevance for understanding developing economies as well (cf. Bates 1997).

2 Of necessity, this summary is brief and slightly stylized. As a result, it does not do full justice to the variety of analyses found within these literatures and neglects some discussions that fall outside them. Note that some of our own prior work can be said to fall within them. For more extensive reviews, see Hall (1999, 2001).

3 An alternative approach to neo-corporatism, closer to our own, which puts less emphasis on the trade union movement and more on the organization of business was also developed by Katzenstein (1985a, 1985b) among others (Offe 1981).

4 One of the pioneering works that some will want to compare is Albert (1993), who develops a contrast between the models of the Rhine and America that parallels ours in some respects. Other valuable efforts to identify varieties of capitalism that have influenced us include Hollingsworth and Boyer (1997), Crouch and Streeck (1997b), and Whitley (1999).

5 There are a few notable exceptions that influence our analysis, including the work of Scharpf (1987, 1997a) and Przeworski and Wallerstein (1982).

6 In other works by the contributors to this volume, 'organized market economy' is sometimes used as a term synonymous with 'coordinated market economy'. Although all of the economies we discuss are 'coordinated' in the general sense of the term, by markets if not by other institutions, the term reflects the prominence of strategic interaction and hence of coordination in the game-theoretic sense in CMEs.

7 Although we do not emphasize it here, this is not meant to deny the observation of Granovetter (1985) and others that market relations are usually underpinned by personal relationships of familiarity and trust.

8 This point applies with particular force to market relationships in which one or more of the participants has substantially more market power than the others, as in cases of oligopoly, oligopsony, and the relations found in some supplier chains. We are not arguing that all markets in LMEs are perfectly competitive.

9 Note that, from time to time, we refer loosely to the 'institutions' or 'organization' of the political economy to refer to both the organizations and institutions found within it.

10 One political economist who has consistently drawn attention to the importance of deliberation is Sabel (1992, 1994) and the issue is now the subject of a growing game-theoretic literature (see Elster 1998).

11 Here we depart from some of our own previous formulations as well (cf. Hall 1986; Soskice 1990*b*).

12 Culpepper documents this problem and explores some solutions to it in this volume and Culpepper (1998).

13 Williamson (1985) himself acknowledges the presence of institutionalized relationships extending beyond markets or hierarchies, albeit without characterizing them precisely as we do here.

14 At the sectoral or regional level, of course, large firms may be able to exercise substantial influence over the development of these institutions, as Hancké shows in this volume (see also Hancké forthcoming).

15 It is possible to apply the general analytical framework of this volume to variations at the regional or sectoral level, as the chapter by Hancké does in some respects. From the perspective of this volume, institutional variation at the regional or sectoral level provides an additional layer of support for particular types of coordination and one that enhances a nation's capacity to support a range of corporate strategies and production regimes.

16 For examples in one sphere, see the essay by Estevez-Abe, Iversen, and Soskice in this volume.

17 Conversely, two institutions can be said to be 'substitutable' if the absence or inefficiency of one increases the returns to using the other. Note that we refer to total returns, leaving aside the question of to whom they accrue, which is a matter of property rights, and we define efficiency as the net returns to the use of an institution given its costs.

18 Of course, there are limits to the institutional isomorphism that can be expected across spheres of the economy. Although efficiency considerations may press in this direction, the presence of functional equivalents for particular arrangements will limit the institutional homology even across similar types of political economies, and the importance to institutional development of historical processes driven by considerations other than efficiency will limit the number of complementarities found in any economy.

19 The employment protection index developed by Estevez-Abe, Iversen, and Soskice in their chapter for this volume is a composite measure of the relative stringency of legislation or collective agreements dealing with hiring and firing, the level of restraint embedded in collective dismissal rules, and the extent of firm-level employment protection. Stock market capitalization is the market value of listed domestic companies as a percentage of GDP.

20 Luxembourg and Iceland have been omitted from this list because of their small size and Mexico because it is still a developing nation.

21 The Gini Index used in Fig. 6.3.2 is a standard measure for income inequality, measured here as post-tax, post-transfer income, reported in the Luxembourg Income Study for the mid- to late 1980s. Full-time equivalent employment is reported as a percentage of potential employment and measured as the total number of hours worked per year divided by full-time equivalent hours per person (37.5 hours at 50 weeks) times the working-age population. It is reported for the latest available of 1993 or 1994.

22 In previous decades, the German banks were also important contributors to such networks by virtue of their control over large numbers of shares in industrial firms (Hall 1986: ch. 9). In recent years, the role of the large commercial banks has declined, as they divest themselves of many holdings (Griffin 2000).

23 'Hold up' is Williamson's (1985) term for the withdrawal of active cooperation to back up demands.

24 Compared to general skills that can be used in many settings, industry-specific skills normally have value only when used within a single industry and firm-specific skills only in employment within that firm.

25 Firms in LMEs tend to rely on bond and equity markets for external finance more heavily than those in CMEs. However, bank lending in such economies also privileges publicly accessible, balance-sheet criteria, since banks find it difficult to monitor the less-obvious dimensions of corporate progress in an environment that lacks the close-knit corporate networks conveying such information in CMEs. Intense monitoring by a loan officer is feasible only when small sums are involved, since it exposes the bank to problems of moral hazard that are especially acute in countries where officers can take advantage of fluid labor markets to move elsewhere.

26 Note that we avoid a distinction often drawn between countries in which firms can raise 'long-term' capital versus those in which only 'short-term' capital is available because this distinction is rarely meaningful. Many companies in LMEs with established market reputations can raise capital for projects promising revenues only in the medium to long term, and firms often finance the bulk of their activities from retained earnings. Of more relevance are the rules governing hostile takeovers, whose prospect can induce firms to pay more attention to corporate earnings and the price of their shares.

27 Partly for this reason, the market valuation of firms in LMEs often depends more heavily on the reputation of its CEO than it does in CMEs.

28 Note that strategic trade theory focuses on a similar set of variables (cf. Krugman 1986; Busch 1999).

References

Aghion, Philippe, and Peter Howitt. 1998. *Endogenous Growth Theory*. Cambridge, Mass.: MIT Press.

Albert, Michel. 1993. *Capitalism against Capitalism*. London: Whurr.

Alvarez, R. Michael, Geoffrey Garret, and Peter Lange. 1991. "Government Partisanship, Labor Organization, and Macroeconomic Performance." *American Political Science Review* 85 (June): 539–56.

Aoki, Masahiko. 1994. "The Japanese Firm as a System of Attributes: A Survey and Research Agenda." In *The Japanese Firm: Sources of Competitive Strength*, ed. Masahiko Aoki and Ronald Dore. Oxford: Clarendon Press: 11–40.

Barro, Robert J., and Xavier Sala-I-Martin. 1995. *Economic Growth*. New York: McGraw-Hill.

Bates, Robert. 1997. *Open-Economy Politics: The Political Economy of the World Coffee Trade*. Princeton: Princeton University Press.

Berger, Suzanne, ed. 1981. *Organizing Interests in Western Europe: Pluralism, Corporatism, and the Transformation of Politics*. Cambridge: Cambridge University Press.

Borrus, Michael and John Zysman. 1997. "Wintelism and the Changing Terms of Global Competition: Prototype of the Future?" BRIE Working Paper 96B (February). Berkeley, Calif.: BRIE.

Boyer, Robert. 1990. *The Regulation School: A Critical Introduction*. New York: Columbia University Press.

Busch, Marc. 1999. *Trade Warriors*. New York: Cambridge University Press.

Calmfors, Lars, and John Driffill. 1988. "Centralisation of Wage Bargaining and Macroeconomic Performance." *Economic Policy* 6 (April): 13–61.

Calvert, R. 1995. "The Rational Choice Theory of Social Institutions: Cooperation, Coordination, and Communication." In *Modern Political Economy*, ed. J. Banks and E. Hanushek. New York: Cambridge University Press: 216–67.

Cameron, David R. 1984. "Social Democracy, Corporatism, Labor Quiescence and the Representation of Economic Interest in Advanced Capitalist Society." In *Order and Conflict in Contemporary Capitalism: Studies in the Political Economy of Western European Nations*, ed. John H. Goldthorpe. New York: Oxford University Press: 143–78.

Campbell, John L., Rogers Hollingsworth, and Leon Lindberg. 1991. *Governance of the American Economy*. New York: Cambridge University Press.

Casper, Steven. 1997. "Reconfiguring Institutions: The Political Economy of Legal Development in Germany and the United States." Ph.D. dissertation, Cornell University, Ithaca, NY.

Chandler, Alfred. 1974. *The Visible Hand*. Cambridge, Mass.: Harvard University Press.

—— and Harold Daems, eds. 1980. *Managerial Hierarchies: Comparative Perspectives on the Rise of the Modern Corporation*. Cambridge, Mass.: Harvard University Press.

Cohen, Stephen. 1997. *Modern Capitalist Planning*. Berkeley and Los Angeles: University of California Press.

Cox, Andrew. 1986. *The State, Finance and Industry*. Brighton: Wheatsheaf.

Crouch, Colin, and Wolfgang Streeck, eds. 1997. *Political Economy of Modern Capitalism: Mapping Convergence and Diversity*. London: Sage.

Culpepper, Pepper D. 1998. "Rethinking Reform: The Politics of Decentralized Cooperation in France and Germany." Ph.D. dissertation, Harvard University.

—— and David Finegold, eds. 1999. *The German Skills Machine*. Oxford: Berghahn.

Deininger, Klaus, and Lyn Squire. 1996. "Measuring Income Inequality: A New Data-Base." Development Discussion Paper No. 537, Harvard Institute for International Development.

DiMaggio, Paul, and Walter Powell. 1991. "Introduction." In *The New Institutionalism in Organizational Analysis*. Chicago: University of Chicago Press: 1–40.

Dore, Ronald. 1986. *Flexible Rigidities*. Stanford, Calif.: Stanford University Press.

Dosi, Giovanni, C. Freeman, R. Nelson, G. Silverberg, and L. Soete. 1988. *Technical Change and Economic Theory*. London: Pinter.

Edquist, Charles. 1997. *Systems of Innovation*. London: Pinter.

Eichengreen, Barry. 1997. "Institutions and Economic Growth after World War II." In *Economic Growth in Europe since 1945*, ed. Nicholas Crafts and Gianni Toniolo. Cambridge: Cambridge University Press: 38–72.

Elster, Jon, ed. 1998. *Deliberative Democracy*. New York: Cambridge University Press.

Estrin, Saul, and Peter Holmes. 1983. *French Planning in Theory and Practice*. London: Allen & Unwin.

Fehn, Rainer. 1998. "Capital Market Imperfections, Greater Volatilities and Rising Unemployment: Does Venture Capital Help?" Working Paper, Baerische Julius-Maximillians-Universität Wurtzbürg.

Finegold, David, and David Soskice. 1988. "The Failure of Training in Britain: Analysis and Prescription." *Oxford Review of Economic Policy* 4(3): 21–53.

Frieden, Jeffry, and Ronald Rogowski. 1996. "The Impact of the International Economy on National Policies: An Analytical Overview." In *Internationalization and Domestic Politics*, ed. Robert Keohane and Helen Milner. New York: Cambridge University Press: 25–47.

Fudenberg, Drew, and Eric Maskin. 1986. "The Folk Theorem in Repeated Games with Discounting and Incomplete Information." *Econometrica* 54(May): 533–54.

Golden, Miriam. 1993. "The Dynamics of Trade Unionism and National Economic Performance." *American Political Science Review* 87(June): 439–54.

Goldthorpe, John H., ed. 1984. *Order and Conflict in Contemporary Capitalism*. New York: Oxford University Press.

Granovetter, Mark. 1985. "Economic Action and Social Structures: The Problem of Embeddedness." *American Journal of Sociology* 91(3): 482–510.

Griffin, John. 2000. "Making Money Talk: A New Bank–Firm Relationship in German Banking?" Paper presented to the Annual Conference of the Society for the Advancement of Socio-economics, London, July.

Grossman, Gene, and Elhanan Helpman. 1992. *Innovation and Growth in the Global Economy*. Cambridge, Mass.: MIT Press.

Hall, Peter A. 1986. *Governing the Economy: The Politics of State Intervention in Britain and France*. New York: Oxford University Press.

———. 1990. "The State and the Market." In *Developments in French Politics*, ed. Peter A. Hall, Jack Hayward, and Howard Machin. London: Macmillan: 171–87.

———. 1999. "The Political Economy of Europe in an Era of Interdependence." In *Continuity and Change in Contemporary Capitalism*, ed. Herbert Kitschelt et al. Cambridge: Cambridge University Press: 135–63.

———. 2001. "The Evolution of Economic Policy in the European Union." In *From Nation-State to European Union*, ed. Anand Menon and Vinvent Wright. Oxford: Oxford University Press: 214–45.

——— and Robert Franzese, Jr. 1998. "Mixed Signals: Central Bank Independence, Coordinated Wage Bargaining, and European Monetary Union." *International Organization* 52(Summer): 502–36.

Helpman, Elhanan. 1984. "Increasing Returns, Imperfect Markets, and Trade Theory." In *Handbook of International Economics,* ed. R. W. Jones and P. B. Kenen. Amsterdam: North Holland: 325–66.

Herrigel, Gary. 1996. *Industrial Constructions: The Sources of German Industrial Power*. Cambridge: Cambridge University Press.

Hollingsworth, J. Rogers, Philippe C. Schmitter, and Wolfgang Streeck, eds. 1994. *Governing Capitalist Economies*. New York: Oxford University Press.

Hollingsworth, J. Rogers, and Robert Boyer, eds. 1997. *Contemporary Capitalism: The Embeddedness of Institutions*. Cambridge: Cambridge University Press.

Jaikumar, R. 1986. "Postindustrial Manufacturing." *Harvard Business Review* (November–December): 69–76.

Johnson, Chalmers. 1982. *MITI and the Japanese Miracle: The Growth of Industrial Policy 1925-1975*. Stanford, Calif.: Stanford University Press.

Katzenstein, Peter J. 1978. "Conclusion: Domestic Sources and Strategies of Foreign Economic Policy." In *Between Power and Plenty: Foreign Economic Policies of Advanced Industrial States*, ed. Peter J. Katzenstein. Madison: University of Wisconsin Press: 295–336.

———. 1985a. *Corporatism and Change*. Ithaca, NY: Cornell University Press.

———. 1985b. *Small States in World Markets*. Ithaca, NY: Cornell University Press.

Knetter, M. 1989. "Price Discrimination by US and German Exporters." *American Economic Review* 79(1): 198–210.

Knight, Jack. 1992. *Institutions and Social Conflict*. New York: Cambridge University Press.

Kreps, David. 1990. "Corporate Culture and Economic Theory." In *Perspectives on Positive Political Economy*, ed. James E. Alt and Kenneth A. Shepsle. New York: Cambridge University Press: 90–143.

Krugman, Paul, ed. 1986. *Strategic Trade Policy and the New International Economics*. Cambridge, Mass.: MIT Press.

Krugman, Paul. 1991. *Geography and Trade*. Cambridge, Mass.: MIT Press.

Lazonick, William. 1991. *Business Organization and the Myth of the Market Economy*. Cambridge: Cambridge University Press.

McArthur, John, and Bruce Scott. 1969. *Industrial Planning in France*. Boston: Harvard Business School.

March, James G. and Johan P. Olsen. 1989. *Rediscovering Institutions: The Organizational Basis of Politics*. New York: Free Press.

Milgrom, Paul, and John Roberts. 1990. "The Economics of Modern Manufacturing: Technology, Strategy and Organization." *American Economic Review* 80: 511–28.

———. 1992. *Economics, Organization and Management*. Englewood Cliffs, NJ: Prentice Hall.

———. 1995. "Complementarities, Industrial Strategy, Structure and Change in Manufacturing." *Journal of Accounting and Economics* 19: 179–208.

Nelson, Richard R., ed. 1993. *National Innovation Systems*. New York: Oxford University Press.

Nordlinger, Eric. 1981. *On the Autonomy of the Democratic State*. Cambridge, Mass.: Harvard University Press.

North, Douglass C. 1990. *Institutions, Institutional Change and Economic Performance*. New York: Cambridge University Press.

OECD. 1996. *OECD Economies at a Glance: Structural Indicators*. Paris: OECD.

Offe, Claus. 1981. "The Attribution of Public Status to Interest Groups: Observations on the West German Case." In *Organizing Interests in Western Europe*, ed. Suzanne Berger. Cambridge: Cambridge University Press.

Olson, Mancur. 1965. *The Logic of Collective Action: Public Goods and the Theory of Groups*. Cambridge, Mass.: Harvard University Press.

Ostrom, Elinor, 1990. *Governing the Commons: The Evolution of Institutions for Collective Action*. New York: Cambridge University Press.

Piore, Michael, and Charles Sabel. 1984. *The Second Industrial Divide*. New York: Basic Books.

Pizzorno, Alessandro. 1978. "Political Exchange and Collective Identity in Industrial Conflict." In *The Resurgence of Class Conflict in Western Europe*, vol. i, ed. Colin Crouch and Alessandro Pizzorno. London: Macmillan: 177–98.

Porter, Michael E. 1990. *The Competitive Advantage of Nations*. New York: Free Press.

Przeworski, Adam, and Michael Wallerstein. 1982. "The Structure of Class Conflict in Democratic Capitalist Societies." *American Political Science Review* 76(2): 215–38.

Regini, Marino. 1984. "The Conditions for Political Exchange: How Concertation Emerged and Collapsed in Britain and Italy." In *Order and Conflict in Contemporary Capitalism: Studies in the Political Economy of Western European Nations*, ed. J. H. Goldthorpe. New York: Oxford University Press: 124–42.

Rhodes, Martin. 1997. "Globalisation, Labour Markets and Welfare States: A Future of 'Competitive Corporatism'?" In *The Future of European Welfare*, ed. Martin Rhodes and Yves Meny. London: Macmillan.

Romer, Paul. 1986. "Increasing Returns and Long-Run Growth." *Journal of Political Economy* 94 (5): 1002–37.

———. 1994. "The Origins of Endogenous Growth." *Journal of Economic Perspectives* 8(1): 3–22.

Sabel, Charles F. 1992. "Studied Trust: Building New Forms of Cooperation in a Volatile Economy." In *Industrial Districts and Local Economic Reorganization*, ed. Frank Pyke and Werner Sengenberger. Geneva: International Institute for Labor Studies: 215–50.

———. 1994. "Learning by Monitoring: The Institutions of Economic Development." In *The Handbook of Economic Sociology*, ed. Neil Smelser and Richard Swedberg. Princeton: Princeton University Press.

Sacks, Paul M. 1980. "State Structure and the Asymmetrical Society." *Comparative Politics* (April): 349–76.

Scharpf, Fritz W. 1987. "Game-Theoretical Interpretations of Inflation and Unemployment in Western Europe." *Journal of Public Policy* 7(3): 227–57.

———. 1991. *Crisis and Choice in European Social Democracy*. Ithaca, NY: Cornell University Press.

———. 1997. *Games Real Actors Play: Actor-Centered Institutionalism in Policy Research*. Boulder, Colo.: Westview Press.

Schmitter, Philippe, and Gerhard Lehmbruch, eds. 1979. *Trends toward Corporatist Intermediation*. Beverly Hills, Calif.: Sage.

Shonfield, Andrew. 1965. *Modern Capitalism*. New York: Oxford University Press.

Skocpol, Theda, and Edwin Amenta. 1985. "Did Capitalists Shape Social Security?" *American Sociological Review* 50(4): 572–5.

Sorge, Arndt, and Michael Warner. 1986. *Comparative Factory Organization*. Aldershot: Gower.

Soskice, David. 1990a. "Wage Determination: The Changing Role of Institutions in Advanced Industrialized Countries." *Oxford Review of Economic Policy* 6(4): 36–61.

———.1990b. "Reinterpreting Corporatism and Explaining Unemployment: Coordinated and Non-coordinated Market Economies." In *Labour Relations and Economic Performance*, ed. Renato Brunetta and Carlo Dell'Aringa. Proceedings of a conference held by the International Economics Association in Venice, Italy. Vol. 95. London: Macmillan: 170–214.

———. 1997. "German Technology Policy, Innovation, and National Institutional Frameworks." *Industry and Innovation* 4(1): 75–96.

Stolper, Wolfgang Friedrich, and Paul Samuelson. 1941. "Protection and Real Wages." *Review of Economic Studies* 9: 58–73.

Streeck, Wolfgang. 1992. *Social Institutions and Economic Performance: Studies on Industrial Relations in Advanced European Capitalist Countries*. London: Sage.

———. 1994. "Pay Restraint without Incomes Policy: Institutionalized Monetarism and Industrial Unionism in Germany?" In *The Return of Incomes Policy*, ed. Ronald Dore, Robert Boyer, and Zoë Mars. London: Pinter: 118–40.

——— and Philip Schmitter, eds. 1986. *Private Interest Government: Beyond Market and State*. Beverly Hills, Calif.: Sage..

Swenson, Peter. 1991. "Bringing Capital Back in, or Social Democracy Reconsidered: Employer Power, Cross-class Alliances, and Centralization of Industrial Relations in Denmark and Sweden." *World Politics* 43(July): 513–44.

———. 1997. "Arranged Alliance: Business Interests in the New Deal." *Politics and Society* 25(March): 66–116.

Swidler, Ann. 1986. "Culture in Action: Symbols and Strategies." *American Sociological Review* 51(2): 273–86.

Teece, David, and Gary Pisano. 1998. "The Dynamic Capabilities of Firms." In *Technology, Organization and Competitiveness*, ed. Giovanni Dosi, David J. Teece, and Josef Chytry. Oxford: Oxford University Press: 193–212.

Thelen, Kathleen. 1991. *Union of Parts: Labor Politics in Postwar Germany*. Ithaca, NY: Cornell University Press.

Vitols, Sigurt, Steven Casper, David Soskice, and Stephen Woolcock. 1997. *Corporate Governance in Large British and German Companies: Comparative Institutional Advantage or Competing for Best Practice*. London: Anglo German Foundation.

Whitley, Richard. 1999. *Divergent Capitalisms: The Social Structuring and Change of Business Systems*. Oxford: Oxford University Press.

Williamson, Oliver. 1975. *Markets and Hierarchies*. New York: Free Press.

———. 1985. *The Economic Institutions of Capitalism: Firms, Markets, Relational Contracting*. New York: Free Press.

Ziegler, J. Nicholas. 1997. *Governing Ideas: Strategies for Innovation in France and Germany*. Ithaca, NY: Cornell University Press.

Zysman, John. 1983. *Governments, Markets, and Growth: Financial systems and the Politics of Industrial Change*. Ithaca, NY: Cornell University Press.

———. 1994. "How Institutions Create Historically Rooted Trajectories of Growth." *Industrial and Corporate Change* 3 (1): 243–83.

Part II

Contemporary Debates

1

Market Reform

Thus far we have reviewed a series of contending perspectives or paradigms that differ in how they understand markets as institutions, and how individuals, societies, and governments interact in the creation and governance of markets. Now we turn to a series of contemporary issues to illustrate how these theoretical perspectives apply to policy debates. Even in rich democracies, where the market tradition is well established, thickly institutionalized, and underpinned by the rule of law, debate persists on how markets should be structured to achieve desired outcomes. In these countries, policy debates have tended to be framed by the dichotomy of government versus market, with the presumption that more of one implies less of the other. In reality, however, the choices are not really about whether to govern markets but rather about *how* to govern them.

For about 25 years after the Second World War, the advanced industrial countries enjoyed a period – often called the "golden age" of capitalism – in which the Keynesian consensus generated a period of rapid growth with high employment, low inflation, and a relatively equitable distribution of income and wealth. Many of these countries moved during this period to expand the welfare state. The postwar era through the mid-1970s thus tended to be an era of bigger government in the rich democracies of the United States and Europe, where the state played numerous roles in the economy, ranging from regulator to service provider. As discussed earlier with respect to the liberal paradigm, however, market liberalism made a comeback in the 1980s both in thought and in policy. The Thatcher–Reagan revolution was animated by a commitment to limiting the role of government in the economy as much as possible. Philosophically, this free-market reform agenda was driven by the liberal mantra of the superiority of individualism over collectivism. This neoliberal revolution was in many ways a reaction to the social democratic welfare states that had developed in Europe since the end of the Second World War, matched to some extent by Lyndon B. Johnson's "Great Society" in the United States.

The neoliberal turn in politics and policy built on the views of scholars like Friedrich Hayek and Milton Friedman, presented earlier in this volume. These scholars understand that markets are complex institutions, and that the government must play a role in facilitating economic activity, particularly in ensuring the rule of law. Yet neoliberals see market reform essentially as a negative exercise: the process of shrinking government and limiting its role in the economy to unfetter the natural forces of the market. Thus Thatcherism and Reaganomics emphasized scaling back the size of the public sector, freeing markets through deregulation, privatizing industries, combatting trade unions, lowering taxes, and cutting welfare state programs.

Deepak Lal illustrates a market-liberal perspective on market governance in advanced industrial countries. Lal follows Hayek in differentiating his view from one of absolute laissez-faire. He not only affirms that markets require a strong legal framework; he also stresses that there is no such thing as a perfectly competitive market. Yet he does not believe that market imperfections – market failures – necessarily justify government intervention. He charges that those who favor government intervention, the "dirigistes," have an unjustifiable faith in the ability of an omnipotent government to govern markets wisely. In contrast, Lal insists that governments are not only highly fallible but also likely to be captured by the very industries they are supposed to be regulating.[1] So Lal, like Hayek, argues that laws must be nondiscriminatory, applying to everyone without regard to their circumstances. For Lal, that rules out government efforts to provide positive justice, such as redistribution in favor of the poor. For the most part, even the imperfect markets of the real world suffice to bestow the core benefits of a market economy: to provide incentives for businesses to produce better goods and services at lower prices.

We can flesh out the distinction between a market-liberal and a market-institutionalist perspective on concrete policy issues by examining how Lal views utility regulation and antitrust policy. His positions resemble those of Friedman and the Chicago School of antitrust policy, named for a prominent group of market-liberal economists and legal scholars at the University of Chicago.[2] Scholars in the Chicago School contend that monopolies tend to be fragile and competition robust because firms that attempt to charge monopoly prices are likely to be challenged by new competitors over time. Moreover, many companies with large market shares have achieved economies of scale by making better products and/or offering lower prices, thereby benefiting consumers. Lal stresses that innovation does not require a large number of firms. Thus a firm's market power should not be judged solely by its market share but also by the "contestability" of the market: the potential for another firm to challenge it. In any case, the government may be incapable of devising an appropriate remedy, or it may be captured by political interests that seek protection from competition, such as small businesses. Lal contends that monopolies are more likely to be the product of government regulation, not the lack of it. So Lal, like Friedman, advocates caution in antitrust enforcement.

Some sectors, such as the traditional landline telephone business, are considered "natural" monopolies because of powerful network effects. It would not be cost-efficient for another company to build a second telephone network, for example, and customers would not want to switch anyway because they could not connect to the customers of the incumbent company. Network sectors exhibit increasing returns to scale, meaning that the network becomes more valuable as the number of subscribers increases. We will see how this concept of network effects applies to the big tech firms of today, such as Facebook, in the section on the Digital Platform Economy. For natural monopoly sectors, Lal proposes that competition within the field be replaced by "competition for the field." By this he means that the government could auction monopoly franchises to service providers, and those franchises would be limited to a fixed period of time.

Steven K. Vogel demonstrates how a market-institutional perspective contrasts with the market-liberal view on market reform in advanced industrial countries, and on sector-specific regulation and antitrust in particular. He stresses that many businesses would rather collude than compete, so the active hand of government is required to press them to compete. He makes this case by evaluating the "deregulation" movement, one of the signature initiatives under the Thatcher and Reagan revolutions. Deregulation was particularly attractive politically because it offered the promise of better economic performance without higher government expenditures. The proponents of deregulation advertised it as a program that would reduce regulation and enhance competition, presuming that those two things were naturally associated. Vogel questions that presumption. He stresses that creating competition in network sectors requires re-regulation rather than deregulation: "freer markets" require more rules.[3] Indeed, some of the boldest deregulation programs, including those of the Thatcher–Reagan era, have been accompanied by a proliferation of rules and regulatory agencies. Market reforms in advanced industrialized countries should be seen as creative processes of enhancing market institutions rather than as negative processes of stripping away government regulation. Vogel also contrasts with Lal on antitrust policy, arguing that governments need strong antitrust enforcement to keep markets competitive. The dominance of the Chicago School approach to antitrust since 1980 has led to a gradual increase in market concentration in the United States, and this process has accelerated with the rise of dominant high-tech firms.[4] Vogel builds on Karl Polanyi in challenging the notion that markets can be "free" or "perfect" and hence questioning the prevailing liberal discourse on the relationship between governments and markets. He introduces the concept of "marketcraft," arguing that market governance constitutes a core function of government roughly comparable to statecraft (the management of foreign affairs).

The contrast between Lal and Vogel highlights some of the core differences between the market-liberal and market-institutionalist worldviews. Lal stresses government failures; Vogel highlights market failures. Lal views free markets as an arena of personal freedom, and government as an agent of constraint. Vogel views real-world markets as riddled with collusion, fraud, and imbalances of power, and government as the agent that enforces competition. Lal views freedom in negative terms, as freedom from government constraint. Vogel views freedom in positive terms, as the freedom to challenge incumbents or to participate in dynamic markets. Lal views government as incapable of governing markets effectively, or captured by special interests. Vogel recognizes that the government can be captured by industry, but stresses that private firms seek "rents" (returns not justified by value added) even in the absence of government protection, and that government regulation can curtail this activity. Lal does not claim that there is such a thing as a free or perfect market, but he does argue that the government role should be limited so as to allow markets to operate as freely as possible. Vogel claims that there is no single market equilibrium, since all markets are governed, and that it is often impossible to tell whether a particular policy option would move toward or away from the hypothetical free market. A move to strengthen antitrust enforcement, for example, could be viewed as a step away from the market because it increases government regulation, or it could be viewed as a move toward the market because it enhances competition. Toward the end of the excerpt, Vogel presents a typology to illustrate the range of market governance mechanisms, including everything from government regulations to business practices and social norms. This typology follows in the tradition of economic sociology in that it goes beyond government regulation to examine the many different types of actors – including industry associations, firms, and individuals – that collectively govern markets.

Notes

1 George Stigler, "The Theory of Economic Regulation," *Bell Journal of Economics and Management Science* 2 (1971): 3–21.

2 Richard Posner, "The Chicago School of Antitrust Analysis," *University of Pennsylvania Law Review* 127 (1979): 925–48. Influential works in the Chicago School include George Stigler, "A Theory of Oligopoly," *Journal of Political Economy* 72 (1964): 44–61; Oliver E. Williamson, "Economies as an Antitrust Defense: The Welfare Tradeoffs," *American Economic Review* 58 (1968): 18–36; and Robert Bork, *The Antitrust Paradox: A Policy At War With Itself* (New York: Basic Books, 1978).

3 See also Steven K. Vogel, *Freer Markets, More Rules: Regulatory Reform in Advanced Industrial Countries* (Ithaca, NY: Cornell University Press, 1996). Vlad Tarko has confirmed this thesis, finding a simultaneous increase in (1) economic liberalization, as measured by economic freedom and doing business indexes, and (2) the number, budgets, and staffing of regulatory agencies, as well as the number of regulations: "Neoliberalism and Regulatory Capitalism: Understanding the 'Freer Markets, More Rules' Puzzle," Social Science Research Network (SSRN) Working Paper, September 2017.

4 Thomas Philippon, *The Great Reversal: How America Gave Up on Free Markets* (Cambridge, MA: Belknap Press, 2019).

Deepak Lal,
Reviving the Invisible Hand (2006)*

2 From *Laissez Faire* to the *Dirigiste Dogma*

The twin pillars of the domestic policy of the British Imperium were the classical liberal policies of "laissez faire" and unilateral free trade. For the classical liberals, Adam Smith and David Hume, these were in the country's national interest, and though free trade would help in promoting understanding between states, they did not believe (as some of their later acolytes like Richard Cobden) that this would lead to international peace. To maintain international order, a balance of power through a network of alliances and treaties is needed.[1] We have seen that the new imperial power—the United States—has instead sought to achieve global free trade through reciprocity, and since the New Deal in the Great Depression, it has also eschewed laissez faire. It has however gradually built up its imperium, though only recently has it begun to use its unprecedented economic and military power to maintain international order. In the following three chapters, dealing with the current discontents with globalization under the U.S. imperium, I want to show that, while most of this discontent is based on simple economic fallacies and invalid empirical assumptions, it has been allowed currency in large part because the United States has eschewed the twin economic principles which underpinned the nineteenth-century LIEO. But what are these principles?

Classical Liberalism and Laissez Faire

Laissez Faire

The laissez faire doctrine has been caricatured as "the night watchman state," as assuming "a harmony of interests," and as assuming utility-maximizing rational actors. But all these are alien to the thought of the fathers of classical liberalism—Hume and Smith.[2] They do not look upon man as a rational utility maximizer with perfect knowledge. Hume talks of the "imperfections and narrow limits of human understanding" and that "reason is, and ought only to be the slave of the passions and can never pretend to any office other than to serve and obey them."[3] Their central claim is that, a free market economy, by promoting the division of labor, and by coordinating the division of knowledge (which necessarily exists in any society) through the price mechanism can goad individuals to become more rational. The specialization that then ensues allows a better allocation of a society's resources and leads to greater national

---

wealth. But, the free market is not considered to be one which has perfect competition as defined by modern-day economists.

Moreover, instead of there being a harmony of interests, a legal framework is needed to mediate between clashing interests and reconcile individual self-interest with the public good. Classical liberals strongly believe in "liberty under the law" and therefore a *qualified*, not an absolutist *laissez faire*.[4] This "liberty under the law" is moreover based on a procedural view of justice, where the latter, as Adam Smith put it, is "but a negative virtue, and merely hinders us from hurting our neighbors."[5] The law must be nondiscriminatory, applying to everyone without regard to particular circumstances. This rules out "positive" notions of justice, for instance of the distributive sort, in part because then the law would be based on the discretion of fallible and most likely corrupt men, to discriminate against some in favor of others.

Thus, the nature of the government is crucial in recommending policy. The great classical liberals from Hume to Smith to Mill were aware of this. If, as I have argued elsewhere,[6] most states are predatory—even democratic ones, where the predators are the median voter and successful pressure groups—concerned more with net revenue maximization than with social welfare maximization, then *normative* analysis based on postulating that the government consists of Platonic Guardians can go horribly wrong.

For the essential problem of political economy is to devise ways in which the state will provide the essential public goods at least cost from taxes. This was clearly recognized by the Classics, whose recommendation of laissez faire was based on a realistic assessment of the nature of governments. The classical policy prescriptions have been caricatured "by Carlisle's phrase anarchy plus the constable, or by LaSalle's simile of the night watchman."[7] But as Robbins (1976) and Myint (1948) have noted, this is a calumny. The classical liberals were not hostile to the state, nor did they believe that governments had only a minor role in economic life. Their view of the state was positive, and as Robbins indicates, Adam Smith's famous statement of the three functions of the state, viz., (i) to protect society from foreign invaders, and (ii) every member, as far as feasible, from oppression and injustice by other members of society, and (iii) provide and maintain various public works and public institutions which provided public goods,[8] is almost identical with Keynes's famous formulation in *The End of Laissez Faire*: "the important thing for government is not to do things which individuals are doing already, but to do those things which at present are not done at all."[9] The ensuing principles of economic liberalism were clearly set out in Mill's *Principles*, and their clearest modern reformulation is set forth in Hayek's *The Constitution of Liberty*. In fact, the current "Washington Consensus" on economic policy is essentially a classical liberal policy package.[10]

However, from Smith to Hayek to Friedman, classical liberals have maintained that "equality" comes into conflict with "liberty," and a true "liberal is not an egalitarian" (Hayek 1960, p. 402). For, as Nozick demonstrated brilliantly with his Wilt Chamberlain example, "no end-state state principle or distributional patterned principle can be continuously realized without continuous interference with people's lives [as any patterned distribution can be upset by people's voluntary actions in exchange]. . . . The socialist society would have to forbid capitalist acts between consenting adults."[11]

Classical liberals have, however, always advocated public transfers if private transfers are unavailable or insufficient to help the "deserving poor,"[12] and also, since Mill, the public *financing* but not *provision* of merit goods, such as health and education for those unable to afford them. Just as in the case of the economic package, the social package promoted by social democrats is increasingly coming to resemble these classical liberal prescriptions, except for merit goods. Thus, eschewing egalitarianism in taxation—in practice if not in rhetoric—and by attempting to reform welfare states to confine the benefits to the "deserving poor," both the New Democrats under President Clinton in the United States and New Labor under Prime Minister Blair in the United Kingdom, are closer to the classical liberal viewpoint than they imagine.

Conservatism

Classical liberalism must also be distinguished from conservatism, though both share some common features. Thus, Hayek, in his magisterial restatement of classical liberal principles in *The Constitution of Liberty*, ended the book with a postscript titled "Why I am not a Conservative."[13]

Hayek distinguishes three points on which classical liberals and conservatives differ. "One of the fundamental traits of the conservative attitude is a fear of change, a timid distrust of the new as such, while the [classical] liberal position is based on courage and confidence, on a preparedness to let change run its course even if we cannot predict where it will lead."[14] This conservative attitude to change is linked, says Hayek, "to two other characteristics of conservatism: its fondness for authority and its lack of understanding of economic forces."[15] These lead conservatives to have strong moral convictions but no political principles which allow them to work with people with different moral values. "The most conspicuous attribute of [classical] liberalism that distinguishes it as much from conservatism as from socialism is the view that moral beliefs concerning matters of conduct which do not directly interfere with the protected sphere of other persons do not justify coercion."[16] Also linked to this fear of the new, says Hayek, "is its propensity to reject well-substantiated new knowledge because it dislikes some of the consequences which seem to follow from it—or, to put it bluntly, its obscurantism,"[17] as well as "its hostility to internationalism and its proneness to a strident nationalism."[18]

The major votaries of classical liberalism today are American conservatives. For, as Hayek noted: "It is the doctrine on which the American system of government is based."[19] But, contemporary American conservatism is a novel brew which, Micklethwait and Wooldridge rightly note, is a mixture of the individualism of classical liberalism and "ubertraditionalism."[20] It represents adherence to the bourgeois organization of society epitomized by that much-maligned word, "Victorian": with its faith in individualism, capitalism, progress, and virtue. Having been silenced by the seemingly endless march of "embedded liberalism" since the New Deal, American conservatism has since the late 1960s regrouped, and under Presidents Reagan and George W. Bush created a new powerful political movement. Thus, apart from the brief period of Margaret Thatcher's ascendancy in Britain,[21] it is only in the United States that the classical liberal tradition continues to have political force.

The End of Laissez Faire

The principles of classical liberalism and laissez faire did not survive the trauma of the First World War, which brought the first LIEO to an end. It was the rise of the "enterprise" voice of socialism and rampant nationalism toward the end of the nineteenth century which led to "the end of laissez faire"—as Keynes called his influential pamphlet. The process began in Europe with Bismarck's social insurance scheme in Germany and the liberal welfare reforms instituted by the Liberal party under Lloyd George in Britain in 1906–14. Following the Great Depression it spread to the United States through Roosevelt's New Deal. The resulting "embedded liberalism,"[22] as it has been called, but which is more appropriately termed "social democratic" became the dominant ideology, not least because of the scribbling of economists. Consequently, by the time of the Second World War the classical liberalism of the nineteenth century was replaced by the Dirigiste Dogma.

[...]

Competition and Monopoly

The trouble with this whole mode of policy analysis lies not only in its neglect of political economy but also in its deviation from the classical liberal concept of competition. As Blaug (1987) notes, there is a "subtle but nevertheless unmistakable difference in the conception of "competition" before and after the "marginal revolution." The modern concept of perfect competition, conceived as a market structure in which all producers are price takers and face perfectly elastic curves for their outputs, was born with Cournot in 1838 and is foreign to the classical conception of competition as a process of rivalry in the search for unrealized profit opportunities, whose outcome is uniformity in both the rate of return on capital invested and the prices of identical goods and services but not because producers are incapable of making prices. In other words, despite a steady tendency throughout the history of economic thought to place the accent on the end-state of competitive equilibrium rather than the process of disequilibrium adjustments leading up to it, this emphasis became remorseless after 1870 or thereabouts, whereas the much looser conception of "free competition" with free but not instantaneous entry to industries is in evidence in the work of Smith, Ricardo, Mill, Marx, and of course Marshall and modern Austrians. For that reason, if for no other, it can be misleading to label classical economics as a species of general equilibrium theory except in the innocuous sense of an awareness that "everything depends on everything else."[23]

From Adam Smith onward, classical liberals also recognized that deviations from free competition (like monopoly) ultimately depend upon government actions which prevent potential rivals from competing. By contrast, the theoretical model, as Demsetz notes: "*assumes* that monopoly power exists, it does not explain *how* monopoly power is exercised and maintained. . . . [N]o good explanation is provided for how present and potential rivals are kept from competing without some governmentally provided restrictions on competitive activities."[24] For we now know from the theory of "contestable markets"[25] that, even with economies of scale and scope which limit the number of firms that can service a particular market, as long as potential rivals can contest the "monopoly," the single eventual incumbent's pricing and output policies need not diverge from those under competition. The only rents such a "monopolist" can acquire are the sunk costs of firm-specific assets essential for production. Thus, antitrust regulations designed to increase competition are unnecessary. Worse, there is evidence of monopolistic capture of regulatory agencies by the companies being regulated.[26] Hence, there is a clear danger that such regulations, instead of promoting competition, will create government-mediated barriers to entry which nurture monopolies.

The dynamic efficiency of capitalism, as Joseph Schumpeter emphasized in his magisterial book *Capitalism, Socialism and Democracy,* does not only depend upon the *imitative* output competition emphasized by perfect competition. In this form of competition, each producer in an industry imitates the products of its competitors and hence the competition is between identical products produced by a large number of producers. Rather, the essence of capitalism Schumpeter notes is the process of creative destruction involving *innovative* competition. He writes:

> In capitalist reality as distinguished from its textbook picture, it is not that kind of [imitative] competition which counts but the competition from the new commodity, the new technology, the new source of supply, the new type of organization—competition which commands a decisive cost or quality advantage and which strikes not at the margins of the profits and the outputs of the existing firms but at their foundations and their very lives. This kind of competition is as much more effective than the other as a bombardment is in a comparison with forcing a door, and so much more important that it becomes a matter of comparative indifference whether competition in the ordinary [imitative] sense functions more or less promptly; the powerful lever that in the long run expands output and brings down prices is in any case made of other stuff. It is hardly necessary to point out that [innovative] competition ... acts not only when in being but also when it is merely an ever-present threat. It disciplines before it attacks ... In many cases, though not all, this will in the long run enforce behavior very similar to the perfectly competitive pattern.[27]

This is as spare and incisive a description of the capitalist process and its dynamics as can be found. It gives the lie to all the dirigiste panaceas being touted by the New Dirigisme based on a myriad of "market failures" within the perfect competition model and the accompanying call for the regulation of a market economy. Thus, for the innovative competition which lies at the heart of the capitalist process, efficiency does not require a large number of firms. Most innovations partake of a race in which the winner takes all. As Demsetz notes: "the competitive intensity of [such] a contest is not always increased by adding more contestants."[28] Patents and other devices to prevent imitative competition allow the winners in innovative competition to secure a big payoff for their innovative effort. This shows that in a dynamic market economy there may be many dimensions of competition, with some of them being inversely related—for example imitative competition requires a large number of firms, while innovative competition requires a small number. Moreover, as the different dimensions of competition relevant for the efficient functioning of a dynamic economy are incommensurable, there can be no single measure of competitiveness (such as market concentration) to judge the efficiency of an actual market economy.

Nor will the "rate of return" or "price cap" regulatory formulae necessarily ensure competition in the large. For, with economies of scale, prices can no longer equal marginal costs and there cannot be perfect competition. Competition will not be merely imitative but have some of the elements of a contest in which some agents will lose and others win. It would be inappropriate to judge the intensity of competition of such a contest by the *ex post* rate of return of the winner. For, as Demsetz notes, "if one were to gauge competitive intensity by the rate of return on investment made by winners in a lottery game, the rate of return would be quite high, but a negative return is obtained if the calculation includes the wagers made by losers."[29] So, if one were to use the rate of return criterion to judge the competitiveness of a particular industry, ideally the calculation should include the costs incurred by those who competed to become incumbents but lost. If, moreover, incumbency depends on government favors, then the "rent seeking" costs of all the contestants associated with competing for political favor would also have to be included. This inclusive rate of return need not be above some competitive norm. But, in practice, it will be impossible to calculate.

But what about natural monopolies? Surely, once a firm acquires one, it will, *faut mieux* exploit its monopoly power, and hence such natural monopolies will require some form of regulation. Most infrastructural services like roads, rail, electricity, and water have elements of natural monopoly. This was the justification used in the past for their nationalization. But, with growing fiscal constraints and the well-known inefficiencies associated with public enterprises, there is a welcome global move toward their privatization. Will this not inevitably lead to natural monopolies being used by private producers to exploit consumers? Hence, should these utilities not be regulated?

The UCLA Industrial Organization school has provided a distinctive and important answer to this question, which unfortunately is not as well known as the various dirigiste regulatory regimes currently being touted by mainstream theorists. The basic idea has been labeled "competition for the field" by Harold Demsetz, following a distinction due to Edwin Chadwick in the nineteenth century between it and "competition within the field."

"Competition for the field" differs from the later development of the notion of "contestability," insofar as the latter is concerned with competition between an existing incumbent and potential entrants to the natural monopoly. By contrast, "competition for the field," as its name suggests, is concerned with the competition for becoming an incumbent in the first place. This has important consequences for the configuration of prices and output and thence the competitive efficiency of the economy. In the theory of contestable markets it has been shown that, in equilibrium, the only rents the incumbent of a natural monopoly can acquire are the incumbent's sunk costs which a new entrant would have to incur in moving in and out of the monopoly. If an outsider can enter and exit a market without incurring any transition costs, the natural monopoly would be perfectly contestable and, despite economies of scale and scope, the incumbent insider would not be able to garner any rents. But, as in many natural monopolies there will be substantial transition costs; insiders will usually be able to extract them as rents from consumers.[30]

The situation is very different from the viewpoint of competition for the field. Here the competition takes place *before* production begins. Would-be natural monopolists would compete for the right to serve the market at the lowest cost, adopting the best technology. In this competition for the field, as Demsetz showed in his famous essay, "Why regulate utilities?" the potential rents of the natural monopoly would be competed away with the best bid amongst the rivals to become the incumbent being accepted by the community. Thereafter, there would be a distinction between insiders and outsiders, and substantial transition costs for the latter—in sharp contrast with the conclusions of contestability theory. For, without these entry barriers, the successful incumbent may not realize the potential cost reductions associated with scale economies. The frequency of competition for the field, or equivalently the length of a franchise to the natural monopoly, will depend upon the particular supply and demand conditions for the output of the natural monopoly.[31] But what cannot be laid down is some ideal form of contract. For, given the ubiquitousness of imperfect information and the associated uncertainty, agents can only search for the best available mutually advantageous contract. In Hayek's felicitous phrase, the market is par excellence "a discovery process."[32]

The Rise of "Embedded Liberalism" in the United States

Why did the United States, the capitalist economy par excellence, pioneer antitrust legislation in the late nineteenth century? The answer lies in its history. Schumpeter noted:

> [I]n the Anglo-American world monopoly has been cursed and associated with functionless exploitation ever since, in the sixteenth and seventeenth centuries, it was English administrative practice to create monopoly positions in large numbers which, on the one hand, answered fairly well to the theoretical pattern of monopolist behavior and, on the other hand, fully justified the wave of indignation that impressed even the great Elizabeth. Nothing is so retentive as a nation's memory.... . That practice made the English-speaking public so monopoly-conscious that it acquired a habit of attributing to that sinister power practically everything it disliked about business. To the typical liberal bourgeois in particular, monopoly became the father of almost all abuses—in fact, it became his pet bogey. Adam Smith, thinking primarily of monopolies of the Tudor and Stuart type, frowned on them in awful dignity ... And in this country [the U.S.] monopoly is being made synonymous with any large- scale business.[33]

The American founding fathers had imbued this attitude from their country of origin.

In a perceptive essay, L. M. Hacker has argued that the anti-capitalist bias emerged in the United States and was amplified by its historians because of a political debate going back to its foundation between the Hamiltonians and Jeffersonians. The former were for a strong interventionist central government, the latter for a weak central government and little or no state intervention. The differences were not based on economic arguments but on moral and political issues. The Jeffersonians believed that a working federation based on states' rights would have emerged but for the Hamiltonian federalists who "won the day, partly by duress and fraud, and the consequences were dire. The establishment of a Supreme Court to override the legislative will and the acceptance of the idea of implied powers in the central government were some of the political results."

Jeffersonian ideas became prominent among historians in the twentieth century. They saw "Jefferson as the champion of natural rights (for natural today read 'human'); Jefferson as the spokesman for equalitarianism; Jefferson as the foe of an established church; Jefferson, notably, who sought to challenge 'monopoly'—this is the advocate whose words (not deeds) are being invoked.... . [T]he broad implications of Jefferson's attack on "monopoly" [were that] only in the wide diffusion of property ownership (i.e., wealth) could social stability and economic progress be found."[34]

The third historical strand was associated with Andrew Jackson. Jacksonianism was also leveling like Jeffersonianism. Jackson "sought to speak for the common man, notably challenging the power of the central government ... Jackson raised the cry of "monopoly" and was successful" (p. 84). After the Civil War, organized farmers took up the anti-capitalist cause by challenging the new industrialists, demanding "Peoples' Land, People's Money and People's Transportation." Their cause became "a moral crusade—they were the victims of those same monopolies against whom Jefferson and Jackson had inveighed."

The opponents of these populist groups were the Hamiltonians, Whigs, and Radical Republicans. They sought "the intervention of government to secure monetary stability and economic progress. A protective tariff system, a national banking program, government support of railroads, homesteads for farmers, easy immigration."[35]

The anti-capitalist bias of American historians was set by Charles Beard in his influential *The Rise of American Civilization*. He "took over the agrarian prejudices of his own Indiana boyhood to the capitalist processes. Late in life he found a remote and mechanical justification for his dislikes. He never showed an interest in these capitalist processes as such or in their economic consequences; but he rejected both for moral rather than for class, ideological, or dialectical reasons."[36]

It was Franklin Roosevelt's genius to knit these various strands together to create the "embedded liberalism" which has remained the dominant economic ideology in the United States Hacker argues:

> Franklin D. Roosevelt assumed the mantle of Jefferson and Jackson as a leveler and defender of human rights. That is to say socially and morally, his identifications were with Jeffersonianism; but not politically. For Roosevelt called upon state interventionism on a grand scale to achieve his intention: the Big State, which Jefferson and Jackson had feared and fought, was his creation. But, because he talked the language of Jefferson, his defenders have turned on the economic ideas of the anti-Roosevelt forces. Capitalism is stagnant and dominated by monopolists; without state intervention the business cycle cannot be resolved, social injustices ameliorated, real wages increased. Once again the anticapitalism of the New Dealers is political and moral; for certainly no case has been made out against capitalism as such.[37]

As such it is the moral critique of capitalism, best epitomized by the hugely influential book *The Robber Barons* by Matthew Josephson, which continues to resonate in America. Its anti-capitalist attitudes being summarized as: "(1) that great fortunes in America were built up by fraud; (2) that the country's natural resources were looted in the process; and (3) that the social consequences of private ownership and wealth were unhappy—in creating classes, in subordinating agriculture, in building slums, etc."[38] These attitudes are still prevalent in the United States, not least in its academies. I deal with this moral repugnance for capitalism in chapter 6. For today, it is the basic reason for the rise of the New Dirigisme.[39]

Notes

1 See Wyatt-Walter (1996).

2 See the excellent book by Razeen Sally (1998) for a clarification of what classical liberalism stands for, and how it has subsequently evolved in discussions of international economic order.

3 D. Hume (1740/1978), part 2.

4 Ibid.

5 Smith (1759/1982), part 2, p. 82.

6 Lal (1988, chap. 13.2); Lal and Myint (1996).

7 Robbins (1952), p. 37.

8 Smith (1759/1982), vol. 2, pp. 184–5.

9 Keynes (1926), pp. 46–7.

10 The "Washington Consensus" was the term coined by Williamson (1990) to describe the policy package which had emerged as best able to promote efficient poverty alleviating growth as a result of the experience of developing countries in the 1970s and 1980s. It is close to that advocated in Harberger (1984) as constituting the best technocratic advice based on experience. It is also the one emerging from the Lal and Myint (1996) study of twenty-five developing countries. Recently Williamson (2000) has sought to partly disown it, as the anti-globalization backlash has used it, particularly in Latin America, as the whipping horse in its denouncement of what it calls the "neo-liberal" policies adopted in Latin America. But, as Vargas Llosa (2000) has argued, there are hardly any countries in Latin America, apart from Chile, who have in fact adopted the full package, and hence to announce its failure on the halfbaked liberalization attempts in many countries is rather premature. Srinivasan (2000) rightly takes Williamson to task for his partial recantation.

11 Nozick (1974), p. 163. Thus, suppose you start off from what is considered a just, say equal, distribution of income. People then voluntarily go to a basketball game and give Wilt Chamberlain, the famous basketball player, a large part of their income to watch him play. The distribution of income will then become unequal. The adherents of a patterned distribution would then have to say this is unjust and force a return to the original distribution of income!

12 See the discussion in Lal and Myint (1996).

13 Conservatism as defined by its major proponent Edmund Burke can, according to John Micklethwaite and Adrian Wooldridge (in their important book *The Right Nation*), be "reduced to six principles: a deep suspicion of the power of the State; a preference for liberty above equality; patriotism; a belief in established institutions and hierarchies; skepticism about the idea of progress; and elitism" Micklethwait and Wooldridge (2004), p. 11. Classical liberals share the first three of these principles but not the last three.

It may also be instructive to see the similarities and differences in the thinking of the leading contemporary conservative thinker Michael Oakeshott and classical liberal Fredrich Hayek. They both agree on the dangerous illusion of constructing social institutions on the basis of a rationalist plan. They also agree on the distinction between the "civil association" and "enterprise view" of the state. Thus, Hayek states in vol. 2 of his *Law, Legislation and Liberty*, "I understand Professor Michael Oakeshott, in his oral teaching, has long used the terms *teleocratic* (and *teleocracy*) and *nomoccratic* (and *nomocracy*) to bring out the same distinction [between an organization and a spontaneous order]. . . . We shall occasionally make use of these terms when we want to stress the end governed character of the organization or the rule-governed character of the spontaneous order" (Hayek 1976, p. 15).

But they differed on the role of ideologies in promoting liberty as well as on the role of liberty in promoting economic efficiency and prosperity. Hayek wished to formulate a classical liberal ideology to combat collectivist ideologies; Oakeshott, however, argued against all doctrines (ideologies). Thus, while agreeing with Hayek's devastating critique of planning in *The Road to Serfdom*, he wrote that the main significance of the book "is not the cogency of the doctrine, but the fact that it is a doctrine. A plan to resist all planning may be better than its opposite but it belongs to the same style of politics" (Oakeshott 1990, p. 26). This is precisely the conservative attitude that Hayek deplored in "Why I am not a Conservative." By its "fear of ideas" and "distrust of theory" conservatism "deprives itself of the weapons needed in the struggle of ideas" (Hayek 1960, p. 404).

Furthermore, though both Hayek and Oakeshott defend free markets, Oakeshott "harbored deep reservations about Hayek's instrumental defense of liberty in terms of its propensity to promote economic efficiency and prosperity" (Franco 2004, p. 12). He looks upon classical liberalism's "plausible ethics of productivity" as a questionable moral ideal, and argues that "the political economy of freedom rests upon the clear acknowledgment that what is being considered is not 'economics' (not the maximization of wealth, not productivity or the standard of life) but *politics* that is, the custody of a manner of living" (Oakeshott 1990, p. 406).

They also disagree about the role of tradition in politics. Hayek notes this adherence to tradition is objectionable as "by its very nature it cannot offer an alternative to the direction in which they are moving" (Hayek 1960, p. 398). Or, as Himmelfarb (1975) observed, if Oakeshott's traditionalism is accepted, how can conservatives criticize the 1960s counterculture when it becomes the dominant culture (the tradition)?

Finally, unlike the classical liberal Hayek who embraces and welcomes change, the conservative Oakeshott seems to be against change. He derides innovation as "almost always an equivocal enterprise, in which gain and loss are so closely interwoven that it is extremely difficult to forecast the final upshot: there is no such thing as an unqualified improvement" (Oakeshott 1990, p. 411). "To be conservative," he writes, "is to prefer the familiar to the unknown, to prefer the tried to the untried, fact to mystery, the actual to the possible, the limited to the unbounded, the near to the distant . . . the convenient to the perfect, present laughter to utopian bliss" (p. 409). This attitude is diametrically opposed to the classical liberal's optimistic view of change, as the quotation in the text from Hayek exemplified.

Franco (2004) provides a judicious account of Oakeshott's philosophy and its relationship to many other philosophers.

14 Hayek (1960), p. 400.

15 Ibid.

16 Hayek (1960), p. 402. He goes on to say, "this may also explain why it seems to be so much easier for the repentant socialist to find a new spiritual home in the conservative fold than in the [classical] liberal."

17 Ibid., p. 404.

18 Ibid., p. 405.

19 Ibid., p. 409.

20 Micklethwait and Wooldridge (2004), p. 348.

21 Who is rightly described as more an American conservative than a traditional British Tory by Micklethwait and Wooldridge (2004), p. 345.

22 Keohane (1984); Ruggie (1983).

23 Blaug (1987), p. 445.

24 Demsetz (1989), p. 94.

25 Baumol, Panzar, and Willig (1982).

26 See Stigler (1988).

27 Schumpeter (1954), pp. 84–5.

28 Demsetz (1995), p. 146.

29 Ibid.

30 I have found this theory particularly useful in thinking of the natural monopoly which is the state. In Lal (1988/2004) I develop a model of the predatory state in which "contestability" plays a central role. The model is used to explain the rise and fall of empires in India over the millennia (see ibid., chap. 13.2).

31 Also, there is no reason why there should not be contractual conditions attached to the possibility of renegotiation of the terms of the franchise before its expiration. In fact, given uncertainty on this account, the rivals bidding for the franchise will take account of these renegotiation costs in their bids. Similarly, if there are likely to be future cost reductions because of technical progress, which would lead to future rents for the incumbent, these too would be taken into account in the rivals' bids for incumbency if they can be forecast, and the best bid again will involve the whittling away of these potential future rents.

Positive or negative windfalls, which are the result of unavoidable uncertainty, need not be inefficient. For instance, even in the near perfect markets for commodities, economic agents suffer positive and negative windfalls all the time, but this does not provide a case for regulation. However, in the case of natural monopolies, as these windfalls could continue for some considerable period of time, there could be political pressure for their curtailment if they are positive, and the danger of bankruptcy for the incumbent and hence of a disruption of supply if they are negative. This would provide a case for some renegotiation clause in the contract granting a franchise to a natural monopoly.

32 In contrast with this UCLA view on regulation, we have the emerging technocratic view on the regulation of natural monopolies. This is based on the frail framework of noncooperative game theory. (See Gilbert and Newberry 1994, which also provides references to this literature.) As the leading lights of game theory recognize, it is of very limited practical relevance because of the plethora of Nash equilibrium which can be generated (Binmore 1990, and Kreps 1990). Though of use in training the intellectual muscles of the young, it has not as yet yielded any robust policy-relevant results in my view. (But see Laffont and Tirole 1993 for an attempt to provide a textbook for the dirigiste technocratic regulator.) Its use in designing the auction for mobile phone licenses in the United Kingdom is better seen as a predatory scheme to transfer potential shareholder wealth to the state than any necessary subserving of efficiency.

33 Schumpeter (1954), p. 100.

34 Hacker (1954), pp. 82–3.

35 Ibid., p. 86.

36 Ibid., p. 79.

37 Ibid., p. 87.

38 Ibid., p. 80.

39 Two excellent accounts of the rise and content of business regulation in the United States are provided in Freyer (2000) and Vietor (2000) in the *Cambridge Economic history of the United States*, vols. 2 and 3. Vietor highlights five chronological stages in the evolution of regulatory policy in the United States. These are "(1) the period between World War I and the Great Depression, in which the growth of nationwide markets and national firms outstripped the power of state and local authorities to fulfill public objectives; (2) the Great Depression through the 1960s, in which New Deal–inspired regulatory regimes shaped most of the industries that comprised the national infrastructure and fostered development and integration in a relatively non-competitive environment; (3) the years from the mid-1960s through the late 1970s, in which a rights revolution extended government controls to a variety of social problems; (4) an overlapping era (1968–1983) of deregulation, in

which New Deal controls on competition were removed or redirected; and (5) the period after 1983, in which government-managed competition and market-oriented controls emerged as the basis for a new regulatory regime" (p. 971). His concluding net historical judgment on regulation is that "it has worked well at times and failed at others. . . . At the very least, regulation during the twentieth century has provided the Untied States with a politically acceptable means for preserving enterprise, while controlling it" (p. 1012). Once again it is the politics not the economics of regulation which has been important in regulating U.S. business.

Bibliography

Baumol, W. J., J. Panzar, and R. Willig (1982): *Contestable Markets*. Harcourt Brace Jovanovich, New York.

Binmore, K. (1990): *Essays in the Foundations of Game Theory*. Blackwell, Oxford.

———. (1994 and 1998): *Game Theory and the Social Contract, Vol. 1: Playing Fair; Vol 2: Just Playing*. MIT Press, Cambridge, Mass.

Blaug, M. (1987): "Classical Economics." In Eatwell, Milgate, and Newman (eds.), *The New Palgrave—A Dictionary of Economics*, vol. 1. Macmillan, London.

Demsetz, H. (1989): "Two Systems of Belief About Monopoly" in his *Efficiency, Competition and Policy*, Blackwell, Oxford.

———. (1995): *The Economics of the Business Firm*. Cambridge Economic Press, Cambridge.

Franco, P. (2004): *Michael Oakeshott—An Introduction*, Yale University Press, New Haven.

Freyer, T. A. (2000): "Business Law and American Economic History." In Engerman and Gallman (eds.) (2000), vol. 2. *The Cambridge Economic History of the United States*, Cambridge University Press, Cambridge.

Gillbert, P. J., and D. M. Newberry (1994): "The Dynamic Efficiency of a Regulatory Constitution." *Rand Journal of Economics* 25: 538–54.

Hacker, L. M. (1954): "The Anti-capitalist Bias of American Historians." In F. Hayek (ed.): *Capitalism and the Historians*. University of Chicago Press, Chicago.

Harberger, A. C. (ed.) (1984): *World Economic Growth*. ICS Press, San Francisco.

Hayek. F. (1960): *The Constitution of Liberty*. Routledge, London.

———. (1976): *Law, Legislation and Liberty*, vol. 2. Routledge, London.

Himmelfarb, G. (1975): "The Conservative Imagination: Michael Oakeshott." *American Scholar* 44 (summer): 405–20.

Hume, D. (1740/1978): *A Treatise on Human Nature*. Clarendon Press, Oxford.

Keohane, R. O. (1984): *After Hegemony*. Princeton University Press, Princeton, N.J.

Keynes, J. M. (1926): *The End of Laissez-Faire*. Hogarth Press, London.

Kreps, D. (1990): *Game Theory and Economic Modelling*. Clarendon Press, Oxford.

Laffont, J. J., and J. Tirole (1993): *A Theory of Incentives in Procurement and Regulation*. MIT Press, Cambridge, Mass.

Lal, D. (1988/2004): *The Hindu Equilibrium, vol. 1*. Clarendon Press, Oxford; revised and abridged edition, Oxford University Press, Oxford.

Lal, D., and H. Myint (1996): *The Political Economy of Poverty, Equity and Growth*. Clarendon Press, Oxford.

Micklethwait, J., and A. Wooldridge. (2004): *The Right Nation—Why America Is Different*. Allen Lane, London.

Myint, H. (1948): *Theories of Welfare Economics*. Harvard University Press, Cambridge, Mass.

Nozick, R. (1974): *Anarchy, State, and Utopia*. Basil Blackwell, Oxford.

Oakeshott, M. (1990): *Rationalism in Politics and Other Essays*, new and expanded ed. Liberty Fund, Indianapolis.

Robbins, L. (1952): *The Theory of Economic Policy in English Classical Political Economy*. Macmillan, London.

———. (1976): *Political Economy: Past and Present*. Macmillan, London.

Ruggie, J. G. (1983): "International Regimes, Transactions and Change: Embedded Liberalism in the Post-war Economic Order." In Stephen D. Krasner (ed.), *International Regimes*, pp. 195–223. Cornell University Press, Ithaca, NY.

Sally, R. (1998): *Classical Liberalism and International Economic Order*. Routledge, London.

Schumpeter, J. A. (1954): *History of Economic Analysis*. Oxford University Press, Oxford.

Smith, A. (1759/1982): *The Theory of Moral Sentiments*. Liberty Fund, Indianapolis.

Srinivasan, T. N. (2000): "The Washington Consensus a Decade Later: Ideology and the Art and Science of Policy Advice." *The World Bank Research Observer* 15 (2): 265–70.

Stigler, G. (ed.) (1988): *Chicago Studies in Political Economy*. University of Chicago Press, Chicago.

Vargas Llosa, Mario (2000): "Liberalism in the New Millennium." In I. Vasquez (ed.), *Global Fortune*. Cato Institute, Washington, D.C.

Vietor, R.H.K. (2000): "Government Regulation of Business." In Engerman and Gallman (eds.) *The Cambridge Economic History of the Untied States*, vol. 3. Cambridge University Press, Cambridge.

Williamson, J. (1990): "What Washington Means by Policy Reform." In J. Williamson (ed.): *Latin American Adjustment: How Much Has Happened?* Institute for International Economics, Washington, D.C.

———. (2000): "What Should the World Bank Think About the Washington Consensus." *World Bank Research Observer* 15 (2): 251–64.

Wyatt-Walter, A. (1996): "Adam Smith and the Liberal Tradition in International Relations." *Review of International Studies* 22 (1).

Steven K. Vogel,
Marketcraft (2018)[*]

1. The Marketcraft Thesis

Markets need rules not only to protect people and the environment from collateral damage, but also to function effectively in the first place. Our real-world choices therefore hinge not on whether markets should be governed, but on *how* they should be governed.[1] Consider the corporation, the institution at the heart of modern capitalism. There is nothing natural about it. The corporation is a construct that is granted legal identity, governing authority, and limited liability by the law. Or consider the stock market, the ultimate embodiment of the capitalist ethos. It is likewise neither free nor natural, but rather elaborately governed. Stock markets require trading rules not only to prevent abuses, but also simply to operate. And they need more extensive rules, such as corporate disclosure requirements and insider trading restrictions, to flourish and to grow. The following chapters review these and other examples in greater detail, demonstrating how and why governments make markets work. But first, this chapter outlines the core thesis of the book.

The argument begins with the basic recognition that real-world markets are *institutions*: humanly devised constraints that shape human interaction.[2] There is no controversy on this point in its most stripped-down form. Yet scholars differ fundamentally in how they understand market institutions. Market liberals acknowledge that markets require some minimal rules of the game: the government must create the basic infrastructure for a modern economy by enforcing the rule of law, protecting private property, and maintaining a monetary system.[3] Beyond that, however, they argue that the government should not "intervene" in market affairs. Other scholars have increasingly stressed that market systems are governed by a far more extensive web of institutions. Institutional economists, for example, view "transaction costs," such as the costs of obtaining information or enforcing contracts, as the friction in the market system, and property rights as the means to reduce these costs. They move beyond the basic legal and financial infrastructure to study institutions such as business groups and labor contracts.[4] Economic sociologists define market institutions even more broadly, including social networks and cultural norms.[5] They stress that markets are always *embedded* in society.[6] In this book, I contend that a more expansive definition of market institutions is not simply more accurate, but that it is a prerequisite for informed policymaking and analysis of real-world markets.

---

[*] From *Marketcraft: How Governments Make Markets Work*, Steven K. Vogel, Copyright © Oxford University Press 2018. (pp. 1–14) Reproduced with permission of Oxford University Press through PLSclear.

I am certainly not the first one to pursue this line of argument. In fact, a "market-institutional" perspective on political economy has emerged as a virtual consensus among policymakers and across social science disciplines when applied to markets everywhere *except* in the advanced industrial countries.[7] Scholars have come to recognize that modern market systems are not natural phenomena that spontaneously arise, but rather complex institutions that must be created and sustained by the visible hand of the government. They make this same basic point with reference to three types of market transition: the historical transition from feudalism to market society in the West, the more recent transition from communism to capitalism in Eastern Europe and East Asia, and the ongoing struggle to create viable market systems in many developing countries.[8] Yet for the most part, scholars have failed to apply this same logic to the subtler transition toward more competitive and more sophisticated market systems in the advanced industrial countries. If markets are institutions, however, then market reform should be more a process of building institutions than one of removing constraints, and this should be no less true for more developed market systems than for less developed ones. Ironically, this point is less obvious for advanced industrial countries because they already have fairly well-developed market institutions. This book explores why viewing markets as institutions—complex combinations of laws, practices, and norms—is essential to understanding recent developments in advanced economies such as the United States and Japan.

Moreover, while some scholars stress that modern markets require effective governance, many policymakers, journalists, and pundits in the advanced economies continue to pretend that they do not. They speak and act as if there were such a thing as a "free market" that thrives without governance. They frame economic debates in terms of the false dichotomy of government versus market.[9] The very language of economic debates—such as the common juxtaposition of "government intervention" versus "market freedom"—betrays these assumptions, and this conceptual confusion can beget some rather serious policy errors, as demonstrated in the chapters to follow.

In this book I seek to advance the conversation in three ways. First, I specify how conventional framing, such as the governments-versus-markets dichotomy, hampers public debate, policy prescription, and scholarly analysis, and I offer some modest suggestions for how to deploy more precise language, enhance conceptual clarity, and refine analysis. Second, I push the logic of the argument further to show how the rather banal assertion that markets are institutions leads logically to some far less obvious propositions, as outlined in the following section. Finally, in the concluding chapter I demonstrate how even the most sophisticated analysts of market institutions sometimes fail to appreciate the full ramifications of their own arguments. They fall into the same linguistic traps as their intellectual adversaries, for example, or they fail to capture the extent to which market behavior is learned, not natural, and market operations are constructed, not free. And I conclude by demonstrating how conceptual misunderstandings can beget policy errors, and by specifying some lessons for both progressives and market liberals.

This chapter presents the logical sequence of the argument, and the following three chapters explore real-world examples. The final chapter reviews the implications for various debates in the fields of rhetoric, economics, political science, sociology, political theory, and public policy.

The Core Propositions

1. There is no such thing as a free or perfect market.

Conceptually, we can imagine the proverbial perfectly competitive market in which buyers and sellers would be seamlessly matched. Economists sometimes assume a perfect market for analytical purposes, and they have made important theoretical and empirical advances by building on such simplifying assumptions. But this perfect market does not exist, and it never has. Even primitive marketplaces were not "free" in that they required some basic rules, such as locations or hours of operation. And the institutions underpinning exchange grew more complex as societies introduced credit and money.[10] Douglass North illustrates this poignantly with his example of buying oranges from his favorite vendor. This simple exchange is governed by a personal relationship, market practices, and social norms, all underpinned by the rule of law.[11]

2. Markets have to be created.

If markets are institutions, then that means that people have to create them. As Karl Polanyi famously quipped, "laissez-faire was planned."[12] The architects of these institutions might be governments, firms, or individuals. And they might create markets deliberately or spontaneously, at one moment in time or over decades or centuries. I am partial to the language of *crafting* markets, as evidenced in the title to this volume, because it highlights the artistry required for effective market governance; it recognizes this as a core government function comparable to statecraft; and it applies to both government and private-sector market governance. But this does not mean that governments always get it right: just as real-world statecraft can be masterful or clumsy, beneficent or disastrous—so it is with marketcraft.

3. Market reform is primarily a constructive enterprise, not a destructive one.

Here we begin to shift from rather banal observations to less obvious implications. Yet this proposition follows logically from the ones preceding it. If markets are institutions, then cultivating markets requires building institutions more than destroying them. In short, liberalizing the economy does not mean liberating it. This simple observation has profound implications for how we understand market reform, and fundamentally challenges some of the most common perspectives on the important issues of our day.[13] It demonstrates how a market-institutional perspective begets both scholarly analysis and policy prescriptions that diverge markedly from the market liberal view. Table 1.1 depicts contrasting analytical perspectives in italics, such as "privatization" versus market transition, and corresponding policy prescriptions below them, such as shock therapy versus gradualism. Market liberals have conceived of market reform as "liberalization" rather than institution building, and therefore they have advocated removing barriers ("privatization" and "liberalization") more than building capabilities (market transition and market development). Yet, as noted earlier, scholars have come to recognize that shifting from

TABLE 1.1 Market Reform: Removing Barriers or Building Institutions?

	The Market-Liberal View: Removing Barriers	The Market-Institutionalist View: Building Institutions
Post-Communist Countries	• *Privatization* • Shock Therapy	• *Market Transition* • Gradualism
Developing Countries	• *Liberalization* • The Washington Consensus	• *Market Development* • Building Market Institutions
Advanced Industrial Countries	• *Deregulation* • Neoliberal Reform	• *Market Reform* • Marketcraft

a planned economy to a market system requires building new institutions more than dismantling old ones, and promoting markets in developing countries requires cultivating the government's ability to sustain market institutions more than just getting overbearing governments out of the way. They have been slower to grasp the implications for the study of market reform in rich countries. Yet even for developed economies, making markets more competitive and expanding them into new realms requires not simply removing regulations that impede competition ("deregulation") but enhancing regulatory capacity and building market institutions, that is, *marketcraft*.

4. There is no single market solution to a policy challenge.

If there is no such thing as a perfect market, then there is no single free-market solution. Any market solution constitutes a particular form of market governance. Real-world market governance varies across many dimensions: not just government versus market, but also public versus private governance, laissez-faire versus pro-competitive regulation, and so on. So this means that there are multiple market solutions to any given challenge, reflecting different combinations of points along these various dimensions.

Some market liberals might accept this proposition, yet insist that the crux of the issue still pits government intervention against market freedom. That is, the question is not whether markets have rules or not, but who sets them—the government or the market players. And the government imposes rules by force, whereas market players devise their rules voluntarily. Yet I would counter that in practice the government must play the leading role in market design, for reasons discussed further in the following section. Moreover, the market liberal perspective underestimates the scale and scope of regulation necessary to make modern markets work and overestimates the level of constraint imposed by government action and the degree of freedom allowed by the market. Reducing the government role would not necessarily unleash markets: in fact, it could just as well constrain market actors more, not less. For example, the government might compromise market freedom by failing to rein in private market power, or by withdrawing regulations that support markets. Chapter 5 returns to this issue of the relationship between government action and market freedom at greater length.

5. There may not even be a more "free-market" or a more market-oriented alternative among policy options.

Even if there is no pure free market, market liberals might argue, we should still posit it as an ideal, a target for policy reform. That is, we should seek to move *toward* the free market, for this would enhance both economic efficiency and personal liberty. Yet most policy choices are not about government versus market, but rather about *how* to govern markets. And if we compare two market designs, it is often not obvious which is more market-like or closer to a free-market solution.

In some cases, it may be possible to judge one option as more market-oriented than another. For example, imposing a tariff implies more government control and less market competition, so removing it could reasonably be viewed as a move toward a hypothetical free market. We should not be surprised that the market liberal worldview fits international trade better than most domestic market governance issues, for it is precisely the issue that motivated Smith and subsequent liberal economists. In most contemporary debates, however, the relevant choices align along dimensions that defy characterization as more or less market oriented. For example, there are complex trade-offs between adversarial versus discretionary styles of government regulation, or open versus closed bidding models for auctions. More fundamentally, it is often not obvious what would constitute a move toward the market. If we shift antitrust policy from a more laissez-faire approach to a more pro-competitive approach, then which is the more market-oriented solution? If we tighten rules over the fair use of copyrighted material, is that a move toward the free market or away from it? The effort to describe these choices in terms of government versus the free market obscures the real choices involved. They involve real trade-offs, but not ones of government versus market. And many contemporary debates take precisely this form, as illustrated in Chapter 2.

6. The government-versus-market dichotomy that animates most debates about economic policy is fundamentally misleading.

The assumption that there is a dichotomy between government and market impedes a more sophisticated understanding of this relationship. As we move from a thin definition of market institutions (the minimal rules of the game) to a thicker one (a broader range of laws, practices, and norms), the relationship between government and market becomes more complementary. Table 1.2 illustrates how the government-versus-market frame leads us to view economic debates in terms of a choice between government protection/regulation and free markets, rather than as a choice between underdeveloped and more developed markets. In practice, government regulation defines and enables markets, so market reform often entails more government (the arrow moving from less developed to more developed markets), not less (the arrow moving from protection/regulation to "free markets"). Moreover, the government-versus-market framing obscures the fact that the government plays a substantial role in the marketplace beyond that of a referee. The government is the largest consumer, employer, lender, borrower, insurer, and property owner in modern market economies.[14]

TABLE 1.2 Two Conceptions of Market Reform

	Less Market	*More Market*
More Government	Protected/Regulated Markets	More Developed Markets
Less Government	Less Developed Markets	"Free Markets"

7. The regulation-versus-competition dichotomy that animates most debates about economic regulation is fundamentally misleading.

The very language of "deregulation" belies this misperception. In conventional discourse, the term refers to less regulation and more competition, as if the two were naturally associated. In fact, generating more competition usually requires more regulation, not less. Thus the dominant trend in advanced industrial countries over the past 40 years has not been one of deregulation (less regulation), but rather one of market reform (more competition) through re-regulation (more regulation): that is, freer markets and more rules.[15]

Deregulation in the literal sense of less regulation and more competition is possible, of course: reducing or eliminating price and entry regulation, for example, should foster more competition. In practice, however, the relationship between regulation and competition tends to be more positive than negative (Figure 1.1). We can refine this point by noting that the relationship between regulation and competition varies across time and across sectors and subsectors. It may be more positive at an early stage of market development, when the government has to create the basic infrastructure to support market competition, and more negative at a later stage, when an incremental increase in the government's role may be more likely to impede than to enhance competition. And it may be more positive in sectors that are conducive to monopoly, such as network industries, and more negative in sectors where barriers to entry are low, such as retail.

Several distinct mechanisms underlie the overall trend toward more regulation with more competition. First, as governments introduce competition in sectors characterized by natural monopoly, such as public utility sectors, they have to deploy pro-competitive regulation to create and sustain competition. Second, as financial markets become more competitive and more sophisticated, governments have to enhance regulation to support these markets, with stricter disclosure requirements, more elaborate trading rules, and more intensive supervision. Third, as product and service markets become more competitive, with a greater number of players, then regulation tends to become more codified and legalistic. Fourth, as transport and product markets become more competitive, governments need to strengthen environmental, health, and safety regulations. If truckers compete more fiercely, for example, governments have to strengthen safety regulation, such as limits on driving hours. In practice, market reform means increasing regulations that enhance competition, such as antitrust rules, and removing regulations that impede it, such as price and entry restrictions. And understanding this process requires carefully differentiating between

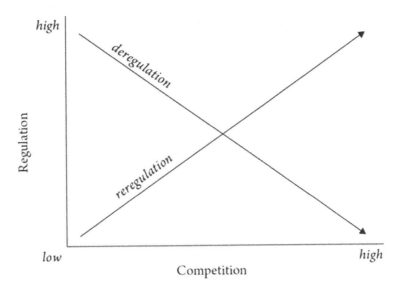

FIGURE 1.1 Deregulation versus reregulation.

the two. Despite the overall trend toward greater regulatory complexity, it may be possible to devise simpler regulatory solutions that are equally or more effective in some
cases. In finance, for example, higher capital reserve requirements, the structural separation of commercial and investment banks, and a financial transaction tax represent
simpler regulatory mechanisms that might reduce the need for some detailed behavioral rules and intensive supervision.

*8. A liberal market economy (LME) like the United States is just as governed as a
coordinated market economy (CME) like Japan, possibly more.*

LMEs feature more competitive labor, financial, and product markets, whereas CMEs
favor greater coordination among firms, banks, and other firms. Scholars of comparative capitalism tend to view LMEs as less institutionalized or less embedded than
CMEs.[16] But if markets are institutions, then all markets are governed by distinct combinations of laws, practices, and norms, so LMEs and CMEs are equally governed.
Chapter 3 examines this proposition via a detailed case study of the United States,
demonstrating how this "freest" of market economies relies on a massive infrastructure of market governance.

  One could even argue that a more liberal market system would actually require a
more elaborate institutional apparatus. Chapters 3 and 5 return to this proposition
in greater detail, but one possible synthesis would hinge on differentiating between
two different meanings of "more governed." LMEs may require more governance
in the limited sense of more laws and regulations to support markets. But with respect
to the private side of governance, such as business practices or social norms, it may
make more sense simply to conclude that all markets are governed, and to leave it
at that.

9. A coordinated market economy like Japan requires more governance,
not less, to shift toward the liberal market model.

This proposition follows logically from propositions 3 and 8. Chapter 4 examines this proposition at length, demonstrating that Japanese leaders publicly vowed to shift in the direction of a more liberal market system beginning in the 1990s, but to do so they had to enact a daunting array of legal and regulatory reforms and to launch campaigns to alter business practices and embrace market values. And despite all of this effort, Japan still did not converge on the liberal market model.

10. The information revolution requires more market governance, not less.

Advances in information technology (IT) have dramatically reduced the cost and increased the speed of many market transactions. Yet technology has also created new challenges of market design that defy the government-versus-market dichotomy. The information economy requires more governance because the core commodity—information—is itself the product of rules, such as patent and copyright protection. So governance becomes more essential to economic performance, and also more complex. IT markets also rely heavily on sectors where regulation is essential, such as telecommunications and finance. The information revolution enables the fabrication of sophisticated markets, such as complex auctions or financial derivatives markets, which in turn rely on more intricate market governance. And the information economy poses new challenges for antitrust enforcement, discussed further in Chapters 2 and 3.

Some of these propositions (1–7) follow logically, whereas others (8–10) will require more empirical evidence for support. The next three chapters review the evidence, but first let us address the critical question of whether governments must govern markets, and define a few key terms.

Market Governance

We have established that markets require governance, but does that mean that governments have to do the governing? Governments have been the central actors in the three transformations noted in the preceding sections: the historical evolution of the market system in the West, the transition from command to market economies in Eastern Europe and East Asia, and the construction of market institutions in developing countries today. Governments play the central role in market governance because they have the unique ability to create and enforce laws and regulations over a given territory.[17] Ronald Coase argues, in his seminal article on "The Problem of Social Cost," that private actors could resolve problems of market governance on their own via private settlements *if* there were no transaction costs.[18] This essay motivated some market liberals to deploy the "Coase theorem" to argue that private contracts could replace government regulation in various arenas.[19] In practical terms, however, governments have to establish the property rights system that undergirds private settlements. Governments also have greater administrative and financial capabilities than private-sector actors, and they tend to be more neutral, legitimate, and accountable. David Moss argues that governments have several critical attributes when it comes to risk-management: for example, the ability to compel participation; a near-perfect credit rating, based on the power to tax and print money; and unparalleled monitoring capabilities, rooted in regulatory and enforcement powers.[20]

Yet governments certainly do not govern markets alone. They sometimes delegate regulation to private-sector "self-regulatory organizations" and standard-setting bodies. A wide range of private-sector organizations contribute to market governance, from industry associations to trade unions. The relationships among private-sector actors—such as management-labor relations, bank-industry relations, supply chains, and distribution networks—also structure markets. Private-sector practices govern markets, from vocational training systems to research and development consortia. And of course societal norms powerfully condition market behavior.

In order to study market governance, therefore, we have to examine both government and private-sector governance, and the interaction between the two. Thus I favor the term *governance* rather than *regulation* because the latter tends to refer more exclusively to government regulation. I define *governance* as follows, following Mark Bevir:

> Governance refers to all processes of governing, whether undertaken by a government, market, or network; whether over a family, tribe, corporation, or territory; and whether by laws, norms, power, or language. Governance is a broader term than government because it focuses not only on the state and its institutions but also on the creation of rule and order in social practices.[21]

Bringing private governance into the analysis is critical for making sense of several of the key propositions in the preceding section. For example, there is no free market (Proposition 1) and the government-versus-markets dichotomy is misleading (Proposition 6) in part because even if we were able to eliminate the laws and regulations that govern markets, this would still leave the private governance of markets in place. And the regulation-versus-competition dichotomy is misleading (Proposition 7) because even if we were able to eliminate anti-competitive laws and regulations, this would leave private anti-competitive practices intact.

Market liberals would contend that government regulation is nonetheless more problematic than private governance not only because it is more threatening to personal liberty (as noted earlier), but also because it is more vulnerable to capture by special interests seeking to game the system for their own benefit. These interests may seek to influence regulation to earn "rents," in the terminology of political economy, meaning unearned income or returns above market value. But if markets are always governed, and market governance includes both government regulation and private-sector practices, then it follows that private firms can seek rents whether or not the government acts. Private firms may seek monopoly profits by anti-competitive behavior in the marketplace as well as by lobbying the government to favor them.[22] In fact, they may be freer to seek rents in the absence of government regulation. To be clear, I am not arguing that government regulation is not vulnerable to capture. Chapters 2–4 will provide many examples of regulatory capture. But I contend that capture is a variable and not a constant; that public sector governance is no more conducive to rent-seeking than private governance; that government failure to act can foster rent-seeking just as much as government action; and that effective government regulation can limit it.

Let me now turn to defining market and market development, before presenting a simple typology of market governance. The *market* can refer to an abstraction, the proverbial perfect market, or to a concrete real-world market: a place of exchange such as a farmers' market, or a product market such as the automobile market. A perfect market would have many buyers and sellers, comparable products, complete information, no enforcement costs, and supply and demand would determine prices. This volume focuses on real-world markets, not perfect markets, so it defines *markets* simply as arenas in which buyers and sellers come together to exchange goods and/ or services.[23]

To move beyond the perfect market ideal to study real-world market institutions, we need to conceive of *market development* in a way that does not rely exclusively on that ideal. Of course the perfectly competitive market provides a valuable metric: more buyers and sellers, better information, and better enforcement of contracts represent elements of market development. The most critical piece is competition, which can be defined by the number of firms in a given product market and the market shares of those firms (market structure), the ability of new entrants to challenge incumbents (contestability), and the ability of challengers to redefine the market. But market development also includes the expansion of the scale of the market (whether measured by trading volume or geographical territory), the expansion of the scope of the market (to more products and services), the creation of new markets (including new marketplaces, such as stock exchanges, as well as the "fabricated" markets discussed in the following chapter), and the increase in the sophistication of markets (including greater speed and accuracy in the transmission and storage of data, more developed financial markets, and more elaborate market design).[24] Chapter 2 explores the myriad ways in which market governance can foster or impede market development broadly defined in this way. It identifies institutional prerequisites for certain types of market development, but it also stresses the diversity of governance arrangements. I do not assume that market development necessarily promotes societal welfare. I set aside for the conclusion a fuller discussion of the normative question of the ultimate goals that markets serve, such as growth, innovation, equity, health, safety, and environmental protection. For present purposes, however, I can simply note that I view markets as means, not ends. We can craft them to achieve whatever purposes we want—and we should.

We can usefully divide market governance into three broad clusters: laws and regulations, practices and standards, and norms and beliefs. Table 1.3 divides these clusters into subcategories with selected examples. *Laws* refer to any legislation passed by the government, from corporate law to labor law. *Regulations* include more detailed rules derived from laws; directives issued by government agencies, courts, or self-regulatory organizations; and enforcement by these agencies, courts, and organizations. *Practices* comprise a wide range of private-sector behavior, including monitoring, such as credit agencies or professional guilds; market design, such as the creation of the mortgage-backed security market; collusion, such as cartels; coordination, such as industry associations or research and development (R&D) consortia; interfirm networks, such as bank groups or supply chains; and business customs, such

TABLE 1.3 Market Governance by Category (With Selected Examples)

Laws and Regulations	Practices and Standards	Norms and Beliefs
• Laws enacted by national or state legislatures • Regulations issued by government agencies, courts, or private-sector organizations • Enforcement of regulations by government agencies, courts, or private-sector organizations • Litigation, such as shareholder or private antitrust suits	• Private-sector monitoring, such as credit agencies or professional guilds • Private-sector market design, such as the mortgage-backed security market • Business collusion, such as cartels • Business coordination, such as industry associations or R&D consortia • Interfirm networks, such as bank groups or supply chains • Business customs, such as recruiting practices • Conventions, such as technical or accounting standards • Codes of conduct, such as corporate governance codes	• Social norms, such as company loyalty • Moral codes, such as minimizing harm or maximizing personal liberty • Legal doctrines, such as the rule of reason for antitrust cases • Ideologies, such as market liberalism or Marxism • Regulatory doctrines, such as fair-value accounting • Policy paradigms, such as the Chicago School of antitrust • Theories, such as the efficient markets hypothesis

as employment or corporate governance systems. *Standards* refer to conventions, such as technical or accounting standards, and codes of conduct, such as corporate governance codes. Laws and regulations differ from practices and standards in that they are binding and enforceable. Laws and regulations also tend to be public and formal, while practices and standards are private and informal—but there are exceptions and hybrid cases that preclude a clear demarcation. For example, private self-regulatory bodies sometimes issue binding and enforceable rules, and public agencies sometimes issue non-binding guidance. *Norms* encompass values, such as company loyalty or shareholder value, and moral codes, such as minimizing harm or maximizing personal liberty. *Beliefs* subsume broad political ideologies, such as market liberalism; legal doctrines, such as the rule of reason; regulatory doctrines, such as fair-value accounting; policy paradigms, such as the Chicago School of antitrust; and theories, such as the efficient markets thesis.

We can also break down market governance by substantive issue area. The examples in Table 1.4 are merely illustrative; they do not represent a comprehensive list, nor do they depict a particular national model. Many analysts of political economy focus on particular types of regulations that constrain markets, such as tariffs and quotas or price and entry controls. This volume shifts attention to the broader range of governance mechanisms that create, define, and empower markets. It focuses primarily on market governance (financial, labor, and industry regulation) and not social regulation (such as health, safety, and environmental regulation) because it seeks to explore the degree to which markets require governance to function and/or to flourish in the first place—not why they require regulation to limit harm to people and to nature. It is far more obvious that markets require regulation to limit collateral damage (social regulation) than that markets require regulation for their own sake to function

TABLE 1.4 Market Governance by Substantive Issue-Area (Selected Examples)

	Laws and Regulations	Practices and Standards	Norms and Beliefs
Corporate Governance	Limited liability	Committee-system corporate boards	Companies should maximize returns to their shareholders.
Accounting	Corporate financial disclosure rules	Accounting standards	Companies should disclose information to investors thoroughly and honestly.
Banking	Capital reserve requirements	Private lending pools	Banks should base lending on the borrower's ability to pay.
Capital Markets	Insider-trading regulation	Stock exchange trading practices	Brokers should act in the best interests of their clients.
Labor Markets	Dismissal rules	Private mediation	Employers should hire on the basis of merit, not relationships.
Antitrust	Merger rules	Price competition strategies	Firms should not be allowed to dominate an industry.
Sector-Specific Regulation	Price and entry regulation	Electricity trading practices	Firms should compete, not collude.
Intellectual Property Rights	Fair-use rules	Cross-licensing	Firms should only receive patents for substantial innovations.

and to flourish (market governance). Market governance and social regulation are interrelated, of course, and the concluding chapter explores this relationship further. For present purposes, however, this remains a useful analytical distinction that allows us to focus on market governance per se.

Notes

1 This chapter builds on Vogel 2007 and Barma and Vogel 2008.
2 North 1990, 3.
3 I use the term "market liberals" to refer to those who advocate free markets with limited government, including classical liberals such as Adam Smith and more recent theorists such as Ludwig von Mises, Friedrich Hayek, and Milton Friedman (Smith 1976; Von Mises 2011; Hayek 1944; Friedman 1962; Friedman and Friedman 1980). I call them "market liberals" to distinguish them from "liberals" as the term is used in US politics, meaning progressives who support active government, including social welfare programs.
4 North 1986; Williamson 2000. Anthologies include Williamson and Master, eds. 1995; Menard 2004; Menard and Shirley, eds. 2005.
5 Granovetter 1985; Fligstein 2001. Anthologies include Biggart, ed. 2002; Dobbin, ed. 2004; Smelser and Swedberg, eds. 2005; and Nee and Swedberg, eds. 2005.

6 I employ this term broadly to mean that markets are inherently part of society and there-fore inseparable from it, following Polanyi 1944, not more narrowly to mean that markets are submerged in interpersonal networks, following Granovetter 1985. See Krippner 2001 for a critique of Granovetter's use of the term.

7 Barma and Vogel 2008, 1–9, define the "market-institutional" perspective as one in which markets are viewed as institutions situated in a particular social and political context. This broad camp includes most of institutional economics, economic sociology, comparative political economy, and economic history, plus much of the work in law and economics, law and society, business administration, economic geography, economic anthropology, and more.

8 See, for example, Polanyi 1944 and North 1981 on the historical evolution of markets; Cohen, Schwartz, and Zysman, eds. 1998 and Stiglitz 2002, 133–165, on post-communist transition, and Chaudhry 1993, World Bank 2002, and Rodrik 2007, especially 16–21, on development.

9 The free-market presumption and the government-versus-market dichotomy are ubiqui-tous in popular discourse, but Greenspan (2007, 15–16) and Forbes (2012, xi) offer typical examples from two influential opinion leaders. Wolf (1988, 1) depicts government versus market as "the cardinal economic choice." Yergin and Stanislaw (1998) and Tanzi (2011) juxtapose governments versus markets in the very titles of their books.

10 See Graeber 2011 on the history of credit.

11 North 1981, 34–37.

12 Polanyi 1944, 141.

13 See Barma and Vogel 2008 on the debates over shock therapy (10–11, 355–423), the Washington consensus (11–13, 425–427), and deregulation (9–10, 329–354).

14 Lindblom 1977, 107–114.

15 Vogel 1996.

16 Crouch and Streeck 1997; Hall and Soskice, eds. 2001.

17 Hodgson 2015, 76–79.

18 Coase 1960.

19 Coase himself did not go this far (McCloskey 1998; Cassidy 2013).

20 Moss 2002, 49–52, 436 (fn 42).

21 Bevir 2013.

22 Fligstein (2001) stresses this dual strategy whereby firms strive to exert control both within the private marketplace and by lobbying government.

23 See Hodgson 2015, 138–139, for a definition that is more thorough but less succinct.

24 Roth (2015, 8–12) describes well-designed markets as thick (many participants), uncongested (not requiring too much time to consummate deals), safe (reliable), and simple.

References

Barma, Naazneen H., and Steven K. Vogel. 2008. "Introduction." In *The Political Economy Reader: Markets as Institutions*, edited by N. Barma and S. Vogel, 1–18. New York: Routledge.

Bevir, Mark. 2013. *A Theory of Governance*. Berkeley and Los Angeles: University of California Press.

Biggart, Nicole W., ed. 2002. *Readings in Economic Sociology*. Oxford: Blackwell.

Cassidy, John. 2013. "Ronald Coase and the Misuse of Economics." *The New Yorker*, September 3, https://www.newyorker.com/news/john-cassidy/ronald-coase-and-the-misuse-of-economics.

Chaudhry, Kiren. 1993. "The Myths of the Market and the Common History of Late Developers." *Politics and Society* 21: 245–274.

Coase, Ronald. 1960. "The Problem of Social Cost." *Journal of Law and Economics* 3: 1–44.

Cohen, Stephen, Andrew Schwartz, and John Zysman, eds. 1998. *The Tunnel at the End of the Light: Privatization, Business Networks, and Economic Transformation in Russia.* Copenhagen: Copenhagen Business School Press.

Crouch, Colin, and Wolfgang Streeck. 1997. "Introduction: The Future of Capitalist Diversity." In *Political Economy of Modern Capitalism*, edited by C. Crouch and W. Streeck, 1–18. London: Sage Publications.

Dobbin, Frank, ed. 2004. *The New Economic Sociology: A Reader.* Princeton, NJ: Princeton University Press.

Fligstein, Neil. 2001. *The Architecture of Markets: An Economic Sociology of Twenty-First Century Capitalist Societies.* Princeton, NJ: Princeton University Press.

Forbes, Steve. 2012. "Foreword." In *Wealth and Poverty: A New Edition for the Twenty-First Century*, by George Gilder, ix–xii. Washington, DC: Regnery Publishing.

Friedman, Milton. 1962. *Capitalism and Freedom.* Chicago: University of Chicago Press.

Friedman, Milton, and Rose Friedman. 1980. *Free to Choose: A Personal Statement.* San Diego: Harcourt.

Graeber, David. 2011. *Debt: The First 5,000 Years.* Brooklyn, NY: Melville House.

Greenspan, Alan. 2007. *The Age of Turbulence: Adventures in a New World.* New York: Penguin Press.

Granovetter, Mark. 1985. "Economic Action and Social Structure: The Problem of Embeddedness." *American Journal of Sociology* 91: 481–510.

Hayek, Friedrich. 1944. *The Road to Serfdom.* Chicago: University of Chicago Press.

Hall, Peter, and David Soskice, eds. 2001. *Varieties of Capitalism: The Institutional Foundations of Comparative Advantage.* New York: Oxford University Press.

Hodgson, Geoffrey M. 2015. *Conceptualizing Capitalism: Institutions, Evolution, Future.* Chicago: University of Chicago Press.

Krippner, Greta R. 2001. "The Elusive Market: Embeddedness and the Paradigm of Economic Sociology." *Theory and Society* 30: 775–810.

Lindblom, Charles E. 1977. *Politics and Markets: The World's Political-Economic Systems.* New York: Basic Books.

Menard, Claude, ed. 2004. *The International Library of New Institutional Economics*, 7 volumes. Cheltenham, UK: Edward Elgar.

Menard, Claude, and Mary M. Shirley, eds. 2005. *Handbook of New Institutional Economics.* Dordrecht: Springer.

McCloskey, Deirdre. 1998. "Other Things Equal: The So-Called Coase Theorem." *Eastern Economic Journal* 24: 367–371.

Moss, David A. 2002. *When All Else Fails: Government as the Ultimate Risk Manager.* Cambridge, MA: Harvard University Press.

Nee, Victor, and Richard Swedberg, eds. 2005. *The Economic Sociology of Capitalism.* Princeton, NJ: Princeton University Press.

North, Douglass C. 1981. *Structure and Change in Economic History.* New York: W. W. Norton.

North, Douglass C. 1986. "The New Institutional Economics." *Journal of Institutional and Theoretical Economics* 142: 230–237.

North, Douglass C. 1990. *Institutions, Institutional Change and Economic Performance.* Cambridge: Cambridge University Press.

Polanyi, Karl. 1944. *The Great Transformation: The Political and Economic Origins of Our Time.* Boston: Beacon Press.

Rodrik, Dani. 2007. *One Economics, Many Recipes: Globalization, Institutions, and Economic Growth*. Princeton, NJ: Princeton University Press.

Roth, Alvin E. 2015. *Who Gets What—and Why*. Boston: Houghton Mifflin Harcourt.

Smelser, Neil J., and Richard Swedberg, eds. 2005. *The Handbook of Economic Sociology*, 2nd ed. Princeton, NJ: Princeton University Press.

Smith, Adam. 1976. *An Inquiry into the Nature and Causes of the Wealth of Nations*, edited by Edwin Cannan. Chicago: University of Chicago Press.

Stiglitz, Joseph E. 2002. *Globalization and Its Discontents*. New York: W. W. Norton.

Tanzi, Vito. 2011. *Government versus Markets: The Changing Economic Role of the State*. Cambridge: Cambridge University Press.

Vogel, Steven K. 1996. *Freer Markets, More Rules: Regulatory Reform in Advanced Industrial Countries*. Ithaca, NY: Cornell University Press.

Vogel, Steven K. 2007. "Why Freer Markets Need More Rules." In *Creating Competitive Markets: The Politics of Regulatory Reform*, edited by Mark K. Landy, Martin A. Levin, and Martin Shapiro, 25–42. Washington, DC: Brookings Institution Press.

Von Mises, Ludwig. 2011. *A Critique of Interventionism*. Auburn, AL: Ludwig von Mises Institute.

Williamson, Oliver E. 2000. "The New Institutional Economics: Taking Stock, Looking Ahead." *Journal of Economic Literature* 38: 595–613.

Williamson, Oliver E., and Scott E. Master, eds. 1995. *Transaction Cost Economics*, 2 volumes. Aldershot, UK: Edward Elgar.

Wolf, Charles. 1988. *Markets or Governments: Choosing between Imperfect Alternatives*. Cambridge, MA: MIT Press.

World Bank. 2002. *World Development Report 2002: Building Institutions for Markets*. Oxford: Oxford University Press.

Yergin, Daniel, and Joseph Stanislaw. 1998. *The Commanding Heights: The Battle between Government and the Marketplace That Is Remaking the Modern World*. New York: Simon & Schuster.

2

Market Transition

The transition from socialism to capitalism across Eastern Europe in the 1990s and in China from the late 1970s onward served as a live experiment for theories of markets and political economy to play out in practice and be tested against each other. Facing enormous stakes in terms of human welfare, policymakers grappled with how to create market systems. Market transition comprises three key sets of economic reforms: liberalization, or moving from command planning to competitive markets and the price mechanism; privatization, that is, transferring state ownership of assets to private ownership; and stabilization of macroeconomic phenomena, such as inflation and exchange rates.[1] In the 1990s, as large parts of the world jettisoned socialist planning and embraced the market, the debate over how quickly and in what sequence the transition was best approached came to be framed as a contest between shock therapy and gradualism. In reality, different countries pursued transition in various sequences and at different speeds, so assessing the merits of shock therapy versus gradualism is not as simple as it may appear. Transition experiences prompted scholars and practitioners to debate whether all components of marketizing reforms must proceed together and the extent to which economic, political, and social transformation are interlinked.

The shock therapy, or "big bang," approach dictates that reformers should take advantage of a window of opportunity for dramatic change and implement a comprehensive and far-reaching set of reforms in unison and as quickly as possible. This prescription rests on the market-liberal perspective that markets emerge spontaneously when allowed to do so and, in turn, bring economic activity to its most efficient equilibrium through the price signal. The rapid, comprehensive approach toward market transition proved successful in some Eastern European countries, most notably Poland, as the whole region moved toward capitalism and democracy in a compressed period of time. The shock therapy logic, as expressed by Jeffrey Sachs, an economist involved in advising governments through such transitions, is that transformation from a planned system to a market economy requires "a leap across the institutional chasm."[2] The prescription is a comprehensive reform package, where price controls are eliminated and market forces are introduced wholesale, and stabilization, liberalization, and privatization are pursued in conjunction. Shock therapy proponents often point to Poland, where liberalizing prices had almost immediate salutary effects, with markets, consumers, and entrepreneurs adjusting in a matter of weeks. While privatization efforts created a period of serious dislocation in the nation's state-owned enterprises and economic pain for many of their employees, Poland emerged with the most successful growth record of any Eastern European post-communist country in the immediate aftermath of market transition.

Gradualism, by contrast, emphasizes the importance of viewing markets as institutions and the necessity of building an institutional infrastructure to support markets and capitalism. Gradualists argue that market transition is not a leap across a chasm but instead a careful process of building a bridge across the chasm that can support both old and new sets of institutions. Gradualists also emphasize the extent to which market transactions are embedded in social relationships and pay careful attention to the relationship between political and economic liberalization. China's reform experience and blistering economic success over the past four decades are viewed as vindication of the gradualist approach. From this perspective, what sequence reforms should be pursued in and whether some elements should be undertaken in tandem are matters to be determined by context and negotiated on an ongoing basis, not dictated by first principles. Deng Xiaoping, the original architect of China's economic reforms, summed up the slow and experimental nature of the Chinese transition to the market in his famous phrase "crossing the river by feeling the stones."

In this section, **Anders Åslund** represents the market-liberal approach to market transition. He argues that comprehensive liberalization, privatization, and stabilization reforms pursued together rapidly achieved the best political–economic results in Central and Eastern Europe. As he outlines, this approach was followed by a key group of radical reformers in the former Soviet bloc, including Poland's Leszek Balcerowicz and Russia's Yegor Gaidar, and championed by the traditional proponents of the "Washington Consensus" on liberal market reforms, including the International Monetary Fund, the World Bank, and the central banks and finance ministries of powerful Western countries, all dominated by neoclassical economists. Radical simplicity characterized the shock therapy economic reform program, as encapsulated in the Polish reforms outlined by Åslund. The state was to be extricated from the market – ending central planning, price-setting, state-ownership, and regulation geared toward social engineering – and refocused on performing its prescribed roles of safeguarding public security, enforcing the rule of law, and providing limited social support to buffer the effects of the transition. Like the market liberals featured through this volume, Eastern European reformers feared state failure more than they did market failure. In their view, earlier attempts to introduce market elements into their economies had failed because they did not go far enough. Shock therapy proponents believed that radical change was necessary to transform the expectations and behavior of economic actors, from individuals and households to bureaucrats and state-owned enterprise managers.

Åslund also makes a forceful case that partial reforms empower entrenched interests at the expense of the collective good. In places where reforms were pursued gradually and piecemeal, he argues, rent-seeking elites were able to extract a great deal of wealth from society by arbitraging the market distortions introduced by slow reform – and these rent-seekers proved to be a lasting hindrance to successful reforms overall. In Åslund's telling, the proponents of gradualism were blind to the corruption and rent-seeking of socialist state actors, which led them to believe erroneously that market failures would be more harmful than state failures and to retain a misplaced faith in state intervention in the economy. He acknowledges that more gradual reforms yielded strong results in China but argues that the preconditions for such experimentalism to succeed – including the political context as well as the power of the party apparatus – were drastically different there compared to Eastern Europe and Russia. Critics of shock therapy, such as Nobel Laureate and former World Bank Chief Economist Joseph Stiglitz, pointed to the pain and dislocation of the rapid economic transformation wrought by "market fundamentalism."[3] Åslund's rejoinder to them is that Russia's 1998 financial crash was a necessary catharsis for Russia to achieve an efficient and productive market economy. Further embracing the market-liberal logic of creative destruction, he argues that the necessary and limited institutions to support markets would arise spontaneously once they were unfettered, thus countering the market-institutionalist prescription of conscious institution-building to manage socioeconomic transition.

In contrast to shock therapy reforms across Eastern Europe, China adopted from 1978 onward a deliberately gradual and experimental set of reforms to make the transition from plan to market. The Chinese Communist Party (CCP) took a distinctive approach to price liberalization by implementing the dual-track price system, with state-set planned prices for a certain quota of production and market prices for the surplus. This had the effect of encouraging households and firms to make economic decisions based on market price signals, achieving the allocative efficiency of the market while maintaining socioeconomic stability and enabling people to adapt to market forces by keeping the plan in place. Scholars dubbed this deliberately transitional approach "reform without losers,"[4] highlighting the fact that gradualism avoided the wrenching socioeconomic dislocation that accompanied big bang reforms in many other instances of transition. In terms of privatization, the CCP adopted the distinct type of community property ownership known as township and village enterprises (TVEs). This hybrid ownership model, neither private nor state-owned, mimicked the function served by private property in a market economy, in a form tailored to the social context. China's gradualist reform experience highlights the social and political embeddedness of markets and manifests Karl Polanyi's observation that one of the crucial roles of the state in relation to markets is to slow down the rate of change to allow society to adjust.

Yuen Yuen Ang's market-institutionalist analysis of China's transition from socialism to capitalism emphasizes the co-evolution and interactive adaptation of states and markets along the country's gradualist pathway. She articulates how the CCP built markets with weak institutions in the first stage of reform from 1978 to 1989 and then preserved markets by crafting strong institutions in the second stage of reform from 1993 onward. Ang's analysis echoes Dani Rodrik's observation that while growth can be ignited in many ways that don't require specific institutional strengths, sustaining growth requires more deliberate attention to building the institutional infrastructure necessary to support markets.

Ang argues that the fact that reforms were gradual and incremental in China does not mean they were modest in scope; they were actually ambitious and wide-ranging. A crucial dimension of Chinese reform success came from leaders recognizing that they had to create the conditions for successful adaptation by enacting complementary sets of market reforms in multiple realms of the economy and then broader institutional measures to support continued market-based success. For Ang, other explanations that highlight neoclassical growth theory, the role of bureaucratic incentives, the incrementalism of reforms, or historical legacies, are only parts of a puzzle and cannot alone explain the broad and bold nature of China's reforms. Ang's narrative of the complex adaptive co-evolution of states and markets in the Chinese reform experience makes the case for a "heterodox" political economy. She emphasizes the value of institutional innovation geared toward pragmatic function rather than orthodox market form and tailored to Chinese reality and context rather than committed to a priori economic principles. This approach, emphasizing pragmatism and context over ideology, is encapsulated in another of Deng Xiaoping's aphorisms about the Chinese reforms he led: "It doesn't matter if a cat is black or white, as long as it catches mice."

Notes

1 The same three imperatives constituted the core of the neoliberal structural adjustment reforms embodied in the Washington Consensus and pursued by the International Monetary Fund and the World Bank in the developing world in the 1980s. See Naazneen Barma, this volume.

2 Jeffrey Sachs, *The End of Poverty: Economic Possibilities for Our Time* (New York: Penguin, 2005), 114.

3 Joseph Stiglitz, *Globalization and Its Discontents* (New York: W. W. Norton, 2002).

4 Laurence J. Lau, Yingyi Qian, and Gerard Roland, "Reform Without Losers: An Interpretation of China's Dual-Track Approach to Transition," *Journal of Political Economy* 108 (2000): 120–43.

Anders Åslund,
How Capitalism Was Built (2013)*

2. Radical Reform versus Gradualism

The end of communism in Europe was the event of a lifetime. Suddenly twenty-eight countries with 400 million people had to choose their political and economic systems anew. Where should they begin? What was most important? What was possible? What theory should be applied? What policy corresponded to their interests? A frequent comment was that no book prescribed how to transition from socialism to capitalism, whereas hundreds elaborated on the opposite, no longer desired direction. A popular joke compared the transition from communism to capitalism to making an aquarium out of a fish soup.

The discussion became heated from the outset because so much was at stake. The fate of a large part of the world was up in the air. Could and should the former Soviet bloc be embraced by the Western world, or should it be shunned? How much economic and social hardship would people in those countries have to suffer? Which ideology would win? Could armed conflicts be avoided?

Intellectuals of all disciplines and convictions, governments, and international organizations geared up to answer the many questions. Although no clear goal was defined, a strong sense of direction prevailed. The popular battle cry was, "We want a 'normal' society!" By "normal," people in the Soviet bloc meant an ordinary Western society – a democracy with a market economy, predominant private property, and the rule of law. Because all these countries had far to go, the final destination did not appear very relevant at the outset of the march, and any specification of the goal could be politically divisive. In the havoc of a collapsing socialist system, Eastern and Central Europeans cared little whether their society would be a Western European social welfare state or a freer American market economy, both being evidently superior to their socialist ruins. These distinctions were left for later.

For Central Europe, Southeastern Europe, and the Baltics, the urge for a normal society was complemented by another battle cry for a "return to Europe," meaning their integration in West European economic and political organizations, notably membership in the European Union (EU) and the North Atlantic Treaty Organization (NATO).

This was a time of liberal triumph. In many ways, the Central European revolutions of 1989 most resembled the European revolutions of 1848 (Ash 1990; Dahrendorf 1990) because late communist society was reminiscent of feudal society, with its hierarchic rule and delegation of partial property rights to vassals, with detailed

---

* From: *How Capitalism Was Built: The Transformation of Central and Eastern Europe, Russia, the Caucasus, and Central Asia, 2nd edition*, Anders Åslund, Copyright © Anders Åslund 2007, 2013. (pp. 36–51, 60–64) Reproduced with permission of Cambridge University Press through PLSclear.

regulation but no rule of law. The instincts were the same. Many saw the state as evil in the tradition of the great liberal thinkers of the mid-nineteenth century, such as John Stuart Mill (1859/1975). The natural response was a demand for the same kind of far-reaching liberalization that occurred in the 1840s with focus on the creation of checks and balances to state power.

Many socialist ideas just died, whereas others reemerged later. "Market socialism," workers' self-management, or a "third way" between capitalism and Soviet-style socialism was no longer discussed. The central issues instead were the speed and strategy of transition to a market economy. How fast and in what order? The dominant intellectual debate over postcommunist transition was between radical and gradual reformers, whereas the outright enemies of market reform kept quiet. The issue was whether the possible reforms – liberalization, macroeconomic stabilization, and privatization – should be undertaken as fast as possible or deliberately more slowly. All purported reformers proclaimed the same objective: to establish a market economy leading to higher economic efficiency, economic growth, and an improved average standard of living. There were other agendas as well, but they were concealed.

At the outset of transition, a broad group of economists and policy makers called for an early, comprehensive, and radical economic reform, which is outlined in the first section of this chapter. The gradual reform proposals of the early transition were much more diverse. They are presented in the long second section. The third section leaps out from the intellectual debate to the conditions that had been created during the Gorbachev reforms for rent seeking and how rent seeking was carried out in the early transition. Initially, the dominance of the radical program was reinforced, but problems in the East, especially in Russia, led to new criticism against radical reform, which culminated around Russia's financial crash in 1998, which is discussed in the final section.

The Radical Reform Program: A Big Bang

The radical program for market economic reforms was supported by three powerful groups. The first group consisted of leading mainstream Western, primarily American macroeconomists, such as Jeffrey Sachs, Stanley Fischer, Lawrence Summers, and David Lipton. Harvard University, the Massachusetts Institute of Technology, and the London School of Economics were focal points of radical reform thinking. A second important set was the best economists in the East, notably Leszek Balcerowicz in Poland, Václav Klaus in Czechoslovakia, and Yegor Gaidar in Russia. They were few but bright, and they knew what they wanted. They were later joined by politicians with economic insights, such as Mart Laar in Estonia and Einars Repše in Latvia. Most of them became leading policy makers. The third group supporting radical reform was the international financial institutions, the International Monetary Fund (IMF) and the World Bank and the ministries of finance and central banks of the major Western governments.

For American macroeconomists, the IMF, the World Bank, and the U.S. government, the Latin American experience with macroeconomic stabilization in the 1980s showed them the way. Their view was that a radical and comprehensive reform program was the best cure (Bruno et al. 1988). This program had been named the

"Washington Consensus" by John Williamson (1990). It can be summarized as "prudent macroeconomic policies, outward orientation, and free-market capitalism," and it drew on neoclassical mainstream economic theory. The choice of name was somewhat unfortunate because it seemed as if Washington dictated economic policies for the world, but the fundamental ten points of this program were pretty obvious because they were not very detailed and avoided ideological controversy:

1. Fiscal discipline is needed.
2. Among public expenditures, discretionary subsidies should be minimized, and education, health, and public investment should be priorities.
3. The tax base should be broad, and marginal tax rates ought to be moderate.
4. Interest rates should be market-determined and real interest rates positive.
5. Exchange rates should be competitive.
6. Foreign trade policy should be rather liberal.
7. Foreign direct investment is beneficial but not a high priority.
8. Privatization is beneficial because private industry is managed more efficiently than state enterprises.
9. Deregulation is a useful means to promote competition.
10. Property rights need to be made secure.

Many economists simultaneously presented similar ideas about the need for radical economic reform.[1] The intellectual development in the East was very sudden. Even the most radical reformers in the Soviet bloc did not think of a full-fledged market economic transformation as a real possibility until the late 1980s. The breakthrough occurred in Moscow in early 1987, when the literary journal *Novy mir* published a couple of articles with devastating criticism of the Soviet economic system (Selyunin and Khanin 1987; Shmelev 1987).

The first truly market economic program to propose large-scale privatization was presented in Poland in 1988 (Dąbrowski et al. 1989). Leszek Balcerowicz (1992) has detailed how the radical economic reform program emerged. It was the result of an economic reform group that he led in Warsaw throughout the late 1980s. Prominent members of his group were Marek Dąbrowski and Stefan Kawalec, later deputy ministers of finance. These Polish liberals were tired of gradual reforms that were reversed. They wanted to break out of market socialism and accomplish a real market economy. Their fundamental insight was that the market reforms had to be truly radical as well as comprehensive. In May 1989, Balcerowicz wrote a summary reform program that included privatization, liberalization of foreign trade, currency convertibility, and an open economy.

Before the Polish reform government was formed in September 1989, the last communist government had liberalized food prices, which led to an inflation of some 40 percent in the month of September. An effective financial stabilization program had to be added to the radical structural reform, which Balcerowicz's advisors, Harvard Professor Jeffrey Sachs and David Lipton, accomplished with their experience of how to defeat high inflation in Latin America. They also assisted by propagating the Polish radical reform program in the West, gaining Western sympathy.

The radical reform program for postcommunist countries followed the Washington Consensus closely, but it went further and was more specific. Therefore, it is not correct, as is often done, to equalize the two. The original radical reform program was adjusted to the prevailing Polish conditions. Moreover, Balcerowicz had not read the Washington Consensus when he drafted his original reform program. Many issues had to be added or reinforced because they had already been done in Latin America – notably, deregulation to create a market and privatization to establish private property. The Balcerowicz program became the standard for a radical, comprehensive reform. Its prescriptions also applied to other countries in similar predicaments. This program was lucid and is easy to summarize[2]:

1. *Macroeconomic stabilization.* The immediate concern was to halt hyperinflation. Fiscal policy had to be centralized and brought under control by a reinforced ministry of finance, which had to swiftly reduce the large budget deficit. The central bank had to be independent and focus on low inflation. Therefore, it needed to tighten monetary policies and introduce positive real interest rates. The exchange rate should be unified and adjusted to the market. The currency needed to be convertible on current account to be freely available for foreign trade.
2. *Deregulation.* The government had to deregulate prices and eliminate most price subsidies to let demand and supply determine prices. It also needed to liberalize domestic trade and break up monopolies to avoid monopolistic pricing. A regime of relatively free foreign trade had to be established. It would eliminate rents in exports as well as imports, and a realistic price structure would be imported. Free trade would alleviate the rampant shortages, facilitate production, and boost living standards.
3. *Privatization.* The government should abolish restrictions on private enterprise and offer new private entrepreneurs a maximum of freedom. It also needed to initiate small-scale privatization early on and start the privatization of large and medium-sized enterprises as soon as possible, but everybody understood that it would take time, and no agreement existed on how to do it.
4. *Reinforcing the social safety net.* The ardors of restructuring required the introduction of a social safety net targeted at new groups in need, especially the unemployed, and an increase of pensions.

Radical reformers wanted to change the role of the state, eliminating the harmful parts of the old state apparatus while building a new democratic government. Jeffrey Sachs (1994, p. 510) summarized the radicals' view of the state in transition:

> A government facing political and economic collapse (the case at hand) must give up responsibility for market prices in order to focus on the core functions of government that are not being met: law and order, public security, a stable monetary system, and basic social welfare. Governments that have reached hyperinflation cannot, *self-evidently,* be expected to develop complex industrial policies or structural policies. After all, they aren't even carrying out their most fundamental tasks.

The state had an important role to play, but it would be very different from what the socialist state had played. Many state functions had to be strengthened – notably, fiscal policy, monetary policy, the rule of law, the registration and defense of private property rights, regulation of banking and financial markets, and targeted social support. Radical reformers supported unemployment insurance and higher pensions as they aspired to stimulate and facilitate structural change (Fischer and Gelb 1991). Any social engineering was out of the question.

The later, so frequent accusations that radical reformers had "forgotten" about institutions and social policy had no base in reality. Indeed, the successful radical reformers undertook the greatest institutional reforms and spent greatly on social assistance.

On all these measures the radical reformers agreed, but their views varied on some other measures, including exchange-rate policy, wage controls, international assistance, and privatization.

- Poland, Czechoslovakia, and Estonia pegged exchange rates early on as nominal anchors for their financial stabilization, whereas others opted for floating exchange rates.
- Poland and Czechoslovakia introduced strict wage controls as an important part of their initial stabilization policy, whereas others had little wage control.
- The role and size of international financial assistance and debt relief varied. Jeffrey Sachs took an international lead as a proponent of aid, whereas others opposed nearly all financial support.
- There were as many views on privatization as there were economists, although the radical reformers considered speedy privatization important.

The differences over exchange rates and wage controls were of a technical nature, whereas the differences over international assistance and especially privatization were profoundly ideological.

The Importance of Speed and Comprehensiveness

The common conviction of the radical reformers was that these major market reforms had to be undertaken as comprehensively and swiftly as possible (Åslund 1992). They were all convinced that a radical and comprehensive reform was needed to bring about a real breakthrough, which would minimize the social costs and render the economic upswing earlier and sharper. This was their prime bone of contention with the gradualists. One popular saying was, "You cannot cross a chasm in two leaps." The leading Estonian reformer, Mart Laar (2002, p. 10), observed, "The only thing we knew was that there was no time to lose."

Still, the protagonists of radical reform had a clear understanding that many measures could not be undertaken instantly and that transition would take at least a decade (notably, Fischer and Gelb 1991). "*Different processes of economic reform have different maximum possible speeds*" (Balcerowicz 1994, p. 82, emphasis in original). Everybody realized that privatization of large enterprises would take years, as would complex reforms, ranging from tax reform, social reforms, civil service reform, and legal reforms to the development of a financial sector.

First, liberal economists in the Soviet bloc had bitter memories of failed and reversed reforms. Characteristically, Balcerowicz (1995, p. 342) concluded that in the 1980s, the Polish "economic reforms failed because they were not radical enough, that is, they did not reach a certain threshold of necessary changes rapidly" so that they achieved "critical mass" of market reforms. If the system did not attain a certain degree of cohesion and consistency, it theoretically could be even more inefficient than the old command economy (Kornai 1990; Boycko 1991; Winiecki 1991a).

Second, the radical reformers were acutely aware of the prevalence of both state and market failure, but they were more fearful of state failure (Shleifer and Vishny 1998). A new market would be imperfect, but the communist state was even more imperfect, so it could not be entrusted with much intervention. The reforms had to deliver a "shock" that could break the hold of the old system to introduce a viable new market economy (Gomułka 1989).

Third, people's expectations had to be changed to render the systemic changes credible and irreversible. Balcerowicz (1995, p. 342) derived from Leon Festinger's theory of cognitive dissonance in social psychology "that people are more likely to change their attitudes and their behaviour if they are faced with radical changes in their environment, which they consider irreversible, than if those changes are only gradual." Otherwise, people would suspect a rollback toward communism and refuse to adjust their behavior.

Fourth, because of the severity of the crisis and the new hope of freedom, the public was prepared to make short-term sacrifices for long-term benefits of society out of sheer idealism. Balcerowicz (1994) emphasized the importance of using this period of "extraordinary politics" to get a full package of reform laws adopted by the parliament while radical economic reforms remained popular. "Both leaders and ordinary citizens feel a stronger-than-normal tendency to think and act in terms of the common good" (Balcerowicz 1995, p. 161).

Fifth, in Central Europe and the Baltics, quick and comprehensive systemic reforms soon changed the intellectual paradigm, whereas slower reforms kept rather parochial economic ideas alive in the post-Soviet countries.

Sixth, standard theories agreed that macroeconomic stabilization had to be done fast to break inflationary expectations.

Seventh, liberalization of prices and trade had to go far enough to generate a critical mass of markets and provide credible incentives. Because the old prices were hopelessly distorted, any gradual adjustment would send inaccurate signals about costs, demand, and supply. Inflationary expectations would be maintained, and entrepreneurs would be unwilling to invest. The profitability of an enterprise would be determined by price regulation, which would render bankruptcies socially unacceptable. Liberalized imports were vital to activate the market and end shortages (Sachs and Lipton 1990).

Eighth, the hardest task was to convince enterprise managers to alter their behavior. Their incentives had to be changed through the introduction of hard budget constraints or a "demand barrier." If they were not convinced that the rules had changed for good, they would not adjust (Sachs and Lipton 1990).

Ninth, corruption, misappropriation of public funds, and rent seeking were ballooning amid the breakdown of communism. Partial liberalization facilitated arbitrage between regulated prices and free prices, but a quick and comprehensive reform could mitigate these distortions.

Tenth, extremely little accurate information was available during the early transition because everything was changing fast and radically, and new statistics were often completely flawed. If little could be measured and few relevant facts could be established, it would have been both pretentious and foolish to attempt anything but a policy based on principle (Balcerowicz 1995).

Finally, the state bureaucracy had numerous reasons to oppose a radical reform program. Under reform, it would lose its prior power, and most of its human capital would become obsolete because the old socialist micromanagement of enterprises would cease. Bureaucrats easily colluded with abundant secret service officers, state enterprise managers, and Communist Party officials. "Populist politicians will try to hook up with coalitions of workers, managers and bureaucrats in hard-hit sectors to slow or reverse the adjustment" (Sachs 1990). It was vital for the sustenance of democracy to disarm the old elite through radical reform. The abortive coup in August 1991 in Moscow and the armed uprising by the predemocratic Russian parliament in October 1993 illustrated the threat of a bureaucratic counterrevolution. As Mart Laar put it, "To wait is to fail."

Gradual Reform Programs

The opponents of radical reform did not form one school but proposed more gradual reform in one or several regards, and no full conceptualization of a gradual reform was apparent. In 1990, the discussion was dominated by contrasts between the just-launched reforms in Poland and Hungary. Gradualists defended the Hungarian methods against the Polish shock therapy with little regard for diverse preconditions. Another source of inspiration was the successful Chinese reform.

The fundamental difference between gradualists and radical reformers was their view of market failure and state failure. First, gradualists thought the old communist economy and state were more viable than radical reformers did. Second, gradualists downplayed the economic crisis after communism, looking at the mild predicament of Hungary rather than the collapse of the Soviet Union. Third, gradualists refused to accept that the communist state was highly corrupt or even "kleptocratic," being more concerned about market failures, such as possible monopoly effects. They favored state intervention and retained a strong belief in social engineering. Fourth, while radical reformers considered the transition a risky task that could stall and fail, gradualists took the success of the market economy for granted because of the strength of the state. They wanted to slow down the transition process and suggested detailed optimal sequencing of reform measures. Fifth, gradualists wanted to stimulate output through demand management, whereas radical reformers saw a systemic lack of supply as the prime problem.

The overt disputes were limited to the speed and order of reforms, but hardly anybody defended a larger public sector than in Western Europe in the early transition debate. In reality, however, many gradualists retained more socialist views than they wanted to reveal at the moment of liberal triumph.

The dominant argument for a more gradual approach was the evident economic successes of the Chinese model of communist reform, which many people of different persuasions wanted to apply to the former Soviet bloc.

A broad group of Western social scientists based their opposition on the contention that radical reform would lead to a greater fall in output and be more socially costly than gradual reform. They wanted to make the reforms less radical and argued for tradeoffs between reform and social costs. On such premises, they developed theoretical models of political economy. Institutional economists wanted to postpone the introduction of a market economy until most institutional reforms had been undertaken.

In the former Soviet Union, reform communists, who had gained considerable authority by calling for market reforms in the early Gorbachev years, now turned against such reforms and refused to accept the reality of a normal market economy.

The Chinese Model

When communism collapsed in the Soviet bloc, East Asia stood out as a shining economic success, and many praised China as a model for the transition countries.[3]

One contention was that Mikhail Gorbachev mistakenly started with democratization in January 1987 and that he should have begun with economic reforms instead (Nolan 1995; Goldman 1996). However, soon after Gorbachev became secretary general of the Communist Party of the Soviet Union in March 1985, he attempted minor economic reforms (Åslund 1991). At that time, Soviet society was utterly petrified. After having attempted economic reforms for two years, Gorbachev realized that the omnipotent party bureaucracy blocked everything, which convinced him to launch partial democratization to undermine it. In China, by contrast, reforms were launched after the devastating Cultural Revolution, which had brought economic decline and terrorized the party apparatus.

To argue that democratization should have followed market economic reform amounted to opposition to any change in the Soviet Union.[4] Russian liberal Vladimir Mau (1999) retorted that "the Chinese path entails leaving power in the hands of the old Nomenklatura in order to preserve a one-party system and the ideological purity of the regime. Economic transformations then are to be undertaken gradually under Nomenklatura control. Any attempt to increase the political activity of individuals must be heavily suppressed." The Soviet Nomenklatura was almighty, and it firmly resisted all reforms.

Another argument was that experimentation was better than full-scale reforms (e.g., Murrell 1992b; Stiglitz 1999a), but no communist country had experimented as much with economic reforms as the Soviet Union. It carried out reforms and experiments in the 1920s, 1950s, 1960s, and 1980s, but the problem was that they were all reversed. The same was largely true of Central Europe (Balcerowicz 1995). Only in Hungary did significant systemic changes persist, but they did not lead to significant growth, and a broad Hungarian consensus advocated more radical reforms (Kornai 1986, 1990). Moreover, economic experiments abounded in the Soviet Union in the 1980s, but they brought no success. The question is rather why experimentation succeeded in China and failed in the Soviet bloc, and the answer lies in the great differences between the Soviet Union and China.

Third, the champions of Chinese reforms agreed that it was right to start the reform with agriculture and small enterprises and leave the large industrial enterprises in state hands, creating a dual economy, with a market economy for the small enterprises and the old state governance for the large state enterprises. The new private or quasi-private sector could generate growth and develop without antagonizing the old state sector (Murrell 1992b; Amsden et al. 1994; Goldman 1996; Nolan 1995). Jeffrey Sachs and Wing Thye Woo (1994) objected that agriculture in China was dominant, whereas it was a small part of the overindustrialized economy in Central Europe and the Soviet Union. Soviet state industry dominated the economy and could not be left aside. Furthermore, Soviet agriculture was industrialized and large scale, too. To break up big state and collective farms was technically difficult. In addition, the huge communist agrarian bureaucracy blocked any progressive economic development for its selfish reasons. Gorbachev tried agricultural reforms in the Soviet Union in the spring of 1985, but he got nowhere. He legalized cooperatives in May 1988, but they became predominantly vehicles of management theft (Åslund 1989, 1991).

Fourth, most proponents of the Chinese model favored gradual price liberalization and opening of the economy (Amsden et al. 1994; Nolan 1995; Goldman 1996). Well, the Soviet Union did so, and the result was truly disastrous: massive rent seeking by prominent members of the Nomenklatura, which is also going on in China (Dąbrowski et al. 2001).

A final argument was that China was right in carrying out a far-reaching decentralization, but the Soviet Union failed to do so. However, Peter Murrell and Mancur Olson (1991) argued convincingly that the decline of the centrally planned economies could be explained by the devolution of power within the party and state hierarchy and the collusion of bureaucrats at lower levels undoing the dictatorship of the secretary general. "The last stage of communism is not the stateless and classless society that Marx forecast, but rule by a rather large aristocracy of upper level bureaucrats" (p. 260). Power was devolved both within the party bureaucracy and to state enterprise managers, but without accountability or responsibility. The Chinese Communist Party maintained some control over its bureaucrats, whereas the Soviet state fell apart. Soviet bureaucrats were relatively more numerous than Chinese bureaucrats and had more flawed incentives, rendering them more harmful. China and Russia used to be deemed similarly corrupt, whereas Russian corruption was perceived as socially more costly, but in the 2000s, Russia has become more corrupt and China less so (Shleifer and Treisman 2000; Transparency International 2010).

In the end, surprisingly little can be compared. Although both China and the Soviet Union were communist dictatorships with socialized economies, most preconditions differed when they launched market economic reforms in 1978 and 1985, respectively. First, the Soviet state and its Communist Party were so petrified that they could no longer reform but only collapse, yet the Chinese state and its Communist Party were still reformable (Åslund 1989). Second, China was dominated by agriculture, but the Soviet Union by large-scale industry (Sachs and Woo 1994). Third, the Soviet Union collapsed in hyperinflation, whereas the Chinese leaders never lost control over macroeconomic stability. China did not need any macroeconomic shock therapy, but the Soviet Union did.

Western Arguments for Gradualism

Four main arguments for gradualism are social democratic political economy, theoretical political economy, the concept of disorganization, and evolutionary or institutional economics.

Przeworski's Political Economy

European social democrats were profoundly uncomfortable during the collapse of communism. Many of them had argued that nothing of the kind could ever happen, and ideologically, they disliked these developments. As the postcommunist output collapse started, left-wingers drew parallels with the Great Depression of 1929–33, the worst crisis of capitalism. In a highly acclaimed book on democracy and the market in Eastern Europe, Adam Przeworski (1991), a leading scholar of comparative politics, laid out the argument. His first postulate was that democracy had to justify itself by material achievements: "To evoke compliance and participation, democracy must generate substantive outcomes: it must offer all the relevant political forces real opportunities to improve their material welfare" (p. 32). Implicitly, he assumed that people opted for democracy for the sake of economic welfare, not for political reasons.

Przeworski's second postulate was that people demanded quick results. "Can structural economic transformation be sustained under democratic conditions, or must either reforms or democracy be sacrificed?" (p. 138). His underlying thought was: "Even if the post-reform system would be more efficient ... a transient deterioration of material conditions may be sufficient to undermine either democracy or the reform process" (p. 137).

Third, Przeworski (1991, p. 163) assumed that "the social cost is higher under the radical strategy, where social cost is defined as the cumulative decline in consumption during the period of transition." "Inflation is likely to flare up again and again under inertial pressures. Unemployment, even if temporary, is difficult to tolerate. Increasing inequality stokes conflicts" (p. 189).

Finally, he presumed that the threat to democracy came from a dissatisfied population. In his 1995 book, Przeworski (1995, p. 85) came back with an even harsher judgment: "[W]e have been critical of the standard neoliberal recipes since we believe that they are faulty in three fundamental ways: they induce economic stagnation, they incur unnecessarily large social costs, and they weaken the nascent democratic institutions." Przeworski assumed that "the continuing material deprivation, the technocratic style of policy making, and the ineffectiveness of the representative institutions undermine popular support for democracy" (1991, pp. 189–90). His assumptions were shared by a large number of political scientists.[5]

But these assumptions did not square with reality. Larry Diamond (1999) debunked Przeworski's first postulate, showing that people see democracy as a value in itself and do not judge it only by economic results. As we shall see, economic reform and democracy were positively correlated, and radical reforms caused less economic decline and social cost. Joel Hellman (1998) made the profound point that the main threat to reforms did not come from the population but from the winning elite. Because of Przeworski's inaccurate assumptions, all his conclusions were faulty as well.

Theoretical Political Economy

A small group of Western economists, primarily Gérard Roland, Mathias Dewatripont, Phillipe Aghion, and Olivier Blanchard, developed an extensive theoretical literature on the political economy of transition.[6] With a cursory look at economic developments in a few transition countries, mostly Poland and Hungary, they made rather heroic assumptions and presented "stylized facts" in line with Przeworski's that were not realistic. The gist of this literature is the assumption that radical reform leads to a sharper decline in output and greater social costs than gradual reform: "Assume that [the] big bang … has a negative expected outcome" (Roland 1993, pp. 534–5). Another assumption was that the population would not tolerate more than a certain decline in output or a certain degree of unemployment. As a tradeoff, they suggested slow liberalization and privatization, as well as more social benefits and subsidies, to make reforms politically possible. They also made the unrealistic assumption that the key political actor was the majority of the population (Dewatripont and Roland 1992b), implying that the nascent democratic institutions were both representative and effective. Then, "gradualism may allow for 'divide and rule' tactics when compensation for the losers from reform is costly, provided the government has enough agenda-setting power" (Roland 1994, p. 1162). They presumed not only a very democratic but also a strong and effective government, assuming nearly perfect social engineering (Dewatripont and Roland 1992b). They also assumed that a more radical reform would lead to higher taxes and, therefore, to a slower growth of the private sector (Aghion and Blanchard 1994; Dewatripont and Roland 1992a).

Economic models can be relevant, even if a few assumptions are not very realistic. The problem with these models, however, was that all their major assumptions contradicted reality, as we shall see in the rest of this book, and their conclusions largely depended on their assumption that more radical reform brought more social hardship. This theoretical literature hangs detached from most empirical research, which has found that radical reforms have been less socially costly. Katz and Owen (2000) have shown that if the assumptions in Dewatripont and Roland (1992b) are changed to the real situation, their article "may be viewed as lending strong support to the big-bang strategy" (Havrylyshyn 2006, pp. 23–4).

Disorganization

Olivier Blanchard and Michael Kremer (1997) developed an alternative model to explain the decline in output with disorganization. Under communism, a typical industry had fewer firms than in the West. For many inputs, firms knew of only one supplier, and for many outputs, only one buyer. During transition, old trade links were disrupted or became uneconomical. With asymmetric information or incomplete contracts, the initial results of bargaining might have been inefficient, implying that market imperfections caused output to fall with the transition. Blanchard and Kremer noticed that shortages persisted because adjustments took time. Looking at Central Europe, the Baltic countries, and Russia, they found empirical evidence for the decline in output having been more pronounced for goods with more complex production processes. They inquired "whether the need to preserve existing production networks provides a justification for gradualism" and whether "a commitment by the government to subsidize state firms for some time may avoid their immediate collapse" (Blanchard and Kremer 1997, p. 1123). However, the authors cautioned that this was only a limited, theoretical case for gradualism, and they acknowledged that it was valid only in the short term because enterprises could be presumed to solve their contract and bargaining problems relatively soon.

Blanchard and Kremer's empirical proof was a regression, showing that more advanced manufacturing industries experienced greater decline, but those also were the greatest value detractors. Therefore, it was desirable that their substandard production plummeted. The systemic disruption prompted every enterprise to review its contracts, which was one of the original arguments for radical reform (Boycko 1991; Murphy et al. 1992). The question is rather which kind of reform minimizes the period of disorganization, and as we shall see, the answer is radical reform.

Institutions First

Nobel Laureate Douglass C. North accused radical reformers of having "forgotten" institutions. North (1994, p. 359) saw radical reform ideas as dominated by neoclassical theory, which he argued "is simply an inappropriate tool to analyze and prescribe policies that will induce development." "While the rules may be changed overnight, the informal norms usually change only gradually ... transferring the formal political and economic rules of successful Western market economies to third-world and Eastern European economies is not a sufficient condition for good economic performance. Privatization is not a panacea for solving poor economic performance." However, he offered no evidence for this alleged forgetfulness of institutions. In reality, all radical reformers were deeply committed to changing the old communist institutions, using Friedrich Hayek (1944/1986, 1960), the leading liberal institutionalist, as the main source of inspiration (Balcerowicz 1992; Klaus 1992; Mau 1999; Akaev 2000).

Peter Murrell (1992a, 1992b, 1992c) tried to develop an *evolutionary theory* for postcommunist economic transition. He observed that in Central Europe "organizations that were expected to change their behavior in response to the new conditions have failed to do so," particularly the dominant large state enterprises (Murrell 1992b, p. 81). He agreed with the radical reformers on the need for a coherent economic environment, but he drew the opposite conclusion: "[L]ittle in the economic record of the past two years suggests that the radical program of reform can be successful. The old cannot be simply destroyed and therefore the radical reform plans have serious problems of coherence" (Murrell 1992b, p. 82). He concluded, "The information and skills of existing personnel are attuned to the existing set of institutions and lose much of their value when those institutions are destroyed" (Murrell 1992c, p. 50). Hence gradual reforms would cause fewer output losses because the old sector would suffer less, whereas the new private market sector would develop better (Murrell and Wang 1993).

Many gradualists insisted that market institutions should be established before the economy was liberalized to avoid market failures. The UN Economic Commission for Europe (1990, p. 23) pleaded, "[L]egal and financial infrastructures of the market economy must be put in place before markets can perform." Only East Germany did so, because West Germany imposed its commercial legislation, but East Germany stands out as one of the most costly and least successful transitions (see Chapter 10). If nothing was done, market reforms certainly would fail, as Belarus has shown. Oleh Havrylyshyn (2006, p. 272) starkly pointed out: "[I]t is easily seen in the time-path of the transition index that those countries which moved most slowly on liberalization elements moved even more slowly on the institution-building elements. This implies that the proclamations of the political elites in these countries that the society was not ready for the market and a gradual evolution was necessary, were not sincere proclamations but masked a hidden agenda." Obviously, institutions could not be built very fast, but the issue was what kind of reform would lead to a faster and better building of institutions.

[...]

Criticism of Radical Reform After the Russian Financial Crash

After the aggressive early debate and a nervous start of transition, policies started to bite, and the international community cheered the successes of radical economic reform in Central Europe and the Baltics. The prevailing sentiment was that Russia and the rest of the post-Soviet countries were eventually getting on the bandwagon.[7] In 1996, the World Bank (1996a) devoted its annual World Development Report to the transition. Its main conclusions read as a credo of radical economic reform (pp. 142–5, emphasis in original):

- *Consistent policies, combining liberalization of markets, trade, and new business entry with reasonable price stability, can achieve a great deal – even in countries lacking clear property rights and strong market institutions.*
- *An efficient response to market processes requires clearly defined property rights – and this will eventually require widespread private ownership.*
- *Major changes in social policy must complement the move to the market.*
- *Institutions that support markets arise both by design and from demand.*
- *International integration can help lock in successful reforms.*

As the years passed by, however, Russia's economic growth failed to take off, although mass privatization had been carried out. Inflation had abated in 1996, and the new stock market skyrocketed. The loans-for-shares privatization in late 1995, which transferred stakes of a dozen of Russia's most valuable oil and metals companies to a handful of oligarchs, aroused an outcry about "original sin" in both Russia and the West. The view that Russia had lapsed into a morass of organized crime and corruption proliferated in vivid journalism.

As the question marks piled up around Russia's transition, the country approached a financial crash in slow motion. On August 17, 1998, the Russian government defaulted on its domestic debt, let the ruble exchange rate plummet, and froze all bank accounts. Roughly half the Russian bank system went bankrupt, and the shock was horrendous. The Russian middle class lost most of its bank savings for the second time. Russian inflation exploded again, and output fell. In an article in the *New York Times,* John Lloyd (1998) famously asked, "Who lost Russia?" Had the attempts to build a market economy in Russia failed? In Russia, the main conclusions were that the long-lasting large budget deficit had to be eliminated and the exchange rate be made competitive.

In the West, however, the left-wing criticism of Joseph Stiglitz came to dominate, especially through his best-selling book, *Globalization and Its Discontents* (2002).[8] Stiglitz (1999a, 1999b, 2000, 2002, 2006) attacked IMF policy on Russia, arguing that the Washington Consensus model did not work there. He reckoned that Russia should have followed China's example, but "the Western advisers, especially from the United States and the IMF, ... marched in so quickly to preach the gospel of the market economy ... arguing for a new religion – market fundamentalism" (Stiglitz 2002, p. 134). Logically, Stiglitz (1999b, p. 4) praised the gradual reforms in truly tyrannical Uzbekistan. In his support of gradualism, Stiglitz lauded Gorbachev's policies: "The Gorbachev-era *perestroika* reforms furnish a good example of incremental institutional reforms" (Stiglitz 1999a, p. 24). The problem was that they had brought about the collapse of the Soviet Union and its economy, a fact on which Stiglitz refrained to comment.

Another criticism was institutional, that the reformers had ignored the importance of the institutional infrastructure of a market economy and dissipated the communist organizational capital. Stiglitz criticized radical reformers for blaming "the failure of the shock therapy on corruption and rent seeking at every turn ... without recognizing any role of the institutional blitzkrieg in destroying but not replacing the old social norms – and thus in removing the last restraints against society-threatening levels of corruption ... Once dissipated, organizational capital is hard to reassemble" (Stiglitz 1999a, p. 9). Stiglitz defended the postcommunist state: "The state is seen as the primary source of the problems: interfering in state firms and preying on private firms. The emphasis is on government failure, not on market failure" (p. 20), while he called radical reformers "market Bolsheviks." The organizational capital he lauded contained the Communist Party and the secret police, which are rarely considered assets in democratic societies.

Stiglitz's third and greatest concern was the Russian privatization. He condemned the Russian loans-for-shares scheme as the main source of corruption. "Russia's oligarchs stole assets, stripped them leaving their country much poorer" (2002, p. 160). "Russia's kind of ersatz capitalism did not provide the incentives for wealth creation and economic growth but rather for asset stripping" (p. 162). Instead, Stiglitz wanted to give away state enterprises to the old elite: "Perhaps trying to discipline spontaneous privatization might have offered the greatest hope" (Stiglitz 1999a, p. 6). Stiglitz largely ignored the macroeconomic crisis, simply arguing that "the rapid liberalization at the beginning had led to the burst of inflation" (2002, p. 156) and that "the tight monetary policies also contributed to the use of barter" (p. 157). He concluded, "Prospects for the future are bleak" (p. 133).

Ironically, this criticism dismissed Russia's economic transformation as a failure just when Russia rose from its ashes, achieving sound macroeconomic stability and an average GDP growth of nearly 7 percent for a decade, whereas the region as a whole recorded even higher growth rates.[9] A nearly unison choir of macroeconomists argued that the problems with Russia's stabilization were not shock therapy but gradualism: "It was not the shock therapy program but the refusal to stick to it that catalyzed many contradictions in Russia's postcommunist development, including its institutional problems" (Mau 1999). "It is said that institutional reforms and privatization should take place first, and liberalization and stabilization should take place later ... but the experiences of those countries that undertook market reforms does not provide a single case to prove such a concept viable" (Mau 1999). Oleh Havrylyshyn (2006, p. 272) underlined, "[T]hose countries which moved most slowly on liberalization elements moved even more slowly on the institution-building elements." Mau (1999) refused to blame the IMF because a "good part of the 'IMF conditions' were developed in Moscow, not in Washington... . This is a typical way for a weak government to launch unpopular reforms." With regard to privatization, Mau and other liberal Russians emphasized that the government could not control state property. "Property manipulation is an important feature of weak state power." Therefore, early and fast privatization with some order was the best option to create a stratum of private owners as a base for a market economy.

The most unabashed rebuttal of the criticism of the Russian economic transformation was presented in a much noticed article by Andrei Shleifer and Daniel Treisman (2004) in *Foreign Affairs*. Their thesis was that "Russia was in 1990, and is today, a middle-income country ... comparable to Argentina in 1991 and Mexico in 1999. Almost all democracies in this income range are rough around the edges: their governments suffer from corruption, their judiciaries are politicized, and their press is almost never entirely free. They have high income inequality, concentrated corporate ownership, and turbulent macroeconomic performance. In all these regards, Russia is quite normal" (p. 22). "In sum, Russia started the 1990s as a disintegrating, centrally planned economy and ended the decade as a market system in a burst of rapid growth" (p. 30). Boldly, Shleifer and Treisman defended the economic performance of the oligarchs in the loans-for-shares companies. "Have the oligarchs stripped assets from the companies they acquired in privatization, rather than investing in them? The audited financial statements of these companies suggest that their assets have grown dramatically, especially since 1998.... And the major oligarchs have been investing hundreds of millions of dollars annually in their companies.... In contrast, the greatest asset-stripping scandals occurred in companies that remained under state control" (p. 29).

As the growth and macroeconomic stability of the post-Soviet countries have become stellar, the interest of international debate has faded away. The two common concerns about the former Soviet Union are high corruption and authoritarianism, whereas the new eastern members of the European Union stand out as successes in these two regards.

Notes

1 Notably Blanchard et al. (1991), Boycko (1991), Brada (1993), Fischer and Gelb (1991), Gelb and Gray (1991), Kornai (1990), and World Bank (1996a). My own contribution to this discussion is Åslund (1992).

2 See Lipton and Sachs (1990a), Sachs and Lipton (1990), and Sachs (1990, 1991, 1993), and Balcerowicz (1992, 1994, 1995).

3 For example, Parkhomenko (1992), Amsden et al. (1994), Nolan (1995), Goldman (1996), and Stiglitz (1999a, 2002, 2006).

4 Marshall Goldman (1991, p. 224) presented a more plausible view of the Gorbachev reforms in 1991: "[E]ven if Gorbachev had adopted a more rational and coherent policy, it is unlikely that he would have succeeded. The Soviet population . . . was too resistant to evolutionary change. For that reason, the odds are that no one else would have done much better." The problem, though, was the Nomenklatura rather than the population.

5 Similar views were expressed by Elster (1990), Offe (1997), Andreas Pickel in Pickel and Wiesenthal (1997), and Stark and Bruszt (1998).

6 See in particular Dewatripont and Roland (1992a, 1992b), Aghion and Blanchard (1994), and Roland (1993, 1994, 2000).

7 A number of quite positive books on the Russian economic transition were published; see Åslund (1995), Granville (1995a), and Layard and Parker (1996).

8 Similar views were expressed by Cohen (2000), Klein and Pomer (2001), Reddaway and Glinski (2001), and Goldman (2003).

9 Two of the sharpest responses were produced by Russian liberal Vladimir Mau (1999) and Polish liberals Marek Dąbrowski, Stanisław Gomułka, and Jacek Rostowski (2001). See also Yevstigneev and Yevstigneeva (1999). Havrylyshyn (2006) offers a later and full criticism. My own contribution was Åslund (1999).

Bibliography

Aghion, Phillipe, and Olivier Blanchard (1994) "On the Speed of Transition in Central Europe," in Stanley Fischer and Julio Rotemberg, eds., *NBER Macroeconomic Annual 1994*. Cambridge, MA: MIT Press, pp. 283–320.

Akaev, Askar A. (2000) *Perekhodnaya ekonomika glazami fizika* [The Transition Economy in the Eyes of a Physicist]. Bishkek: Uchkun.

Amsden, Alice H., Jacek Kochanowicz, and Lance Taylor (1994) *The Market Meets Its Match: Restructuring the Economies of Eastern Europe*. Cambridge, MA: Harvard University Press.

Ash, Timothy Garton (1990) *We the People: The Revolution of '89 Witnessed in Warsaw, Budapest, Berlin & Prague*. Cambridge, UK: Granta Books.

Åslund, Anders (1989) "Soviet and Chinese Reforms – Why They Must Be Different," *The World Today* 45(11): 188–91.

——— (1991) *Gorbachev's Struggle for Economic Reform*, 2nd ed. Ithaca, NY: Cornell University Press.

——— (1992) *Post Communist Economic Revolutions: How Big a Bang?* Washington, DC: Center for Strategic and International Studies.

——— (1995) *How Russia Became a Market Economy*. Washington, DC: Brookings Institution.

Balcerowicz, Leszek (1992) *800 dni skontrolowanego szoku* [800 Days of Controlled Shock]. Warsaw: Polska Oficyna Wydawnicza "BGW."

——— (1994) "Understanding Postcommunist Transitions," *Journal of Democracy* 5(4): 75–89.

——— (1995) *Socialism, Capitalism, Transformation*. Budapest: Central European University Press.

Blanchard, Olivier, Rudiger Dornbusch, Paul Krugman, Richard Layard, and Lawrence Summers (1991) *Reform in Eastern Europe.* Cambridge, MA: MIT Press.

Blanchard, Olivier and Michael Kremer (1997) "Disorganization," *Quarterly Journal of Economics* **112**(4): 1091–126.

Boycko, Maxim (1991) "Price Decontrol: The Microeconomic Case for the 'Big Bang' Approach," *Oxford Review of Economic Policy* **7**(4): 35–45.

Brada, Josef C. (1993) "The Transformation from Communism to Capitalism: How Far? How Fast?" *Post-Soviet Affairs* **9**(1): 87–110.

Bruno, Michael, Guido di Tella, Rudiger Dornbusch, and Stanley Fischer, eds. (1988) *Inflation Stabilization: The Experiences of Israel, Argentina, Brazil, Bolivia, and Mexico.* Cambridge, MA: MIT Press.

Dąbrowski, Marek, Stanisław Gomułka, and Jacek Rostowski (2001) "Whence Reform? A Critique of the Stiglitz Perspective," *Policy Reform* **4**: 291–324.

Dąbrowski, Marek, Marcin Swięcicki, Stefan Kawalec, Janusz Lewandowski, Jan Szomburg, Janusz Beksiak, and Ryszard Bugaj (1989) *Propozycie Przekształcenie Polskiej Gospodarki* [Proposals for the Transformation of the Polish Economy]. Warsaw: PTE.

Dahrendorf, Ralf (1990) *Reflections on the Revolution in Europe.* London: Chatto & Windus.

Dewatripont, Mathias, and Gérard Roland (1992a) "The Virtues of Gradualism and Legitimacy in the Transition to a Market Economy," *Economic Journal* **102**: 291–300.

—— (1992b) "Economic Reform and Dynamic Political Constraints," *Review of Economic Studies* **59**: 703–30.

Diamond, Larry (1999) *Developing Democracy: Towards Consolidation.* Baltimore, MD: John Hopkins University Press.

Fischer, Stanley, and Alan Gelb (1991) "The Process of Socialist Economic Transformation," *Journal of Economic Perspectives* **5**(4): 91–105.

Gelb, Alan H., and Cheryl W. Gray (1991) *The Transformation of Economies in Central and Eastern Europe: Issues, Progress and Prospects.* Washington, DC: World Bank.

Goldman, Marshall I. (1991) *What Went Wrong with Perestroika.* New York: Norton.

—— (1996) *Lost Opportunity: What Has Made Economic Reform in Russia So Difficult?* New York: Norton.

Gomułka, Stanisław (1989) "Shock Needed for Polish Economy," *The Guardian,* August 19.

Granville, Brigitte (1995a) *The Success of Russian Economic Reforms.* London: Royal Institute for International Affairs.

Havrylyshyn, Oleh (2006) *Diverging Paths in Post-Communist Transformation: Capitalism for All or Capitalism for the Few?* Basingstoke, UK: Palgrave Macmillan.

Hayek, Friedrich A. [1944] (1986) *Road to Serfdom.* Chicago: The University of Chicago Press.

—— (1960) *The Constitution of Liberty.* London: Routledge & Kegan Paul.

Hellman, Joel S. (1998) "Winners Take All: The Politics of Partial Reform in Postcommunist Transitions," *World Politics* **50**(2): 203–34.

Katz, Barbara G., and Joel Owen (2000) "Choosing Between Big Bang and Gradual Reform: An Option Price Approach," *Journal of Comparative Economics* **28**(1): 95–107.

Klaus, Václav (1992) *Dismantling Socialism: A Preliminary Report.* Prague: Top Agency.

—— (1994) *Rebirth of a Country: Five Years After.* Prague: Ringier.

Kornai, János (1990) *The Road to a Free Economy. Shifting from a Socialist System: The Example of Hungary.* New York: Norton.

Laar, Mart (2002) *Little Country That Could.* London: Centre for Research into Post-Communist Economies.

Layard, Richard, and John Parker (1996) *The Coming Russian Boom.* New York: Free Press.

Lipton, David, and Jeffrey D. Sachs (1990a) "Creating a Market in Eastern Europe: The Case of Poland," *Brookings Papers on Economic Activity* **20**(1): 75–147.

Lloyd, John (1998) "Who Lost Russia?" *New York Times,* August 15.

Mau, Vladimir (1999) "*Rossiiskie ekonomicheskie reformy glazami zapadnykh kritikov*" [Russian Economic Reforms in the Eyes of Western Critics], *Voprosy ekonomiki* **71**(11): 4–23.

Mill, John Stuart [1859] (1975) *On Liberty.* New York: Norton.

Murphy, Kevin A., Andrei Shleifer, and Robert W. Vishny (1992) "The Transition to a Market Economy: Pitfalls of Partial Reform," *Quarterly Journal of Economics* **57**(3): 889–903.

Murrell, Peter (1992a) "Conservative Political Philosophy and the Strategy of Economic Transition," *East European Politics and Societies* **6**(1): 3–16.

—— (1992b) "Evolutionary and Radical Approaches to Economic Reform," *Economics of Planning* **25**(1): 79–95.

—— (1992c) "Evolution in Economics and in the Economic Reform of the Centrally Planned Economies," in Christopher Clague and Gordon C. Rausser, eds., *The Emergence of Market Economies in Eastern Europe.* Cambridge, MA: Blackwell, pp. 35–53.

Murrell, Peter, and Mancur Olson (1991) "The Devolution of Centrally Planned Economies," *Journal of Comparative Economics* **15**(2): 239–65.

Murrell, Peter, and Yijang Wang (1993) "When Privatization Should Be Delayed: The Effect of Communist Legacies on Organizational and Institutional Reforms," *Journal of Comparative Economics* **17**(2): 385–406.

Nolan, Peter (1995) *China's Rise, Russia's Fall: Politics, Economics and Planning in the Transition from Stalinism.* New York: St. Martin's Press.

North, Douglass C. (1994) "Economic Performance Through Time," *American Economic Review* **84**(3): 359–68.

Parkhomenko, Sergei (1992) "*Volsky sozdaet partiyu pragmatikov*" [Volsky Creates a Party of Pragmatists], *Nezavisimaya gazeta,* May 13, p. 2.

Przeworski, Adam (1991) *Democracy and the Market.* Cambridge, UK: Cambridge University Press.

—— (1995) *Sustainable Democracy.* Cambridge, UK: Cambridge University Press.

Roland, Gérard (1993) "Political Economy of Restructuring and Privatization in Eastern Europe," *European Economic Review* **37**(2–3): 533–40.

—— (1994) "On the Speed and Sequencing of Privatisation and Restructuring," *Economic Journal* **104**(426): 1158–68.

—— (2000) "*Corporate Governance Systems and Restructuring: The Lessons from the Transition Experience,*" Washington, DC: World Bank, Annual Bank Conference on Development Economics, April 18–20.

Sachs, Jeffrey D. (1990) "What Is to Be Done?" *The Economist,* January 13, pp. 19–24.

—— (1991) "Crossing the Valley of Tears in East European Reform," *Challenge* **34**(5): 26–34.

—— (1993) *Poland's Jump to the Market Economy.* Cambridge, MA: MIT Press.

—— (1994) "Life in the Economic Emergency Room," in John Williamson, ed., *The Political Economy of Policy Reform.* Washington, DC: Institute for International Economics, pp. 501–23.

Sachs, Jeffrey D., and David A. Lipton (1990) "Poland's Economic Reform," *Foreign Affairs* **63** (3): 47–66.

Sachs, Jeffrey D., and Wing Thye Woo (1994) "Reform in China and Russia," *Economic Policy* **18**: 101–45.

Selyunin, Vasili, and Grigori I. Khanin (1987) "*Lukovaya tsifra*" [Cunning Number], *Novy mir* **63**(2): 181–201.

Shleifer, Andrei, and Daniel Treisman (2000) *Without a Map: Political Tactics and Economic Reform in Russia.* Cambridge, MA: MIT Press.

—— (2004) "A Normal Country," *Foreign Affairs* **83**(2): 20–38.

Shleifer, Andrei, and Robert W. Vishny (1998) *The Grabbing Hand: Government Pathologies and Their Cures.* Cambridge, MA: Harvard University Press.

Shmelev, Nikolai P. (1987) "*Avansy i dolgi*" [Advances and Debts], *Novy mir* **63**(6): 142–58.

Stiglitz, Joseph E. (1999a) "Whither Reform? Ten Years of Transition," presented at the Annual Bank Conference on Development Economics, Washington, DC, April 28–30.

—— (1999b) "*Quis Custociet Ipsos Custodes?* Corporate Governance Failures in the Transition," presented at the Annual Bank Conference on Development Economics—Europe, Paris, June 21–3.

—— (2000) "The Insider: What I Learned at the World Economic Crisis," *New Republic,* April 17 and **24,** pp. 56–60.

—— (2002) *Globalization and Its Discontents.* New York: Norton.

—— (2006) *Making Globalization Work.* New York: Norton.

Transparency International (2010) "Corruption Perceptions Index." Available http://www.transparency.org/policy_research/surveys_indices/cpi/2010 (accessed June 2011).

United Nations Economic Commission for Europe (1990) *Economic Survey of Europe in 1989–1990.* New York: United Nations.

Williamson, John (1990) *Latin American Adjustment: How Much Has Happened?* Washington, DC: Institute for International Economics.

Winiecki, Jan (1991a) *Resistance to Change in the Soviet Economic System.* New York: Routledge.

World Bank (1996a) *World Development Report 1996: From Plan to Market.* Oxford, UK: Oxford University Press.

Yuen Yuen Ang,
How China Escaped the Poverty Trap (2016)*

Introduction: How Did Development *Actually* Happen?

Providence has not created the human race either entirely independent or perfectly slave. It traces, it is true, a fatal circle around each man that he cannot leave; but within its vast limits man is powerful and free; so too with peoples.

— Alexis de Tocqueville, *Democracy in America*

The greatest fever of all was aspiration, a belief in the sheer possibility to remake a life. Some who tried succeeded; many others did not. More remarkable was that they defied a history that told them never to try.

— Evan Osnos, *The Age of Ambition*

Imagine a pauper who turns to two finance gurus for advice. Not only is he broke, this pauper is poorly educated and lives in a rough neighborhood. The first guru urges, "Earn your first paycheck. Once you start making money, your circumstances will improve, and you will eventually escape poverty." The second guru counsels differently: "Start by doing as my rich clients do: attend college, move to a safe town, and buy health insurance. You can only escape poverty by first creating the prerequisites for wealth."

The two gurus mean well, but the advice of both experts clearly falls short. The first guru provides no clue as to how the pauper might earn his first paycheck, much less how to sustain a stable income. Conversely, the second guru ignores the realities of poverty. If the pauper could afford to, he would have obtained the prerequisites for a better life long ago. Attaining such prerequisites is not the solution to poverty; the difficulty of attaining them is itself the problem.

The parable of the pauper and two gurus reflects a fundamental problem of development in the real world. All wealthy capitalist economies feature institutions of good governance, such as protection of private property rights, professional bureaucracies, modern courts, formal accountability, and pluralistic participation, which all seem necessary for successful markets.[1] Yet attaining these preconditions also appears to depend on the level of economic wealth.

So how can poor and weak societies escape poverty traps? Which comes first in development—economic growth or good governance?

Answers have been sharply divided. Modernization theory holds that "growth → good governance." The argument goes that as countries grow rich, a burgeoning middle class will demand greater accountability and protection of individual rights, leading eventually to capitalist democracies.[2] Similarly, others argue that countries succeed in modernizing public administrations and eradicating corruption only after they become sufficiently wealthy.[3]

Mirroring the first guru's shortfall, however, modernization theory does not explain the origins of economic growth. According to the Harrod-Domar model in classical economics, growth comes from capital investments. But how do impoverished countries secure investments? Economist Jeffrey Sachs argues that such investments should come from developed nations in the form of massive foreign aid.[4] He believes that once the Third World economy is jump-started, "all good things" will follow.[5] Yet many studies find the link between foreign aid and prosperity tenuous.[6] Some even contend that foreign aid has actually worsened corruption and brought more harm than good to the poor.[7]

A second widely embraced theory forcefully advances a reverse causal claim: "good governance → growth." International agencies like the World Bank and IMF, joined by many Western policy makers and academics, maintain that it is necessary to "get governance right" before markets can grow.[8] The logic is intuitive. All prosperous economies share a common set of strong, law-bound governmental institutions. Therefore, aspiring developers should first replicate the checklist of best practices found in wealthy democracies. Then, it is expected, growth will naturally blossom from good institutional soil.

Reminiscent of the second guru, however, this paradigm ignores the problem of how poor and weak states can meaningfully attain good governance. The term "meaningfully" deserves emphasis, for it is one thing to adopt the formality of best practices but another to actually implement them.[9] For instance, at the behest of international agencies, some developing countries have built courts and have written laws in books, but they have frequently lacked professional judges to adjudicate disputes, and citizens have routinely distrusted and avoided the legal system even after new laws were promulgated.[10] If achieving good governance were a mere technicality of copying best practices from the developed West, then late developers would have accomplished it long ago. In fact, as Pritchett and Woolcock, two leading voices on international development, lament, the imposition of good governance standards has been "a root cause of the deep problems encountered by developing countries."[11]

Going further, a third school points to history as the underlying cause of good governance or state capacity. This approach may be abbreviated as "history → good governance → growth." Following a path-dependent logic, several scholars posit colonialization as the root of present-day national inequalities.[12] In *Why Nations Fail,* Acemoglu and Robinson trace the stark divide between North and South America to their contrasting colonial legacies.[13] According to them, English colonizers founded settlements of equal opportunity and limited government on North American soil, paving the way for future capitalist success, whereas Spanish conquerors imposed unequal and exploitive structures in Latin America, stunting prosperity over the long term.

Although this third school reminds us of the enduring effects of history, it does not point a way out of poverty traps.[14] Rather, the authors of *Why Nations Fail* conclude that "different patterns of institutions today are deeply rooted in the past because once society gets organized in a particular way, this tends to persist." And they add, "This persistence and the forces that create it also explain why it is so difficult to remove world inequality and to make poor countries prosperous."[15] Their conclusion raises a troubling question: If the seeds of national successes and failures were indeed planted long ago and became rooted over time, what can nations lacking the right history do today?[16]

The observation that many poor nations fail *because* they suffer troubled histories and bad starts is correct, but by itself not particularly surprising. What is harder and more useful, instead, is to explain why some nations succeed *despite* ominous starting points and daunting odds, as witnessed most dramatically in China's rise from a socialist backwater to a global powerhouse since market reforms began in 1978.[17]

This book investigates how China escaped the poverty trap and made the Great Leap from a barren communist political economy into the middle-income, capitalist dynamo that it is today. More broadly, grounded in my analysis of China's metamorphosis, this is a study about how development *actually* happens. Is it really the institutions of good governance so keenly proffered to developing countries today that launch markets? Or is it growth that enables good governance? Or is history destiny?

My answer begins with a simple observation: development *is* a coevolutionary process. States and markets interact and adapt to each other, changing mutually over time. Neither economic growth nor good governance comes first in development. China's experience provides an especially rich illustration of the coevolutionary process of development, but this process is not unique to China. As we shall see by the end of this book, the rise of Western societies, too, actually followed a coevolutionary pattern,[18] as did the astonishing boom of the movie industry in contemporary Nigeria.

Although development as a coevolutionary process is intuitively observed (in my experience, it appears that the less formal training one receives, the more intuitive it is), analyzing mutual changes among many moving parts is far from easy. To this end, I lay out a framework for systematically mapping the coevolution of states and markets. This approach reveals surprising insights into the causal sequence of development and raises new questions about the sources of societal adaptation.

My answers to how China—and poor and weak societies in general—escaped the poverty trap are twofold. The first: build markets *with* weak institutions. My analysis reveals that the institutions, strategies, and state capacities that promote growth vary over the course of development, among countries and even among localities within countries. Even more surprisingly, I show that the practices and features that *defy* norms of good governance—normally viewed as "weak" institutions—are paradoxically the raw materials for *building* markets when none exist. By contrast, the "good" or "strong" institutions found in wealthy economies are institutions that *preserve* existing markets.

The idea that we can harness weak institutions to build markets carries tremendous political and practical import. Perhaps the one thing poor countries possess in abundance are so-called weak institutions. Examples of weak institutions featured in this study include the fusion of public and private interests (vs. bureaucratic professionalism), partial (vs. impartial) regulation, campaign-style (vs. routine) policy implementation, indiscriminate and uncoordinated (vs. selective) industrial promotion policies, incentives for petty fee extractions (vs. eradicating corruption), to name some.[19] Normally, we believe that the way out of poverty traps is to "quickly" replace such weak institutions with strong institutions that define advanced industrialized economies.[20] This book points to a different path. It illuminates the development potential that may lie hidden within apparently weak institutions.

The second answer: create the right conditions for adaptation. History is not destiny. Although past encounters determine starting points, any given legacy may be reshaped for destructive or constructive ends. Instead of attributing national successes and failures only to history or geography,[21] I emphasize instead the efforts of reformers to foster improvisation among ground-level agents, such that they may effectively utilize existing resources to tackle the problems of the poor, and thereby turn the typical *problems* of underdevelopment into the *solutions* to development.

Yet while improvisation is essential to the development process, improvisation does not occur automatically and indeed often fails. Instead of dispensing obvious advice like "avoid mimicry," "promote innovation," and "embrace experimentation," fashionable among some development pundits who invoke adaptive language,[22] I underscore the inherent challenges of achieving these goals. By studying how China tackled these challenges, we'll learn about some actions that may be taken to spur the coevolution of states and markets as well as the effects of particular measures deployed. Also, by unpacking the processes through which China escaped the poverty trap, we will also understand how China arrived at the particular problems that it faces today.

How Did China Escape the Poverty Trap?

Today, with news of China's spectacular rise repeated ad nauseam, it is easy to forget the dire circumstances confronting its reformers following the death of Mao.[23] It is also convenient to attribute China's transformation to the misimpression of a "strong state" or that China was perhaps not so poor at the start of reforms. So a basic reality check is in order.

In 1980 China's GDP per capita was only US$193, lower than that of Bangladesh, Chad, and Malawi,[24] present-day "bottom-billion" countries.[25] In practical terms, an income per capita of US$193 means that average food consumption fell below basic nutritional standards. The Chinese people did not eat more or better food during the 1970s than they had in the 1930s, before the Chinese Communist Party (CCP) took power.[26]

Not only was China abjectly poor, the regime had oscillated between extreme dictatorship and political anarchy. In three decades under Mao's rule, China suffered two major political disasters. The Great Leap Forward (1958–1961) was Mao's frenzied scheme to accelerate economic production by political command, a campaign that culminated in mass starvation and claimed an estimated thirty million lives. Mao then tried to reconsolidate power by unleashing the Cultural Revolution (1966–1976), also nicknamed "ten years of madness."[27] Young red guards loyal to Mao went on a purge against alleged class enemies at all levels of government, including national leaders like Deng Xiaoping. In many official yearbooks, statistics during the period of the Cultural Revolution are missing,[28] for the bureaucracy was so devastated that it literally stopped counting. Mass killings spread to society and descended into what Walder describes as "virtual civil wars."[29] An entire generation of young people was deprived of formal education. Reflecting on the state of anarchy, MacFarquhar and Schoenhals conclude, "For a decade, the Chinese political system was first turned into chaos and then paralyzed."[30]

Granted, China was at least unified under the CCP when Deng and his reformist team took power. Nonetheless, the state apparatus they inherited hardly fit the description of a strong state. Add the fact that China was poorer than bottom-billion countries like Chad, and the starting point in 1978 bode ill.

Now, fast forward thirty-five years. China has become the world's second largest economy, the world's largest exporter, and America's largest foreign creditor. By 2012 China's GDP per capita had jumped thirty-fold from US\$193 to US\$6,091, leaving other bottom-billion countries far in the dust (in Malawi, GDP per capita nudged up by only \$50 in thirty-two years, a typical case of being stuck).[31] Undergirding these impressive growth statistics is a radical restructuring of the economy. China today boasts legions of private firms, Fortune 500 companies, multinational investors, a booming middle class, and capitalist institutions like securities, e-commerce, and corporate governance standards.[32]

Politically, power remains firmly and solely in the hands of the CCP. Yet the absence of multiparty elections does not mean the absence of political change. Inside the dictatorial regime, the bureaucracy has undergone several makeovers that have altered the role of the government, its delivery of public services, and citizens' daily encounters with the state. In particular, although the reform-era bureaucracy remains notorious for corruption,[33] it is equally famous for being adaptive and entrepreneurial. China ranks among the world's most decentralized administrations. Local governments embrace capitalism, advance policy innovations, and compete to produce economic results. Under Mao, the bureaucracy was ossified and doggedly anticapitalist. But, today, as one Chinese official declared with a dash of irony, "Our nation cares about businesses. In fact, I feel that no capitalist state can match our devotion to the capitalist sector."[34]

For mainstream political economists, China's great transformation—both economic and bureaucratic—is intriguing but also troubling.[35] In *Why Nations Fail*, Acemoglu and Robinson struggle to make sense of China's rise. According to them, growth is preconditioned on the establishment of nonextractive and inclusive institutions, essentially, democratic institutions. But even today China is not a democracy. National elections are barred. Members of the judicial and legislative bodies are handpicked by the ruling party. Extractive practices are still rife in parts of China. During the early phase of reforms, there was no formal protection of private property rights.

In defense, Acemoglu and Robinson surmise that sooner or later, China's hypergrowth will run out of steam.[36] Yet even if growth slows, which is expected for any economy that reaches middle-income status, the burning question remains: how did China come *this* amazingly far? Their reply is that "a critical juncture," namely Mao's death, followed by Deng's efforts to build a reform coalition, turned China around. Furthermore, they claim, growth under extractive institutions was possible because an extremely poor country like China had plenty of "catching up" to do. Finally, they sum up: "Some luck is key, because history always unfolds in a contingent way."[37]

Luck, of course, influences any outcome. But assigning three decades of sustained economic and institutional remaking to luck is hardly satisfying. Moreover, all poor countries have ample room for "catching up," so why didn't they catch up the way China did?

Looking beyond luck and easy explanations, specialists of China have proposed a wealth of theories to account for its astonishing turnaround. All of these theories are valid and valuable, but, as we shall see, they form only parts of the grand picture of China's political-economic transformation that has been missing thus far. Let us first review some pieces of the puzzle.

For a start, some credit China's boom to loosened restrictions on capitalism in an economy that possesses basic growth factors, for example, abundant cheap labor and coastal cities poised to export.[38] There is no doubt that inputs like capital and labor are necessary for growth, but to conclude that such factors on their own will produce an economic miracle is like believing that eggs, sugar, and flour will turn into cake if left overnight in a mixing bowl.[39] Especially in a late-developing, communist context, how basic inputs are mobilized and distributed by the state is critical to the rise and shape of markets.

Shifting from economic to political factors, another set of explanations cites changes in bureaucratic incentives as the key to China's growth spurt. Under Deng's reformist agenda, local leaders who delivered prosperity were promoted,[40] and local governments were allowed to retain a sizable share of revenue earned.[41] These changes in incentives, it is argued, sparked local officials nationwide to pursue growth. These incentives, however, did *not* work equally throughout China. It is well-known that while some localities, concentrated on the coast, grew rich and built competent administrations, others remained poor and predatory.[42] These geographically limited theories not only mask wide variation in local outcomes within China, but more significantly, they underplay the role of regional inequalities in China's national reform success. As my study will show, unequal rates of political-economic coevolution across regions served to accelerate early takeoffs on the coast and late takeoffs among inland locales.

Still a third explanation looks to the incremental quality of China's reforms. As is well-known, Chinese reformers rejected the shock therapy approach of the former Soviet Union and instead chose to modify pre-existing institutions on the margins, such as by creating dual-track pricing and a system of hybrid property rights.[43] Some argue that such "second-best" and "transitional" institutional forms are sufficient to stimulate markets in the beginning.[44] Then, as predicted, once markets mature, early institutions "should eventually be replaced by more conventional, best-practice institutions."[45] My book extends this crucial idea that conventionally good institutions may not be necessary for early growth. But whereas the previous literature stopped at asserting that initial institutions "should" eventually be replaced,[46] this study presents historical evidence to identify *when, why,* and *how* institutional replacement occurs.

Yet a fourth body of literature lists various adaptive actions taken by the CCP-state as a cause of "authoritarian resilience" and reform success.[47] Examples include policy experiments,[48] eliciting and incorporation of social feedback,[49] party co-optation of private entrepreneurs,[50] bureaucratic initiatives in generating revenue,[51] and efforts to study the experiences of other countries.[52] This abundant literature describes various adaptive or entrepreneurial actions,[53] but it does not explain *why* China displays such exceptional inventiveness, especially in contrast to many other stagnant postcommunist systems and failed states. Moreover, China's apparent adaptive capacity cannot explain authoritarian resilience because such adaptability itself needs to be explained.

One notable effort to trace the sources of China's adaptability is Heilmann and Perry's *Mao's Invisible Hand*. They propose that post-Mao leaders inherited "guerrilla" norms of flexibility from the CCP's revolutionary past and applied these norms to market reforms.[54] I completely agree that the Maoist legacy has contributed to the current leadership's cache of rhetoric and tools.[55] Still it doesn't explain why reformers were persistently keen to reconfigure various elements, whether from the past or the present, to formulate new solutions and why many of these solutions successfully propelled change. A revolutionary legacy can lead down many paths. And the particular path China has taken—with distinct steps, achievements, and pains—is not neatly dictated by the past.

In short, existing accounts each highlight a different piece of the grand puzzle: basic growth factors, bureaucratic incentives, incremental reforms, historical legacies, and more. Every piece is essential, yet none can explain how the other pieces interacted and aggregated to remake an entire political economy within the span of a single generation.

Nor can existing theories account for three distinct patterns of China's capitalist revolution. First, the changes are *broad*. China's reforms are famously incremental; yet they culminate in a drastic economic and bureaucratic restructuring nationwide. Second, the methods are *bold*. State actors seemed unfazed by the use of extreme and unorthodox methods to achieve goals. Third, local outcomes are *uneven*. Coastal locales like Shanghai and Shenzhen sped ahead, growing markets and modernizing governance ahead of others. In China, national success is coupled with sharp regional inequalities not seen in East Asia or in other large countries like the United States.

Evidently, numerous factors were simultaneously at play in China's great transformation. A dynamic and comprehensive account, however, will have to go further to consider the underlying conditions that allowed multiple factors to interact and coevolve and to explain the distinctively broad, bold, and uneven patterns of change. To draw generalizable lessons from China's unique experiences, we must also answer this question: What is exceptional and not exceptional about the nature of adaptation in China?

Building this new and integrative account of how China escaped the poverty trap requires that we rethink some of the foundations of traditional social science analyses.

Complexity: An Alternative Paradigm

Development is more than a problem of growing from poor to rich. As the scholarship on poverty traps emphasizes,[56] the poor are simultaneously beset by problems of instability, corruption, patrimonialism, and weak policy enforcement that arise from and deepen poverty. No doubt, wealthy nations have their own share of problems too, such as obesity and aging populations, but these are problems that stem from material abundance. Cast more precisely in game theoretic terms, development is a problem of making the transition from one self-reinforcing equilibrium (poverty traps) to another equilibrium (rich and modern), a process that may be termed the Great Leap.

Existing frameworks and tools in social science are extremely useful for answering certain questions where endogeneity (mutual causation) is irrelevant, but they do not take us very far in understanding an inherently interactive and complex process like political-economic development.

Take for instance a state-of-the-art study by North, Wallis, and Weingast, which tries to explain how underdeveloped societies can make the transition to capitalism and modernity. They argue that this process requires several "doorstep conditions," including rule of law among elites and centralized control of the military. Once such doorstep conditions are in place, they hold, it is possible but not inevitable that "a transition proper ensues."[57] Needless to say, we must first arrive at the doorstep before we can step past any door. Although North, Wallis, and Weingast take us one major step back in the causal chain, their conclusion is still critically missing insights into the "incremental changes" that led to the doorstep or,[58] in Krasner's term, "the empty middle."[59]

Then consider the abundance of quantitative analyses that attempt to prove either the modernization theory or good governance as the primary cause of growth.[60] A debate between Kaufmann, Kraay, and Mastruzzi (creators of the Worldwide Governance Indicators or WGI) and political scientists Kurtz and Schrank is especially instructive.[61] Kaufmann and his colleagues have used the WGI, the most widely accepted measure of governance in the world, in many regression analyses to prove that "governance matters, in the sense that there is a strong causal relationship from good governance to better development outcomes."[62] Kurtz and Schrank refute this claim. Running regressions using the same data but with different empirical specifications, they reach the opposite conclusion: "good governance is in all likelihood a consequence, rather than a cause, of economic growth."[63] So who's right and who's wrong?[64]

Both conclusions are partial. The big, commonsense picture is lost in debates about whether growth or good governance comes first in development, as Przeworski acutely underscores in his sweeping review of the literature. He writes, "In the end, the motor of history is endogeneity. From some initial circumstances and under some invariant conditions, wealth, its distribution, and the institutions that allocate factors and distribute incomes are *mutually interdependent* and *evolve together.*"[65]

My book takes the reality of "mutual interdependence" between growth and governance as the starting point and pursues two objectives:

1. Develop an analytic template and data-collection strategy to systematically map the coevolution of states and markets over time and across space.
2. Explore the conditions that allow and foster coevolutionary processes of radical change.

I adopt a paradigm that is different from the one we currently embrace. Our conventional paradigm (meaning the way we view the world) assumes a *complicated*—rather than *complex*—reality. The terms "complicated" and "complex" are often conflated in daily language, but in fact they describe two completely different worlds.[66] In a complicated world, collectives are made up of many separate parts that do not interact and change with one another, of which a toaster is a good example. A toaster is a machine made up of many separate parts. Press a button and it will produce a predictable action: toasted bread pops up. To study complicated worlds, we can parse out the different parts into separate categories of cause and effect and then try to pin down the linear effects of a hypothesized independent variable on a dependent variable. Much of our analyses have proceeded as if social worlds are complicated. In this view of the world, it makes sense to debate whether it is growth that causes good governance or the reverse.

Yet we all know that social worlds are not complicated; they are almost always complex. Complex systems comprise many moving parts that interact with one another and change together, triggering outcomes that cannot be precisely controlled or predicted in advance. Human bodies are an example of complex systems. Political economies, comprising many players, many institutions, and many interactions, are complex.

Traditional assumptions of causality and tools of analysis serve us well when studying complicated worlds, but "using these same tools to understand complex worlds fails," state Miller and Page, two leading theorists of the booming and interdisciplinary field of complex adaptive systems (which I term "complexity"). Why is that? They elaborate with an apt metaphor: "Because it becomes impossible to reduce the system without killing it. The ability to collect and pin to a board all of the insects that live in the garden does little to lend insight into the ecosystem contained therein."[67]

Fortunately, just as we don't always have to kill insects in order to study natural habitats, we don't have to reduce complexity in order to make sense of complex worlds. This book applies some concepts and tools from complexity studies to the political economy of development.[68]

Mapping Coevolution

My first and easier—but not easy—task is to develop a method for *systematically* mapping the coevolution of states and markets. As Pierson observes, "contemporary social scientists typically take a 'snapshot' view of political life."[69] For example, those who follow China may be inclined to draw conclusions from the most current events. The present, however, gives only a temporally limited view. Hence Pierson urges researchers to "shift from snapshots to moving pictures" by " *systematically* situating particular moments (including the present) in a temporal sequence."[70] My work extends this emphasis on time, and I seek to enrich this agenda by adding several new dimensions.

Without going into methodological details that will later be elaborated, here is a sketch of my approach. (1) I select two institutions or domains of activities (e.g., markets and bureaucratic functions, markets and state development strategies). (2) I specify the significant time periods of analysis, since we cannot obviously regress infinitely to the starting point of human development. In the case of China, the year of 1978, the official launch of market reforms, is a clear place to start. (3) I collect data to track the institutional traits of each domain studied. For example, to trace the market conditions of a city, I examine not only quantitative but also qualitative patterns, such as industrial makeup and the focus of economic reforms, at each significant time period.[71] My approach of recording state and market features over time generates a qualitative panel dataset for each case (observations of multiple dimensions repeated over time), rather than cross-sectional snapshots of several cases. (4) My final step is to locate and trace evidence of mutual feedbacks, where relevant, among the domains of concern in each case.

In examining mutual feedbacks, I focus on three signature mechanisms of coevolution:[72]

1. *Variation*: generation of alternatives
2. *Selection*: selection among and assembly of alternatives to form new combinations
3. *Niche creation*: crafting of distinct and valuable roles among heterogeneous units within a system

Each of these mechanisms raises concrete questions that guide our mapping of coevolutionary paths, as follows. *Variation*: Were new options and strategies being produced, and by whom? *Selection*: What shaped the motivation for selection at a given juncture? Was an adaptive choice retained or abandoned for a new selection, and why? *Niche creation*: Was a unit in question trying to differentiate from other members of the system or blindly replicating the strategies of others? Are their roles competitive or complementary? By attending to these signature mechanisms, we have a grounded basis for examining whether—and *exactly* how—states and markets coevolve.

One key distinction between my approach and the seminal work of Thelen, Mahoney, and other historical institutionalists on "institutional evolution" and "gradual institutional change" is my focus on mapping sequences of mutual adaptations.[73] I start with a precise understanding of evolution as an *adaptive* process that occurs through the mechanisms outlined above. As Holland, another leading complexity theorist, defines, adaptation is the process by which an agent "fits itself to its environment," including other agents.[74] A process of gradual change may *not* involve adaptation. For example, aging occurs gradually, but it is not the result of our adaptive responses to the environment. Nor are evolutionary processes always slow-moving;[75] microcosms can adapt and evolve within minutes. My analysis examines the processes of mutual adaptation—coevolution—among two or more populations or institutional domains in political economies, a process that is *not* synonymous with gradual or slow changes.

My empirical approach generates multiple snapshots of reciprocal feedbacks between states and markets. When these snapshots are strung in sequence, it reveals a causal logic that integrates and yet departs sharply from the conclusions of conventional theories. To get a feel for what I mean, consider five snapshots taken from my historical study of one coastal county in China,[76] reviewed in reverse order from its most current status.

Snapshot 1: Around 2002, the county government planned the construction of a central business district (CBD) and relocated businesses into state-designated zones. This forceful effort paved the way for an unprecedented economic boom.

For proponents of the developmental state, this snapshot illustrates the indispensable role of strong and autonomous states in accelerating growth among late-developing economies.[77]

Snapshot 2: During the late 1990s, as local industries flourished and the county became congested and chaotic, there was an increasing demand for urban zoning.

Now we learn that county officials initiated an aggressive zoning program in response to an earlier economic contingency and bottom-up demand for state interventions to address the problem, not because autonomous state planners came up with the initiative on their own.[78]

Snapshot 3: Between 1993 and 1995, collectively owned enterprises were privatized en masse. The state, at that time, limited its role to facilitating the creation of private property rights. It did not pick winners (favor some industries over others) nor had it conceived the idea of constructing a CBD.

This evidence would cheer the proponents of good governance, who advocate limited government and private property rights protection.[79] Looking at this snapshot in isolation, we would mistakenly conclude that the developmental state school was proven wrong.

Snapshot 4: Prior to 1993, the county achieved an initial growth spurt, but the expansion of existing collective enterprises were constrained by vestiges of state control and the lack of clear private property rights.

Again, proponents of good governance would cheer. Even prior to privatization, though, industrial production had already grown at a phenomenal rate (thirty-three-fold since 1978!), which disproves their assumption that private property rights are necessary for growth.

Snapshot 5: From 1978 onward, the county promoted the establishment of collectively owned township and village enterprises (TVEs), which sparked rural industrialization and early growth.

This snapshot illustrates that early growth can occur in the absence of private property rights and that "small initial changes can have a large impact."[80] With the benefit of hindsight, however, we know that such "small initial changes" were soon replaced by new institutions and development strategies.

So, depending on when (which year) and where (coastal or inland) we look in China, there is evidence for a whole variety of competing explanations for successful reforms: developmental vs. minimalist states, private vs. collective property rights, orthodox vs. unorthodox institutions.

What happens if we string the five snapshots in sequence, starting from 1978? Generically expressed, we obtain this causal sequence of *mutual feedbacks*: Preexisting "weak" institutions (e.g., communes rather than private individuals and centralized states as political units)[81] → creatively adapted to build markets (e.g., creation of hybrid enterprises based on collective property rights) → market emerges → generates new pressures and resources for institutional change → market consolidates → generates new pressures and resources for institutional change again → market takes off and matures.[82]

Compressing the causal chain above, we arrive at a succinct three-step formula:

harness weak institutions to build markets → emerging markets stimulate strong institutions → strong institutions preserve markets.

Although the particulars vary wildly from case to case, this is the long-term pattern of political-economic coevolution that I find at the national and subnational levels in China. And as I will explore in the concluding chapter, such a pattern also emerges in the expansion of trade in late medieval Europe, the revolution of public finance in the antebellum United States, and the flourishing of Nollywood in contemporary Nigeria. To be clear, the causal pattern that emerges from my analyses does not suggest a teleological process that converges at the same end point. As is already well-known, even among advanced economies, good governance and strong institutions do not function and look the same.[83]

Rather, the value of extracting a coevolutionary causal chain lies in making clear what the study of development has critically missed. The third step of "strong institutions preserve markets" has been firmly established by the work of North,[84] North and Weingast,[85] Weingast,[86] and Acemoglu and Robinson,[87] among other leading political economists. The second step of "markets stimulate strong institutions" constitutes the domain of modernization theory.[88]

By comparison, with few exceptions,[89] we know woefully little about the *first* step of the causal chain: build markets *with* weak institutions. Even less is known about how these three essential steps connect in sequence. These are the gaps I seek to fill through a coevolutionary approach to development.

Fostering Adaptation

Mapping the coevolution of states and markets is the easier part of the book. Addressing the harder question comes next: What are the conditions that enable a continuously adaptive process of coevolution? Do these conditions result from exogenous forces or can they be created? In his thought-provoking book *Understanding the Process of Economic Change*, Douglass North raises a similar question: "It is not sufficient to describe societal change; rather we must attempt to find the underlying forces shaping the process of change."[90] He dubs these underlying forces "adaptive efficiency." In his words, "Put simply the richer the artifactual structure the more likely are we to confront novel problems successfully. That is what is meant by adaptive efficiency; creating the necessary artifactual structure is an essential goal of public policy."[91]

What does this "necessary artifactual structure" look like? And how can we go about creating it? North proposes a causal link between individual beliefs at the cognitive level and adaptive efficiency at the societal level, but he does not indicate how we can bridge the overwhelming gap between the extremely micro and the extremely macro levels. Nevertheless, North's probing ruminations clearly indicate that the quest for understanding the underlying sources of adaptive efficiency is not wishful thinking. It marks the next frontier of development theories and practices, waiting to be explored.

To embark on a new intellectual journey to explore the creation of adaptive efficiency, we must find a different guide. Axelrod and Cohen's *Harnessing Complexity* provides an especially useful and concrete framework. Two founding thinkers of complexity, Axelrod and Cohen begin with the observation that adaptation is "both promising and problematic."[92] Not everyone would immediately agree with this observation. Normally we are inclined to think about adaptation itself as the solution to all problems. Thus popular literature readily invokes buzzwords from complexity and adaptation to accessorize slogans: "Embrace experimentation! Muddle through purposively! Promote innovation! Celebrate diverse solutions! And above all, don't fear change!"

Although adaptation is universally desirable, people often fail to adapt, and even if they try they may still fail. Experimentation and muddling through may not produce useful solutions or indeed any solution. Bottom-up participation may degenerate into shouting matches and gridlock, as is sometimes seen in democratic settings. And if promoting innovation were easy, then we would all have done it long ago, and all our problems would have been magically solved. Obviously it is easier said than done to adapt and to adapt effectively.

What precisely are some obstacles against effective adaptation? And what can we do about them? Drawing on the complexity paradigm, this book highlights three universal problems of adaptation, grouped into the themes of variation, selection, and niche creation. Interpreted in the context of reform China, these problems manifest as follows.

> *Variation*: Central reformers want local agents to flexibly implement central mandates according to local conditions. But too much leeway may generate chaos. So one enduring problem in China's policy making and implementation is how to strike a balance between flexibility and conformity, variety and uniformity.

> *Selection*: How agents adapt to particular situations is shaped by their criteria of success. In the corporate sector, success is defined by financial performance, so corporate agents adapt to make profits. Governments, on the other hand, typically have to cater to multiple and even conflicting goals and demands.[93] So how does the CCP state clearly define and reward success in the bureaucracy?

> *Niche creation*: Diversity provides raw material for innovation and allows for niche creation.[94] In China, however, the sheer diversity of conditions across regions also leads to huge disparities that may impede national economic progress and foment political discontent. This generates a third problem of how regional diversity may be turned from a liability into a collective advantage.

China is not exceptional in the adaptive problems it faced; rather it is unique in the way it tackled these problems. Each of the remaining chapters in the book will be devoted to examining how the Chinese state, national and local, responded to the three adaptive problems named above.

Through this analysis, we will arrive at a dynamic picture of how China escaped the poverty trap. We will also understand why its transformative process has displayed three distinct patterns: systemic changes despite incremental reforms (broad), unusually entrepreneurial but also corruption-prone bureaucrats (bold), and wide regional disparities coexisting with national prosperity (uneven).

The Argument in Brief

Authors are often asked to give a one-line summary of their argument. Here is mine: Poor and weak countries can escape the poverty trap by first building markets with weak institutions and, more fundamentally, by crafting environments that facilitate improvisation among the relevant players.

It is tempting to search for a single "model"—a package of particular institutions and policies—that can be replicated across all contexts and believed to produce equal success. If such a model were to exist, it would be delightfully convenient. But this is a search for a mirage. In fact, whether in the capitalist-democratic West, the East Asian developmental states, or China at different periods of reform, no particular solution is universally effective or ideal. Particular solutions work only when they *fit* the needs and resources of particular contexts and the success criteria of the players involved.

Instead of aspiring to copy the exact actions taken by others, what is fundamentally needed for development are conditions that spur a productive and sustained search for solutions that fit different and evolving environments. Stated in North's terms, such conditions are "the necessary artifactual structure" that enables economic and political agents to "confront novel problems successfully."[95] And as Axelrod and Cohen emphasize, this process of confronting novel problems may produce endless possible solutions, "even without knowing in advance just what will change, or just what will be learned."[96]

China escaped the poverty trap by constructing a set of underlying conditions that fostered an adaptive, bottom-up search *within* the state for localized solutions. As China is a late-developing, single-party authoritarian regime, the state plays an oversized role in shaping adaptive processes and outcomes. Condensing various elements of its adaptive approach into a pithy maxim, I call it *directed improvisation*. Central reformers direct; local state agents improvise. The center does not direct by precisely dictating what local agents must do. Instead, it directs by tackling the problems of adaptation earlier outlined: authorizing yet delimiting the boundaries of localization (variation), clearly defining and rewarding bureaucratic success (selection), and encouraging mutual exchanges between highly unequal regions (niche creation). Within these centrally drawn parameters, local authorities improvise a variety of solutions to locally specific and ever-changing problems. It is this paradoxical mixture of top-down direction and bottom-up improvisation that lays the foundation for coevolutionary processes of radical change.

In other words, generalizable from China's market reforms are insights into the process of building markets with weak institutions and the strategies of directing improvisation, not the particular solutions that were improvised to solve particular problems at various times and places. Furthermore, such lessons need not apply only narrowly to other countries. Numerous organizations and groups share similar challenges of improvising with existing resources and making adaptation work.[97]

Notes

1 Different disciplines employ different but overlapping terms in reference to the quality of governance and institutions. Most economists adopt the term "institutions," defined by North as "rules of the game" that structure social behavior (North 1990). Three common measures of institutions used by economists are "risk of expropriation by the government, government effectiveness, and constraints on the executive" (Glaeser et al. 2004, 273), which are all measures of governance. The term "good governance" has been widely used in the policy and aid community (Grindle 2004; IMF 1997; Jomo and Chowdhury 2012b). Invoking Douglass North's seminal work, the creators of the Worldwide Governance Indicators (WGI) at the World Bank define good governance as "norms of limited government that protect private property from predation by the state" (Kaufmann, Kraay, and Mastruzzi 2007a, 555). The WGI measures six dimensions of governance: voice and accountability, political stability, government effectiveness, regulatory quality, rule of law, and control of corruption. Political scientists and sociologists refer more commonly to state capacity and stress the ability of governments to actualize goals (Evans, Rueschemeyer, and Skocpol 1985; Migdal, Kohli, and Shue 1994). A recent volume, *States in the Developing World,* defines state capacity as "the organizational and bureaucratic ability to implement governing projects" (Centeno, Kohli, and Yashar, forthcoming). Some political scientists disagree that limited government defines good governance (Kurtz and Schrank 2007a, 2007b). Yet regardless of the different terms used and disagreements about definition, the general consensus is that the institutions found among successfully developed economies are a universal benchmark of good or strong institutions, also widely believed to be necessary for economic growth.

2 Boix and Stokes 2003; Inglehart and Welzel 2005; Lipset 1959.

3 For a case study, see Goldsmith 2012. For quantitative studies, see Glaeser et al. 2004; Kurtz and Schrank 2007b.

4 Sachs 2005; Sachs et al. 2004.

5 Sachs 2005, 73.

6 Burnside and Dollar 2000.

7 Deaton 2013; Easterly 2006b; Hubbard and Duggan 2009.

8 IMF 1997; 1998, 39–42; World Bank 1992, 1994, 2002b.

9 The belief that growth is preconditioned on good governance has provided strong rationale for conditional aid. As Collier sharply points out, however, "Conditionality turned out to be a paper tiger: governments discovered they only needed to *promise* to reform, not actually do it" (2007, 67). See also Pritchett and de Weijer 2011; Riggs 1964.

10 Andrews 2013, 35; Hendley 1999; Jensen 2003.

11 Pritchett and Woolcock 2004, 193. For similar views, see Riggs 1964; Fukuyama 2004; Lansing 2006; Rodrik 2007; Pritchett and de Weijer 2011; Andrews 2013.

12 Acemoglu, Johnson, and Robinson 2002; Handley 2008; Kohli 2004; Lange 2009; Mahoney 2010. Also see arguments about the long-lasting effects of state formation moments on economic and political outcomes (Levitsky and Murillo 2013; Vu 2010).

13 Acemoglu and Robinson 2012. For an earlier articulation, see Sokoloff and Engerman 2000.

14 See Przeworski's critique of the deterministic overtones of path-dependent arguments in a review of the literature. As he observes, "Indeed, I cannot find an explicit specification of alternative paths in any of the institutionalist writings" (2004, 172).

15 Acemoglu and Robinson 2012, 44.

16 Acemoglu and Robinson assert that countries can "break the mold" by "*quickly* developing inclusive economic and political institutions" (2012, 409–410, italics added), citing the

case of postindependence Botswana, one of the few sub-Saharan African countries that are thriving today. Pushing their logic back one step, the obvious question is: why could Botswana "quickly" achieve good governance while many others could not? The authors reply, "Botswana *already* had tribal institutions that had achieved some amount of centralized authority and contained important pluralistic features" (413, italics added). They further compare this tribal system to the Magna Carta, a celebrated agreement of limited government between King John and the barons of England in the thirteenth century (407). So we are rerouted back to the original problem: if nations don't *already* have prototypes of good institutions like the Magna Carta, then how can they *quickly* develop good institutions in order to achieve economic success? Clearly, according to the logic of Acemoglu and Robinson, absent a long history of good institutions, poverty and weak governance will persist. And this, as the title of their book declares, is "why nations fail."

17 China's policy of "reform and opening" (*gaige kaifang*) was officially inaugurated under Deng's leadership at the Third Plenum held in December of 1978.

18 Also, see work by John Padgett and his collaborators for extraordinarily intricate accounts of the coevolution of political and economic networks during various periods of European history (Padgett and McLean 2011; Padgett and Powell 2012). Similarly, in an incisive historical analysis, Chang (2002) argues that developed countries did not in fact use "good" policies and institutions when they were in the process of developing. And as Ginsburg (2015), a legal scholar, points out, even the Magna Carta, popularly revered as an exemplary liberal institution, was in fact "a failure," "hardly constrained the monarch," and limited the rights of women and minorities.

19 More examples include personal patron-client ties, communal affiliations, rampant piracy, profit-oriented rather than service-oriented public administration, and taxless public finance (paying for public projects without formal taxation or transparent rules of public borrowing).

20 Acemoglu and Robinson recommend that the way to escape vicious cycles is by "*quickly* developing inclusive economic and political institutions" (2012, 409–410, italics added).

21 See Diamond (2005) on geography as the "ultimate" cause of divergence in human development.

22 Owen Barder, "The Implications of Complexity for Development," Kapuscinski Lecture, May 2012, http://www.owen.org/blog/5723.

23 Furthermore, prior to the establishment of the People's Republic of China in 1949, China had suffered more than a century of dynastic decline, foreign invasion, civil war, and famines (Schell and Delury 2013).

24 In 1980, measured by current U.S. dollars, China's GDP per capita was equivalent to Malawi's and only about 88 percent of Chad's and Bangladesh's. World Bank Database, http://data.worldbank.org/indicator/.

25 The "bottom billion" refers to the world's poorest countries (Collier 2007).

26 Brandt and Rawski 2008, 5; Lardy 1983, 148.

27 Feng 1996.

28 One example is the Organizational History Statistics (*zuzhishi ziliao*), an authoritative statistical source compiled by the Central Organization Department on the size of public employment.

29 Walder 2009, 1. See also Su 2011.

30 MacFarquhar and Schoenhals 2006, 2.

31 World Bank database, http://data.worldbank.org/indicator/.

32 Whether these institutions work like they do in the capitalist West is a different matter; the dramatic structural transformation of the economic system since 1978 is beyond doubt.

33 Manion 2004; Wedeman 2012.

34 Fujian city official, interview (REG-2012–020). To maintain the anonymity of my respondents, I do not identify their names or particular location. Instead, I identify the interviewees by the year in which the first interview was conducted, followed by an ID. For more on my coverage of interviews and citation protocol, see appendix B.

35 Also, in contradiction to Sachs's policy advice, China did not escape the poverty trap through massive foreign assistance.

36 Naysayer predictions about China's imminent collapse have long been made by others (Chang 2001; Pei 2006).

37 Acemoglu and Robinson 2012, 423, 440, 427.

38 See Woo 1999. For a similar argument in the context of East Asia, see Krugman 1994.

39 It would be equally simplistic to attribute China's turnaround solely to high investments. As Barry Naughton, an expert on the Chinese economy, explained, "High investment rates 'cause' economic growth, in a mechanical sense, but are also themselves a symptom of productivity improvements that are the ultimate source of economic growth" (2007, 148). Such "productivity improvements" were highly dependent on state policies and institutions. Moreover, whereas high investment rates during the socialist period reflected almost only state investments, investment decisions during the reform period were made by households, businesses, and government in response to "new areas in the dynamic Chinese economy" (Naughton 2015, 114).

40 Landry 2008; H. Li and Zhou 2005; Maskin, Qian, and Xu 2000.

41 Montinola, Qian, and Weingast 1995; Oi 1992, 1999; Walder 1995; Whiting 2001.

42 As Tsai observed, "Within a single province, evidence can be mustered for market preserving federalism, local state corporatism, and even klepto-patrimonialism" (2004, 18). See also Baum and Shevchenko 1999; Bernstein & Lü 2003.

43 Coase and Wang 2012; Lin, Cai, and Li 2003; Naughton 1995; Oi and Walder 1999; Rawski 1995; Shirk 1993.

44 Hausmann, Pritchett, and Rodrik 2005; Oi and Walder 1999; Qian 2003; Rodrik 2008.

45 Qian 2003, 323.

46 Also, this literature does not notice that so-called transitional institutions worked better in some parts of China than others and were replaced at different times. In chapters 1 and 6, I show and explain why the rate of institutional replacement varied across regions.

47 The term "authoritarian resilience" was coined by Nathan 2003.

48 Florini, Lai, and Tan, 2012; Gallagher 2005; Heilmann 2008.

49 Dimitrov 2013a; Mertha 2008; Nathan 2003; Tsai 2007.

50 Dickson 2008; Tsai 2007.

51 Duckett 2001; Lee 2014; Stockmann 2012.

52 Shambaugh 2008.

53 For recent edited volumes on adaptive governance and innovation in China, see Dimitrov 2013b; Heilmann and Perry 2011b; Teets and Hurst 2015; Naughton and Tsai 2015.

54 Heilmann and Perry 2011a.

55 In particular, see Perry's (2011) insightful discussion of the reconfiguration of Maoist campaigns for present-day economic policy implementation, which I find similar to the phenomenon of en masse investment recruitment by local agencies (more in chapter 1).

56 The literature on poverty traps is large enough to constitute an entire subfield. For a review, see Bowles, Durlauf, and Hoff 2006.

57 North, Wallis, and Weingast 2009, 26.

58 Ibid., 167.

59 Krasner 2014.

60 There had been efforts to introduce alternative regression models to capture highly inter-active, nonlinear relationships (for example, in international conflict, see Beck, King, and Zeng [2000]), but such models have not generally entered mainstream analyses and graduate training. Statistical (or machine) learning offers a promising array of new tools for modeling nonparametric relationships. This book seeks to provide a qualitative-historical foundation for studying complex interactions and reciprocal causation on a macro level that would complement the micro tools of statistical learning.

61 This is a series of essays published in *The Journal of Politics* (Kaufmann, Kraay, and Mastruzzi 2007a, 2007b; Kurtz and Schrank 2007a, 2007b). For another debate, see Kaufmann and Kraay 2002; Lora 2002; Pritchett 2002.

62 Kaufmann, Kraay, and Zoido-Lobatón 1999, 1. For other econometric analyses offering evidence that good governance or institutions cause growth, see Acemoglu, Johnson, and Robinson 2002; Kaufmann and Kraay 2002; Kaufmann, Kraay, and Mastruzzi 2007b; Knack and Keefer, 1995; Mauro 1995; Rodrik, Subramanian, and Trebbi 2004.

63 Kurtz and Schrank 2007b, 540.

64 Kaufmann, Kraay, and Mastruzzi rebut by faulting their critics for not complying with "the best-practice frontier" in growth empirics (2007a, 555). Tellingly, their rebuttal was focused on the technicalities of regression analysis rather than the process of political-economic change. Despite acknowledging that growth regressions are "intrinsically dynamic," feedbacks between growth and governance were treated as an endogeneity problem that could be statistically fixed (2007a, 561).

65 Przeworski 2004, 185, emphasis added.

66 Axelrod and Cohen 1999, 7–15; Page 2011, 7.

67 Miller and Page 2007, 10.

68 Introductory guides to complex adaptive systems include Axelrod and Cohen 1999; Holland 1996; Miller and Page 2007; Mitchell 2009. The Santa Fe Institute is a center dedicated to the study of complexity.

69 Pierson 2004, 2; see also Hall 2003.

70 Pierson 2004, 2.

71 Fine-grained insights into actual practices and structural patterns are not conveniently recorded in available datasets. Thus my study relies heavily on interviews with more than four hundred veteran bureaucrats and businesses and in-depth fieldwork in selected local-ities that cover coastal, central, and western regions.

72 Axelrod and Cohen 1999; Holland 1996; Ostrom and Basurto 2011. Yet another mechanism of coevolution is retention, namely, propagation and abandonment of previous selections. Retention will feature prominently in my micro-level analyses of coevolutionary paths (in particular, see chapters 1, 5 and 6). Retention, however, is set aside in my current exam-ination of meta-institutions that structure adaptive processes. Instead, this book focuses on the meta-institutions that influence the processes of variation (chapter 3), selection (chapter 4), and niche creation (chapters 5 and 6). I discuss the conditions that influence the retention and replacement of initial selections in a separate work.

73 Mahoney and Thelen 2015; Mahoney and Thelen 2010; Streeck and Thelen 2005; Thelen 2004.

74 Holland 1996, 9. In complexity terms, an agent "has the ability to interact with its envir-onment, including other agents" (Axelrod and Cohen 1999, 4). Thus, a cog in a machine is not an agent, but a human is an agent. Organizations and communities may be considered populations of agents.

75 Pierson 2004, 82.

76 This is Blessed County from Zhejiang Province, which is featured in chapter 6.

77　Amsden 1989; Evans 1995; Johnson 1982; Wade 1990; Woo-Cumings 1999.

78　In *Bringing the State Back In,* Evans, Rueschemeyer, and Skocpol highlight state autonomy as essential to state capacity. By autonomous states, they mean "collectivities of career officials . . . [who] are likely to launch distinctive new state strategies in times of crisis" (1985, 9). In this instance of the Chinese county, however, state actors did not respond to an externally imposed crisis, but rather to an endogenous consequence of their earlier development strategies.

79　Kaufmann, Kraay, and Mastruzzi 2007b; Kaufmann, Kraay, and Zoido-Lobatón 1999.

80　Oi & Walder 1999, 24.

81　This use of communal affiliations to create property rights finds striking parallels with the case of medieval Europe, as originally documented by Greif (2006a) and which I discuss in chapter 7.

82　To clarify, this instance does not indicate that coevolutionary processes must start with communal institutions and end with activist state interventions. The particular contents of each step are unique to each place. What is generalizable is the pattern of mutual causation that emerges from the particulars.

83　Aoki 2010; Hall and Soskice 2001.

84　North 1990.

85　North and Weingast 1989.

86　Weingast 1995.

87　Acemoglu and Robinson 2012.

88　Inglehart and Welzel 2005.

89　One notable exception is the literature on various measures of partial market reforms in China prior to 1993.

90　North 2005, 13.

91　Ibid., 70.

92　Axelrod and Cohen 1999, xiv.

93　This is apparent from a common saying in politics: "You can't please everyone." See, for example, "In Challenger, a Chastening for Emanuel," *New York Times,* Feb. 25, 2015.

94　Page 2011.

95　North 2005, 70.

96　Axelrod and Cohen 1999, 114.

97　On the challenges of localizing foreign aid, see Ang 2014b.

References

Acemoglu, Daron, Johnson, Simon, and Robinson, James. 2002. Reversal of fortune: Geography and institutions in the making of the modern world income distribution. *Quarterly Journal of Economics, 117*(4), 1231–1294.

Acemoglu, Daron, and Robinson, James.. 2012. *Why nations fail: The origins of power, prosperity and poverty.* New York: Crown Publishers.

Amsden, Alice H. 1989. *Asia's next giant: South Korea and late industrialization.* New York: Oxford University Press.

Andrews, Matt. 2013. *The limits of institutional reform in development: Changing rules for realistic solutions.* Cambridge: Cambridge University Press.

Ang, Yuen Yuen. 2014b. Making details matter: How to reform aid agencies to generate contextual knowledge. Winning Essay of the GDN Essay Competition on The Future of Development Assistance, available on the website of Global Development Network.

Aoki, Masahiko. 2010. *Corporations in evolving diversity: Cognition, governance, and institutions.* Oxford: Oxford University Press.

Axelrod, Robert M., and Cohen, Michael D. 1999. *Harnessing complexity: Organizational implications of a scientific frontier.* New York: Free Press.

Baum, Richard, and Shevchenko, Alexei. 1999. The "state of the state." In M. Goldman and R. MacFarquhar (Eds.), *The paradox of China's post-Mao reforms.* Cambridge, Mass.: Harvard University Press.

Beck, Nathaniel, King, Gary, and Zeng, Langche. 2000. Improving quantitative studies of international conflict: A conjecture. *American Political Science Review, 94*(1), 21–35.

Bernstein, Thomas P., and Lü, Xiaobo. 2003. *Taxation without representation in rural China.* Cambridge: Cambridge University Press.

Boix, Carles, and Stokes, Susan C. 2003. Endogenous democratization. *World Politics, 55*(4), 517–549.

Bowles, Samuel, Durlauf, Steven, and Hoff, Karla Ruth. 2006. *Poverty traps.* Princeton, N.J.: Princeton University Press.

Brandt, Loren, and Rawski, Thomas G. 2008. *China's great economic transformation.* Cambridge: Cambridge University Press.

Burnside, Craig, and Dollar, David. 2000. Aid, policies, and growth. *The American Economic Review, 90*(4), 847–868.

Centeno, Miguel, Kohli, Atul, and Yashar, Deborah. Forthcoming. States in the developing world: Cambridge: Cambridge University Press.

Chang, Gordon. 2001. *The coming collapse of China.* New York: Random House.

Chang, Ha-Joon. 2002. *Kicking away the ladder: Development strategy in historical perspective.* London: Anthem.

Coase, Ronald, and Wang, Ning. 2012. *How China became capitalist.* Houndmills, Basingstoke: Palgrave Macmillan.

Collier, Paul. 2007. *The bottom billion: Why the poorest countries are failing and what can be done about it.* Oxford: Oxford University Press.

Deaton, Angus. 2013. *The great escape: Health, wealth, and the origins of inequality.* Princeton, N.J.: Princeton University Press.

Diamond, Jared M. 2005. *Guns, germs, and steel: The fates of human societies.* New York: Norton.

Dickson, Bruce J. 2008. *Wealth into power: The Communist Party's embrace of China's private sector.* Cambridge: Cambridge University Press.

Dimitrov, Martin. 2013a. Vertical accountability in communist regimes: The role of citizen complaints in Bulgaria and China. In M. Dimitrov (Ed.), *Why communism did not collapse.* New York: Cambridge University Press.

———. 2013b. *Why communism did not collapse: Understanding authoritarian regime resilience in Asia and Europe.* New York: Cambridge University Press.

Duckett, Jane. 2001. Bureaucrats in business, Chinese-style: The lessons of market reform and state entrepreneurialism in the People's Republic of China. *World Development, 29*(1), 23–37.

Easterly, William. 2006b. *The white man's burden: Why the West's efforts to aid the rest have done so much ill and so little good.* New York: Penguin Press.

Evans, Peter. 1995. *Embedded autonomy: States and industrial transformation.* Princeton, N.J.: Princeton University Press.

Evans, Peter, Rueschemeyer, Dietrich, and Skocpol, Theda. 1985. *Bringing the state back in.* Cambridge: Cambridge University Press.

Feng, Jicai. 1996. *Ten years of madness: Oral histories of China's Cultural Revolution.* San Francisco: China Books and Periodicals.

Florini, Ann, Lai, Hairong, and Tan, Yeling. 2012. *China experiments: From local innovations to national reform.* Washington, D.C.: Brookings Institution Press.

Fukuyama, Francis. 2004. *State-building: Governance and world order in the 21st century.* Ithaca, N.Y.: Cornell University Press.

Gallagher, Mary. 2005. *Contagious capitalism: Globalization and the politics of labor in China.* Princeton, N.J.: Princeton University Press.

Ginsburg, Tom. 2015. Stop revering Magna Carta. *The New York Times,* June 14.

Glaeser, Edward, La Porta, Rafael, Lopez-De-Silanes, Florencio, and Shleifer, Andrei. 2004. Do institutions cause growth? *Journal of Economic Growth, 9*(3), 271–303.

Greif, Avner. 2006a. History lessons: The birth of impersonal exchange: The community responsibility system and impartial justice. *The Journal of Economic Perspectives, 20*(2), 221–236.

Grindle, Merilee. 2004. Good enough governance: Poverty reduction and reform in developing countries. *Governance, 17*(4), 525–548.

Hall, Peter. 2003. Aligning ontology and methodology in comparative research. In J. Mahoney and D. Rueschemeyer (Eds.), *Comparative historical analysis in the social sciences.* New York: Cambridge University Press.

Hall, Peter, and Soskice, David. 2001. *Varieties of capitalism: The institutional foundations of comparative advantage.* Oxford: Oxford University Press.

Handley, Antoinette. 2008. *Business and the state in Africa: Economic policy-making in the neo-liberal era.* Cambridge: Cambridge University Press.

Hausmann, Ricardo, Pritchett, Lant, and Rodrik, Dani. 2005. Growth accelerations. *Journal of Economic Growth, 10*(4), 303–329.

Heilmann, Sebastian. 2008. From local experiments to national policy: The origins of China's distinctive policy process. *China Journal, 59*(59), 1–30.

Heilmann, Sebastian, and Perry, Elizabeth. 2011a. Embracing uncertainty: Guerilla policy style and adaptive governance in China. In S. Heilmann and E. Perry (Eds.), *Mao's invisible hand: The political foundations of adaptive governance in China.* Cambridge, Mass: Harvard University Press.

Heilmann, Sebastian, and Perry, Elizabeth.——. 2011b. *Mao's invisible hand: The political foundations of adaptive governance in China.* Cambridge, Mass: Harvard University Press.

Hendley, Kathryn. 1999. Rewriting the rules of the game in Russia: The neglected issue of demand for law. *East European Constitutional Review, 8*(4), 89–95.

Holland, John H. 1996. *Hidden order: How adaptation builds complexity.* Cambridge, Mass.: Perseus Books.

Hubbard, R. Glenn, and Duggan, William R. 2009. *The aid trap: Hard truths about ending poverty.* New York: Columbia Business School Pub.

IMF (International Monetary Fund). 1997. *Good governance: The IMF's role.* Washington, D.C.: IMF.

———. 1998. *Annual report 1998.* Washington, D.C.: IMF.

Inglehart, Ronald, and Welzel, Christian. 2005. *Modernization, cultural change, and democracy: The human development sequence.* Cambridge: Cambridge University Press.

Jensen, Erik G. 2003. The rule of law and judicial reform: The political economy of diverse institutional patterns and reformers' responses. In E. G. Jensen and T. C. Heller (Eds.), *Beyond common knowledge: Empirical approaches to the rule of law.* Stanford, Calif.: Stanford University Press.

Johnson, Chalmers. 1982. *MITI and the Japanese miracle: The growth of industrial policy, 1925–1975.* Stanford, Calif.: Stanford University Press.

Jomo, K. S., and Chowdhury, Anis. 2012b. *Is good governance good for development?* London: Bloomsbury Academic. Published in association with the United Nations.

Kaufmann, Daniel, and Kraay, Aart. 2002. Growth without governance. *Economia: Journal of the Latin American and Caribbean Economic Association, 3*(1), 169–229.

Kaufmann, Daniel, Kraay, Aart, and Mastruzzi, Massimo. 2007a. Growth and governance: A reply. *The Journal of Politics, 69*(2), 555–562.

———. 2007b. Growth and governance: A rejoinder. *The Journal of Politics, 69*(2), 570–572.

Kaufmann, Daniel, Kraay, Aart, and Zoido-Lobatón, Pablo. 1999. Governance matters. World Bank Policy Research Working Paper 2196. http://info.worldbank.org/governance/wgi/pdf/govmatters1.pdf.

Knack, Stephen, and Keefer, Philip. 1995. Institutions and economic performance: Cross-country tests using alternative institutional measures. *Economics and Politics, 7*(3), 207.

Kohli, Atul. 2004. *State-directed development: Political power and industrialization in the global periphery.* Cambridge: Cambridge University Press.

Krasner, Stephen. 2014. State building outside in: Development theories and policy implications. Paper presented at the University of Michigan Center for Chinese Studies Annual Conference on "Building State Capacity in China and Beyond," Oct. 17, 2014.

Krugman, Paul. 1994. The myth of Asia's miracle. *Foreign Affairs, 73*, 62.

Kurtz, Marcus, and Schrank, Andrew. 2007a. Growth and governance: Models, measures, and mechanisms. *The Journal of Politics, 69*(2), 538–554.

———. 2007b. Growth and governance: A defense. *The Journal of Politics, 69*(2), 563–569.

Landry, Pierre. 2008. *Decentralized authoritarianism in China: The Communist Party's control of local elites in the post-Mao era.* Cambridge: Cambridge University Press.

Lange, Matthew. 2009. *Lineages of despotism and development: British colonialism and state power.* Chicago: University of Chicago Press.

Lansing, Stephen. 2006. *Perfect order: Recognizing complexity in Bali.* Princeton, N.J.: Princeton University Press.

Lardy, Nicholas R. 1983. *Agriculture in China's modern economic development.* Cambridge: Cambridge University Press.

Lee, Charlotte. 2014. *Training the party: Party adaptation and elite training in reform-era China.* Cambridge: Cambridge University Press.

Levitsky, Steven, and Murillo, Victoria. 2013. Building institutions on weak foundations. *Journal of Democracy, 24*(2), 93–107.

Li, Hongbin, and Zhou, Li-An. 2005. Political turnover and economic performance: The incentive role of personnel control in China. *Journal of Public Economics, 89*(9), 1743–1762.

Lin, Justin Yifu, Cai, Fang, and Li, Zhou. 2003. *The China miracle: Development strategy and economic reform.* Rev. ed. Hong Kong: Chinese University Press.

Lipset, Seymour Martin. 1959. Some social requisites of democracy: Economic development and political legitimacy. *The American Political Science Review, 53*(1), 69–105.

Lora, Eduardo. 2002. Growth without governance: Comments. *Economia: Journal of the Latin American and Caribbean Economic Association, 3*(1), 216.

MacFarquhar, Roderick, and Schoenhals, Michael. 2006. *Mao's last revolution.* Cambridge, Mass.: Harvard University Press.

Mahoney, James, and Thelen, Kathleen. 2010. *Explaining institutional change: Ambiguity, agency, and power.* Cambridge: Cambridge University Press.

———. 2015. *Advances in comparative-historical analysis.* Cambridge: Cambridge University Press.

Manion, Melanie. 2004. *Corruption by design: Building clean government in mainland China and Hong Kong.* Cambridge, Mass.: Harvard University Press.

Maskin, Eric, Qian, Yingyi, and Xu, Chenggang. 2000. Incentives, information, and organizational form. *The Review of Economic Studies, 67*(231), 359.

Mauro, Paulo. 1995. Corruption and Growth. *Quarterly Journal of Economics, 110*(3), 681–712.

Mertha, Andrew. 2008. *China's water warriors: Citizen action and policy change.* Ithaca, N.Y.: Cornell University Press.

Migdal, Joel S., Kohli, Atul, and Shue, Vivienne. 1994. *State power and social forces: Domination and transformation in the Third World.* Cambridge: Cambridge University Press.

Miller, John H., and Page, Scott E. 2007. *Complex adaptive systems: An introduction to computational models of social life.* Princeton, N.J.: Princeton University Press.

Mitchell, Melanie. 2009. *Complexity: A guided tour.* Oxford: Oxford University Press.

Montinola, Gabriella., Qian, Yingyi, and Weingast, Barry. 1995. Federalism, Chinese style— The political basis for economic success in China. *World Politics, 48*(1), 50–81.

Nathan, Andrew. 2003. Authoritarian resilience. *Journal of Democracy, 14*(1), 6–17.

Naughton, Barry. 1995. *Growing out of the plan: Chinese economic reform, 1978–1993.* New York: Cambridge University Press.

———. 2007. *The Chinese economy: Transitions and growth.* Cambridge, Mass.: MIT Press.

———. 2015. Economic rebalancing. In J. deLisle and A. Goldstein (Eds.), *China's challenges.* Philadelphia: University of Pennsylvania Press.

Naughton, Barry, and Tsai, Kellee. 2015. *State capitalism, institutional adaptation, and the Chinese miracle.* New York: Cambridge University Press.

North, Douglass. 1990. *Institutions, institutional change, and economic performance.* Cambridge; New York: Cambridge University Press.

———. 2005. *Understanding the process of economic change.* Princeton, N.J.: Princeton University Press.

North, Douglass, Wallis, John, and Weingast, Barry. 2009. *Violence and social orders: A conceptual framework for interpreting recorded human history.* Cambridge: Cambridge University Press.

North, Douglass, and Weingast, Barry. 1989. Constitutions and commitment: The evolution of institutional governing public choice in seventeenth-century England. *The Journal of Economic History, 49*(4), 803–832.

Oi, Jean. 1992. Fiscal reform and the economic foundations of local state corporatism in China. *World Politics, 45*(1), 99–126.

———. 1999. *Rural China takes off: Institutional foundations of economic reform.* Berkeley: University of California Press.

Oi, Jean, and Walder, Andrew. 1999. *Property rights and economic reform in China.* Stanford, Calif.: Stanford University Press.

Osnos, Evan. 2014. *Age of ambition: Chasing fortune, truth, and faith in the new China.* New York: Farrar, Straus and Giroux.

Ostrom, Elinor, and Basurto, Xavier. 2011. Crafting analytical tools to study institutional change. *Journal of Institutional Economics, 7*(3), 317–343.

Padgett, John, and McLean, Paul. 2011. Economic credit in renaissance Florence. *Journal of Modern History, 83*(1), 1–47.

Padgett, John, and Powell, Walter. 2012. *The emergence of organizations and markets.* Princeton, N.J.: Princeton University Press.

Page, Scott E. 2011. *Diversity and complexity.* Princeton, N.J.: Princeton University Press.

Pei, Minxin. 2006. *China's trapped transition: The limits of developmental autocracy.* Cambridge, Mass.: Harvard University Press.

Perry, Elizabeth. 2011. From mass campaigns to managed campaigns: "Constructing a new socialist countryside." In S. Heilmann (Ed.), *Mao's invisible hand: The political foundations of adaptive governance in China* (viii). Cambridge, Mass: Harvard University Asia Center. Distributed by Harvard University Press.

Pierson, Paul. 2004. *Politics in time: History, institutions, and social analysis.* Princeton, N.J.: Princeton University Press.

Pritchett, Lant. 2002. Growth without governance: Comments. *Economia: Journal of the Latin American and Caribbean Economic Association, 3*(1), 224.

Pritchett, Lant, and de Weijer, Frauke 2011. Fragile states: Stuck in a capability trap? World Development Report 2011 Background Paper.

Pritchett, Lant, and Woolcock, Michael. 2004. Solutions when the solution is the problem: Arraying the disarray in development. *World Development, 32*(2), 191–212.

Przeworski, Adam. 2004. The last instance: Are institutions the primary cause of economic development? *European Journal of Sociology, 45*(2), 165–188.

Qian, Yingyi. 2003. How Reform Worked in China. In D. Rodrik (Ed.), *In search of prosperity: Analytic narratives on economic growth.* Princeton, N.J.: Princeton University Press.

Rawski, Thomas G. 1995. Implications of China's reform experience. *China Quarterly, 144,* 1150–1173.

Riggs, Fred Warren. 1964. *Administration in developing countries: The theory of prismatic society.* Boston: Houghton Mifflin.

Rodrik, Dani. 2007. *One economics, many recipes: Globalization, institutions, and economic growth.* Princeton, N.J.: Princeton University Press.

———. 2008. Second-best institutions. *American Economic Review, 98*(2), 100–104.

Rodrik, Dani, Subramanian, Arvind, and Trebbi, Francesco. 2004. Institutions rule: The primacy of institutions over geography and integration in economic development. *Journal of Economic Growth, 9*(2), 131–165.

Sachs, Jeffrey. 2005. *The end of poverty: Economic possibilities for our time.* London: Penguin.

Sachs, Jeffrey, McArthur, John, Schmidt-Traub, Guido, Kruk, Margaret, Bahadur, Chandrika, Faye, Michael, and McCord, Gordon. 2004. Ending Africa's poverty trap. *Brookings Papers on Economic Activity, 2004*(1), 117–216.

Schell, Orville, and Delury, John. 2013. *Wealth and power: China's long march to the twenty-first century.* New York: Random House.

Shambaugh, David L. 2008. *China's Communist Party: Atrophy and adaptation.* Washington, D.C.: Berkeley: Woodrow Wilson Center Press; University of California Press.

Shirk, Susan L. 1993. *The political logic of economic reform in China.* Berkeley: University of California Press.

Sokoloff, Kenneth, and Engerman, Stanley. 2000. History lessons: Institutions, factor endowments, and paths of development in the New World. *Journal of Economic Perspectives, 14*(3), 217–232.

Stockmann, Daniela. 2012. *Media commercialization and authoritarian rule in China.* Cambridge: Cambridge University Press.

Streeck, Wolfgang, and Thelen, Kathleen. 2005. Introduction: Institutional change in advanced political economies. In W. Streeck and K. Thelen (Eds.), *Beyond continuity: Institutional change in advanced political economies.* Oxford: Oxford University Press.

Su, Yang. 2011. *Collective killings in rural China during the cultural revolution.* New York: Cambridge University Press.

Teets, Jessica, and Hurst, William. 2015. *Local governance innovation in China: Experimentation, diffusion, and defiance.* New York: Routledge.

Thelen, Kathleen. 2004. *How institutions evolve: The political economy of skills in Germany, Britain, the United States, and Japan.* Cambridge: Cambridge University Press.

Tsai, Kellee. 2004. Off Balance: The unintended consequences of fiscal federalism in China. *Journal of Chinese Political Science, 9*(2), 1–27.

———. 2007. *Capitalism without democracy: The private sector in contemporary China.* Ithaca, N.Y.: Cornell University Press.

Vu, Tuong. 2010. *Paths to development in Asia: South Korea, Vietnam, China, and Indonesia.* New York: Cambridge University Press.

Wade, Robert. 1990. *Governing the market: Economic theory and the role of government in East Asian industrialization.* Princeton, N.J.: Princeton University Press.

Walder, Andrew G. 1995. Local governments as industrial firms: An organizational analysis of China's transitional economy. *American Journal of Sociology, 101*(2), 263–301.

———. 2009. *Fractured rebellion: The Beijing Red Guard movement.* Cambridge, Mass.: Harvard University Press.

Wedeman, Andrew. 2012. *Double paradox: Rapid growth and rising corruption in China.* Ithaca, N.Y.: Cornell University Press.

Weingast, Barry. 1995. The economic role of political institutions: Market-preserving federalism and economic development. *Journal of Law, Economics, and Organization, 11*(1), 1–31.

Whiting, Susan. 2001. *Power and wealth in rural China: The political economy of institutional change.* New York: Cambridge University Press.

Woo-Cumings, Meredith. 1999. *The developmental state.* Ithaca, N.Y.: Cornell University Press.

Woo, Wing Thye. 1999. The real reasons for China's growth. *China Journal* (41), 115–137.

World Bank. 1992. *Governance and Development.* Washington, D.C.: World Bank.

———. 1994. *Governance: The World Bank's experience.* Washington, D.C.: World Bank.

———. 2002b. *World development report 2002: Building institutions for markets.* New York: Oxford University Press.

3

Market Development

The appropriate relationship between states and markets in the pursuit of industrialization and economic growth has been hotly contested in developing countries. Discourse about the economics of development rose to a renewed prominence in the 1990s, propelled by such intellectuals as the Nobel Prize-winning economist Amartya Sen and other theorist–practitioners like Joseph Stiglitz and Jeffrey Sachs, as well as by household names such as Bono and Bill Gates. Debate permeates both theoretical and practical realms in a high-stakes battle to achieve economic growth, reduce poverty, and improve human welfare, and spans the merits of microlevel grassroots aid programs all the way through to prescriptions for reforming the international political economy architecture. In this section, we focus on how the concept of markets as institutions informs discussions of economic development, looking at perspectives on how developing countries should connect to the global economy, what types of growth-enhancing reforms they should put in place, the consequences of orthodox and heterodox economic strategies for development track records, and the very nature of development itself.

One of the major debates surrounding development strategies for poor countries is about what terms of connection to the global economy are most beneficial. **Arvind Panagariya** articulates a "full-throated and focused" market-liberal position, arguing that openness to trade, along with a general commitment to free-market competition, is the surest route to economic growth in the developing world. He cites the extraordinary economic success in the latter half of the twentieth century of the export-oriented East Asian "tigers," in contrast to the torpid trajectories of countries, like India, that chose the route of protectionist self-sufficiency and a dominant state role in domestic production.[1] He defends the track record of the structural adjustment programs of the International Monetary Fund and World Bank – which caused so many to eventually turn against neoliberal policies – by arguing that these reforms often led to undesirable outcomes because many leaders in the developing world failed, sometimes willfully, to implement them properly. Panagariya claims that the revisionist view of the East Asian Miracle, which attributed the region's economic success to industrial policy and state intervention, unfairly contributed to a general hostility to trade liberalization – in reality, he argues, the East Asian industrializers relied on trade openness for their success.

Many countries in the developing world opened their economies to trade and foreign investment in the 1990s, for a range of reasons that Panagariya discusses. He credits this openness, in turn, with economic growth and poverty alleviation across the board in the developing world. Even as he makes the case for the free market's superior efficiency, he states that liberal policies are necessary but not sufficient for economic success – other policies and factors must also be in place, such as macroeconomic stability, well-functioning infrastructure, and an absence of conflict. Overall, he delivers an updated version of the classical liberal stance on the gains from free trade, echoing Adam Smith and David Ricardo, and emphasizes that the protectionist policies of the past led to resource misallocation and overall inefficiency. Panagariya cautions, however, that a political case must continue to be made for liberal trade policies by demonstrating that they are more likely than protectionist policies to be linked to sustained, rapid growth and poverty reduction. He is cognizant of the political costs of liberalizing trade reforms but argues that they are not as high as critics of free trade would have us believe, an assertion he supports by pointing to the many developing countries that have moved in this direction over the past three decades. Panagariya rebuts a series of critiques of free trade and makes the case for continued openness and defense against protectionism in the developing world, emphasizing the need to communicate clearly about the gains from openness and the costs of protectionism. The burden of proof, he argues, is on the critics of openness to demonstrate that protectionism fares better in terms of growth and poverty alleviation, something he holds they have been unable to do.

In a nuanced counterpoint to the neoliberal orthodoxy espoused by Panagariya, **Dani Rodrik** delivers a heterodox economic perspective on growth and the policies and institutions necessary to initiate and sustain growth in the developing world. Grounded in and echoing some of the tenets of market-liberalism, Rodrik emphasizes that there are certain robust economic principles that any country must achieve in order to ignite and sustain growth – including market-based competition, integration with the global economy, macro-fiscal and financial stability, and institutional capacity for enforcing contracts and protecting property rights. The orthodox viewpoint holds that such principles can only be achieved through a certain set of neoliberal policies that emphasize, in particular, the importance of a laissez-faire approach to markets and a reduced role for the state in the economy – hence the generalized dictums of the Washington Consensus. The core of Rodrik's heterodox argument is that it is the first-order principles themselves that matter, not the policies employed to achieve them, and the principles can be achieved through a range of economic strategies, some of which appear antithetical to the Washington Consensus. He illustrates how the countries that have been most successful over the past half-century, such as the East Asian tigers followed by China, have not hewn very closely to the policy prescriptions of the Washington Consensus, while those that attempted or were forced into conformity with those policies, including much of Latin America, fared nowhere near as well.

Rodrik also emphasizes that context is crucial, making his a market-institutionalist perspective at its core. Market-enhancing institutions must perform certain functions and achieve certain goals to support sustained growth. Yet recognizing that does not, contra the neoliberal consensus, dictate their form – what they look like, how they are designed, in what order they are sequenced, and so on. Rodrik attributes China's economic success, for example, to a series of policy innovations that diverged significantly from Anglo-American economic norms but that delivered, in practice, very familiar economic foundations essential to supporting markets and growth.[2] Echoing Alexander Gerschenkron, Rodrik argues that the first-order principles that support markets and economic growth can be produced by a range of institutional arrangements, which are to some extent the result of path dependence in a country's historical trajectory. Successful strategies often mix orthodox and heterodox policies in unconventional and experimental ways that can only be transplanted across borders in ways that fit with local context and incentives.

Naazneen Barma charts the evolution of how theories on economic development and their implications for policy in the developing world have evolved over the past half-century. She explores, in particular, the move from different strands of development orthodoxy, including Marxism-inspired dependency theory as well as neoliberal structural adjustment programs, to a more eclectic and heterodox approach to development. Although the two main waves of development dogma came to opposite conclusions and prescriptions about the appropriate role for the state in the economy, Barma argues that they both rested on a faulty conception of the public and private sector as antithetical to each other. She counters that states and markets should be viewed as complementary in the process of economic development – and that it is not the degree but the type of government involvement in conceptualizing and implementing development strategies that is the central determinant of whether poor countries have been able to improve their economic lot. In contrast to Arvind Panagariya's rosy view of trade openness and liberalizing reforms as the panacea for economic development, Barma points to some of the gains of the import-substituting protectionist wave of the 1960s and 1970s in many developing countries, while acknowledging the inefficiencies and setbacks that accompanied that form of heavy state involvement in the economy. She is also much more critical of the neoliberal-inspired structural adjustment policies imposed on the developing world in the 1980s, pointing to the poor economic outcomes as well as the socioeconomic dislocation that came about as a result of the attempt to move to freer markets without complementary institutional infrastructure or state capacity.

Using the experience of the East Asian developmental state, Barma argues that economic development in poor countries requires an appropriate balance between states and markets, with a particular role for market-enhancing state capacity. In her review of the scholarship on the East Asian Miracle, the governments in question chose to engage in active economic transformation as the pathway to industrialization and growth. At the same time, well-functioning and competitive markets were also crucial to provide signals to producers and generate efficiency gains overall. For Barma – echoing Dani Rodrik's emphasis on the unconventional mix of orthodox and heterodox that often ignites and sustains growth – the heart of the East Asian success story was an adaptive, evolving process of states attempting to support and nudge private economic actors via a series of market-conforming, as opposed to market-distorting, interventions. This developmental strategy, in turn, rested on a particular political–economic alliance between mostly authoritarian political elites and their capitalist corporate counterparts. The model was extremely successful in raising the economic fortunes of much of East Asia. Yet it was a developmental strategy specific to the late-industrialization challenge in a very particular and timebound global economic context. And it also came with non-negligible social costs to the groups not squarely part of the growth alliance, with lasting consequences for the political economy of the region and the relationship of its states to its societies.

Amartya Sen is a renowned development economist whose body of work has spanned a number of central topics in the study of economic development. He was awarded the Nobel Prize in Economics in 1998 for his contributions to the study of welfare economics, social choice, and poverty, including his extensive research on famines. In *Development As Freedom*, Sen brought into mainstream development thinking the perspective that measures of economic growth, poverty reduction, industrialization, and technological advance are too narrow to fully capture the concept of development, serving as some of the means to development but not fully reflecting its ends. He articulated an expanded notion of economic development as encompassing non-material human well-being and individual lived experience, which include social and political criteria in addition to the material successes that can be captured with measures of aggregate economic output.

For Sen, freedom is both the ultimate goal of development and its crucial means. He made the case that poverty can be thought of as "unfreedom" – or a lack of economic, political, and social capabilities. Development removes those sources of unfreedom, thereby expanding freedom or the range of human choice; in turn, these earned freedoms are constitutive of true development. In the selection presented, he portrays markets as both a source of economic progress and representative, intrinsically, of the human right to freedom of exchange and transition, thus reflecting the market-liberal viewpoint of Adam Smith and Friedrich Hayek. At the same time, he cautions that markets require "social support, public regulation, or statecraft" to truly and equitably enrich human lives, echoing the market-institutionalist ethos of Karl Polanyi, Steven Vogel, and others in this reader. Sen's perspective embeds economic well-being in the social and political sphere and reconceptualizes development as the process of expanding freedoms across those spheres. Thought of in this way, material improvements may be necessary but are not sufficient for development as freedom – which requires the interlinking of social and economic arrangements oriented toward the collective good as well as political and civic rights. In Sen's expansive perspective, human well-being is no longer simply a beneficial consequence of economic success; it becomes, instead, the intrinsically valuable basis for expanded possibilities for action and leading "the kind of lives we value."

Notes

1 See also Jagdish Bhagwati and Arvind Panagariya, *Why Growth Matters: How Economic Growth in India Reduced Poverty and the Lessons for Other Developing Countries* (New York: Council on Foreign Relations, 2013).

2 See Yuen Yuen Ang, this volume, and Yingyi Qian, "How Reform Worked in China," in Dani Rodrik, ed., *In Search of Prosperity: Analytical Narratives on Economic Growth* (Princeton, NJ: Princeton University Press, 2003), 297–333. For an orthodox neoliberal viewpoint on China's reform success, see Wing Thye Woo, "The Real Reasons for China's Growth," *The China Journal* 41 (January 1999): 115–37.

Arvind Panagariya,
Free Trade & Prosperity (2019)[*]

1. Setting the Stage

No nation was ever ruined by trade, even seemingly the most disadvantageous one.
—Benjamin Franklin, 1774

Immediately following the Second World War, there was consensus that trade liberalization would help speed up the reconstruction and recovery of war-torn European economies while also helping North America grow faster. Ironically, there was also consensus that trade would not serve well the cause of economic development in the emerging independent Third World countries. Consequently, whereas both intellectuals and policymakers rallied behind the efforts to liberalize trade among Western industrial countries under the auspices of the General Agreement on Tariffs and Trade, they simultaneously blessed without qualification indiscriminate trade barriers and import substitution in Third World countries, which today we call "developing countries."

It so happened, however, that the British had maintained their colony Hong Kong as a free port with no tariffs or other trade barriers since its acquisition in the early 1840s. Additionally, in the late 1950s and early 1960s, farsighted political leadership in three East Asian nations—Taiwan, Singapore, and South Korea—recognized that import substitution in labor-intensive products in which they enjoyed comparative advantage had been largely exhausted. Their options were to either continue with import substitution by moving into progressively more capital-intensive products or, discarding the conventional wisdom, switch to greater reliance on exports, which would permit them to expand further the production of labor-intensive products in which they enjoyed comparative advantage but had exhausted the scope for import substitution. They chose the latter.

The results of the turn to this outward-oriented strategy were spectacular. Taking advantage of the vast global markets, these three countries managed to grow at rates of 8 to 10 percent on a sustained basis, a feat never before accomplished in human history. Alongside them, Hong Kong continued to flourish under its free trade regime. The four "Asian tigers," or newly industrialized economies (NIEs), as they eventually came to be called, achieved in three decades the kind of prosperity that Western industrial economies had taken a century or longer to achieve.

By contrast, the two largest countries of the world by population, China and India, remained staunchly wedded to protectionist, even near-isolationist, trade policies. The

---

entire effort of these countries was geared toward replacing more and more imports by domestic production, with the state playing a direct and dominant role in the production activity. Both countries performed poorly economically, with their per capita incomes becoming a small fraction of those of the four tiger economies by 1980. Lack of sustained rapid growth was also the fate of other developing countries in Asia, Africa, and Latin America that broadly followed the path of industrialization through import substitution.

The success of the East Asian tiger economies and the relatively poor performance of many other developing countries that remained wedded to import substitution led numerous economists to reassess their views. Large-scale multicountry studies conducted in the 1970s eventually replaced the existing conventional wisdom, which promoted industrialization through import substitution, with one that saw outward orientation as the key to growth and development.

Armed with this new conventional wisdom, in the 1980s the International Monetary Fund (IMF) and the World Bank aggressively used their considerable financial resources to induce debt-ridden developing countries, especially in Africa and Latin America, to rapidly drop protection against imports. In a large number of countries, the local leadership saw this liberalization as having been externally imposed under fiscal stress, and therefore they either subverted the recommendation of the IMF and the World Bank at the implementation level or eventually reversed liberalization once the crisis situation had been overcome.[1] The recommendation generally failed to produce the promised results.

Alongside these developments, influential authors began to reinterpret the success of the East Asian tigers as the result of clever industrial policies by their governments. They contended that well-calibrated interventions targeting specific sectors, infant industry protection, and coordination of interrelated investment activities by governments were behind the success of these countries. This revisionist view went some distance toward complementing the hostility to trade liberalization that had accompanied the failure of IMF- and World Bank—led trade liberalization to produce recovery in Africa and Latin America during the 1980s.

Notwithstanding the economic failures during the 1980s and the revisionist critique, during the 1990s country after country in the developing world went on to embrace outward-oriented policies. In part this happened because the Uruguay Round of trade negotiations brought the developing countries into the center of multilateral trade talks. Breaking from past practice, the developed countries insisted in this round of negotiations that the developing countries too must undertake liberalization obligations if they wished to maintain access to developed-country markets on a nondiscriminatory basis.

But this was not the only factor at work. At least three additional developments led the developing countries themselves to come to the view that trade openness was good for them. First, the Soviet Union, which once had been seen as embodying the success of autarkic policies, saw a steady decline of its economy throughout the 1980s and finally collapsed spectacularly in 1991. Second, China, which had voluntarily, rather than under pressure from the IMF and the World Bank, adopted outward-oriented policies beginning in the late 1970s, saw its economy grow at double-digit rates during the 1980s. Finally, countries such as India also came to appreciate that decades of efforts at import substitution had delivered outcomes far poorer than what the NIEs had been able to achieve through outward orientation.

This change of mind meant that developing countries' leaders came to own these policies of liberalization. Furthermore, in numerous cases liberalization was supported by complementary policies that helped translate openness into faster growth. Today the developing world is far more open to trade and foreign investment than at any other time in post—Second World War history.

Nonetheless, with the threat of protectionism constantly lurking in the background, those with a stake in greater prosperity for the developing countries can ill afford to be complacent. Left-leaning intellectuals, including many economists, staff at nongovernmental organizations (NGOs), and journalists, rarely pass up the opportunity to blame any country's economic failure on "neoliberal" prescriptions, foremost among them liberal trade. Moreover, thanks to the liberalization that has already taken place, the share of imports in gross domestic product (GDP) has risen substantially in recent decades in nearly all developing countries. As a result, the scope for import substitution is once again quite large. As the brilliant French economist Frédéric Bastiat reminded us 170 years ago, the expansion of industry that receives import protection is visible to all, but the damage from such protection, which is spread throughout the economy, is not.[2] As a result, import substitution remains a tempting target for politicians keen on demonstrating the successes of their policies to an unsuspecting electorate.

If outward-oriented policies are to be sustained in the developing countries, it is important that their benefits and the damage done by protection are exposed in ways that allow the public at large to see them. During the last two centuries, many volumes advocating the case for free trade and exposing the fallacies underlying the arguments by protectionists in the context of the developed countries have appeared.[3] But it is remarkable that despite the passage of seventy years since the former colonies began winning independence, a similar volume devoted to a systematic defense of openness in the context of the developing countries has been lacking. While vast amounts of research have been done on the importance of pro-free-trade policies in the developing countries, a full-throated and focused defense of trade openness as applied to the developing countries has not been attempted to date. It is this glaring gap that the present volume aims to fill.

During the past two decades, skeptics have written extensive critiques of outward-oriented policies and extolled the benefits of industrial policies reinforced by import substitution. I make an effort to systematically analyze their arguments and point out the logical flaws in them. Among other things, building on the seminal work of economist Robert Baldwin, published half a century ago, I pinpoint the conceptual flaws in arguments advocating infant industry protection. I also explain why a logical case for infant industry protection cannot be made, just as Baldwin concluded.[4]

I go on to argue that the one-time benefits of freeing up trade, though worthwhile, are insufficient to overcome political hurdles to the removal of protectionist policies in the developing countries. Instead, under most circumstances, the ability of economists and policy analysts to convince policymakers to adopt and sustain outward-oriented policies depends on establishing a link between these policies, on the one hand, and growth and poverty alleviation, on the other. A large part of the book is devoted to examining this link. This is done at both the aggregate level and the individual-country level. I present voluminous evidence showing that whenever countries have seen sustained rapid growth, low or declining barriers to trade and a high or rising share of trade in GDP have accompanied it. At the aggregate, cross-country level, we now have persuasive evidence causally connecting trade to per capita income. Individual country experiences reinforce this evidence.

The remainder of this chapter is organized as follows. In the first section, I briefly discuss the contrasting experiences of South Korea and India to set the tone for the book. In the second section, I explain how the study of these and other contrasting experiences led to a switch in the conventional wisdom on trade policy for the developing countries from import substitution to an outward orientation. In the third section, I briefly introduce the revisionist critique of the new conventional wisdom. In the fourth section, I address the common allegation that advocates of free trade are motivated by ideological impulses instead of by logical arguments and evidence. In the final section, I provide an outline of the book.

India and South Korea: An Elephant and a Tiger

In the 1950s, the official view in the United States was that while countries such as India would rapidly grow out of poverty, there was a big question mark about countries in the Far East. The prospect of South Korea turning into a basket case was seen as realistic. In a speech delivered on October 4, 2004, to African governors of the IMF, economist Anne O. Krueger, who at the time was the IMF's first deputy managing director, described the South Korea of the late 1950s in these terms:

> Picture a poor, largely rural peasant economy, almost wholly lacking in natural resources. So poor, in fact, that this economy is crucially dependent on foreign aid transfers—amounting to more than 10% of GDP. It is so poor and so dependent on outside help that some economists doubt it is a viable economy without those large aid inflows. It has the highest density of people on arable land anywhere in the world; the highest rate of inflation in the world; and its exports are 3% of GDP, 88% of which are primary commodities…. And I am not exaggerating the situation. There was genuine alarm [among South Koreans] when it became clear that the United States had decided to scale down the financial assistance it was providing Korea, on the grounds that Korea would not grow, so only providing support to maintain very low consumption levels was appropriate.[5]

In contrast, the United States had been favorably inclined toward India as it kicked off its development program in the early 1950s, largely because India was a democracy and Prime Minister Jawaharlal Nehru was a charismatic leader who commanded wide respect. The recognition that India was experimenting with economic and political ideas that were widely shared in the West led U.S. scholars throughout the 1950s and early 1960s to champion India as the model from which lessons would be gleaned for other developing countries.

Yet by the early 1970s, the tables had turned. India lost its shine, and a wide gulf in relations appeared between it and the United States. The first major failure came in agriculture, with the country's food grain production failing to keep pace with its rapidly rising population. Between 1961 and 1964, India had to import 25 million tons of food grain. Then followed two back-to-back droughts in 1965 and 1966, during which 19 million tons of food grain had to be imported. The United States provided a large part of this food grain via its aid program under Public Law 480. Seeking to leverage the aid in order to get India to change its policies, President Lyndon Johnson kept the country on what he himself called "ship-to-mouth" existence.[6] In turn, this produced outrage in India toward the United States.

As the years went on, India's general economic failure became further apparent. The country turned progressively inward, with its imports-to-GDP ratio declining from a peak of nearly 10 percent in the 1950s to below 5 percent in the early 1970s. This decline cut off Indian manufacturing firms from access to high-quality inputs and the latest technology, which is often embedded in imported machinery. That resulted in poor-quality products, for which there were few takers in the export markets. Poor export performance in turn reinforced the need for import controls. The vicious circle of import restrictions leading to poor export performance and poor export perform-ance necessitating import controls was thus complete. Efficiency and productivity growth suffered.

Prime Minister Indira Gandhi, who came to office in 1966 and ruled until 1984, with a short break from 1977 to 1980, repeatedly called for the elimination of poverty, but little progress was achieved. In what was perhaps the first comprehensive study of poverty in the developing countries, economist Gary Fields described the state of poverty in India in the late 1970s in these stark terms:

> India is a miserably poor country. Per-capita yearly income is under $100. Of the Indian people, 45 percent receive incomes below $50 per year and 90 percent below $150 ... . India's poverty problem is so acute and her resources so limited that it is debatable whether any internal policy change short of a major administrative overhaul and radical redirection of effort might be expected to improve things substantially.[7]

In contrast to India, South Korea, which had been predicted to have no realistic prospects of economic growth in the 1950s, shot up like a rocket beginning in the early 1960s. In the 1950s and early 1960s, both India and South Korea had grown approximately 4 percent per year. In the 1950s, both had pursued import substitu-tion. But, unlike India, South Korea began to shift toward an export-oriented policy in the late 1950s and early 1960s. Rather than go deeper into import substitution in products in which it lacked comparative advantage, it chose to expand the output of labor-intensive products in which it had comparative advantage and sell them in the export markets. This approach allowed it to benefit from scale economies, com-petition in the global marketplace, and access to high-quality inputs and the latest technologies. During the years that followed, its performance turned out to be dra-matically different from India's.

The contrasting strategies of India and South Korea produced contrasting outcomes. Whereas India's trade expansion could barely keep pace with its abysmal growth in GDP, that of South Korea exploded. Exports of goods and services as a proportion of GDP in South Korea rose from a paltry 4.6 percent in 1963 to a hefty 28.7 percent in 1973. Over the same period, the ratio fell from 4.5 percent to just 4.0 percent in India. Import performance exhibited the same contrast. Imports of goods and services as a proportion of GDP in South Korea rose from 15.7 percent in 1960 to 31.8 percent in 1973. In India, the ratio fell from 6 percent in 1963 to 4.7 percent in 1973.

The differences in the performance in trade were mirrored in the differences in GDP growth. In the period 1963–73, South Korea registered an impressive growth rate of 9.5 percent. During the same period, India grew barely 3.4 percent annually. The proportion of the population living below the poverty line remained unchanged in India, with the absolute number of poor growing on account of increased population. In contrast, poverty fell dramatically in South Korea.

At a personal level, in 1974 I came to Princeton University to do my doctorate in economics. Studies of the success of the East Asian tigers had just begun to emerge at the time, and so there was at best limited awareness of the success of these countries in India. Indeed, even scholars and teachers who may have known about it were probably unwilling to give the countries due credit or admit that India had much to learn from their experience. Until as late as the end of the 1980s, most Indian scholars and policymakers could be heard arguing that these countries were too small to be relevant to a populous country such as India.

Therefore, my first effective introduction to the dramatic difference between the economic performances of India and South Korea took place in the supermarkets and shopping malls of the United States. On my visits to these stores, I discovered that products of daily use such as stationery, clothing, furniture, and kitchen utensils invariably came from South Korea or other Asian tiger economies. Anytime I randomly picked a product in the shops, there was a non-negligible probability that it would bear a "Made in Korea" stamp and a near-zero probability that it was imported from India. Even a careful combing of the store for items made in India yielded no results.

A Turnaround in the Conventional Wisdom

As I have already noted, South Korea was not the only developing country that broke away from the conventional wisdom of the time to achieve an unconventionally high growth rate on a sustained basis. During the years 1963–73, Taiwan and Singapore were also successful in sustaining GDP growth rates of over 10 percent. Hong Kong missed the double-digit mark by a tiny margin, growing 9.8 percent per year.[8] These countries more or less maintained this exceptional performance in the 1970s.

As more and more data on the experience of the developing countries became available, economists began to analyze these countries to better understand the sources of sustained rapid growth. The 1970s saw the publication of two large-scale cross-country studies. The first of them, conducted under the auspices of the Organisation for Economic Co-operation and Development (OECD) and summarized by project directors Ian Little, Tibor Scitovsky, and Maurice Scott, produced detailed narratives of six countries: Brazil, India, Mexico, Pakistan, Philippines, and Taiwan.[9] The second study, sponsored by the National Bureau of Economic Research (NBER) and synthesized by its co-directors, Jagdish Bhagwati and Anne Krueger, in two separate volumes, focused on the experiences of ten countries: Brazil, Chile, Colombia, Egypt, Ghana, India, Israel, Philippines, South Korea, and Turkey.[10] Complementing these large-scale studies was a study done at the World Bank. Edited by Bela Balassa, this study covered six semi-industrialized economies: Argentina, Colombia, Israel, South Korea, Singapore, and Taiwan.[11]

These studies led economists to rethink the prevailing consensus on economic development. Little, Scitovsky, and Scott noted that the conventional wisdom of the time had overemphasized industry relative to agriculture and underestimated the importance of exports as against import substitution in promoting industrialization. They reasoned that support to industry could be provided in ways that did not discourage the exports of either industrial or agricultural products. They concluded that this would "promote greater efficiency in the use of resources" and "create less unequal distribution of income and higher levels of employment in both industry and agriculture."[12]

The evidence gathered by the Bhagwati-Krueger NBER project considerably strengthened the view that outward orientation had not received the attention it deserved. The project's case study of South Korea's success, prepared by Charles Frank, Kwang Suk Kim, and Larry Westphal, offered compelling evidence in favor of the superiority of outward-oriented policies over import substitution.[13] The authors drew the following contrast between the contributions of export expansion and import substitution to South Korean growth:

> The most striking result of this analysis is the predominance of export expansion over import substitution. From 1955 to 1968, 20.2 percent of total growth was attributable directly and indirectly to export expansion, while –0.6 percent was due to import substitution. Thus, on balance, there was negative import substitution but substantial export expansion.... From 1960 to 1968, export expansion was relatively even more important, and accounted for 22.4 percent of growth compared with –1.4 percent for import substitution.
>
> Another striking conclusion to be drawn ... is that export expansion generated considerable domestic backward linkages while import substitution did not. The average contribution of export expansion for either the 1955–68 or 1960–68 period almost doubles when indirect effects are taken into account.[14]

In parallel, reporting on the impact of inward-looking policies on growth in the NBER case study on India, Bhagwati and T. N. Srinivasan reached the conclusion that the country's "foreign trade regime led to a wasteful misallocation of investible resources among alternative industries and also accentuated the under-utilization of investment within these industries." They further found that the trade regime had undermined competition among the firms in these industries and "practically eliminated the incentive that such competition normally provides for reducing costs."[15]

The Balassa study of six semi-industrialized countries reinforced the findings of the OECD and NBER projects. It found that the incentive systems in Korea, Singapore, and Taiwan had discriminated least between nontraditional primary and manufacturing activities and between sales in export and domestic markets. The bias in favor of import substitution and against exports within the manufacturing sector was the greatest in Argentina, followed by Colombia and Israel, in that order. The first set of countries had clearly outperformed those in the second set.

By the early 1980s, the conventional wisdom among economists had shifted away from import substitution and in favor of outward orientation. This change coincided with the election of Ronald Reagan as president of the United States. Reagan, who firmly believed in free trade and markets, went on to deploy the United States' considerable influence to press the World Bank and the IMF to use their financial clout to promote free trade policies in the developing countries. Acting under U.S. pressure, these institutions considerably accelerated the use of conditionality in loans to the developing countries to coerce them into adopting liberal trade policies. They also sponsored numerous country-specific studies that broadly concluded in favor of outward-oriented policies.

With the evidence of the failure of import substitution policies accumulating, a handful of countries other than the four Asian tigers had begun to partially dismantle their protectionist policies during the second half of the 1970s. In Latin America the most notable example was Chile, which began the process in 1974, and in Asia it was China, which launched its open-door policy in December 1978.[16] Even in India, the protectionist regime had peaked by the mid-1970s, and the liberalization process got under way to a certain extent in the second half of the 1970s.[17] But the process accelerated greatly during the 1980s as the World Bank and IMF began to actively promote it. These institutions were especially successful in getting many small, crisis-ridden developing countries to liberalize.

Revisionists Strike Back

But as Paul Samuelson has famously said, fighting protectionism is like fighting a skin disease—no sooner do you cure it in one place than it appears in another. As it became increasingly accepted that outward-oriented policies promised outcomes superior to those of import substitution, critics regrouped and mounted a counter-attack. Careful early work by Westphal had emphasized the importance of industrial policy and infant industry promotion in South Korea.[18] But he had always taken pains to emphasize the centrality of outward orientation to the Korean experience. In his subsequent writings, he was also cautious about drawing any sweeping lessons in favor of targeting and promoting infant industries in other developing countries.[19]

In contrast, in what were zealous attempts to resuscitate the case for protection as a means to foster rapid growth in the developing countries, political scientists Alice Amsden and Robert Wade went on to reinterpret the successful experiences of South Korea and Taiwan as the triumph of not just industrial policy but also import substitution.[20] Subsequently, economist Dani Rodrik widened the scope of those claims to include the experience of a wide spectrum of developing countries that he claimed had flourished under import substitution industrialization in the 1960s and early 1970s. He also argued that trade liberalization in Africa and Latin America in the late 1970s and beyond had met with systematic economic failure.[21] More recently, Joseph Stiglitz, Andrew Charlton, Erik Reinert, Ha-Joon Chang, and influential NGOs such as Oxfam and Christian Aid have thrown their weight against trade liberalization in the developing countries.[22]

Free Trade Advocates, Not Free Trade Ideologues

Critics of free trade policies often like to discredit proponents of free trade by labeling them as ideologues. While this characterization may fit certain individuals, the vast majority of the first-generation scholars who began to refocus attention on outward-oriented policies in preference to import substitution arrived at this position through careful study and analysis. It is often forgotten that at one time these proponents had been actually sympathetic to—even advocates of—import substitution and infant industry protection. After all, with truly rare exceptions, there were no economists prescribing pro-free-trade policies for the developing countries in the 1950s and 1960s despite the fact that most saw free trade as a worthy goal for the developed countries. Virtually all of them gave a nod to not just tariffs but also quantitative restrictions in the developing countries. This virtual consensus in favor of a positive role for protection was most likely the reason that even the General Agreement on Tariffs and Trade, signed in 1947, gave the developing countries free rein to impose quantitative restrictions and did not ask them to liberalize trade in the early negotiating rounds.

The conversion of two specific scholars, Jagdish Bhagwati and Ian Little, to a pro-free-trade view illustrates this point. After completing his studies at Cambridge and Oxford, Bhagwati returned to India in 1961. Though on-the-ground reality in India and elsewhere would gradually turn him into the world's foremost advocate of free trade, in 1961 he shared the intellectual attitudes that had shaped India's increasingly inward-looking trade policies. Motivated by those attitudes and nationalistic instincts common among Indians of his generation, upon his return to India Bhagwati was appalled by the craze for foreign products he observed among his fellow citizens. He happened to share this sentiment in a letter with Harry Johnson, his teacher and a distinguished trade economist at Cambridge who by then had moved to the University of Chicago. Johnson, a quick wit, shot back in his reply to Bhagwati that if the paper on which his letter was written was any indication of the quality of Indian products, he found the craze for foreign products by Indians quite rational.

This episode might conceivably have been a turning point in the conversion of Bhagwati into a free trade advocate. But it was not. Instead, the process was a gradual one, as illustrated by his 1970 book on India, co-authored with Padma Desai and published as a part of the OECD project mentioned earlier. For one thing, the title of the book—*India: Planning for Industrialization*—scarcely points to any ideological adherence to free trade. More substantively, a modern-day critic of free trade would likely find the trade policy recommendations in the book wholly acceptable.

The book recommends dismantling the import licensing regime and either replacing fixed exchange rates with a flexible exchange rate regime or moving to a system of competitive auctions of foreign exchange, with a small fraction of the foreign exchange reserved for high-priority sectors. The recommendations explicitly allow the use of tariffs for protection of domestic industries. In explaining what a more rational trade policy regime would have looked like, the authors note, "These arrangements [relating to the removal of import licensing and reform of the foreign exchange system] would have been consistent with protection of domestic industries, where necessary, since it would have always been open to use tariff policy for this purpose."[23] Today Bhagwati goes much further, advocating a trade policy that is significantly closer to free trade and eliminates protection aimed at import substitution.

The second example is equally dramatic. Economist Ian Little, who co-directed the OECD project, had been an active advocate of import substitution in the early 1960s. In a 1960 article on the policy choices facing India, he expressed export pessimism and a preference for import substitution in these words:

> The present pattern of exports … is a most unpromising basis for expansion. Any major expansion of exports could come about only if India deliberately set about producing new manufactures for exports on a large scale. This would seem to be unjustifiably risky … . It would be surprising if it did not turn out to be economical for her to produce something of almost everything, and surprising if international trade should ever come to more than a small fraction of national income.

In the next paragraph, he went on to explicitly defend import substitution:

> Thus, the relative attractions of import substitution are great. There is no doubt about the demand being there. One can, as it were, see what to produce. There are the obvious advantages of goodwill for domestic products, and transport costs act in favor not against them. Lower quality goods can be more easily absorbed. In short, the risks of failure are much less.[24]

As with Bhagwati, Little's thinking evolved gradually. Though his OECD study, published in 1970, questioned the old conventional wisdom, it did not entirely reject import substitution. Its main thrust was against policies that discouraged exports. From a policy perspective, it mainly advocated granting exporters a free trade regime through tariff-free availability of imported machines and raw materials. Much later, in the 1990s, he shifted to a view that favored complete free trade. In an article published five years after India launched its liberalizing reforms, he wrote:

> I believe there was in 1991, and still is, a wide consensus that the Indian Economic Model that prevailed from 1947 to 1991 did not well serve the objective of a rapid rate of growth in which all, especially the poor, would share. To put it crudely, the regime was too dirigiste and too autarkic.[25]

When he described the type of economic system toward which reforms should be directed, the first element was this: "There is virtual free trade, and freedom of foreigners to invest in India, and Indians to invest abroad."

Both Bhagwati and Little arrived at their free trade positions after long journeys through failed efforts to promote industrialization behind a protective wall.

[…]

5. Trade Openness, Growth, and Poverty

Exposing the Critics' Specious Arguments

> Those who cavalierly reject the Theory of Evolution as not being adequately supported by facts seem to forget that their own theory is supported by no facts at all.
>
> —Herbert Spencer, 1852

The static gains from trade based on differences in productivity and factor endowment between countries, economies of scale, and product variety arise from improved allocation of the existing world resources and efficient international exchange. According to available estimates, these gains can lead to one-time permanent increases in national incomes of at most 5 percent. While such gains may be significant and desirable, often they prove insufficient to persuade political leadership in the developing countries to abandon protectionist policies.

A wider political acceptance of the case for trade openness in the developing countries must be based on two related arguments: the indispensability of liberal trade policies to sustained rapid growth and the centrality of growth to combating poverty. If low or declining trade barriers can help accelerate per capita income growth by even 2 percentage points per annum for two to three decades, the accumulated increase in income can greatly contribute to the overall process of development through urbanization and building of infrastructure while also leading to substantial reductions in abject poverty. Growth helps create gainful employment, which places ever-rising wages in the hands of the poor while also generating revenue for the government that it can use to finance anti-poverty programs.

Against this background, the critical question we must address from a policy standpoint is whether low or declining barriers to trade are more conducive to faster growth and poverty alleviation than high or rising barriers. This is the central point of contention between proponents and opponents of trade openness when it comes to trade policies in the developing countries. It requires a careful study of cross-country experience over the past several decades as well as within-country experiences of countries that have followed markedly different trade policies during different time periods. This is the task we now undertake.

The question of the relationship of trade openness with growth and poverty alleviation is largely an empirical one. Unlike theory, the empirical world can be messy. In theory, free trade is the state of no trade barriers, while autarky is the state of prohibitive trade barriers. But in the real world, we are almost always somewhere between these two extremes, with some trade barriers present. Moreover, trade openness is only one of several policies that must come together to yield sustained rapid growth and poverty alleviation. Therefore, teasing out the role of trade openness empirically can be a challenge. Indeed, this factor has been at the heart of much of the confusion that prevails in the policy space on the role of trade openness. To avoid this confusion, I begin by first stating in the clearest possible terms how trade openness is to be defined and what role should be established for it in delivering growth and poverty alleviation.

Setting the Bar Right

Regrettably, when offering free trade as the key to rapid growth, some free trade advocates have fallen into the trap of setting the bar for themselves far higher than necessary. In turn, this has made the task of successfully challenging their case relatively easy for free trade critics. For example, in their otherwise well-argued and well-researched contribution to the debate, free trade advocates Deepak Lal and Sarath Rajapatirana state, "It seems to be as firm a stylized fact as any in the economics of developing countries: a sustained movement to an outward-oriented trade regime leads to faster growth of both exports and incomes."[26] The suggestion in this statement that trade openness on its own leads to sustained rapid growth is easily challenged: one does not have to look too far or too hard to find examples of countries failing to achieve either significant progress in export expansion or accelerated growth upon opening to foreign trade.

It is not my intention to defend the relationship between trade openness and growth in this strong form. Instead, the view taken in this volume is that the defense of the pro-free-trade position only requires establishing that liberal trade policies offer better prospects for sustained rapid growth than do protectionist trade policies. In a nutshell, liberal trade policies, which I identify with low or declining barriers to trade, are necessary for sustained rapid growth and poverty alleviation but not sufficient. That liberal trade policies are not sufficient for faster growth is readily seen by considering situations in which either world markets are closed or internal infrastructure linking the centers of production to ports is nonexistent. Under such circumstances, autarky would obtain even if there were no formal barriers to trade whatsoever. The removal of barriers would not hurt the country, but it would also not yield a positive benefit.

While sufficiency conditions may vary according to countries' individual circumstances, I propose to demonstrate in this volume that liberal trade policies are an integral part of nearly every policy package that has delivered sustained rapid growth and poverty alleviation. I will present empirical evidence based on cross-country experience as well as individual country experiences over time. Furthermore, I will show that an econometric analysis using cross-country data allows us to establish a causal relationship between trade openness and growth with a high degree of confidence.

Does the lack of sufficiency of trade openness for sustaining rapid growth negate the economist's case for free trade? Hardly. It still remains true that between low and high barriers, a country is better off opting for the former, since low barriers confer some immediate gains from efficient exchange and possibly specialization according to comparative advantage. And, of course, as other policies are put in place, low barriers also improve the country's prospects for sustained rapid growth. Protection offers neither advantage.

Opponents of free trade sometimes argue that if trade liberalization does not guarantee sustained rapid growth, why should a government pay its political cost? The response is that if we care enough about the country's future economic prospects, it is worth persuading its leaders to move toward a regime that promises improved economic prospects. Moreover, if done gradually and in conjunction with appropriate adjustments in the exchange rate, trade liberalization is among the least contentious reforms. Small, across-the-board tariff cuts make imports marginally more attractive relative to similar domestically produced goods. A simultaneous depreciation of the domestic currency (e.g., a change in the exchange rate from 60 rupees per dollar to 65 rupees per dollar) temporarily offsets the decline in the prices of imports and softens the blow to producers of liberalized products. Additionally, the depreciation makes the country's export goods more attractive to foreigners. This helps export sectors to expand and absorb the resources gradually released by the liberalized import-competing sectors, thus minimizing unemployment in transition.

That the political costs of broad-based trade liberalization are not as high as the critics would have us believe is evidenced by the considerable liberalization undertaken on a unilateral basis by a large number of countries in Asia, Africa, and Latin America at various points in time during the last three decades.[27] Despite continued voices of dissent, support for liberal trade policies in the developing countries today is much stronger than at any time prior to 1990.

Trade and Growth: Debunking Some Specious Arguments

In the context of the relationship between trade and growth, critics offer several arguments against freeing up trade that seem superficially plausible but turn out to be false upon careful scrutiny. Because these arguments often cloud and confuse the debate, it is best to get them out of the way at the outset.

Trade Liberalization Failed to Catalyze and Sustain Growth in Many Instances

Free trade critics frequently cite countries that opened their economies to foreign trade but failed to achieve higher growth on a sustained basis. This was true of many countries in Latin America and Africa in the 1980s. In some cases the failure is explained either by the liberalization's lack of credibility or by outright reversal. But there remain cases in which liberalization was not reversed and yet no significant jump in the growth rate was observed. At a slightly more sophisticated level, critics argue that the existing econometric evidence fails to establish a *causal* link between removal of barriers to trade and growth.[28]

A moment's reflection should convince the reader that these examples and arguments neither undermine the case for liberalization nor strengthen the case for protection. For starters, free trade advocates can cite an even larger number of examples of countries failing to stimulate growth through protectionism. They can also point out that opponents of free trade have not even *attempted* to establish a causal link between sustained rapid growth and protection. The quotation from Herbert Spencer at the beginning of this chapter is instructive in this respect.

The flaw in the argument is that a country must base its trade policy choices not on whether openness by itself will lead to higher growth but whether it will be more conducive to sustained rapid growth than protectionism would be. Few trade economists offer free trade as a cure-all. They recognize that a lack of policy credibility, macroeconomic instability, an overvalued exchange rate, structural rigidities in product or factor markets, external or internal conflicts, and poor infrastructure may block the positive growth effects of an open trade regime from being realized. What we simultaneously need to keep in mind is that beneficial internal policies will fall well below their potential without low or declining barriers to trade.

Writing as far back as 1985, Vittorio Corbo, Anne Krueger, and Fernando Ossa explicitly stated in the introduction to their book *Export-Oriented Development*

Strategies that the experiences they reviewed revealed "a set of basic conditions for sustained export-led growth."[29] They went on to identify five such conditions: a stable macroeconomic framework, an appropriate real exchange rate, a free trade regime for exporters, timely financing for exporters at domestically competitive rates, and non-discrimination against savings. One can take issue with the specific elements in this list, but the essential point is that thoughtful trade economists do not claim that trade liberalization by itself will ensure sustained rapid growth.

When Countries Have Achieved Sustained Rapid Growth, the Catalyst Has Not Been Trade Liberalization

Critics also attack the case for liberal trade polices on the ground that certain successful experiences of sustained growth were actually catalyzed by alternative policies, such as land reform in the case of China, government-engineered increase in investment demand in the case of South Korea and Taiwan, and incremental domestic policy reform in the case of India.[30]

While the assertion that trade was not a catalyst to rapid growth in these countries is highly questionable, for now it suffices to note that even if this is true, open trade policies remain critical because they are necessary to *sustain* such growth.[31] Even if growth is initially stimulated by land reform, incremental domestic policy reform, or government-led expansion of investment demand, it is unlikely to be sustained if the trading environment is autarkic. A careful study of a large number of successful cases, including Hong Kong, Singapore, South Korea, and Taiwan in the 1960s and 1970s and India, China, Chile, and Vietnam in the 1980s and beyond, reveals that whatever the source of the initial stimulus, low or declining barriers to trade have almost always accompanied sustained rapid growth. Indeed, under Mao Zedong, China had tried a variety of land reforms at different points in time, but they failed to deliver rapid growth because the overall policy framework was anti-growth, with a high level of protection being a part of that framework.

High Protection Does Not Preclude Rapid Growth

Critics cite examples of countries that managed to register high growth rates behind high walls of protection to conclude that protection works. Again, high *initial* trade barriers do not preclude the *onset* of rapid growth, especially in large countries such as Brazil, China, and India. Sometimes the growth process itself may be kicked off by gradual liberalization of an initially highly protected regime. But the available evidence shows that even if protection is high and the initial stimulus comes from an alternative policy change, growth sustains and accelerates only if the country responds by undertaking liberalization that accommodates the pressures for the expansion of trade that such growth generates. Evidence pointing to the fact that a country grew rapidly while still behind a high wall of protection does not prove the efficacy of protection. The critical question for such an economy is whether it was lowering or further raising the protection during the period of rapid growth.

Import Substitution Has Preceded Outward Orientation

Free trade critics point to countries such as South Korea, Taiwan, and even Singapore, which went through a phase of import substitution before turning outward, to bolster the case for import substitution industrialization. Purely as a matter of historical record, import substitution prior to turning outward has been an integral part of the development experience of virtually all developing countries except Hong Kong. Given the conventional wisdom in the immediate postcolonial era that import substitution offered the only route to industrialization to the developing countries, this outcome was inevitable. But the key policy question is whether this phase of import substitution was a necessary condition for the success of outward-oriented policies later. For one thing, we do have the example of Hong Kong, which achieved sustained rapid growth without even a short period of import substitution. Moreover, the periods of import substitution varied greatly across countries that eventually achieved sustained rapid growth through opening up. For example, Singapore went through a very brief and mild period of import substitution, South Korea pursued it for a longer but still relatively short period, and India and China stayed with it for a very long time. The fact that each of these countries succeeded in achieving sustaining rapid growth only after turning outward suggests that import substitution was not essential to its success. The critics' argument remains a case of post hoc fallacy.

An argument can perhaps be made that the *first* stage of import substitution, during which a country replaces imports of labor-intensive non-durable consumer goods such as apparel and footwear and intermediate inputs used in them by domestic products, may not be overly costly. And if followed by a switch to outward-oriented policies, as was the case with Singapore, South Korea, and Taiwan, such import substitution may even appear to have contributed positively to sustained rapid growth. The cost is likely to be low because the country essentially encourages the production of goods in which it has a comparative advantage. But as the production structure begins to become more complex, the risks of choosing the wrong industries rise exponentially, as illustrated by the Indian experience.

In the present-day context, references to the success or otherwise of the first-stage import substitution must be seen as largely academic. Nearly every developing country is now past pursuing first-stage import substitution. As such, references to its success in the 1950s and 1960s cannot serve as the basis for continued import substitution today.

Industrial Policy Was Central to Many Growth Miracles

Some critics question the importance of outward-oriented policies on the ground that most successful countries relied on industrial policy, including targeting of certain industries. They reject the importance of reduced trade barriers by appeal to interventions in the domestic market. The efficacy of industrial policy itself constitutes a separate subject of debate among economists, but even if we accept that such policies made a positive contribution to the growth of South Korea and Taiwan, we cannot reject the contribution made by openness. Indeed, it can be argued that it is the presence of low or declining trade barriers that either minimized the damage from industrial policies or maximized their benefits. The contrasting experiences of South Korea and India during the first three decades of their development (1950–80) vividly illustrate this.

Trade Openness and Poverty: Debunking Yet More Specious Arguments

When confronted with persuasive evidence that sustained rapid growth has almost always been achieved under outward-oriented trade policies and rapidly expanding trade, anti-globalization critics often change the subject, arguing instead that the movement toward greater trade openness must still be resisted because it hurts the poor. Some scholars, most notably Robert Wade, explicitly side with the NGOs and journalists in their assault on openness as a source of increased poverty, while others, such as Ravi Kanbur, express sympathy without necessarily joining them.[32]

Before examining the arguments offered by critics, it is necessary to explain how poverty is measured. In principle, measures of poverty can be based on consumption expenditures, income, nutrition, life expectancy, infant mortality, educational attainments, and various other indicators considered relevant to human welfare. But the commonest metric is defined in terms of income or expenditure.

To measure poverty, we first define the "poverty consumption bundle" as the bundle of commodities and services necessary for a representative household, defined in terms of size and age-gender composition, to achieve a minimal acceptable living standard. We then define the poverty line as the minimum expenditure (or income) necessary to buy the poverty consumption bundle at a given set of prices. The proportion of a country's population with expenditure (or income) below this poverty line is called the country's poverty ratio or headcount ratio. Though the academic literature offers a number of additional, technically more sophisticated measures of poverty, much of the policy debate is centered on the poverty ratio.[33]

We may now examine some key claims of the critics regarding the impact of openness on poverty.

Rising Numbers of Poor Have Accompanied Rising Trade Openness

Many NGOs, international institutions, and scholars critical of openness as an instrument of promoting poverty alleviation have resorted to citing the changes in the absolute number of poor to argue that increased openness has failed the poor, even impoverished them. In the late 1990s, as part of the World Bank's effort to promote the so-called Comprehensive Development Framework, invented by its president, James Wolfensohn, the Bank played up the notion that poverty in the world had gone up during the age of globalization and economic reforms. For example, in its *1999 Annual Review of Development Effectiveness*, the World Bank noted, "The number of poor people living on less than US$ 1 a day rose from 1,197 million in 1987 to 1,214 million in 1998. Excluding China, there are 100 million more poor people in developing countries than a decade ago." This evidence in turn served as the justification for the assertion in the foreword to the report, "Despite the potential benefits of globalization and technological change, world poverty has increased and growth prospects have dimmed for developing countries."[34] Similar statements can be found in numerous other contemporary documents from the World Bank, as well as those from the United Nations and its affiliated organizations, which traditionally have been skeptical of outward-oriented policies. In turn, antitrade NGOs have seized on these assertions, prominently citing them on their websites.[35]

There are, of course, many problems with the assertions in that World Bank document. Counting the global poor using a common global poverty line lacks proper conceptual foundation. And if one nevertheless insists on engaging in such an exercise, there is no reason China, which made huge strides in bringing poverty down during the period 1987–98 through increased outward orientation complemented by other pragmatic reforms, should be excluded from the calculation of global poor. But above all, we must question the wisdom of using the absolute number of poor instead of the poverty ratio as the correct indicator for evaluating a policy's effectiveness in combating poverty.

To explain why the reliance on the absolute number of poor is problematic, consider the case of India. According to official estimates by the government of India, in 1983 the poverty ratio in the country was 44.5 percent and the absolute number of poor was 323 million. Between 1983 and 2004, India's population rose by 375 million to 1.1 billion. A reasonable assumption would be that absent an effective poverty alleviation strategy, 44.5 percent of the additional 375 million individuals would have been poor. That is to say, in 2004 the absolute number of poor would have risen by 166.9 million to reach 489.9 million. So if the absolute number of poor in 2004 remained unchanged at 323 million, it would imply a reduction in the number of poor by 166.9 million. The conclusion that any increase in the number of poor represents increased poverty follows only if we make the silly assumption that none of the new additions to the population were born in poverty. In reality, the number of poor in 2004 turned out to be 302 million, implying that India had successfully pulled 187.9 million people out of poverty. This substantial decline is properly captured by the poverty ratio, which fell to 27.5 percent in 2004 from 44.5 percent in 1983.

A more dramatic way to make this point is to consider the absolute number of those living above the poverty line. Suppose this number rises over time. Does this unambiguously imply that poverty has gone down? The answer is an unequivocal no. In a country with rising population, it is highly likely that the number of poor and the number of non-poor would rise simultaneously. A reasonable way to determine whether poverty has risen or fallen under such circumstances is to look at the distribution of the population between the poor and non-poor.

Rising Number of Absolute Poor Shows Openness Has Failed the Poor

All, including such critics as Wade, agree that the poverty ratio has declined globally.[36] Dissent on the efficacy of globalization in combating poverty is based on the contention that the poor rose in absolute numbers alongside the opening up of the global economy. I have already argued that the appropriate index to measure poverty when evaluating the impact of alternative policies on poverty is the poverty ratio. But even ignoring this fact, the conclusion that the rising number of poor in an era of opening up to trade represents a failure of outward-oriented policies is problematic. For one thing, as T. N. Srinivasan has cogently argued, the measurement of global poverty using a common poverty line such as $1 per day at purchasing power parity (PPP) is fraught with serious conceptual and data problems.[37] But more important from our viewpoint, the indictment of openness on the grounds that it accompanies a rise in the absolute number of the poor suffers from a serious logical problem.

I have argued that openness is a necessary condition for growth but not a sufficient one. Therefore, even if the global poverty ratio or the absolute number of poor worldwide is shown to have risen during the 1990s and beyond, it proves little against the necessity of openness to combating poverty. In countries where the absence of complementary conditions resulted in a failure to sustain growth, there is no reason to expect that openness by itself would have led to a sustained reduction in poverty. For instance, sustained rapid growth is unlikely to have been achieved in many African countries suffering from civil war during the 1990s. Indeed, the number of poor in such countries is likely to have risen on account of conflict and war. Inclusion of these countries will then bias the outcome toward an increased absolute number of poor in the world despite increased openness.

As far back as four decades ago, economist Walter Galenson offered compelling evidence demonstrating that whenever a country achieved sustained rapid growth, it also succeeded in bringing poverty down.[38] Using the data available to him at the time, he reached the conclusion that "rapid sustained growth has had positive effects on the living standards of all economic groups of those countries that experienced it." He went on to add, "Growth has not 'failed'; there has simply not been enough of it in the great majority of the less developed nations."[39]

Finally, critics do not provide evidence that protectionism has done better than openness in combating global poverty. If they are to be believed, they must show that higher or rising protection in the past has delivered better outcomes for a similar increase in population. Not only have they not done it, but even the thought that this is what is required to clinch their case has not occurred to them.

Globalization Has Bypassed the Core Poor

Sometimes critics of trade openness refer to specific groups that have not been lifted out of poverty or have even been impoverished during a period of trade liberalization accompanied by sustained rapid growth and then make the sweeping claim that openness and growth do not help the poor. They point to the continued or worsened plight of the "core poor," defined as the poorest among the poor, and proceed to conclude that openness and growth hurt the poor. This claim is reminiscent of the claim that growth does not "trickle down" to the truly poor.

Three factors make it particularly easy to focus asymmetrically on losers or non-winners rather than outright winners during periods of sustained rapid growth under increased openness. First, those lifted out of poverty are often invisible, but those still remaining poor may be highly visible. This is akin to the phenomenon in which an import-competing sector that shrinks as a result of liberalization is clearly identifiable, but sectors that expand the production of export goods to pay for increased imports are not identified in the same way, because they are not subject to direct policy action. Indeed, when these sectors expand, the credit may readily be given to alternative, directly observable factors such as the entrepreneurship of specific individuals, improved infrastructure, or even some direct government initiative.

Second, liberalization works by moving workers from less efficient sectors to more efficient ones. This means that the adverse impact on liberalized sectors in the form of workers being dislocated is immediate, whereas the impact in terms of reemployment in more productive jobs in the expanding sectors takes time.

Finally, most countries have geographically remote and hard-to-reach areas, often inhabited by groups that are among the poorest. Being physically separated, they are easily identified and are also among those usually unaffected by growth in the mainstream of the economy. Any positive impact of growth reaches them only through targeted anti-poverty programs.

Indictment of growth on the grounds that it bypasses many poverty-stricken groups, without recognition that it yields greater *aggregate* reduction in poverty than alternative policies, is not new. In his important 1980 book, economist Gary Fields cites the work of Keith Griffin, which foreshadowed the current skepticism of many toward openness and poverty. Fields summarizes Griffin's study:

> Drawing on a series of earlier studies, Griffin gives evidence of persistent poverty for *selected groups in particular countries, even rapidly growing ones. The indicators of poverty differ from country to country*: proportion of the rural poor below an absolute poverty line in several Asian countries; income share of the poorest 20 percent in the Philippines and 80 percent in Bangladesh; incomes of smallholders and landless workers in Malaysia and Sri Lanka; average real incomes of cocoa producers in Ghana; incomes of informal sector workers and smallholder farmers in the poorest regions of Tanzania; "pure labor share" of national income in Colombia; and so on. (Emphasis added)[40]

Two decades later, the World Bank (2000) also played up the damage done to selected groups by openness and, more generally, pro-market reforms. The following excerpt gives a flavor of the examples it cited:

> Evidence from a study of six African countries highlights how different groups fared differently under reforms. Poverty was more likely to decline in countries that improved their macroeconomic balances than in those that did not. But the evidence also shows that in three countries—Kenya, Nigeria, and Tanzania—real spending by the poorest segment of the population declined, even though the incidence of poverty [poverty ratio] fell nationwide. The decline in spending was particularly marked in Tanzania, where the poorest 10 percent were worse off in 1991 than they were in 1983. In Kenya the incidence of hard core poverty increased by four percentage points. In Nigeria, where overall poverty declined markedly, the incidence of hard core poverty rose 2.5 percentage points between 1985 and 1992.[41]

Prior to enumerating examples of reforms hurting specific groups such as these, the draft report is explicit in stating that the objective of the exercise is to sensitize policymakers to the need for determining beforehand "whether the reforms (or the way in which they are implemented) can be modified to reduce the costs to the poor without sacrificing much efficiency." While this is an eminently sensible reason for analyzing in detail the impact on specific groups, the draft report winds up injecting a heavy dose of skepticism about the desirability of reforms themselves, concluding, "These examples reveal that poor people can be hurt by reforms. It is little wonder, then, that in many civil society forums one hears voices of discontent about reform."

The problem with the argument that openness and other reforms must be resisted because they have not helped specific groups or even have hurt them is that in practice there is no policy that has been shown to benefit every poor individual. Even policies designed to directly assist the poverty-stricken can and do fail to aid many of the poor. Such anti-poverty initiatives in India as above-market procurement prices for food grains, subsidized fertilizer prices, rural electrification, and publicly provided primary education have left the poorest of the poor untouched because they lack the resources necessary to access these programs. After all, who but the richer farmers with plenty of farmland can effectively access fertilizer subsidies and above-market prices for the grain they produce? Leftist parties in India resisted the Green Revolution in the 1960s because they saw it as anti-poor. The argument was that the Green Revolution would benefit well-to-do farmers by raising their productivity but leave small farmers worse off because food grain prices would decline in response to the increase in productivity.

Therefore, the critical issue is not whether openness and growth help all of the poor but whether they help more of them than protection would. To be convincing, critics must offer persuasive evidence of protectionist policies delivering better outcomes. This they have not done. In contrast, sustained rapid growth, to which openness contributes handsomely, has almost always helped reduce aggregate poverty and, given a sufficiently long period of time, eliminated it altogether, as in the cases of Taiwan and South Korea.

In the end, the overall criterion for choosing among alternative policy packages has to be the decline in aggregate poverty. Arguments such as those offered by Kanbur that "for an NGO working with street children in Accra, or for a local official coping with increased poverty among indigenous peoples in Chiapas, it is cold comfort to be told, 'but national poverty has gone down'" are misplaced.[42] In making national policy, it is aggregate poverty that should count for more than what any specific NGO seeks for the constituency it represents.

Practically speaking, only a policy that generates enough income to bring down poverty overall has the potential to then address the plight of specific groups that are otherwise left out. The policy has to target aggregate poverty, with the interests of specific, hard-to-reach groups addressed through direct anti-poverty programs and social safety nets—just as the fifteen-year plan for India prepared by Pitamber Pant of the Perspective Division of the Planning Commission recommended as far back as 1962. A policy that delivers rapid growth and helps bring down aggregate poverty also generates more revenue for the government, which it can use to finance direct anti-poverty programs aimed at assisting the "core poor."

Churning at the Bottom of the Distribution

Economist Martin Ravallion has drawn attention to the process of "churning," whereby positions get swapped between poor and non-poor over two or more time periods with no change in aggregate poverty.[43] Such churning will naturally make those falling into poverty unhappy and those escaping it happy. From a policy perspective, however, the issue is whether such churning is yet one more reason for skepticism toward openness. There are at least three reasons why the answer to this question is in the negative.

First, churning at all levels is an integral part of dynamic economies. Economist John Haltiwanger reports that in the United States between 1980 and 2009, every year 15 percent of the jobs existing in the previous year were destroyed while 17 percent of all jobs were new jobs.[44] This churning in jobs is bound to be associated with some churning in incomes as well. In contrast, economies exhibiting stability are also likely to be associated with economic stagnation. Such economies will offer very little hope of poverty alleviation.

Second, even holding the poverty ratio constant, it is not altogether clear that churning is necessarily harmful. For one thing, over time it implies a more equal distribution of income. As an example, compare two countries that are identical in all respects except that in one of them there is no churning while in the other the bottom 20 percent and the next 20 percent of the population annually exchange their positions. Then the distribution of income among the bottom 40 percent of the population over any two-year period will be more equal in the second country than in the first.

Finally, and perhaps most important, when there is no churning, fatalism is likely to afflict those experiencing poverty year in and year out. In contrast, when churning takes place, it brings hope to those at the bottom of the distribution. A family that comes out of poverty one year but falls back into it the next year is more likely to struggle to break the cycle permanently than one that stays in poverty permanently.

Concluding Remarks

In assessing the liberal trade policy framework against protectionism, the question we must ask is which of these two regimes offers better prospects for growth and poverty alleviation. Critics have often pointed to this or that deficiency of outcomes from trade liberalization without making any effort to show that protectionism yields a superior outcome on average. Critics rest their case on many specious arguments, which turn out to be false upon close examination.

They argue, for example, that trade liberalization has failed to stimulate growth in many cases; that it cannot be credited with having catalyzed many of the growth miracles; that every successful country has pursued import substitution in the early stages of development; that high protection has not been inconsistent with rapid growth; and that industrial policy has been a part of many success stories. Each of these criticisms of openness as an engine of growth distracts from the main point: there are no examples of countries having experienced sustained rapid growth without low or declining barriers to trade. Indeed, free trade critics have never even attempted to offer empirical evidence showing that high and rising protection can yield sustained rapid growth.

When confronted with compelling evidence of liberal trade policies being a part of nearly all experiences of sustained rapid growth, critics switch to arguing that trade openness has failed to help the poor. For example, they argue that poverty has risen alongside opening to trade; that even if the poverty ratio has fallen, the rise in the absolute number of poor testifies to the failure of openness; that opening to trade and the accompanying growth have done precious little for the core poor; and that increased openness has been associated with churning, whereby poor come out of poverty but fall back into it after a while. A closer examination of each of these arguments reveals its hollowness. In particular, critics do not show that where trade openness has failed, protectionism has succeeded. To persuade, they must demonstrate that on average protectionism yields a superior outcome with respect to poverty alleviation. This they have not done.

Notes

1 In this context, see Yatawara 2000.
2 Bastiat 1845.
3 Two old classics are Bastiat 1845 [1996] and George 1886 [1949]; a more recent one is lrwin 2005. In modern times, the focus has shifted to globalization, of which free trade is merely a part, albeit an important one. Several volumes on globalization have appeared during the past two decades. In particular, see the excellent volumes by Bhagwati (2004) and Wolf (2004), which also address many issues related to developing countries.
4 Baldwin 1969.
5 Krueger 2004.
6 Richard Solomon and Nigel Quinney state, "Ignoring the pleas of Agriculture Secretary Orville Freeman and Secretary of State Dean Rusk, Johnson continued to impose on India what he himself called a 'ship-to-mouth' existence" (2010, 260).
7 Fields 1980, 204.
8 Little 1979, 448–49.
9 Little, Scitovsky, and Scott 1970.
10 Bhagwati 1978; Krueger 1978.
11 Balassa 1982.
12 Little, Scitovsky, and Scott 1970, 1.
13 Frank, Kim, and Westphal 1975.
14 Frank, Kim, and Westphal 1975, 92.
15 Bhagwati and Srinivasan 1975, 191.
16 Edwards and Lederman 2002 on Chile; Panagariya 1993 for China.
17 Panagariya 2008, ch.4.
18 Westphal 1978, 1982.
19 Westphal 1990.
20 Amsden 1989; Wade 1990.
21 Rodrik 1999.
22 Stiglitz 2002; Stiglitz and Charlton 2005; Reinert 2007; Chang 2002, 2007.
23 Bhagwati and Desai 1970, 495.
24 Little 1960, 25.

25 Little 1996a, 162.

26 Lal and Rajapatirana 1987, 208.

27 This is systematically documented in the excellent volume on unilateral trade liberalization edited by Bhagwati 2002.

28 For example, Rodriguez and Rodrik 2000.

29 Corbo, Krueger, and Ossa 1985.

30 For example, Rodrik 1995 on South Korea and Taiwan, and Rodrik 2003 on India and China.

31 The issue of the initial catalyst to growth in South Korea and Taiwan is analyzed in greater detail in Part III.

32 For instance, see Wade 2002 and Kanbur 2001.

33 Occasionally analysts also track the evolution of income of the bottom three or four deciles of the population to assess whether the lot of the poor is improving over time.

34 World Bank 1999, 1, ix.

35 For example, see *IFG Bulletin* 1, no. 3 (2001) by the International Forum on Globalization at http://www.thirdworldtraveler.com/Globalization/GlobalizationFactsFigures.html (accessed November 26, 2017).

36 Wade 2002.

37 To quote Srinivasan from one of his many writings on this subject, "A poverty bundle common to all regions within a geographically and culturally diverse country such as India, let alone for all countries of the world, cannot be meaningfully defined. If such a bundle could be defined, then the national poverty line at any point in time would be the value of that bundle at the prices in *local currency* that households face in that nation at that point in time. There is no need for any exchange rate in such a calculation. [Angus] Deaton is absolutely right in arguing that, because such an internationally accepted bundle does not exist, it does not make sense to simply convert $1/day to local currency values using purchasing power parity (PPP) exchange rates with commodities weighted by their shares in the consumption of the poor. The reason is that doing so makes poverty lines move around with changes in PPP exchange rates arising from world market price changes that have no relevance to the poor. For example, the poverty line for one country would be shifted by a change in the world price of a commodity that is not consumed by the poor in that country but consumed by the poor in some other country, because such a price change affects the PPP exchange rate. In any case, global poverty counts are based on neither a common global poverty bundle nor conversions to local currency values using PPP exchange rates with commodity weights more relevant to the poor" (2008, 14). Additional problems characterizing global figures on poverty include non-comparability of sample surveys across countries and over time and sampling and non-sampling errors in them.

38 Galenson (1977).

39 Quoted in Fields 1980, 167. Galenson defined fast-growing economies as those exhibiting annual GDP growth rates of 7 percent or more.

40 Fields 1980, 167–68.

41 World Bank 2000, 8.14. I have suppressed a footnote from the above quotation following the expression "hard core poverty" in the Kenya. The footnote states, "Based on a poverty line that defines approximately 10 percent of the relevant population as poor in the base year. This line is kept constant in real terms in estimating the incidence in the terminal year."

42 Kanbur 2001, 1087.

43 Ravallion 2003.

44 Haltiwanger 2012.

References

Amsden, Alice. 1989. *Asia's Next Giant: South Korea and Late Industrialization*. New York: Oxford University Press.

Balassa, B. 1982. "Development Strategies and Economic Performance: A Comparative Analysis of Eleven Semi-industrialized Economies." In *Development Strategies in Semi-industrialized Economies*, edited by B. Balassa, 38–62. Baltimore: Johns Hopkins University Press.

Baldwin, R. F. 1969. "The Case Against Infant-Industry Tariff Protection." *Journal of Political Economy* 77, nos. 5–6: 295–305.

Bastiat, Frederic. 1845 (1996). *Economic Sophisms*, edited and translated by Arthur Goddard. Irvington-on-Hudson, NY: Foundation for Economic Education.

Bhagwati, Jagdish. 1978. *Foreign Trade Regimes and Economic Development: Anatomy and Consequences of Exchange Rate Regimes*. New York: National Bureau of Economic Research.

Bhagwati, Jagdish. 2002. *Going Alone: The Case for Relaxed Reciprocity in Freeing Trade*. Cambridge, MA: MIT Press.

Bhagwati, Jagdish. 2004. *In Defense of Globalization*. New York: Oxford University Press.

Bhagwati Jagdish, and Padma Desai. 1970. *India: Planning for Industrialization*. London: Oxford University Press.

Bhagwati, Jagdish, and T. N. Srinivasan. 1975. *Foreign Trade Regimes and Economic Development: India*. New York: National Bureau of Economic Research.

Chang, Ha-Joon. 2002. *Kicking Away the Ladder: Development Strategy in Historical Perspective*. London: Anthem World Economics.

Chang, Ha-Joon. 2007. *Bad Samaritans: Rich Nations, Poor Policies and the Threat to the Developing World*. London: Random House Business Books.

Corbo, V., Anne Krueger, and Fernando Ossa. 1985. "Introduction." In *Export-Oriented Development Strategies: The Success of Five Newly Industrializing Countries*, edited by V. Corbo, Anne Krueger, and Fernando Ossa. Boulder, CO: Westview Press.

Edwards, Sebastian, and Daniel Lederman. 2002. "The Political Economy of Unilateral Liberalization: The Case of Chile." In *Going Alone: The Case of Relaxed Reciprocity in Freeing Trade*, edited by Jagdish Bhagwati. Cambridge, MA: MIT Press.

Fields, Gary. 1980. *Poverty, Inequality and Development*. Cambridge: Cambridge University Press.

Frank, Charles R. Jr., Kwang Suk Kim, and Larry E. Westphal. 1975. *Foreign Trade Regimes and Economic Development: South Korea*. New York: National Bureau of Economic Research.

Galenson, Walter. 1977. "Economic Growth, Income and Employment." Paper presented at the conference on Poverty and Development in Latin America, Yale University, April.

George, Henry. 1886 (1949). *Protection or Free Trade: An Examination of the Tariff Question, with Special Reference to the Interests of Labor*. New York: Robert Schalkenbach Foundation.

Haltiwanger, John. 2012. "Job Creation and Firm Dynamics in the United States." In *Innovation and the Economy*, edited by Josh Lerner and Scott Stern, 12:17-38. Chicago: University of Chicago Press.

Kanbur, Ravi. 2001. "Economic Policy; Distribution and Poverty: The Nature of the Disagreements." *World Development* 29, no. 6: 1083–94.

Krueger, Anne. 1978. *Foreign Trade Regime and Economic Development: Liberalization Attempts and Consequences*. New York: National Bureau of Economic Research.

Krueger, Anne. 2004. "Opening Remarks." Speech delivered to the African Governors of the International Monetary Fund, October 4. http://www.imforg/external/np/speeches/2004/100404.htm.

Lal, Deepak, and Sarath Rajapatirana. 1987. "Foreign Trade Regimes and Economic Growth in Developing Countries." *World Bank Research Observer* 2, no. 2: 189–217.

Little, I. M. D. 1960. "The Strategy of lndian Development." *National Institute Economic Review* 9, no. 1: 20–29.

Little, I. M. D. 1979. "An Economic Reconnaissance." In *Economic Growth and Structural Change in Taiwan: The Postwar Experience of the Republic of China*, edited by Walter Galenson. Ithaca, NY: Cornell University Press.

Little, I. M. D. 1996a. "India's Economic Reforms 1991–96." *Journal of Asian Economics* 7, no. 2: 161–76.

Little, Ian, Tibor Scitovsky, and Maurice Scott. 1970. *Industry and Trade in Some Developing Countries*. London: Oxford University Press.

Panagariya, Arvind. 1993. "Unravelling the Mysteries of China's Foreign Trade Regime." *World Economy* 16, no. 1: 51–68.

Panagariya, Arvind. 2008. *India: The Emerging Giant*. New York: Oxford University Press.

Ravallion, Martin. 2003. "The Debate on Globalization, Poverty and Inequality: Why Measurement Matters." World Bank Development Research Group Working Paper 3038.

Reinert, Erik. 2007. *How Rich Countries Got Rich and Why Poor Countries Stay Poor*. London: Constable and Robinson.

Rodriguez, Francisco, and Dani Rodrik. 2000. "Trade Policy and Economic Growth: A Skeptic's Guide to the Cross-National Evidence." In *NBER Macroeconomics Annual 2000*, edited by Ben S. Bernanke and Kenneth Rogoff. Cambridge, MA: MIT Press.

Rodrik, Dani. 1995. "Getting Interventions Right: How South Korea and Taiwan Grew Rich." *Economic Policy* 20: 55–107.

Rodrik, Dani. 1999. *The New Global Economy and Developing Countries: Making Openness Work*. Washington, DC: Overseas Development Council.

Rodrik, Dani. 2003. "Institutions, Integration, and Geography: In Search of the Deep Determinants of Economic Growth." In *In Search of Prosperity: Analytic Narratives of Economic Growth*, edited by Dani Rodrik. Princeton, NJ: Princeton University Press.

Solomon, Richard H., and Nigel Quinney. 2010. *American Negotiating Behavior: Wheeler-Dealers, Legal Eagles, Bullies, and Preachers*. Washington, DC: United States Institute of Peace.

Srinivasan, T. N. 2008. "Globalization and Poverty." In *Trade, Growth and Poverty*, edited by Elias Dinopoulos, Pravin Krishna, Arvind Panagariya, and Kar-yiu Wong. New York: Routledge.

Stiglitz, Joseph. 2002. *Globalization and Its Discontents*. New York: W. W. Norton.

Stiglitz, Joseph, and Andre Charlton. 2005. *Fair Trade For All—How Trade Can Promote Development*. Oxford: Oxford University Press.

Wade, Robert. 1990. *Governing the Market: Economic Theory and the Role of the Government in East Asian Industrialization*. Princeton, NJ: Princeton University Press, 1990.

Wade, Robert. 2002. "Globalization, Poverty and Income Distribution: Does the Liberal Argument Hold?" Working Paper 02–33. London School of Economics.

Westphal, Larry E. 1978. "The Republic of Korea's Experience with Export-Led Industrial Development." *World Development* 6: 347–82.

Westphal, Larry E. 1990. "Industrial Policy in an Export-Propelled Economy: Lessons from South Korea's Experience." *Journal of Economic Perspectives* 4, no. 3: 41–59.

Wolf, Martin. 2004. *Why Globalization Works*. New Haven, CT: Yale University Press.

World Bank. 1999. *1999 Annual Review of Development Effectiveness*. Washington, DC: World Bank.

World Bank. 2000. *World Development Report 2000: Consultation Draft.* January. Washington, DC: World Bank.

Yatawara, Ravindra. 2000. "Timing Is Everything: On the Determinants of Commercial Policy Changes." In *Essays on the Reform of Trade and Exchange*, 1–57. PhD dissertation, Columbia University, New York.

Dani Rodrik,
One Economics, Many Recipes (2007)[*]

1. Fifty Years of Growth (and Lack Thereof):
An Interpretation

Real per capita income in the developing world grew at an average rate of 2.1 percent per annum during the four and a half decades between 1960 and 2004.[1] This is a high growth rate by almost any standard. At this pace incomes double every 33 years, allowing each generation to enjoy a level of living standards that is twice as high as the previous generation's. To provide some historical perspective on this performance, it is worth noting that Britain's per capita GDP grew at a mere 1.3 percent per annum during its period of economic supremacy in the middle of the nineteenth century (1820–70) and that the United States grew at only 1.8 percent during the half century before World War I when it overtook Britain as the world's economic leader (Maddison 2001, table B-22, 265). Moreover, with few exceptions, economic growth in the last few decades has been accompanied by significant improvements in social indicators such as literacy, infant mortality, and life expectation.[2] So on balance the recent growth record looks quite impressive.

However, since the rich countries themselves grew at a very rapid clip of 2.5 percent during the period 1960–2004, few developing countries consistently managed to close the economic gap between them and the advanced nations. As figure 1.1 indicates, the countries of East and Southeast Asia constitute the sole exception. Excluding China, this region experienced pretty consistent per capita GDP growth of 3.7 percent over 1960–2004. Despite the Asian financial crisis of 1997–98 (which shows as a slight dip in figure 1.1), countries such as South Korea, Thailand, and Malaysia ended the century with productivity levels that stood significantly closer to those enjoyed in the advanced countries.

Elsewhere, the pattern of economic performance has varied greatly across different time periods. China has been a major success story since the late 1970s, experiencing a stupendous growth rate of 8.0 percent since 1978. Less spectacularly, India has roughly doubled its growth rate since the early 1980s, pulling South Asia's growth rate up to 3.3 percent in 1980–2000 from 1.1 percent in 1960–1980. The experience in other parts of the world was the mirror image of these Asian growth take-offs. Latin America and sub-Saharan Africa both experienced robust economic growth prior to the late 1970s and early 1980s—2.9 percent and 2.2 percent respectively—but then lost ground subsequently in dramatic fashion. Latin America's growth rate

---

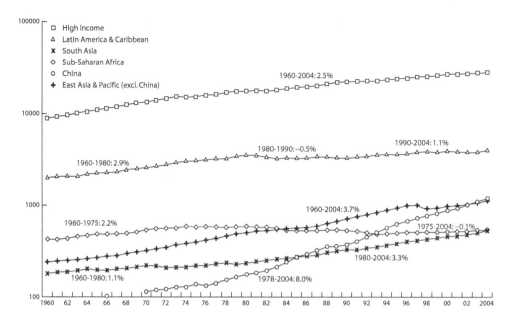

FIGURE 1.1 GDP per capita by country groupings (in 2000 US$)

Source: World Bank, World Development Indicators.

collapsed in the "lost decade" of the 1980s, and has remained anemic despite some recovery in the 1990s. Africa's economic decline, which began in the second half of the 1970s, continued throughout much of the 1990s and has been aggravated by the onset of HIV/AIDS and other public-health challenges. Measures of total factor productivity run parallel to these trends in per capita output (see, for example, Bosworth and Collins 2003).

Hence the aggregate picture hides tremendous variety in growth performance, both geographically and temporally. We have high-growth countries and low-growth countries; countries that have grown rapidly throughout, and countries that have experienced growth spurts for a decade or two; countries that took off around 1980 and countries whose growth collapsed around 1980.

This chapter is devoted to the question, what do we learn about growth strategies from this rich and diverse experience? By *growth strategies* I refer to economic policies and institutional arrangements aimed at achieving economic convergence with the living standards prevailing in advanced countries. My emphasis will be less on the relationship between specific policies and economic growth—the stock-in-trade of cross-national growth empirics—and more on developing a broad understanding of the contours of successful strategies. Hence my account harks back to an earlier generation of studies that distilled operational lessons from the observed growth experience, such as Albert Hirschman's *The Strategy of Economic Development* (1958), Alexander Gerschenkron's *Economic Backwardness in Historical Perspective* (1962), and Walt Rostow's *The Stages of Economic Growth* (1965). This chapter follows an unashamedly inductive approach in this tradition.

A key theme in these works, as well as in the present analysis, is that growth-promoting policies tend to be context specific. We are able to make only a limited number of generalizations on the effects on growth, say, of liberalizing the trade regime, opening up the financial system, or building more schools. As I will stress throughout this book, the experience of the last two decades has frustrated the expectations of policy advisors who thought we had a good fix on the policies that promote growth. And despite a voluminous literature, cross-national growth regressions ultimately do not provide us with much reliable and unambiguous evidence on such operational matters.[3] An alternative approach, the one I adopt here, is to shift our focus to a higher level of generality and to examine the broad design principles of successful growth strategies. This entails zooming away from the individual building blocks and concentrating on how they are put together.

The chapter revolves around two key arguments. One is that neoclassical economic analysis is a lot more flexible than its practitioners in the policy domain have generally given it credit for. In particular, first-order economic principles—protection of property rights, contract enforcement, market-based competition, appropriate incentives, sound money, debt sustainability—do not map into unique policy packages. Good institutions are those that deliver these first-order principles effectively. There is no unique correspondence between the *functions* that good institutions perform and the *form* that such institutions take. Reformers have substantial room for creatively packaging these principles into institutional designs that are sensitive to local constraints and take advantage of local opportunities. Successful countries are those that have used this room wisely.

The second argument is that igniting economic growth and sustaining it are somewhat different enterprises. The former generally requires a limited range of (often unconventional) reforms that need not overly tax the institutional capacity of the economy. The latter challenge is in many ways harder, as it requires constructing a sound institutional underpinning to maintain productive dynamism and endow the economy with resilience to shocks over the longer term. The good news is that this institutional infrastructure does not have to be constructed overnight. Ignoring the distinction between these two tasks—starting and sustaining growth—leaves reformers saddled with impossibly ambitious, undifferentiated, and impractical policy agendas.

The plan for the chapter is as follows. The next section sets the stage by evaluating the standard recipes for economic growth in light of recent economic performance. The third section develops the argument that sound economic principles do not map into unique institutional arrangements and reform strategies. The fourth section reinterprets recent growth experience using the conceptual framework of the previous section. The fifth section discusses a two-pronged growth strategy that differentiates between the challenges of igniting growth and the challenges of sustaining it. Concluding remarks are presented in the final section.

What We Know that (Possibly) Ain't So

Development policy has always been subject to fads and fashions. During the 1950s and 1960s, "big push," planning, and import-substitution were the rallying cries of economic reformers in poor nations. These ideas lost ground during the 1970s to more market-oriented views that emphasized the role of the price system and an outward

TABLE 1.1 Rules of Good Behavior for Promoting Economic Growth

Original Washington Consensus	"Augmented" Washington Consensus (additions to the original 10 items)
1. Fiscal discipline	11. Corporate governance
2. Reorientation of public expenditures	12. Anticorruption
3. Tax reform	13. Flexible labor markets
4. Interest rate liberalization	14. Adherence to WTO disciplines
5. Unified and competitive exchange rates	15. Adherence to international financial codes and standards
6. Trade liberalization	16. "Prudent" capital-account opening
7. Openness to direct foreign investment	17. Nonintermediate exchange rate regimes
8. Privatization	18. Independent central banks/inflation targeting
9. Deregulation	19. Social safety nets
10. Secure property rights	20. Targeted poverty reduction

orientation.[4] By the late 1980s a remarkable convergence of views had developed around a set of policy principles that John Williamson (1990) infelicitously termed the "Washington Consensus." These principles remain at the heart of conventional understanding of a desirable policy framework for economic growth, even though they have been greatly embellished and expanded in the years since.

The left panel in table 1.1 shows Williamson's original list, which focused on fiscal discipline, "competitive" currencies, trade and financial liberalization, privatization and deregulation. These were perceived to be the key elements of what Krugman (1995, 29) has called the "Victorian virtue in economic policy," namely "free markets and sound money."

Toward the end of the 1990s, this list was augmented in the thinking of multilateral agencies and policy economists with a series of so-called second-generation reforms that were more institutional in nature and targeted at problems of "good governance." A complete inventory of these Washington Consensus–plus reforms would take too much space, and in any case the precise listing differs from source to source.[5] I have shown a representative sample of 10 items (to preserve the symmetry with the original Washington Consensus) in the right panel of table 1.1. They range from anticorruption and corporate governance to "flexible" labor markets and social safety nets.

The perceived need for second-generation reforms arose from a combination of sources. First, there was growing recognition that market-oriented policies might be inadequate without more serious institutional transformation, in areas ranging from the bureaucracy to labor markets. For example, trade liberalization will not reallocate an economy's resources appropriately if the labor markets are "rigid" or insufficiently "flexible." Second, there was a concern that financial liberalization might lead to crises and excessive volatility in the absence of a more carefully delineated macroeconomic framework and improved prudential regulation. Hence arose the focus on nonintermediate exchange-rate regimes, central bank independence, and adherence to international financial codes and standards. Finally, in response to the complaint that the Washington Consensus represented a trickle-down approach to poverty, the policy framework was augmented with social policies and antipoverty programs.

It is probably fair to say that a list along the lines of table 1.1 captures in broad brushstrokes mainstream post–Washington Consensus thinking on the key elements of a growth program. How does such a list fare when held against the light of contemporary growth experience? Imagine that we gave table 1.1 to an intelligent Martian and asked him to match the growth record displayed in figure 1.1 with the expectations that the list generates. How successful would he be in identifying which of the regions adopted the standard policy agenda and which did not?

Consider first the high-performing East Asian countries. Since this region is the only one that has done consistently well since the early 1960s, the Martian would reasonably guess that there is a high degree of correspondence between the region's policies and the list in table 1.1. But he would be at best half right. South Korea's and Taiwan's growth policies, to take two important illustrations, exhibit significant departures from the mainstream consensus. Neither country undertook significant deregulation or liberalization of its trade and financial systems well into the 1980s. Far from privatizing, they both relied heavily on public enterprises. South Korea did not even welcome direct foreign investment. And both countries deployed an extensive set of industrial policies that took the form of directed credit, trade protection, export subsidization, tax incentives, and other nonuniform interventions. Using the minimal scorecard of the original Washington Consensus (left panel of table 1.2), the Martian would award South Korea a grade of 5 (out of 10) and Taiwan perhaps a 6 (Rodrik 1996a).

The gap between the East Asian "model" and the more demanding institutional requirements shown in the right panel of table 1.1 is, if anything, even larger. I provide a schematic comparison between the mainstream "ideal" and the East Asian reality in table 1.2 for a number of different institutional domains, such as corporate governance, financial markets, business-government relationships, and public ownership. Looking at these discrepancies, the Martian might well conclude that South Korea, Taiwan, and (before them) Japan stood little chance to develop. Indeed, so strong were the East Asian anomalies that when the Asian financial crisis of 1997–98 struck, many observers attributed the crisis to the moral hazard, "cronyism," and other problems created by East Asian–style institutions (see MacLean 1999; Frankel 2000a).

The Martian would also be led astray by China's boom since the late 1970s and by India's less phenomenal, but still significant growth pickup since the early 1980s. While both of these countries have transformed their attitudes toward markets and private enterprise during this period, their policy frameworks bear very little resemblance to what is described in table 1.1. India deregulated its policy regime slowly and undertook very little privatization. Its trade regime remained heavily restricted late into the 1990s. China did not even adopt a private property rights regime, and it merely appended a market system to the scaffolding of a planned economy (as discussed further below). It is hardly an exaggeration to say that had the Chinese economy stagnated in the last couple of decades, the Martian would be in a better position to rationalize it using the policy guidance provided in table 1.1 than he is to explain China's *actual* performance.[6]

TABLE 1.2 East Asian Anomalies

Institutional Domain	Mainstream Ideal	"East Asian" Pattern
Property rights	Private, enforced by the rule of law	Private, but government authority occasionally overrides the law (esp. in Korea)
Corporate governance	Shareholder ("outsider") control, protection of shareholder rights	Insider control
Business-government relations	Arm's length, rule based	Close interactions
Industrial organization	Decentralized, competitive markets, with tough antitrust enforcement	Horizontal and vertical integration in production (*chaebol*); government-mandated "cartels"
Financial system	Deregulated, securities based, with free entry. Prudential supervision through regulatory oversight.	Bank based, restricted entry, heavily controlled by government, directed lending, weak formal regulation
Labor markets	Decentralized, deinstitutionalized, "flexible" labor markets	Lifetime employment in core enterprises (Japan)
International capital flows	"Prudently" free	Restricted (until the 1990s)
Public ownership	None in productive sectors	Plenty in upstream industries

The Martian would be puzzled that the region that made the most determined attempt at remaking itself in the image of table 1.1, namely Latin America, has reaped so little growth benefit out of it. Countries such as Mexico, Argentina, Brazil, Colombia, Bolivia, and Peru did more liberalization, deregulation, and privatization in the course of a few years than East Asian countries have done in four decades. Figure 1.2 shows an index of structural reform for these and other Latin American countries, taken from Lora (2001a). The index measures on a scale from 0 to 1 the extent of trade and financial liberalization, tax reform, privatization, and labor-market reform undertaken. The regional average for the index rises steadily from 0.34 in 1985 to 0.58 in 1999. Yet the striking fact from figure 1.1 is that Latin America's growth rate has remained a fraction of its pre-1980 level. The Martian would be at a loss to explain why growth is now lower given that the quality of Latin America's policies, as judged by the requirements in table 1.1, have improved so much.[7] A similar puzzle, perhaps of a smaller magnitude, arises with respect to Africa, where economic decline persists despite an overall (if less marked) "improvement" in the policy environment.[8]

The Martian would recognize that the growth record is consistent with some of the *higher-order* economic principles that inspire the standard policy consensus. A semblance of property rights, sound money, fiscal solvency, market-oriented incentives—these are elements common to all successful growth strategies.[9] Where they have been lacking, economic performance has been lackluster at best. But the Martian would also have to conclude that the mapping from our more detailed policy preferences (such as those in table 1.1) to economic success is quite imperfect. He would wonder if we could not do better.

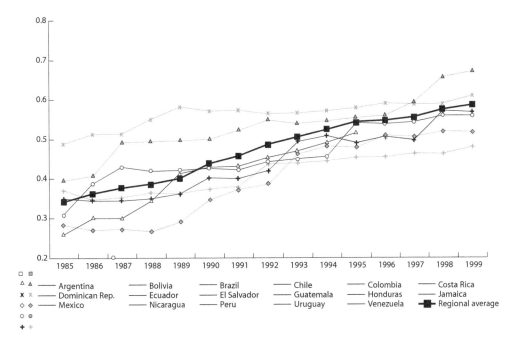

FIGURE 1.2 Structural reform index for Latin American Countries

Source: Lora 2001a.

Indeterminate Mapping From Economic Principles To Institutional Arrangements

Here is another thought experiment. Imagine a Western economist was invited to Beijing in 1978 in order to advise the Chinese leadership on a reform strategy. What would she recommend, and why?

The economist would recognize that reform must start in the rural areas since the vast majority of the poor live there. An immediate recommendation would be the *liberalization of agricultural markets* and the *abolition of the state order system* under which peasants had to make obligatory deliveries of crops at low, state-controlled prices. But since price liberalization alone would be inadequate to generate the appropriate supply incentives under a system of communal land ownership, the economist would also recommend the *privatization of land.* Next, the economist would have to turn her attention to the broader implications of price liberalization in agriculture. Without access to cheap grains, the state would be left without a source of implicit tax revenue, so *tax reform* must be on the agenda as well. And in view of the rise of food prices, there must be a way to respond to urban workers' demand for higher wages. State enterprises in urban areas must be *corporatized*, so that their managers are in a position to adjust their wages and prices appropriately.

But now there are other problems that need attention. In an essentially closed and noncompetitive economy, price-setting autonomy for large state enterprises entails

TABLE 1.3 The Logic of the Washington Consensus and a Chinese Counterfactual

Problem		Solution
Low agricultural productivity	→	Price liberalization
Production incentives	→	Land privatization
Loss of fiscal revenues	→	Tax reform
Urban wages	→	Corporatization
Monopoly	→	Trade liberalization
Enterprise restructuring	→	Financial sector reform
Unemployment	→	Social safety nets

the exercise of monopoly power. So the economist would likely recommend *trade liberalization* in order to "import" price discipline from abroad. Openness to trade in turn calls for other complementary reforms. There must be *financial sector reform* so that financial intermediaries are able to assist domestic enterprises in the inevitable adjustments that are called forth. And, of course, there must be *social safety nets* in place so that those workers who are temporarily displaced have some income support during the transition.

The story can be embellished by adding other required reforms, but the message ought to be clear. By the time the Western economist is done, the reform agenda she has formulated looks very similar to the Washington Consensus (see table 1.3). The economist's reasoning is utterly plausible, which underscores the point that the consensus is far from silly: it is the result of systematic thinking about the multiple, often complementary reforms needed to establish property rights, put market incentives to work, and maintain macroeconomic stability. But while this particular reform program represents a logically consistent way of achieving these end goals, it is not the only one that has the potential of doing so. In fact, in view of the administrative and political constraints that such an ambitious agenda is likely to encounter, there may be better ways of getting there.

How can we be sure of this? We know this because China took a very different approach to reform—one that was experimental in nature and relied on a series of policy innovations that departed significantly from Western norms. What is important to realize about these innovations is that in the end they delivered—for a period of a couple of decades at least—the very same goals that the Western economist would have been hoping for: market-oriented incentives, property rights, macroeconomic stability. But they did so in a peculiar fashion that, given the Chinese historical and political context, had numerous advantages.

For example, the Chinese authorities liberalized agriculture only *at the margin* while keeping the plan system intact. Farmers were allowed to sell surplus crops freely at a market-determined price only after they had fulfilled their obligations to the state under the state order system. As Lau, Qian, and Roland (2000) explain, this ingenious system generated efficiency without creating any losers. In particular, it was a shortcut that neatly solved a conundrum inherent in wholesale liberalization: how to provide microeconomic incentives to producers while insulating the central government from the fiscal consequences of liberalization. As long as state quotas were set below the fully liberalized market outcome (so that transactions were conducted at market prices at the margin) and were not ratcheted up (so that producers did not have to worry about the quotas creeping up as a result of marketed surplus), China's dual-track reform in effect achieved full allocative efficiency. But it entailed a different inframarginal distribution—one that preserved the income streams of initial claimants. The dual-track approach was eventually employed in other areas as well, such as industrial goods (e.g., coal and steel) and labor markets (employment contracts). Lau et al. (2000) argue that the system was critical to achieve political support for the reform process, maintain its momentum, and minimize adverse social implications.

Another important illustration comes from the area of property rights. Rather than privatize land and industrial assets, the Chinese government implemented novel institutional arrangements such as the household responsibility system (under which land was "assigned" to individual households according to their size) and township and village enterprises (TVEs). The TVEs were the growth engine of China until the mid-1990s (Qian 2003), with their share in industrial value added rising to more than 50 percent by the early 1990s (Lin, Cai, and Li 1996, 180), so they deserve special comment. Formal ownership rights in TVEs were vested not in private hands or in the central government, but in local communities (townships or villages). Local governments were keen to ensure the prosperity of these enterprises, as their equity stake generated revenues directly for them. Qian (2003) argues that in the environment characteristic of China, property rights were effectively more secure under direct local government ownership than they would have been under a private-property-rights legal regime. The efficiency loss caused by the absence of private control rights was probably outweighed by the implicit security guaranteed by local government control. It is difficult to explain otherwise the remarkable boom in investment and entrepreneurship generated by such enterprises.

Qian (2003) discusses other examples of "transitional institutions" China employed to fuel economic growth—fiscal contracts between central and local governments, anonymous banking—and one may expand his list by including arrangements such as special economic zones. The main points to take from this experience are the following. First, China relied on highly unusual, nonstandard institutions. Second, these unorthodox institutions worked precisely because they produced orthodox results, namely market-oriented incentives, property rights, macroeconomic stability, and so on. Third, it is hard to argue, in view of China's stupendous growth, that a more standard, "best-practice" set of institutional arrangements would have necessarily done better. Of course, it is entirely possible that these Chinese-style institutions will turn out to be dysfunctional in the longer run and therefore in need of reform themselves. My point is simply that they sparked an unprecedented rate of economic growth in a manner that is hard to envisage the mainstream alternatives accomplishing.

China's experience helps lay out the issues clearly because its institutional innovations and growth performance are both so stark. But the Chinese experience with nonstandard growth policies is hardly unusual; in fact, it is more the rule than the exception. The (other) East Asian anomalies noted previously (table 1.2) can be viewed as part of the same pattern: nonstandard practices in the service of sound economic principles. I summarize a few non-Chinese illustrations in table 1.4.

TABLE 1.4 How to Understand and Rationalize Institutional Anomalies: Four Illustrations

Objective	What is the Problem?	Institutional Response	Prerequisites	Institutional Complements
Financial deepening (saving mobilization and efficient intermediation)	Asymmetric information (investors know more about their projects than lenders do) and limited liability	"Financial restraint" (Hellmann et al. 1997): controlled deposit rates restricted entry; creation of rents to induce better portfolio risk management, better monitoring of firms, and increased deposit mobilization by banks	Ability to maintain restraint at *moderate* levels; positive real interest rates; macroeconomic stability; avoid state capture by financial interests	*Finance:* highly regulated financial markets (absence of security markets and closed capital accounts to prevent cherry picking and rent dissipation); *politics:* state "autonomy" to prevent capture and decay into "crony capitalism"
Spurring investment and entrepreneurship in nontraditional activities	Economies of scale together with interindustry linkages depress private return to entrepreneurship/investment below social return.	"Industrial policy as a coordination device" (Rodrik 1995a): credit subsidies (Korea) and tax incentives (Taiwan) for selected sectors; protection of home market coupled with export subsidies; public enterprise creation for upstream products; arm-twisting and cajoling by political leadership; socialization of investment risk through implicit investment guarantees	High level of human capital relative to physical capital; relatively competent bureaucracy to select investment projects	*Trade:* need to combine import protection (in selected sectors) with exposure to competition in export markets to distinguish high-from low-productivity firms; *business-government relations:* "embedded autonomy" (Evans 1995) to enable close interactions and information exchange while preventing state capture and decay into "crony capitalism"
Productive organization of the workplace	Trade-off between information sharing (working together) and economies of specialization (specialized tasks)	"Horizontal hierarchy" (Aoki 1997)	(Unintended) fit with prewar arrangements of military resource mobilization in Japan	*Corporate governance:* insider control to provide incentive for accumulating long-term managerial skills; *labor markets:* lifetime employment and enterprise unionism to generate long-term collaborative teamwork; *financial markets:* main bank system to discipline firms and reduce the moral hazard consequences of insider control; *politics:* "bureau-pluralism" (regulation protection) to redistribute benefits to less productive, traditional sectors
Reduce antiexport bias	Import-competing interests are politically powerful and opposed to trade liberalization	Export-processing zone (Rodrik 1999a)	Saving boom; elastic supply of foreign investment; preferential market access in EU	*Dual labor markets:* segmentation between male and female labor force, so that increased female employment in the EPZ does not drive wages up in the rest of the economy

Consider, for example, the case of financial controls. I noted earlier that few of the successful East Asian countries undertook much financial liberalization early in their development process. Interest rates remained controlled below market-clearing levels, and competitive entry (by domestic or foreign financial intermediaries) was typically blocked. It is easy to construct arguments as to why this was beneficial from an economic standpoint. Table 1.4 summarizes the story laid out by Hellmann, Murdock, and Stiglitz (1997), who coin the term *financial restraint* for the Asian model. Where asymmetric information prevails and the level of savings is suboptimal, Hellman et al. argue that creating a moderate amount of rents for incumbent banks can generate useful incentives. These rents induce banks to do a better job of monitoring their borrowers (since there is more at stake) and to expand efforts to mobilize deposits (since there are rents to be earned on them). Both the quality and the level of financial intermediation can be higher than under financial liberalization. These beneficial effects are more likely to materialize when the preexisting institutional landscape has certain properties—for example, when the state is not "captured" by private interests and the external capital account is restricted (see last two columns of table 1.4). When these preconditions are in place, the economic logic behind financial restraint is compelling.

The second illustration in table 1.4 comes from South Korea's and Taiwan's experiences with industrial policy. The governments in these countries rejected the standard advice that they take an arm's length approach to their enterprises and actively sought to coordinate private investments in targeted sectors. Once again, it is easy to come up with economic models that provide justification for this approach. I have argued (Rodrik 1995a) that the joint presence of scale economies and interindustry linkages can depress the private return to investment in nontraditional activities below the social return. Industrial policy can be viewed as a "coordination device" to stimulate socially profitable investments. In particular, the socialization of investment risk through implicit bailout guarantees may be economically beneficial despite the obvious moral hazard risk it poses. However, once again, there are certain prerequisites and institutional complements that have to be in place for this approach to make sense (see table 1.4).

The third illustration in table 1.4 refers to Japan and concerns the internal organization of the workplace, drawing on Aoki's (1997) work. Aoki describes the peculiar institutional foundations of Japan's postwar success as having evolved from a set of arrangements originally designed for wartime mobilization and centralized control of resources. He presents Japan's team-centered approach to work organization and its redistribution of economic resources from advanced to backward sectors—arrangements that he terms "horizontal hierarchy" and "bureau-pluralism," respectively—as solutions to particular informational and distributive dilemmas the Japanese economy faced in the aftermath of World War II. Unlike the previous authors, however, he views this fit between institutions and economic challenges as having been unintended and serendipitous.

Lest the reader think this is solely an East Asian phenomenon, an interesting example of institutional innovation comes from Mauritius (Rodrik 1999a). Mauritius owes a large part of its success to the creation in 1970 of an export-processing zone (EPZ), which enabled an export boom in garments to European markets. Yet instead of liberalizing its trade regime across the board, Mauritius combined this EPZ with a domestic sector that was highly protected until the mid-1980s, a legacy of the policies of import-substituting industrialization (ISI) followed during the 1960s. The industrialist class that had been created with these policies was naturally opposed to the opening up of the trade regime. The EPZ scheme provided a neat way around this difficulty (Wellisz and Saw 1993). The creation of the EPZ generated new profit opportunities, without taking protection away from the import-substituting groups. The segmentation of labor markets was particularly crucial in this regard, as it prevented the expansion of the EPZ (which employed mainly female labor) from driving wages up in the rest of the economy, and thereby disadvantaging import-substituting industries. New profit opportunities were created at the margin, while leaving old opportunities undisturbed. At a conceptual level, the story here is essentially very similar to the two-track reforms in China described earlier. To produce the results it did, however, the EPZ also needed a source of investible funds, export-oriented expertise, and market access abroad, which were in turn provided by a terms-of-trade boom, entrepreneurs from Hong Kong, and preferential market access in Europe, respectively (Rodrik 1999a; Subramanian and Roy 2003).

In reviewing cases such as these, we may read too much into them after the fact. In particular, we need to avoid several fallacies. First, we cannot simply assume that institutions take the form that they do *because* of the functions that they perform (the functionalist fallacy). Aoki's account of Japan is a particularly useful reminder that a good fit between form and function might be the unintended consequence of historical forces. Second, it is not correct to ascribe the positive outcomes in the cases just reviewed only to their anomalies (the ex post rationalization fallacy). Many accounts of East Asian success emphasize the standard elements—fiscal conservatism, investment in human resources, and export orientation (see, for example, World Bank 1993). As I will discuss below, East Asian institutional anomalies have often produced perverse results when employed in other settings. And it is surely not the case that all anomalies are economically functional.

The main point I take from these illustrations is robust to these fallacies, and has to do with the "plasticity" of the institutional structure that neoclassical economics is capable of supporting. All of the above institutional anomalies are compatible with, and can be understood in terms of, neoclassical economic reasoning ("good economics"). Neoclassical economic analysis does not determine the form that institutional arrangements should or do take. What China's case and other examples discussed above demonstrate is that the higher-order principles of sound economic management do not map into unique institutional arrangements.

In fact, principles such as appropriate incentives, property rights, sound money, and fiscal solvency all come institution-free. We need to operationalize them through a set of policy actions. The experiences above show us that there may be multiple ways of packing these principles into institutional arrangements. Different packages have different costs and benefits depending on prevailing political constraints, levels of administrative competence, and market failures. The preexisting institutional landscape will typically offer both constraints and opportunities, requiring creative shortcuts or bold experiments. From this perspective, the "art" of reform consists of selecting appropriately from a potentially infinite menu of institutional designs.

A direct corollary of this line of argument is that there is only a weak correspondence between the higher-order principles of neoclassical economics and the specific policy recommendations in the standard list (as enumerated in table 1.1). Once again, an example may clarify the point. Consider one of the least contentious recommendations in the list, having to do with trade liberalization. Can the statement "Trade liberalization is good for economic performance" be derived from first principles of neoclassical economics? Yes, but only if a *large* number of side conditions are met:

- The liberalization must be complete or else the reduction in import restrictions must take into account the potentially quite complicated structure of substitutability and complementarity across restricted commodities.[10]
- There must be no microeconomic market imperfections other than the trade restrictions in question, or if there are some, the second-best interactions that are entailed must not be adverse.[11]
- The home economy must be "small" in world markets, or else the liberalization must not put the economy on the wrong side of the "optimum tariff."[12]
- The economy must be in reasonably full employment, or if not, the monetary and fiscal authorities must have effective tools of demand management at their disposal.
- The income redistributive effects of the liberalization should not be judged undesirable by society at large, or if they are, there must be compensatory tax-transfer schemes with low enough excess burden.[13]
- There must be no adverse effects on the fiscal balance, or if there are, there must be alternative and expedient ways of making up for the lost fiscal revenues.
- The liberalization must be politically sustainable and hence credible so that economic agents do not fear or anticipate a reversal.[14]

All these theoretical complications could be sidestepped if there were convincing evidence that in practice trade liberalization systematically produces improved economic performance. But even for this relatively uncontroversial policy, it has proved difficult to generate unambiguous evidence (see Rodríguez and Rodrik 2001; Vamvakidis 2002; and Yanikkaya 2003).[15]

The point is that even the simplest of policy recommendations—"liberalize foreign trade"—is contingent on a large number of judgment calls about the economic and political context in which it is to be implemented.[16] Such judgment calls are often made implicitly. Rendering them explicit has a double advantage: it warns us about the potential minefields that await the standard recommendations, and it stimulates creative thinking on alternatives (as in China) that can sidestep those minefields. By contrast, when the policy recommendation is made unconditionally, as in the mainstream consensus (Washington or post-Washington), the gamble is that the policy's prerequisites will coincide with our actual draw from a potentially large universe of possible states of the world.

I summarize this discussion with the help of tables 1.5, 1.6, and 1.7, dealing with microeconomic policy, macroeconomic policy, and social policy, respectively. Each table contains three columns. The first column displays the ultimate goal that is targeted by the policies and institutional arrangements in the three domains. Hence

TABLE 1.5 Sound Economics and Institutional Counterparts: Microeconomics

Objective	Universal Principles	Plausible Diversity in Institutional Arrangements
Productive efficiency (static and dynamic)	*Property rights*: Ensure potential and current investors can retain the returns to their investments.	What type of property rights? Private, public, cooperative?
	Incentives: Align producer incentives with social costs and benefits.	What type of legal regime? Common law? Civil law? Adopt or innovate?
	Rule of law: Provide a transparent, stable, and predictable set of rules.	What is the right balance between decentralized market competition and public intervention?
		Which types of financial institutions/corporate governance are most appropriate for mobilizing domestic savings?
		Is there a public role to stimulate technology absorption and generation (e.g., "protection" of intellectual property rights)?

TABLE 1.6 Sound Economics and Institutional Counterparts: Macroeconomics

Objective	Universal Principles	Plausible Diversity in Institutional Arrangements
Macroeconomic and Financial Stability	*Sound money*: Do not generate liquidity beyond the increase in nominal money demand at reasonable inflation.	How independent should the central bank be? What is the appropriate exchange-rate regime (dollarization, currency board, adjustable peg, controlled float, pure float)?
	Fiscal sustainability: Ensure public debt remains "reasonable" and stable in relation to national aggregates.	Should fiscal policy be rule-bound, and if so, what are the appropriate rules?
	Prudential regulation: Prevent financial system from taking excessive risk.	Size of the public economy. What is the appropriate regulatory apparatus for the financial system? What is the appropriate regulatory treatment of capital account transactions?

TABLE 1.7 Sound Economics and Institutional Counterparts: Social Policy

Objective	Universal Principles	Plausible Diversity in Institutional Arrangements
Distributive justice and poverty alleviation	*Targeting*: Redistributive programs should be targeted as closely as possible to the intended beneficiaries.	How progressive should the tax system be? Should pension systems be public or private?
	Incentive compatibility: Redistributive programs should minimize incentive distortions.	What are the appropriate points of intervention: educational system? access to health? access to credit? labor markets? tax system?
		What is the role of "social funds"?
		Redistribution of endowments (land reform, endowments-at-birth)?
		Organization of labor markets: decentralized or institutionalized?
		Modes of service delivery: NGOs, participatory arrangements., etc.

microeconomic policies aim to achieve static and dynamic efficiency in the allocation of resources. Macroeconomic policies aim for macroeconomic and financial stability. Social policies target poverty reduction and social protection.

The next column displays some of the key higher-order principles that economic analysis brings to the table. Allocative efficiency requires property rights, the rule of law, and appropriate incentives. Macroeconomic and financial stability requires sound money, fiscal solvency, and prudential regulation. Social inclusion requires incentive compatibility and appropriate targeting. These are the "universal principles" of sound economic management. They are universal in the sense that it is hard to see what any country would gain by systematically defying them. Countries that have adhered to these principles—no matter how unorthodox their manner of doing so—have done well, while countries that have flouted them have typically done poorly.

From the standpoint of policymakers, the trouble is that these universal principles are not operational as stated. In effect, the answers to the real questions that preoccupy policymakers—how far should I go in opening up my economy to foreign competition, should I free up interest rates, should I rely on payroll taxes or the VAT, and the others listed in the third column of each table—cannot be directly deduced from these principles. This opens up space for a multiplicity of institutional arrangements that are compatible with the universal, higher-order principles.

These tables clarify why the standard recommendations (table 1.1) correlate poorly with economic performance around the world. The Washington Consensus, in its various forms, has tended to blur the line that separates column 2 from column 3. Policy advisors have been too quick in jumping from the higher-order principles in column 2 to taking unconditional stands on the specific operational questions posed in column 3. And as their policy advice has yielded disappointing results, they have moved on to recommendations with even greater institutional specificity (as with "second-generation reforms"). As a result, sound economics has often been delivered in unsound form.

I emphasize that this argument is not one about the advantages of gradualism over shock therapy. In fact, the set of ideas I have presented is largely orthogonal to the long-standing debate between the adherents of the two camps (see for example Lipton and Sachs 1990; Aslund, Boone, and Johnson 1996; Williamson and Zagha 2002). The strategy of gradualism presumes that policymakers have a fairly good idea of the institutional arrangements that they want to achieve ultimately, but that for political and other reasons they can proceed only step by step in that direction. The argument here is that there is typically a large amount of uncertainty about what those institutional arrangements are, and therefore that the process required is more one of "search and discovery" than one of gradualism. The two strategies may coincide when policy changes reveal information *and* small-scale policy reforms have a more favorable ratio of information revelation to risk of failure.[17] But it is best not to confuse the two strategies. What stands out in the cases of real success, as I will further illustrate below, is not gradualism per se but an unconventional mix of standard and nonstandard policies well attuned to the reality on the ground.

Notes

1 This figure refers to the exponential growth rate of GDP per capita (in constant 2000 US$) for the group of low- and middle-income countries. The data come from the World Development Indicators of the World Bank.

2 According to the World Bank's World Development Indicators, even in sub-Saharan Africa life expectancy rose from 41 in the early 1960s to 50 by the early 1990s, and then fell back to 46 by 2003 under the influence of the AIDS scourge.

3 Easterly (2005) provides a good overview of these studies. See also Temple 1999; Brock and Durlauf 2001; Rodríguez and Rodrik 2001; and Rodríguez 2005.

4 Easterly (2001) provides an insightful and entertaining account of the evolution of thinking on economic development. See also Lindauer and Pritchett 2002; and Krueger 1997.

5 For diverse perspectives on what the list should contain, see Stiglitz 1998; World Bank 1998; Naim 1999; Birdsall and de la Torre 2001; Kaufmann 2002; Ocampo 2002; and Kuczynski and Williamson 2003.

6 Vietnam, a less well known case than China, has many of the same characteristics: rapid growth since the late 1980s as a result of heterodox reform. Vietnam has benefited from a gradual turn toward markets and greater reliance on private entrepreneurship, but as Van Arkadie and Mallon (2003) argue, it is hard to square the extensive role of the state and the nature of the property rights regime with the tenets of the Washington Consensus.

7 Lora (2001b) finds that structural reforms captured by this index do correlate with growth rates in the predicted manner, but that the impacts (taking the decade of the 1990s as a whole) are not strong. Another econometric study by Loayza, Fajnzylber, and Calderón (2002) claims that Latin America's reforms added significantly to the region's growth.

However, the latter paper uses outcome variables such as trade/GDP and financial depth ratios as its indicators of "policy," and therefore is unable to link economic performance directly to the reforms themselves. This paper also finds a strongly negative dummy for the 1990s—i.e., an unexplained growth reduction.

8 See also Milanovic 2003 for a closely related Martian thought experiment. Milanovic emphasizes that economic growth has declined in most countries despite greater globalization.

9 Here is how Larry Summers (2003) summarizes the recent growth evidence: "[The] rate at which countries grow is substantially determined by three things: their ability to integrate with the global economy through trade and investment; their capacity to maintain sustainable government finances and sound money; and their ability to put in place an institutional environment in which contracts can be enforced and property rights can be established. I would challenge anyone to identify a country that has done all three of these things and has not grown at a substantial rate." Note how these recommendations are couched not in terms of specific policies (maintain tariffs below x percent, raise the government primary surplus above y percent, privatize state enterprises, and so on), but in terms of "abilities" and "capacities" to get certain outcomes accomplished. I will suggest below that these "abilities" and "capacities" do not map neatly into the standard policy preferences, and can be generated in a variety of ways.

10 There is a large theoretical literature on partial trade reform, which shows the difficulty of obtaining unambiguous characterizations of the welfare effects of incomplete liberalization. See Hatta 1977a and 1977b; Anderson and Neary 1992; and Lopez and Panagariya 1992. For an applied general equilibrium analysis of how these issues can complicate trade reform in practice, see Harrison, Rutherford, and Tarr 1993.

11 For an interesting empirical illustration on how trade liberalization can interact adversely with environmental externalities, see Lopez 1997.

12 This is not a theoretical curiosum. Gilbert and Varangis (2003) argue that the liberalization of cocoa exports in West African countries has depressed world cocoa prices, with most of the benefits being captured by consumers in developed countries.

13 The standard workhorse model of international trade, the factor-endowments model and its associated Stolper-Samuelson theorem, comes with sharp predictions on the distributional effects of import liberalization (the "magnification effect").

14 Calvo (1989) was the first to point out that lack of credibility acts as an intertemporal distortion. See also Rodrik 1991.

15 Recent empirical studies have begun to look for nonlinear effects of trade liberalization. In a study of India's liberalization, Aghion et al. (2003) find that trade liberalization appears to have generated differentiated effects across Indian firms depending on prevailing industrial capabilities and labor market regulations. Firms that were close to the technological frontier and in states with more "flexible" regulations responded positively, while others responded negatively. See also Helleiner 1994 for a useful collection of country studies that underscores the contingent nature of economies' response to trade liberalization.

16 This is one reason why policy discussions on standard recommendations such as trade liberalization and privatization now often take the formulaic form, "Policy x is not a panacea; in order to work, it must be supported by reforms in the areas of a, b, c, d, and so on."

17 For example, Dewatripont and Roland (1995) and Wei (1997) present models in which gradual reforms reveal information and affect subsequent political constraints.

References

Aghion, Philippe, Robin Burgess, Stephen Redding, and Fabrizio Zilibotti. 2003. "The Unequal Effects of Liberalization: Theory and Evidence from India." Department of Economics, London School of Economics, March.

Anderson, James E., and J. Peter Neary. 1992. "Trade Reform with Quotas, Partial Rent Retention, and Tariffs." *Econometrica* 60: 57–76.

Aoki, Masahiko. 1997. "Unintended Fit: Organizational Evolution and Government Design of Institutions in Japan." In *The Role of Government in East Asian Economic Development: Comparative Institutional Analysis*. Ed. M. Aoki et al. Oxford: Clarendon Press.

Aslund, Anders, Peter Boone, and Simon Johnson. 1996. "How to Stabilize: Lessons from Post-Communist Countries." *Brookings Papers on Economic Activity* 1: 217–313.

Birdsall, Nancy, and Augusto de la Torre. 2001. *Washington Contentious: Economic Policies for Social Equity in Latin America*. Washington, DC: Carnegie Endowment for International Peace.

Bosworth, Barry, and Susan M. Collins. 2003. "The Empirics of Growth: An Update." Brookings Institution, March 7.

Brock, William A., and Steven N. Durlauf. 2001. "Growth Empirics and Reality." *World Bank Economic Review* 15.2: 229–72.

Calvo, Guillermo. 1989. "Incredible Reforms." In *Debt, Stabilization and Development*. Ed. Calvo et al. New York: Basil Blackwell.

Dewatripont, Mathias, and Gerard Roland. 1995. "The Design of Reform Packages Under Uncertainty." *American Economic Review* 85.5: 1207–23.

Easterly, William. 2001. *The Elusive Quest for Growth*. Cambridge: MIT Press.

———. 2005. "National Policies and Economic Growth: A Reappraisal." In *Handbook of Economic Growth*. Ed. Philippe Aghion and Steven Durlauf. Vol. 1. Amsterdam: Elsevier.

Evans, Peter. 1995. *Embedded Autonomy: States and Industrial Transformation*. Princeton, NJ: Princeton University Press.

Frankel, Jeffrey. 2000a. "The Asian Model, the Miracle, the Crisis, and the Fund." In *Currency Crises*. Ed. Paul Krugman. Chicago: University of Chicago Press.

Gerschenkron, Alexander. 1962. *Economic Backwardness in Historical Perspective: A Book of Essays*. Cambridge: Harvard University Press.

Gilbert, Christopher L., and Panos Varangis. 2003. "Globalization and International Commodity Trade with Specific Reference to the West African Cocoa Producers." NBER Working Paper no. W9668. National Bureau of Economic Research, May.

Harrison, Glenn W., Thomas F. Rutherford, and David G. Tarr. 1993. "Trade Reform in the Partially Liberalized Economy of Turkey." *World Bank Economic Review* 7.2: 191–218.

Hatta, Tatsuo. 1977a. "A Recommendation for a Better Tariff Structure." *Econometrica* 45: 1859–69.

———. 1977b. "A Theory of Piecemeal Policy Recommendations." *Review of Economic Studies* 44: 1–21.

Helleiner, Gerald K. ed. 1994. *Trade Policy and Industrialization in Turbulent Times*. London: Routledge.

Hellmann, Thomas, Kevin Murdock, and Joseph Stiglitz. 1997. "Financial Restraint: Toward a New Paradigm." In *The Role of Government in East Asian Economic Development: Comparative Institutional Analysis*. Eds. M. Aoki et al. Oxford: Clarendon Press.

Hirschman, Albert O. 1958. *The Strategy of Economic Development*. New Haven: Yale University Press.

Kaufmann, Daniel. 2002. "Rethinking Governance." World Bank Institute, World Bank, Washington, DC, December.

Krueger, Anne O. 1997. "Trade Policy and Development: How We Learn" *American Economic Review* 87.1: 1–22.

Krugman, Paul. 1995. "Dutch Tulips and Emerging Markets." *Foreign Affairs* 74.4: 36–37.

Kuczynski, Pedro-Pablo, and John Williamson, eds. 2003. *After the Washington Consensus: Restarting Growth and Reform in Latin America.* Washington, DC: Institute for International Economics.

Lau, Lawrence, J., Yingyi Qian, and Gerard Roland. 2000. "Reform Without Losers: An Interpretation of China's Dual-Track Approach to Transition." *Journal of Political Economy* 108.1: 120–43.

Lin, Justin Yifu, Fang Cai, and Zhou Li. 1996. *The China Miracle: Development Strategy and Economic Reform,* Shatin, NT, Hong Kong: Chinese University Press.

Lindauer, David L., and Lant Pritchett. 2002. "What's the Big Idea? The Third Generation of Policies for Economic Growth." *Economia* 3.1: 1–40.

Lipton, David, and Jeffrey Sachs. 1990. "Creating a Market Economy in Eastern Europe: The Case of Poland." *Brookings Papers on Economic Activity* 1: 75–133.

Loayza, Norman, Pablo Fajnzylber, and Cesar Calderón. 2002. "Economic Growth in Latin America and the Caribbean: Stylized Facts, Explanations, and Forecasts." World Bank, Washington, DC, June.

Lopez, Ramon. 1997. "Environmental Externalities in Traditional Agriculture and the Impact of Trade Liberalization: The Case of Ghana." *Journal of Development Economics* 53.1: 17–39.

Lopez, Ramon, and Arvind Panagariya. 1992. "On the Theory of Piecemeal Tariff Reform: The Case of Pure Imported Intermediate Inputs." *American Economic Review* 82.3: 615–25.

Lora, Eduardo. 2001a. "Structural Reforms in Latin America: What Has Been Reformed and How to Measure It." Inter-American Development Bank, Washington, DC, December.

———. 2001b. "El crecimiento económico en América Latina después de una década de reformas estructurales." Research Department, Inter-American Development Bank, Washington, DC.

MacLean, Brian K. 1999. "The Rise and Fall of the 'Crony Capitalism' Hypothesis: Causes and Consequences." Department of Economics, Laurentian University, Ontario, March.

Maddison, Angus. 2001. *The World Economy: A Millennial Perspective.* Paris: OECD.

Milanovic, Branko. 2003. "The Two Faces of Globalization: Against Globalization as We Know It." *World Development* 31.4: 667–83.

Naim, Moises. 1999. "Fads and Fashion in Economic Reforms: Washington Consensus or Washington Confusion?" Paper prepared for the IMF Conference on Second Generation Reforms, Washington, DC, October.

Ocampo, José Antonio. 2002. "Rethinking the Development Agenda." United Nations Economic Commission for Latin America and the Caribbean (ECLAC), Santiago, Chile.

Qian, Yingyi. 2003. "How Reform Worked in China." In *In Search of Prosperity: Analytic Narratives of Economic Growth.* Ed. Dani Rodrik. Princeton, NJ: Princeton University Press.

Rodríguez, Francisco. 2005. "Cleaning up the Kitchen Sink: On the Consequences of the Linearity Assumption for Cross-Country Growth Empirics." Department of Economics, Wesleyan University, September.

Rodríguez, Francisco, and Dani Rodrik. 2001. "Trade Policy and Economic Growth: A Skeptic's Guide to the Cross-National Evidence." In *NBER Macroeconomics Annual 2000.* Ed. Ben Bernanke and Kenneth S. Rogoff. Cambridge: MIT Press.

Rodrik, Dani. 1991. "Policy Uncertainty and Private Investment in Developing Countries." *Journal of Development Economics* 36: 229–42.

———. 1995a. "Getting Interventions Right: How South Korea and Taiwan Grew Rich." *Economic Policy* 20: 55–107.

———. 1996a. "Understanding Economic Policy Reform." *Journal of Economic Literature* 34.1: 9–41.

———. 1999a. *The New Global Economy and Developing Countries: Making Openness Work.* Washington, DC: Overseas Development Council.

Rostow, Walt W. 1965. *The Stages of Economic Growth: A Non-Communist Manifesto.* Cambridge: Cambridge University Press.

Stiglitz, Joseph E. 1998. "More Instruments and Broader Goals Moving toward the Post-Washington Consensus." United Nations University/WIDER, Helsinki.

Subramanian, Arvind, and Devesh Roy. 2003. "Who Can Explain the Mauritian Miracle? Meade, Romer, Sachs, or Rodrik?" *In Search of Prosperity: Analytic Narratives of Economic Growth.* Ed. Dani Rodrik. Princeton, NJ: Princeton University Press.

Summers, Lawrence H. 2003. Godkin Lectures. John F. Kennedy School of Government, Harvard University, April.

Temple, Jonathan. 1999. "The New Growth Evidence." *Journal of Economic Literature* 37.1: 112–56.

Vamvakidis, Athanasios. 2002. "How Robust is the Growth-Openness Connection? Historical Evidence." *Journal of Economic Growth* 7.1: 57–80.

Van Arkadie, Brian, and Raymond Mallon. 2003. *Vietnam: A Transition Tiger?* Canberra: Asia Pacific Press.

Wei, Shang-Jin. 1997. "Gradualism versus Big Bang: Speed and Sustainability of Reforms." *Canadian Journal of Economics* 30.4B: 1234–47.

Wellisz, Stanislaw, and Philippe Lam Shin Saw. 1993. "Mauritius." In *The Political Economy of Poverty, Equity, and Growth: Five Open Economies.* Ed. Ronald Findlay and Stanislaw Wellisz. New York: Oxford University Press.

Williamson, John. 1990. "What Washington Means by Policy Reform." In *Latin American Adjustment: How Much Has Happened?* Ed. J. Williamson. Washington, DC: Institute for International Economics.

Williamson, John, and Roberto Zagha. 2002. "From Slow Growth to Slow Reform." Institute for International Economics, Washington, DC, July.

World Bank. 1993. *The East Asian Miracle: Economic Growth and Public Policies.* New York: Oxford University Press.

———. 1998. "Beyond the Washington Consensus: Institutions Matter." World Bank, Washington, DC.

Yanikkaya, Halit. 2003. "Trade Openness and Economic Growth: A Cross-Country Empirical Investigation." *Journal of Development Economics* 72.1: 57–89.

Naazneen H. Barma,
"Economic Development: From Orthodoxy to Heterodoxy" (2021)*

How have some poor countries become quite rich and improved their societal welfare, while others have remained quite poor in terms of both incomes and quality of life? The answer lies in great part on the role that the state has played in conceptualizing and implementing development strategies. The two main waves of development orthodoxy after the Second World War came to opposite conclusions about the appropriate role for the state in the economy but both rested on a faulty conception of the public and private sectors as antithetical to each other. The interventionist wave that came first, from the 1950s through the early 1970s, aimed to solve market failures, advocating for the state to play a heavy role in economic development to substitute for nascent markets and a weak private sector and to adopt a nationalist approach to deliberate industrial transformation. The neoliberal wave that followed from the mid-1970s through the late 1990s took the opposite tack and aimed to solve government failures, demanding that the state be extricated from the economy to enable free markets to flourish and private economic incentives to dictate efficiency and spur growth.

Instead, states and markets should be viewed as complementary in the process of economic development. The key issue is not *how much* state involvement exists in the economy in the pursuit of development – instead, it is *what type* of government involvement is pursued. State capacity must be employed to support markets by securing basic political–economic order and credibly enforcing property rights, and to formulate and implement predictable, accountable, and legitimate public policy that enables markets to flourish in ways that underpin economic growth and benefit society. These forms of state capacity can be built incrementally even in poor countries and be used in a way that prioritizes certain core government functions to aid in equitable and sustainable economic development.

Development Dogmas

Why some countries have become rich while others remain poor is the central political–economic question of our times. The development economist Lant Pritchett coined the phrase "the Great Divergence" to encapsulate two stylized insights about global growth rates and income levels over the twentieth century.[1] The first pattern is a convergence among rich countries and a divergence of rich countries from poor. The

---

* Written especially for *The Political Economy Reader,* Second Edition. The author is indebted to Jennifer Brass, Martha Johnson, Rachel Sigman, and Steven Vogel for invaluable feedback on this piece.

poor world as a whole has grown more slowly than the rich world and fallen further behind, with some countries' economies stagnating or even declining. The second pattern is that growth levels have not been uniform in the developing world. Growth has varied a great deal across poor countries and has been more volatile within them. Some emerging economies have experienced explosive growth rates and caught up with the rich world: for example, the East Asian industrializers in the 1960s and 1970s, Chile in the 1970s, China since the 1980s, and Brazil in the late 1990s. Others have grown more slowly, in fits and starts, including India along with many Latin American and some sub-Saharan African countries. And an unfortunate few, especially those mired in conflict and prone to natural disasters, such as the Democratic Republic of the Congo, Haiti, and Yemen, have experienced declining per capita incomes at various points.

Poor countries have attempted a range of developmental strategies since the end of the Second World War in the quest to become rich. On the core question of the role of the state in the economy, the pendulum has swung back and forth in developing countries over the past 75 years.[2] The postwar period offered the competing political–economic models of capitalism in the First World and socialism in the Second World. In most of the Third World, a phenomenon known as statism or "dirigisme" took hold. In the 1950s and 1960s, Keynesian intervention in markets was ascendant even in the capitalist West. Statism in the Third World, as in the industrialized world, involved both Keynesian macroeconomic management as well as some measure of government ownership of the means of production in strategic sectors of the economy.[3] Markets were thought to be weak and private sector actors to be immature in poor countries; thus the state needed to step in to provide capital and administer the economy. Such intervention was not an outright rejection of market capitalism, like socialism, but a deliberate attempt to manage the economy in the belief that statism was better for the economy. Statism was also advantageous for political and strategic reasons in the many newly independent countries across the developing world. Left with economies that had been stunted, warped, and impoverished as a result of exploitative colonial practices, political elites exercising their independence were keen to overthrow colonial legacies and channel the full force of the state toward rapid industrialization and socioeconomic progress.

An extreme manifestation of the statist inclination came in the form of import substitution industrialization prompted by dependency theory, a structuralist school of thought that was especially influential in Latin America in the 1960s and 1970s.[4] Dependency theory was grounded in a Marxist, historical materialist understanding of a country's economic situation. Different strands of dependency theory emphasized different causal dynamics but shared the foundational perspective that a country's stage of (under)development is conditioned by its place in the global capitalist system.[5] Dependency theorists characterized the international system as comprising two sets of states: the dominant or core states, that is, the advanced industrialized nations of the world; and the dependent or periphery states, that is, those in the underdeveloped world, in the parlance of the time. *Dependencistas* argued that the international capitalist system had created a rigid international division of labor that was responsible for poverty and underdevelopment in the periphery: the dependent states' role was to supply cheap minerals, agricultural commodities, and cheap labor; while the industrialized core extracted the surplus from what was produced in the periphery. Compounding underdevelopment, some dependency theorists argued, the terms of trade would constantly decline for dependent countries (i.e., they would have to export successively more commodities to sustain their import levels), making them even worse off over time.[6] Third World countries would not, as modernization theory would have it, catch up to the richer countries once their socio-cultural systems evolved and they put the right policies in place. They were poor because they were coercively integrated into the global capitalist system led by the industrialized nations, in most cases via violent and unjust colonial exploitation.

The prescriptive implications of dependency theory encouraged poor countries to pursue policies of self-sufficiency that would allow them to control their interaction with the global economy and alter their economic production structures. One of the most important of such policies was the statist practice known as import substitution industrialization (ISI). Across the developing world, governments restricted imports through tariffs and non-tariff trade barriers, while giving domestic industries favorable terms through subsidies and cheap credit to build their competitiveness. Political and economic elites sought to implement autonomous national development strategies that made the state the agent of industrial transformation. Governments mobilized the capital necessary for industrialization and growth, implementing five-year state planning targets to shift their countries up the economic value chain from agriculture to manufacturing. In some parts of the developing world, this state-led industrialization started out fairly successfully – resulting in high growth rates in some countries, for example 7 percent in Turkey and 6.5 percent in Mexico from the 1950s to the 1970s, as well as some particular industrial successes, such as a six-fold steel production increase in India over the same period.[7] The developing world also achieved food self-sufficiency by the 1970s, helped along by the increased crop yields achieved in the Green Revolution of the 1960s and 1970s.

Yet these successes relied to some extent on favorable international conditions. Demand for commodities from the developing world was driven by the high postwar growth rates of 5–6 percent in the industrialized world. The global economic stability and favorable interest rates engendered by the United States' economic hegemony and the new international financial architecture incarnated in the Bretton Woods regime also aided growth globally. In the 1970s, several economic shocks – including the 1973 oil crisis, interest rate hikes in the industrialized world, and collapsing commodity prices – derailed progress in the developing world, culminating in the nadir of the Latin American debt crisis of the late 1970s and early 1980s.

By the 1970s, too, the accumulating economic inefficiencies and political–economic consequences of state-led and managed production that substituted for markets had become apparent. In many developing countries, a lack of competition with imported goods led to inefficiency and waste, eventually slowing growth. Heavy government involvement in the economy and ownership and management of an extensive range of state-owned enterprises led to rent-seeking and entrenched political interests that made reform near impossible. One common tactic, for example, had been the use of agricultural and commodity marketing boards, which set primary sector prices artificially low domestically and then sold goods at the global market price to siphon surplus from the agricultural sector and channel it into the manufacturing sector. This attempt to accelerate the natural process of industrialization with a heavy state hand undermined rural economies. The political logics that often drove pseudo-economic decisions about pricing created adverse incentives for rural farmers that led to poorer economic outcomes.[8]

The pendulum had already begun to swing in the industrialized world away from Keynesianism and toward the ascendance of neoliberal economic prescriptions. This occurred for practical reasons, since government intervention had failed to rein in stagflation in the 1970s, in which both unemployment and inflation steadily increased. The motivation was also conceptual, as a new group of leaders came to power across the world who leaned toward market liberalism in their beliefs that free markets were a cornerstone of liberty as well as the correct route to efficiency, economic growth, and collective welfare. Margaret Thatcher, for example, who became the British Prime Minister in 1979, often declared, "There is no alternative" to capitalist market economics. Her beliefs and policies were soon matched in the United States with the onset of Reaganomics in the early 1980s.

Mainstream neoclassical economists started viewing economic policy in developing countries through the same lens. Deepak Lal summarized much of the criticism against the statist paradigm, arguing that development economics wrongly propagated the "dirigiste dogma," or the view that governments must intervene in the economy to aid development.[9] He recognized that governments must provide the foundation on which markets rest – but argued that the dirigiste dogma falsely maintained that government intervention to supplant the price mechanism in markets could improve welfare. In Lal's perspective, the most serious distortions in developing economies came not from the inevitable imperfections of the market but from government intervention in those markets.

The neoliberal approach to development was premised on the need to remove the obstacles in place, many of them believed to be created by government, that were preventing markets and rational individual incentives from achieving efficient gains. Extricating the state from the economy in order to improve economic efficiency became the central development agenda pursued by the World Bank and the International Monetary Fund (IMF). Developing countries that sought their help, suffering stagnation and debt crisis, had no choice but to follow their prescriptions. A wave of structural adjustment thus took hold in the developing world, sometimes implemented by domestic elites (e.g., the "Chicago Boys" in Chile, trained in neoclassical economics in the United States) but most often imposed as conditionalities for financial and technical assistance from the international financial institutions. This ascendant neoliberal view of markets and economic development was dubbed the Washington Consensus, after the location of its three biggest proponents, the World Bank, the IMF, and the United States Treasury Department.[10] The core spirit of the Washington Consensus was encapsulated in three dictums of reform: *stabilize the macroeconomy*, by enacting fiscal austerity measures to get a grip on inflation and runaway unproductive state-spending, which was thought to "crowd out" private investment and stifle the economy; *liberalize prices and the economy*, by removing price controls and deregulating the economy in both domestic and trade realms, thereby enabling markets to function freely; and *privatize property ownership*, by shedding state-owned enterprises and direct state involvement in the economy and putting property ownership into the hands of private economic actors.

As with earlier waves of development dogma, the results of the neoliberal turn were mixed.[11] Structural adjustment policies resulted in a great deal of socioeconomic dislocation, as governments across the developing world slashed their budgets by downsizing the public sector workforce and cutting government spending in the social sectors. Structural adjustment programs were found, as a result, to have increased poverty and inequality in many instances. Facing contradictory incentives, political elites often only implemented partial reforms to their own benefit, which led to even higher degrees of rent-seeking and corruption as economies underwent reform.[12] In some countries, such as Mexico, Chile, Ghana, and later India, the short-term socioeconomic pain imposed by liberalization and structural adjustment is believed to have been followed by positive long-term economic outcomes resulting from deep reforms, although inequality persists. Overall, however, structural adjustment did not lead to the enhanced growth and economic success it promised. Instead, the neoliberal principles intended to usher in market efficiency introduced new and unanticipated inefficiencies.[13] The macroeconomic stability prized by market liberals, for example, proved necessary but not at all sufficient for growth. Some dimensions of government spending often work to "crowd in" private economic activity: infrastructure investments, in particular, can be crucial to igniting productivity and growth in nascent sectors of the economy. Similarly, some types of public enterprise enable necessary economies of scale and confer positive externalities and public goods that the market would not provide on its own.

Crucially, markets require complementary market infrastructure to work well, which in turn calls for some form of government involvement.[14] Yet, as Kiren Aziz Chaudhry observed, developing country governments are often too weak to create this institutional infrastructure.[15] She argued that dirigisme in the developing world was a result of this administrative crisis: governments that were unable to adequately provide rules and regulate the market took the relatively easier route of directly producing and distributing goods and services. In Chaudhry's analysis, the problem in developing countries was not too much government intervention but too little government capacity and hence too little market infrastructure. In this context, the market-liberal impulse to undo statist mechanisms for governing developing economies "without replacing them with effective alternatives encourages economic, administrative, and even political fragmentation."[16] In the worst-case scenario, blindly following neoliberal economic orthodoxy without considering the consequences could lead to state collapse in the developing world. The harshest critiques of structural adjustment viewed it as neocolonialism, deliberately designed to oppress the developing world.[17]

States and Markets Intertwined: The Developmental State

In the aftermath of the waves first of statist intervention in developing economies, followed by the neoliberal push for less government and more markets, the pendulum swing between states and markets started to settle in the mid to late 1990s. Development economists came to emphasize what was unique about low-income countries, especially the fact that they experienced more market failures and needed greater capacity and infrastructure to facilitate markets. In part, this meant recognizing developing countries as industrial and technological latecomers that needed the state to assist in overcoming the hurdles associated with industrialization and development.[18] It had become apparent that both the statist impulse to substitute for weak markets and private sector capacity, as well as the "more markets, less state" dictum of the neoliberal era, had framed the relationship between states and markets incorrectly. The more appropriate approach was achieving the right balance between the two, with a particular emphasis on employing state capacity to support and enhance markets.

This realization was prompted, in no small part, by the East Asian Miracle, in which a number of newly industrializing countries (NICs) in the region had by the 1980s effectively escaped the capitalist periphery and joined the ranks of the industrialized world.[19] The strategies adopted by these East Asian governments – especially Japan, South Korea, and Taiwan, as well as Singapore and Hong Kong – were striking and the region became fertile ground for the states-versus-markets debate. The most successful East Asian economies had moved in the 1960s from ISI to an export-oriented industrialization strategy that embraced global markets and resulted in two decades of rapid industrialization and blistering growth. Some attributed the success of these countries to their having implemented the core prescriptions of neoclassical economics.[20] Other scholars challenged how true to free-market economics the East Asian NICs really were, pointing to the unique political–economic compact between governments and industrial capitalist concerns that came to be known as the "developmental state."[21] Clearly, in the East Asian industrialization and development experience, the state played a more active role in the economy than that advocated by neoclassical theory. The real debate was over to what degree the East Asian state was involved in the economy, in what manner, and to what ends – and whether those forms of government management were truly the key to the success story.

The East Asian economic experience delivered a vivid counterpoint to the experiences of many other developing regions in the 1980s – contrasting directly, for example, with Latin America's "lost decade" and relative stagnation in most of sub-Saharan Africa. Why had East Asian nations succeeded while other developing countries remained mired in underdevelopment in the periphery? Stephan Haggard argued that one of the problems with dependency theory is that, in its structuralism, it missed the wide variety of state responses to "dependence."[22] He laid out a comparative analysis of two types of development strategies – one focused on self-reliance and domestic industrialization through ISI in developing countries such as India, Brazil, Argentina, and Mexico, and the other the East Asian model of an initial period of ISI followed by a deliberate transition beginning in the early 1960s to export-led growth. Haggard's analysis of why these different strategies were chosen and how they were implemented rejects the notion that the East Asian NICs embraced neoclassical prescriptions. He points instead to the importance of understanding how developmental alliances emerged and the institutions through which state involvement in the market took place. Stronger, more centralized states in the East Asian NICs – in part resting on their authoritarian control – adopted the mercantilist strategy of pursuing national economic interest on the global stage.[23] East Asian governments were better able to structure their partnership with domestic capitalist concerns, finding ways to incentivize and reward efficiency gains and, eventually, performance on global markets. In contrast, landed elites and other vested interests in Latin America protected domestic infant industries, which remained relatively inefficient and vulnerable to being used as sources of patronage and rent distribution to favored social groups.

In short, the East Asian governments were thought to have found the right recipe for active economic transformation, pursuing existential survival through economic success via a deliberate move up the economic value chain and technology ladder – especially timely as American aid and economic openness to the region were beginning to wind down in the 1960s. The most revisionist takes on the East Asian Miracle, such as Alice Amsden's, held that governments "led the market," using industrial policy and intervention in financial markets to guide capital to where it would generate the highest overall return for the whole economy and using other policy and institutional measures to deliberately alter market incentive structures and boost specific industries and firms within them.[24] Yet such arguments did not give quite enough credit to the role of the market in providing signals to producers and generating efficiency gains overall. Instead, the heart of the story was an adaptive, evolving process of states attempting to support and nudge private economic actors.

In this vein, Robert Wade proposed "the governed market theory of East Asian success," in which elements of both state-direction and market-based resource allocation complemented each other.[25] The South Korean and Taiwanese governments, according to Wade, treated particular industries as public goods, too critical for the general welfare to be left to the market – especially, in mercantilist fashion, those industries necessary for military self-sufficiency and national survival – and guided the market processes of resource allocation to produce different investment and production outcomes than would otherwise have occurred. At the same time, however, the focus was on achieving results in export markets: it was the targeted, market-*conforming* interventions (e.g., performance-based export credits, subsidies, tax incentives, and duty-free imports for exporters) that worked, not those that were blunt and intentionally market-*distorting* (e.g., direct credit and devalued exchange rates).

These policies were supported by a specific growth alliance between authoritarian political and corporatist business actors, whose interests and very survival were supported by productive investment and industrialization. Although governments were committed to broad-based public education to support the developmental project and ensure that society shared in its fruits, the region's authoritarian governments generally limited societal input into policymaking. Insulated from the demands of societal interest groups and embedded in partnerships with the domestic capitalist class, technocratic government agencies focused on implementing the necessary policies to advance nationalist economic goals without the same political constraints experienced in many other developing countries.[26] Meritocratic bureaucracies with centralized economic policymaking powers pursued a dynamic approach to creating comparative advantage in their economies, shaping both the macro-structure or industrial profile of the economy as well as the micro-operations of specific sectors and firms. Chalmers Johnson described this complex of political and economic arrangements dedicated to industrialization and growth as the *plan-rational* or *developmental state*, identifying it firmly as a capitalist system while distinguishing it from the market-rational or regulatory state thought to be the norm in capitalism.[27] Johnson argued that the developmental state rested on a "soft authoritarian–capitalist nexus" – a strong state, insulated from societal pressures, focused on industrialization and development with a market orientation and a capitalist base in society.[28] The crucial underpinning of success in the East Asian economies was a state–market partnership with a shared long-term commitment to growth, a "cohesive-capitalist" pattern of state intervention that Atul Kohli described as two horses acting in harmony to pull along the chariot of the economy.[29]

Yet the developmental state was not meant to be seen as a new orthodoxy of its own, as was clear in the analyses of the original scholars of the phenomenon. Johnson explicitly identified the developmental state as an approach for late industrialization and catch-up development.[30] In East Asia, the developmental state was a feature of its time and its place. It was enabled by a particular moment in the international economy, with an industrialized world willing to keep markets relatively open, transfer technology, and invest increasing flows of foreign capital, as well as a particular geopolitical moment marked by the hegemony and protective security umbrella of the United States in the region. Domestically, too, the colonial history of much of the region followed by its devastation in the Second World War enabled the particular brand of right-wing, capitalist authoritarianism that served as the political basis for the developmental regimes.[31] Once the East Asian economies had caught up and claimed their place in the industrialized world, they were forced to restructure their economic strategies to be nimbler on global markets. The single-minded pursuit of growth also came with its own social costs, especially for unskilled labor, unfavored regions, immigrants, and the environment. More recently, from the 1997–1998 Asian Financial Crisis onward, East Asian governments have had to pay more attention to, and invest more resources in, the societal groups whose interests had been downplayed.[32]

Redefining Development

The statist, neoliberal, and developmental state approaches were all primarily focused on industrialization and economic transformation to generate growth in gross domestic product (GDP). Increasingly, scholars and practitioners advocate for a definition of development that encompasses more than simply increases in per capita income. Some believe that GDP is an entirely imperfect measure of development. Marilyn Waring, for example, observed that GDP does not count most housework or carework, the vast majority of which is carried out by women, nor is the environmental cost of economic activity factored into GDP.[33] Simon Kuznets, an originator of the concept of GDP, argued in his 1971 Nobel Prize acceptance speech that national accounts like GDP fail to measure pollution and the other negative effects of industrial production and that the production of military armaments should be discounted in GDP because of their destructive intent.[34] Critiques like these have led to a number of alternative indexes being designed to measure societal welfare in ways that are not encapsulated in GDP, including, for example, the UN's Human Development Index, which captures health and education outcomes as crucial elements of development.

Other critical perspectives have directly challenged the "development model" and its focus on industrialization and growth. The "post-development" school, for example, rejects the development paradigm itself as a Euro-centric universalist view, centered around material accumulation, that maintains the global capitalist division of labor. The goal, instead, should be to find more sustainable and equitable alternatives to development that call on the benefits of traditional political–economic practices.[35] Other scholars call for the decolonization of the study and the practice of development aid and the adoption of more race-conscious lenses in development studies.[36] Growth in the developing world has also traveled hand in hand with environmental degradation and the climate crisis. The contemporary de-growth movement has emerged out of the recognition that the pursuit of growth above all else has come with damaging consequences to the environment and human well-being. De-growthists advocate for slowing down our economic systems to both produce and consume less, making the case that putting bounds on material accumulation will improve ecological and societal welfare.[37]

Even from the more common epistemological perspective that views economic growth as necessary for improvements in the quality of life, albeit far from sufficient, it is incontrovertible that the pursuit of increased per capita income has unequal consequences for different social groups. In any developing country success story, there are women, people of color, ethnic and regional groups, migrants, disabled people, and other marginalized groups, who have not shared in the full fruits of economic development, even when it is relatively equitable in the aggregate. It is essential to recognize that development is not simply a process of capital accumulation and industrialization. Amartya Sen's concept of "development as freedom," for example, emphasizes capability expansion – for which core freedoms such as social justice and political rights are necessary in addition to economic well-being.[38] More attention is paid today in development circles to the importance of inclusive growth that is as equitable as possible across social groups. As with achieving progress on earlier definitions of development, strategies more attuned toward the impact of growth on economic and social justice require particular forms of political settlement and state capacity.

From Development Orthodoxy to Heterodoxy

A government role in the economy and some degree of state capacity are necessary for growth and development – and, eventually, to mitigate the negative consequences of, and inequalities associated with, development and to achieve its more expansive aims. The more technocratic notions of governance and institutional capacity that were a central feature of the scholarship on the East Asian developmental state have become major elements of contemporary development thinking.[39] As Jennifer Brass describes, the "good governance" paradigm that took hold at the World Bank and other development agencies in the 1990s has largely displaced the earlier dogma of the Washington Consensus and represents a sort of synthesis between the statist and neoliberal dogmas that preceded it.[40] In this line of thinking, where countries are on the state intervention spectrum is less important than how the core governance functions that bolster markets – for example, predictability, credibility, and accountability – are served.

The insight that market development in poor countries requires a state-provided institutional infrastructure has also become more prevalent since the early 1990s. The World Bank's *World Development Report* of 2002 imported the concept into conventional development wisdom, declaring that market-enhancing institutions are necessary to make markets more effective in delivering growth and reducing poverty in developing countries.[41] Others have elaborated similar recipes for market development in poor countries that hinge on the reduction of transaction costs to facilitate economic activity. Hernando De Soto, for example, observed that in the developing world, many assets have not been converted into productive capital because of a lack of formal property rights.[42] If states could formalize property rights – often established via customary norms rather than title in developing countries – and establish the legal systems to regulate them, De Soto argues, the economic potential of those assets could be unleashed. Other scholars have cautioned that formalized property rights are not likely to make a dramatic difference in the absence of other necessary market infrastructure.[43]

An emphasis on the institutional foundations of markets, the tailoring of institutions to different national environments, and even the role of government in building market institutions, is a far cry from the neoliberal prescriptions of the 1980s. It is also a much more subtle and targeted view of the appropriate role of the state in the economy than that represented in the dirigiste wave that dominated the 1960s. Equally important in contemporary development thinking is the need to get incentives right, along with the recognition that states can distort incentives no matter how laissez-faire or interventionist they are with economic policy.[44]

Some development economists and agencies have taken a radically micro tack in the way they think about development and poverty reduction, focusing on individual-level incentives and analyzing how various interventions affect those incentives through randomized, controlled experiments.[45] Such work focuses on understanding the decision-making calculus of poor people in low-income countries, with the goal of shifting incentives to lead to more optimal outcomes. More macro thinkers have countered that the effects of such interventions can only be marginal – and that what is necessary to transform developing countries is high-capacity institutions that support markets along with concerted government policymaking oriented toward the collective good.[46]

Looking at the experience of the East Asian NICs, what might appear to be optimized institutional solutions have actually emerged from a long process of trial and error, accompanied by political struggle and settlement. The appropriate forms of state involvement in the market, and the growth coalition that ties the state to corporate and societal interests in developing countries in shaping that involvement, are the consequences of country-specific, path-dependent processes that reflect distinct pathways to political–economic order in different states.[47] In other words, timing and context is crucial and the outcomes will necessarily be heterodox. Institutions must perform certain functions and achieve certain goals in terms of supporting markets and promoting industrialization and development – but that does not dictate their form, or what they look like and how they are designed, in any given place at any given time.[48]

Most countries in the developing and emerging world have weak state capacity. Matt Andrews, Lant Pritchett, and Michael Woolcock observe that these low levels of capability in turn make building more state capability a slow and uneven process.[49] They offer two reasons for this capability trap in the developing world. First, echoing Dani Rodrik on the issue of form versus function, they identify the problem of "iso-morphic mimicry," whereby development agencies have spent a great deal of resources making states in the developing world "look like" states in the advanced world, on the assumption that if they look the same they will perform the same. Second is the burden of "premature load-bearing," or placing too much responsibility on the state before it is ready, which reflects Kiren Chaudhry's analysis of administrative weakness in the developing world. These unrealistic and premature expectations set states up for failure in terms of outcomes and the stresses placed on them actually compromise their capacity even more. Compounding these more technocratic considerations is the fact that – as noted by Chaudhry and many scholars of the East Asian develop-mental state – building state capacity is equally, if not more, a political challenge that requires the sustained commitment of a political coalition.[50]

Although the reality of a low-level capability trap is sobering, it leaves the possibility that state capacity can be built incrementally. The key is that tasks must remain within the bounds of what the state is actually capable of doing and be sequenced in a way that prioritizes what states must absolutely be able to do. Yuen Yuen Ang demonstrates one example of how this is possible when there is political commitment to do so via the example of China's decades-long reform experience, which she describes as a result of the gradual "co-evolution" of states and markets.[51] What do developing countries need their states to be able to do in order to support and sustain markets in the pur-suit of industrialization and economic growth? State capacity is necessary to secure a foundational level of political–economic order and to credibly enforce property rights. Governments must also be capable of formulating and implementing predictable, accountable, and legitimate public policy to support private sector activity and safe-guard societal interest. If markets are nascent, then state capacity, too, can be basic; as the economy evolves, so, too, can the state's role in enhancing it in ways geared toward the collective good. Developing countries must approach this task not via the orthodox impulse to order and engineer but in the heterodox spirit of humility and flexibility to enable experimentation.[52] When we view the state–market balance in developing countries through this lens it becomes clear that how states can successfully support and intervene in markets to promote economic growth and improve societal welfare is constantly evolving and adapting in ways that are specific to time and context.

Notes

1 Lant Pritchett, "Divergence, Big Time," *Journal of Economic Perspectives* 11 (1997): 3–17. See, also, Angus Deaton, *The Great Escape: Health, Wealth, and the Origins of Inequality* (Princeton, NJ: Princeton University Press, 2013).

2 John Rapley, *Understanding Development: Theory and Practice in the Third World* (3rd edition) (Boulder, CO: Lynne Rienner, 2007); Jennifer Brass, "Development Theory," in Christopher Ansell and Jacob Torfing, eds., *Handbook on Theories of Governance* (Cheltenham: Edward Elgar Publishing, 2016), 115–25.

3 Albert O. Hirschman, *The Strategy of Economic Development* (New Haven, CT: Yale University Press, 1958); Albert O. Hirschman, *Essays in Trespassing: Economics to Politics and Beyond* (New York: Cambridge University Press, 1981).

4 Andre Gunder Frank, *Capitalism and Underdevelopment in Latin America* (New York: Monthly Review Press, 1967); Fernando H. Cardoso and Enzo Falleto, *Dependency and Development in Latin America* (Berkeley, CA: University of California Press, 1979); Stephan Haggard, *Pathways from the Periphery: The Politics of Growth in the Newly Industrializing Countries* (Ithaca, NY: Cornell University Press, 1990).

5 For a recasting of dependency theory as a still relevant research program focused on a global historical approach to the polarizing tendencies of global capitalism and the constraints faced by peripheral economies, see Ingrid Harvold Kvangraven, "Beyond the Stereotype: Restating the Relevance of the Dependency Research Programme," *Development and Change* (2020): 1–37. https://doi.org/10.1111/dech.12593.

6 Raul Prebisch, *The Economic Underdevelopment of Latin America and its Principal Problems* (New York: United Nations, 1950).

7 Rapley, *Understanding Development*, 41–2.

8 Robert H. Bates, *Markets and States in Tropical Africa* (Berkeley, CA: University of California Press, 1981). For a critique of the neopatrimonialism lens often applied to economic outcomes in African and other developing countries, see Thandika Mkandawire, "Neopatrimonialism and the Political Economy of Economic Performance in Africa: Critical Reflections," *World Politics* (May 2015): 1–50.

9 Deepak Lal, *The Poverty of "Development Economics"* (London: Institute of Economic Affairs, 1983).

10 The phrase is attributed to John Williamson, at the time an IMF official, who enumerated a list of ten key policies that made up the endorsed reforms. John Williamson, "What Washington Means by Policy Reform," in John Williamson, ed., *Latin American Adjustment: How Much Has Happened?* (Washington, DC: Institute for International Economics, 1990).

11 Rapley, *Understanding Development*, 87–92.

12 Nicolas van de Walle, *African Economies and the Politics of Permanent Crisis, 1979–1999* (Cambridge: Cambridge University Press, 2001).

13 William Easterly, *The Elusive Quest for Growth: Economists' Adventures and Misadventures in the Tropics* (Cambridge, MA: MIT Press, 2001).

14 Douglass C. North, *Structure and Change in Economic History* (New York: W. W. Norton, 1981); Karl Polanyi, *The Great Transformation: The Political and Economic Origins of our Time* (Boston, MA: Beacon Press, 2001).

15 Kiren Aziz Chaudhry, "The Myths of the Market and the Common History of Late Developers," *Politics and Society* 21 (1993): 245–74.

16 Chaudhry, "Myths of the Market," 265.

17 One vocal proponent of this view was the Malaysian Prime Minister, Dr. Mahatir Mohamed, in the context of the conditions imposed on IMF bailouts during the Asian Financial Crisis of 1997–1998. See *Commanding Heights: The Battle for the World Economy* documentary. Available at: https://www.pbs.org/wgbh/commandingheights/hi/story/index.html.

18 Alexander Gerschenkron, "Economic Backwardness in Historical Perspective," in B. F. Hoselitz, ed., *The Progress of Underdeveloped Areas* (Chicago, IL: University of Chicago Press, 1962).

19 Haggard, *Pathways from the Periphery.*

20 Bela Belassa, "The Lessons of East Asian Development: An Overview," *Economic Development and Cultural Change* 36 (1988): S273–S290; Helen Hughes, ed., *Achieving Industrialization in East Asia* (Cambridge: Cambridge University Press, 1988).

21 Chalmers Johnson, *MITI and the Japanese Miracle: The Growth of Industrial Policy, 1925–75* (Stanford, CA: Stanford University Press, 1982).

22 Haggard, *Pathways from the Periphery.*

23 James Fallows, "How the World Works," *The Atlantic* (December 1993): 1–16.

24 Alice Amsden, *Asia's Next Giant: South Korea and Late Industrialization* (Oxford: Oxford University Press, 1989).

25 Robert Wade, *Governing the Market: Economic Theory and the Role of Government in East Asian Industrialization* (Princeton, NJ: Princeton University Press, 1990).

26 Peter Evans, *Embedded Autonomy: States and Industrial Transformation* (Princeton, NJ: Princeton University Press, 1995).

27 Johnson, *MITI and the Japanese Miracle.*

28 Chalmers Johnson, "Political Institutions and Economic Performance: The Government–Business Relationship in Japan, South Korea, and Taiwan," in Frederic C. Deyo, ed., *The Political Economy of the New Asian Industrialism* (Ithaca, NY: Cornell University Press, 1987), 136–47.

29 Atul Kohli, *State-Directed Development: Political Power and Industrialization in the Global Periphery* (Cambridge: Cambridge University Press, 2004).

30 Johnson, *MITI and the Japanese Miracle.*

31 Minxin Pei, "Constructing the Political Foundations of an Economic Miracle," in Henry S. Rowen, ed., *Behind East Asian Growth: The Political and Social Foundations of Prosperity* (New York: Routledge, 1998), 39–59.

32 Stephan Haggard, *Developmental States* (Cambridge: Cambridge University Press, 2018).

33 Marilyn Waring, *If Women Counted* (New York: Harper & Row, 1988).

34 Adam Davidson, "The Economy's Missing Metrics," *The New York Times* (July 1, 2015).

35 Aram Ziai, "Post-Development 25 Years after the *Development Dictionary*," *Third World Quarterly* 38 (2017): 2547–58.

36 Olivia U. Rutazibwa, "On Babies and Bathwater: Decolonizing International Development Studies," in R. Icazwa, O. Rutazibwa, and S. de Jong, eds., *Decolonization and Feminisms in Global Teaching and Learning* (New York: Routledge, 2018); Kamna Patel, "Race and a Decolonial Turn in Development Studies," *Third World Quarterly* 41 (2020): 1463–75.

37 See, for example, Giacomo D'Alisa, Federico Demaria, and Giorgos Kallis, *Degrowth: A Vocabulary for a New Era* (New York: Routledge, 2015).

38 Amartya Sen, *Development As Freedom* (New York: Anchor, 1999).

39 The World Bank, *World Development Report 1997: The State in a Changing World* (New York: Oxford University Press, 1997); Commission on Growth and Development, *The Growth Report: Strategies for Sustained Growth and Inclusive Development* (Washington, DC: The World Bank, 2008).

40 Brass, "Development Theory."

41 The World Bank, *World Development Report 2002: Building Institutions for Markets* (New York: Oxford University Press, 2002).

42 Hernando De Soto, *The Mystery of Capital: Why Capitalism Triumphs in the West and Fails Everywhere Else* (New York: Basic Books, 2003).

43 Singumbe Muyeba, "Does Strength of Tenure Rights among the Urban Poor Improve Household Economies? Contrasting Matero and George in Lusaka City," *International Journal of Urban Sustainable Development* 10 (2018): 16–31.

44 Easterly, *Elusive Quest for Growth.*

45 Abhijit V. Banerjee and Esther Duflo, *Poor Economics: A Radical Rethinking of the Way to Fight Global Poverty* (New York: Public Affairs, 2011).

46 Timothy Besley, "Poor Choices: Poverty from the Ground Level," *Foreign Affairs* 91 (2012): 160–7.

47 Dan Slater, *Ordering Power: Contentious Politics and Authoritarian Leviathans in Southeast Asia* (New York: Cambridge University Press, 2010).

48 Dani Rodrik, "Fifty Years of Growth (and Lack Thereof): An Interpretation," in Dani Rodrik, ed., *One Economics, Many Recipes: Globalization, Institutions, and Economic Growth* (Princeton, NJ: Princeton University Press, 2007), 13–55.

49 Matt Andrews, Lant Pritchett, and Michael Woolcock, *Building State Capability: Evidence, Analysis, Action* (Oxford: Oxford University Press, 2017).

50 See, also, Miguel Angel Centeno, Atul Kohli, Deborah J. Yashar, and Dinsha Mistree, eds., *States in the Developing World* (Cambridge: Cambridge University Press, 2017).

51 Yuen Yuen Ang, *How China Escaped the Poverty Trap* (Ithaca, NY: Cornell University Press, 2017).

52 See James Scott, *Seeing Like a State: How Certain Schemes to Improve the Human Condition Have Failed* (New Haven, CT: Yale University Press, 1999); and Albert O. Hirschman, "The Principle of the Hiding Hand," *The Public Interest* 6 (1967): 10–23.

Amartya Sen,
Development as Freedom (1999)[*]

Introduction

Development as Freedom

Development can be seen, it is argued here, as a process of expanding the real freedoms that people enjoy. Focusing on human freedoms contrasts with narrower views of development, such as identifying development with the growth of gross national product, or with the rise in personal incomes, or with industrialization, or with technological advance, or with social modernization. Growth of GNP or of individual incomes can, of course, be very important as *means* to expanding the freedoms enjoyed by the members of the society. But freedoms depend also on other determinants, such as social and economic arrangements (for example, facilities for education and health care) as well as political and civil rights (for example, the liberty to participate in public discussion and scrutiny). Similarly, industrialization or technological progress or social modernization can substantially contribute to expanding human freedom, but freedom depends on other influences as well. If freedom is what development advances, then there is a major argument for concentrating on that overarching objective, rather than on some particular means, or some specially chosen list of instruments. Viewing development in terms of expanding substantive freedoms directs attention to the ends that make development important, rather than merely to some of the means that, inter alia, play a prominent part in the process.

Development requires the removal of major sources of unfreedom: poverty as well as tyranny, poor economic opportunities as well as systematic social deprivation, neglect of public facilities as well as intolerance or overactivity of repressive states. Despite unprecedented increases in overall opulence, the contemporary world denies elementary freedoms to vast numbers—perhaps even the majority—of people. Sometimes the lack of substantive freedoms relates directly to economic poverty, which robs people of the freedom to satisfy hunger, or to achieve sufficient nutrition, or to obtain remedies for treatable illnesses, or the opportunity to be adequately clothed or sheltered, or to enjoy clean water or sanitary facilities. In other cases, the unfreedom links closely to the lack of public facilities and social care, such as the absence of epidemiological programs, or of organized arrangements for health care or educational facilities, or of effective institutions for the maintenance of local peace and order. In still other cases,

---

the violation of freedom results directly from a denial of political and civil liberties by authoritarian regimes and from imposed restrictions on the freedom to participate in the social, political and economic life of the community.

Effectiveness and Interconnections

Freedom is central to the process of development for two distinct reasons.

1) *The evaluative reason:* assessment of progress has to be done primarily in terms of whether the freedoms that people have are enhanced;
2) *The effectiveness reason:* achievement of development is thoroughly dependent on the free agency of people.

I have already signaled the first motivation: the evaluative reason for concentrating on freedom. In pursuing the second, that of effectiveness, we have to look at the relevant empirical connections, in particular at the mutually reinforcing connections between freedoms of different kinds. It is because of these interconnections, which are explored in some detail in this book, that free and sustainable agency emerges as a major engine of development. Not only is free agency itself a "constitutive" part of development, it also contributes to the strengthening of free agencies of other kinds. The empirical connections that are extensively explored in this study link the two aspects of the idea of "development as freedom."

The relation between individual freedom and the achievement of social development goes well beyond the constitutive connection—important as it is. What people can positively achieve is influenced by economic opportunities, political liberties, social powers, and the enabling conditions of good health, basic education, and the encouragement and cultivation of initiatives. The institutional arrangements for these opportunities are also influenced by the exercise of people's freedoms, through the liberty to participate in social choice and in the making of public decisions that impel the progress of these opportunities. These interconnections are also investigated here.

Some Illustrations: Political Freedom and Quality of Life

The difference that is made by seeing freedom as the principal ends of development can be illustrated with a few simple examples. Even though the full reach of this perspective can only emerge from a much more extensive analysis (attempted in the chapters to follow), the radical nature of the idea of "development as freedom" can easily be illustrated with some elementary examples.

First, in the context of the narrower views of development in terms of GNP growth or industrialization, it is often asked whether certain political or social freedoms, such as the liberty of political participation and dissent, or opportunities to receive basic education, are or are not "conducive to development." In the light of the more foundational view of development as freedom, this way of posing the question tends to miss the important understanding that these substantive freedoms (that is, the liberty of political participation or the opportunity to receive basic education or health care) are among the *constituent components* of development. Their relevance for development does not have to be freshly established through their indirect contribution to the growth of GNP or to the promotion of industrialization. As it happens, these freedoms and rights are *also* very effective in contributing to economic progress; this connection will receive extensive attention in this book. But while the causal relation is indeed significant, the vindication of freedoms and rights provided by this causal linkage is over and above the directly constitutive role of these freedoms in development.

A second illustration relates to the dissonance between income per head (even after correction for price variations) and the freedom of individuals to live long and live well. For example, the citizens of Gabon or South Africa or Namibia or Brazil may be much richer in terms of per capita GNP than the citizens of Sri Lanka or China or the state of Kerala in India, but the latter have very substantially higher life expectancies than do the former.

To take a different type of example, the point is often made that African Americans in the United States are relatively poor compared with American whites, though much richer than people in the third world. It is, however, important to recognize that African Americans have an *absolutely* lower chance of reaching mature ages than do people of many third world societies, such as China, or Sri Lanka, or parts of India (with different arrangements of health care, education, and community relations). If development analysis is relevant even for richer countries (it is argued in this work that this is indeed so), the presence of such intergroup contrasts within the richer countries can be seen to be an important aspect of the understanding of development and underdevelopment.

Transactions, Markets and Economic Unfreedom

A third illustration relates to the role of markets as part of the process of development. The ability of the market mechanism to contribute to high economic growth and to overall economic progress has been widely—and rightly—acknowledged in the contemporary development literature. But it would be a mistake to understand the place of the market mechanism only in derivative terms. As Adam Smith noted, freedom of exchange and transaction is itself part and parcel of the basic liberties that people have reason to value.

To be *genetically against* markets would be almost as odd as being generically against conversations between people (even though some conversations are clearly foul and cause problems for others—or even for the conversationalists themselves). The freedom to exchange words, or goods, or gifts does not need defensive justification in terms of their favorable but distant effects; they are part of the way human beings in society live and interact with each other (unless stopped by regulation or fiat). The contribution of the market mechanism to economic growth is, of course, important, but this comes only after the direct significance of the freedom to interchange—words, goods, gifts—has been acknowledged.

As it happens, the rejection of the freedom to participate in the labor market is one of the ways of keeping people in bondage and captivity, and the battle against the unfreedom of bound labor is important in many third world countries today for some of the same reasons the American Civil War was momentous. The freedom to enter markets can itself be a significant contribution to development, quite aside from whatever the market mechanism may or may not do to promote economic growth or industrialization. In fact, the praise of capitalism by Karl Marx (not a great admirer of capitalism in general) and his characterization (in *Das Kapital*) of the American Civil War as "the one great event of contemporary history" related directly to the importance of the freedom of labor contract as opposed to slavery and the enforced exclusion from the labor market. As will be discussed, the crucial challenges of development in many developing countries today include the need for the freeing of labor from explicit or implicit bondage that denies access to the open labor market. Similarly, the denial of access to product markets is often among the deprivations from which many small cultivators and struggling producers suffer under traditional arrangements and restrictions. The freedom to participate in economic interchange has a basic role in social living.

To point to this often neglected consideration is not to deny the importance of judging the market mechanism comprehensively in terms of all its roles and effects, including those in generating economic growth and, under many circumstances, even economic equity. We must also examine, on the other side, the persistence of deprivations among segments of the community that happen to remain excluded from the benefits of the market-oriented society, and the general judgments, including criticisms, that people may have of lifestyles and values associated with the culture of markets. In seeing development as freedom, the arguments on different sides have to be appropriately considered and assessed. It is hard to think that any process of substantial development can do without very extensive use of markets, but that does not preclude the role of social support, public regulation, or statecraft when they can enrich—rather than impoverish—human lives. The approach used here provides a broader and more inclusive perspective on markets than is frequently invoked in *either* defending *or* chastising the market mechanism.

I end this list of illustrations with another that draws directly on a personal recollection from my own childhood. I was playing one afternoon—I must have been around ten or so—in the garden in our family home in the city of Dhaka, now the capital of Bangladesh, when a man came through the gate screaming pitifully and bleeding profusely; he had been knifed in the back. Those were the days of communal riots (with Hindus and Muslims killing each other), which preceded the independence and partitioning of India and Pakistan. The knifed man, called Kader Mia, was a Muslim daily laborer who had come for work in a neighboring house—for a tiny reward—and had been knifed on the street by some communal thugs in our largely Hindu area. As I gave him water while also crying for help from adults in the house, and moments later, as he was rushed to the hospital by my father, Kader Mia went on telling us that his wife had told him not to go into a hostile area in such troubled times. But Kader Mia had to go out in search of work and a bit of earning because his family had nothing to eat. The penalty of his economic unfreedom turned out to be death, which occurred later on in the hospital.

The experience was devastating for me. It made me reflect, later on, on the terrible burden of narrowly defined identities, including those firmly based on communities and groups (I shall have occasion to discuss that issue in this book). But more immediately, it also pointed to the remarkable fact that economic unfreedom, in the form of extreme poverty, can make a person a helpless prey in the violation of other kinds of freedom. Kader Mia need not have come to a hostile area in search of a little income in those terrible times had his family been able to survive without it. Economic unfreedom can breed social unfreedom, just as social or political unfreedom can also foster economic unfreedom.

Organizations and Values

Many other examples can be given to illustrate the pivotal difference that is made by pursuing a view of development as an integrated process of expansion of substantive freedoms that connect with one another. It is this view that is presented, scrutinized and utilized in this book to investigate the development process in inclusive terms that integrate economic, social and political considerations. A broad approach of this kind permits simultaneous appreciation of the vital roles, in the process of development, of many different institutions, including markets and market-related organizations, governments and local authorities, political parties and other civic institutions, educational arrangements and opportunities of open dialogue and debate (including the role of the media and other means of communication).

Such an approach also allows us to acknowledge the role of social values and prevailing mores, which can influence the freedoms that people enjoy and have reason to treasure. Shared norms can influence social features such as gender equity, the nature of child care, family size and fertility patterns, the treatment of the environment and many other arrangements and outcomes. Prevailing values and social mores also affect the presence or absence of corruption, and the role of trust in economic or social or political relationships. The exercise of freedom is mediated by values, but the values in turn are influenced by public discussions and social interactions, which are themselves influenced by participatory freedoms. Each of these connections deserves careful scrutiny.

The fact that the freedom of economic transactions tends to be typically a great engine of economic growth has been widely acknowledged, even though forceful detractors remain. It is important not only to give the markets their due, but also to appreciate the role of other economic, social, and political freedoms in enhancing and enriching the lives that people are able to lead. This has a clear bearing even on such controversial matters as the so-called population problem. The role of freedom in moderating excessively high fertility rates is a subject on which contrary views have been held for a long time. While that great eighteenth-century French rationalist Condorcet expected that fertility rates would come down with "the progress of reason," so that greater security, more education and more freedom of reflected decisions would restrain population growth, his contemporary Thomas Robert Malthus differed radically with this position. Indeed, Malthus argued that "there is no reason whatever to suppose that anything beside the difficulty of procuring in adequate plenty the necessaries of life should either indispose this greater number of persons to marry early, or disable them from rearing in health the largest families." The comparative merits of the two different positions—relying respectively on reasoned freedom and economic compulsion—will be investigated later on in this study (the balance of evidence, I shall argue, is certainly more on Condorcet's side). But it is especially important to recognize that this particular controversy is just one example of the debate between profreedom and antifreedom approaches to development that has gone on for many centuries. That debate is still very active in many different forms.

Institutions and Instrumental Freedoms

Five distinct types of freedom, seen in an "instrumental" perspective, are particularly investigated in the empirical studies that follow. These include (1) *political freedoms,* (2) *economic facilities,* (3) *social opportunities,* (4) *transparency guarantees* and (5) *protective security.* Each of these distinct types of rights and opportunities helps to advance the general capability of a person. They may also serve to complement each other. Public policy to foster human capabilities and substantive freedoms in general can work through the promotion of these distinct but interrelated instrumental freedoms. In the chapters that follow, each of these different types of freedom—and the institutions involved—will be explored, and their interconnections discussed. There will be an opportunity also to investigate their respective roles in the promotion of overall freedoms of people to lead the kind of lives they have reason to value. In the view of "development as freedom," the instrumental freedoms link with each other and with the ends of enhancement of human freedom in general.

While development analysis must, on the one hand, be concerned with objectives and aims that make these instrumental freedoms consequentially important, it must also take note of the empirical linkages that tie the distinct types of freedom *together,* strengthening their joint importance. Indeed, these connections are central to a fuller understanding of the instrumental role of freedom.

A Concluding Remark

Freedoms are not only the primary ends of development, they are also among its principal means. In addition to acknowledging, foundationally, the evaluative importance of freedom, we also have to understand the remarkable empirical connection that links freedoms of different kinds with one another. Political freedoms (in the form of free speech and elections) help to promote economic security. Social opportunities (in the form of education and health facilities) facilitate economic participation. Economic facilities (in the form of opportunities for participation in trade and production) can help to generate personal abundance as well as public resources for social facilities. Freedoms of different kinds can strengthen one another.

These empirical connections reinforce the valuational priorities. In terms of the medieval distinction between "the patient" and "the agent," this freedom-centered understanding of economics and of the process of development is very much an agent-oriented view. With adequate social opportunities, individuals can effectively shape their own destiny and help each other. They need not be seen primarily as passive recipients of the benefits of cunning development programs. There is indeed a strong rationale for recognizing the positive role of free and sustainable agency—and even of constructive impatience.

4

Climate Change

Climate change is the most critical contemporary existential challenge to human well-being. The debate in this section between the ecomodernists and the de-growthists starts from the shared premise that climate change is real, that it is a present threat to human and planetary welfare, and that some major and concerted effort to combat it is necessary for both moral and practical reasons. Where the two perspectives diverge is on the role of the market and industrial technology and, at heart, the merits of privileging economic growth while enacting environmental policy.

The debate between them reflects how the policy pendulum has swung on environmental protection in the United States and how perspectives on the market itself influence environmental policy.[1] Presidents Richard Nixon and Jimmy Carter recognized and acted upon the imperative to safeguard the environment in the 1970s, in the same way that they moved toward more government management of the market through macroeconomic and regulatory policy. In turn, environmental policy was not immune to the deregulation pursued by President Ronald Reagan when he took office in the 1980s with an emphasis on unconstrained economic growth as the route to expanded prosperity. Today, a broad swathe of policymakers, businesses, and the public recognize that poor environmental quality is a negative externality that hampers growth, yet a core debate persists about how much growth should be sacrificed to address the climate crisis.

The ecomodernist manifesto written by **John Asafu-Adjaye et al.** is rooted in many of the first principles of the market-liberal paradigm. The central argument rests on a faith, like that of Adam Smith, in inevitable gains in economic efficiency and technological progress as long as markets are free, in the power of innovation to fix socioeconomic ills, and in the basic universalism of human history. The manifesto is also grounded in the market-liberal logic that spontaneously occurring and unencumbered markets achieve the best possible outcome for humanity given how the relative scarcities of resources are managed most efficiently by market price signals. Echoing Smith and Eric Hobsbawm, the ecomodernists write that increasing economic specialization – from agriculturally intensive and rural to industrial and urban economies – has resulted in continuous improvements in efficiency, growth, and technological innovation. These forms of progress, in their view, will lead inevitably to further relative decoupling of environmental impact from economic growth and thus to less environmental stress over time. The ecomodernists are not doctrinaire market-liberals; echoing Alexander Gerschenkron, they recognize that technological solutions to environmental problems must take into account the broader economic, social, and political context and that, as a result, environmental policy will necessarily vary across different political–economic systems. At its heart, though, the ecomodernist manifesto is an expression of the optimistic belief that humans can and will avert ecological crisis without having to sacrifice economic growth.

The de-growthists, **Jeremy Caradonna et al.**, offer a direct rebuttal to the ecomodernists, critiquing their techno-optimism as overly rosy and identifying inaccuracies in their empirical evidence and analysis. Moreover, the de-growthists criticize the ecomodernists for what their narrative omits: the very real tolls of industrial capitalism and the adverse effects of modern technologies. They argue that the ecomodernists have glossed over how periods of unfettered economic growth have led to social, ecological, and environmental devastation, resulting in a net loss for human well-being. Echoing Karl Polanyi, the de-growthists observe that any improvements on the social, ecological, and environmental fronts have come as a result of conscious, deliberate societal and government action. They share with the ecomodernists the emphasis on the varied contexts facing countries at different levels of industrialization and development. Yet the de-growthists take the pessimistic view that decoupling economic growth from its environmental impacts is a "fantasy," hence we must essentially abandon the goal of growth to adequately address climate change. This zero-sum nature of the relationship between growth and the environment is illustrated with the observation that only major economic shocks – as a result of war, pandemics, and financial crises – have ever resulted in outright reductions in carbon emissions. In the estimation of the de-growthists, even the effects of environment-preserving technological innovation that emerge as a result of growth have been outweighed by the environment-harming effects of aggregate growth.

The ecomodernist and de-growthist perspectives lead to different prescriptions regarding the question of how the state should intervene to address climate change and safeguard the environment. As reflected in the general spirit of the ecomodernist manifesto, the policies that are most palatable to market-liberals revolve around market-based solutions. Both the European Union and the state of California have, for example, adopted variants of a cap and trade model that effectively sets a market price on carbon emissions. A straightforward carbon tax, which has been adopted in a number of Scandinavian countries, is another essentially market-based solution to the negative externality of carbon emissions. These approaches are rooted in the market-liberal logic that price signals will effectively change incentives, leading consumers and producers to make decisions that reduce carbon emissions over time. Such carbon-pricing programs have achieved results – but nowhere near the scale that would be required to effectively halt the alarming pace of climate change. The programs that exist fall very short of capturing the negative externalities of carbon, pricing it far below even the most conservative estimates of its true social cost and contributing to a false sense that enough action is being taken.[2] Carbon-pricing also embeds within itself adverse political economy incentives: it makes the public very aware of the short-term costs of climate action by raising energy bills, while failing to make clear the long-term benefits of mitigation for the environment, public health, and the economy.[3]

More market-institutionalist perspectives on climate change, such as that of the de-growthists, emphasize the embeddedness of the market in society and in the physical environment in which human society exists. They go so far as to link climate change with the other contemporary fault lines of modernity – racial injustice, socioeconomic inequality, intolerance toward immigration, propensity to conflict – via the common connection of such societal challenges to market-liberal capitalism and the commodification of the earth and its resources.[4] The prescription, in turn, is something along the lines of a Green New Deal, undergirded by the principle that solving these challenges requires more regulation and investment from government, in partnership with the private sector, to actively cut carbon emissions across society – and, crucially, to jointly address issues of environmental policy and social justice. Yet even the Green New Deal, with a major element of green industrial policy, does not give up on the goal of growth as much as the de-growthists would advocate.[5] Meaningful climate policy with tangible collective benefits has been elusive for more than a generation because of the political power and deep pockets of the industrial interests in favor of the status quo. Fossil fuel energy companies are emblematic of the privileged position enjoyed by big business that Charles Lindblom diagnosed in capitalist democracies. The potential for a policy that harnesses a public sector–private sector partnership to address the environmental, economic, and social ills associated with climate change will hinge on whether a broad, winning coalition can be formed across government, business, and society and the extent to which these groups see markets and society as embedded in the climate realm.

Notes

1 Daniel Immerwahr, "Growth vs. the Climate," *Dissent* (Spring 2015).
2 Jessica F. Green, "It's Time to Abandon Carbon Pricing," *Jacobin* (September 24, 2019).
3 Matto Mildenberger and Leah C. Stokes, "The Trouble with Carbon Pricing," *Boston Review* (September 24, 2020).
4 E.g., Naomi Klein, *This Changes Everything: Capitalism vs. the Climate* (New York: Simon & Schuster, 2014).
5 Robert Pollin, "De-Growth vs. a Green New Deal," *New Left Review* 112 (July/August 2018).

John Asafu-Adjaye et al., "An Ecomodernist Manifesto" (2015)*

To say that the Earth is a human planet becomes truer every day. Humans are made from the Earth, and the Earth is remade by human hands. Many earth scientists express this by stating that the Earth has entered a new geological epoch: the Anthropocene, the Age of Humans.

As scholars, scientists, campaigners, and citizens, we write with the conviction that knowledge and technology, applied with wisdom, might allow for a good, or even great, Anthropocene. A good Anthropocene demands that humans use their growing social, economic, and technological powers to make life better for people, stabilize the climate, and protect the natural world.

In this, we affirm one long-standing environmental ideal, that humanity must shrink its impacts on the environment to make more room for nature, while we reject another, that human societies must harmonize with nature to avoid economic and ecological collapse.

These two ideals can no longer be reconciled. Natural systems will not, as a general rule, be protected or enhanced by the expansion of humankind's dependence upon them for sustenance and well-being.

Intensifying many human activities — particularly farming, energy extraction, forestry, and settlement — so that they use less land and interfere less with the natural world is the key to decoupling human development from environmental impacts. These socioeconomic and technological processes are central to economic modernization and environmental protection. Together they allow people to mitigate climate change, to spare nature, and to alleviate global poverty.

Although we have to date written separately, our views are increasingly discussed as a whole. We call ourselves ecopragmatists and ecomodernists. We offer this statement to affirm and to clarify our views and to describe our vision for putting humankind's extraordinary powers in the service of creating a good Anthropocene.

1.

Humanity has flourished over the past two centuries. Average life expectancy has increased from 30 to 70 years, resulting in a large and growing population able to live in many different environments. Humanity has made extraordinary progress in

---

* From: Document originally published at Ecomodernism.org (http://www.ecomodernism.org/manifesto-english) in 2015 signed by John Asafu-Adjaye, Linus Blomqvist, Stewart Brand, Barry Brook, Ruth Defries, Erle Ellis, Christopher Foreman, David Keith, Martin Lewis, Mark Lynas, Ted Nordhaus, Roger Pielke, Jr., Rachel Pritzker, Joyashree Roy, Mark Sagoff, Michael Shellenberger, Robert Stone, Peter Teague. Permission to republish granted by Ted Nordhaus on behalf of the signers.

reducing the incidence and impacts of infectious diseases, and it has become more resilient to extreme weather and other natural disasters.

Violence in all forms has declined significantly and is probably at the lowest per capita level ever experienced by the human species, the horrors of the 20th century and present-day terrorism notwithstanding. Globally, human beings have moved from autocratic government toward liberal democracy characterized by the rule of law and increased freedom.

Personal, economic, and political liberties have spread worldwide and are today largely accepted as universal values. Modernization liberates women from traditional gender roles, increasing their control of their fertility. Historically large numbers of humans — both in percentage and in absolute terms — are free from insecurity, penury, and servitude.

At the same time, human flourishing has taken a serious toll on natural, nonhuman environments and wildlife. Humans use about half of the planet's ice-free land, mostly for pasture, crops, and production forestry. Of the land once covered by forests, 20 percent has been converted to human use. Populations of many mammals, amphibians, and birds have declined by more than 50 percent in the past 40 years alone. More than 100 species from those groups went extinct in the 20th century, and about 785 since 1500. As we write, only four northern white rhinos are confirmed to exist.

Given that humans are completely dependent on the living biosphere, how is it possible that people are doing so much damage to natural systems without doing more harm to themselves?

The role that technology plays in reducing humanity's dependence on nature explains this paradox. Human technologies, from those that first enabled agriculture to replace hunting and gathering, to those that drive today's globalized economy, have made humans less reliant upon the many ecosystems that once provided their only sustenance, even as those same ecosystems have often been left deeply damaged.

Despite frequent assertions starting in the 1970s of fundamental "limits to growth," there is still remarkably little evidence that human population and economic expansion will outstrip the capacity to grow food or procure critical material resources in the foreseeable future.

To the degree to which there are fixed physical boundaries to human consumption, they are so theoretical as to be functionally irrelevant. The amount of solar radiation that hits the Earth, for instance, is ultimately finite but represents no meaningful constraint upon human endeavors. Human civilization can flourish for centuries and millennia on energy delivered from a closed uranium or thorium fuel cycle, or from hydrogen-deuterium fusion. With proper management, humans are at no risk of lacking sufficient agricultural land for food. Given plentiful land and unlimited energy, substitutes for other material inputs to human well-being can easily be found if those inputs become scarce or expensive.

There remain, however, serious long-term environmental threats to human well-being, such as anthropogenic climate change, stratospheric ozone depletion, and ocean acidification. While these risks are difficult to quantify, the evidence is clear today that they could cause significant risk of catastrophic impacts on societies and ecosystems. Even gradual, non-catastrophic outcomes associated with these threats are likely to result in significant human and economic costs as well as rising ecological losses.

Much of the world's population still suffers from more-immediate local environmental health risks. Indoor and outdoor air pollution continue to bring premature death and illness to millions annually. Water pollution and water-borne illness due to pollution and degradation of watersheds cause similar suffering.

2.

Even as human environmental impacts continue to grow in the aggregate, a range of long-term trends are today driving significant decoupling of human well-being from environmental impacts.

Decoupling occurs in both relative and absolute terms. *Relative* decoupling means that human environmental impacts rise at a slower rate than overall economic growth. Thus, for each unit of economic output, less environmental impact (e.g., deforestation, defaunation, pollution) results. Overall impacts may still increase, just at a slower rate than would otherwise be the case. *Absolute* decoupling occurs when total environmental impacts — impacts in the aggregate — peak and begin to decline, even as the economy continues to grow.

Decoupling can be driven by both technological and demographic trends and usually results from a combination of the two.

The growth *rate* of the human population has already peaked. Today's population growth rate is one percent per year, down from its high point of 2.1 percent in the 1970s. Fertility rates in countries containing more than half of the global population are now below replacement level. Population growth today is primarily driven by longer life spans and lower infant mortality, not by rising fertility rates. Given current trends, it is very possible that the size of the human population will peak this century and then start to decline.

Trends in population are inextricably linked to other demographic and economic dynamics. For the first time in human history, over half the global population lives in cities. By 2050, 70 percent are expected to dwell in cities, a number that could rise to 80 percent or more by the century's end. Cities are characterized by both dense populations and low fertility rates.

Cities occupy just 1 to 3 percent of the Earth's surface and yet are home to nearly four billion people. As such, cities both drive and symbolize the decoupling of humanity from nature, performing far better than rural economies in providing efficiently for material needs while reducing environmental impacts.

The growth of cities along with the economic and ecological benefits that come with them are inseparable from improvements in agricultural productivity. As agriculture has become more land and labor efficient, rural populations have left the countryside for the cities. Roughly half the US population worked the land in 1880. Today, less than 2 percent does.

As human lives have been liberated from hard agricultural labor, enormous human resources have been freed up for other endeavors. Cities, as people know them today, could not exist without radical changes in farming. In contrast, modernization is not possible in a subsistence agrarian economy.

These improvements have resulted not only in lower labor requirements per unit of agricultural output but also in lower land requirements. This is not a new trend: rising harvest yields have for millennia reduced the amount of land required to feed the average person. The average per-capita use of land today is vastly lower than it was 5,000 years ago, despite the fact that modern people enjoy a far richer diet. Thanks to technological improvements in agriculture, during the half-century starting in the mid-1960s, the amount of land required for growing crops and animal feed for the average person declined by one-half.

Agricultural intensification, along with the move away from the use of wood as fuel, has allowed many parts of the world to experience net reforestation. About 80 percent of New England is today forested, compared with about 50 percent at the end of the 19th century. Over the past 20 years, the amount of land dedicated to production forest worldwide declined by 50 million hectares, an area the size of France. The "forest transition" from net deforestation to net reforestation seems to be as resilient a feature of development as the demographic transition that reduces human birth rates as poverty declines.

Human use of many other resources is similarly peaking. The amount of water needed for the average diet has declined by nearly 25 percent over the past half-century. Nitrogen pollution continues to cause eutrophication and large dead zones in places like the Gulf of Mexico. While the total amount of nitrogen pollution is rising, the amount used per unit of production has declined significantly in developed nations.

Indeed, in contradiction to the often-expressed fear of infinite growth colliding with a finite planet, demand for many material goods may be saturating as societies grow wealthier. Meat consumption, for instance, has peaked in many wealthy nations and has shifted away from beef toward protein sources that are less land intensive.

As demand for material goods is met, developed economies see higher levels of spending directed to materially less-intensive service and knowledge sectors, which account for an increasing share of economic activity. This dynamic might be even more pronounced in today's developing economies, which may benefit from being late adopters of resource-efficient technologies.

Taken together, these trends mean that the total human impact on the environment, including land-use change, overexploitation, and pollution, can peak and decline this century. By understanding and promoting these emergent processes, humans have the opportunity to re-wild and re-green the Earth — even as developing countries achieve modern living standards, and material poverty ends.

3.

The processes of decoupling described above challenge the idea that early human societies lived more lightly on the land than do modern societies. Insofar as past societies had less impact upon the environment, it was because those societies supported vastly smaller populations.

In fact, early human populations with much less advanced technologies had far larger individual land footprints than societies have today. Consider that a population of no more than one or two million North Americans hunted most of the continent's large mammals into extinction in the late Pleistocene, while burning and clearing forests across the continent in the process. Extensive human transformations of the environment continued throughout the Holocene period: as much as three-quarters of all deforestation globally occurred *before* the Industrial Revolution.

The technologies that humankind's ancestors used to meet their needs supported much lower living standards with much higher per-capita impacts on the environment. Absent a massive human die-off, any large-scale attempt at recoupling human societies to nature using these technologies would result in an unmitigated ecological and human disaster.

Ecosystems around the world are threatened today because people over-rely on them: people who depend on firewood and charcoal for fuel cut down and degrade forests; people who eat bush meat for food hunt mammal species to local extirpation. Whether it's a local indigenous community or a foreign corporation that benefits, it is the continued dependence of humans on natural environments that is the problem for the conservation of nature.

Conversely, modern technologies, by using natural ecosystem flows and services more efficiently, offer a real chance of reducing the totality of human impacts on the biosphere. To embrace these technologies is to find paths to a good Anthropocene.

The modernization processes that have increasingly liberated humanity from nature are, of course, double-edged, since they have also degraded the natural environment. Fossil fuels, mechanization and manufacturing, synthetic fertilizers and pesticides, electrification and modern transportation and communication technologies, have made larger human populations and greater consumption possible in the first place. Had technologies not improved since the Dark Ages, no doubt the human population would not have grown much either.

It is also true that large, increasingly affluent urban populations have placed greater demands upon ecosystems in distant places — the extraction of natural resources has been globalized. But those same technologies have also made it possible for people to secure food, shelter, heat, light, and mobility through means that are vastly more resource- and land-efficient than at any previous time in human history.

Decoupling human well-being from the destruction of nature requires the conscious acceleration of emergent decoupling processes. In some cases, the objective is the development of technological substitutes. Reducing deforestation and indoor air pollution requires the *substitution* of wood and charcoal with modern energy.

In other cases, humanity's goal should be to use resources more productively. For example, increasing agricultural yields can reduce the conversion of forests and grasslands to farms. Humans should seek to liberate the environment from the economy.

Urbanization, agricultural intensification, nuclear power, aquaculture, and desalination are all processes with a demonstrated potential to reduce human demands on the environment, allowing more room for non-human species. Suburbanization, low-yield farming, and many forms of renewable energy production, in contrast, generally require more land and resources and leave less room for nature.

These patterns suggest that humans are as likely to spare nature because it is not needed to meet their needs as they are to spare it for explicit aesthetic and spiritual reasons. The parts of the planet that people have not yet profoundly transformed have mostly been spared because they have not yet found an economic use for them — mountains, deserts, boreal forests, and other "marginal" lands.

Decoupling raises the possibility that societies might achieve peak human impact without intruding much further on relatively untouched areas. Nature unused is nature spared.

4.

Plentiful access to modern energy is an essential prerequisite for human development and for decoupling development from nature. The availability of inexpensive energy allows poor people around the world to stop using forests for fuel. It allows humans to grow more food on less land, thanks to energy-heavy inputs such as fertilizer and tractors. Energy allows humans to recycle waste water and desalinate sea water in order to spare rivers and aquifers. It allows humans to cheaply recycle metal and plastic rather than to mine and refine these minerals. Looking forward, modern energy may allow the capture of carbon from the atmosphere to reduce the accumulated carbon that drives global warming.

However, for at least the past three centuries, rising energy production globally has been matched by rising atmospheric concentrations of carbon dioxide. Nations have also been slowly decarbonizing — that is, reducing the carbon intensity of their economies — over that same time period. But they have not been doing so at a rate consistent with keeping cumulative carbon emissions low enough to reliably stay below the international target of less than 2 degrees Centigrade of global warming. Significant climate mitigation, therefore, will require that humans rapidly accelerate existing processes of decarbonization.

There remains much confusion, however, as to how this might be accomplished. In developing countries, rising energy consumption is tightly correlated with rising incomes and improving living standards. Although the use of many other material resource inputs such as nitrogen, timber, and land are beginning to peak, the centrality of energy in human development and its many uses as a substitute for material and human resources suggest that energy consumption will continue to rise through much if not all of the 21st century.

For that reason, any conflict between climate mitigation and the continuing development process through which billions of people around the world are achieving modern living standards will continue to be resolved resoundingly in favor of the latter.

Climate change and other global ecological challenges are not the most important immediate concerns for the majority of the world's people. Nor should they be. A new coal-fired power station in Bangladesh may bring air pollution and rising carbon dioxide emissions but will also save lives. For millions living without light and forced to burn dung to cook their food, electricity and modern fuels, no matter the source, offer a pathway to a better life, even as they also bring new environmental challenges.

Meaningful climate mitigation is fundamentally a technological challenge. By this we mean that even dramatic limits to per capita global consumption would be insufficient to achieve significant climate mitigation. Absent profound technological change there is no credible path to meaningful climate mitigation. While advocates differ in the particular mix of technologies they favor, we are aware of no quantified climate mitigation scenario in which technological change is not responsible for the vast majority of emissions cuts.

The specific technological paths that people might take toward climate mitigation remain deeply contested. Theoretical scenarios for climate mitigation typically reflect their creators' technological preferences and analytical assumptions while all too often failing to account for the cost, rate, and scale at which low-carbon energy technologies can be deployed.

The history of energy transitions, however, suggests that there have been consistent patterns associated with the ways that societies move toward cleaner sources of energy. Substituting higher-quality (i.e., less carbon-intensive, higher-density) fuels for lower-quality (i.e., more carbon-intensive, lower-density) ones is how virtually all societies have decarbonized, and points the way toward accelerated decarbonization in the future. Transitioning to a world powered by zero-carbon energy sources will require energy technologies that are power dense and capable of scaling to many tens of terawatts to power a growing human economy.

Most forms of renewable energy are, unfortunately, incapable of doing so. The scale of land use and other environmental impacts necessary to power the world on biofuels or many other renewables are such that we doubt they provide a sound pathway to a zero-carbon low-footprint future.

High-efficiency solar cells produced from earth-abundant materials are an exception and have the potential to provide many tens of terawatts on a few percent of the Earth's surface. Present-day solar technologies will require substantial innovation to meet this standard and the development of cheap energy storage technologies that are capable of dealing with highly variable energy generation at large scales.

Nuclear fission today represents the only present-day zero-carbon technology with the demonstrated ability to meet most, if not all, of the energy demands of a modern economy. However, a variety of social, economic, and institutional challenges make deployment of present-day nuclear technologies at scales necessary to achieve significant climate mitigation unlikely. A new generation of nuclear technologies that are safer and cheaper will likely be necessary for nuclear energy to meet its full potential as a critical climate mitigation technology.

In the long run, next-generation solar, advanced nuclear fission, and nuclear fusion represent the most plausible pathways toward the joint goals of climate stabilization and radical decoupling of humans from nature. If the history of energy transitions is any guide, however, that transition will take time. During that transition, other energy technologies can provide important social and environmental benefits. Hydroelectric dams, for example, may be a cheap source of low-carbon power for poor nations even though their land and water footprint is relatively large. Fossil fuels with carbon capture and storage can likewise provide substantial environmental benefits over current fossil or biomass energies.

The ethical and pragmatic path toward a just and sustainable global energy economy requires that human beings transition as rapidly as possible to energy sources that are cheap, clean, dense, and abundant. Such a path will require sustained public support for the development and deployment of clean energy technologies, both within nations and between them, through international collaboration and competition, and within a broader framework for global modernization and development.

5.

We write this document out of deep love and emotional connection to the natural world. By appreciating, exploring, seeking to understand, and cultivating nature, many people get outside themselves. They connect with their deep evolutionary history. Even when people never experience these wild natures directly, they affirm their existence as important for their psychological and spiritual well-being.

Humans will always materially depend on nature to some degree. Even if a fully synthetic world were possible, many of us might still choose to continue to live more coupled with nature than human sustenance and technologies require. What decoupling offers is the possibility that humanity's material dependence upon nature might be less destructive.

The case for a more active, conscious, and accelerated decoupling to spare nature draws more on spiritual or aesthetic than on material or utilitarian arguments. Current and future generations could survive and prosper materially on a planet with much less biodiversity and wild nature. But this is not a world we want nor, if humans embrace decoupling processes, need to accept.

What we are here calling nature, or even wild nature, encompasses landscapes, seascapes, biomes and ecosystems that have, in more cases than not, been regularly altered by human influences over centuries and millennia. Conservation science, and the concepts of biodiversity, complexity, and indigeneity are useful, but alone cannot determine which landscapes to preserve, or how.

In most cases, there is no single baseline prior to human modification to which nature might be returned. For example, efforts to restore landscapes to more closely resemble earlier states ("indigeneity") may involve removing recently arrived species ("invasives") and thus require a net *reduction* in local biodiversity. In other circumstances, communities may decide to sacrifice indigeneity for novelty and biodiversity.

Explicit efforts to preserve landscapes for their non-utilitarian value are inevitably anthropogenic choices. For this reason, all conservation efforts are fundamentally anthropogenic. The setting aside of wild nature is no less a human choice, in service of human preferences, than bulldozing it. Humans will save wild places and landscapes by convincing our fellow citizens that these places, and the creatures that occupy them, are worth protecting. People may choose to have some services — like water purification and flood protection — provided for by natural systems, such as forested watersheds, reefs, marshes, and wetlands, even if those natural systems are more expensive than simply building water treatment plants, seawalls, and levees. There will be no one-size-fits-all solution.

Environments will be shaped by different local, historical, and cultural preferences. While we believe that agricultural intensification for *land-sparing* is key to protecting wild nature, we recognize that many communities will continue to opt for *land-sharing*, seeking to conserve wildlife within agricultural landscapes, for example, rather than allowing it to revert to wild nature in the form of grasslands, scrub, and forests. Where decoupling reduces pressure on landscapes and ecosystems to meet basic human needs, landowners, communities, and governments still must decide to what aesthetic or economic purpose they wish to dedicate those lands.

Accelerated decoupling alone will not be enough to ensure more wild nature. There must still be a conservation politics and a wilderness movement to demand more wild nature for aesthetic and spiritual reasons. Along with decoupling humankind's material needs from nature, establishing an enduring commitment to preserve wilderness, biodiversity, and a mosaic of beautiful landscapes will require a deeper emotional connection to them.

6.

We affirm the need and human capacity for accelerated, active, and conscious decoupling. Technological progress is not inevitable. Decoupling environmental impacts from economic outputs is not simply a function of market-driven innovation and efficient response to scarcity. The long arc of human transformation of natural environments through technologies began well before there existed anything resembling a market or a price signal. Thanks to rising demand, scarcity, inspiration, and serendipity, humans have remade the world for millennia.

Technological solutions to environmental problems must also be considered within a broader social, economic, and political context. We think it is counterproductive for nations like Germany and Japan, and states like California, to shutter nuclear power plants, recarbonize their energy sectors, and recouple their economies to fossil fuels and biomass. However, such examples underscore clearly that technological choices will not be determined by remote international bodies but rather by national and local institutions and cultures.

Too often, modernization is conflated, both by its defenders and critics, with capitalism, corporate power, and laissez-faire economic policies. We reject such reductions. What we refer to when we speak of modernization is the long-term evolution of social, economic, political, and technological arrangements in human societies toward vastly improved material well-being, public health, resource productivity, economic integration, shared infrastructure, and personal freedom.

Modernization has liberated ever more people from lives of poverty and hard agricultural labor, women from chattel status, children and ethnic minorities from oppression, and societies from capricious and arbitrary governance. Greater resource productivity associated with modern socio-technological systems has allowed human societies to meet human needs with fewer resource inputs and less impact on the environment. More-productive economies are wealthier economies, capable of better meeting human needs while committing more of their economic surplus to non-economic amenities, including better human health, greater human freedom and opportunity, arts, culture, and the conservation of nature.

Modernizing processes are far from complete, even in advanced developed economies. Material consumption has only just begun to peak in the wealthiest societies. Decoupling of human welfare from environmental impacts will require a sustained commitment to technological progress and the continuing evolution of social, economic, and political institutions alongside those changes.

Accelerated technological progress will require the active, assertive, and aggressive participation of private sector entrepreneurs, markets, civil society, and the state. While we reject the planning fallacy of the 1950s, we continue to embrace a strong public role in addressing environmental problems and accelerating technological innovation, including research to develop better technologies, subsidies, and other measures to help bring them to market, and regulations to mitigate environmental hazards. And international collaboration on technological innovation and technology transfer is essential in the areas of agriculture and energy.

7.

We offer this statement in the belief that both human prosperity and an ecologically vibrant planet are not only possible but also inseparable. By committing to the real processes, already underway, that have begun to decouple human well-being from environmental destruction, we believe that such a future might be achieved. As such, we embrace an optimistic view toward human capacities and the future.

It is our hope that this document might contribute to an improvement in the quality and tenor of the dialogue about how to protect the environment in the 21st century. Too often discussions about the environment have been dominated by the extremes, and plagued by dogmatism, which in turn fuels intolerance. We value the liberal principles of democracy, tolerance, and pluralism in themselves, even as we affirm them as keys to achieving a *great* Anthropocene. We hope that this statement advances the dialogue about how best to achieve universal human dignity on a biodiverse and thriving planet.

Jeremy Caradonna et al.,
"A Call to Look Past *An Ecomodernist Manifesto*: A Degrowth Critique" (2015)[*]

One of the counties within the province of sustainable development is now called "ecomodernism," and it has come to prominence over the past few years, in part because of the figures associated with it, including prominent environmental thinkers such as Ted Nordhaus, Michael Shellenberger, and Stewart Brand. The *New York Times* recently praised the ecomodernist message in an article called, misleadingly, "A Call to Look Past Sustainable Development."[1] Why is the article's title so misleading? For the simple reason that the figures within ecomodernism want cultural and economic change that is sustainable, just like the rest of us; they simply want to move the focus of development in a new direction, even though this "new" direction seems surprisingly and troublingly conventional at times. The *New York Times* article mentions a new statement of principles that the ecomodernists published this year. It is called *An Ecomodernist Manifesto* (2015) and is co-authored by eighteen leading lights of the sustainability movement, including Nordhaus, Shellenberger, and Brand, but also the physicist David Keith, the scientist, Nobel Prize Winner, and Indian economist Joyashree Roy, and the filmmaker Robert Stone. Many of the authors are associated with The Breakthrough Institute, a think tank whose mission has been described as "'neoliberal conservation' guided by economic rationality and human-centered managerialism."[2]

Given the level of attention that ecomodernism has received, it seems worthwhile to analyze critically the ecomodernists' manifesto, and to offer those criticisms from a county on the other side of the province—namely, from the point of view of "degrowth."[3] Degrowth has also risen to prominence in recent years, ever since the Great Recession (2008-2009) forced a reappraisal of the growth-addicted, deregulated, neo-liberal economic policies that have dominated national governments and international financial institutions since the 1980s.[4] Indeed, degrowth has also had its moment in the sun—that is, in the *New York Times*—as it has been the subject of a heated public debate between the economist Paul Krugman and ecological economists. Krugman's article, "Errors and Emissions" (18 September 2014) triggered an impassioned exchange between Krugman, Richard Heinberg, and others involved in degrowth and the economics of sustainability.[5] It would appear that the debate over growth is back in fashion for the first time since the 1970s.[6]

Sustainable degrowth has been defined by numerous authors over the past five years, but François Schneider, Joan Martinez-Alier, and Georgios Kallis offer perhaps the simplest and clearest definition: "Sustainable degrowth is defined as an equitable downscaling of production and consumption that increases human wellbeing and enhances ecological conditions."[7] Those who populate the degrowth county are equally interested in sustainable development (or developing towards sustainability), but diverge from ecomodernism and the denizens of other counties in some crucial ways. While ecomodernists, as we shall see, tend to promote the necessity of endless economic growth and the role that new technologies will play in creating a sustainable global society, the backers of degrowth see the transition to sustainability (or a steady-state economy) occurring through less impactful economic activities and a voluntary contraction of material throughput of the economy—at least, in the more developed and wealthier parts of the globe[8]— to reduce humanity's aggregate demands on the biosphere. From a degrowth perspective, technology is not viewed as a magical savior since many technologies often accelerate environmental decline.[9]

After careful analysis, those in the degrowth camp have come to the conclusion that the only way for humanity to live within its biophysical limits and mitigate the effects of climate change is to *reduce* economic activity, to downscale consumerist lifestyles, to move beyond conventional energy sources, to give up on the fantasy of "decoupling" economic and population growth from environmental impacts, and to rethink the technologies that have gotten us into our current predicament. There has been no known society that has simultaneously expanded economic activity and reduced absolute energy consumption.[10] All efforts to decouple growth of gross domestic product (GDP) from environmental destruction through technological innovations and renewable energies have failed to achieve the absolute reductions necessary for a livable planet. There has only been a handful of instances over the past century during which global or regional carbon dioxide (CO_2) emissions have actually declined. Notable instances include: 1) the Great Depression of the 1930s, 2) the economic recession following the second oil shock in the early 1980s, 3) the collapse of Soviet economies after the end of the Cold War, and 4) the two years of recession following the financial crisis triggered in 2008. That is, from all that we know, only a less "busy" economy can actually achieve lower emissions.[11] Likewise, the ecological economist Peter A. Victor has shown through modeling the Canadian economy that economic growth makes the job of fighting climate change all the more difficult. He writes that "for example, if an economy grows at 3% per year for 40 years, an average annual reduction in GHG [greenhouse gas] intensity of 7.23% is required if GHG emissions are to be reduced by 80%. This compares with an average annual reduction in GHG intensity of 4.11% if there is no economic growth during that period."[12]

The following is a critique of the *Ecomodernist Manifesto* from the point of view of degrowth, which draws on a biophysical and ecological perspective, as well as the science of thermodynamics, and rejects the idea that industrial modernity provides a simple blueprint to a future, sustainable society. It is written, however, with the recognition that at least *some* of the claims in the *Manifesto* are accurate and worth supporting. Indeed, there is much to admire in it, including the optimistic tone of its authors and the genuine affinity for the natural world that leaps off the page. Further, it must be acknowledged that the different counties within sustainable development want fundamentally the same thing, which is a world that respects ecological realities; enhances public health, human wellbeing, equity, justice, democracy, and life satisfaction; and creates the conditions for resilient ecosystems and a stable and prosperous global civilization. Debate among different schools of thought is healthy and ultimately beneficial for the broader sustainability movement.

In some ways, the disagreements between ecomodernists and degrowthists revive long-standing disagreements among sustainable development proponents about the twin role played by economic growth and modern technological innovation in ameliorating humanity's conditions—disagreements that have existed ever since the United Nations began to endorse sustainability in the 1980s.[13] Should development occur in a top-down fashion, brokered by powerful international nongovernmental organizations (NGOs), governments, and industry, or bottom-up, in organic, low-impact, and community-led efforts? Does one create a sustainable society via deregulated financial institutions and growth-based economics, or through regulated economic systems and the abandonment of pro-growth policies? These questions have elicited wildly different answers. Indeed, the two flagship documents of sustainable development, the *World Conservation Strategy* (1980) and the more well-known *Our Common Future* (the Brundtland Report, 1987), while helping tremendously to provide the concept of sustainable development with an identity, contain, in certain places, contradictory or at least inconsistent ideas about the role that technology and economic growth should play in future development.[14]

Not only does the *Manifesto* rehash the belief that yet more growth and yet more technology will save us, but it also suffers from a range of other problems, including factually incorrect statements, deficient and contradictory argumentation, dubious environmental claims, and shocking omissions. The purpose of this short essay is to deconstruct the statements, arguments, and vision of the ecomodernists' manifesto, while offering, where appropriate, counterclaims and counterarguments that can hopefully better illuminate the challenges of sustainable development moving forward.

The manifesto, which does not include sources or references, is divided into seven sections (*The Communist Manifesto*, by contrast, had only four) that puts forth a vision of a future society, or a pathway to that society, that is driven by the creation of new technologies, as well as the "intensification" of human activities, that together would "decouple [e] human development from environmental impacts (7).[15] In short, the manifesto rehashes the fantastical goal, long pursued by neoclassical economists, of separating out the apparently desirable stuff (more people, more affluence, more consumption) from the undesirable stuff (waste, pollution, environmental degradation, and declines in energy stocks). Key to the ecomodernist argument is the narrative of modernity, or in more technocratic language, "modernization." The ecomodernists do not romanticize low-impact indigenous or pre-industrial societies, and do not seem to value anything about global societies that existed before, say, 1750, or those in the present that retain non-industrial practices. These people are simply and backwardly "undeveloped."[16] The ecomodernists view the Industrial Revolution as a largely positive phase of human history that increased life expectancy, allowed for technologies that increased human wellbeing, produced modern medicine and the ability to more effectively fight disease, and created systems that mitigated the effects of natural disasters (8).

At times, the manifesto reads like a chapter from a Herbert Spencer tract; the love, admiration, and faith in science and technology borders on the Victorian, and the mythos of Progress, so essential to industrialism since the 19th century, is bizarrely juxtaposed against more sober acknowledgements of humankind's toll on the planet. Here's one example of this rather saccharine metanarrative of Progress: "Personal, economic, and political liberties have spread worldwide and are today largely accepted as universal values. Modernization liberates women from traditional gender roles, increasing their control of their fertility. Historically large numbers of humans—both in percentage and in absolute terms—are free from insecurity, penury, and servitude" (8-9).

One does not need a degrowth perspective to understand that this statement is highly questionable and that the effects of "modernization" have been more complex than this liberationist narrative would suggest. The "liberation" of women from "traditional gender roles" was due in large part to the work of twentieth-century suffragettes and feminists, and had relatively little to do with industrialism in the narrow sense. (And what about women in the non-Western industrialized world?) It is important to acknowledge, moreover, that child labor and 16-hour days for adults fuelled the Industrial Revolution and were ended only by strike action taken by trade unions in the face of strong opposition by industrialists. In these cases, technology and industrial production were the problem, for which collective, grass-roots action and resistance was the solution. Further, the idea that there are fewer people in "servitude" in 2015 than there were in the past is also a debatable point. New research sponsored by the United Nations suggests that over 20 million people are currently working as modern-day slaves.[17] The *total* number of African slaves brought to the Americas by Europeans between 1500 and 1850 was 12 million, although many millions more died in waiting or in transit.[18] At no single point, however, did the population of African (or aboriginal) slaves come close to 20 million. Slaves and subjugation certainly existed in other parts of the world, too, but the notion that servitude has declined in real numbers over time ultimately rests on the subjective interpretation on the word "servitude." But the raw numbers are, here, beside the point. The point is that ecomodernism offers a peculiarly whitewashed and sugary interpretation of industrial modernism, and fails to acknowledge that the interrelated problems of overconsumption and environmental decline were *not* coincidental byproducts of those modern industrial processes. Industrial modernity has certainly brought numerous benefits to humankind, but it has come at a heavy toll, and one that jeopardizes the possibility of creating a sustainable society.[19]

The technology-will-save-us thesis of the ecomodernists merely restates the optimism of industrialists and many futurists going back two centuries or more, but also borrows from the technocratic school of thought within sustainability that is often associated with Amory Lovins.[20] The ecomodernists paper over the highly destructive nature of modern technologies throughout the manifesto, or else exaggerate the benefits of emergent technologies, such as the dubious and largely untested systems for carbon capture and storage (24). "Given that humans are completely dependent on the living biosphere, how is it possible that people are doing so much damage to natural systems without doing more harm to themselves?"(9). It comes as news to us that humans are not doing harm to themselves. The World Health Organization reported recently that in 2012 around 7 million people died—that is, one in eight of total global deaths—"as a result of air pollution exposure," the vast majority of which was emitted via "modern" technologies.[21] In the 1970s, Paul Ehrlich developed the metric I = PAT, in which the overall impact of a society is determined by the factors of population, affluence, and technology.[22] This metric was invented as a caution toward overly simplistic acceptance of technologies, but the ecomodernists set aside this concern (28) and assume that more technology is necessarily the solution. The *Manifesto* is silent on the topic of geoengineering, but one worries that the ecomodernists support this fraught and highly risky response to climate change.[23]

The ecomodernists scoff at the idea of "limits to growth," arguing that technology will always find a way to overcome those limits. "Despite frequent assertions starting in the 1970s of fundamental 'limits to growth,' there is still remarkably little evidence that human populations and economic expansion will outstrip the capacity to grow food or procure critical material resources in the foreseeable future" (9).[24] Here is one of the first clues that the ecomodernists agree with George H. W. Bush that the limits to growth are, in the words of the former president, "contrary to human nature."[25] But what additional evidence do the ecomodernists need to appreciate that the limits to growth *are* being reached?

Graham Turner, Ugo Bardi, and numerous others have shown through empirical research that many of the modeled scenarios, and the fundamental thesis, of the Club of Rome remain as relevant as ever—that is, that the human endeavor is bumping up against natural limits.[26] Richard Heinberg has demonstrated that the production of conventional oil, natural gas, and heavy oil all peaked around 2010, despite, but also due to, continued global reliance on fossil fuels, which still comprise over 80% of the world's primary source of energy.[27] The so-called Green Revolution and chemically intensive conventional farming has polluted many of the world's waterways and lakes, and has caused a New Jersey-sized dead zone in the Gulf of Mexico. In North America, the vast majority of the original humus content on arable land has been lost to agriculture and monocultures.[28] There are 7 million tons of accumulated non-biodegradable plastic debris caught in the eastern and western gyres of the Pacific Ocean, and half of the fish biomass in the world's oceans show traces of microplastic contamination.[29] Copper will be in short supply by as early as the 2030s, and a number of rare Earth minerals will not be far behind.[30] Perhaps the absolute limits to growth have not yet been reached, but mounting evidence suggests that they are not far off, and it behooves ecomodernists to consider that yet more growth might *not* be the answer. The history of industrialism to date suggests that more growth will be coupled with increasing environmental costs.[31] It is also worth realizing that many once-thriving societies, from the Anasazi to the Maya, collapsed due to demographic, ecological, and social pressures.[32] The limits to growth are real, even if their exact nature differs over time and space.

Moreover, the ecomodernists' disregard for ecology and natural systems is disturbingly anthropocentric. That is, they ignore or externalize the non-human casualties of growth. Even if technology and human ingenuity enabled miraculously the endless growth of "human populations and economic expansion"—why would we want this, again?—this Biggering would still generate manifold environmental impacts. The collapse of the Atlantic northwest cod fishery in the 1980s and early 1990s is merely one example of ecological ruin that was facilitated by industrial technologies (refrigeration, new kinds of ships, new harvesting material, and so forth) and the naive contempt for natural limits.[33] When the Canadian Federal Minister of Fisheries and Oceans declared a much-belated moratorium on the cod fishery in 1992, it brought to an end 500 years of intensive cod harvesting, destroyed many Canadian maritime communities, and put paid to the debate on natural limits. It is true that humanity survived the decline of the Northern cod, but does the precipitous decline of this fishery matter in the Story of Modern Progress?

One of the central arguments of the *Manifesto* is that human-induced environmental impacts could one day become "decoupled" from economic growth. As noted, this has long been the fantasy of neoclassical economists, who want to have their cake and eat it, too.[34] But rather than addressing the fundamental flaws of a growth-obsessed economy, the ecomodernists assume that economic growth is both necessary and possible in the long term and that, therefore, technology will have to do the work of decoupling. "Decoupling of human welfare from environmental impacts will require a sustained commitment to technological progress and the continuing evolution of social, economic, and political institutions alongside those changes" (29). The authors argue that the *relative* environmental impact of humans has decreased in some domains, even though there has not been an absolute decoupling of these aggregated impacts (11). They cite as evidence the fact that many countries have reduced their carbon intensity over the past few decades, meaning that they get more economic bang for their energy buck (20), partly because of increases in energy efficiency. However, to hold aggregate ecological impact over time constant with growth, eco-efficiency would need to improve at the same rate as the economy grows, which places a heavy burden on engineers and inventors. More troublingly, the ecomodernists fail to address the deeper problem that absolute, aggregated impacts have continued to climb—the concentration of GHGs in the atmosphere is increasing, the extinction of species chugs along at an alarming rate, the Human Appropriation of Net Primary Production (HANPP) remains staggeringly high, and the world's major ecosystems have only become more degraded since the middle of the last century.[35] Moreover, there is no hint of the Jevons Paradox—the long-recognized enigma that increases in technological and energy efficiency almost always *increase* consumption, not decrease it, due to various rebound effects.[36] But the more profound dilemma is that ecomodernism is still locked inside the business-as-usual, growth paradigm.[37] It is certainly true that a growing global economy will mean greater impacts on the natural world and human health, which is why we question the necessity of this growth.

Even the most anti-growth and pro-steady-state economists, from Herman Daly to Daniel O'Neil, argue that some parts of the world, namely Sub-Saharan Africa, could benefit from more economic growth.[38] Many other parts of the planet would benefit from less growth, or in any case, will have to make do with a less busy economy. The point is that there needs to be a more critical and qualitative approach to growth, and one that jettisons GDP as a meaningful measure of economic well-being. But the ecomodernists seem to assume that all growth is good, in contradistinction to the degrowthists, who recognize that much of the growth in the developed world, with its high levels of material throughput and energy consumption, is "uneconomic" and leads to long-term costs and environmental impacts. In other words, growth backfires. Rather than leaving the developing world to play an impossible game of catch-up with levels of energy and material consumption in the developed world, what is needed is for the high-consumption countries to cease treating the present growth model as a limitless aspiration for others to follow.[39]

One of the most unfortunate results of this technophilism and Biggering-Is-Better attitude is the ecomodernists' adoration of nuclear power. The environmental thinkers behind the *Manifesto* seem to have followed James Lovelock into the misguided belief that nuclear power is the only hope for humanity.[40] Some passages rival H. G. Wells' *Anticipations* (1901) in their gushing optimism in Scientific Progress. Consider the following:

> "Human civilization can flourish for centuries and millennia on energy delivered from a closed uranium or thorium fuel cycle, or from hydrogen-deuterium fusion" (10).

> "Nuclear fission presents the only present-day zero-carbon technology with the demonstrated ability to meet most, if not all, of the energy demands of a modern economy." (23)

> "We think it is counterproductive for nations like Germany and Japan, and states like California, to shutter nuclear power plants, recarbonize their energy sectors, and recouple their economies to fossil fuels and biomass." (28)

The reality is that nuclear power has never played a major role in meeting the world's energy demands, despite the fact that it was touted throughout much of the middle and late twentieth century as a panacea for our energy woes. According to the Intergovernmental Panel on Climate Change (IPCC), nuclear provides only 2 percent of the world's energy, although the International Energy Association puts the number at 5.7 percent.[41] These numbers are still well below those of renewables, which are pushing 15 percent of global energy consumption.[42]

Indeed, there are at least eight reasons that nuclear power should not be seen as a positive contribution from the standpoint of sustainable development, and it is worth dwelling on them in detail, since ecomodernism places so much emphasis on nuclear. First, nuclear power has never lived up to its expectations as a major energy source, especially when compared to its *immense* impacts and costs. Second, the building of nuclear power plants is hugely capital intensive, which seems to contradict the *Manifesto*'s call for "cheap, clean, dense, and abundant" energy sources (24). Third, nuclear power is a nonrenewable resource since uranium is finite, and some energy analysts project that low-cost and accessible stocks could become quite scarce by 2080. Fourth, most countries do not possess uranium deposits, and therefore nuclear power prevents many countries from achieving energy independence. Fifth, most countries do not currently have (or want, or could even consider) a nuclear power plant. As of 2013, only 31 countries had this capacity. Sixth, nuclear power and nuclear weapons are inherently linked since the ability to produce nuclear power also establishes the material basis and expertise for making nuclear weapons. It is not an energy source that creates the conditions for long-term peace, as we have learned recently, once again, in the standoff between Iran and the West. Seventh, nuclear waste is dangerously radioactive and essentially impossible to store safely in the long term, since the waste takes thousands of years to lose its radioactivity. The 440 or so nuclear power plants that function today generate enormous amounts of waste, much of which is still sitting on the grounds of the power plants, while some has been stored in caves or dumped in the ocean. Eighth, and finally, nuclear power plants are prone to catastrophic disasters—that is, environmental impacts—such as the ones that occurred in 1986 at Chernobyl, and in 2011 at the Fukushima Daiichi plant in Japan.[43] Even with future breakthroughs in nuclear technology, the reality is that a nuclear power will always remain an ecologically reckless endeavor.

As a result of these disasters, and these concerns, public confidence in nuclear power has waned considerably in most countries around the world, and some governments, such as in Germany, have begun phasing out their remaining facilities. As seen above, the ecomodernists do not like that citizens in Germany or Japan are questioning nuclear power. Yet this indignation is insensitive in the extreme. For starters, Japan is still coping with a major power plant calamity, and one that has led to much soul-searching over the future of energy in Japan. In Germany, the effects of the Chernobyl disaster were direct and impactful. In West Berlin, for instance, the prevalence of Down syndrome rose dramatically in the nine months following the incident, which blanketed much of Western Europe in radioactive fallout. It may very well be true, as the *Manifesto* notes, that nuclear power is a low-carbon technology (at least, in the direct production phases of the energy), but there are *many* other health and environmental impacts to consider, not to mention the political and economic ramifications of this technology. More nuclear power plants will almost inevitably mean more disasters and more long-term storage headaches. The ecomodernists seem particularly miffed that Germans want to "recarbonize" their economy, since reducing nuclear will, according to the *Manifesto*, require filling the void with coal (along with wind, biomass, and solar), although this, too, is a complicated matter. Renewable energy production has, so far, overcompensated for the decline in production in nuclear energy, and there is every indication that it could continue to do so. It is true that Germany, along with many other countries, is still powered in part by coal. But Germany, unlike national governments in Canada or the United States, has a long-term energy plan to wean itself from fossil fuels.[44] Why abandon those gains in favor of nuclear power (a proven liability) and carbon capture and storage (which reinforces the fossil-fueled status quo)?

Rather than ramping up on dangerous forms of energy production to meet increased economic activity, the world needs less (and also different) economic activity and a sustainable population, which could then create the possibility of powering the world via renewable resources. That is, degrowthists and ecomodernists agree that economic growth creates energy problems, but the two camps differ starkly in their response to this dilemma. For the ecomodernists, population and economic growth are taken as givens, and thus governments are forced into making difficult decisions about energy, including support for conventional, hard energies, from coal and gas to nuclear power. For degrowthists, population growth and continued economic expansion are seen as undesirable and essentially impossible in the medium term, and thus the solution is to live within biophysical limits, and reduce global energy demands to a level that could be safely met by renewables. To borrow a book title from Ted Trainer, *Renewable Energy Cannot Sustain a Consumer Society.*[45]

The ecomodernists also assume that the increasing urbanization of the planet is fundamentally positive. Dehli now counts 25. million people. Beijing has over 21 million smog-chocked inhabitants. Mexico City, 20 million. Cities now occupy an astounding three percent of the Earth's surface and house around four billion people (12), leading to historically unprecedented densities of human clusterings. While urban dwellers tend to have higher incomes and better access to societal services than their rural counterparts, looking only at the average number hides the deep inequalities within and across cities worldwide. A city such as Mumbai has stunning inequalities, human suffering, public health crises, slums, and dilapidated infrastructure. The relative affluence of urban dwellers comes at a cost for the environment. Cities are home to about half of the global population, but contribute about 80 percent of global GHG emissions.[46] It is hard to see how yet more urbanization will necessarily increase human wellbeing, as the ecomodernists credulously contend. Economic growth has been accompanied by mounting income inequalities in urban areas and beyond. In contrast to the three decades of rapid growth following World War II, the little growth that has been squeezed out of the economic system in recent years has largely benefitted the richer strata of society, while cramming the world's poor into densely packed cities, from China to Brazil.[47] The bright and powerful vision of economic growth—to provide the material basis for a better life for all—bears little resemblance to the current prospects of only accumulating the wealth of the richest while destroying the environment and livelihoods of future generations and the poorest and most vulnerable today.

Further, ecomodernism is patently condescending toward peasants, farmers, and those who support agrarian values. This *Manifesto* is not for Wendell Berry. The authors note that only two percent of Americans are today engaged in farming, whereas half the population lived and worked on farms in the 1880s (12)—a demographic shift, it should be noted, that was facilitated by access to cheap and abundant fossil fuels. The authors go so far as to say that humans need to be "liberated" from agricultural labor, as though the production of food were not an essential good in and of itself. This very westernized and industrialized snobbery toward agrarianism is redolent of Nicholas Kristof and Sheryl WuDunn's infamous and repugnant *New York Times* article, entitled "Two Cheers for Sweatshops," which assumed that working in a wretched factory in industrial China was perforce a better fate than working in a rice paddy, as farmers in China have done for "forty centuries."[48] From the point of view of degrowth, a lower impact and less consumerist world will require an *increase* in farming (and gardening) and greater reconnections to the natural world. A sustainable global society will need more than two percent of the population engaged in food production. More generally, the *Manifesto* has literally nothing to say about the impacts of conventional farming, monoculture, pesticide-resistant insects, genetically modified organisms (GMOs), and the increasing privatization of seeds and genetic material. It implicitly implies that the Green Revolution was an unqualified positive for humankind. The CEOs of Monsanto and Nestlé would no doubt endorse this manifesto.

The issue of condescension toward indigenous cultures is particularly stark in the *Manifesto*. There is not a word about religion, spirituality, or indigenous ecological practices, even though the authors throw a bone to the "cultural preferences" for development (26). But the core assumption is that "development" has only one true trajectory, and that is to "modernize" along the lines of Western, industrialized countries. The conceit that technological modernity is Progress is hugely favorable to the development path of the Global North, but also quasi-imperialist in its assumption that the rest of the world needs to reproduce, in fast forward, the European and Neo-European Industrial Revolution. How is it simultaneously true that industrial modernity is both the problem and the solution? If the authors acknowledge, as they do, that industrialism has produced manifold negative impacts on the natural world, then why assume that yet more industrialism will magically reverse this trend? Furthermore, the ecomodernists do not seem to believe that the "developed" North has anything to learn from the "less developed" Global South. Is it possible that indigenous societies that lived sustainably for long periods of time might have important lessons to teach the rest of the world? The ecomodernists do not seem to think so.

Finally, the *Manifesto* often uses misleading (if not downright false) language in making its case. The passages on deforestation are especially greenwashed. For instance, the ecomodernists claim that three quarters of deforestation occurred before the Industrial Revolution (16). This may be true, but as Williams (2002) has shown, this is not really saying much.[49] Anatomically modern homo sapiens have been around for 200,000 years, and it has taken only 250 years to produce one quarter of all recorded deforestation. This fact does not strike us as particularly laudable, nor is it laudable that pollutive fossil fuels replaced forest resources as the world's primary form of energy. Also, on page 13, the *Manifesto* manages to imply that there is currently "net reforestation" occurring on the globe, but since the text has no sources, it is hard to know the origin or particulars of this claim. The 2014 *Millennium Development Report* shows that a combination of afforestation and reforestation efforts has slowed deforestation rates, but that the world still suffered a net loss of forested land between 2000 and 2010 by many millions of hectares.[50] Certainly, the vast majority of those who study deforestation, including the World Wide Fund for Nature and the United Nations, contend unequivocally that deforestation is an ongoing concern. "For example, in the Amazon around 17 percent of the forest has been lost in the last 50 years."[51] The United Nations Food and Agriculture Organization's 2005 *Forest Resources Assessment* paints a pretty bleak picture for the world's tropical forests, and many of the temperate ones, too, noting that loss of woodland jeopardizes essential ecosystem services, a concept that never appears in the *Manifesto*.[52]

The authors of *An Ecomodernist Manifesto* have their collective hearts in the right place. There is no argument that the human economy needs to "decarbonize" or that growth will create new energy challenges. There is no argument that "humans are completely dependent on the living biosphere" and that ecosystems need to be protected and strengthened. We agree that climate change, ozone depletion, and the acidification of the ocean constitute real threats to the prospects of a sustainable future. Further, there is no argument that a sustainable society is one that would promote human well-being, public health, and life satisfaction. But unfortunately, the vision put forth by the ecomodernists, with its technophilia and support for endless economic growth, falls well short of crafting a set of objectives that can or should be adopted globally. There is nothing really "eco" about ecomodernism, since its base assumptions violate everything we know about ecosystems, energy, population, and natural resources. Fatally, the ecomodernists neglect to identify the ultimate ill that plagues us—to wit, the addiction to growth-based economics, rooted in finite and polluting fossil fuels, and the sprawling industrial society that these energy sources and policies have facilitated over the past two hundred and fifty years; deeper still, they subscribe to the pig-headed belief that all of this necessarily equates to a desirable mode of development. To be clear, there are alternative conceptions of development and modernity that do not perpetuate the destructive mindset and practices of economic growth, extractivism, exploitation, and technological dependency, but which open up pathways to a good life based on real sustainability, equality, justice, and ecological wisdom.[53]

Notes

1 Porter, E. (2015, April 14). A call to look past sustainable development. *New York Times.* Retrieved from http://www.nytimes.com/2015/04/15/business/an-environmentalist-call-to-look-past-sustainable-development.html? r=0

2 Collard, R-C., Dempsey, J. Sundberg, J. (2014). A manifesto for abundant futures. *Annals of the Association of American Geographers,* DOI. 10.1080/00045608.2014.973007. See page 2. The authors of this manifesto for abundant futures anticipate some of the critiques offered here, including the neocolonial orientation of ecomodernism.

3 Some of the responses to the manifesto have been published on the Ecomodernist's own website: http://www.ecomodernism.org/responses/.

4 Harvey, D. (2007) *A brief history of neoliberalism.* New York: Oxford Univ. Press.

5 Krugman, P. (2014, September 18). Errors and emissions. *New York Times.* Retrieved from http://www.nytimes.com/2014/09/19/opinion/paul-krugman-could-fighting-global-warming-be-cheap-and-free.html; Heinberg, R. (2014, September 22). Paul Krugman's Errors and Omissions. *Post Carbon Institute.* Retrieved from http://www.postcarbon.org/paul-krugmans-errors-and-omissions/; Also see Krugman, P. (2014, October 7). Slow steaming and the supposed limits to growth. *New York Times.* Retrieved from http://krugman.blogs.nytimes.com/2014/10/07/slow-steaming-and-the-supposed-limits-to-growth/; Also see Heinberg, R. (2014, October 10)Paul Krugman and the Limits of Hubris. *Post Carbon Institute.* Retrieved from http://www.postcarbon.org/paul-krugman-and-the-limits-of-hubris/.

6 Caradonna, J. (2014). *Sustainability: a history.* New York: Oxford Univ. Press, ch.4.

7 F. Schneider, J. Martinez-Alier, G. Kallis. (2011, October 5). "Sustainable Degrowth." *Journal of Industrial Ecology.* 15 (5), 654; The literature on degrowth has become voluminous. Many of the recent articles are inspired by the work of ecological economists over the past few decades, including seminal books by Herman Daly, William Rees, Peter A. Victor, Tim Jackson, and Richard Heinberg. For Heinberg and Daly, see footnotes below. Victor, Peter A. (2008). *Managing without growth. Slower by design, not disaster.* United Kingdom: Edward Elgar.; Jackson, Timothy. (2009). *Prosperity without growth.* United States: Earthscan.; D'Alisa, G., Demaria, F., and Kallis, G. Routledge.(Eds.). (2014). *Degrowth: a vocabulary for a new era.* Milton Park: Routledge.; Some of the recent articles on degrowth include the following: F. Sekulova, G. Kallis, B. Rodriguez-Labajos, F. Schneider. (2013). Degrowth: from theory to practice. *Journal of Cleaner Production.* 38. 1-6.; Schenider, F., Kallis, G., Martinez-Alier, J. (2010). Crisis or opportunity? Economic degrowth for social equity and ecological sustainability. Introduction to this special issue. *Journal of Cleaner Production.* 18, 511-518; G. Kallis, C. Kerschner, J. Martinez-Alier. (2012). The economics of degrowth. *Ecological Economics.* 84, 172-180.

8   *Toward a Steady-State Economy.* (1973). Ed. Daly. H. Freeman; Daly, H. E. (1977). *Steady-State Economics.* Freeman; Daly, H. E. (1996). *Beyond Growth: The Economics of Sustainable Development.* Boston: Beacon Press; O'Neil. D. W. (2012). Measuring progress in the degrowth transition to a steady state economy. *Ecological Economics* 84, 221-231. Note, too, that there is ongoing discussion about the term "degrowth," as some prefer "postgrowth" or other terms.

9   Steffen, W., Broadgate, W., Deutsch, L., Gaffney, O., Ludwig, C. (2015). The trajectory of the Anthropocene: The great acceleration. *The Anthropocene Review.* January, 2015: http://anr.sagepub.com/content/early/2015/01/08/2053019614564785.abstract

10 Caradonna. (2014); Heinberg, R. (2011). *The End of Growth: Adapting to Our New Economic Reality.* New Society Publishers.

11 See Schneider, Martinez, Kallis. (2011). See also Broder. J. M. (2009, February 16). Emissions fell in 2009, showing impact of recession. *New York Times.*

12 Peter A. Victor. (2011). Growth, degrowth and climate change: A scenario analysis. *Ecological Economics,* 1-7: 2. See also K. Anderson and A. Bows-Larkin (2013). Avoiding dangerous climate change demands demands de-growth strategies from wealthier nations. (Web log comment). Retrieved from http://kevinanderson.info/blog/avoiding-dangerous-climate-change-demands-de-growth-strategies-from-wealthier-nations/.

13 The concept of sustainable development emerged at a time (late 1970s-1980s) of relative global consensus about the need for a new development path, in which catastrophic events at Minamata, Seveso, Bhopal, and Chernobyl made it impossible to overlook the social and environmental costs of the conventional modernization model. The common refrain in the United Nations was that there was need for a theory that combined the promise of material improvements with the promise of increasing social equality without destroying the environmental bases on which human life depended. See Caradonna. (2014). *Sustainability: a history.* New York: Oxford Univ. Press; Robinson, John A. (2004). Squaring the circle? Some thoughts on the idea of sustainable development. *Ecological Economics,* 48 (4), 369–384; Borowy, I. (2014). *Defining sustainable development: The world commission on environment and development (Brundtland Commission).* Milton Park: Routledge.; See, also, Rist, who criticizes the coupling of "development" and "sustainable." Rist, G. (2010). Is 'development' a panacea? How to think beyond obsolete categories. *Canadian Journal of Development Studies/Revue d'études du développement* (30), 345-354.

14 IUCN. (1980). *World Conservation Strategy: Living Resource Conservation for Sustainable Development.*; UNWCED. (1987). *Report of the World Commission on Environment and Development: Our Common Future.*

15 From here on, in-text page citations of the manifesto. *An Economist Manifesto.* (2015).

16 The *Manifesto's* assertion (16) that Native peoples hunted "most of the continent's large mammals to extinction in the late Pleistocene, while burning and clearing forests across the continent in the process" is a thesis that is subject to intense debate. The early-natives-as-genocidal-killers-of-the-megafauna has been rejected by new studies, and questioned by others. Recent research on mastodons, using carbon dating of fossil remains, adds more evidence to the argument that the extinction of the megafauna predates human presence in North America. See Zazula, D. G., et. al. (2014). American mastodon extirpation in the arctic and subarctic predates human colonization and terminal pleistocene climate change. *PNAS* 111 (52), 18460-18465. See, more generally, Flores, J. C. (2014). Modelling Late Pleistocene megafaunal extinction and critical cases: A simple pre-predator perspective. *Ecological Modelling* (291), 218-223; Braje, T. J. and Erlandson, J. M. (2013). *Human acceleration of animal and plant extinctions: A Late Pleistocene, Holocene, and Anthropocene continuum.* Anthropocene, 2013. Moreover, the *Manifesto* suggests that native use of fire was necessarily unsustainable, which is another highly debatable point. See Pyne, S. J. (2001).

Fire: A Brief History. University of Washington and British Museum. Many native groups managed and even created ecosystems largely through strategic use of fire, and managed to do so successfully for millennia.

17 See for a discussion of The International Labour Organization's report: J. Nelson (2014, May 20). Modern-day slavery generates billions: UN report. *The Globe and Mail.* Retrieved from http://www.theglobeandmail.com/report-on-business/international-business/modern-day-slavery-generates-billions-according-to-new-report/article18768332/

18 Richardson, D. (2011). Involuntary migration in the early modern world. *The Cambridge World History of Slavery,* Vol. 3. Eds. Bradley, K. and Cartledge, P. Cambridge: Cambridge Univ. Press.

19 Latour, B. (2010). An attempt at a 'Compositionist Manifesto'. *New Literary History* 41, 471-490, asks, on p.486, what it is that Modernists, with their capital 'P' conception of Progress, are actually fleeing from, given that pre-industrial societies had much less of a destructive and lasting impact on the natural world.

20 Lovins, A. (1977). *Soft Energy Paths: Toward a Durable Peace.* Penguin; Hawken, P., Lovins, A. and Hunter, L. (1999/2000). *Natural Captialism: Creating the Next Industrial Revolution.* New York: Little, Brown and Company.

21 See World Health Organization (2014). 7 million premature deaths annually linked to air pollution [press release]. Retrieved from http://www.who.int/mediacentre/news/releases/2014/air-pollution/en/

22 Ehrlich, P. R. and Holdren, J. P. (1971, March 26). Impact of population growth. *Science, New Series,* 171 (3977), 1212-1217.

23 There are real concerns that geoengineering could create untold ecological problems, including severe disruptions to the hydrological cycle. See Tilmoes, Simone, et. al. (2013). The hydrological impact of geoengineering in the geoengineering model intercomparison project (GeoMIP). *Journal of Geophysical Research.* 118 (19), 11,036-11,058.; See also Charles Mann's recent and illuminating discussion of the threat of billionaires going rogue on geoengineering: C. C. Mann (2014, September). How to talk about climate change so people will listen. *The Atlantic.* Retrieved from http://www.theatlantic.com/magazine/archive/2014/09/how-to-talk-about-climate-change-so-people-will-listen/375067/.

24 Here the authors are implicitly critiquing the Club of Rome (1972). *The Limits to Growth.* New York: Universe. See also the 30-year update to *Limits* (2004). There is an extensive literature on the Club of Rome's modeling and scenarios for the future, although the ecomodernists minimize the extensive research on ecological limits. See footnotes below for sources by Turner and Bardi.

25 Bush, G. H. W. (1990). *Public Papers of the Presidents of the United States: George Bush, 1990.* Best Books. 520.

26 See, for instance, Turner, G. M. (2012). On the cusp of global collapse? Updated comparison of the *Limits to Growth* with historical data. *Gaia* (21), 116-124; Turner, F. M. (2008). A comparison of the *Limits to Growth* with 30 years of reality. *Global Environmental Change* (18), 397-411; Bardi, U. (2011). *The Limits to Growth Revisited.* Springer, New York; Higgs, K. (201). *Collision course: Endless growth on a finite planet.* Cambridge, MA: MIT Press.

27 Heinberg (2011): 3-5, 16.; Caradonna (2014): 192; IPCC. (2011). *Renewable Energy Sources and Climate Change Mitigation,* 10.

28 Roberts, P. (2008). *The End of Food.* New York; Fromartz, S. (2007). *Organic, Inc.* New York; Montgomery, D. (2007). *Dirt: The Erosion of Civilizations.* Berkeley; Keith, Lierre. (2009). *The Vegetarian Myth: Food, Justice, and Sustainability.* PM Press; Tasch, W. (2008). *Inquiries into the Nature of Slow Money: Investing as if Food, Farms, and Fertility Mattered.* Chelsea Green.

29 Costa, M. F. and Ivar, J. A. (2014). The present and future of microplastic pollution in the marine environment. *Environmental Pollution,* 185, 352-364.

30 Brown, L. (2006). *Plan B 2.0: Rescuing a Planet Under Stress and a Civilization in Trouble.* New York: W.W. Norton, 109. Brown cites U.S. Geological Survey data to argue that low-cost natural reserves of lead could be exhausted by 2024; tin by 2026, copper by 2031, iron ore by 2070, and bauxite by 2075.

31 Ecological Footprint Analysis suggests that the world has been living in a state of global overshoot for several years now. Wackernagel, M., et. al. (2002, July 9). Tracking the ecological over-shoot of the human economy. *Proceedings of the National Academy of Sciences,* 9266-9271. See also Turner (2012), Turner (2008), and Bardi (2011).

32 Diamond, J. (2005). *Collapse: How Societies Choose to Fail or Succeed.* New York: Viking Press.

33 Kurlansky, M. (1997). *Cod: a biography of the fish that changed the world.* Penguin, 2010.

34 See Caradonna, (2014), ch.4 for background. On the problems with decoupling, see Worldwatch Institute. (2015). *The state of the world report 2015: Hidden threats to sustainability.* London: Island Press, and especially ch.3, Victor, P.A. and Jackson, T. "The trouble with growth," 37-50; Wiedmann, T.O., et. al. (2013, September 3). The material footprint of nations. *PNAS,* 1-6; Smil, V. (2013). *Making the Modern World: Materials and Dematerialization.* Wiley; Murphy, D. J. and Hall, C. A. S. (2011). Energy return on investment, peak oil, and the end of economic growth in Ecological Economics Review. Robert Constanza, Karin Limburg & Ida Kubiszewski, eds. *Ann. N.Y. Acad. Sci.* (1219), 52-72.

35 IPCC (2014). *The Synthesis Report of the Fifth Assessment Report; Millennium Ecosystem Assessment.* (2005). For the HANNP, see O'Neil (2012), 225. The more basic problem is the assumption that what happened in a few Northern countries can be repeated in the rest of the world. The ecological footprint or carbon intensity in high-income countries has increased in part because a lot of extraction and production has been exported to other continents. Global trade obscures and complicates the notion of national carbon intensity and the real responsibility for consumption.

36 Jevons, W. S. (1866). *The Coal Question.* Second edition. London: Macmillan; Daly (1977); Jackson, T. (2009). *Prosperity Without Growth: Economics for a Finite Planet.* London: Earthscan.

37 See Schmelzer, M. (forthcoming, 2016). *The hegemony of growth. The making of the economic growth paradigm and the OECD, 1948-2010.* Cambridge.

38 Daly (1977); Daly (1996); O'Neil (2012).

39 See Kubiszewski, I., et. al. (2013). Beyond GDP: Measuring and achieving global genuine progress. *Ecological Economics* (93), 57-68.

40 See J. Lovelock. (2004, May 24). Nuclear power is the only green solution. *The Independent.* Retrieved from http://www.independent.co.uk/voices/commentators/james-lovelock-nuclear-power-is-the-only-green-solution-6169341.html.

41 See Caradonna (2014), 284, which cites and summarizes reports from the IPCC (2011) and the International Energy Agency. (2012). *Key World Energy Statistics.*

42 IPCC (2011).

43 Most of this material is taken from Caradonna (2014), 284.

44 See, for instance, Federal Ministry for the Environment, Nature Conservation and Nuclear Safety (Germany). *Development of Renewable Energy Sources in Germany 2012.* Online at http://www.erneuerbare-energien.de/fileadmin/Daten_EE/Dokumente_PDFs_/20130328 hgp_e_ppt_2012_fin_bf.pdf; see also Baake, R. (2014, December 12). Saubere Wende. *Die Zeit.* Retrieved from http://www.zeit.de/2014/51/energiewende-klimawandel. Also, note that, in Canada, provinces and territories wield considerable power in determining their own energy policies. The Province of Ontario has done more than most provinces or

American states in moving away from fossil fuels, which it did by closing its coal-fired generating plants and prohibiting the construction of new ones. The reason that Germany, and also Denmark, are unique is in the commitment from national governments in moving away from hard energies.

45 Trainer, T. (2007). *Renewable Energy Cannot Sustain a Consumer Society*. Dordrecht: Springer. Along the same lines, see Zehner, O. (2012). *Green Illusions: The Dirty Secrets of Clean energy and the Future of Environmentalism*. Lincoln: Univ. of Nebraska Press.

46 Sovacool, B.K., Brown, M.A. (201). Twelve metropolitan carbon footprints: a preliminary comparative global assessment. *Energy Policy* 38 (9), 4856-4869.

47 See, for example, Picketty, T. 2013. *Le capital au XXIe siècle*. Éditions du Seuil; Streeck, W. 2014. *Buying time: the delayed crisis of democratic capitalism*. New York: Verson; Milanovic, B. 2005. *Worlds apart: measuring international and global inequality*. Princeton: PUP; OECD. 2014. *How was life? Global wellbeing since 1820*. Paris: OECD.

48 Kristoff, N. and WuDunn, S. (2000, September 24). Two cheers for sweatshops. *New York Times*. Retrieved from http://www.nytimes.com/2000/09/24/magazine/two-cheers-for-sweatshops.html.; King, F. H. (1911). *Farmers of Forty Centuries or Permanent Agriculture in China, Korea and Japan*. King.

49 Williams, M. (2002). *Deforesting the Earth: From Prehistory to Global Crisis*. Chicago: Univ. of Chicago Press.

50 UN. (2014). *Millennium Development Goals*, 240.

51 See the WWF report here: https://www.worldwildlife.org/threats/deforestation

52 UNFAO. (2005). *Forest Resources Assessment*.

53 In addition to the many useful and visionary sources cited in this essay, see the Degrowth Declaration from Barcelona, 2010: http://www.barcelona.degrowth.org/Barcelona-2010-Declaration.119.0.html.

5

The Global Financial Crisis

The global financial crisis of 2007–08 began in the United States and spread to the rest of the world, with a crash in real estate and financial markets, the widespread failure or near-failure of financial institutions, and a "great recession" that devastated homeowners, workers, and citizens. Many economists and financial analysts were caught by surprise. The crisis exposed fundamental flaws in contemporary capitalism, raising profound questions for scholarship in political economy and for policy debates on everything from macroeconomic management to housing policy and financial regulation.

Market liberals and market institutionalists draw different lessons from the crisis. They agree that modern financial markets require effective regulation. The commercial banking sector requires deposit insurance schemes to prevent bank runs, reserve requirements to make banks keep sufficient cash in hand, and prudential regulation to preclude banks from taking excessive risks. And stock markets need disclosure rules to make companies provide accurate information and trading rules to prevent fraud and to ensure orderly market operations. Yet market liberals tend to have greater faith that financial institutions will act prudently on their own; that private actors can take responsibility for some elements of regulation, such as credit ratings or accounting standards; that sophisticated investors can take big risks without threatening the financial system more broadly; that complex financial instruments make markets more efficient and diffuse risk; and that markets have a considerable ability to self-correct. In contrast, market institutionalists tend to believe that banks will take excessive risks and seek outsized "rents" (returns not justified by value added) if not constrained by regulation; that private sector actors cannot be trusted to regulate themselves; that financial derivatives are more likely to increase risk than to moderate it; and that financial markets are inherently unstable. Market liberals tend to blame the crisis on too much government intervention in financial markets, whereas market institutionalists fault insufficient government regulation.

Peter Wallison presents a primary line of argument on the market-liberal side. He contends that the U.S. government's housing policies caused the financial crisis. The government fostered the creation of subprime and other risky loans by pressing financial institutions to extend credit to low-income borrowers and thereby encouraging them to lower their mortgage approval standards. And many of those borrowers ultimately defaulted when the housing bubble deflated. The Community Reinvestment Act (CRA) of 1977 required insured banks and savings and loan (S&L) banks to extend loans to borrowers at or below 80 percent of the median income in the areas the banks serviced. Then in 1992 the government required the two government-chartered mortgage finance firms, Fannie Mae and Freddie Mac, to allocate at least 30 percent of their loans to low-income borrowers. This policy put Fannie and Freddie in competition with the Federal Housing Administration, which had a mandate to serve low-income borrowers, and with private subprime lenders, which also specialized in serving those borrowers. This competition gradually undermined mortgage lending standards so that by 2008 about one-half of all mortgages were subprime or otherwise risky. Government housing policy also affected the private market in securitized loans indirectly by fueling the unusually long ten-year (1997–2007) housing bubble.

Joseph Stiglitz directly rebuts this line of argument. He counters that government housing policy cannot possibly account for investors who gambled on derivative financial instruments or overinvestment in commercial real estate. The government did not constrain Fannie Mae and Freddie Mac much in practice, and it certainly did not encourage lenders to engage in predatory lending aimed at short-term profits. In fact, default rates on the CRA loans were comparable to other areas of lending. Instead, Stiglitz blames the crisis on a combination of macroeconomic policies that fueled the asset bubble, flaws in financial regulation that permitted banks to engage in risky behavior, and financial professionals who engaged in rent-seeking and took excessive risks. He stresses that low interest rates alone would not have produced a crisis if stronger banking regulation had been in place. Moreover, Stiglitz notes that the financial sector failed to perform its core functions of providing value to borrowers and investors in the run-up to the crisis. It did not develop inexpensive and safe mortgage products, but rather products like mortgage-backed securities with high transaction costs, variable interest rates, and no protection from the risks of a drop in housing value or the loss of a job. Meanwhile, Wall Street financial innovations were designed to circumvent regulations, not to provide value for the broader public over the long run. In fact, financial institutions did not even serve their own shareholders and bondholders very well, because they misjudged and mispriced risk to boost short-term returns. Stiglitz argues that this is due to a misalignment of incentives rooted in corporate governance. Finance executives were rewarded based on their banks' stock prices more than long-term performance, so they focused on how to generate higher fees rather than how to deliver long-term value to their clients and their shareholders. And sometimes this drove them to look for creative ways to circumvent accounting rules and financial regulations. Moreover, Stiglitz highlights how the financial sector used its political power to lobby the government to alter regulations in its favor, thereby enabling its predatory strategies.

Let's briefly unpack the pieces to this story.[1] As Stiglitz notes, the Federal Reserve Bank certainly fueled the housing bubble by keeping interest rates low before the crisis. Defenders of the Fed, including Chairman Alan Greenspan himself, argue that the Bank's primary mission is to combat price inflation, not asset inflation; that it is particularly difficult to distinguish an asset bubble from legitimate appreciation of the underlying value of assets; that it is tricky to deflate a bubble by raising interest rates; and that any move to offset a bubble would be unpopular politically.[2] Yet the Fed's mission is to oversee the overall health of the U.S. economy and the global economy more broadly, and as such it has a duty to watch for asset bubbles. It had other tools to combat asset inflation in addition to interest rates, including limiting banks' exposure to risky mortgages or raising capital requirements. Evidence available at the time indicated that the U.S. housing and stock markets were dangerously inflated, and some experts warned of a looming financial crisis.[3] Global imbalances in capital flows also inflated the housing bubble. High savings in China and other Asian and Middle Eastern countries generated a glut of assets, searching the globe for attractive investments, yet not finding ample opportunities due to surplus funds in many markets. So global savings poured into the United States, and targeted the housing market for investment. This drove global interest rates lower, pressing investors to seek riskier assets and greater leverage to maximize returns.

A shortlist of the specific developments that contributed to the crisis would include financial liberalization; the failure to regulate derivatives; the development of a market for mortgage-backed securities that broke the direct link between borrower and lender; failures by private sector monitors, including credit agencies, accountants, and financial analysts; and irresponsible behavior by investment banks, lenders, and borrowers. In the last two decades of the twentieth century, the U.S. government moved the earliest and the furthest among major industrial countries to liberalize financial markets. American financial institutions drove financial reforms through marketplace challenges to the regulatory regime combined with political appeals for legal and regulatory changes. Congress phased out deposit interest ceilings under the Depository Institutions Deregulatory and Monetary Control Act of 1980. It then sought to strengthen the competitive position of S&Ls and other banks by allowing them to make riskier investments and to offer adjustable-rate mortgages under the Garn–St. Germain Depository Institutions Act of 1982. The Clinton administration permitted interstate banking in 1994, fueling consolidation in the financial sector. And the large commercial banks and investment banks aggressively lobbied Congress to repeal the Glass–Steagall Act – which prevented banks, securities firms, and insurance companies from crossing into each other's business lines – prevailing in 1999 with the Financial Services Modernization (Gramm–Leach–Bliley) Act. This facilitated the emergence of the "shadow" banking sector made up of non-banks that offered banking services, such as investment banks that financed mortgages through mortgage-backed securities.

The government's deference to Wall Street shaped specific government regulatory policies, including the non-regulation of over-the-counter (OTC) derivative securities markets. Derivatives – such as futures, options, and warrants – are financial instruments whose price is derived from the value of underlying assets, such as bonds, stocks, or real estate. In a futures contract, for example, one party agrees to sell a given asset to another party at a given price at some future date. Derivatives were originally designed to hedge risk, but they could also be used for speculation. They were often traded over-the-counter, meaning that there was no central market that governed the transactions, with less regulation of the transactions and the assets that underpinned them. Likewise, the authorities left hedge funds and similar operations largely unregulated because these funds targeted high-worth individuals and institutions with professional advisers, not ordinary consumers. Yet these funds created systemic risk through opaque derivatives, interlocking portfolios, and a lack of market transparency.[4]

These various regulatory decisions and non-decisions set the stage for the drama to follow, with the market for mortgage-backed securities taking center stage. By collecting many mortgages into large pools, securitizing them, and then selling them off to investors, these instruments broke the direct link between the lender and the borrower. The investment banks divided the mortgages into tiers, with the lowest-rated tranches (the subprime mortgages) earning the highest returns. This gave them an incentive to favor subprime loans, because it allowed them to expand the mortgage market and earn higher profits.[5] To make matters worse, the investment banks increased their leverage ratios to maximize their ability to profit from high volume with small trading margins. In essence, they used their ability to borrow more funds to make bigger bets. But this higher leverage left them vulnerable to even a small drop in housing prices. Meanwhile, the investment banks used derivative instruments to design elaborate hedging strategies to insure themselves against default risk. In theory this should have reduced risk, but in practice the hedging strategies enabled the financial institutions to take greater risks and to overwhelm the capacity of the insurers in the case of a systemic crisis. The credit rating agencies continued to give mortgage-backed securities AAA ratings, judging that these were relatively safe investments that pooled risk. The government granted authority to private rating agencies to assess creditworthiness and credit risk. The credit agencies wielded enormous power in financial markets because their ratings determined the ability of firms and other institutions to raise capital. The agencies charged fees for assessing the creditworthiness of specific firms or assets. Yet this generated a conflict of interest, since the firms paying those fees desired high ratings.

With the benefit of hindsight, we can recognize that the market-liberal worldview itself contributed to the financial crisis.[6] Many scholars and practitioners put too much faith in the ability of financial institutions to manage risks, financial markets to self-correct, and financial executives to act prudently. They were convinced that more sophisticated financial markets would enhance the efficiency of markets and the performance of the economy, and elaborate hedging strategies would deliver a combination of efficiency and stability. Many abided by the "efficient markets" hypothesis that financial markets are rational in that they take into account all available information about the value of shares. And they believed that private sector actors would not take excessive risks because they would want to preserve their reputations, since these reputations are so critical in finance. Greenspan famously conceded that his own ideology misled him in testimony to Congress:

Greenspan: Those of us who have looked to the self-interest of lending institutions to protect shareholder's equity (myself especially) are in a state of shocked disbelief ...

Chairman [Henry] Waxman: The question I had for you is you had an ideology. You had a belief that free, competitive – and this is shown – your statement, "I do have an ideology. My judgment is that free, competitive markets are by far the unrivaled way to organize economies. We have tried regulation, none meaningfully worked." That was your quote. You have the authority to prevent irresponsible lending practices that led to the subprime mortgage crisis. You were advised to do so by many others. Now, our whole economy is paying its price. You feel that your ideology pushed you to make decisions that you wish you had not made? …

Greenspan: What I am saying to you is, yes, I found a flaw …[7]

The market-institutional view does not imply that more financial regulation is always better. But it does suggest that financial systems are delicate ecosystems governed by laws, practices, and norms, and they deliver more value to the public at a lower cost when they are governed well.

Notes

1 This section builds on Steven K. Vogel, *Marketcraft: How Governments Make Markets Work* (Oxford: Oxford University Press, 2018), 69–76.

2 Alan Greenspan, *The Age of Turbulence: Adventures in a New World* (New York: The Penguin Press, 2007), 200–2.

3 Raghuram G. Rajan, "Has Financial Development Made the World Riskier?" Paper Presented at Federal Reserve Bank of Kansas City Symposium, Jackson Hole, Wyoming, August 27, 2005. Also: Dean Baker, "Bush's House of Cards," *The Nation* (August 9, 2004); Robert J. Shiller, "Bubble Trouble," *Project Syndicate* (September 17, 2007); Nouriel Roubini, "The Rising Risk of a Systemic Financial Meltdown: The Twelve Steps to Financial Disaster," *EconoMonitor* (February 5, 2008).

4 Barry Eichengreen reviews the regulatory origins of the crisis and discusses possible remedies in "Origins and Regulatory Consequences of the Subprime Crisis," in Edward J. Balleisen and David A. Moss, eds., *Government and Markets: Toward a New Theory of Regulation* (Cambridge: Cambridge University Press, 2010), 419–42.

5 Neil Fligstein and Alexander Roehrkasse, "The Causes of Fraud in the Financial Crisis of 2007 to 2009: Evidence from the Mortgage-Backed Securities Industry," *American Sociological Review* 81 (2016): 617–43.

6 John L. Campbell, 2010. "Neoliberalism in Crisis: Regulatory Roots of the U.S. Financial Meltdown," in Michael Lounsbury and Paul M. Hirsch, eds., *Markets on Trial: The Economic Sociology of the U.S. Financial Crisis* (Bingley: Emerald Group, 2010), 367–403.

7 Alan Greenspan, Testimony to the Committee of Government Oversight and Reform of the United States House of Representatives, October 23, 2008.

Peter Wallison,
"The True Story of the Financial Crisis" (2011)*

What Caused the Financial Crisis?

George Santayana is often quoted for the aphorism that "Those who cannot remember the past are condemned to repeat it." Looking back on the financial crisis, we can see why the study of history is often so contentious and why revisionist histories are so easy to construct. There are always many factors that could have caused a historical event; the difficult task is to discern which, among a welter of possible causes, were the significant ones — the ones without which history would have been different.

Using this standard, I believe that the *sine qua non* of the financial crisis was U.S. government housing policy, which led to the creation of 27 million subprime and other risky loans — half of all mortgages in the United States — which were ready to default as soon as the massive 1997–2007 housing bubble began to deflate. If the U.S. government had not chosen this policy path — fostering the growth of a bubble of unprecedented size and an equally unprecedented number of weak and high-risk residential mortgages — the great financial crisis of 2008 would never have occurred.

In this article, I will outline the logical process that I followed in coming to the conclusion that it was the U.S. government's housing policies — and nothing else — that were responsible for the 2008 financial crisis.

The inquiry has to begin with what everyone agrees was the trigger for the crisis — the so-called mortgage meltdown that occurred in 2007. That was the relatively sudden outbreak of delinquencies and defaults among mortgages, primarily in a few states — California, Arizona, Nevada, and Florida — but to a lesser degree everywhere in the country. No one disputes that the losses on these mortgages and the decline in housing values that resulted from the ensuing foreclosures weakened financial institutions in the U.S. and around the world and were the precipitating cause of the crisis.

This raised a significant question. The U.S. had experienced housing bubbles in the past. Since the Second World War, there had been two — beginning in 1979 and 1989 — but when these bubbles deflated they had triggered only local losses. Why was the deflation of the housing bubble in 2007 so destructive?

The Commission's answer was that there were weaknesses in the financial system — failures of regulation and risk management, excessive leverage and risk-taking — that were responsible for the ensuing devastation. To establish this idea, the Commission had to show that these weaknesses were something new. It didn't attempt to do this, although that was an essential logical step in establishing its point. And the Commission ignored a more obvious answer: the quality of the mortgages in the bubble. As I noted earlier — and as the Commission never acknowledged or disputed — by 2008, half all mortgages in the U.S. — 27 million — were subprime or otherwise risky loans. If the Commission had really been looking for the reasons that the collapsing bubble was so destructive, the poor quality of the mortgages in the bubble was a far more likely hypothesis than that there had been a previously undetected weakening in the way the U.S. financial system operated.

This in turn raised two other major questions. Why were there so many weak and risky loans in this bubble? What had happened to mortgage underwriting standards in the preceding years that caused such a serious deterioration in mortgage quality?

"Affordable Housing Goals" and the Deterioration in Underwriting Standards

Research showed that the turning point came in 1992, with the enactment by Congress of what were called "affordable housing goals" for Fannie Mae and Freddie Mac. These two firms, which were shareholder-owned, had been chartered by Congress more than 20 years earlier to operate a secondary market in mortgages. The original idea was that they would buy mortgages from banks and other originators (Fannie and Freddie were not permitted to originate mortgages), standardize the mortgage document, resell those mortgages to institutional and other investors, and in that way create a national market for U.S. mortgages.

From the beginning, Fannie and Freddie's congressional charters required them to buy only mortgages that would be acceptable to institutional investors — in other words, prime mortgages. At the time, a prime mortgage was a loan with a 10–20 percent down payment, made to a borrower with a good credit record who had sufficient income to meet his or her debt obligations after the loan was made. Fannie and Freddie operated under these standards until 1992.

The 1992 affordable housing goals required that, of all mortgages Fannie and Freddie bought in any year, at least 30 percent had to be loans made to borrowers who were at or below the median income in the places where they lived. Over succeeding years, the Department of Housing and Urban Development (HUD) increased this requirement, first to 42 percent in 1995, to 50 percent in 2000, and finally to 55 percent in 2007. It is important to note, accordingly, that this occurred during both Democratic and Republican administrations.

At the 50 percent level, Fannie and Freddie had to acquire at least one goal-eligible loan for every prime loan that they acquired, and since not all subprime loans were goals-eligible Fannie and Freddie were in effect required to buy many more subprime loans than prime loans to meet the goals. As a result of this process, by 2008, Fannie and Freddie held the credit risk of 12 million subprime or otherwise risky loans — almost 40 percent of their single-family book of business.

But this was not by any means the full extent of the problem. HUD took Congress's enactment of the affordable housing goals as an expression of a congressional policy to reduce underwriting standards so that low-income borrowers would have greater access to mortgage credit. As outlined in my dissent, by tightening the affordable housing goals, HUD put Fannie and Freddie into competition with the Federal Housing

Administration (FHA), a government agency with an explicit mission to provide credit to low-income borrowers, and with subprime lenders such as Countrywide, that had pledged to reduce underwriting standards in order to make more mortgage credit available to low-income borrowers. Moreover, all these organizations were joined by insured banks and S&Ls, which as noted above were required under the CRA to make mortgage credit available to borrowers who are at or below 80 percent of the median income in the areas where they live.

Of course, it is possible to find borrowers who meet prime loan standards among low-income families, but it is far more difficult to find such loans among these borrowers than among middle-income groups. And when Fannie, Freddie, FHA, subprime lenders like Countrywide, and insured banks and S&Ls are all competing to find loans to borrowers in the low-income category, the inevitable result was a significant deterioration in underwriting standards.

So, for example, while one in 200 mortgages involved a down payment of 3 percent or less in 1990, by 2007 it was one in less than three. Other credit standards had also declined. As a result of this government-induced competition, by 2008 19.2 million out of the total of 27 million subprime and other weak loans in the U.S. financial system could be traced directly or indirectly to U.S. government housing policies.

Private Sector Securitization of Subprime Loans

If the government was responsible for 19.2 million of the 27 million subprime and other risky loans, that leaves 7.8 million similar loans that came from other sources. These were mortgages securitized by the private sector (often called Wall Street in the Commission's report) and held by financial institutions around the world. How were these mortgages the result of U.S. government housing policy?

This is an important question. Even though these privately securitized mortgages were less than one-third of the total number of subprime and other risky loans outstanding, they are the reason that banks and other loan originators generally have been blamed — in the media, in most books and films about the financial crisis, and of course by the Commission — for the financial crisis.

The securitization of subprime and other risky loans was also a new phenomenon in the housing bubble that ended in 2007, and it was a direct result of the extraordinary growth of the bubble itself. Most bubbles in the past lasted three or four years. In that time, delinquencies begin to appear and the inflow of speculative funds begins to dry up. The bubble that deflated in 2007, however, had an unprecedentedly long 10-year life. The reason was that the money flow into that bubble was not from private speculators looking for profit, but primarily from the government pursuing a social policy by directing the investments of companies or agencies it regulated or otherwise controlled.

Housing bubbles tend to suppress defaults. As housing prices rise, people who can't meet their obligations can sell the house for more than they paid, or can refinance, so delinquencies are limited. By 2002, five years into the bubble that began in 1997, investors were beginning to notice that subprime and other risky loans — which usually carried higher than normal interest rates because of their risk — were not showing delinquencies or defaults commensurate with their risks. In other words, the data suggested that mortgage-backed securities (MBS) made of these loans were offering unusually high risk-adjusted yields. This stimulated the development of a private market in securitized subprime loans — something that had never existed before.

This market was about 4 percent of all mortgages made in 2002, but by 2004 had grown to 15 percent. It kept growing through 2005 and 2006, but completely collapsed in 2007, when the 10-year bubble finally topped out and began to deflate.

Thus, the 7.8 million subprime and other risky loans that were securitized during the 2000s and still outstanding in 2008 were also the indirect result of U.S. government housing policies, which had built an unprecedented bubble in the late 1990s. The bubble created the necessary conditions — a long run of subprime loans without the expected losses — for the growth of a huge securitization market in subprime and other risky loans in the mid-2000s.

Before leaving this subject, it is important to address one statement that has appeared again and again in the mainstream media, in statements by members of the Obama administration, and was repeated in the Commission report. This is the claim that Fannie and Freddie became insolvent because, seeking profits or market share, they "followed Wall Street" into subprime lending. This idea neatly avoids the question of why Fannie and Freddie became insolvent in the first place, and focuses the blame again on the private sector. The statement, however, as the following quote from Fannie's 2006 10-K report makes clear, is untrue:

> [W]e have made, and continue to make, significant adjustments to our mortgage loan sourcing and purchase strategies in an effort to meet HUD's increased housing goals and new subgoals. These strategies include entering into some purchase and securitization transactions with lower expected economic returns than our typical transactions. We have also relaxed some of our underwriting criteria to obtain goals-qualifying mortgage loans and increased our investments in higher-risk mortgage loan products that are more likely to serve the borrowers targeted by HUD's goals and subgoals, which could increase our credit losses.

Subprime and Other Risky Loans Cause the Financial Crisis

With half of all mortgages weak and of low quality by late 2007, an eventual financial crisis was a foregone conclusion. No financial system could withstand the huge losses that occurred when the delinquencies and defaults associated with 27 million subprime and other risky loans began to appear. Alarmed by these unexpected and unprecedented numbers of these delinquencies and defaults, investors fled the multitrillion dollar market for MBS, dropping MBS values — and especially those MBS backed by subprime and other risky loans — to fractions of their former prices.

Mark-to-market accounting then required financial institutions to write down the value of their assets — reducing their capital positions and causing great investor and creditor unease. In this environment, the government's rescue of Bear Stearns in March of 2008 temporarily calmed investor fears but created significant moral hazard; investors and other market participants reasonably believed after the rescue of Bear that all large financial institutions would also be rescued if they encountered financial difficulties.

However, when Lehman Brothers — an investment bank even larger than Bear — was allowed to fail, market participants were shocked; suddenly, they were forced to consider the financial health of their counterparties, many of which appeared weakened by losses and the capital writedowns required by mark-to-market accounting.

This caused a halt to lending and a hoarding of cash — a virtually unprecedented period of market paralysis and panic that we know as the financial crisis of 2008.

The Policy Stakes

The failure of the Financial Crisis Inquiry Commission to do its job is one more obstacle to persuading the American people that the Dodd-Frank Act is illegitimate and should be repealed. The act is far and away the most restrictive piece of legislation ever imposed on the U.S. economy, and it will have a long-term effect in slowing economic growth, just as the uncertainties it has created have already slowed the recovery from the recession. The DFA was sold to the American people by the media and the Obama administration as necessary to prevent another financial crisis, but as outlined in this article and made very clear in my dissent, the financial crisis was not caused by weak or ineffective regulation. On the contrary, the financial crisis of 2008 was caused by government housing policies — sponsored and promoted by many of the same people who framed and ultimately enacted the DFA. If we don't learn that important lesson, we will make the same mistake again, and then we really *will* have another financial crisis.

Works Cited

Pinto, Edward J. 2010. "Triggers of the Financial Crisis." Memorandum. American Enterprise Institute. https://www.aei.org/research-products/report/triggers-of-the-financial-crisis/.

———. 2011. "Government Housing Policies in the Lead-up to the Financial Crisis: A Forensic Study." American Enterprise Institute. https://www.aei.org/research-products/report/government-housing-policies-in-the-lead-up-to-the-financial-crisis-a-forensic-study/.

Wallison, Peter J. 2011. *Dissent from the Majority Report of the Financial Crisis Inquiry Commission*. American Enterprise Institute (AEI) Press. https://www.aei.org/research-products/book/dissent-from-the-majority-report-of-the-financial-crisis-inquiry-commission-2/.

Joseph E. Stiglitz,
Freefall: America, Free Markets, and The Sinking of The World Economy (2010)[*]

Chapter One

The Making of A Crisis

The only surprise about the economic crisis of 2008 was that it came as a surprise to so many. For a few observers, it was a textbook case that was not only predictable but also predicted. A deregulated market awash in liquidity and low interest rates, a global real estate bubble, and skyrocketing subprime lending were a toxic combination. Add in the U.S. fiscal and trade deficit and the corresponding accumulation in China of huge reserves of dollars—an unbalanced global economy—and it was clear that things were horribly awry.

What *was* different about this crisis from the multitude that had preceded it during the past quarter century was that this crisis bore a "Made in the USA" label. And while previous crises had been contained, this "Made in the USA" crisis spread quickly around the world. We liked to think of our country as one of the engines of global economic growth, an exporter of sound economic policies—not recessions. The last time the United States had exported a major crisis was during the Great Depression of the 1930s.[1]

The basic outlines of the story are well known and often told. The United States had a housing bubble. When that bubble broke and housing prices fell from their stratospheric levels, more and more homeowners found themselves "underwater." They owed more on their mortgages than what their homes were valued. As they lost their homes, many also lost their life savings and their dreams for a future—a college education for their children, a retirement in comfort. Americans had, in a sense, been living in a dream.

The richest country in the world was living beyond its means, and the strength of the U.S. economy, and the world's, depended on it. The global economy needed ever-increasing consumption to grow; but how could this continue when the incomes of many Americans had been stagnating for so long?[2] Americans came up with an ingenious solution: borrow and consume as if their incomes *were* growing. And borrow they did. Average savings rates fell to zero—and with many rich Americans saving substantial amounts, that meant poor Americans had a large negative savings rate. In other words, they were going deeply into debt. Both they and their lenders

---

[*] From: *Freefall: America, Free Markets, and The Sinking of The World Economy*, Joseph E. Stiglitz, Copyright © 2010 Joseph E. Stiglitz. (pp. 1–26) Used by permission of W. W. Norton & Company, Inc. and Penguin Books, UK.

could feel good about what was happening: they were able to continue their consumption binge, not having to face up to the reality of stagnating and declining incomes, and lenders could enjoy record profits based on ever-mounting fees.

Low interest rates and lax regulations fed the housing bubble. As housing prices soared, homeowners could take money out of their houses. These mortgage equity withdrawals—which in one year hit $975 billion, or more than 7 percent of GDP[3] (gross domestic product, the standard measure of the sum of all the goods and services produced in the economy)—allowed borrowers to make a down payment on a new car and still have some equity left over for retirement. But all of this borrowing was predicated on the risky assumption that housing prices would continue to go up, or at least not fall.

The economy was out of kilter: two-thirds to three-quarters of the economy (of GDP) was housing related: constructing new houses or buying contents to fill them, or borrowing against old houses to finance consumption. It was unsustainable—and it wasn't sustained. The breaking of the bubble at first affected the worst mortgages (the subprime mortgages, lent to low-income individuals), but soon affected all residential real estate.

When the bubble popped, the effects were amplified because banks had created complex products resting on top of the mortgages. Worse still, they had engaged in multibillion-dollar bets with each other and with others around the world. This complexity, combined with the rapidity with which the situation was deteriorating and the banks' high leverage (they, like households, had financed their investments by heavy borrowing), meant that the banks didn't know whether what they owed to their depositors and bondholders exceeded the value of their assets. And they realized accordingly that they couldn't know the position of any other bank. The trust and confidence that underlie the banking system evaporated. Banks refused to lend to each other—or demanded high interest rates to compensate for bearing the risk. Global credit markets began to melt down.

At that point, America and the world were faced with both a financial crisis and an economic crisis. The economic crisis had several components: There was an unfolding residential real estate crisis, followed not long after by problems in commercial real estate. Demand fell, as households saw the value of their houses (and, if they owned shares, the value of those as well) collapse and as their ability—and willingness—to borrow diminished. There was an inventory cycle—as credit markets froze and demand fell, companies reduced their inventories as quickly as possible. And there was the collapse of American manufacturing.

There were also deeper questions: What would replace the unbridled consumption of Americans that had sustained the economy in the years before the bubble broke? How were America and Europe going to manage their restructuring, for instance, the transition toward a service-sector economy that had been difficult enough during the boom? Restructuring was inevitable—globalization and the pace of technology demanded it—but it would not be easy.

The Story in Short

While the challenges going forward are clear, the question remains: How did it all happen? This is not the way market economies are *supposed* to work. Something went wrong—badly wrong.

There is no natural point to cut into the seamless web of history. For purposes of brevity, I begin with the bursting of the tech (or dot-com) bubble in the spring of 2000—a bubble that Alan Greenspan, chairman of the Federal Reserve at that time, had allowed to develop and that had sustained strong growth in the late 1990s.[4] Tech stock prices fell 78 percent between March 2000 and October 2002.[5] It was hoped that these losses would not affect the broader economy, but they did. Much of investment had been in the high-tech sector, and with the bursting of the tech stock bubble this came to a halt. In March 2001, America went into a recession.

The administration of President George W. Bush used the short recession following the collapse of the tech bubble as an excuse to push its agenda of tax cuts for the rich, which the president claimed were a cure-all for any economic disease. The tax cuts were, however, not designed to stimulate the economy and did so only to a limited extent. That put the burden of restoring the economy to full employment on monetary policy. Accordingly, Greenspan lowered interest rates, flooding the market with liquidity. With so much excess capacity in the economy, not surprisingly, the lower interest rates did not lead to more investment in plant and equipment. They worked—but only by replacing the tech bubble with a housing bubble, which supported a consumption and real estate boom.

The burden on monetary policy was increased when oil prices started to soar after the invasion of Iraq in 2003. The United States spent hundreds of billions of dollars importing oil—money that otherwise would have gone to support the U.S. economy. Oil prices rose from $32 a barrel in March 2003 when the Iraq war began to $137 per barrel in July 2008. This meant that Americans were spending $1.4 billion per day to import oil (up from $292 million per day before the war started), instead of spending the money at home.[6] Greenspan felt he could keep interest rates low because there was little inflationary pressure,[7] and without the housing bubble that the low interest rates sustained and the consumption boom that the housing bubble supported, the American economy would have been weak.

In all these go-go years of cheap money, Wall Street did not come up with a good mortgage product. A good mortgage product would have low transaction costs and low interest rates and would have helped people manage the risk of homeownership, including protection in the event their house loses value or borrowers lose their job. Homeowners also want monthly payments that are predictable, that don't shoot up without warning, and that don't have hidden costs. The U.S. financial markets didn't look to construct these better products, even though they are in use in other countries. Instead, Wall Street firms, focused on maximizing their returns, came up with mortgages that had high transaction costs and variable interest rates with payments that could suddenly spike, but with no protection against the risk of a loss in home value or the risk of job loss.

Had the designers of these mortgages focused on the ends—what we actually wanted from our mortgage market—rather than on how to maximize *their* revenues, then they might have devised products that would have *permanently* increased homeownership. They could have "done well by doing good." Instead their efforts produced a whole range of complicated mortgages that made them a lot of money in the short run and led to a slight *temporary* increase in homeownership, but at great cost to society as a whole.

The failings in the mortgage market were symptomatic of the broader failings throughout the financial system, including and especially the banks. There are two core functions of the banking system. The first is providing an efficient payments mechanism, in which the bank facilitates transactions, transferring its depositors' money to those from whom they buy goods and services. The second core function is assessing and managing risk and making loans. This is related to the first core function, because if a bank makes poor credit assessments, if it gambles recklessly, or if it puts too much money into risky ventures that default, it can no longer make good on its promises to return depositors' money. If a bank does its job well, it provides money to start new businesses and expand old businesses, the economy grows, jobs are created, and at the same time, it earns a high return—enough to pay back the depositors with interest and to generate competitive returns to those who have invested their money in the bank.

The lure of easy profits from transaction costs distracted many big banks from their core functions. The banking system in the United States and many other countries did not focus on lending to small and medium-sized businesses, which are the basis of job creation in any economy, but instead concentrated on promoting securitization, especially in the mortgage market.

It was this involvement in mortgage securitization that proved lethal. In the Middle Ages, alchemists attempted to transform base metals into gold. Modern alchemy entailed the transformation of risky subprime mortgages into AAA-rated products safe enough to be held by pension funds. And the rating agencies blessed what the banks had done. Finally, the banks got directly involved in gambling—including not just acting as middlemen for the risky assets that they were creating, but actually holding the assets. They, and their regulators, might have thought that they had passed the unsavory risks they had created on to others, but when the day of reckoning came—when the markets collapsed—it turned out that they too were caught off guard.[8]

Parsing Out Blame

As the depth of the crisis became better understood—by April 2009 it was already the longest recession since the Great Depression—it was natural to look for the culprits, and there was plenty of blame to go around. Knowing who, or at least what, is to blame is essential if we are to reduce the likelihood of another recurrence and if we are to correct the obviously dysfunctional aspects of today's financial markets. We have to be wary of too facile explanations: too many begin with the excessive greed of the bankers. That may be true, but it doesn't provide much of a basis for reform. Bankers acted greedily because they had incentives and opportunities to do so, and that is what has to be changed. Besides, the basis of capitalism is the pursuit of profit: should we blame the bankers for doing (perhaps a little bit better) what everyone in the market economy is supposed to be doing?

In the long list of culprits, it is natural to begin at the bottom, with the mortgage originators. Mortgage companies had pushed exotic mortgages on to millions of people, many of whom did not know what they were getting into. But the mortgage companies could not have done their mischief without being aided and abetted by the banks and rating agencies. The banks bought the mortgages and repackaged them, selling them on to unwary investors. U.S. banks and financial institutions had boasted about their clever new investment instruments. They had created new products which, while touted as instruments for managing risk, were so dangerous that they threatened to bring down the U.S. financial system. The rating agencies, which should have checked the growth of these toxic instruments, instead gave them a seal of approval, which encouraged others—including pension funds looking for safe places to put money that workers had set aside for their retirement—in the United States and overseas, to buy them.

In short, America's financial markets had failed to perform their essential societal functions of managing risk, allocating capital, and mobilizing savings while keeping transaction costs low. Instead, they had created risk, misallocated capital, and encouraged excessive indebtedness while imposing high transaction costs. At their peak in 2007, the bloated financial markets absorbed 41 percent of profits in the corporate sector.[9]

One of the reasons why the financial system did such a poor job at managing risk is that the market mispriced and misjudged risk. The "market" badly misjudged the risk of defaults of subprime mortgages, and made an even worse mistake trusting the rating agencies and the investment banks when they repackaged the subprime mortgages, giving a AAA rating to the new products. The banks (and the banks' investors) also badly misjudged the risk associated with high bank leverage. And risky assets that normally would have required substantially higher returns to induce people to hold them were yielding only a small risk premium. In some cases, the seeming mispricing and misjudging of risk was based on a smart bet: they believed that if troubles arose, the Federal Reserve and the Treasury would bail them out, and they were right.[10]

The Federal Reserve, led first by Chairman Alan Greenspan and later by Ben Bernanke, and the other regulators stood back and let it all happen. They not only claimed that they couldn't tell whether there was a bubble until after it broke, but also said that even if they had been able to, there was nothing they could do about it. They were wrong on both counts. They could have, for instance, pushed for higher down payments on homes or higher margin requirements for stock trading, both of which would have cooled down these overheated markets. But they chose not to do so. Perhaps worse, Greenspan aggravated the situation by allowing banks to engage in ever-riskier lending and encouraging people to take out variable-rate mortgages, with payments that could—and did—easily explode, forcing even middle-income families into foreclosure.[11]

Those who argued for deregulation—and continue to do so in spite of the evident consequences—contend that the costs of regulation exceed the benefits. With the global budgetary and real costs of this crisis mounting into the trillions of dollars, it's hard to see how its advocates can still maintain that position. They argue, however, that the real cost of regulation is the stifling of innovation. The sad truth is that in America's financial markets, innovations were directed at circumventing regulations, accounting standards, and taxation. They created products that were so complex they had the effect of both increasing risk and information asymmetries. No wonder then that it is impossible to trace any sustained increase in economic growth (beyond the bubble to which they contributed) to these financial innovations. At the same time, financial markets did not innovate in ways that would have helped ordinary citizens with the simple task of managing the risk of homeownership. Innovations that would have helped people and countries manage the other important risks they face were actually resisted. Good regulations could have redirected innovations in ways that would have increased the efficiency of our economy and security of our citizens.

Not surprisingly, the financial sector has attempted to shift blame elsewhere— when its claim that it was just an "accident" (a once-in-a- thousand-years storm) fell on deaf ears.

Those in the financial sector often blame the Fed for allowing interest rates to remain too low for too long. But this particular attempt to shift blame is peculiar: what other industry would say that the reason why its profits were so low and it performed so poorly was that the costs of its inputs (steel, wages) were too low? The major "input" into banking is the cost of its funds, and yet bankers seem to be complaining that the Fed made money too cheap! Had the low-cost funds been used well, for example, if the funds had gone to support investment in new technology or expansion of enterprises, we would have had a more competitive and dynamic economy.

Lax regulation without cheap money might not have led to a bubble. But more importantly, cheap money with a well-functioning or well-regulated banking system could have led to a boom, as it has at other times and places. (By the same token, had the rating agencies done their job well, fewer mortgages would have been sold to pension funds and other institutions, and the magnitude of the bubble might have been markedly lower. The same might have been true even if rating agencies had done as poor a job as they did, if investors themselves had analyzed the risks properly.) In short, it is a combination of failures that led the crisis to the magnitude that it reached.

Greenspan and others, in turn, have tried to shift the blame for the low interest rates to Asian countries and the flood of liquidity from their excess savings.[12] Again, being able to import capital on better terms should have been an advantage, a blessing. But it is a remarkable claim: the Fed was saying, in effect, that it can't control interest rates in America anymore. Of course, it can; the Fed *chose* to keep interest rates low, partly for reasons that I have already explained.[13]

In what might seem an outrageous act of ingratitude to those who rescued them from their deathbed, many bankers blame the government—biting the very hand that was feeding them. They blame the government for not having stopped them—like the kid caught stealing from the candy store who blamed the storeowner or the cop for looking the other way, leading him to believe he could get away with his misdeed. But the argument is even more disingenuous because the financial markets had *paid* to get the cops off the beat. They successfully beat back attempts to regulate derivatives and restrict predatory lending. Their victory over America was total. Each victory *gave* them more money with which to influence the political process. They even had an argument: deregulation had led them to make more money, and money was the mark of success. Q.E.D.

Conservatives don't like this blaming of the market; if there is *a* problem with the economy, in their hearts, they know the true cause must be government. Government wanted to increase household ownership, and the bankers' defense was that they were just doing their part. Fannie Mae and Freddie Mac, the two private companies that had started as government agencies, have been *a* particular subject of vilification, as has the government program called the Community Reinvestment Act (CRA), which encourages banks to lend to underserved communities. Had it not been for these efforts *at* lending to the poor, so the argument goes, all would have been well. This litany of defenses is, for the most part, sheer nonsense. AIG's almost $200 billion bailout (that's *a* big amount by *any* account) was based on derivatives (credit default swaps)—banks gambling with other banks. The banks didn't need *any* push for egalitarian housing to engage in excessive risk-taking. Nor did the massive overinvestment in commercial real estate have anything to do with government homeownership policy. Nor did the repeated instances of bad lending around the world from which the banks have had to be repeatedly rescued. Moreover, default rates on the CRA lending were actually comparable to other areas of lending—showing that such lending, if done well, does not pose greater risks.[14] The most telling point though is that Fannie Mae and Freddie Mac's mandate was for "conforming loans," loans to the middle class. The banks jumped into subprime mortgages—an *area* where, *at* the time, Freddie Mac and Fannie Mae were not making loans—without *any* incentives from the government. The president *may* have given some speeches about the ownership society but there is little evidence that banks snap to it when the president gives *a* speech. A policy has to be accompanied by carrots and sticks, and there weren't any. (If *a* speech would do the trick, Obama's repeated urging of banks to restructure more mortgages and to lend more to small businesses would have had some effect.) More to the point, advocates of homeownership meant permanent, or at least long-term, ownership. There was no point of putting someone in a home for a few months and then tossing him out after having stripped him of his life savings. But that was what the banks were doing. I know of no government official who would have said that lenders should engage in predatory practices, lend beyond people's ability to pay, with mortgages that combined high risks and high transaction costs. Later on, years after the private sector had invented the toxic mortgages (which I discuss at greater length in chapter 4), the privatized and under-regulated Fannie Mae and Freddie Mac decided that they too should join in the fun. Their executives thought, Why couldn't they enjoy bonuses akin to others in the industry? Ironically, in doing so, they helped save the private sector from some of its own folly: many of the securitized mortgages wound up on their balance sheet. Had they not bought them, the problems in the private sector arguably would have been far worse, though by buying so many securities, they may also have helped fuel the bubble.[15]

As I mentioned in the preface, figuring out what happened is like "peeling an onion": each explanation raises new questions. In peeling back the onion, we need to ask, Why did the financial sector fail so badly, not only in performing its critical social functions, but even in serving shareholders and bondholders well?[16] Only executives in financial institutions seem to have walked away with their pockets lined—less lined than if there had been no crash, but still better off than, say, the poor Citibank shareholders who saw their investments virtually disappear. The financial institutions complained that the regulators didn't *stop* them from behaving badly. But aren't firms supposed to behave well on their own? In later chapters I will give a simple explanation: flawed incentives. But then we must push back again: Why were there flawed incentives? Why didn't the market "discipline" firms that employed flawed incentive structures, in the way that standard theory says it should? The answers to these questions are complex but include a flawed system of corporate governance, inadequate enforcement of competition laws, and imperfect information and an inadequate understanding of risk on the part of the investors.

While the financial sector bears the major onus for blame, regulators didn't do the job that they should have done—ensuring that banks don't behave badly, as is their wont. Some in the less regulated part of the financial markets (like hedge funds), observing that the worst problems occurred in the highly regulated part (the banks), glibly conclude that regulation is the problem. "If only they were unregulated like us, the problems would never have occurred," they argue. But this misses the essential point: The reason why banks are regulated is that their failure can cause massive harm to the rest of the economy. The reason why there is less regulation needed for hedge funds, at least for the smaller ones, is that they can do less harm. The regulation did not cause the banks to behave badly; it was deficiencies in regulation and regulatory enforcement that failed to prevent the banks from imposing costs on the rest of society as they have repeatedly done. Indeed, the one period in American history when they have not imposed these costs was the quarter century after World War II when strong regulations were effectively enforced: it can be done.

Again, the failure of regulation of the past quarter century needs to be explained: the story I tell below tries to relate those failures to the political influence of special interests, particularly of those in the financial sector who made money from deregulation (many of their economic investments had turned sour, but they were far more acute in their political investments), and to ideologies—ideas that said that regulation was not necessary.

Market Failures

Today, after the crash, almost everyone says that there is a need for regulation—or at least for more than there was before the crisis. Not having the necessary regulations has cost us plenty: crises would have been less frequent and less costly, and the cost of the regulators and regulations would be a pittance relative to these costs. Markets on their own evidently fail—and fail very frequently. There are many reasons for these failures, but two are particularly germane to the financial sector: "agency"—in today's world scores of people are handling money and making decisions on behalf of (that is, as agents of) others—and the increased importance of "externalities."

The agency problem is a modern one. Modern corporations with their myriad of small shareholders are fundamentally different from family-run enterprises. There is a separation of ownership and control in which management, owning little of the company, may run the corporation largely for its own benefit.[17] There are agency problems too in the process of investment: much was done through pension funds and other institutions. Those who make the investment decisions—and assess corporate performance—do so not on their behalf but on behalf of those who have entrusted their funds to their care. All along the "agency" chain, concern about performance has been translated into a focus on *short-term returns*.

With its pay dependent not on long-term returns but on stock market prices, management naturally does what it can to drive up stock market prices—even if that entails deceptive (or creative) accounting. Its short-term focus is reinforced by the demand for high quarterly returns from stock market analysts. That drive for short-term returns led banks to focus on how to generate more fees—and, in some cases, how to circumvent accounting and financial regulations. The innovativeness that Wall Street ultimately was so proud of was dreaming up new products that would generate more income in the short term for its firms. The problems that would be posed by high default rates from some of these innovations seemed matters for the distant future. On the other hand, financial firms were not the least bit interested in innovations that might have helped people keep their homes or protect them from sudden rises in interest rates.

In short, there was little or no effective "quality control." Again, in theory, markets are supposed to provide this discipline. Firms that produce excessively risky products would lose their reputation. Share prices would fall. But in today's dynamic world, this market discipline broke down. The financial wizards invented highly risky products that gave about normal returns for a while—with the downside not apparent for years. Thousands of money managers boasted that they could "beat the market," and there was a ready population of shortsighted investors who believed them. But the financial wizards got carried away in the euphoria—they deceived themselves as well as those who bought their products. This helps explain why, when the market crashed, they were left holding billions of dollars' worth of toxic products.

Securitization, the hottest financial-products field in the years leading up to the collapse, provided a textbook example of the risks generated by the new innovations, for it meant that the relationship between lender and borrower was broken. Securitization had one big advantage, allowing risk to be spread; but it had a big disadvantage, creating new problems of imperfect information, and these swamped the benefits from increased diversification. Those buying a mortgage-backed security are, in effect, lending to the homeowner, about whom they know nothing. They trust the bank that sells them the product to have checked it out, and the bank trusts the mortgage originator. The mortgage originators' incentives were focused on the quantity of mortgages originated, not the quality. They produced massive amounts of truly lousy mortgages. The banks like to blame the mortgage originators, but just a glance at the mortgages should have revealed the inherent risks. The fact is that the bankers *didn't want to know.* Their incentives were to pass on the mortgages, and the securities they created backed by the mortgages, as fast as they could to others. In the Frankenstein laboratories of Wall Street, banks created new risk products (collateralized debt instruments, collateralized debt instruments squared, and credit default swaps, some of which I will discuss in later chapters) without mechanisms to manage the monster they had created. They had gone into the moving business—taking mortgages from the mortgage originators, repackaging them, and moving them onto the books of pension funds and others—because that was where the fees were the highest, as opposed to the "storage business," which had been the traditional business model for banks (originating mortgages and then holding on to them). Or so they thought, until the crash occurred and they discovered billions of dollars of the bad assets on their books.

Externalities

The bankers gave no thought to how dangerous some of the financial instruments were to the rest of us, to the large externalities that were being created. In economics, the technical term *externality* refers to situations where a market exchange imposes costs or benefits on others who aren't party to the exchange. If you are trading on your own account and lose your money, it doesn't really affect anyone else. However, the financial system is now so intertwined and central to the economy that a failure of one large institution can bring down the whole system. The current failure has affected everyone: millions of homeowners have lost their homes, and millions more have seen the equity in their homes disappear; whole communities have been devastated; taxpayers have had to pick up the tab for the losses of the banks; and workers have lost their jobs. The costs have been borne not only in the United States but also around the world, by billions who reaped no gains from the reckless behavior of the banks.

When there are important agency problems and externalities, markets typically fail to produce efficient outcomes—contrary to the widespread belief in the efficiency of markets. This is one of the rationales for financial market regulation. The regulatory agencies were the last line of defense against both excessively risky and unscrupulous behavior by the banks, but after years of concentrated lobbying efforts by the banking industry, the government had not only stripped away existing regulations but also failed to adopt new ones in response to the changing financial landscape. People who didn't understand why regulation was necessary—and accordingly believed that it was unnecessary—became regulators. The repeal in 1999 of the Glass-Steagall Act, which had separated investment and commercial banks, created ever larger banks that were too big to be allowed to fail. Knowing that they were too big to fail provided incentives for excessive risk-taking.

In the end, the banks got hoisted by their own petard: The financial instruments that they used to exploit the poor turned against the financial markets and brought them down. When the bubble broke, most of the banks were left holding enough of the risky securities to threaten their very survival—evidently, they hadn't done as good a job in passing the risk along to others as they had thought. This is but one of many ironies that have marked the crisis: in Greenspan and Bush's attempt to minimize the role of government in the economy, the government has assumed an unprecedented role across a wide swath—becoming the owner of the world's largest automobile company, the largest insurance company, and (had it received in return for what it had given to the banks) some of the largest banks. A country in which socialism is often treated as an anathema has socialized risk and intervened in markets in unprecedented ways.

These ironies are matched by the seeming inconsistencies in the arguments of the International Monetary Fund (IMF) and the U.S. Treasury before, during, and after the East Asian crisis—and the inconsistencies between the policies then and now. The IMF might claim that it believes in market fundamentalism—that markets are efficient, self-correcting, and accordingly, are best left to their own devices if one is to maximize growth and efficiency—but the moment a crisis occurs, it calls for massive government assistance, worried about "contagion," the spread of the disease from one country to another. But contagion is a quintessential externality, and if there are externalities, one can't (logically) believe in market fundamentalism. Even after the multibillion-dollar bailouts, the IMF and U.S. Treasury resisted imposing measures (regulations) that might have made the "accidents" less likely and less costly—because they believed that markets fundamentally worked well on their own, even when they had just experienced repeated instances when they didn't.

The bailouts provide an example of a set of inconsistent policies with potentially long-run consequences. Economists worry about incentives—one might say it is their number-one preoccupation. One of the arguments put forward by many in the financial markets for not helping mortgage owners who can't meet their repayments is that it gives rise to "moral hazard"—that is, incentives to repay are weakened if mortgage owners know that there is some chance they will be helped out if they don't repay. Worries about moral hazard led the IMF and the U.S. Treasury to argue vehemently against bailouts in Indonesia and Thailand—setting off a massive collapse of the banking system and exacerbating the downturns in those countries. Worries about moral hazard played into the decision not to bail out Lehman Brothers. But this decision, in turn, led to the most massive set of bailouts in history. When it came to America's big banks in the aftermath of Lehman Brothers, concerns about moral hazard were shunted aside, so much so that the banks' officers were allowed to enjoy huge bonuses for record losses, dividends continued unabated, and shareholders and bondholders were protected. The repeated rescues (not just bailouts, but ready provision of liquidity by the Federal Reserve in times of trouble) provide part of the explanation of the current crisis: they encouraged banks to become increasingly reckless, knowing that there was a good chance that if a problem arose, they would be rescued. (Financial markets referred to this as the "Greenspan/Bemanke put.") Regulators made the mistaken judgment that, because the economy had "survived" so well, markets worked well on their own and regulation was not needed—not noting that they had survived *because* of massive government intervention. Today, the problem of moral hazard is greater, by far, than it has ever been.

Agency issues and externalities mean that there is a role for government. If it does its job well, there will be fewer accidents, and when the accidents occur, they will be less costly. When there are accidents, government will have to help in picking up the pieces. But how the government picks up the pieces affects the likelihood of future crises—and a society's sense of fairness and justice. Every successful economy—every successful society—involves both government and markets. There needs to be a balanced role. It is a matter not just of "how much" but also of "what." During the Reagan and both Bush administrations, the United States lost that balance—doing too little then has meant doing too much now. Doing the wrong things now may mean doing more in the future.

Recessions

One of the striking aspects of the "free market" revolutions initiated by President Ronald Reagan and Prime Minister Margaret Thatcher of England was that perhaps the most important set of instances when markets fail to yield efficient outcomes was forgotten: the repeated episodes when resources are not fully utilized. The economy often operates below capacity, with millions of people who would like to find work not being able to do so, with episodic fluctuations in which more than one out of twelve can't find jobs—and numbers that are far worse for minorities and youth. The official unemployment rate doesn't provide a full picture: Many who would like to work full-time are working part-time because that's the only job they could get, and they are not included in the unemployment rate. Nor does the rate include those who join the rolls of the disabled but who would be working if they could only get a job. Nor does it include those who have been so discouraged by their failure to find a job that they give up looking. This crisis though is worse than usual. With the broader measure of unemployment, by September, 2009, more than one in six Americans who would have liked to have had a full-time job couldn't find one, and by October, matters were worse.[18] While the market is self-correcting—the bubble eventually burst—this crisis shows once again that the correction may be slow and the cost enormous. The cumulative gap between the economy's actual output and potential output is in the trillions.

Who Could Have Foreseen the Crash?

In the aftermath of the crash, both those in the financial market and their regulators claimed, "Who could have foreseen these problems?" In fact, many critics had—but their dire forecasts were an inconvenient truth: too much money was being made by too many people for their warnings to be heard.

I was certainly not the only person who was expecting the U.S. economy to crash, with global consequences. New York University economist Nouriel Roubini, financier George Soros, Morgan Stanley's Stephen Roach, Yale University housing expert Robert Shiller, and former Clinton Council of Economic Advisers/National Economic Council staffer Robert Wescott all issued repeated warnings. They were all Keynesian economists, sharing the view that markets were not self-correcting. Most of us were worried about the housing bubble; some (such as Roubini) focused on the risk posed by global imbalances to a sudden adjustment of exchange rates.

But those who had engineered the bubble (Henry Paulson had led Goldman Sachs to new heights of leverage, and Ben Bernanke had allowed the issuance of subprime mortgages to continue) maintained their faith in the ability of markets to self-correct—until they *had* to confront the reality of a massive collapse. One doesn't have to have a Ph.D. in psychology to understand why they wanted to pretend that the economy was going through just a minor disturbance, one that could easily be brushed aside. As late as March 2007, Federal Reserve Chairman Bernanke claimed that "the impact on the broader economy and financial markets of the problems in the subprime market seems likely to be contained."[19] A year later, even after the collapse of Bear Stearns, with rumors swirling about the imminent demise of Lehman Brothers, the official line (told not only publicly but also behind closed doors with other central bankers) was that the economy was already on its way to a robust recovery after a few blips.

The real estate bubble that had to burst was the most obvious symptom of "economic illness." But behind this symptom were more fundamental problems. Many had warned of the risks of deregulation. As far back as 1992, I worried that the securitization of mortgages would end in disaster, as buyers and sellers alike underestimated the likelihood of a price decline and the extent of correlation.[20]

Indeed, anyone looking closely at the American economy could easily have seen that there were major "macro" problems as well as "micro" problems. As I noted earlier, our economy had been sustained by an unsustainable bubble. Without the bubble, aggregate demand—the sum total of the goods and services demanded by households, firms, government, and foreigners—would have been weak, partly because of the growing inequality in the United States and elsewhere around the world, which shifted money from those would have spent it to those who didn't.[21]

For years, my Columbia colleague Bruce Greenwald and I had drawn attention to the further problem of a *global* lack of aggregate demand—the total of all the goods and services that people throughout the world want to buy. In the world of globalization, global aggregate demand is what matters. If the sum total of what people around the world want to buy is less than what the world can produce, there is a problem—a weak global economy. One of the reasons for weak global aggregate demand is the growing level of reserves—money that countries set aside for a "rainy day."

Developing countries put aside hundreds of billions of dollars in reserves to protect themselves from the high level of global volatility that has marked the era of deregulation, and from the discomfort they feel at turning to the IMF for help.[22] The prime minister of one of the countries that had been ravished by the global financial crisis of 1997 said to me, "We were in the class of '97. We learned what happens if you don't have enough reserves."

The oil-rich countries too were accumulating reserves—they knew that the high price of crude was not sustainable. For some countries, there was another reason for reserve accumulation. Export-led growth had been lauded as the best way for developing countries to grow; after new trade rules under the World Trade Organization took away many of the traditional instruments developing countries used to help create new industries, many turned to a policy of keeping their exchange rates competitive. And this meant buying dollars, selling their own currencies, and accumulating reserves.

These were all good reasons for accumulating reserves, but they had a bad consequence: there was insufficient global demand. A half trillion dollars, or more, was being set aside in these reserves every year in the years prior to the crisis. For a while, the United States had come to the rescue with debt-based profligate consumption, spending well beyond its means. It became the world's consumer of last resort. But that was not sustainable.

The Global Crisis

This crisis quickly became global—and not surprisingly, as nearly a quarter of U.S. mortgages had gone abroad.[23] Unintentionally, this helped the United States: had foreign institutions not bought as much of its toxic instruments and debt, the situation here might have been far worse.[24] But first the United States had exported its deregulatory philosophy—without that, foreigners might not have bought so many of its toxic mortgages.[25] In the end, the United States also exported its recession. This was, of course, only one of several channels through which the American crisis became global: the U.S. economy is still the largest, and it is hard for a downturn of this magnitude not to have a global impact. Moreover, global financial markets have become closely interlinked—evidenced by the fact that two of the top three beneficiaries of the U.S. government bailout of AIG were foreign banks.

In the beginning, many in Europe talked of decoupling, that they would be able to maintain growth in their economies even as America went into a downturn: the growth in Asia would save them from a recession. It should have been apparent that this too was just wishful thinking. Asia's economies are still too small (the entire consumption of Asia is just 40 percent of that of the United States),[26] and their growth relies heavily on exports to the United States. Even after a massive stimulus, China's growth in 2009 was some 3 to 4 percent below what it had been before the crisis. The world is too interlinked; a downturn in the United States could not but lead to a global slowdown. (There is an asymmetry: because of the immense internal and not fully tapped market in Asia, it might be able to return to robust growth even though the United States and Europe remain weak—a point to which I return in chapter 8.)

While Europe's financial institutions suffered from buying toxic mortgages and the risky gambles they had made with American banks, a number of European countries grappled with problems of their own design. Spain too had allowed a massive housing bubble to develop and is now suffering from the near-total collapse of its real estate market. In contrast to the United States, however, Spain's strong banking regulations have allowed its banks to withstand a much bigger trauma with better results—though, not surprisingly, its overall economy has been hit far worse.

The United Kingdom too succumbed to a real estate bubble. But worse, under the influence of the city of London, a major financial hub, it fell into the trap of the "race to the bottom," trying to do whatever it could to attract financial business. "Light" regulation did no better there than in the United States. Because the British had allowed the financial sector to take on a greater role in their economy, the cost of the bailouts was (proportionately) even greater. As in the United States, a culture of high salaries and bonuses developed. But at least the British understood that if you give taxpayer money to the banks, you have to do what you can to make sure they use it for the purposes intended—for more loans, not for bonuses and dividends. And at least in the U.K., there was some understanding that there had to be accountability—the heads of the bailed-out banks were replaced—and the British government demanded that the taxpayers get fair value in return for the bailouts, not the giveaways that marked both the Obama and Bush administrations' rescues.[27]

Iceland is a wonderful example of what can go wrong when a small and open economy adopts the deregulation mantra blindly. Its well-educated people worked hard and were at the forefront of modern technology. They had overcome the disadvantages of a remote location, harsh weather, and depletion of fish stocks—one of their traditional sources of income—to generate a per capita income of $40,000. Today, the reckless behavior of their banks has put the country's future in jeopardy.

I had visited Iceland several times earlier in this decade and warned of the risks of its liberalization policies.[28] This country of 300,000 had three banks that took on deposits and bought assets totaling some $176 billion, eleven times the country's GDP.[29] With a dramatic collapse of Iceland's banking system in the fall of 2008, Iceland became the first developed country in more than thirty years to turn to the IMF for help.[30] Iceland's banks had, like banks elsewhere, taken on high leverage and high risks. When financial markets realized the risk and started pulling money out, these banks (and especially Landsbanki) lured money from depositors in the U.K. and Netherlands by offering them "Icesaver" accounts with high returns. The depositors foolishly thought that there was a "free lunch": they could get higher returns without risk. Perhaps they also foolishly thought their own governments were doing their regulatory job. But, as everywhere, regulators had largely assumed that markets would take care of themselves. Borrowing from depositors only postponed the day of reckoning. Iceland could not afford to pour hundreds of billions of dollars into the weakened banks. As this reality gradually dawned on those who had provided funds to the bank, it became only a matter of time before there would be a run on the banking system; the global turmoil following the Lehman Brothers collapse precipitated what would in any case have been inevitable. Unlike the United States, the government of Iceland knew that it could not bail out the bondholders or shareholders. The only questions were whether the government would bail out the Icelandic corporation that insured the depositors, and how generous it would be to the foreign depositors. The U.K. used strong-arm tactics—going so far as to seize Icelandic assets using anti-terrorism laws—and when Iceland turned to the IMF and the Nordic countries for assistance, they insisted that Icelandic taxpayers bail out U.K. and Dutch depositors even beyond the amounts the accounts had been insured for. On a return visit to Iceland in September 2009, almost a year later, the anger was palpable. Why should Iceland's taxpayers be made to pay for the failure of a private bank, especially when foreign regulators had failed to do their job of protecting their own citizens? One widely held view for the strong response from European governments was that Iceland had exposed a fundamental flaw in European integration: "the single market" meant that any European bank could operate in any country. Responsibility for regulation was put on the "home" country. But if the home country failed to do its job, citizens in other countries could lose billions. Europe didn't want to think about this and its profound implications; better to simply make little Iceland pick up the tab, an amount some put at as much as 100 percent of the country's GDP.[31]

As the crisis worsened in the United States and Europe, other countries around the world suffered from the collapse in global demand. Developing countries suffered especially, as remittances (transfers of money from family members in developed countries) fell and capital that had flowed into them was greatly diminished—and in some cases reversed. While America's crisis began with the financial sector and then spread to the rest of the economy, in many of the developing countries—including those where financial regulation is far better than in the United States—the problems in the "real economy" were so large that they eventually affected the financial sector. The crisis spread so rapidly partly because of the policies, especially of capital and financial market liberalization, the IMF and the U.S. Treasury had foisted on these countries—based on the same free market ideology that had gotten the United States into trouble.[32] But while even the United States finds it difficult to afford the trillions in bailouts and stimulus, corresponding actions by poorer countries are well beyond their reach.

The Big Picture

Underlying all of these symptoms of dysfunction is a larger truth: the world economy is undergoing seismic shifts. The Great Depression coincided with the decline of U.S. agriculture; indeed, agricultural prices were falling even before the stock market crash in 1929. Increases in agricultural productivity were so great that a small percentage of the population could produce all the food that the country could consume. The transition from an economy based on agriculture to one where manufacturing predominated was not easy. In fact, the economy only resumed growing when the New Deal kicked in and World War II got people working in factories.

Today the underlying trend in the United States is the move away from manufacturing and into the service sector. As before, this is partly because of the success in increasing productivity in manufacturing, so that a small fraction of the population can produce all the toys, cars, and TVs that even the most materialistic and profligate society might buy. But in the United States and Europe, there is an additional dimension: globalization, which has meant a shift in the locus of production and comparative advantage to China, India, and other developing countries.

Accompanying this "microeconomic" adjustment are a set of macroeconomic imbalances: while the United States should be saving for the retirement of its aging baby-boomers, it has been living beyond its means, financed to a large extent by China and other developing countries that have been producing more than they have been consuming. While it is natural for some countries to lend to others—some to run trade deficits, others surpluses—the pattern, with poor countries lending to the rich, is peculiar and the magnitude of the deficits appear unsustainable. As countries get more indebted, lenders may lose confidence that the borrower can repay—and this can be true even for a rich country like the United States. Returning the American and global economy to health will require the restructuring of economies to reflect the new economics and correcting these global imbalances.

We can't go back to where we were before the bubble broke in 2007. Nor should we want to. There were plenty of problems with that economy—as we have just seen. Of course, there is a chance that some new bubble will replace the housing bubble, just as the housing bubble replaced the tech bubble. But such a "solution" would only postpone the day of reckoning. Any new bubble could pose dangers: the oil bubble helped pushed the economy over the brink. The longer we delay in dealing with the underlying problems, the longer it will be before the world returns to robust growth.

There is a simple test of whether the United States has made sufficient strides in ensuring that there will not be another crisis: If the proposed reforms had been in place, could the current crisis have been avoided? Would it have occurred anyway? For instance, giving more power to the Federal Reserve is key to the proposed Obama regulatory reform. But as the crisis began, the Federal Reserve had more powers than it used. In virtually every interpretation of the crisis, the Fed was at the center of the creation of this and the previous bubble. Perhaps the Fed's chairman has learned his lesson. But we live in a country of laws, not of men: should we have a system requiring that the Fed first be burned by fire to ensure that another won't be set? Can we have confidence in a system that can depend so precariously on the economic philosophy or understanding of one person—or even of the seven members of the Board of Governors of the Fed? As this book goes to press, it is clear that the reforms have not gone far enough.

We cannot wait until *after the crisis*. Indeed, the way we have been dealing *with* the crisis may be making it all the more difficult to address these deeper problems. The next chapter outlines what we should have done to address the crisis—and why what we did fell far short.

Notes

1 See Milton Friedman and Anna Schwartz, *A Monetary History of the United States, 1867–1960* (Princeton: Princeton University Press, 1971), and Barry Eichengreen, *Golden Fetters: Gold Standard and the Great Depression, 1919–1939* (Oxford: Oxford University Press, 1995).

2 From 2000 to 2008, real median household income (that is, adjusting for inflation) decreased by almost 4 percent. At the end of the last expansion, in 2007, incomes were still some 0.6 percent below the level attained before the end of the previous expansion, in 2000. See U.S. Census Bureau, "Income, Poverty, and Health Insurance Coverage in the United States: 2008," *Current Population Reports*, September 2009, available at http://www.census.gov/prod/2009pubs/p60-236.pdf.

3 James Kennedy, "Estimates of Mortgage Originations Calculated from Data on Loans Outstanding and Repayments" (not seasonally adjusted), November 2008, available at http://www.wealthscribe.com/wp-content/uploads/2008/11/equity-extraction-data-2008-q2.pdf. Updated estimates from Alan Greenspan and James Kennedy, "Estimates of Home Mortgage Originations, Repayments, and Debt on One-to-Four-Family Residences," Finance and Economics Discussion Series, Division of Research and Statistics and Monetary Affairs, Federal Reserve Board, Working Paper 2005-4 1, September 2005.

4 The tech bubble itself is another story, told more fully in Joseph E. Stiglitz, *Roaring Nineties: A New History of the World's Most Prosperous Decade* (New York: W. W. Norton, 2003).

5 The NASDAQ Composite Index (generally used as a measure of the performance of technology stocks) closed at a high of 5,046.86 on March 9, 2000. On October 9, 2002, the NASDAQ Composite closed at a low of 1,114.11. Google Finance, NASDAQ Composite Historical Prices, available at http://www.google.com/finance/historical?q=INDEXNASDAQ:COMPX.

6 U.S. Energy Information Administration, "Petroleum Navigator" database, U.S. Imports of Crude Oil (Thousand Barrels per Day) [accessed on August 28, 2009] and Weekly All Countries Spot Price FOB Weighted by Estimated Export Volume (Dollars per Barrel) [accessed on September 2, 2009], available at http:// tonto.eia.doe.gov/dnav/pet/pet_pri_top.asp.

7 Alan Greenspan is often given credit for the era of low inflation, but many other countries around the world had low inflation—it was not a distinctively American phenomenon. The fact that China was supplying the world with manufactured goods at low and even declining prices was one of the common critical factors.

8 How this could have happened is a matter of extensive debate. Part of the problem was that like any trading firm, they held "inventory." Part of the problem too was that, in the complicated repackagings, they may have been fooled by their own calculations; they held on to some securities and absorbed some risk. Some of these were held off-balance sheet—they could record fees from the repackaging without recording the risks associated with the parts that had not been sold. Their incentives to engage in these off-balance-sheet activities are discussed in later chapters.

9 See Bureau of Economic Analysis, National Income and Product Accounts Table, "Table 6.16D. Corporate Profits by Industry," available at http://www.bea.gov/National/nipaweb/SelectTable.asp.

10 One of the standard arguments for why the market put such a low price on risk was that with interest rates on safe assets so low, the market clamored for assets with slightly higher yields, driving up the price of the assets and driving down the returns. Some in Wall Street make a parallel argument: when the spread between the long rate and the short rate was

reduced when the Federal Reserve raised its interest rates, beginning in June 2004, many said they "had" to take on more risk to get the earnings that they had previously had. That's like a robber saying in his defense, when honest ways of making a living disappeared, I had to turn to a life of crime. Regardless of the interest rate, investors should have insisted on adequate compensation for the risk borne. (The Fed raised the interest rate seventeen times by 25 basis points from June 2004 to June 2006, moving the intended federal funds rate from 1.25 percent to 5.25 percent over that period. Federal Reserve, "Intended Federal Funds Rate, Change and Level, 1990 to Present," December 16, 2008, available at http://www.federalreserve.gov/fomc/fundsrate.htm. During that period, the rate on ten-year U.S. Treasury bonds fell from 4.7 percent in June 2004 to as low as 3.9 percent in June 2005 before rising to 5.1 percent in June 2006. See 10-year Treasury Note, TNX, on finance.yahoo.com. Thus, the yield curve flattened significantly and actually inverted by June 2006.)

11 Alan Greenspan, "Understanding Household Debt Obligations," remarks at the Credit Union National Association 2004 Governmental Affairs Conference, Washington, DC, February 23, 2004, available at http://www.federalreserve.gov/boarddocs/speeches/2004/20040223/default.htm. See also the discussion in chapter 4.

12 Alan Greenspan, "The Fed Didn't Cause the Housing Bubble," *Wall Street Journal*, March 11, 2009, p. A15.

13 The Fed normally focuses its attention on short-term government interest rates, allowing the market to determine long-term interest rates. But this is a self-imposed restraint: during the crisis, the Fed showed its ability and willingness to determine other interest rates.

14 Community Reinvestment Act (CRA) loans perform comparably to other subprime loans. In fact, loans originated under NeighborWorks America, a typical CRA program, had a lower delinquency rate than subprime loans. See Glenn Canner and Neil Bhutta, "Staff Analysis of the Relationship between the CRA and the Subprime Crisis," memorandum, Board of Governors of the Federal Reserve System, Division of Research and Statistics, November 21, 2008 available at http://www.federalreserve.gov/newsevents/speech/20081203_analysis.pdf, and Randall S. Kroszner, "The Community Reinvestment Act and the Recent Mortgage Crisis," speech at Confronting Concentrated Poverty Policy Forum, December 3, 2008, available at http://www.federalreserve.gov/newsevents/speech/kroszner2008l203a.htm.

15 Freddie Mac purchased a total of $ 158 billion, or 13 percent, of all subprime and Alt-A securities created in 2006 and 2007, and Fannie Mae purchased an additional 5 percent. The biggest suppliers of the securities to Fannie and Freddie included Countrywide Financial Corp. of Calabasas, California, as well as Irvine, California–based New Century Financial Corp. and Ameriquest Mortgage Co., lenders that either went bankrupt or were forced to sell themselves. Fannie and Freddie were the biggest buyers of loans from Countrywide, according to the company. See Jody Shenn, "Fannie, Freddie Subprime Spree May Add to Bailout," *Bloomberg.com*, September 22, 2009.

16 One reason why the financial sector may have failed to perform its critical social functions is that those in the sector didn't understand what they were. But in a well-functioning market economy, markets are supposed to provide the incentives that lead individuals to do what is in society's interest, even if individual market participants may not understand what that is.

17 Adolf Berle and Gardiner Means emphasized the separation of ownership and control in their classic book, *The Modern Corporation and Private Property* (New York: Harcourt, Brace and World, 1932), seventy-eight years ago, but since then matters have become much worse, with so much of savings generated by pension funds. Those who manage these

funds typically do not even attempt to exercise control over the behavior of the firm. John Maynard Keynes worried extensively about the shortsighted behavior of investors. He suggested that they were much like a judge in a beauty contest, trying to judge not who was the most beautiful person but who others would think was (chapter 12 of *General Theory of Employment Interest and Money* [Cambridge, UK: Macmillan Cambridge University Press, 1936]). Again, matters have almost surely become worse since he wrote. Some of my own research helped put Berle and Means's theory on sounder theoretical grounds. See J. E. Stiglitz, "Credit Markets and the Control of Capital," *Journal of Money, Banking, and Credit,* vol. 17, no. 2 (May 1985), pp. 133–152, and A. Edlin and J. E. Stiglitz, "Discouraging Rivals: Managerial Rent-Seeking and Economic Inefficiencies," *American Economic Review,* vol. 85, no. 5 (December 1995), pp. 1301–1312.

18 The seasonally adjusted rate of "Total unemployed, plus all marginally attached workers plus total employed part time for economic reasons, as a percent of all civilian labor force plus all marginally attached workers" was 17.5 percent in October 2009. Bureau of Labor Statistics, "Current Population Survey: Labor Force Statistics, Table U-6," available at http://www.bls.gov/news.release/empsit.tl2.htm.

19 Statement of Ben S. Bernanke, Chairman, Board of Governors of the Federal Reserve System, before the Joint Economic Committee, U.S. Congress, Washington, DC, March 28, 2007.

20 Buyers and sellers of mortgages failed to recognize that if interest rates rose or the economy went into recession, the housing bubble might break, and most would be in trouble. That is precisely what happened. As I note below, securitization also created problems of information asymmetries, attenuating incentives for good credit assessments. See Joseph E. Stiglitz, "Banks versus Markets as Mechanisms for Allocating and Coordinating Investment," in J. Roumasset and S. Barr (eds.), *The Economics of Cooperation* (Boulder, CO: Westview Press, 1992).

21 In the years immediately preceding the crisis, as noted earlier, domestic demand had also been weakened by high oil prices. The problems of high oil prices and growing inequality —reducing domestic aggregate demand—afflicted many other countries. Income inequality increased in more than three-quarters of OECD countries from the mid-1980s to the mid-2000s, and the past five years saw growing poverty and inequality in two-thirds of OECD countries. See Organisation for Economic Co-operation and Development (OECD), *Growing Unequal? Income Distribution and Poverty in OECD Countries,* Paris, October 2008.

22 In *Globalization and Its Discontents* (op. cit.), I explain more fully the reasons for this discomfort: the IMF's policies (often based on the flawed market fundamentalism that I have discussed in this chapter) led downturns into recessions, recessions into depression, and imposed unpalatable (and often unnecessary) structural and macro-policies that impeded growth and contributed to poverty and inequality.

23 Daniel O. Beltran, Laurie Pounder, and Charles P. Thomas, "Foreign Exposure to Asset-Backed Securities of U.S. Origin," Board of Governors of the Federal Reserve System, International Finance Discussion Paper 939, August 1, 2008. At the same time, foreign purchases of U.S. mortgages and mortgage-backed products fueled the bubble.

24 As I explain later, the issue is more complex, since the supply of foreign funds may itself have fed the bubble.

25 To be fair, some other countries (such as the United Kingdom under Margaret Thatcher) had bought into the deregulatory philosophy on their own. For later U.K. governments, "light regulation" was used as a competitive instrument to attract financial firms. In the end, the country surely lost more than it gained.

26 "An Astonishing Rebound," *Economist,* August 13, 2009, p. 9.

27 In spite of its efforts, lending in the United Kingdom remained constricted. It is not easy to determine precisely what "fair value" means. But it entails receiving enough of the shares (claims on the future income of the banks) to compensate the government for the money provided and the risk borne. As I note later, a careful study of the U.S. bailout has shown that the U.S. taxpayer did not get fair value.

28 See Joseph E. Stiglitz, "Monetary and Exchange Rate Policy in Small Open Economies: The Case of Iceland," Central Bank of Iceland, Working Paper 15, November 2001, available at http://www.sedlabanki.is/uploads/files/WP-15.pdf.

29 Willem H. Buiter and Anne Sibert, "The Icelandic Banking Crisis and What to Do about It: The Lender of Last Resort Theory of Optimal Currency Areas," Centre for Economic Policy Research (CEPR) Policy Insight 26, October 2008, available at http://www.cepr.org/pubs/PolicyInsights/PolicyInsight26.pdf.

30 Britain turned to the International Monetary Fund (IMF) for help in 1976.

31 The total combined foreign liabilities of Iceland's banks were in excess of $100 billion, dwarfing the country's GDP of $14 billion. "Iceland Agrees Emergency Legislation," *Times Online (UK),* October 6, 2008, available at http://www.timesonline.co.uk/tol/news/world/europe/article4889832.ece. Iceland's parliament passed legislation in late August 2009 to repay the United Kingdom and the Netherlands about $6 billion that those governments had given depositors who lost money in Icelandic savings accounts during the financial crisis. See Matthew Saltmarsh, "Iceland to Repay Nations for Failed Banks' Deposits," *New York Times,* August 29, 2009, p. B2. However, the United Kingdom and the Netherlands objected to terms in the law that the repayment guarantee ran out in 2024. Iceland agreed to a new deal in October 2009 which said that if the money is not repaid by 2024, the guarantee will be extended in five-year blocks. The release of IMF funds to Iceland had been held up by the disagreement on the repayment. See "Iceland Presents Amended Icesave Bill, Eyes IMF Aid," Reuters, October 20, 2009.

32 Capital market liberalization meant allowing short-term money to flow freely into and out of the country. One can't build factories and schools with such hot money; but such hot money can wreak havoc on an economy. Financial market liberalization entails opening up an economy to foreign financial institutions. There is increasing evidence that foreign banks do less lending to small and medium-sized enterprises and, in some instances, respond more strongly to global shocks (like the current crisis), thereby generating more volatility. There is also evidence that capital market integration did not lead to reduced volatility and higher growth in the manner expected. See Eswar Prasad, Kenneth Rogoff, Shang-Jin Wei, and M. Ayhan Kose, "Effects of Financial Globalisation on Developing Countries: Some Empirical Evidence," *Economic and Political Weekly,* vol. 38, no. 41 (October 2003), pp. 4319–4330; M. Ayhan Kose, Eswar S. Prasad, and Marco E. Terrones, "Financial Integration and Macroeconomic Volatility." *IMF Staff Papers,* vol. 50 (Special Issue, 2003), pp. 119–142; Hamidur Rashid, "Evidence of Financial Disintermediation in Low Income Countries: Role of Foreign Banks," Ph.D. dissertation, Columbia University, New York, 2005; and Enrica Detragiache, Thierry Tressel, and Poonam Gupta, "Foreign Banks in Poor Countries: Theory and Evidence," International Monetary Fund Working Paper 06/18, Washington, DC, 2006.

6

Inequality

Economic inequality has risen substantially since the 1970s in most industrial countries, and particularly sharply in the United States.[1] This severe inequality denies ordinary workers the fruits of their labor, constrains economic opportunities, impedes economic growth, and compromises the legitimacy of political and economic systems.[2] **Thomas Piketty**, a French economist, recasts the debate over inequality in his magisterial work, *Capital in the Twenty-First Century*. He documents trends in inequality from the mid-nineteenth century through the present in major industrial economies. He demonstrates that inequality has risen in these countries throughout this era, with the important exception of the 1910–80 period. He argues that if the rate of return to capital (r) exceeds the growth rate (g), as it did through most of this period, then inequality will rise. Those with substantial capital will earn a return on this capital of 4–5 percent, while those without capital will remain relatively poor given slow growth. The 1910–80 period is distinctive because the two world wars eliminated so much wealth, and governments raised taxes on income and inheritance to pay for World War I and did not lower those rates substantially until about 1980. Piketty enhances our understanding of inequality because he generates and analyzes new historical data; he clarifies the distinction between wealth and income inequality; and he differentiates several epochs of inequality. He also identifies national variations within the broader trends he observes, stressing that the U.S. rise in wage income inequality over the past few decades exceeds that of other countries by a substantial margin. His main policy recommendation is to raise taxes in a progressive direction, primarily by imposing a substantial wealth tax. He contends that this would be the only policy measure with a large enough impact to alter the propensity for inequality to increase over time. He explicitly recognizes the primacy of politics and institutions but does not flesh out that side of the argument.[3] A market-institutionalist perspective could fill this gap by specifying how political forces, government policies, and market institutions augment or moderate economic inequality, as outlined below.

N. Gregory Mankiw provides a sophisticated version of the market-liberal perspective on inequality. Mankiw is a professor of economics at Harvard University who served as the Chair of the Council of Economic Advisors under President George W. Bush. He believes that economic actors generally engage in voluntary exchanges meant to benefit both parties. And he feels that pay should reflect the value of the marginal product from labor. He proposes a "just deserts" approach to inequality: people should receive the compensation they deserve based on skill and effort. We should accept inequality that reflects just desserts, and we should not seek to transfer these rewards to others. Mankiw acknowledges, however, that inequalities also may reflect "rents," or excess returns above value added. That is, some people may receive more than their just rewards because they benefit from government policies that favor them. In that case, he would support amending those policies. Nonetheless, he concludes that rising inequality in the United States is primarily due to variations in economic contributions that have been exacerbated by technological advances, and not by rent-seeking. He rejects charges from the Left that high incomes do not reflect greater contributions to society; that the U.S. tax system is regressive; or that the rich should pay higher taxes because they benefit from government investment in physical, legal, and social infrastructure.

A market-institutional perspective would challenge Mankiw's presumption that inequality reflects differential economic contributions rather than rent-seeking, and scholars have been amassing evidence to support this view. It would stress that there is no free-market equilibrium, only an infinite variety of ways to govern markets, including government regulations and private sector practices. For example, wages depend heavily on the specific regulations on union formation and practices for wage bargaining.[4] There is no natural free-market equilibrium, only a field of possibilities from employer-friendly to worker-friendly, and from collaborative to more adversarial approaches. This market-institutional perspective does not deny that skill and effort affect economic rewards in a market economy, but it suggests that they do so in combination with the specifics of market governance at particular times in particular places. It stresses that inequality reflects the minutiae of market governance, including financial regulation, corporate governance, antitrust, and intellectual property rights as well as labor regulation. Some have referred to reforms in these realms as a "predistribution" policy agenda because they address inequalities at their source rather than redistributing wealth after the fact via taxation and welfare benefits.[5]

We can grasp how market governance affects inequality more concretely by examining how these various elements of market governance have evolved in the United States since the 1980s, and how those changes have in turn contributed to the growth in inequality, especially wage income inequality. This also highlights how politics shapes inequality and how government policy decisions have fueled the rise of inequality.[6] For labor market governance, the decline of labor power has been driven more by changes in the implementation of labor law and in labor practices than in changes in the law itself, at least at the federal level. Congress failed to pass measures to preserve union strength; national leaders took steps to undermine it; state governments passed laws hostile to labor; and employers increasingly deployed practices to discourage union organization. This contributed to wage stagnation for the majority of Americans, mass layoffs, greater employment insecurity, and a decline in labor compensation as a share of national income. Meanwhile, financial reforms facilitated financial innovation, propelled industry consolidation, increased market volatility, and augmented the ability of financial institutions and their executives to capture rents at the expense of borrowers and investors. The financial sector seized a growing share of the economy without delivering greater benefits to consumers.[7]

Piketty attributes skyrocketing executive pay to corporate governance, as top managers have been able to set their own compensation, and to social norms that allowed this.[8] He is right that the U.S. corporate governance model is characterized by distinctive norms, but he misses how the transition since the 1980s has been driven by specific legal and regulatory battles. Since the 1980s, developments in government regulation and business practices have shifted U.S. corporations from a managerial model of corporate governance, in which managers control their companies without deference to shareholders, toward a shareholder model, in which they seek to maximize short-term returns for shareholders and for themselves (since they are compensated via stock options). This has contributed not only to higher shareholder returns, but also to a lower labor share of income and to stagnant investment. Over the long run, these management practices have impaired corporate performance and weakened the U.S. economy overall.[9]

In antitrust, as noted in the Market Reform section, the United States shifted from fairly aggressive enforcement during the Warren Court era to a much more laissez-faire stance with the Reagan revolution and the ascendance of the Chicago School of antitrust. Chicago School scholars believed that firms with large market shares often attained that status by providing better goods and services at better prices, rather than by unfair practices; that these firms often faced viable competition; and that antitrust remedies, such as breaking up dominant firms, could very well cause more harm than good. This shift in policy led to a gradual increase in market concentration. And that in turn exacerbated inequality because dominant firms could charge higher prices, which boosted higher profits, higher pay for executives, and higher returns for shareholders. Dominant firms also face less competition in hiring workers, so they can pay lower wages and provide worse working conditions without losing workers.[10]

The U.S. intellectual property (IP) rights regime has contributed to growing inequality by enabling firms that enjoy the benefits of IP protection to increase their profits and salaries for managers and core workers at the expense of other firms, consumers, and workers. The U.S. government since 1980 has expanded patent protection to cover software and business practices, and extended copyright protection in duration. The IP regime has contributed to the polarization of the economy, with high-profit firms with IP that share their rents with a relatively small core of managers and workers, and a broader sector in more competitive industries that tend to squeeze their workers with lower wages and less favorable work conditions. The U.S. firms with the highest level of profits are concentrated in those sectors characterized by a high reliance on IP, especially pharmaceuticals and high technology.[11] Market governance has shifted in a neoliberal direction in other advanced industrial countries over this same period, but not to the same degree.[12] Germany and Japan, for example, have enacted market reforms, but they have moved more incrementally and have not fueled the same surge in income inequality.

This then raises the question of *why* market governance has shifted in a direction that exacerbates inequality. To put it simply, those with wealth and power have actively lobbied for policy reforms that favor themselves at the expense of the broader public, and the neoliberal turn has particularly favored these interests. But understanding the recent surge in income inequality in the United States also requires going back to historic roots, including the profound disparities in wealth, status, and power grounded in racial and ethnic differences. The legacy of slavery left deeply entrenched patterns of inequality in power and wealth between whites and African Americans. The United States has a long history of unequal treatment under the law beyond slavery, from the Jim Crow laws to voting restrictions and criminal justice. And these legal and regulatory barriers have been compounded by marketplace discrimination, from labor to finance to housing markets. Racial discrimination in hiring has reinforced occupational segregation and perpetuated the racial wage gap. In financial markets, minority consumers have had more trouble getting credit; they are more likely to fall victim to predatory lending; and to pay more for financial services overall.[13] Minority business owners are less likely to apply for loans and more likely to be denied, and they pay higher interest rates when they do borrow. This disparity in financial access has contributed to a stunning racial wealth gap. Moreover, those who oppose policies that could promote economic equality and opportunity have leveraged race to make their case, implying that benefits would go disproportionately to minorities who are lazy rather than structurally disadvantaged.[14] The acceleration of inequality in America in recent decades is not simply a matter of differential returns from capital and labor, but the result of the mutual reinforcement of political, social, and economic inequities over time.

Notes

1 Some parts of this introduction build on Steven K. Vogel, "The Regulatory Roots of Inequality in America," *Journal of Law and Political Economy* 1 (2021).

2 Anthony B. Atkinson, 2015. *Inequality: What Can Be Done?* (Cambridge, MA: Harvard University Press, 2015), 9–14; Heather Boushey, *Unbound: How Inequality Constricts Our Economy and What We Can Do About It* (Cambridge, MA: Harvard University Press, 2019), 194–5.

3 Thomas Piketty, *Capitalism in the Twenty-First Century*, translated by Arthur Goldhammer (Cambridge, MA: Belknap Press, 2017). Piketty examines politics and institutions in greater depth, and ideology in particular, in *Capital and Ideology*, translated by Arthur Goldhammer (Cambridge, MA: Belknap Press, 2020).

4 Anna Stansbury and Lawrence H. Summers, 2020. "The Declining Worker Power Hypothesis: An Explanation for the Recent Evolution of the American Economy," National Bureau of Economic Research Working Paper 27193 (May 2020).

5 Matt Bai originally coined this term in "The Poverty Platform," *New York Times Magazine* (June 10, 2007).

6 Jacob S. Hacker and Paul Pierson. *Winner-Take-All Politics: How Washington Made the Rich Richer and Turned Its Back on the Middle Class* (New York: Simon and Schuster, 2010).

7 Thomas Philippon, *The Great Reversal: How America Gave Up on Free Markets* (Cambridge, MA: Belknap Press, 2019).

8 Thomas Piketty, *Capitalism in the Twenty-First Century* (Cambridge, MA: Belknap Press, 2017), 32–3, 417–20.

9 William Lazonick, "The Fragility of the U.S. Economy: The Financialized Corporation and the Disappearing Middle Class," in Dan Breznitz and John Zysman, eds., *The Third Globalization: Can Wealthy Nations Stay Rich in the Twenty-First Century?* (New York: Oxford University Press, 2013), 232–76.

10 Boushey, *Unbound*, 115–16. Philippon, *The Great Reversal*, also identifies increasing market concentration as a source of inequality in the United States, and contrasts this to Western Europe, where antitrust enforcement has been tougher and competition stronger.

11 Herman Mark Schwartz, "Wealth and Secular Stagnaton: The Role of Industrial Organization and Intellectual Property Rights," *RSF: The Russell Sage Foundation Journal of the Social Sciences* (2016): 226–49.

12 Steven K. Vogel, *Freer Markets, More Rules: Regulatory Reform in Advanced Industrial Countries* (Ithaca, NY: Cornell University Press, 1996); Steven K. Vogel, *Japan Remodeled: How Government and Industry Are Reforming Japanese Capitalism* (Ithaca, NY: Cornell University Press, 2006).

13 Mehrsa Badaradan, *The Color of Money: Black Banks and the Racial Wealth Gap* (Cambridge, MA: Belknap Press, 2017).

14 Ian Haney López, *Dog Whistle Politics: Strategic Racism, Fake Populism, and the Dividing of America* (Oxford: Oxford University Press, 2014).

N. Gregory Mankiw,
"Defending the One Percent" (2013)[*]

Imagine a society with perfect economic equality. Perhaps out of sheer coincidence, the supply and demand for different types of labor happen to produce an equilibrium in which everyone earns exactly the same income. As a result, no one worries about the gap between the rich and poor, and no one debates to what extent public policy should make income redistribution a priority. Because people earn the value of their marginal product, everyone has the appropriate incentive to provide the efficient amount of effort. The government is still needed to provide public goods, such as national defense, but those are financed with a lump-sum tax. There is no need for taxes that would distort incentives, such as an income tax, because they would be strictly worse for everyone. The society enjoys not only perfect equality but also perfect efficiency.

Then, one day, this egalitarian utopia is disturbed by an entrepreneur with an idea for a new product. Think of the entrepreneur as Steve Jobs as he develops the iPod, J. K. Rowling as she writes her Harry Potter books, or Steven Spielberg as he directs his blockbuster movies. When the entrepreneur's product is introduced, everyone in society wants to buy it. They each part with, say, $100. The transaction is a voluntary exchange, so it must make both the buyer and the seller better off. But because there are many buyers and only one seller, the distribution of economic well-being is now vastly unequal. The new product makes the entrepreneur much richer than everyone else.

The society now faces a new set of questions: How should the entrepreneurial disturbance in this formerly egalitarian outcome alter public policy? Should public policy remain the same, because the situation was initially acceptable and the entrepreneur improved it for everyone? Or should government policymakers deplore the resulting inequality and use their powers to tax and transfer to spread the gains more equally?

In my view, this thought experiment captures, in an extreme and stylized way, what has happened to US society over the past several decades. Since the 1970s, average incomes have grown, but the growth has not been uniform across the income distribution. The incomes at the top, especially in the top 1 percent, have grown much faster than average. These high earners have made significant economic contributions, but they have also reaped large gains. The question for public policy is what, if anything, to do about it.

This development is one of the largest challenges facing the body politic. A few numbers illustrate the magnitude of the issue. The best data we have on the upper tail of the income distribution come from Piketty and Saez's (2003, with updates)

* From: article originally published in the *Journal of Economic Perspectives,* vol. 27, no. 3, Summer 2013, Copyright © American Economic Association. (pp. 21–34) Reproduced with permission of the *Journal of Economic Perspectives.*

tabulations of individual tax returns. (Even these numbers, though, are subject to some controversy: the tax code changes over time, altering the incentives to receive and report compensation in alternative forms.) According to their numbers, the share of income, excluding capital gains, earned by the top 1 percent rose from 7.7 percent in 1973 to 17.4 percent in 2010. Even more striking is the share earned by the top 0.01 percent—an elite group that, in 2010, had a membership requirement of annual income exceeding $5.9 million. This group's share of total income rose from 0.5 percent in 1973 to 3.3 percent in 2010. These numbers are not easily ignored. Indeed, they in no small part motivated the Occupy movement, and they have led to calls from policymakers on the left to make the tax code more progressive.

At the outset, it is worth noting that addressing the issue of rising inequality necessarily involves not just economics but also a healthy dose of political philosophy. We economists must recognize not only the limits of what we know about inequality's causes, but also the limits on the ability of our discipline to prescribe policy responses. Economists who discuss policy responses to increasing inequality are often playing the role of amateur political philosopher (and, admittedly, I will do so in this essay). Given the topic, that is perhaps inevitable. But it is useful to keep in mind when we are writing as economists and when we are venturing beyond the boundaries of our professional expertise.

Is Inequality Inefficient?

It is tempting for economists who abhor inequality to suggest that the issue involves not just inequality per se, but also economic inefficiency. Discussion of inequality necessarily involves our social and political values, but if inequality also entails inefficiency, those normative judgments are more easily agreed upon. The Pareto criterion is the clearest case: if we can make some people better off without making anyone worse off, who could possibly object? Yet for the question at hand, this criterion does not take us very far. As far as I know, no one has proposed any credible policy intervention to deal with rising inequality that will make everyone, including those at the very top, better off.

More common is the claim that inequality is inefficient in the sense of shrinking the size of the economic pie. (That is, inefficiency is being viewed through the lens of the Kaldor–Hicks criterion.) If the top 1 percent is earning an extra $1 in some way that reduces the incomes of the middle class and the poor by $2, then many people will see that as a social problem worth addressing. For example, suppose the rising income share of the top 1 percent were largely attributable to successful rent-seeking. Imagine that the government were to favor its political allies by granting them monopoly power over certain products, favorable regulations, or restrictions on trade. Such a policy would likely lead to both inequality and inefficiency. Economists of all stripes would deplore it. I certainly would.

Joseph Stiglitz's (2012) book, *The Price of Inequality*, spends many pages trying to convince the reader that such rent-seeking is a primary driving force behind the growing incomes of the rich. This essay is not the place for a book review, but I can report that I was not convinced. Stiglitz's narrative relies more on exhortation and anecdote than on systematic evidence. There is no good reason to believe that rent-seeking by the rich is more pervasive today than it was in the 1970s, when the income share of the top 1 percent was much lower than it is today.

I am more persuaded by the thesis advanced by Claudia Goldin and Lawrence Katz (2008) in their book *The Race between Education and Technology*. Goldin and Katz argue that skill-biased technological change continually increases the demand for skilled labor. By itself, this force tends to increase the earnings gap between skilled and unskilled workers, thereby increasing inequality. Society can offset the effect of this demand shift by increasing the supply of skilled labor at an even faster pace, as it did in the 1950s and 1960s. In this case, the earnings gap need not rise and, indeed, can even decline, as in fact occurred. But when the pace of educational advance slows down, as it did in the 1970s, the increasing demand for skilled labor will naturally cause inequality to rise. The story of rising inequality, therefore, is not primarily about politics and rent-seeking, but rather about supply and demand.

To be sure, Goldin and Katz focus their work on the broad changes in inequality, not on the incomes of the top 1 percent in particular. But it is natural to suspect that similar forces are at work. The income share of the top 1 percent exhibits a U-shaped pattern: falling from the 1950s to the 1970s, and rising from the 1970s to the present. The earnings differentials between skilled and unskilled workers studied by Goldin and Katz follow a similar U-shaped pattern. If Goldin and Katz are right that the broad changes in inequality have been driven by the interaction between technology and education, rather than changes in rent-seeking through the political process, then it would seem an unlikely coincidence that the parallel changes at the top have been driven by something entirely different. Rather, it seems that changes in technology have allowed a small number of highly educated and exceptionally talented individuals to command superstar incomes in ways that were not possible a generation ago. Erik Brynjolfsson and Andrew McAfee (2011) advance this thesis forcefully in their book *Race Against the Machine*. They write, "Aided by digital technologies, entrepreneurs, CEOs, entertainment stars, and financial executives have been able to leverage their talents across global markets and capture reward that would have been unimaginable in earlier times (p. 44)."

Nonetheless, to the extent that Stiglitz is right that inefficient rent-seeking is a driving force behind rising inequality, the appropriate policy response is to address the root cause. It is at best incomplete and at worst misleading to describe the situation as simply "rising inequality," because inequality here is a symptom of a deeper problem. A progressive system of taxes and transfers might make the outcome more equal, but it would not address the underlying inefficiency. For example, if domestic firms are enriching themselves at the expense of consumers through quotas on imports (as is the case with some agribusinesses), the solution to the problem entails not a revision of the tax code, but rather a change in trade policy. I am skeptical that such rent-seeking activities are the reason why inequality has risen in recent decades, but I would support attempts to reduce whatever rent-seeking does occur.

An especially important and particularly difficult case is the finance industry, where many hefty compensation packages can be found. On the one hand, there is no doubt that this sector plays a crucial role. Those who work in commercial banks, investment banks, hedge funds, and other financial firms are in charge of allocating capital and risk, as well as providing liquidity. They decide, in a decentralized and competitive way, which firms and industries need to shrink and which will be encouraged to grow. It makes sense that a nation would allocate many of its most talented and thus highly compensated individuals to this activity. On the other hand, some of what occurs in financial firms does smack of rent-seeking: when a high-frequency trader figures out a way to respond to news a fraction of a second faster than a competitor, the vast personal reward may well exceed the social value of what is produced. Devising a legal and regulatory framework to ensure that we get the right kind and amount of financial activity is a difficult task. While the solution may well affect the degree of equality and the incomes of the 1 percent, the issue is primarily one of efficiency. A well-functioning economy needs the correct allocation of talent. The last thing we need is for the next Steve Jobs to forgo Silicon Valley in order to join the high-frequency traders on Wall Street. That is, we shouldn't be concerned about the next Steve Jobs striking it rich, but we want to make sure he strikes it rich in a socially productive way.

Equality of Opportunity as a Desideratum

Closely related to the claim of inefficiency is concern about inequality of opportunity. Equality of opportunity is often viewed as a social goal in itself, but economists recognize that the failure to achieve such equality would normally lead to inefficiency as well. If some individuals are precluded from pursuing certain paths in life, then they might be unable to contribute fully to growing the economic pie. To be specific, if children from poor families are unable to continue their education because of financial constraints, they do not accumulate the optimal amount of human capital. The outcome from underinvestment in education is both unequal and inefficient.

Measuring the degree of equality of opportunity is difficult. In his book, Stiglitz (2012) proposes a metric: the intergenerational transmission of income. He writes (p. 18), "If America were really a land of opportunity, the life chances of success—of, say, winding up in the top 10 percent—of someone born to a poor or less educated family would be the same as those of someone born to a rich, well-educated, and well-connected family." In other words, under this definition of equality of opportunity, people's earnings would be uncorrelated with those of their parents. Needless to say, in the data, that is not at all the case, which leads Stiglitz to conclude that we are falling short of providing equal opportunity.

Yet the issue cannot be settled so easily, because the intergenerational transmission of income has many causes beyond unequal opportunity. In particular, parents and children share genes, a fact that would lead to intergenerational persistence in income even in a world of equal opportunities. IQ, for example, has been widely studied, and it has a large degree of heritability. Smart parents are more likely to have smart children, and their greater intelligence will be reflected, on average, in higher incomes. Of course, IQ is only one dimension of talent, but it is easy to believe that other dimensions, such as self-control, ability to focus, and interpersonal skills, have a degree of genetic heritability as well.

This is not to say that we live in a world of genetic determinism, for surely we do not. But it would be a mistake to go to the other extreme and presume no genetic transmission of economic outcomes. A recent survey of the small but growing field of genoeconomics by Benjamin et al. (2012) reports, "Twin studies suggest that economic outcomes and preferences, once corrected for measurement error, appear to be about as heritable as many medical conditions and personality traits." Similarly, in his study of the life outcomes of adopted children, Sacerdote (2007) writes, "While educational attainment and income are frequently the focus of economic studies, these are among the outcomes least affected by differences in family environment." (He reports that family background exerts a stronger influence on social variables, such as drinking behavior.) This evidence suggests that it is implausible to interpret generational persistence in income as simply a failure of society to provide equal opportunities. Indeed, Sacerdote estimates (in his table 5) that while 33 percent of the variance of family income is explained by genetic heritability, only 11 percent is explained by the family environment. The remaining 56 percent includes environmental factors unrelated to family. If this 11 percent figure is approximately correct, it suggests that we are not far from a plausible definition of equality of opportunity—that is, being raised by the right family does give a person a leg up in life, but family environment accounts for only a small percentage of the variation in economic outcomes compared with genetic inheritance and environmental factors unrelated to family.

To the extent that our society deviates from the ideal of equality of opportunity, it is probably best to focus our attention on the left tail of the income distribution rather than on the right tail. Poverty entails a variety of socioeconomic maladies, and it is easy to believe that children raised in such circumstances do not receive the right investments in human capital. By contrast, the educational and career opportunities available to children of the top 1 percent are, I believe, not very different from those available to the middle class. My view here is shaped by personal experience. I was raised in a middle-class family; neither of my parents were college graduates. My own children are being raised by parents with both more money and more education. Yet I do not see my children as having significantly better opportunities than I had at their age.

In the end, I am led to conclude that concern about income inequality, and especially growth in incomes of the top 1 percent, cannot be founded primarily on concern about inefficiency and inequality of opportunity. If the growing incomes of the rich are to be a focus of public policy, it must be because income inequality is a problem in and of itself.

The Big Tradeoff

In the title of his celebrated book, Arthur Okun (1975) told us that the "big tradeoff" that society faces is between equality and efficiency. We can use the government's system of taxes and transfers to move income from the rich to the poor, but that system is a "leaky bucket." Some of the money is lost as it is moved. This leak should not stop us from trying to redistribute, Okun argued, because we value equality. But because we are also concerned about efficiency, the leak will stop us before we fully equalize economic resources.

The formal framework that modern economists use to address this issue is that proposed by Mirrlees (1971). In the standard Mirrlees model, individuals get utility from consumption C and disutility from providing work effort L. They differ only according to their productivity W. In the absence of government redistribution, each person's consumption would be WL. Those with higher productivity would have higher consumption, higher utility, and lower marginal utility.

The government is then introduced as a benevolent social planner with the goal of maximizing total utility in society (or, sometimes, a more general social welfare function that could depend nonlinearly on individual utilities). The social planner wants to move economic resources from those with high productivity and low marginal utility to those with lower productivity and higher marginal utility. Yet this redistribution is hard to accomplish, because the government is assumed to be unable to observe productivity W; instead, it observes only income WL, the product of productivity and effort. If it redistributes income too much, high-productivity individuals will start to act as if they are low-productivity individuals. Public policymakers are thus forced to forgo the first-best egalitarian outcome for a second-best incentive-compatible solution. Like a government armed with Okun's leaky bucket, the Mirrleesian social planner redistributes to some degree but also allows some inequality to remain.

If this framework is adopted, then the debate over redistribution turns to questions about key parameters. In particular, optimal redistribution depends on the degree to which work effort responds to incentives. If the supply of effort is completely inelastic, then the bucket has no leak, and the social planner can reach the egalitarian outcome. If the elasticity is small, the social planner can come close. But if work effort responds substantially to incentives, then the bucket is more like a sieve, and the social planner should attempt little or no redistribution. Thus, much debate among economists about optimal redistribution centers on the elasticity of labor supply.

Even if one is willing to accept the utilitarian premise of this framework, there is good reason to be suspicious of particular numerical results that follow from it. When researchers implement the Mirrlees model, they typically assume, as Mirrlees did, that all individuals have the same preferences. People are assumed to differ only in their productivity. For purposes of illustrative theory, that assumption is fine, but it is also false. Incomes differ in part because people have different tastes regarding consumption, leisure, and job attributes. Acknowledging variation in preferences weakens the case for redistribution (Lockwood and Weinzierl 2012). For example, many economics professors could have pursued higher-income career paths as business economists, software engineers, or corporate lawyers. That they chose to take some of their compensation in the form of personal and intellectual freedom rather than cold cash is a personal lifestyle choice, not a reflection of innate productivity. Those who made the opposite choice may have done so because they get greater utility from income. A utilitarian social planner will want to allocate greater income to these individuals, even apart from any incentive effects.

Another problem with the Mirrlees framework as typically implemented is that it takes a simplistic approach to tax incidence. Any good introductory student of economics knows that when a good or service is taxed, the buyer and seller share the burden. Yet in the Mirrlees framework, when an individual's labor income is taxed, only the seller of the services is worse off. In essence, the demand for labor services is assumed to be infinitely elastic. A more general set of assumptions would acknowledge that the burden of the tax is spread more broadly to buyers of those services (and perhaps to sellers of complementary inputs as well). In this more realistic setting, tax policy would be a less well-targeted tool for redistributing economic well-being.

The harder and perhaps deeper question is whether the government's policy toward redistribution is best viewed as being based on a benevolent social planner with utilitarian preferences. That is, did Okun and Mirrlees provide economists with the right starting point for thinking about this issue? I believe there are good reasons to doubt this model from the get-go.

The Uneasy Case for Utilitarianism

For economists, the utilitarian approach to income distribution comes naturally. After all, utilitarians and economists share an intellectual tradition: early utilitarians, such as John Stuart Mill, were also among the early economists. Also, utilitarianism seems to extend the economist's model of individual decision making to the societal level. Indeed, once one adopts the political philosophy of utilitarianism, running a society becomes yet another problem of constrained optimization. Despite its natural appeal (to economists, at least), the utilitarian approach is fraught with problems.

One classic problem is the interpersonal comparability of utility. We can infer an individual's utility function from the choices that individual makes when facing varying prices and levels of income. But from this revealed-preference perspective, utility is not inherently measurable, and it is impossible to compare utilities across people. Perhaps advances in neuroscience will someday lead to an objective measure of happiness, but as of now, there is no scientific way to establish whether the marginal dollar consumed by one person produces more or less utility than the marginal dollar consumed by a neighbor.

Another more concrete problem is the geographic scope of the analysis. Usually, analyses of optimal income redistribution are conducted at the national level. But there is nothing inherent in utilitarianism that suggests such a limitation. Some of the largest income disparities are observed between nations. If a national system of taxes and transfers is designed to move resources from Palm Beach, Florida, to Detroit, Michigan, shouldn't a similar international system move resources from the United States and Western Europe to sub-Saharan Africa? Many economists do support increased foreign aid, but as far as I know, no one has proposed marginal tax rates on rich nations as high as the marginal tax rates imposed on rich individuals. Our reluctance to apply utilitarianism at the global level should give us pause when applying it at the national level.

In a 2010 paper, Matthew Weinzierl and I emphasized another reason to be wary of utilitarianism: it recommends a greater use of "tags" than most people feel comfortable with. As Akerlof (1978) pointed out, if the social planner can observe individual characteristics that are correlated with productivity, then an optimal tax system should use that information, in addition to income, in determining an individual's tax liability. The more the tax system is based on such fixed characteristics rather than income, the less it will distort incentives. Weinzierl and I showed that one such tag is height. Indeed, the correlation between height and wages is sufficiently strong that the optimal tax on height is quite large. Similarly, according to the utilitarian calculus, the tax system should also make a person's tax liability a function of race, gender, and perhaps many other exogenous characteristics. Of course, few people would embrace the idea of a height tax, and Weinzierl and I did not offer it as a serious policy proposal. Even fewer people would be comfortable with a race-based income tax (although Alesina, Ichin, and Karabarbounis, 2011, propose in earnest a gender-based tax). Yet these implications cannot just be ignored. If you take from a theory only the conclusions you like and discard the rest, you are using the theory as a drunkard uses a lamp post—for support rather than illumination. If utilitarianism takes policy in directions that most people don't like, then perhaps it is not a sound foundation for thinking about redistribution and public policy.

Finally, in thinking about whether the utilitarian model really captures our moral intuitions, it is worth thinking for a moment about the first-best outcome for a utilitarian social planner. Suppose, in contrast to the Mirrlees model, the social planner could directly observe productivity. In this case, the planner would not need to worry about incentives, but could set taxes and transfers based directly on productivity. The optimal policy would equalize the marginal utility of consumption across individuals; if the utility function is assumed to be additively separable in consumption and leisure, this means everyone consumes the same amount. But because some people are more productive than others, equalizing leisure would not be optimal. Instead, the social planner would require more-productive individuals to work more. Thus, in the utilitarian first-best allocation, the more-productive members of society would work more and consume the same as everyone else. In other words, in the allocation that maximizes society's total utility, the less-productive individuals would enjoy a higher utility than the more productive.

Is this really the outcome we would want society to achieve if it could? A true utilitarian would follow the logic of the model and say "yes." Yet this outcome does not strike me as the ideal toward which we should aspire, and I suspect most people would agree. Even young children have an innate sense that merit should be rewarded (Kanngiesser and Warneken 2012)—and I doubt it is only because they are worried about the incentive effects of not doing so. If I am right, then we need a model of optimal government taxes and transfers that departs significantly from conventional utilitarian social planning.

Listening to the Left

In recent years, the left side of the political spectrum has focused much attention on the rising incomes of the top 1 percent. This includes President Obama's proposals to raises taxes on higher incomes, the Occupy Wall Street movement, and a rash of books about economic inequality. Even though I don't share the Left's policy conclusions, I find it is worthwhile to listen carefully to their arguments to discern what set of philosophical principles and empirical claims underlie their concerns.

It is, I believe, hard to square the rhetoric of the Left with the economist's standard framework. Someone favoring greater redistribution along the lines of Okun and Mirrlees would argue as follows: "The rich earn higher incomes because they contribute more to society than others do. However, because of diminishing marginal utility, they don't get much value from their last few dollars of consumption. So we should take some of their income away and give it to less-productive members of society. While this policy would cause the most productive members to work less, shrinking the size of the economic pie, that is a cost we should bear, to some degree, to increase utility for society's less-productive citizens."

Surely, that phrasing of the argument would not animate the Occupy crowd! So let's consider the case that the Left makes in favor of greater income redistribution. There are three broad classes of arguments.

The first is the suggestion that the tax system we now have is regressive. Most famously, during the presidential campaign of 2008, at a fund-raiser for Hillary Clinton, the billionaire investor Warren E. Buffett said that the rich were not paying enough. Mr. Buffett used himself as an example. He asserted that his taxes in the previous year equaled only 17.7 percent of his taxable income, while his receptionist paid about 30 percent of her income in taxes (Tse 2007). In 2011, President Obama proposed the "Buffett rule," which would require taxpayers with income over a million dollars to pay at least 30 percent of their income in federal income taxes.

There are, however, good reasons to be skeptical of Buffett's calculations. If his receptionist was truly a middle-income taxpayer, then to get her tax rate to 30 percent, he most likely added the payroll tax to the income tax. Fair enough. But for Buffett's tax rate to be only 17.7 percent, most of his income was likely dividends and capital gains, and his calculation had to ignore the fact that this capital income was already taxed at the corporate level. A complete accounting requires aggregating not only all taxes on labor income but also all taxes on capital income.

The Congressional Budget Office (2012) does precisely that when it calculates the distribution of the federal tax burden—and it paints a very different picture than did Buffett's anecdote. In 2009, the most recent year available, the poorest fifth of the population, with average annual income of $23,500, paid only 1.0 percent of its income in federal taxes. The middle fifth, with income of $64,300, paid 11.1 percent. And the top fifth, with income of $223,500, paid 23.2 percent. The richest 1 percent, with an average income of $1,219,700, paid 28.9 percent of its income to the federal government. To be sure, some taxpayers aggressively plan to minimize taxes, and this may result in some individual cases where those with high incomes pay relatively little in federal taxes. But the CBO data make clear that these cases are the exceptions. As a general rule, the existing federal tax code is highly progressive.

A second type of argument from the Left is that the incomes of the rich do not reflect their contributions to society. In the standard competitive labor market, a person's earnings equal the value of his or her marginal productivity. But there are various reasons that real life might deviate from this classical benchmark. If, for example, a person's high income results from political rent-seeking rather than producing a valuable product, the outcome is likely to be both inefficient and widely viewed as inequitable. Steve Jobs getting rich from producing the iPod and Pixar movies does not produce much ire among the public. A Wall Street executive benefiting from a taxpayer-financed bailout does.

The key issue is the extent to which the high incomes of the top 1 percent reflect high productivity rather than some market imperfection. This question is one of positive economics, but unfortunately not one that is easily answered. My own reading of the evidence is that most of the very wealthy get that way by making substantial economic contributions, not by gaming the system or taking advantage of some market failure or the political process. Take the example of pay for chief executive officers. Without doubt, CEOs are paid handsomely, and their pay has grown over time relative to that of the average worker. Commentators on this phenomenon sometimes suggest that this high pay reflects the failure of corporate boards of directors to do their job. Rather than representing shareholders, the argument goes, boards are too cozy with the CEOs and pay them more than they are worth to their organizations. Yet this argument fails to explain the behavior of closely-held corporations. A private equity group with a controlling interest in a firm does not face the alleged principal–agent problem between shareholders and boards, and yet these closely-held firms also pay their CEOs handsomely. Indeed, Kaplan (2012) reports that over the past three decades, executive pay in closely-held firms has outpaced that in public companies. Cronqvist and Fahlenbrach (2013) find that when public companies go private, the CEOs tend to get paid more rather than less in both base salaries and bonuses. In light of these facts, the most natural explanation of high CEO pay is that the value of a good CEO is extraordinarily high (a conclusion that, incidentally, is consistent with the model of CEO pay proposed by Gabaix and Landier 2008).

A third argument that the Left uses to advocate greater taxation of those with higher incomes is that the rich benefit from the physical, legal, and social infrastructure that government provides and, therefore, should contribute to supporting it. As one prominent example, President Obama (2012) said in a speech, "If you were successful, somebody along the line gave you some help. There was a great teacher somewhere in your life. Somebody helped to create this unbelievable American system that we have that allowed you to thrive. Somebody invested in roads and bridges. If you've got a business—you didn't build that. Somebody else made that happen. The Internet didn't get invented on its own. Government research created the Internet so that all the companies could make money off the Internet. The point is that when we succeed, we succeed because of our individual initiative, but also because we do things together."

In the language of traditional public finance, President Obama was relying less on the ability-to-pay principle and more on the benefits principle. That is, higher taxation of the rich is not being justified by the argument that their marginal utility of consumption is low, as it is in the frameworks of Okun and Mirrlees. Rather, higher taxation is being justified by the claim that the rich achieved their wealth in large measure because of the goods and services the government provides and therefore have a responsibility to finance those goods and services.

This line of argument raises the empirical question of how large the benefit of government infrastructure is. The average value is surely very high, as lawless anarchy would leave the rich (as well as most everyone else) much worse off. But like other inputs into the production process, government infrastructure should be valued at the margin, where the valuation is harder to discern. As I pointed out earlier, the average person in the top 1 percent pays more than one-quarter of income in federal taxes, and about one-third if state and local taxes are included. Why isn't that enough to compensate for the value of government infrastructure?

A relevant fact here is that, over time, an increasing share of government spending has been for transfer payments, rather than for purchases of goods and services. Government has grown as a percentage of the economy not because it is providing more and better roads, more and better legal institutions, and more and better educational systems. Rather, government has increasingly used its power to tax to take from Peter to pay Paul. Discussions of the benefits of government services should not distract from this fundamental truth.

In the end, the Left's arguments for increased redistribution are valid in principle but dubious in practice. If the current tax system were regressive, or if the incomes of the top 1 percent were much greater than their economic contributions, or if the rich enjoyed government services in excess of what they pay in taxes, then the case for increasing the top tax rate would indeed be strong. But there is no compelling reason to believe that any of these premises holds true.

The Need for an Alternative Philosophical Framework

A common thought experiment used to motivate income redistribution is to imagine a situation in which individuals are in an "original position" behind a "veil of ignorance" (as in Rawls 1971). This original position occurs in a hypothetical time before we are born, without the knowledge of whether we will be lucky or unlucky, talented or less talented, rich or poor. A risk-averse person in such a position would want to buy insurance against the possibility of being born into a less-fortunate station in life. In this view, governmental income redistribution is an enforcement of the social insurance contract to which people would have voluntarily agreed in this original position.

Yet take this logic a bit further. In this original position, people would be concerned about more than being born rich or poor. They would also be concerned about health outcomes. Consider kidneys, for example. Most people walk around with two healthy kidneys, one of which they do not need. A few people get kidney disease that leaves them without a functioning kidney, a condition that often cuts life short. A person in the original position would surely sign an insurance contract that guarantees him at least one working kidney. That is, he would be willing to risk being a kidney donor if he is lucky, in exchange for the assurance of being a transplant recipient if he is unlucky. Thus, the same logic of social insurance that justifies income redistribution similarly justifies government-mandated kidney donation.

No doubt, if such a policy were ever seriously considered, most people would oppose it. A person has a right to his own organs, they would argue, and a thought experiment about an original position behind a veil of ignorance does not vitiate that right. But if that is the case, and I believe it is, it undermines the thought experiment more generally. If imagining a hypothetical social insurance contract signed in an original position does not supersede the right of a person to his own organs, why should it supersede the right of a person to the fruits of his own labor?

An alternative to the social insurance view of the income distribution is what, in Mankiw (2010), I called a "just deserts" perspective. According to this view, people should receive compensation congruent with their contributions. If the economy were described by a classical competitive equilibrium without any externalities or public goods, then every individual would earn the value of his or her own marginal product, and there would be no need for government to alter the resulting income distribution. The role of government arises as the economy departs from this classical benchmark. Pigovian taxes and subsidies are necessary to correct externalities, and progressive income taxes can be justified to finance public goods based on the benefits principle. Transfer payments to the poor have a role as well, because fighting poverty can be viewed as a public good (Thurow 1971).

This alternative perspective on the income distribution is a radical departure from the utilitarian perspective that has long influenced economists, including Okun and Mirrlees. But it is not entirely new. It harkens back about a century to the tradition of "just taxation" suggested by Knut Wicksell (1896, translated 1958) and Erik Lindahl (1919, translated 1958). More important, I believe it is more consistent with our innate moral intuitions. Indeed, many of the arguments of the Left discussed earlier are easier to reconcile with the just-deserts theory than they are with utilitarianism. My disagreement with the Left lies not in the nature of their arguments, but rather in the factual basis for their conclusions.

The political philosophy one adopts naturally influences the kind of economic questions that are relevant for determining optimal policy. The utilitarian perspective leads to questions such as: How rapidly does marginal utility of consumption decline? What is the distribution of productivity? How much do taxes influence work effort? The just-deserts perspective focuses instead on other questions: Do the high incomes of the top 1 percent reflect extraordinary productivity, or some type of market failure? How are the benefits of public goods distributed across the income distribution? I have my own conjectures about the answers to these latter questions, and I have suggested them throughout this essay, but I am the first to admit that they are tentative. Fortunately, these are positive questions to which future economic research may provide more definitive answers.

To highlight the difference between these approaches, consider how each would address the issue of the top tax rate. In particular, why shouldn't we raise the rate on high incomes to 75 percent, as France's President Hollande has recently proposed, or to 91 percent, where it was through much of the 1950s in the United States? A utilitarian social planner would say that perhaps we should and would refrain from doing so only if the adverse incentive effects were too great. From the just-deserts perspective, such confiscatory tax rates are wrong, even ignoring any incentive effects. By this view, using the force of government to seize such a large share of the fruits of someone else's labor is unjust, even if the taking is sanctioned by a majority of the citizenry.

In the final analysis, we should not be surprised when opinions about income redistribution vary. Economists can turn to empirical methods to estimate key parameters, but no amount of applied econometrics can bridge this philosophical divide. I hope my ruminations in this essay have convinced some readers to see the situation from a new angle. But at the very least, I trust that these thoughts offer a vivid reminder that fundamentally normative conclusions cannot rest on positive economics alone.

References

Akerlof, George A. 1978. "The Economics of 'Tagging' as Applied to the Optimal Income Tax, Welfare Programs, and Manpower Planning." *American Economic Review* 68(1): 8–19.

Alesina, Alberto, Andrea Ichin, and Loukas Karabarbounis, 2011. "Gender-Based Taxation and the Division of Family Chores." *American Economic Journal: Economic Policy* 3(2): 1–40.

Benjamin, Daniel J., David Cesarini, Christopher F. Chabris, Edward L. Glaeser, David I. Laibson, Vilmundur Guðnason, Tamara B. Harris, Lenore J. Launer, Shaun Purcell, Albert Vernon Smith, Magnus Johannesson, Patrik K. E. Magnusson, Jonathan P. Beauchamp, Nicholas A. Christakis, Craig S. Atwood, Benjamin Hebert, Jeremy Freese, Robert M. Hauser, Taissa S. Hauser, Alexander Grankvist, Christina M. Hultman, and Paul Lichtenstein. 2012. "The Promises and Pitfalls of Genoeconomics." *Annual Review of Economics* vol. 4, pp. 627–62.

Brynjolfsson, Erik, and Andrew McAfee. 2011. *Race Against the Machine.* Lexington, MA: Digital Frontier Press.

Congressional Budget Office. 2012. "The Distribution of Household Income and Federal Taxes, 2008 and 2009." July. Available at: http://www.cbo .gov/publication/43373.

Cronqvist, Henrik, and Rudiger Frahlenbrach. 2013. "CEO Contract Design: How Do Strong Principals Do It?" *Journal of Financial Economics* 108(3): 659–74.

Gabaix, Xavier, and Augustin Landier. 2008. "Why Has CEO Pay Increased So Much?" *Quarterly Journal of Economics* 123(1): 49–100.

Goldin, Claudia, and Lawrence F. Katz. 2008. *The Race between Education and Technology.* Cambridge, MA Harvard University Press.

Kanngiesser Patricia, and Felix Warneken. 2012. "Young Children Consider Merit when Sharing Resources with Others." *PLoS ONE* 7(8): e43979.

Kaplan, Steven N. 2012. "Executive Compensation and Corporate Governance in the U.S.: Perceptions, Facts, and Challenges." NBER Working Paper 18395.

Lindahl, Erik. 1958. "Just Taxation—A Positive Solution." In *Classics in the Theory of Public Finance,* edited by Richard Musgrave and Alan Peacock, 98–123. London: Macmillan.

Lockwood, Benjamin, and Matthew Weinzierl. 2012. *"De Gustibus non est Taxandum:* Theory and Evidence on Preference Heterogeneity and Redistribution." Harvard Business School Working Paper 12-063.

Mankiw, N. Gregory. 2010. "Spreading the Wealth Around: Reflections Inspired by Joe the Plumber." *Eastern Economic Journal* 36(3): 285–98.

Mankiw, N. Gregory, and Matthew Weinzierl. 2010. "The Optimal Taxation of Height: A Case Study of Utilitarian Income Redistribution." *American Economic Journal: Economic Policy* 2(1): 155–76.

Mirrlees, James A. 1971. "An Exploration in the Theory of Optimal Income Taxation." *Review of Economic Studies* 38(2): 175–208.

Obama, Barack. 2012. "Remarks by the President at a Campaign Event in Roanoke, Virginia." July 13. http://www.whitehouse.gov/the-press-office/2012/07/13/remarks-president-campaign-event-roanoke-virginia.

Okun, Arthur. 1975. *Equality and Efficiency: The Big Tradeoff.* Brookings Institution.

Piketty, Thomas, and Emmanuel Saez. 2003. "Income Inequality in the United States, 1913–1998." *Quarterly Journal of Economics* 118(1): 1–39. (Tables and figures updated to 2011 at Saez's website: http://elsa.berkeley.edu/~saez/.)

Rawls, John. 1971. *A Theory of Justice.* Belknap Press.

Sacerdote, Bruce. 2007. "How Large Are the Effects from Changes in Family Environment? A Study of Korean American Adoptees." *Quarterly Journal of Economics* 122 (1): 119–157.

Stiglitz, Joseph E. 2012. *The Price of Inequality: How Today's Divided Society Endangers Our Future.* W. W. Norton and Company.

Thurow, Lester C. 1971. "The Income Distribution as a Pure Public Good." *Quarterly Journal of Economics* 85(2): 327–36.

Tse, Tomoeh Murakami. 2007. "Buffett Slams Tax System Disparities." *Washington Post,* June 27.

Wicksell, Knut. 1958. "A New Principle of Just Taxation." In *Classics in the Theory of Public Finance*, edited by Richard Musgrave and Alan Peacock, 72–118. London: Macmillan.

Thomas Piketty,
Capital in the Twenty-First Century (2014)*

Introduction

"Social distinctions can be based only on common utility."
—Declaration of the Rights of Man and the Citizen, article 1, 1789

The distribution of wealth is one of today's most widely discussed and controversial issues. But what do we really know about its evolution over the long term? Do the dynamics of private capital accumulation inevitably lead to the concentration of wealth in ever fewer hands, as Karl Marx believed in the nineteenth century? Or do the balancing forces of growth, competition, and technological progress lead in later stages of development to reduced inequality and greater harmony among the classes, as Simon Kuznets thought in the twentieth century? What do we really know about how wealth and income have evolved since the eighteenth century, and what lessons can we derive from that knowledge for the century now under way?

These are the questions I attempt to answer in this book. Let me say at once that the answers contained herein are imperfect and incomplete. But they are based on much more extensive historical and comparative data than were available to previous researchers, data covering three centuries and more than twenty countries, as well as on a new theoretical framework that affords a deeper understanding of the underlying mechanisms. Modern economic growth and the diffusion of knowledge have made it possible to avoid the Marxist apocalypse but have not modified the deep structures of capital and inequality—or in any case not as much as one might have imagined in the optimistic decades following World War II. When the rate of return on capital exceeds the rate of growth of output and income, as it did in the nineteenth century and seems quite likely to do again in the twenty-first, capitalism automatically generates arbitrary and unsustainable inequalities that radically undermine the meritocratic values on which democratic societies are based. There are nevertheless ways democracy can regain control over capitalism and ensure that the general interest takes precedence over private interests, while preserving economic openness and avoiding protectionist and nationalist reactions. The policy recommendations I propose later in the book tend in this direction. They are based on lessons derived from historical experience, of which what follows is essentially a narrative.

A Debate without Data?

Intellectual and political debate about the distribution of wealth has long been based on an abundance of prejudice and a paucity of fact.

To be sure, it would be a mistake to underestimate the importance of the intuitive knowledge that everyone acquires about contemporary wealth and income levels, even in the absence of any theoretical framework or statistical analysis. Film and literature, nineteenth-century novels especially, are full of detailed information about the relative wealth and living standards of different social groups, and especially about the deep structure of inequality, the way it is justified, and its impact on individual lives. Indeed, the novels of Jane Austen and Honoré de Balzac paint striking portraits of the distribution of wealth in Britain and France between 1790 and 1830. Both novelists were intimately acquainted with the hierarchy of wealth in their respective societies. They grasped the hidden contours of wealth and its inevitable implications for the lives of men and women, including their marital strategies and personal hopes and disappointments. These and other novelists depicted the effects of inequality with a verisimilitude and evocative power that no statistical or theoretical analysis can match.

Indeed, the distribution of wealth is too important an issue to be left to economists, sociologists, historians, and philosophers. It is of interest to everyone, and that is a good thing. The concrete, physical reality of inequality is visible to the naked eye and naturally inspires sharp but contradictory political judgments. Peasant and noble, worker and factory owner, waiter and banker: each has his or her own unique vantage point and sees important aspects of how other people live and what relations of power and domination exist between social groups, and these observations shape each person's judgment of what is and is not just. Hence there will always be a fundamentally subjective and psychological dimension to inequality, which inevitably gives rise to political conflict that no purportedly scientific analysis can alleviate. Democracy will never be supplanted by a republic of experts—and that is a very good thing.

Nevertheless, the distribution question also deserves to be studied in a systematic and methodical fashion. Without precisely defined sources, methods, and concepts, it is possible to see everything and its opposite. Some people believe that inequality is always increasing and that the world is by definition always becoming more unjust. Others believe that inequality is naturally decreasing, or that harmony comes about automatically, and that in any case nothing should be done that might risk disturbing this happy equilibrium. Given this dialogue of the deaf, in which each camp justifies its own intellectual laziness by pointing to the laziness of the other, there is a role for research that is at least systematic and methodical if not fully scientific. Expert analysis will never put an end to the violent political conflict that inequality inevitably instigates. Social scientific research is and always will be tentative and imperfect. It does not claim to transform economics, sociology, and history into exact sciences. But by patiently searching for facts and patterns and calmly analyzing the economic, social, and political mechanisms that might explain them, it can inform democratic debate and focus attention on the right questions. It can help to redefine the terms of debate, unmask certain preconceived or fraudulent notions, and subject all positions to constant critical scrutiny. In my view, this is the role that intellectuals, including social scientists, should play, as citizens like any other but with the good fortune to have more time than others to devote themselves to study (and even to be paid for it—a signal privilege).

[...]

The Major Results of This Study

What are the major conclusions to which these novel historical sources have led me? The first is that one should be wary of any economic determinism in regard to inequalities of wealth and income. The history of the distribution of wealth has always been deeply political, and it cannot be reduced to purely economic mechanisms. In particular, the reduction of inequality that took place in most developed countries between 1910 and 1950 was above all a consequence of war and of policies adopted to cope with the shocks of war. Similarly, the resurgence of inequality after 1980 is due largely to the political shifts of the past several decades, especially in regard to taxation and finance. The history of inequality is shaped by the way economic, social, and political actors view what is just and what is not, as well as by the relative power of those actors and the collective choices that result. It is the joint product of all relevant actors combined.

The second conclusion, which is the heart of the book, is that the dynamics of wealth distribution reveal powerful mechanisms pushing alternately toward convergence and divergence. Furthermore, there is no natural, spontaneous process to prevent destabilizing, inegalitarian forces from prevailing permanently.

Consider first the mechanisms pushing toward convergence, that is, toward reduction and compression of inequalities. The main forces for convergence are the diffusion of knowledge and investment in training and skills. The law of supply and demand, as well as the mobility of capital and labor, which is a variant of that law, may always tend toward convergence as well, but the influence of this economic law is less powerful than the diffusion of knowledge and skill and is frequently ambiguous or contradictory in its implications. Knowledge and skill diffusion is the key to overall productivity growth as well as the reduction of inequality both within and between countries. We see this at present in the advances made by a number of previously poor countries, led by China. These emergent economies are now in the process of catching up with the advanced ones. By adopting the modes of production of the rich countries and acquiring skills comparable to those found elsewhere, the less developed countries have leapt forward in productivity and increased their national incomes. The technological convergence process may be abetted by open borders for trade, but it is fundamentally a process of the diffusion and sharing of knowledge—the public good par excellence—rather than a market mechanism.

From a strictly theoretical standpoint, other forces pushing toward greater equality might exist. One might, for example, assume that production technologies tend over time to require greater skills on the part of workers, so that labor's share of income will rise as capital's share falls: one might call this the "rising human capital hypothesis." In other words, the progress of technological rationality is supposed to lead automatically to the triumph of human capital over financial capital and real estate, capable managers over fat cat stockholders, and skill over nepotism. Inequalities would thus become more meritocratic and less static (though not necessarily smaller): economic rationality would then in some sense automatically give rise to democratic rationality.

Another optimistic belief, which is current at the moment, is the idea that "class warfare" will automatically give way, owing to the recent increase in life expectancy, to "generational warfare" (which is less divisive because everyone is first young and then old). Put differently, this inescapable biological fact is supposed to imply that the accumulation and distribution of wealth no longer presage an inevitable clash between dynasties of rentiers and dynasties owning nothing but their labor power. The governing logic is rather one of saving over the life cycle: people accumulate wealth when young in order to provide for their old age. Progress in medicine together with improved living conditions has therefore, it is argued, totally transformed the very essence of capital.

Unfortunately, these two optimistic beliefs (the human capital hypothesis and the substitution of generational conflict for class warfare) are largely illusory. Transformations of this sort are both logically possible and to some extent real, but their influence is far less consequential than one might imagine. There is little evidence that labor's share in national income has increased significantly in a very long time: "nonhuman" capital seems almost as indispensable in the twenty-first century as it was in the eighteenth or nineteenth, and there is no reason why it may not become even more so. Now as in the past, moreover, inequalities of wealth exist primarily within age cohorts, and inherited wealth comes close to being as decisive at the beginning of the twenty-first century as it was in the age of Balzac's *Père Goriot*. Over a long period of time, the main force in favor of greater equality has been the diffusion of knowledge and skills.

Forces of Convergence, Forces of Divergence

The crucial fact is that no matter how potent a force the diffusion of knowledge and skills may be, especially in promoting convergence between countries, it can nevertheless be thwarted and overwhelmed by powerful forces pushing in the opposite direction, toward greater inequality. It is obvious that lack of adequate investment in training can exclude entire social groups from the benefits of economic growth. Growth can harm some groups while benefiting others (witness the recent displacement of workers in the more advanced economies by workers in China). In short, the principal force for convergence—the diffusion of knowledge—is only partly natural and spontaneous. It also depends in large part on educational policies, access to training and to the acquisition of appropriate skills, and associated institutions.

I will pay particular attention in this study to certain worrisome forces of divergence—particularly worrisome in that they can exist even in a world where there is adequate investment in skills and where all the conditions of "market efficiency" (as economists understand that term) appear to be satisfied. What are these forces of divergence? First, top earners can quickly separate themselves from the rest by a wide margin (although the problem to date remains relatively localized).

More important, there is a set of forces of divergence associated with the process of accumulation and concentration of wealth when growth is weak and the return on capital is high. This second process is potentially more destabilizing than the first, and it no doubt represents the principal threat to an equal distribution of wealth over the long run.

To cut straight to the heart of the matter: in Figures I.I and I.2 I show two basic patterns that I will try to explain in what follows. Each graph represents the importance of one of these divergent processes. Both graphs depict "U-shaped curves," that is, a period of decreasing inequality followed by one of increasing inequality. One might assume that the realities the two graphs represent are similar. In fact they are not. The phenomena underlying the various curves are quite different and involve distinct economic, social, and political processes. Furthermore, the curve in Figure I.I represents income inequality in the United States, while the curves in Figure I.2 depict the capital/income ratio in several European countries (Japan, though not shown, is similar). It is not out of the question that the two forces of divergence will ultimately come together in the twenty-first century. This has already happened to some extent and may yet become a global phenomenon, which could lead to levels of inequality never before seen, as well as to a radically new structure of inequality. Thus far, however, these striking patterns reflect two distinct underlying phenomena.

The US curve, shown in Figure I.I, indicates the share of the upper decile of the income hierarchy in US national income from 1910 to 2010. It is nothing more than an extension of the historical series Kuznets established for the period 1913–1948. The top decile claimed as much as 45–50 percent of national income in the 1910s–1920s before dropping to 30–35 percent by the end of the 1940s. Inequality then stabilized

FIGURE I.I Income inequality in the United States, 1910–2010

The top decile share in US national income dropped from 45–50 percent in the 1910s–1920s to less than 35 percent in the 1950s (this is the fall documented by Kuznets); it then rose from less than 35 percent in the 1970s to 45–50 percent in the 2000s–2010s.

Sources and series: see piketty.pse.ens.fr/capital21c.

at that level from 1950 to 1970. We subsequently see a rapid rise in inequality in the 1980s, until by 2000 we have returned to a level on the order of 45–50 percent of national income. The magnitude of the change is impressive. It is natural to ask how far such a trend might continue.

I will show that this spectacular increase in inequality largely reflects an unprecedented explosion of very elevated incomes from labor, a veritable separation of the top managers of large firms from the rest of the population. One possible explanation of this is that the skills and productivity of these top managers rose suddenly in relation to those of other workers. Another explanation, which to me seems more plausible and turns out to be much more consistent with the evidence, is that these top managers by and large have the power to set their own remuneration, in some cases without limit and in many cases without any clear relation to their individual productivity, which in any case is very difficult to estimate in a large organization. This phenomenon is seen mainly in the United States and to a lesser degree in Britain, and it may be possible to explain it in terms of the history of social and fiscal norms in those two countries over the past century. The tendency is less marked in other wealthy countries (such as Japan, Germany, France, and other continental European states), but the trend is in the same direction. To expect that the phenomenon will attain the same proportions elsewhere as it has done in the United States would be risky until we have subjected it to a full analysis—which unfortunately is not that simple, given the limits of the available data.

The Fundamental Force for Divergence: r > g

The second pattern, represented in Figure I.2, reflects a divergence mechanism that is in some ways simpler and more transparent and no doubt exerts greater influence on the long-run evolution of the wealth distribution. Figure I.2 shows the total value of private wealth (in real estate, financial assets, and professional capital, net of debt) in Britain, France and Germany, expressed in years of national income, for the period 1870–2010. Note, first of all, the very high level of private wealth in Europe in the late nineteenth century: the total amount of private wealth hovered around six or seven years of national income, which is a lot. It then fell sharply in response to the shocks of the period 1914–1945: the capital/income ratio decreased to just 2 or 3. We then observe a steady rise from 1950 on, a rise so sharp that private fortunes in the early twenty-first century seem to be on the verge of returning to five or six years of national income in both Britain and France. (Private wealth in Germany, which started at a lower level, remains lower, but the upward trend is just as clear.)

This "U-shaped curve" reflects an absolutely crucial transformation, which will figure largely in this study. In particular, I will show that the return of high capital/income ratios over the past few decades can be explained in large part by the return to a regime of relatively slow growth. In slowly growing economies, past wealth naturally takes on disproportionate importance, because it takes only a small flow of new savings to increase the stock of wealth steadily and substantially.

If, moreover, the rate of return on capital remains significantly above the growth rate for an extended period of time (which is more likely when the growth rate is low,

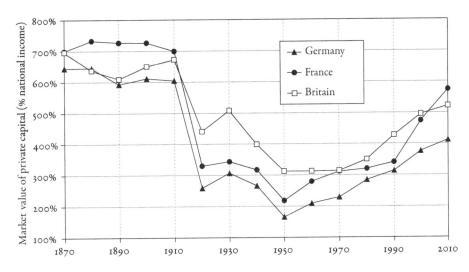

FIGURE I.2 The capital/income ratio in Europe, 1870–2010

Aggregate private wealth was worth about six to seven years of national income in Europe in 1910, between two and three years in 1950, and between four and six years in 2010.

Sources and series: see piketty.pse.ens.fr/capital21c.

though not automatic), then the risk of divergence in the distribution of wealth is very high.

This fundamental inequality, which I will write as $r > g$ (where r stands for the average annual rate of return on capital, including profits, dividends, interest, rents, and other income from capital, expressed as a percentage of its total value, and g stands for the rate of growth of the economy, that is, the annual increase in income or output), will play a crucial role in this book. In a sense, it sums up the overall logic of my conclusions.

When the rate of return on capital significantly exceeds the growth rate of the economy (as it did through much of history until the nineteenth century and as is likely to be the case again in the twenty-first century), then it logically follows that inherited wealth grows faster than output and income. People with inherited wealth need save only a portion of their income from capital to see that capital grow more quickly than the economy as a whole. Under such conditions, it is almost inevitable that inherited wealth will dominate wealth amassed from a lifetime's labor by a wide margin, and the concentration of capital will attain extremely high levels— levels potentially incompatible with the meritocratic values and principles of social justice fundamental to modern democratic societies.

What is more, this basic force for divergence can be reinforced by other mechanisms. For instance, the savings rate may increase sharply with wealth.[1] Or, even more important, the average effective rate of return on capital may be higher when the individual's initial capital endowment is higher (as appears to be increasingly common). The fact that the return on capital is unpredictable and arbitrary, so that wealth can be enhanced in a variety of ways, also poses a challenge to the meritocratic model. Finally, all of these factors can be aggravated by the Ricardian scarcity principle: the high price of real estate or petroleum may contribute to structural divergence.

To sum up what has been said thus far: the process by which wealth is accumulated and distributed contains powerful forces pushing toward divergence, or at any rate toward an extremely high level of inequality. Forces of convergence also exist, and in certain countries at certain times, these may prevail, but the forces of divergence can at any point regain the upper hand, as seems to be happening now, at the beginning of the twenty-first century. The likely decrease in the rate of growth of both the population and the economy in coming decades makes this trend all the more worrisome.

My conclusions are less apocalyptic than those implied by Marx's principle of infinite accumulation and perpetual divergence (since Marx's theory implicitly relies on a strict assumption of zero productivity growth over the long run). In the model I propose, divergence is not perpetual and is only one of several possible future directions for the distribution of wealth. But the possibilities are not heartening. Specifically, it is important to note that the fundamental $r > g$ inequality, the main force of divergence in my theory, has nothing to do with any market imperfection. Quite the contrary: the more perfect the capital market (in the economist's sense), the more likely r is to be greater than g. It is possible to imagine public institutions and policies that would counter the effects of this implacable logic: for instance, a progressive global tax on capital. But establishing such institutions and policies would require a considerable degree of international coordination. It is unfortunately likely that actual responses to the problem—including various nationalist responses—will in practice be far more modest and less effective.

[...]

Note

1 This destabilizing mechanism (the richer one is, the wealthier one gets) worried Kuznets a great deal, and this worry accounts for the title of his 1953 book *Shares of Upper Income Groups in Income and Savings*. But he lacked the historical distance to analyze it fully. This force for divergence was also central to James Meade's classic *Efficiency, Equality, and the Ownership of Property* (London: Allen and Unwin, 1964), and to Atkinson and Harrison, *Distribution of Personal Wealth in Britain,* which in a way was the continuation of Meade's work. Our work follows in the footsteps of these authors.

7

The Digital Platform Economy

How have market institutions shaped the digital platform economy of today? We have already reviewed several distinct perspectives on the nature of innovation. For Adam Smith and for most market liberals, the market provides the primary motivation for innovation. The proverbial bakers seek better ways to bake bread out of their own self-interest. In addition, as Douglass North stresses, property rights generate a powerful incentive for innovation. As the private return (profit) from innovation increases relative to the social return (the benefits to society) due to better-defined and enforced property rights, entrepreneurs have a more powerful motive to innovate. Thus intellectual property rights – patents, copyrights, and trademarks – are critical to innovation. Eric Hobsbawm problematizes the market-liberal view of innovation, stressing that entrepreneurs seek to increase profits, not innovation. So most entrepreneurs will try to squeeze out more profits with existing technology rather than to risk investment in technological advancement to increase productivity.

Mariana Mazzucato brings this debate up to date, arguing that the U.S. government played a critical role in fostering the digital revolution. She directly challenges the market-liberal presumption that the government is sluggish and bureaucratic whereas the business sector is dynamic and innovative. She stresses the government's entrepreneurial role in launching bold programs of research and investment and underwriting the risks that propel breakthrough innovation. She questions the prevalent image of independent entrepreneurs operating out of their garages to produce the technology underpinning this revolution. She notes that the U.S. government funded the research that produced much of the relevant technology, and provided early-stage capital for many of the most successful high-tech firms. She illustrates this argument via a case study of Apple, demonstrating how the government enabled the company to succeed. Specifically, the government provided funds to Apple at an early stage. It drove some of the key technological advances embedded in Apple products by funding research and development and providing a launch market via procurement contracts. And government tax, trade, and technology policies enhanced Apple's ability to compete in global markets.

U.S. government-supported research fostered the exponential increase in computing power from semiconductors, plus key technical advances in transmission, networking, and applications that propelled the digital revolution. Information became a commodity that could be expressed in binary form and transmitted at virtually no cost. The U.S. government "created" the Internet in the sense that the Defense Department's Advanced Research Projects Agency (DARPA) funded the development of the ARPANET, which provided the underlying architecture. The government also promoted the digital revolution in some less obvious ways, such as antitrust policy and regulatory reform. U.S. antitrust policy shaped the information revolution by preventing vertically integrated firms like IBM and AT&T from dominating the electronics sector. This left more room for new entrants and facilitated the bottom-up nature of innovation in the early years of the Internet era. The breakup of AT&T and subsequent pro-competitive regulation also fostered competition in telecommunications. This brought lower communications costs, including flat-rate local service, which enabled venture firms to offer value-added services and household consumers to experiment with new applications at a reasonable cost. These government policies contributed to some of the key features of the digital economy: a breakdown of the hierarchical value chain; greater value creation and technological leadership from upstream industries, such as software and component producers; dynamic innovation by startups in software, data communications, and e-commerce; innovative information technology deployment strategies from large corporate users; and mass experimentation by consumers. Moreover, different national governments combined these policies in different ways, leading the digital revolution to roll out along distinct trajectories.[1]

The digital revolution set the stage for the emergence of the digital platform economy. Digital "platforms" provide a set of shared techniques, technologies, and interfaces for a broad array of users, which can then build on that foundation. Some of the most powerful platform companies, like Google and Amazon, host their own digital marketplaces.[2] These firms not only dominate their respective niches within the digital economy, but they exercise market power as gatekeepers over their own market infrastructure. The emergence of these firms has recast the antitrust policy debate, with reformers calling for a major overhaul of antitrust enforcement to tame these big tech firms.

Tyler Cowen provides a rigorous defense of the market-liberal view and its continued relevance to the big tech firms of today. Cowen is a well-known economist, columnist, and blogger who has popularized a libertarian view on economic issues. In this excerpt from his book, *Big Business: A Love-Letter to an American Anti-Hero*, he defends the tech giants against critics who argue that they are too dominant, they have too much power over consumers and markets, and they stifle innovation. Cowen stresses that these companies have grown so large because they have delivered extraordinary value to consumers at a low price, or for free. Google, for example, revolutionized the way that we access information, and has allowed people to find valuable resources or to locate old friends more efficiently. Apple transformed the smartphone into a critical personal resource, and this has prompted other firms to produce better phones at lower prices and to develop a dizzying array of applications. Moreover, the big tech firms have not rested on their laurels: they have continued to invest their resources in more innovation. While these firms have sometimes bought out smaller competitors, the possibility of being acquired provides startups with a powerful incentive to innovate and a mechanism to finance their growth. Cowen (like Lal in the Market Reform section) argues that while these firms may dominate a particular niche at a given moment, they remain vulnerable to challengers who could displace them with disruptive innovations. And consumers may prefer the dominant platforms, but they still have other options.

Nonetheless, a growing chorus of voices has emerged to warn that the big tech firms pose a fundamental threat to the dynamism of the American economy.[3] **Lina Khan** wrote an influential article on Amazon as a student at Yale Law School, and then went on to be appointed chair of the Federal Trade Commission (FTC) in the Biden administration. In that article, Khan argues that the dominant paradigm on antitrust policy that evaluates competition by reference to a consumer welfare standard is ill-equipped to address digital platform firms like Amazon because it focuses on consumer prices. Amazon has not used its market power to raise prices, but rather has engaged in predatory pricing to pursue growth over profits.[4] In the shorter article included here, Khan breaks down big tech power into three main elements. First, digital platform firms exercise gatekeeper power because they control a part of the market infrastructure for the digital economy. Many businesses have virtually no choice but to sell through Amazon or to advertise through Google because those platforms are so dominant. And that leaves the platform firms with the ability to leverage their market power to extract favorable terms from these businesses and to fend off potential competitors. Second, these firms can leverage their dominance as platforms to benefit their other lines of business. For example, Amazon can privilege the sale of its own products over third-party goods, or Google can favor its affiliated businesses in search results. And third, they can exploit the huge amount of data they accumulate as platforms. Google and its business clients can use data to target advertisements or to engage in price discrimination, offering different prices to different customers. Likewise, Amazon can use the data it gathers about businesses that sell on its platform to compete with those businesses, or to inform decisions about buying out or squeezing out those competitors.[5]

Khan proposes distinct policy solutions for each of these different challenges. For the gatekeeper issue, she proposes common carriage regulation. These platforms provide a vital infrastructure for the current-day economy, roughly akin to the railways or the telephone lines of an earlier era. So common carriage regulation would treat this infrastructure as a public good, subject to government regulation regarding pricing and terms. The policy of net neutrality – whereby Internet service providers must provide access to all users on equal terms – subjected the Internet to common carriage regulation. The Obama administration adopted net neutrality in 2015, and the Trump administration repealed it in 2017. For the leverage problem, Khan advocates a structural solution. For example, firms could be allowed to provide a marketplace or to compete on that marketplace – but not both. Khan suggests that data power is the most radical challenge of the digital platform model, and the one the least amenable to traditional remedies. The European Union has sought to tackle this via its General Data Protection Regulation (GDPR), which prohibits platform firms from favoring their own lines of business on their platforms. Yet Khan suggests that data regulation will not be effective unless combined with antitrust solutions. Many observers are concerned about big tech's control over data not only as an antitrust issue, but also as one of personal privacy. Shoshana Zuboff, for example, evokes Karl Polanyi in referring to our era as one of surveillance capitalism that turns human experience into a fourth fictitious commodity, in addition to labor, land, and money. The surveillance capitalists gather extensive personal data – including our voices, personalities, and emotions – and use this data to *predict* and to *shape* our behavior, such as making purchasing decisions.[6]

Notes

1 Abraham Newman and John Zysman, "Transforming Politics in the Digital Era," in Zysman and Newman, eds., *How Revolutionary Was the Digital Revolution? National Responses, Market Transitions and Global Technology* (Stanford, CA: Stanford University Press, 2006), 391–411.
2 Martin Kenney and John Zysman, "The Rise of the Platform Economy," *Issues in Science and Technology* 32 (March 2016): 61–9.
3 Tim Wu, *The Curse of Bigness: Antitrust in the New Gilded Age* (New York: Columbia Global Reports, 2018); Thomas Philippon, *The Great Reversal: How America Gave Up on Free Markets* (Cambridge, MA: Belknap Press, 2019).
4 Lina Khan, "Amazon's Antitrust Paradox," *Yale Law Review* 126 (2017): 710–805.
5 Carl Shapiro, a veteran antitrust economist, shares Khan's concern about big tech power, but cautions that Khan and other "antitrust populists" exaggerate the novelty of the phenomenon and overestimate the threat: "Antitrust in a Time of Populism," *International Journal of Industrial Organization* 61 (November 2018): 714–48. Herbert Hovenkamp defends the consumer welfare standard in "Progressive Antitrust," *University of Illinois Law Review* (2018): 71–113.
6 Shoshana Zuboff, *The Age of Surveillance Capitalism: The Fight for a Human Future at the New Frontier of Power* (New York: Public Affairs, 2019), 514.

Tyler Cowen,
Big Business: A Love Letter to an American Anti-Hero (2019)*

6 Are the Big Tech Companies Evil?

Google's original motto, which endeared it to many geeks, was "Don't be evil." And indeed, for a long time it seemed the company realized this aspiration. People under thirty may not know how hit-or-miss it was to search the web prior to Google. It has greatly enhanced our ability to find the right restaurant reviews, look up medical information, research dating or business partners, and track down old friends, not to mention that it provides the means for good, link-based blogging, among many other advances. Google changed our lives, and very much for the better, even if we sometimes misuse it, such as consulting it as a substitute for serious medical advice. And for a long time we held the company in high esteem for supplying these services without charging us any dollars whatsoever.

But somewhere along the way, the story changed. Google still supplies high-quality search for free, but a growing number of people believe that Google and many of the other major tech companies are evil. They describe a company that has invested so heavily in superior data that no competitor can come near it, thereby giving the company a dominant position in the online advertising market. And they say that its supposedly free offerings come at the cost of our privacy and vulnerability to the surveillance state. (By the way, since often I am referring to the slightly distant past, most of the time I will use the word "Google" to refer to what is now Google and its parent company Alphabet combined, with Google as a subsidiary of Alphabet since 2015.)

Coming from another direction, Nicholas Carr wrote a book arguing that Google is partly responsible for the decline in our memories—why remember facts when you can just search for them? He asserted outright that Google makes us stupider. More recently, social media companies have been blamed for the ascent of Donald Trump, the renaissance of racism, "fake news," and the collapse of appropriate democratic discourse. The framing of "great stuff for free" has been replaced by "the product is us."

Hostility toward American big business is nothing new, but of course the key question is to what extent the critics are correct. For the most part, to continue my love letter to American business, I would like to speak up for the tech companies, especially the big ones. They have brought human beings into closer contact with each other than ever before, whether emotionally or intellectually, mostly through social media. They also have placed so much of the world's information at our fingertips, and more often than not it is accessible within minutes or even seconds. Whatever problems these developments may have brought in their wake, they are unparalleled achievements and

---

arguably the greatest advances of the contemporary world. And, speaking on a purely personal basis, I find that the existence of a well-functioning, searchable, shareable, and mobile internet has given me public audiences far greater than anything I ever expected to have. The internet and the ease of use enabled by the big tech companies drove the single biggest revolution that ever has come to my career.

So what's not to love? Well, there are some drawbacks, and I'll focus the second part of this chapter on where some future and present problems might lie—namely, our privacy. I don't necessarily mind that tech companies store information about us, but the terms of that storage and its use are opaque, it is not always easy to opt out, and the companies do not always keep that information sufficiently private and secure, as evidenced by multiple hacking episodes, including a major information hack of Yahoo emails in 2013 and a hack of Equifax, a credit bureau (and not really a tech company), in 2017, not to mention various illegitimate drains of information from Facebook. I'll lay out these criticisms in more detail, but for now I'll just say that I think the benefits of the tech companies still far outweigh their costs, as evidenced by how few Americans are trying very hard to opt out.

In any case, first I'd like to turn to the charges of monopoly and the disappearance of competition. It is easy enough to see that the contemporary tech industry has plenty of firms that seem to dominate a particular area—just consider Google, Facebook, eBay, Netflix, Apple, Snapchat, Twitter, and Microsoft, among others. But what are we to make of this? Are these new tech monopolies as bad as the price-gouging monopolies of yore? At least so far, it hardly seems so.

Many of these "monopolists," if that is even the right word, charge either nothing or much lower fees than their pre-internet counterparts. eBay takes a commission and never has been connected to a zero-charge model, but typically it is much cheaper to put a lot of items on eBay than to cart them around to resale or antique stores and arrange for their disposition by consignment or outright sale. Microsoft charges for its software, but once you take multiple copies, educational discounts, and piracy into account, the company hardly seems like an extortionist. For each copy of Microsoft Word that is sold, other copies are pirated or otherwise reproduced in a way that does not result in a traditional fee for sale at the price set by Microsoft. Apple is the company on this list that charges luxury prices, at least for its hardware. But before the iPhone, you couldn't buy something like that at any price. And within a few years after the debut of the iPhone, there were plenty of cheaper smartphone models on the market, and since that time those models have gained most of the market share. As of this writing, smartphones are becoming cheaper yet, due to imports from China, and the quality of those products is likely to improve rapidly. Apple helped enable these cheaper products, whether it wanted to or not, and all along the company knew it would end up creating competitors. So it is inaccurate and unjust to attack the big tech companies on the grounds of price, most of all compared to the counterfactual in which those tech companies did not exist.

A new set of charges, however, comes from another direction: that the major tech companies dominate their platforms and therefore may be stifling innovation. For instance, if Google controls search and Facebook dominates one segment of social networking, maybe those companies won't work so hard to introduce new services. Furthermore, those large and successful companies may be evolving into stultifying bureaucracies, afraid that new ideas might transform the market and threaten their dominance. To cite a possible example, if social networking becomes the primary means for accessing artificial intelligence (AI), maybe Facebook would lose its dominant market position to some other company better at AI, and in turn Facebook might steer the market away from AI to protect its current position. A related fear is that large, monopolizing tech companies will buy up potential upstart competitors, with the foreclosing of potential competition. Indeed, we've seen Google buy over 190 companies, including Deja-News, YouTube, Android, Motorola Mobile, and Waze, while Facebook has bought up Instagram, Spool, Threadsy, and WhatsApp, among numerous others, and purchased intellectual property from former rival Friendster.

In theory, you can imagine how those arguments might carry some weight. Yet in practice the major tech companies have proven to be vigorous innovators. Furthermore, the prospect of being bought up by Google or one of the other tech giants has boosted the incentive for others to innovate, and it has given struggling companies access to capital and expertise when they otherwise might have folded or never started in the first place.

Has Competition Really Disappeared?

First, I'd like to challenge the premise that competition has disappeared from tech markets, as has been suggested by numerous commentators. Recently, Alex Shephard wrote in the *New Republic*, "Giants like Google and Facebook and Amazon don't have meaningful competitors." *New York Times* tech columnist Farhad Manjoo told us that "smartphones and social networks might be ruining the world," which of course requires the presumption that we have no easy way to get away from their influences. I won't cover every possible example or complaint, but let's consider what are sometimes nominated as the two most egregious tech monopolies, Google and Facebook, with Google coming first.[1]

One rating of the top eight search engines goes as follows:

Google
Bing
Yahoo
Ask.com
AOL
Baidu
WolframAlpha
DuckDuckGo

That's actually plenty of choice, and even includes DuckDuckGo, whose chief selling point is that it attempts to offer complete confidentiality and doesn't store or sell data on your browsing history.[2]

You might argue that Google is the best of the lot and that the company holds a kind of natural monopoly due to the data it has accumulated over the years. That is a plausible argument, but still, a natural monopoly based on higher quality of service is the way a lot of markets are supposed to work. Google keeps that leading position only by having, at least in the minds of most users, the best product, and indeed the best overall suite of associated products, such as its email, chat, and Google Docs services.

Furthermore, a natural monopoly through data is unlikely to last forever. As the years pass, search engines will compete across new and hitherto unforeseen dimensions, just as Apple and many other competitors knocked out Nokia cell phones. There is no particular reason to think Google will dominate those new dimensions, and in fact Google's success may stop it from seeing the new paradigms when they come along. I don't pretend I am the one who can name those new dimensions of competition, but what about search through virtual or augmented reality? Search through the Internet of Things? Search through the offline "real world" in some manner? Search through an assemblage of AI capabilities, or perhaps in some longer-run brain implants or genetic information? I genuinely don't know. What I do know is that new dimensions of product quality arise all the time, and supposed natural monopolies find out their monopolies are not so natural after all. The internet is still in its early years, and whatever is required to succeed ten or twenty years from now likely will be quite different from what is required now. In the meantime, Google is doing a great job with search and advertising, and that is why the company is leading those markets.

Alternatively, you might ask whether Google (or for that matter Facebook) has some kind of monopoly power over advertising markets. While Google offers search for free, of course advertising on its platform costs money. As we know, advertising is a major source of the company's income, and if you sell something to a searcher clicking on your Google ad, Google gets a share of the proceeds. In 2017, for instance, Alphabet took in $95 billion from its advertisements and search advertising services. And other than Facebook, Google doesn't have a close, comparably scaled competitor in the online advertising market.[3]

Nonetheless, I'm not very worried about monopoly in this context. First, Google still competes with Facebook, television, radio, circulars, direct mail, and many other sources of information, and if you wish, you can throw email and word of mouth onto that list; instead of searching for where to buy something, very often I email one of my friends and ask. Second, insofar as Google has taken on a big share of the market, it is because its ads are cheaper and better targeted than alternatives. In the longer run, Google cannot charge higher prices than the status quo ex ante, because users would go back to previous methods of advertising, such as television or radio, or maybe try something better yet. That limits Google's monopoly power and constrains Google's ads to be a price-lowering institution. In other words, when it comes to advertising, the main source of the company's revenue, Google has to offer a better deal than what went before it, and indeed it has consistently done so, thus accounting for most of the company's revenue.

So what about Facebook? Doesn't the company have a kind of monopoly on social networks?

Well, I belong to or have considered belonging to the following social networks: LinkedIn, Twitter, Snapchat, email, various chat services, contacts lists in my cell phone, Pinterest, Instagram, and WhatsApp, the last two owned by Facebook (I'll come back to that). Facebook's main personal page has to compete with all of those. I also use my blog as a means of social networking, and believe it or not, sometimes I circulate in the physical world as well.

Facebook is the biggest player on that list, but one lesson is simply that it is possible to start new social media services, provided they offer something useful to users. Another lesson is that a lot of the communication that is now on Facebook could jump to another social network, even if users could not take their photos and old posts with them. People seem to feel quite comfortable using multiple social networks, and in their minds those networks compete against each other for usefulness and convenience. It's actually not that hard to imagine Facebook becoming less of a major player on some future list of the major social networks that people use. Users still could keep access to their old Facebook photos, just as people might use Linked In for some concrete purposes, including some purely friendly purposes, yet without necessarily making it their major means of social networking. Again, there is plenty of competition and rivalry for the market.

For a moment, I'd like to consider both Instagram and WhatsApp, both of which are owned by Facebook. Both compete against Facebook's main service in a way that improves the quality of that main service. Facebook has not turned either of these services into appendages of the Facebook page proper, in part because the company realizes that users value some version of those services in their current form. To make them too Facebook-like would invite potential entrants to in some way copy or improve upon what Instagram and WhatsApp have been, and a new and growing upstart rival social network is the last thing Facebook wants. So those services continue to exist as alternatives to the main Facebook page, and thus they are indirect competition for that page, *even though they are owned by Facebook.* My ability to have a multiperson chat with geographically dispersed friends on WhatsApp, for instance, limits how many ads or other forms of clutter the company is willing to place on my main Facebook page. And while I would not be shocked if, over time, Facebook lowered the quality of my Instagram and WhatsApp services, doing so would in essence be inviting new competition in those service areas. I would in fact be quite happy to use a better version of WhatsApp, and I don't care whether or not it is connected to Facebook the company.

I really do get that Facebook is the elephant in the room. If I ask the more practical question of whether I can choose from a lot of high-quality services—usually free—doing some pretty nifty things, the answer clearly is yes. That too is the result of competition.

Have The Big Tech Companies Stopped Innovating?

Other than giving me the best free search in the world, what does Google do for me? Well, I use Gmail, one of the best and biggest email services in the world, and it is completely free. Anyone can set up a Gmail account and begin using it immediately. That possibility would have astonished us as recently as the 1980s.

Google also has taken a lead role in developing self-driving vehicles. While I don't expect Google to become a major manufacturer of such cars, they put in key work on the underlying artificial intelligence, scanners, road mapping, programs, and other features of the service. They also helped make the idea publicly acceptable, in part by having driverless Google cars take people to work for years. While it is debated exactly when driverless cars, trucks, and buses will be ready for regular use, by now it is a debate over when rather than whether. Twenty years ago, or maybe even ten years ago, very few people expected that, and Google has helped pave the way for this progress.

Self-driving vehicles arguably will be the biggest and most important technological breakthrough since the internet. They hold out the promise of seriously limiting the number of car deaths, easing commutes, and making many of the elderly, the disabled, and the young far more mobile across space.

Another innovation, still a work in progress and from Alphabet rather than Google more narrowly, is the use of hot-air balloons to give an area internet access, also known as Project Loon. This was used after Hurricane Maria in 2017 to restore internet access in Puerto Rico and may end up being important in remote areas of Africa as well. Perhaps the value proposition here remains uncertain, but it is a bold attempt to create a better and more connected living situation for some of the world's more vulnerable people. It does seem that the technology works, though at what cost or sustainability we do not yet know. The work of Google and Alphabet on robotics also has not yet shown a real payoff, as far as outsiders can tell.

Even some of Google's failures will likely prove to be of use. Google Glass, the wearable device intended to integrate a goggles experience with internet access and viewing, failed. Still, this was a learning step in the broader development of wearable devices and a stepping-stone for others, or maybe Google/Alphabet itself, to build on.

Google significantly upgraded YouTube after buying the company. At the time, it was considered a very risky purchase, and many commentators suggested that Google was crazy to pay $1.65 billion for a company that, at the time, had very little revenue. Furthermore, YouTube appeared to be a cesspool for comments and a bottomless pit for copyright violation suits.

What did Google do? They cleaned up the legal issues, using their advanced software capabilities to spot potential copyright violations, and they enforced takedown requests. They also improved search on YouTube. Perhaps most important, Google invested heavily in the technology that made video so widely used on the internet today. When Google bought YouTube, video on the internet often was slow, interruptions were frequent, and you had to engage in a process of buffering, which meant you either had to preload the video or put up with starts and stops in your watching experience. By figuring out and investing in ways of shortening the path of video transmission, Google made video watching on the internet far more efficient. Many different parts of the internet benefited from these advances.

Today YouTube is also a leader for academic video and online education, far beyond what it was before the Google purchase. When Alex Tabarrok and I started our online economics education site, Marginal Revolution University (MRUniversity.com), do you know where we decided to place the content? You probably can guess: YouTube. How much did Google charge us for this service? Absolutely nothing, nor does it charge the users anything, nor is our product connected with advertisements, either for Google, for us, or for any third party. This means that users around the world, in any non-censoring country, can access all kinds of video-based educational resources for free.

Google and cell phones for a long time did not seem to be an obvious combination. Yet in 2005 Google purchased Android and elevated the company's open-source system to the most commonly used cell phone software in the entire world. Other companies have since modified and arguably improved this software, so Google probably has not been the major beneficiary of its own actions. Because of the Google-Android combination, hundreds of millions of people have enjoyed better and cheaper smartphones. More generally, Google has made most of their software open-source, enabling others to build upon it with additional advances; there are entire companies devoted to helping other companies build upon Google's open-source software.

And all that from a company that is just twenty years old. The astonishing thing, to my mind, is how many people attack and condemn Google. After I wrote that the anti-trust authorities should not go after Google, one commentator on my blog, *Marginal Revolution,* had the following gripe: "They show zero interest in calendar innovation, for instance, and have a half-broken to-do list product, but both are protected by Gmail integration." *That's* your complaint? Those are some pretty high standards.

OK, so Google looks pretty strong as an innovator. What about Facebook?

Facebook has consistently upgraded the quality and diversity of its product since its inception. In 2006, Yahoo offered to buy out Facebook for $1 billion, and at the time many commentators thought this was a no-brainer offer for Mark Zuckerberg. Of course, he declined it and proceeded to invest further, making the company worth many times more than that—more than $50 billion as of 2017. Arguably Zuckerberg has done a better job allocating capital within his company than any other recent American CEO. Most of those increases in value have sprung from service and quality upgrades, innovations at the time they were instituted.

The idea of the News Feed, for instance, was introduced in 2006, and now it is seen as a standard and indeed central feature of Facebook. Facebook also has been a leader in the development of targeted advertising, and now the company and Google command the two largest shares (by a wide margin) of the advertising market. The big advantage of Facebook is that you can reach demographics or individuals with particular interests. For instance, do you wish to advertise a product or service and target individuals with interests in economics? In the old days that was hard to do, but Facebook has made it cheap and easy. You place the ad and Facebook ensures it is sent to individuals whose feed reflects an interest in economics. This has revolutionized how companies communicate information about their products to individuals. Furthermore, Facebook has made the advertising market work for mobile. When the company went public it was not doing mobile ads, and many industry observers wondered whether mobile ads ever could succeed. These days, mobile ads are by far the biggest part of their revenue stream.

Facebook also has revolutionized how media companies deliver stories to their readers, and the reality is that Facebook became the world's largest and most important media company within a small number of years. I have some reservations about that development, and I will get to those, but if we are looking for innovation, this is unquestionably a significant example. Finally, Facebook is seeking to improve the quality of AI services and integrate those into its pages. It remains to be seen how well they will succeed in this endeavor, but at the very least they are helping to drive this highly competitive race.

Just to be up-front, I should note that, in my own personal life, I am not a fan of Facebook in the same way that I am a fan of Google. I consider it to be an amazing company and believe that Mark Zuckerberg has been one of the most impressive CEOs of our time. Still, I have two complaints. The first is mostly personal and subjective: I find their page confusing to look at and use, and their changes in page organization over time have confused me as well (too much innovation, from my point of view). That said, I recognize that the Facebook page seems to be working very well for most users.

My second complaint about Facebook is my belief that the company is not elevating the quality of news consumed by the American public. More and more people use Facebook as a means of accessing news items and sharing those items with their friends. The net incentive is that news producers come much closer to "giving the people what they want," which in this context means many pieces that are partisan, personality driven, cutesy, glib, or some mix of those qualities. The news organizations have in a rather undignified fashion run after this traffic as rapidly as possible, obliging market demand. One observer described the archetypical social media sharing story as being titled "What Could Possibly Even Happen, My Goodness. Baby Ducks See Water for the First Time, Can You BELIEVE What They Do?" In fact what they do is sip water from the pool, but I suppose you have to click to find that out.

To put it bluntly, it is quite easy to waste time on Facebook. The services of Google, in contrast, are more tailored for specific uses, such as querying for information, looking for how to buy a movie ticket, or maybe using Google Maps to get from one place to another. There is a clearer beginning and ending of tasks, which is one reason I think Google does more social good than cultural harm.

When it comes to Facebook news stories, Russian-manipulated content has received a lot of attention in recent times. I view that as a minor problem; the amount of money spent on such ads seems to have been quite small, at the time about 0.1 percent of Facebook's *daily* advertising revenue. Many of the reports of "fake news" following the 2016 election strike me as misrepresentations. Most of us probably saw the clickbait headlines about how many people clicked on or liked totally false stories on Facebook, but as a share of total interactions with Facebook, under generous assumptions, that was only about 0.0006 percent of user actions. That's bad, but there are also plenty of misrepresentations on television, in tabloids, in forwarded emails, in dinner table conversations, and in personal gossip. There simply hasn't been serious evidence presented that Russian activity on Facebook influenced election outcomes.[4]

The "more serious" mainstream media sources ran innumerable stories about the Hillary Clinton email scandal, even when there wasn't much there, and that probably hurt her chances more than anything on Facebook. Maybe each story was factually accurate, but the overall impression was more negative than was appropriate. Very often, misleading frequencies for reporting (or not reporting) true news are a bigger problem in the media than outright lies and falsehoods. By one estimate from *Columbia Journalism Review*, over a six-day period near the end of the campaign, the *New York Times* ran as many front page stories about Clinton's emails as it did about all policy issues over the sixty-nine days immediately preceding the election.[5]

I don't think we ever will have a fully clear idea of the impact of "fake news" during the last presidential election, but keep in mind that only 14 percent of Americans reported that social media was their main source of electoral news. When it comes to opinions about elections, Facebook has nothing close to a monopoly, as it competes with family influences, private conversations, cable news, talk radio, email, books, and many other sources. Or look at the broader electoral picture. The Democratic Party did quite poorly with respect to governorships and state legislatures, and it does not seem that Facebook fake news or Russian-bought propaganda played a major role in those races. A recent study shows that the most politically polarized Americans are the elderly, the group least likely to be getting its reporting from social media and the most frequent watchers of cable television news. The problems of media bias and polarization—in various directions— are real, but they are not mainly about Russian-bought content on Facebook.[6]

For all the criticism Facebook has been receiving on this issue, keep in mind that for-profit publishing houses have a long history of publishing the works of Marx, Mao, Hitler, and Stalin, thinkers whose ideas have led to the deaths of many millions. These books hardly had a neutral impact in the West, as they commanded the imaginations and loyalties of a big chunk of several generations of the Western intelligentsia. These books continue to be sold on the open market, and I am happy about this, as much as I disapprove of the embodied ideas. I save my criticisms for the bad ideas, not for, say, Penguin Random House or the owners of the printing presses. Yet Facebook has become the whipping boy du jour, perhaps because it is such a visible part of our lives. The truth is simply that an open publishing environment is going to lead to the communication of a lot of bad ideas; that is part of free speech, and there is nothing new about this dilemma. This time around it is supposed to be "really different" because Facebook is a kind of monopoly, or because Facebook uses algorithms to order articles, or for whatever reason. From my naive, long-term historical perspective, Facebook hasn't come anywhere near to doing the damage that the printing press (and radio) did by helping to communicate the ideas of fascism, Marxism, communism, and so on.

I should add that I have personal experience buying "propagandistic" ads on Facebook—namely, for my free online education program MRUniversity.com, mentioned earlier in connection with YouTube. The purpose of these ads was to target Facebook users who showed an interest in economics or were connected to universities and to encourage those individuals to click on the videos. I can't say I was unhappy with these expenditures, as they did drive some traffic to our site. But it was hardly possible to manipulate people like zombies, and we have moved away from buying the ads, even though they helped give us an early boost. That is a much more typical Facebook advertising story than what you might hear about these days.

The idea of a "filter bubble" is another criticism of Facebook, but it is not supported by the facts. So many times I have heard that Facebook or other social media put us in worlds where conservatives listen only to conservatives and progressives only to progressives, or some such similar complaint about echo chambers. Maybe at times that feels true, but the numbers just don't support the fear, at least not so far. As far as we can tell, ideological segregation in online news is relatively low, inasmuch as conservatives visit a lot of fairly left-wing news sources and those on the left consume a reasonable degree of conservative media. For instance, the best available data show that the average conservative on the internet is exposed to about 60 percent conservative sources, hardly an overwhelming number. Liberals are exposed to about

53 percent relatively conservative sites. Those same data also show that there is far more ideological segregation in our face-to-face interactions with family, friends, and coworkers than happens online.[7]

I do have a very specific concern about Facebook: I worry that it is making us a little too sociable—in the online sense, of course—and taking scarce time away from other things we might be doing, like talking to our spouse or children. I don't doubt the sociability is what the users want, but the ability of Facebook to command our attention so effectively may pull human attention away from other endeavors—in my view, not always for the better.[8]

This concern is related to some broader problems with relatively open online media. Facebook is a medium, and therefore it will channel user preferences in many regards. That will include nasty notes to friends, racist sentiments, and organizing for harmful or inefficient political causes. Any highly successful medium will carry along a lot of the bad along with the good, and Facebook is no exception. Most of the blame I put on Facebook's users, and to some extent on the media companies that, in a shortsighted manner, decided to chase Facebook traffic too intently. Still, I don't think we should be entirely happy about a medium that allows so many base or simply banal instincts to be channeled so effectively. I understand that fixing this problem would require Facebook to be much more paternalistic and big brotherish, and the cure could be worse than the disease.

As I am writing this chapter, the big controversy is whether Facebook and YouTube will too heavily censor controversial sources of news and information. Overall, this is a stronger concern on the right than on the left. I frequently hear right-wing, conservative, and Republican thinkers and analysts worry that so many of the employees in the big tech companies are left-wing and one way or another will put the other side's ideas at a disadvantage.

This issue is developing as I write, and my discussion might be out of date by the time you are reading this, but I'd still like to make a few points. First, the major tech companies for the most part have not wanted to censor content. It is expensive for them, and they know better than anyone how hard it is to find clear lines in this area. To the extent that censorship has arisen as an issue, it is because the public and some politicians have demanded a response (with tech company employees exercising some pressure as well). So maybe our beef should be with the intrinsic difficulty of the problem, and not with the tech companies per se.

Second, Facebook and YouTube carry so much content we should not be surprised if some number of their take-down decisions turn out to be mistakes. As I write, their overall record seems remarkably good, no matter how much some people may howl over anecdotal evidence of mistakes. With the exception of some small number of overt fascists and racists who have been banned from some social networks, the rest of us are free to post our opinions as we see fit.

Finally, we have to compare the present to the past. Let's say that Facebook and YouTube unjustly took you off their platform and would not let you back on. That is indeed a bad development. But were you so much better off in the "good old days," when you had basically zero chance of getting on the three major networks or the big radio stations or of writing for the major newspapers? Dissident voices have more outlets than ever before, even if a few of them receive tough treatment from the big tech companies.

Overall, this is an area where we need to be careful, and I do in fact share the concerns of people who worry that public pressure will push the major tech companies into too many take-down or "no service" decisions. But it's also not an easy problem to fix. Given that we've already decided they have the right not to carry images of beheadings and child porn, we really can't deny them some discretion. And would it help to split either Facebook or YouTube into two or three entities? I don't think so. That simply means that a slightly larger number of entities would face the same public pressures and quite possibly arrive at the very same content-carry decisions. Your real options are to find corners of the internet that will be interested in your ideas, and adjust accordingly. It's still a far freer intellectual world than what we knew only a short time ago.

To consider a third major tech company: Apple too continues to be a major innovator, in spite of its reputation to the contrary. Not only does Apple have three truly major developments under its belt—personal computers, smartphones, and smart tablets—but the company continues to try to drive further advances. The future of the Apple Watch remains uncertain, but at the very least it is a major achievement along the path of developing higher-quality and more practical internet-connected wearables; its millions of users already find it a convenient way to receive messages and track and measure certain aspects of their behavior. Apple Pay is a major player in fintech, and millions of people use it to pay for goods and services with a simple swipe at a terminal. Even if that doesn't prove to be the winning technology, it is a stepping-stone for the later improvements of others.

Or look at Amazon. The company started off selling books but moved to many different sectors of retail. It innovated by showing that it made sense to allow used books to compete alongside new product, thereby lowering prices for the millions of customers wishing to buy the used copies. Amazon has constructed what is arguably the world's best logistics network ever and these days is working on the use of drones to deliver packages. Whether or not that succeeds, or is allowed by the regulators, it is a bold attempt at innovation. Amazon's work in cloud computing has driven that market and made it much easier for other innovators to rapidly scale their businesses. Amazon also pioneered home artificial intelligence with Alexa: just speak to it and it will do your bidding as well as the software allows. Expect upgrades. And Kindle—well, that was an Amazon innovation too. Amazon's cell phone didn't work out, but as with the other tech companies, Amazon's overall record shows how hard it is trying to improve our lives with better products. It's now trying to innovate, if that is the correct word, by showing that brick-and-mortar bookstores can still make good economic sense. The principles Amazon uses for choosing and displaying titles are very different from those of traditional bookstores, as they rely more on data generated through Amazon. We'll see if they succeed.

Overall, I am astonished at just how varied the innovations of the major tech companies have been. It seems they have a core capacity for assembling, motivating, and coordinating human talent above and beyond the particular business lines where they won their earliest victories.

Notes

1 See Shephard 2018; Manjoo 2017.
2 The list is from Chris 2017.
3 On Alphabet and Google and related ad revenues, see Stambor 2018.
4 On the numbers, see Watts and Rothschild 2017.
5 See Watts and Rothschild 2017.
6 On those estimates, see Allcott and Gentzkower 2017. On polarization, see Boxell, Gentzkow, and Shapiro 2017.
7 See Gentzkow and Shapiro 2014; Boxell, Gentzkow, and Shapiro 2017.
8 I also see Facebook as taking a lot of culture, such as music, out of its broader social context. Since social media allow people to bond so quickly and effectively, we don't, for instance, need music for this end nearly so much anymore. Formerly, young people used music to signal who they were and to which social circles they wanted to belong. If you were a feminist in the late 1990s, you might listen to Indigo Girls and trade Sarah McLachlan CDs and go to Lilith Fair concerts. Today you can use Facebook to show your views with a Planned Parenthood support banner or maybe post something on Instagram. Arguably, the result is that music is less connected to our social attachments, and it doesn't seem to have the cultural force, social influence, or political meaning of earlier times. Pop music has been in the ascendant, and, outside of rap, protest music is less important, even in a time with a highly controversial president (namely, Donald Trump). The above passage draws from Cowen 2017d.

Selected Bibliography

Allcott, Hunt, and Matthew Gentzkower. 2017. "Social Media and Fake News in the 2016 Election." NBER Working Paper No. 23089. National Bureau of Economic Research, Washington, DC.

Boxell, Levi, Matthew Gentzkow, and Jesse M. Shapiro. 2017. "Is the Internet Causing Political Polarization? Evidence from Demographics." NBER Working Paper No. 23258. National Bureau of Economic Research, Washington, DC.

Chris, Alex. 2017. "Top 10 Search Engines in the World." Reliablesoft.net. Accessed December 6, 2017. https://www.reliablesoft.net/top-10-search-engines-in-the -world/.

Cowen, Tyler. 2017d. "Facebook's Harm Is Taking Life out of Context." *Bloomberg View,* September 20, 2017.

Gentzkow, Matthew, and Jesse M. Shapiro. 2014. "Ideological Segregation Online and Offiine." Chicago Booth Research Paper No. 10-19. Booth School of Business, University of Chicago.

Manjoo, Farhad. 2017. "Why Tech Is Starting to Make Me Uneasy." *New York Times,* October 11, 2017.

Shephard, Alex. 2018. "Don't Look to Democrats to Regulate Big Tech." *New Republic,* March 13, 2018.

Stambor, Zak. 2018. "Google's Ad Revenue Jumps Nearly 25% in 2017," Digital-Commerce360, February 1, 2018. https://www.digitalcommerce360.com/2018/02/0l/googles-ad-revenue-jumps-nearly-25-in-2017.

Watts, Duncan J., and David M. Rothschild. 2017. "Don't Blame the Election on Fake News. Blame It on the Media." *Columbia Journalism Review,* December 5, 2017.

Mariana Mazzucato,
The Entrepreneurial State (2013)[*]

Introduction

Thinking Big Again
   [...]

A Discursive Battle

What is the role of the public sector in economic growth? After the financial crisis, with public budgets bloated, mainly due to their role in 'saving' the private sector, across the globe we are hearing that in order for nations to be competitive, innovative and dynamic, we must have more market and less State. At best, we are told, governments merely facilitate the economic dynamism of the private sector; at worst, their lumbering, heavy-handed, and bureaucratic institutions actively inhibit it. The fast-moving, risk-loving and pioneering private sector, by contrast, is what really drives the type of innovation that creates economic growth.

According to this view, the secret behind an engine of innovation like Silicon Valley lies in its entrepreneurs and venture capitalists. The State can intervene in the economy—but only to fix 'market failures' or *level the playing field*. It can regulate the private sector in order to account for the external costs companies may impose on the public (such as pollution), and it can invest in public goods such as basic scientific research or the development of drugs with little market potential. To some on the political right even fixing market failures would be a sin, because such attempts would lead to a worse outcome in the form of 'government failures'.

What all these views have in common is the assumption that the State should stick to fixing markets, not directly trying to create and shape them. A 2012 *Economist* article on the future of manufacturing encapsulated this common conception. 'Governments have always been lousy at picking winners, and they are likely to become more so, as legions of entrepreneurs and tinkerers swap designs online, turn them into products at home and market them globally from a garage', the article stated. 'As the revolution rages, governments should stick to the basics: better schools for a skilled workforce, clear rules and a level playing field for enterprises of all kinds. Leave the rest to the revolutionaries'.

This book is committed to dismantling this false image, which underpins a global trend—promoted by conservative economists, politicians and the media—of bashing and diminishing the importance of the State. It focuses on what Tony Judt called a 'discursive battle': how we talk about the State matters. Depicting private business as the innovative force, while the State is cast as the inertial one—necessary for the 'basics', but too large and heavy to be the dynamic engine—is a description that can become a self-fulfilling prophecy. If we continue to depict the State as only a facilitator and administrator, and tell it to stop dreaming, in the end that is what we get, and ironically it also then becomes easier to criticize it for being lame and inefficient.

The book argues that the fabricated image of a lazy State and a dynamic private sector is one that has allowed some agents in the economy to describe themselves as the 'wealth creators', and in doing so, extract an enormous amount of value from the economy—in the name of 'innovation'. Indeed, the biggest fall in capital gains tax in US history happened at the end of the 1970s when the National Venture Capital Association managed to succeed in their lobbying for a 50 per cent fall (from 40 to 20 per cent) in just five years (Lazonick and Mazzucato, 2013). All on the back of a narrative of the venture capitalists being the true entrepreneurs and risk takers—a story we will see is far from the truth.

This biased story line, describing some actors in the economy as the true 'innovators', wealth creators and risk takers, and the others—including the State—as wealth extractors or just distributors, is hurting the possibility of building dynamic and interesting public-private partnerships today. To put it bluntly, this fabricated story hurts innovation and increases inequality. And the problem goes beyond innovation. The story has been used to downsize the State through an increased number of public activities being outsourced to the more 'dynamic and efficient' private sector, chopping away at the very brains of the State—with fewer and fewer resources aimed at building its own internal competencies and capabilities—and reducing what was once a wholesome notion of public 'value' as something to aspire to into a narrow notion of 'public good' used only to delineate the narrow areas that merit some government intervention (e.g. infrastructure, etc.).

Thinking Big

This conventional view of a boring, lethargic State versus a dynamic private sector is as wrong as it is widespread. The book concentrates on telling a very different story: in countries that owe their growth to innovation—and in regions within those countries, like Silicon Valley—the State has historically served not just as an administrator and regulator of the wealth creation process, but a key actor in it, and often a more daring one, willing to take the risks that businesses won't. This has been true not only in the narrow areas that economists call 'public goods' (like funding of basic research) but across the entire innovation chain, from basic research to applied research, commercialization and early-stage financing of companies themselves. Such investments (yes governments invest, not only 'spend') have proved transformative, creating entirely new markets and sectors, including the Internet, nanotechnology, biotechnology and clean energy. In other words, the State has been key to creating and shaping markets not only 'fixing' them. Indeed, as is described in one of the longest chapters of the book (Chapter 5), every technology that makes the iPhone smart and not stupid owes its funding to both basic and applied research funded by the State. This of course does not mean that Steve Jobs and his team were not crucial to Apple's success, but that ignoring the 'public' side of that story will prevent future Apples from being born.

Transformational public investments were often fruits of 'mission-oriented' policies, aimed at thinking big: going to the moon or fighting climate change. Getting governments to think big again about innovation is not just about throwing more taxpayer money at more activities. It requires fundamentally reconsidering the traditional role of the State in the economy. In the remainder of this introduction I delineate what this entails.

First, it means empowering governments to envision a *direction* for technological change and invest in that direction. Creating markets not only fixing them. Different from narrow attempts to identify and pick winners, envisioning a direction for economic development and technical change broadens the technological opportunity landscape and requires that the State creates a network of willing (not necessarily 'winning') agents that are keen to seize this opportunity through public-private partnerships. Second, it means abandoning the shortsighted way public spending is usually evaluated. Public investment should be measured by its courage in pushing markets into new areas, rather than the usual assumption of an existing market that the public and private actors must bump elbows in (one 'crowding out' the other). Third, it means allowing public organizations to experiment, learn and even fail! Fourth, precisely because failure is part of the trial and error process of trying to push markets into new areas, it means figuring out ways for governments and taxpayers to reap some of the rewards from the upside, rather than just de-risking the downside. Only once policymakers move past the myths about the State's role in innovation will they stop being, as John Maynard Keynes put it in another era, 'the slaves of some defunct economist'.

Creating Markets Not Only Fixing Them

According to neoclassical economic theory that is taught in most economics departments, the goal of government policy is simply to correct market failures. In this view, once the sources of failure have been addressed—a monopoly reined in, a public good subsidized, or a negative externality taxed—market forces will efficiently allocate resources, enabling the economy to follow a path to growth. But that view forgets that markets are blind, so to speak. They may neglect societal or environmental concerns. And they often head in suboptimal, path-dependent directions that are self-reinforcing. Energy companies, for example, would rather invest in extracting oil from the deepest confines of the Earth than in clean energy. In other words, our energy system moves along a carbon-intensive path that was set up more than a century ago. This is not just about market failure, it's about the wrong kind of market getting stuck.

The path-dependent direction that the economy follows under 'free-market' conditions is problematic, particularly when the world is confronted with great societal challenges such as climate change, youth unemployment, obesity, aging and inequality. In addressing these challenges, the State must lead—not by simply fixing market failures but by actively creating and shaping (new) markets, while regulating existing ones. It must direct the economy towards new 'techno-economic paradigms', in the words of the technology and innovation scholar Carlota Perez. Usually, these directions are not generated spontaneously from market forces; they are largely the result of strategic public-sector decision making.

Indeed, nearly all the technological revolutions in the past—from the Internet to today's green tech revolution—required a massive push by the State. Silicon Valley's techno-libertarians might be surprised to find out that Uncle Sam funded many of the innovations behind the information technology revolution. The iPhone is often heralded as the quintessential example of what happens when a hands-off government allows genius entrepreneurs to flourish, and yet the development of the features that make the iPhone a smartphone rather than a stupid phone was publicly funded. The iPhone depends on the Internet; the progenitor of the Internet was ARPANET, a program funded in the 1960s by the Defense Advanced Research Projects Agency (DARPA), which is part of the Defense Department. The Global Positioning System (GPS) began as a 1970s US military program called NAVSTAR. The iPhone's touchscreen technology was created by the company FingerWorks, which was founded by a professor at the publicly funded University of Delaware and one of his doctoral candidates, who received grants from the National Science Foundation and the CIA. Even SIRI, the iPhone's cheery, voice-recognizing personal assistant, can trace its lineage to the US government: it is a spinoff of a DARPA artificial-intelligence project.

And this is not just about the military-industrial complex. It is just as true in health and energy. As the physician Marcia Angell has shown, many of the most promising new drugs trace their origins to research done by the taxpayer-funded National Institutes of Health (NIH), which has an annual budget of some $30 billion. Private pharmaceutical companies, meanwhile, tend to focus more on the D than the R part of R&D, and some slight variations of existing drugs and marketing.

And more recently, despite the myths about the shale gas boom being driven by wildcatting entrepreneurs operating independently from the State, the US federal government invested heavily in the technologies that unleashed it (Shellenberger, Nordhaus, Trembath and Jenkins, 2012). When in 1976, the Morgantown Energy Research Center (owned and operated by the US Department of Energy) and the Bureau of Mines launched the Eastern Gas Shales Project, which demonstrated how natural gas could be recovered from shale formations, the federal government opened the Gas Research Institute, funded through a tax on natural gas production, and spent billions of dollars on research into shale gas. In this same period, the Sandia National Laboratories, also part of the US Department of Energy, developed the 3-D geologic mapping technology used for fracking operations.

The story of State-funded energy innovation is being repeated today, not just in renewable energy but even in the 'green' companies themselves. Tesla Motors, SolarCity and Space X, all led by entrepreneur Elon Musk, are currently surfing a new wave of state technology. Together, these high-tech ventures have benefited from $4.9 billion in local, state and federal government support, such as grants, tax breaks, investments in factory construction and subsidized loans. The State also forges demand—*creates the market*—for their products by granting tax credits and rebates to consumers for solar panels and electric vehicles and by contracting $5.5 billion worth of procurement contracts with SpaceX and $5.5 billion for the National Aeronautics and Space Administration (NASA) and the US Air Force. While some of this governmental support has recently been the focus of news articles, two things have passed relatively unnoticed (Hirsch 2015). First, that Tesla Motors also benefitted for a massive publicly funded guaranteed loan of $465 million. Secondly Tesla, SolarCity, and SpaceX have also benefitted from *direct investments* in radical technologies by the US Department of Energy, in the case of battery technologies and solar panels, and by NASA, in the case of rocket technologies. Technologies that SpaceX is now using in its business dealings with the International Space Station. This shouldn't come as a surprise—the State has been behind the development of many key technologies that are later integrated by the private sector into breakthrough innovations. These companies are of course helping to push the innovation frontier by further developing State-funded technologies, and, crucially, contributing to a transition to a more environmentally sustainable economy. But all we hear in the media is the one-sided myth of the lone entrepreneur.

The role of the State is massive not only on the supply side, but also on the demand side, that is, the deployment and diffusion of new technologies. Even in cases where private markets seemed to play a leading role, such as in the automobile revolution, it was the State that established the enabling conditions for car *diffusion* (new street regulations, road construction works, licensing and traffic rules, etc.). In the mass-production revolution, for instance, the State invested in both the underlying technologies and their diffusion across the economy. On the supply side, defence investments in the United States, beginning in World War II, led to improvements in aerospace, electronics and materials. On the demand side, the US government's post–World War II subsidization of suburban living—by building roads, backing mortgages and guaranteeing incomes through the welfare state—enabled workers to own homes, buy cars and consume other mass-produced goods. And today, more of Tesla's electric cars are sold in Norway than in the United States due to the Norwegian government's policies stimulating the purchase of 'green' products. Supply-side support from the US government, demand-side support by the Norwegian government. Hardly a lone entrepreneur!

For policymakers, then, the question should not be whether to pick winners or not. Everything of relevance has been picked! From the Internet to fracking technology. What should become more central to the policy debate is *how* to pick broadly defined directions, within which bottom-up experimentation can take place. But private investments will only kick in after those directions have been picked, creating expectations in business about future growth opportunities in particular areas. Such directionality will of course involve some failures here and there, but the advantages that result from those supply-side and demand-side pushes will be more than worth the wait—creating decades of growth. Rather, the question should be how to do so in a way that is democratically accountable and that solves the most pressing social and technological challenges.

[...]

Chapter 5

The State Behind The iPhone

Stay hungry, stay foolish.

Steve Jobs (2005)

In his now well-known Stanford University commencement address, delivered on 12 June 2005, Steve Jobs, then CEO of Apple Computer and Pixar Animation Studios, encouraged the graduating class to be innovative by 'pursuing what you love' and 'staying foolish'. The speech has been cited worldwide as it epitomizes the culture of the 'knowledge' economy, whereby what are deemed important for innovation are not just large R&D labs but also a 'culture' of innovation and the ability of key players to change the 'rules of the game'. By emphasizing the 'foolish' part of innovation, Jobs highlights the fact that underlying the success of a company like Apple—at the heart of the Silicon Valley revolution—is not (just) the experience and technical expertise of its staff, but (also) their ability to be a bit 'crazy', take risks and give 'design' as much importance as hardcore technology. The fact that Jobs dropped out of school, took calligraphy classes and continued to dress all his life like a college student in sneakers is all symbolic of his own style of staying young and 'foolish'.

While the speech is inspiring, and Jobs has rightly been called a 'genius' for the visionary products he conceived and marketed, this story creates a myth about the origin of Apple's success. Individual genius, attention to design, a love for play and foolishness were no doubt important characteristics. But without the massive amount of public investment behind the computer and Internet revolutions, such attributes might have led only to the invention of a new toy—not to cutting-edge revolutionary products like the iPad and iPhone which have changed the way that people work and communicate. As in the discussion of venture capital in Chapter 2, whereby venture capital has entered industries like biotechnology only after the State had done the messy groundwork, the genius and 'foolishness' of Steve Jobs led to massive profits and success, largely because Apple was able to ride the wave of massive State investments in the 'revolutionary' technologies that underpinned the iPhone and iPad: the Internet, GPS, touch-screen displays and communication technologies. Without these publicly funded technologies, there would have been no wave to foolishly surf.

This chapter is dedicated to telling the story of Apple, and in doing so, asks questions that provocatively challenge the ways in which the role of the State and Apple's success are viewed. In Chapter 8, we ask whether the US public benefited, in terms of employment and tax receipts, from these major risks taken by such an investment of US tax dollars. Or were the profits siphoned off and taxes avoided? Why is the State eagerly blamed for failed investments in ventures like the American Supersonic Transport (SST) project (when it 'picks losers'), and not praised for successful early-stage investments in companies like Apple (when it 'picks winners')? And why is the

State not rewarded for its direct investments in basic and applied research that lead to successful technologies that underpin revolutionary commercial products such as the iPod, the iPhone and the iPad?

The 'State' Of Apple Innovation

Apple has been at the forefront of introducing the world's most popular electronic products as it continues to navigate the seemingly infinite frontiers of the digital revolution and the consumer electronics industry. The popularity and success of Apple products like the iPod, iPhone and iPad have altered the competitive landscape in mobile computing and communication technologies. In less than a decade the company's consumer electronic products have helped secure its place among the most valuable companies in the world, making record profits of $39.5 billion in 2014 for its owners. Apple's new iOS family of products brought great success to the company, but what remains relatively unknown to the average consumer is that the core technologies embedded in Apple's innovative products are in fact the results of decades of federal support for innovation. While the products owe their beautiful design and slick integration to the genius of Jobs and his large team, nearly every state-of-the-art technology found in the iPod, iPhone and iPad is an often overlooked and ignored achievement of the research efforts and funding support of the government and military.

TABLE 3. Apple's net sales, income and R&D figures between 1999 and 2011 (US$, millions)

Year	Global	Americas	iPod	iPhone	iPad	Net Income	R&D	Sales/ R&D (%)
2014	182,795	65,232	2,286	101,991	30,283	39,510	6,041	3.30
2013	170,910	62,739	4,411	91,279	31,980	37,037	4,475	2.62
2012	156,508	57,512	5,615	78,692	30,495	41,733	3,381	2.16
2011	108,249	38,315	7,453	47,057	19,168	25,922	2,429	2.24
2010	65,225	24,498	8,274	25,179	4,958	14,013	1,782	2.73
2009	36,537	16,142	8,091	6,754	n/a	5,704	1,333	3.65
2008	32,479	14,573	9,153	1,844	n/a	4,834	1,109	3.41
2007	24,006	11,596	8,305	123	n/a	3,495	782	3.26
2006	19,315	9,307	7,676	n/a	n/a	1,989	712	3.69
2005	13,931	6,590	4,540	n/a	n/a	1,335	534	3.83
2004	8,279	4,019	1,306	n/a	n/a	276	489	5.91
2003	6,207	3,181	345	n/a	n/a	69	471	7.59
2002	5,742	3,088	143	n/a	n/a	65	430	7.49
2001	5,363	2,996	n/a	n/a	n/a	(25)	430	8.02
2000	7,983	4,298	n/a	n/a	n/a	786	380	4.76
1999	6,134	3,527	n/a	n/a	n/a	601	314	5.12

NOTE: Apple's annual net sales, income and R&D figures were obtained from the company's annual SEC 10-K filings.

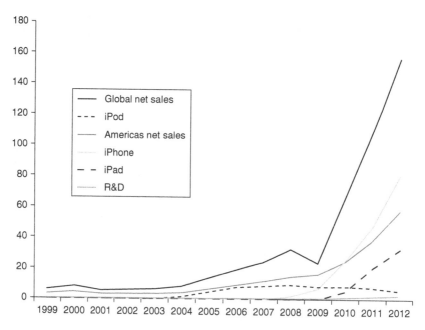

FIGURE 10 Apple net sales by region and product (US$, billions)

Only about a decade ago Apple was best known for its innovative personal computer design and production. Established on 1 April 1976 in Cupertino, California, by Steve Jobs, Steve Wozniak and Ronald Wayne, Apple was incorporated in 1977 by Jobs and Wozniak to sell the Apple I personal computer.[1] The company was originally named Apple Computer, Inc. and for 30 years focused on the production of personal computers. On 9 January 2007, the company announced it was removing the 'Computer' from its name, reflecting its shift in focus from personal computers to consumer electronics. This same year, Apple launched the iPhone and iPod Touch featuring its new mobile operating system, iOS, which is now used in other Apple products such as the iPad and Apple TV. Drawing on many of the technological capabilities of earlier generations of the iPod, the iPhone (and iPod Touch) featured a revolutionary multi-touch screen with a virtual keyboard as part of its new operating system.

While Apple achieved notable success during its 30-year history by focusing on personal computers, the success and popularity of its new iOS products have far exceeded any of its former achievements in personal computing. In the 5-year period following the launch of the iPhone and iPod Touch in 2007, Apple's global net sales increased nearly 460 per cent. As Table 3 illustrates, the new iOS product line represented on average 72 per cent of the overall net sales of Apple in 2011–2014.

The success and popularity of Apple's new products were quickly reflected in the company's revenues. In 2011, Apple's revenue ($76.4 billion) was so big that it surpassed the US government's operating cash balance ($73.7 billion), according to the latest figures from the US Treasury Department available at that time (BBC News 2011). In 2014, according to figures in Apple's Form 10-K (submitted to the US Securities and Exchange Commission), its revenues reached the impressive figure of

$182.8 billion. This surge in Apple's revenues was quickly translated into better market valuations and increased popularity of shares of Apple stock listed on the NASDAQ. As shown in Figure 11, Apple's stock price has increased from $8/share to $700/share since the iPod was first introduced by Steve Jobs on 23 October 2001. The launch of iOS products in 2007 enabled the company to secure a place among the most valuable companies in the US.[2]

As indicated by Figure 10 and documented in company financial reports, the rampant growth in product sales following the launch of the iOS family of products paved the way for Apple's successful comeback from its wobbly conditions in the late 1980s. Interestingly, as the company continued to launch one new product after the next with increasing success, the company's financial reports reveal a steady decline in the global sales/R&D ratios, which indicate the portion of funds allocated to R&D activities in comparison to global product sales was falling over time (see Table 3). It could be argued that this is simply a testament to how unprecedented and exponential growth in product sales was relative to the annual growth of R&D expenditures. It could also be interpreted as the expected outcome of steady investment in R&D efforts. However, when viewed in the context of just how competitive the product markets are for consumer electronic products, these rather unimpressive R&D figures stand out. Longtime Apple analyst Horace Schmidt approaches this issue from a different angle by comparing Apple's R&D figures against those of the company's rivals. According to the data compiled by Dediu and Schmidt (2012) and presented in Figure 12, Apple ranks in the bottom three in terms of the portion of sales allocated for supporting R&D activities among 13 of its top rivals.

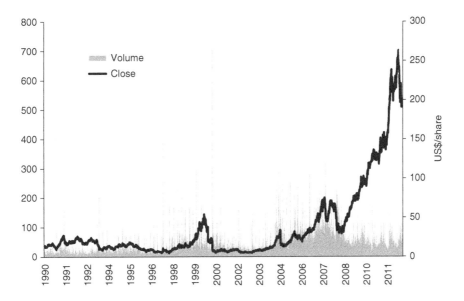

FIGURE 11 Apple stock prices between 1990 and 2012

SOURCE: Yahoo! Finance, available online at http://finance.yahoo.com/charts?s=AAPL#symbol=aapl;range=19900102,20121231;compare=;indicator=split+volume;charttype=area;crosshair=on;ohlcvalues=0; logscale=off;source=undefined;Charts/Interactive (from 1 January 1990 to 31 December 2012).

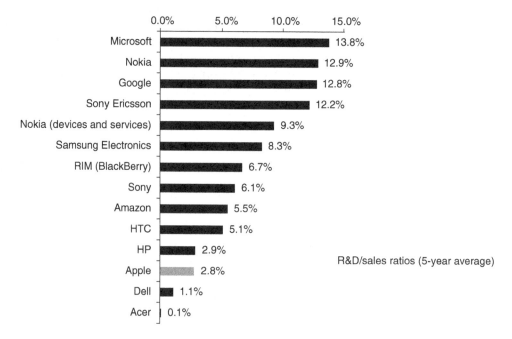

FIGURE 12 Productive R&D or free lunch?

SOURCE: Retrieved from Dediu and Schmidt (2012), 'You Cannot Buy Innovation', *Asymco*, 30 January. Note: The author's calculations are based on the leading smartphone developers' 5-year average R&D figures between 2006 and 2011.

Schmidt therefore inquires how Apple manages to get away with such a relatively low rate of R&D (as a percentage of sales ratios) in comparison to its competitors while still outpacing them in product sales. Many Apple experts explain this marginal R&D productivity as the company's success in implementing effective R&D programmes in a fashion that can only be seen in small technology start-ups. There is no doubt that Apple's ingenuity in engineering design, combined with Steve Jobs' commitment to simplicity, certainly contributed to its efficiency. But, the most crucial facts have been omitted when explaining this figure, which is that Apple concentrates its ingenuity not on *developing* new technologies and components, but on *integrating* them into an innovative architecture: its great in-house innovative product designs are, like those of many 'smart phone' producers, based on technologies that are mostly invented somewhere else, often backed by tax dollars.[3] The following section will provide historical background on technologies that enabled the future glory of the company.

Surfing Through The Waves of Technological Advancements

From its humble beginnings selling personal computer kits to its current place as the leader in the global information and communications industry, Apple has mastered designing and engineering technologies that were first developed and funded by the US government and military. Apple's capabilities are mainly related to their ability to (a) recognize emerging technologies with great potential, (b) apply complex engineering skills that successfully integrate recognized emerging technologies and (c) maintain a clear corporate vision prioritizing design-oriented product development for ultimate user satisfaction. It is these capabilities that have enabled Apple to become a global powerhouse in the computer and electronics industry. During this period prior to launching its popular iOS platform products, Apple received enormous direct and/or indirect government support derived from three major areas:

1) Direct equity investment during the early stages of venture creation and growth.
2) Access to technologies that resulted from major government research programmes, military initiatives, public procurement contracts, or that were developed by public research institutions, all backed by state or federal dollars.
3) Creation of tax, trade or technology policies that supported US companies such as Apple that allowed them to sustain their innovation efforts during times when national and/or global challenges hindered US companies from staying ahead, or caused them to fall behind in the race for capturing world markets.

[…]

Fostering an Indigenous Sector

In addition to government efforts nurturing the science base and fostering innovation in the US, the US government has played a critical role in protecting the intellectual 'property' of companies like Apple, and ensuring that it is protected against other trade right violations. The federal government has actively fought on behalf of companies like Apple to allow it secure access to the global consumer market, and it is a crucial partner in establishing and maintaining global competitive advantage for these companies (Prestowitz 2012). Although US-based corporations define themselves as transnational entities whose existence transcends political borders, Washington is the first place they usually turn to when conflicts in the global market arise. Accessing foreign markets protected by trade restrictions was only possible with the US government acting as a backer and vanguard. For example, in the 1980s Apple had difficulties entering the Japanese market. The company called on the US government for assistance, arguing that it was the government's obligation to assist the company in opening the Japanese market to US products by appealing to the Japanese government (Lyons 2012). When unfettered global competition hit home, companies such as Apple were backed by the government to ensure that intellectual property laws were carefully enforced all over the world. The added protection created for Apple by local and federal authorities continues to provide this form of subsidy, which allows the company to continue innovating.

Additionally, the US government has been providing various other-types of tax and procurement support that greatly benefits American companies such as Apple. According to a Treasury Department document, companies (including Apple) overall claimed $8.3 billion in research and experiment (R&E) tax credits in 2008 (Office of Tax Policy 2011). Additionally, California provides generous R&D tax packages for which computer and electronics companies are the largest applicants (Ibele 2003).[4] Since 1996, Apple has reportedly claimed $412 million in R&D tax credits of all kinds (Duhigg and Kocieniewski 2012).

Government procurement policies have supported Apple through various critical stages, which made it possible for the company to survive in the midst of ferocious competition against its competitors. Public schools in the US have been loyal Apple customers, purchasing their computers and software each year since the 1990s.[5] Klooster (2009) argues that public schools were a critical market for Apple as it reeled from its Apple III and Lisa product flops in the late 1980s. Provisions in the (post-financial crisis) 2009 American Recovery and Reinvestment Act (ARRA) provided incentives to benefit computer and electronics companies in the US. For instance, among various other incentives, through a small change in the scope of IRS 529 plans, 'computer technology and equipment' purchases were defined as a qualified education expense, which is expected to boost up Apple's computer, tablet and software sales.[6]

In sum, 'finding what you love' and doing it while also being 'foolish' is much easier in a country in which the State plays the pivotal serious role of taking on the development of high-risk technologies, making the early, large and high-risk investments, and then sustaining them until such time that the later-stage private actors can appear to 'play around and have fun'. Thus, while 'free market' pundits continue to warn of the danger of government 'picking winners', it can be said that various US government policies laid the foundation that provided Apple with the tools to become a major industry player in one of the most dynamic high-tech industries of the twenty-first century so far. Without the frequent targeted investment and intervention of the US government it is likely that most would-be 'Apples' would be losers in the global race to dominate the computing and communications age. The company's organizational success in integrating complex technologies into user-friendly and attractive devices supplemented with powerful software mediums should not be marginalized; however, it is indisputable that most of Apple's best technologies exist because of the prior collective and cumulative efforts driven by the State, which were made in the face of uncertainty and often in the name of, if not national security, then economic competitiveness.

Notes

1 In 1977, at the time of incorporation, Ronald Wayne sold his stake in the company to Jobs and Wozniak for $800. When Apple first went public in 1980, its initial public offering generated more capital than any IPO since Ford Motor Company in 1956. This created more instant millionaires (around 300) than any other company in history (Malone 1999).

2 When Apple stocks were traded at peak levels on 10 April 2012, the surge in the stock prices pushed the company's overall market value to $600 billion. Only a few companies in the US, such as General Electric ($600 billion in August 2000) and Microsoft ($619 billion, on 30 December 1999), have ever seen this incredible level of valuation (Svensson 2012). On 25 November 2014, Apple's market capitalization surpassed $700 billion, a (nominal) level that no other company in American history ever reached (Microsoft still holds the record for market capitalization in real terms).

3 The type of 'architectural innovation' with which Apple engages is not a riskfree enterprise, and in one seminal typology of innovations (Abernathy and Clark 1985) it is considered the most radical type of innovation, for it may disrupt existing markets and competences. Yet the point of this chapter is not to praise Apple for its innovation prowess, which is

extensively done by all kinds of publics—from Mac enthusiasts through the media and Hollywood to politicians—but to tell the part of Apple's story that has not been told elsewhere: that its 'architectural innovations' have been enabled by State-led investments in R&D and technological inventions.

4 According to a 2003 state of California legislative report assessing the results of California's research and development tax credit (RDC) programme, SMEs are the largest applicants in terms of number of claims (over 60 per cent of the applicants), while larger companies have the largest share of claims in total value (over 60 per cent of the total value of RDC claims).

5 Apple's share of the total educational computer purchases of US elementary and high schools reached 58 per cent in 1994 (Flynn 1995). Educators have also welcomed Apple's new 'textbook initiative', which is expected to reduce textbook prices significantly by increasing school use of virtual textbooks. These virtual textbooks would require iPad use and would be expected to increase Apple's iPad sales in the coming years.

6 Section 529 of the Internal Revenue Code (US tax code) includes certain tax advantages, also known as 'qualified tuition programs' or 'college savings plans'. A legislative amendment in 2011 allowed parents and students to use the funds in their college savings accounts for purchasing computers, computer equipment and accessories (including iPads). None of these purchases were considered eligible school expenses for account withdrawals before (Ebeling 2011).

Bibliography

Abernathy, W. J. and K B. Clark. 1985 'Innovation: Mapping the Winds of Creative Destruction'. *Research Policy* 14, no. 1: 3–22. https://d0i.0rg/10.1016/0048-7333(85)90021-6.

Angell, M. 2004. *The Truth about the Drug Companies*. New York: Random House.

BBC News. 2011. 'Apple Holding More Cash Than USA'. BBC News, 29 July. Available online at http://www.bbc.co.uk/news/technology-14340470 (accessed 13 July 2012).

Dediu, H. and D. Schmidt. 2012. 'You Cannot Buy Innovation'. *Asymco*, 30 January. Available online at http://www.asymco.com/2012/01/30/you-cannot-buy-innovation/?utm_source=feedburner&utm_medium=feed&utm_campaign = Feed%3A+Asymco+%about 28asymco%29 (accessed 12 June 2012).

Duhigg, C. and D. Kocieniewski. 2012. 'How Apple Sidesteps Billions in Taxes'. *New York Times*, 'The iEconomy Series', 28 April. Available online at http://www.nytimes.com/2012/04/29/business/apples-tax-strategy-aims-at-low-tax-states-and-nations.html (accessed 1 July 2012).

Ebeling, A. 2011. 'Get Uncle Sam to Help You Buy an iPad in 2011'. *Forbes*, 'Taxes', 16 August. Available online at http://www.forbes.com/sites/ashleaebeling/2011/08/16/get-uncle-sam-to-help-you-buy-an-ipad-in-2011/ (accessed 3 September 2012).

Economist. 2012. 'The Third Industrial Revolution'. 21 April. Available online at http://www.economist.com/node/21553017 (accessed 30 April 2012).

Flynn, L. 1995. 'Apple Holds School Market, Despite Decline'. *New York Times*, 'Technology', 11 September. Available online at http://www.nytimes.com/1995/09/11/business/apple-holds-school-market-despite-decline.html?pagewanted=print&src=pm (accessed 19 July 2012).

Hirsch, Jerry. 2015. 'Elon Musk's Growing Empire Is Fueled by $4.9 Billion in Government Subsidies'. *LA Times*. 20 May. Available online at http://www .latimes.com/business/la-fi-hy-musk-subsidies-20150531-story.html (accessed 29 June 2015).

Ibele, M. 2003. 'An Overview of California's Research and Development Tax Credit'. Legislative Analyst's Office, November. Available online at http://www.lao.ca.gov/2003/randd_credit/113003_research_development.html (accessed 22 January 2013).

Jobs, S. 2005. '"You've got to find what you love," Jobs says'. *Stanford Report*, 14 June. Commencement address delivered on 12 June 2005, Stanford University. Available online at http://news.stanford.edu/news/2005/june15/jobs-061505.html (accessed January 2013).

Judt, T. 2010. *Ill Fares the Land*. New York: Penguin Press.

Keynes, J. M. 1926. *The End of Laissez-Faire*. London: L & V Woolf.

———. 1934. *The General Theory of Employment, Interest and Money*. New York: Harcourt, Brace & Company.

———. 1937. 'The General Theory of Employment'. *Quarterly Journal of Economics* 51, no. 2 (February): 209–23.

Klooster, J. W. 2009. *Icons of Invention: The Makers of the Modern World from Gutenberg to Gates*. Santa Barbara, CA: Greenwood Press.

Lazonick, W. and M. Mazzucato. 2013. 'The Risk-Reward Nexus in the Innovation-Inequality Relationship: Who Takes the Risks? Who Gets the Rewards?' *Industrial and Corporate Change* 22, no. 4.

Lyons, D. 2012. 'Apple Caves on Audits'. The Daily Beast, 13 February. Available online at http://www.thedailybeast.com/newsweek/2012/02/12/apple-s-hypocrisy-on-u-s-jobs.html (accessed 7 July 2012).

Malone, M. S. 1999. *Infinite Loop: How the World's Most Insanely Great Computer Company Went Insane*. New York: Currency Press.

OTP (Office of Tax Policy). 2011. 'Investing in U.S. Competitiveness: The Benefits of Enhancing the Research and Experimentation (R&E) Tax Credit'. A report from the Office of Tax Policy, United States Department of the Treasury, 25 March.

Perez, C. 2002. *Technological Revolutions and Financial Capital: The Dynamics of Bubbles and Golden Ages*. Cheltenham: Edward Elgar.

———. 2012. 'Financial Crises, Bubbles and the Role of Government in Unleashing Golden Ages'. FINNOV Discussion Paper D2.12.

Prestowitz, C. 2012. 'Apple Makes Good Products but Flawed Arguments'. *Foreign Policy*, 23 January.

Shellenberger, M., Nordhaus, T., Trembath, A. and Jenkins, J. 'Where the Shale Gas Revolution Came From: Government's Role in the Development of Hydraulic Fracturing in Shale'. The Breakthrough Institute. Available online at http://thebreakthrough.org/images/main_image/Where_the_Shale_ Gas_Revolution_Came_From2.pdf (accessed 29 June 2015).

Svensson, P. 2012. 'Apple Closing in on Microsoft Record as Valuation Hits $600B'. Metro News, 10 April. Available at http://metronews.ca/news/world/98144/apple-closing-in-on-microsoft-record-as-valuation-hits-600b/ (accessed 10 September 2012).

Lina M. Khan,
"Sources of Tech Platform Power" (2018)[*]

A handful of tech platforms mediate a large and growing share of our commerce and communications. Over the last year, the public has come to realize that the power these firms wield may pose significant hazards. Elected leaders ranging from Senator Elizabeth Warren (D-MA) to Senator Ted Cruz (R-TX) have expressed alarm at the level of control that firms like Amazon, Alphabet (Google's parent company), and Facebook enjoy. In a recent poll, a majority of Americans voiced concern that the government wouldn't do enough to regulate U.S. tech companies.[1] As the editor of *BuzzFeed* observed, a "major trend in American politics" is "the palpable, and perhaps permanent, turn against the tech industry," now viewed as "sinister new centers of unaccountable power."[2]

New revelations continue to expose the degree of power these firms wield and the consequences that flow from that power. The potential effects range from stifling startups and undermining innovation to manipulating the flow of information and enabling foreign interference in our elections. Despite growing recognition of platform power, public conversation about why this power exists and what to do about it is still in its early stages. This essay seeks to advance that discussion. Part I identifies forms of platform power, identifying gatekeeper power, vertical integration, and information asymmetries, and explores how this power is being or could be exploited. Part II examines historical analogies for these forms of power and identifies legal hooks that could help us tackle it.

I. Forms And Sources of Platform Power and Its Abuses

Amazon, Google, and Facebook share key forms and sources of power. Generalizing these forms of power helps identify a toolkit for tackling platform power, even as the specific mechanics of their business models vary. While more extensive studies of platform power would benefit from being platform-specific, identifying the common bases of their dominance helps place them within existing legal frameworks.

The first is gatekeeper power. This power stems from the fact that these companies serve effectively as infrastructure for digital markets—they are distribution channels, the arteries of commerce.[3] They have captured control over technologies that other firms rely on to do business in the online economy. Fifty-five percent of online shopping searches, for example, now begin on Amazon's platform; last year the

---

[*] From: article first published in the *Georgetown Law Technology Review,* Vol 2.2, (2018). (pp.325–334). Republished with permission.

company enjoyed over 40 percent of online sales revenue in the United States. Google and Facebook together capture 73 percent of all digital advertising in the country and 83 percent of all growth, while Apple and Google's Android jointly account for 99 percent of the world's smartphone operating systems. For producers, retailers, advertisers, and app developers looking to reach users and consumers, these platforms are vital intermediaries, the railroads of the 21st century. Newcomers that have attempted to compete with a platform in a platform market (like Jet.com) have been acquired by other giants (Walmart).

The degree of market control enjoyed by dominant platforms is protected both by network effects and the self-reinforcing advantages of acquired data, which serve as barriers to entry. This means that not only are the platforms vital intermediaries, but—in many instances—they are the only real option. Even when producers, retailers, advertisers, publishers, and app developers manage to find alternate channels to reach consumers, those narrower paths can only really supplement access on the margins. The platforms generate too much business and attract too many eyeballs for firms to bypass them entirely. This renders businesses highly dependent on the platforms for access to users—a finding confirmed by a recent study undertaken by the European Commission (EC). The EC wrote,

> Many of the business users have indicated that they try to avoid any conflict with platforms, fearing a negative impact on their business. This applies especially to conflicts with the largest platforms, as business users indicate that often no viable alternative for these major platforms exists due to their scale, geographic range and the number of (potential) customers active on the platforms.[4]

Platforms can use their gatekeeper power to extort and extract better terms from the business users that depend on their infrastructure. For example, Amazon has disabled the "buy-buttons" for book publishers in order to extract better terms; executives have also described how the company tweaks algorithms during negotiations to remind firms of its power to sink their sales, through demoting their rank below where users usually look when making purchases.[5] Recently, the company has started offloading costs onto suppliers by subsidizing shipping costs through increased fees for the companies that sell through its platform. Merchants attempting to negotiate with Amazon risk seeing their accounts suspended, and getting kicked off its platform often means not just seeing lower revenue, but having to lay off employees.[6] Google and Facebook, meanwhile, capture such an outsized share of user attention online that publishers and digital advertisers feel compelled to sell there. Their duopoly position gives these two firms power to raise prices. Last quarter, Facebook hiked the average price per ad by 43 percent.[7]

Platforms also use their gatekeeper power to entrench their gatekeeper power, limiting the ability of third-party merchants to reach users independently—and thereby cultivating deeper business dependence on their infrastructure. Amazon, for example, closely monitors communications between third-party Marketplace merchants and consumers, penalizing merchants who direct consumers to their own independent websites or other sales channels.[8] Gatekeeper power now also risks shaping the content and production of news. Dependence on Facebook and Google for traffic has led publishers to package news according to the dictates of the platforms' algorithms. As a bill recently introduced by House Representative David Cicilline stated,[9] "[a]n entity with the power to dictate the terms of distribution of news has the power to dictate the content of news." The head of the Newspaper Association of America noted,[10] "Facebook and Google are our primary regulators."

A second form of power is leveraging. The source of this power is the fact that the platforms not only serve as critical infrastructure, but are also integrated across markets. This enables a platform to leverage its platform dominance to establish an advantageous position in a separate or ancillary market. By placing a platform in direct competition with the firms using its infrastructure, this form of integration also creates a core conflict of interest, incentivizing a platform to privilege its own goods and services over those offered by third parties. Amazon, for example, sells Amazon-branded apparel alongside apparel by independent designers; an independent study found that Amazon prioritizes its own brands on and restricts rivals' access to certain prominent promotional areas on its website.[11]

Last year, the European Commission announced that this form of self-bias or discrimination violates European competition laws. It fined Google $2.7 billion for "systematically giv[ing] prominent placement to its own comparison shopping service" and "demot[ing] rival comparison shopping services in its search results," leading traffic to third-party websites to plummet.[12] The EU competition authority is also conducting investigations into potentially anticompetitive leveraging tactics Google engaged in through its Android operating system and AdSense.[13] Apple, meanwhile, has previously blocked updates to Spotify from the App Store—a tactic that Spotify alleges Apple pursued to undermine Spotify as a rival to Apple Music.[14] If gatekeeper power gives platforms the ability to extort, leveraging power gives platforms the incentive to discriminate in favor of their own goods, services, and applications over those offered by other businesses.

A third form of power is information exploitation. The source of this power is the various forms of data that platforms collect on consumers and business users. Platforms gather enormous amounts of information, ranging from the amount of time you hover your mouse over a particular button and the number of days an item sits in your shopping basket, to every location you've visited with your phone and how you psychologically react to different posts and words. In some cases, platforms also track user activity on third-party websites and applications. Platforms can exploit this data in a host of ways, altering what information you see based on your profile. For example, Facebook may display certain job postings only to younger workers, or certain housing advertisements only to non-minorities.[15] Platforms can also harness this data to engage in first-degree price discrimination,[16] charging each consumer a different price for the same good or service. Uber,[17] for example, has admitted that it engages in personalized price discrimination. The degree to which other platforms are engaging in similar practices has not been publicly documented. Separate from the risks of discrimination, the extent of platforms' data-gathering creates significant privacy threats. Even robust privacy controls would only go so far to protect users, given the security vulnerabilities that inevitably arise when data is concentrated in a single entity.

Platforms also engage in information exploitation against the businesses that use their services to reach markets. Amazon, for example, collects swaths of information on the merchants selling through its Marketplace. It routinely uses this data to inform its own sales and products, exploiting insights generated by third-party retailers and producers to go head-to-head with them, rolling out replica products that it can rank higher in search results or price below-cost.[18] In this way Amazon's platform functions as a petri dish, where independent firms undertake the initial risks of bringing products to market and Amazon gets to reap from their insights, often at their expense.[19] Notably, it is the other forms of power—the fact that Amazon is a gatekeeper and integrated across lines of business—that enable it to exploit information in this way; those two forms of power enhance its ability to leverage the third.

Facebook has similarly developed the systematic ability to exploit information. A few years ago it acquired Onavo, a virtual private network that disguises browsing traffic to ensure users greater privacy. But news reports document that Onavo also lets Facebook closely track which competing applications are diverting attention from Facebook's own app.[20] Using this information, Facebook can either make an aggressive acquisition bid, taming the nascent threat by bringing it in-house, or can introduce an identical app, eating into its business.[21] The issue here is not that the platforms introduce rival goods—thereby increasing competition—but that their strategies are based on a significant information asymmetry that exists between the platforms and everyone else. The ability to intervene at the very earliest stages of a rival's growth means platforms can effectively eliminate competition before it becomes a threat.

To be sure, platforms exhibit other forms and mechanisms of power. But these three sources—gatekeeper power, leveraging power, and information exploitation power—explain to a good extent the current dominance these firms enjoy.

II. Addressing Platform Power

Breaking down platform power into its specific forms and sources allows us to distill what about platform power, if anything, is actually new. In other words, we can understand which facets of platform power we have grappled with in the past, and which aspects present new issues that require new thinking and/or new policy action.

Two of these forms of power—gatekeeper power and leveraging power—we have tackled in the past. Gatekeeper power can arise any time there is a network monopoly, a feature of industries with high fixed costs and network effects, or the phenomenon whereby a product or service becomes more valuable the more that users use it. Indeed, the gatekeeper power of the railroads—and the railroads' abuse of this power—gave rise to the anti-monopoly movement in the late 1800s, ultimately leading to the creation of the Interstate Commerce Commission in 1887 and the passage of the Sherman Antitrust Act in 1890.[22] Railroads abused their power through a host of practices, including, for example, imposing discriminatory pricing schemes, extorting the merchants and producers reliant on their infrastructure, and privileging the transportation of their own goods and services[23]. Determining that breaking up the railroads would hamper our national transportation system, Congress designed a regime to prevent railroads from exploiting their power. Most notably, railroads had to abide by common carriage (or equal access) rules providing equal access on equal terms, and had to publicly list their prices. This helped scale back their power to arbitrarily hike prices and extort the farmers and suppliers reliant on the railroads to get to market.[24]

Indeed, common carriage has been a traditional tool for maintaining the benefits of network monopoly while preventing the private firms who manage this monopoly from exploiting their power. Mandating nondiscriminatory access in the form of common carriage has also been applied to inns, ports, stockyards, and grain elevators, to name a few. Most recently, the Federal Communications Commission under the Obama administration adopted common carriage rules in the form of "network neutrality," prohibiting discrimination by Internet service providers. Specifically, net neutrality rules prevented broadband providers from blocking or slowing down access to content, or from charging more for certain content, as a way of creating equal access. Introducing common carriage for platforms would be one way to tackle their gatekeeper power. A platform neutrality regime could require a platform to treat all commerce flowing through its infrastructure equally, preventing a platform from using the threat of discrimination to extract and extort. Platform neutrality would prohibit Google, for example, from ranking less-popular Google properties above more-popular services offered by independent businesses.[25]

A set of tools also exists to tackle leveraging power. Structural remedies and prophylactic bans could limit the ability of dominant platforms to enter certain distinct lines of business.[26] Amazon, for example, would be prohibited from operating both as a platform for online commerce and as a producer of goods; Alphabet, meanwhile, would be prohibited from owning both an operating system and applications that run on it. This separations approach, in turn, would limit the ability of dominant platforms to leverage their platform advantage into other areas. As with common carriage, structural separations have been a mainstay tool for tackling the power of network monopolies and other firms that play an infrastructure-like role in the economy. Structural bans have been applied to railroads, telecommunications carriers, television networks, and banks. Introducing a separations regime for platforms would help prevent leveraging and eliminate a core conflict of interest currently embedded in the business model of dominant platforms.

Information exploitation power presents more of a challenge. To some extent, we have addressed information exploitation in the past through disclosure regimes and laws requiring public auditing of privately collected information. But two aspects of platforms' information exploitation power seem new. One is the sheer volume of information that these firms collect, and the security vulnerabilities created when a handful of platforms capture swaths of data. Partly the issue is structural: concentrated data is often more vulnerable to security breaches than is that same data dispersed. Partly it comes down to business model: as digital advertising firms, Google and Facebook make money through collecting information. So long as their business models are surveillance-based, they will continue to collect as much information as possible. The other challenge that information exploitation poses is not to privacy but to competition. Gathering data on business activity that relies on the platform gives the platform an information advantage it can use to extort value from those businesses by harvesting their insights, or to thwart nascent rivals in ancillary lines of business.

Tackling information exploitation power is not straightforward. One idea is to regulate their conduct, limiting what information platforms collect and how they use it. This would include introducing privacy regulations like those adopted by Europe in its General Data Protection Regulation (GDPR) and prohibiting platforms from using information collected on their platforms to advantage distinct lines of business. But these forms of regulation risk proving ineffective unless we also address the structure of platforms—namely, those that target the underlying incentive and ability of these businesses. These reforms would include, for example, structuring competition in platform markets (by creating a presumption against future acquisitions and undoing past acquisitions where necessary) and ending surveillance-based business models (by requiring platforms to spin off their ad networks).[27]

The discussion around how to tackle platform power is just beginning. As the debate develops, it's worth recalling that certain facets of platform power are not new, and that existing levers and concepts can be retooled to ensure that the platforms are structured to align with—and not undermine—open markets, fair competition, and the democratic oversight over and safe use of information.

Notes

1 Ali Breland, *Americans Want Tougher Regulations for Tech Companies: Poll,* HILL (Apr. 20, 2018) http://thehill.com/policy/technology/384144-poll-americans-want-tougher-regulations-for-technology-companies [https://perma.cc/3DN9-GLDB]

2 Ben Smith, *There's Blood in the Water in Silicon Valley,* BUZZFEED (Sept. 12, 2017, 3:37 PM), https://www.buzzfeed.com/bensmith/theres-blood-in-the-water-in-silicon-valley [https://perma.cc/C9ZJ-SVA8].

3 For a detailed account of how platforms serve as infrastructure, see K. Sabeel Rahman, *Private Power, Public Values: Regulating Social Infrastructure in a Changing Economy,* 39 CARDOZO L. REV. 5 (2017).

4 ECORYS, *Business-to-Business Relations in the Online Platform Environment* (May 22, 2017), http://businessdocbox.com/Marketing/69772826-Business-to-business-relations- in-the-online-platform-environment.html [https://perma.cc/QDB8-LMXW].

5 George Packer, *Cheap Words,* NEW YORKER (Feb. 17, 2014) https://www.newyorker.com/magazine/2014/02/17/cheap-words [https://perma.cc/Z73Q- Q3WM].

6 For accounts describing the relationship between Amazon and third-party sellers, see Olivia LaVecchia & Stacy Mitchell, *Amazon's Stranglehold: How the Company's Tightening Grip Is Stifling Competition, Eroding Jobs, and Threatening Communities,* INST. FOR LOC. SELF-RELIANCE 10 (Nov. 2016), http://ilsr.org/wp-content/uploads/2016/11/ILSR_AmazonReport_final.pdf [https://perma.cc/6KAS-2GUY]; Olivia Solon & Julia Carrie Wong, *Jeff Bezos v the World: Why All Companies Fear 'Death By Amazon',* GUARDIAN (Apr. 24, 2018, 11:32 AM), https://www.theguardian.com/technology/2018/apr/24/amazon-jeff-bezos-customer-data- industries [https://perma.cc/AB7A-ABDX]; Angel Gonzalez, *Third-Party Sellers Giving Amazon a Huge Boost,* SEATTLE TIMES (May 31, 2016, 8:26 PM), https://www.seattletimes.com/business/amazon/amazon-to-host-forum-for-its-marketplace-merchants [https://perma.cc/V8F3-H9ES] ("'There's a whole class of businesses out there who live in fear of going out of business as a result of the fiat of Amazon and their algorithms,' said a seller who declined to be named"); Lina M. Khan, *Amazon's Antitrust Paradox,* 127 YALE L. J. 710 (2017).

7 Max A. Cherney, *Facebook Earnings Send Stock to Record After Massive Ad Price Increase,* MKT. WATCH (Feb. 1, 2018, 12:58 PM), https://www.marketwatch.com/story/facebook-earnings-stock-touches-record-after-massive-ad-price-increase-2018-01-31 [https://perma.cc/YW32-J4E5].

8 Amazon Seller Central, "Prohibited seller activities and actions," https://sellercentral. amazon.com/gp/help/external/200386250 ("Any attempt to circumvent the established Amazon sales process or to divert Amazon users to another website or sales process is prohibited.") [https://perma.cc/4Y8J-SWLM].

9 Journalism Competition and Preservation Act of 2018, H.R. 5190, 115th Cong. § 2 (2018).

10 Nitasha Tiku, *Publishers Could Get a New Weapon Against Facebook and Google*, WIRED (Mar. 7, 2018, 7:00 AM), https://www.wired.com/story/bill-would-let-publishers-gang-up-versus-facebook-and-google [https://perma.cc/9NFX-EVH5].

11 *Amazon: By Prioritizing Its Own Fashion Label Brands in Product Placement on Its Increasingly Dominant Platform, Amazon Risks Antitrust Enforcement by a Trump Administration*, CAPITOL F. (Dec. 13, 2016), https://thecapitolforum.com/wp-content/uploads/2016/07/Amazon-2016.12.13.pdf [https://perma.cc/L654-WLTQ].

12 European Commission Press Release IP/17/1784, Antitrust: Commission Fines Google 2.42 Billion Euros for Abusing Dominance as a Search Engine by Giving Illegal Advantage to Own Comparison Shopping Service (June 27, 2017).

13 Foo Yun Chee, *EU Antitrust Chief Says Investigation of Google's Android, AdSense is Advancing*, REUTERS (Apr. 18, 2018, 4:25 PM), https://www.reuters.com/article/us-eu-google-antitrust/eu-antitrust-chief-says-investigation-of-googles-android-adsense-is-advancing-idU SKBN1HP2YL [https://perma.cc/LH7U-Y2CW].

14 Peter Kafka, *Spotify Says Apple Won't Approve a New Version of Its App Because It Doesn't Want Competition for Apple Music*, RECODE (June 13, 2016, 12:45 PM), https://www.recode.net/2016/6/30/12067578/spotify-apple-app-store-rejection   [https://perma.cc/VE6B-4B5W].

15 Julia Angwin, et al., *Dozens of Companies Are Using Facebook to Exclude Older Workers from Job Ads*, PROPUBLICA (Dec. 20, 2017, 5:45 PM), https://www.propublica.org/article/facebook-ads-age-discrimination-targeting [https://perma.cc/4SPZ-VZ7F]; Julia Angwin & Terry Parris Jr., *Facebook Lets Advertisers Exclude Users by Race*, PROPUBLICA (Oct. 28, 2016, 1:00 PM), https://www.propublica.org/article/facebook-lets-advertisers-exclude-users-by-race [https://perma.cc/U6S2-CVCY].

16 Firms that engage in first-degree price discrimination charge different consumers different prices for the same good or service. Although this form of price discrimination previously existed largely as a thought experiment for economists, surveillance-based data collection enables companies today to determine the maximum price that each consumer will be willing to pay for a product. Neil Howe, *A Special Price Just for You*, FORBES (Nov. 17, 2017, 5:56 PM), https://www.forbes.com/sites/neilhowe/2017/11/17/a-special-price-just-for-you/.

17 Eric Newcomer, *Uber Starts Charging What It Thinks You're Willing to Pay*, BLOOMBERG TECH. (May 19, 2017, 3:19 PM), https://www.bloomberg.com/news/articles/2017-05-19/uber-s-future-may-rely-on-predicting-how-much-you-re-willing-to-pay   [https://perma.cc/QNX3-EHSA].

18 Julie Creswell, *Amazon, the Brand Buster*, N.Y. TIMES (June 23, 2018), https://www.nytimes.com/2018/06/23/business/amazon-the-brand-buster.html   [https://perma.cc/QM8A-D3CW]; Spencer Soper, *Got a Hot Seller on Amazon? Prepare for E-Tailer To Make One Too*, BLOOMBERG (Apr. 20, 2016), http://www.bloomberg.com/news/articles/2016-04-20/got-a-hot-seller-on-amazon-prepare-for-e-tailer-to-make-one-too [http://perma.cc/79GL-5A8E].

19 Greg Bensinger, *Competing with Amazon on Amazon*, WALL ST. J. (June 27, 2016), https://www.wsj.com/articles/SB10001424052702304441404577482902055882264 [https://perma.cc/353H-YPRH].

20 Deepa Seetharaman & Betsy Morris, *Facebook's Onavo Gives Social-Media Firm Inside Peek at Rivals' Users,* WALL ST. J. (Aug. 13, 2017) https://www.wsj.com/articles/facebooks-onavo-gives-social-media-firm-inside-peek-at-rivals-users-1502622003 [https://perma.cc/WU9E-Z9ZN]; Elizabeth Dwoskin, *Facebook's Willingness to Copy Rivals' Apps Seen as Hurting Innovation,* WASH. POST (Aug. 10, 2017), https://www.washingtonpost.com/business/economy/facebooks-willingness-to-copy-rivals-apps-seen-as-hurting-innovation/2017/08/10/ea7188ea-7df6-11e7-a669-b400c5c7e1cc_story.html [https://perma.cc/A2YM-GJHD].

21 *Id.*

22 Susan P. Crawford, CAPTIVE AUDIENCE: THE TELECOM INDUSTRY AND MONOPOLY POWER IN THE NEW GILDED AGE 15 (2013).

23 Joseph D. Kearney & Thomas W. Merrill, *The Great Transformation of Regulated Industries Law,* 98 COLUM. L. REV. 1323, 1333–34 (1998).

24 *Id.*

25 For one take on how to implement platform neutrality, see Frank Pasquale, *Platform Neutrality: Enhancing Freedom of Expression,* 17 THEORETICAL INQUIRIES IN L. 487 (2016).

26 For a detailed account of why structural remedies and prophylactic bans should be applied in the context of dominant tech platforms, see Lina M. Khan, *The Separation of Platforms and Commerce,* COLUM. L. REV. (forthcoming 2019).

27 For arguments explaining why platforms should be forced to change their business model, see Roger McNamee, *How to Fix Facebook: Make Users Pay for It,* WASH. POST (Feb. 21, 2018), https://www.washingtonpost.com/opinions/how-to-fix-facebook-make-users-pay-for-it/2018/02/20/a22d04d6-165f-11e8-b681-2d4d462a1921_story.html [https://perma.cc/W32Q-TEEJ]; Barry Lynn & Matt Stoller, *Facebook Must Be Restructured. The FTC Should Take These Nine Steps Now,* GUARDIAN (Mar. 22, 2018, 10:28 AM), https://www.theguardian.com/commentisfree/2018/mar/22/restructure-facebook-ftc-regulate-9-steps-now [https://perma.cc/55TE-26YS].

8

The COVID-19 Pandemic

The COVID-19 virus pandemic originated in Wuhan, China in late 2019 and rapidly spread through much of the world. It posed one of the most acute challenges for governments and societies around the world in recent history, one that threatened both lives and livelihoods. And it starkly revealed vulnerabilities in political systems and market institutions. This crisis requires us not only to rethink government policies and social practices, but also the intellectual models we use to think about those policies and practices.[1]

The initial responses and health outcomes varied cross-nationally in ways that defied much of the conventional wisdom about the superiority or inferiority of certain political, economic, and healthcare systems. The United States and Britain struggled, for example, while Vietnam and Ghana fared better. The pandemic is bound to generate a rich scholarly literature explaining the variation in policy responses, social behavior, and public health and economic outcomes. The complex interaction of multiple variables – such as political institutions, social norms, and the characteristics of the disease itself – mandates a certain modesty in taking on this intellectual challenge. We must recognize, for example, that idiosyncratic factors such as individual personalities, past experiences with pandemics, weather, and travel patterns all played a part – thus making it impossible to identify any structural forces that fully account for government policy, public behavior, or health and economic outcomes.

Nonetheless, scholars and commentators have proposed some intriguing hypotheses. Joel Selway, for example, argues that countries with proportional representation electoral systems fared better because they have broader and more inclusive coalitions that design more efficient health systems.[2] Steven Levitsky and Daniel Ziblatt suggest that countries with "radical right illiberal populist" leaders fared worse because they discount scientific expertise.[3] The Free Exchange columnist at *The Economist* builds on Hall and Soskice to suggest that coordinated market economies (CMEs) such as Germany coordinated policy responses better than liberal market economies (LMEs) like the United States and Britain, but the liberal market economies excelled in developing vaccines.[4] Steven Weber and Nils Gilman contend that governments with operational expertise, long-term planning, and socialization of risks coped better – irrespective of political regime type.[5] Constantin Manuel Bosancianu et al. find that government capacity and interpersonal and institutional trust correlated with lower mortality rates, while bureaucratic corruption and ethnic fragmentation correlated with higher mortality rates.[6]

Scholars have also examined factors that affect economic policy responses more specifically. For example, Jérémie Cohen-Setton and Jean Pisani Ferry contend that France and many European countries were able to save more jobs at a lower cost than the United States because they deployed a job retention scheme that kept workers attached to their employers instead of a family support and unemployment benefits scheme that presumed that workers would be laid off.[7] Likewise, Elsa Massoc asserts that France was able to allocate financial support to small businesses more efficiently and effectively than Germany due to close collaborative ties between the government and the banks. The French government induced banks to comply with its state-guaranteed credit program with less government support and on better terms for the borrowers.[8] While no single hypothesis is likely to unravel the puzzle of differential national experiences with the pandemic, this growing research stream should provide some novel insights for the study of comparative political economy.

The two readings included here focus more on the intellectual mission of this volume than on specific policy debates. They suggest ways in which the COVID-19 pandemic mandates nothing less than a rethinking of our prevalent intellectual paradigms. The authors represent two very different traditions: one a libertarian, closer to what we have called a market liberal, and the other two more heterodox, closer to what we have called market institutionalists. Together they provide a particularly fitting way to conclude this volume by reconsidering prevalent schools of thought in political economy.

Brink Lindsey is a vice president at the Niskanen Center, a center-right think tank based in Washington D.C. Lindsey comes from a libertarian perspective, but he is willing to challenge libertarian principles as well as to defend them – as he does in this short article. He begins by recognizing that a pandemic exposes the limits of a libertarian view in that the government has to take the lead when public safety is threatened. The government has to step in to contain the outbreak; to assure supply and distribution of tests, treatments, and vaccines; and to support businesses and workers that are unable to conduct normal economic activity. At the same time, Lindsey stresses that the pandemic does not undermine the core libertarian case for limited government and free markets. Governments can over-reach and over-regulate. They can be incompetent, inefficient, or captured by political interests. So libertarians are right to insist on careful scrutiny of government action. Yet Lindsey calls for a transformation of the libertarian cause from one of *less* government to one of more *effective* government. He contends that the primary failures of the U.S. response to the COVID-19 pandemic were errors of omission (what the government failed to do) and not commission (what it did). The governments of South Korea, Taiwan, Hong Kong, Australia, New

Zealand, and Germany, among others, demonstrated greater government capacity in their policy responses to the pandemic. In a companion piece to the one included here, Lindsey declares that libertarians should embrace something like the market-institutionalist perspective advocated in this volume. "[In] appreciating the world-transforming virtues of the market system," he concludes, "it is vitally important for us to keep in mind this qualification: *a well-functioning market system is neither self-executing nor self-sustaining.* To achieve what they are capable of, markets need to be embedded in and supplemented by supportive legal, political, and social institutions."[9]

Carolina Alves and **Ingrid Harvold Kvangraven** also link policy failures in national responses to the pandemic to analytical lapses, but they represent a different scholarly tradition and they focus on Britain rather than the United States. Some of their conclusions overlap with those of Lindsey, nonetheless. Alves and Kvangraven present their position as one of "heterodox" economics in contrast with mainstream or neoclassical economics. Their argument resembles the market-institutional critique of market-liberal thought presented in this volume in that they stress that markets are deeply embedded in society and politics. They contend that the COVID-19 pandemic has exposed the distinct vulnerabilities of countries such as Britain with limited state capacities, underfunded health systems, and precarious labor markets. The British government pursued decades of market reforms and austerity measures that undermined the country's ability to weather such a crisis. In contrast, countries as diverse as Ghana, New Zealand, Vietnam, Singapore, and South Korea responded more promptly and more effectively with rigorous testing and contact tracing, full or partial lockdown, support for unemployed workers, and clear public communication. Moreover, Alves and Kvangraven claim that the flawed conceptual models of mainstream economics contributed to Britain's unpreparedness for the pandemic and its inadequate responses to it. Specifically, mainstream economists tended to vilify the state and to celebrate the market, to value efficiency over resilience, and to study markets in relative isolation from their broader social and political context. So policymakers who followed these precepts sought to boost profits and lower wages, to restrain social spending, and to eschew long-term planning or investment in surge capacity. Alves and Kvangraven charge that British authorities relied too heavily on specific types of scientific evidence and consulted too narrow a range of advisors. They advocate for a heterodox economics that focuses on systems of production and distribution, recognizes the central role of power in market relations, and studies economic systems beyond just markets. They maintain that this approach enables a deeper understanding of the causes and consequences of the COVID-19 pandemic. For example, feminist economists have long noted the centrality of social reproduction as a core activity that keeps the economy going, yet the school and business closures after the pandemic hit have brutally exposed the vulnerabilities of child and elder care regimes. A heterodox approach is better equipped to analyze how a crisis like this can expose societal inequalities, including those based on gender, class, and race. Alves and Kvangraven conclude that analysts must move beyond the state–market dichotomy and recognize that the government is itself integral to the economy and powerfully affects the public good.

Notes

1 Neil Fligstein and Steven Vogel, "Political Economy after Neoliberalism," *Boston Review* (October 6, 2020).

2 Joel Selway, "Which Kind of Democracies Respond More Effectively to a Pandemic?" *Washington Post* Monkey Cage (May 19, 2020).

3 David Leonhardt and Lauren Leatherby, "Where the Virus is Growing Most," *The New York Times* (June 2, 2020).

4 "Which is the Best Market Model?" *The Economist* (September 12, 2020).

5 Steven Weber and Nils Gilman, "The Long Shadow of the Future," *Noema* (June 10, 2020).

6 Constantin Manuel Bosancianu et al., "Political and Social Correlates of Covid-19 Mortality," WZB Berlin Social Science Center Working Paper (June 2020).

7 Jérémie Cohen-Setton and Jean Pisani Ferry, "When More Delivers Less: Comparing the US and French COVID-19 Crisis Responses," Peterson Institute for International Economics (PIIE) Policy Brief 20-9, June 2020.

8 Elsa Massoc, "Having Banks 'Play Along': State–Bank Coordination and State-Guaranteed Credit Programs During the COVID-19 Crisis in France and Germany," *Journal of European Public Policy* (2021).

9 Brink Lindsey, "Free Markets and Limited Government Reconceived," *Niskanen Center Commentary* (June 23, 2020).

Brink Lindsey,
"What the Pandemic Revealed" (2020)*

On March 3, in response to reports that some Republican lawmakers favored free testing and treatments for COVID-19, Derek Thompson of *The Atlantic* tweeted, "There are no libertarians in a pandemic (Thompson 2020)." The witticism bounced all over social media during the ensuing days and weeks – and with good reason, since the jab hit its target squarely on the nose.

When public safety is threatened, whether by war or disease, our dependence on government becomes immediately and viscerally obvious. There are no Centers for Disease Control in the private sector. There is no possibility of swiftly identifying the virus, and launching a crash program to develop tests, treatments, and vaccines, without massive government support for medical research. And for those tests, treatments, and vaccines to be effective, their distribution cannot be restricted by ability to pay; government must step in to ensure wide availability.

In addition, vigorous use of the government's emergency powers – banning large public gatherings, temporarily shutting down schools and businesses, issuing stay-at-home orders, quarantining the sick and those exposed to them – has been needed to help contain the outbreak. When a highly contagious and fatal disease can spread before its victims even show symptoms, the libertarian ethos of personal responsibility – do what you want, and bear the consequences for good or ill – leads not to mass flourishing but to mass death. Only the government has the power and resources to internalize the externalities of contagion and coordinate a rational response (Bethune and Korinek 2020).

Despite being put on the defensive, supporters of free markets and limited government were able to respond with some fairly effective counterpunching. In the first place, the fact that certain kinds of government action are necessary under the extraordinary conditions of a public health emergency – a fact freely acknowledged by many libertarians and partisans of small government – does not mean that expansive government across the board is a good idea in normal times. Further, in the emergency now upon us, overweening government has contributed significantly to the scale of the pandemic here in the United States. Effective responses to the outbreak have been badly hampered by inadequate supplies of test kits and equipment, and primary responsibility for this failure rests with the Food and Drug Administration and its heavy-handed regulatory approach (Stapp 2020). A key blunder was the decision in early February to allow only the CDC to produce and conduct tests; problems with the CDC's initial test then led to weeks of disastrous delay.

---

* From: document originally published by the Niskanen Center in 2020 at https://www.niskanencenter .org/what-the-pandemic-revealed/ under a Creative Commons Attribution 4.0 International License (https://creativecommons.org/licenses/by/4.0/). Republished here under the terms of that license with minor editing to convert hyperlinked sources to in-text parenthetical citations with a bibliography.

Meanwhile, responding to the crisis has necessitated a string of regulatory waivers at the federal and state levels – to allow doctors and nurses to work out of state, to facilitate telemedicine, to expand the scope of work that non-M.D. health professionals can do, to allow restaurants and bars to sell alcohol to takeout customers, and more (Polumbo 2020). The relevant rules have been put aside temporarily as obviously dysfunctional now – but perhaps that means at least some of them are dysfunctional, if less obviously, all the time (Weissmann et al. 2020; Broughel 2020)?

And although emergency measures to slow transmission of the virus were clearly called for, the actual restrictions imposed were certainly not above criticism (Dalmia 2020). As we have learned more about how the virus spreads, it appears that bans on outdoor activities went too far and may have been counterproductive. Where to draw the line between permitted and proscribed was never going to be an exact science in the fog of crisis, but there were plenty of cases of seemingly arbitrary distinctions (for example, one jurisdiction banned use of motorboats but not nonmotorized boats) that did nothing to advance public safety but did undermine the legitimacy of necessary restrictions.

The points scored on both sides in this back-and-forth hold profoundly important implications for the intellectual future of the political right. To begin with, the pandemic makes clear that there will always be a vital need for critical scrutiny of government's actions, and thus an important role to play for those with a skeptical view of government power and competence. Even in the middle of a public health emergency, when the case for broad government powers is overwhelming, there is no guarantee that those powers will be used wisely or effectively. The CDC and the FDA both have thousands of employees and multi-billion-dollar annual budgets; notwithstanding those considerable resources at their disposal, and the obvious importance of controlling infectious diseases to their missions, those two agencies failed in the relatively simple task of developing viral infection tests in a timely manner – with a staggering cost in lives and dollars lost as a result of their incompetence.

Just because we give government the requisite authority and funding to perform some task, we cannot assume that the result will be mission accomplished. Indeed, there are sound reasons to assume otherwise. Overconfidence and the lure of technocratic control provide an ever-present temptation for governments to overreach; the lack of clear feedback signals about the effectiveness of government actions dulls incentives to recognize problems and improve performance; there is always a risk that government authority, no matter that its exercise is unquestionably called for, will be misappropriated by insiders to benefit them at the public's expense. Placing and defending limits on government, preventing and rolling back excesses, are therefore jobs that will always be with us.

But if the pandemic has shown that a critical stance toward government is always needed in formulating and evaluating policy, it has demonstrated even more forcefully the limitations and shortcomings of libertarians' exclusive focus on government excess. The gravest failures in the government response to the pandemic were sins of omission, not commission – not unnecessary and ill-advised interference with the private sector, but the inability to accomplish tasks for which only government is suited. Yes, at the outset of the crisis the FDA was disastrously over-restrictive in permitting labs to develop their own tests for the virus, but it is flatly risible to suggest that everything would have worked out fine if only government had gotten out of the way. Leaving aside the decades of government support for medical research that made it technologically possible to identify the virus and test for its presence in a human host, there is no way that private, profit-seeking firms would ever develop and conduct the testing, contact tracing, and isolation of the infected needed to slow the spread of the virus. Government funding and coordination are irreplaceable. Looking ahead, there is no prospect for rapid development and wide distribution of treatments and vaccines without a heavy dose of government involvement.

The pandemic produced not only a public health crisis, but an economic crisis as well – the sharpest and most severe contraction of economic activity since the Great Depression. While the economic collapse was doubtless aggravated at the margins by forced business closures and stay-at-home orders, those interventions largely codified the public's spontaneous response to the uncontrolled outbreak of a highly infectious and potentially fatal disease. It's quite simply impossible to run a modern economy at anything near its potential level of output when people are afraid that going to work or going shopping might kill them or their loved ones.

Government excess, in other words, was not the fundamental problem. On the contrary, a large and activist government was all that stood between us and mass privation and suffering on a mind-boggling scale. Only government can mitigate the economic effects of the pandemic – in the same way it responds to other shocks that lead to other, less drastic slumps – by acting as insurer of last resort, using its taxing, spending, borrowing, and money-creating powers to sustain household spending and keep businesses afloat until resumption of something approaching normal economic activity is possible.

Unfortunately, the patchwork "kludgeocracy" that is the American welfare state was poorly suited to meet the challenge of the coronavirus shock (Teles 2013). Our employment-based health insurance system left people abandoned in their hour of need as layoffs spiked into the tens of millions. The absence of any well-designed system of automatic stabilizers sent states and localities hurtling toward fiscal collapse. Many state unemployment insurance systems fell victim to antiquated software based on long-defunct programming languages – while one state's system was exposed as having been designed purposefully to discourage people from claiming benefits (Kelly 2020; Fineout and Caputo 2020). Policymakers flailed in their efforts to extend emergency aid to businesses, forced to go through banks with improvised lending programs that too often funneled money to where it was needed least (Kurtzleben et al. 2020).

In the current double crisis, what has been lacking is not restraints on government power. What has been lacking – shockingly, shamefully, tragically lacking – is the capacity to exercise government power effectively. Of course that incapacity has been most obvious at the top, with the shambolic failures of the Trump administration to prepare for the outbreak and lead a coordinated, coherent national response (Frum 2020; Rucker et al. 2020). But the backwardness and incompetence of American government have been visible at all levels – especially in contrast to the sophisticated and efficient governance on display in places as diverse as South Korea, Taiwan, Hong Kong, Australia, New Zealand, and Germany.

How far we've fallen is truly shocking: The country that beat the Nazis, conquered the atom, and put a man on the moon now struggles to produce enough masks for its doctors and nurses. "Over more than two centuries, the United States has stirred a very wide range of feelings in the rest of the world: love and hatred, fear and hope, envy and contempt, awe and anger," wrote Irish columnist Fintan O'Toole, voicing the emerging and humiliating verdict of global public opinion (O'Toole 2020). "But there is one emotion that has never been directed towards the U.S. until now: pity."

As to how to close America's deficit in state capacity, a question with millions of lives in the balance, libertarianism has nothing to say. The libertarian project is devoted exclusively to stopping government from doing things it ought not to do; its only advice about how to improve government is "less." When it comes to making government strong enough and capable enough to do the things it needs to do, libertarianism is silent.

Actually, worse than silent. It is quite simply impossible to lead any institution capably without believing in the fundamental integrity of that institution and the importance of its mission. And the modern libertarian movement, which has done so much to shape attitudes on the American right about the nature of government and its proper role, is dedicated to the proposition that the contemporary American state is illegitimate and contemptible. In the libertarian view, government is congenitally incapable of doing anything well, the public sphere is, by its very nature, dysfunctional and morally tainted, and therefore the only thing to do with government is – in the famous words of activist Grover Norquist – "to shrink it down to the size where we can drown it in the bathtub."

The gradual diffusion of these anti-government attitudes through the conservative movement and the Republican Party has rendered the American right worse than irrelevant to the project of restoring American state capacity. It has become actively hostile, undermining the motivations needed to launch such a project and the virtues needed to pull it off.

As I've already argued, none of this means that libertarians are wrong about everything, or that libertarian ideas are worthless. But it does mean that skepticism about government, standing alone, is an insufficient foundation for good governance. The insights of libertarian thought – suspicion of centralized power, alertness to how even the best-intended government measures can still go horribly wrong, recognition of the enormous fertility of the marketplace's decentralized, trial-and-error experimentation – are genuine and abiding. But they are not sufficient.

The ideology of libertarianism claims otherwise: It asserts that a set of important but partial and contingent truths are in fact a comprehensive and timeless blueprint for the ideal political order. The error of this assertion has been made painfully obvious by the pandemic, but it was increasingly evident for many years beforehand. The overlap between genuine libertarian insights and the pressing challenges facing the American polity has been steadily shrinking since the end of the 20th century.

I say this as someone who discovered libertarian ideas in the 1970s. Back then, the intellectual orthodoxy tilted heavily in favor of top-down, technocratic management of economic life. Paul Samuelson's bestselling economics textbook was still predicting that the Soviet Union would soon overtake us in GDP. John Kenneth Galbraith argued that competition was as passé here as it was behind the Iron Curtain; the "technostructure" of central planning reigned supreme, whether it took the form of the Politburo or Big Business. As to the newly independent countries of the postcolonial world, there was widespread confidence that a "big push" of state-led investment would put them on the fast track to prosperity. Here at home, the dominant economic analysis of regulation continued to assume that its scope and content were guided purely by considerations of the public interest as opposed to any political factors. And inflation was widely assumed to be an affliction endemic to advanced economies that could be subdued only with price controls.

The intellectual turn against markets had derived enormous momentum from events. The catastrophic collapse of the Great Depression had seriously discredited capitalism, while the energetic experimentation of the New Deal showcased government activism favorably. Belief in the benevolence and effectiveness of American government, and the crucial importance of collective action for collective welfare, gained further strength from the experience of World War II. And the glittering economic performance of the postwar decades under the Big Government-Big Business-Big Labor triumvirate seemed to confirm that government management and economies of scale had permanently displaced upstart entrepreneurship and creative destruction as the primary engines of progress.

But by the 1970s, events had turned. Stagflation, the combination of soaring prices and slumping output, was afflicting the country despite the fact that its very existence was a baffling mystery to the reigning practitioners of macroeconomic "fine-tuning." In cruel mockery of the noble goals and soaring rhetoric of the "War on Poverty," a major expansion of anti-poverty programs had been followed by waves of urban riots, a soaring crime rate, and the catastrophic breakdown of intact families among African-Americans. The auto and steel industries, pillars of the economy and only recently world leaders in efficiency and innovation, were buckling under the competitive challenge of imports from Europe and Japan. Gas lines and periodic rationing suggested a grim future of ever more tightly binding "limits to growth (Meadows et al. 1974)."

Against this backdrop, the rising movement of libertarian thought and free-market economics represented a much-needed corrective. The information processing and incentive alignment performed by markets had been seriously underappreciated, as had the gap between the theoretical possibilities of government activism and what was actually achievable in practice. Under the circumstances, it mattered little that the new movement's philosophical foundations were shaky and its empirical claims overstated. At the relevant margins, the critics of Big Government had the better of the argument overall and were pushing in the right direction. After a massive increase in the size and scope of government over the course of decades, the nation was reeling from multiplying economic and social ills. The time was ripe for a thoroughgoing critique of top-down, centralized, technocratic policymaking.

During the 1980s and 1990s, the return of boom times at home, the collapse of communism and the rise of globalization abroad, and the entrepreneur-led information technology revolution seemed to affirm the conclusion that "the era of big government is over (Clinton [1996] 2014)." But with the dawn of a new century, the tide of events shifted again. The failure of another round of tax cutting to unleash dynamism and growth; the incompetent response to Hurricane Katrina; the bursting of the housing bubble and the ensuing financial and economic meltdown; the opening of a yawning class divide along educational lines; the spread of social problems once identified with the urban "underclass" to broad swaths of the country; the rise of "deaths of despair;" and now the coronavirus pandemic – in the face of all this, the one-size-fits-all prescription of cutting taxes, government spending, and regulatory costs imposed on business looked increasingly irrelevant, if not like outright quackery.

The ideals of free markets and limited government remain vital, and vitally important. But the times have made plain that the dominant conceptions of these ideals, rooted in libertarian ideology, are fatally flawed. That ideology is based on fundamental intellectual errors about the nature of politics and the conditions that make individual freedom and competitive markets possible. And as that ideology has moved beyond theoretical inquiry to exert real influence over political actors, its effects on American political culture have ultimately been nothing short of poisonous.

For those of us who continue to believe in the indispensability of a critical stance toward government power, the task before us is one of intellectual reconstruction. We must reject minimal government as the organizing principle of policy reform. Making or keeping government as small as possible is an ideological fixation, not a sound principle of good governance. Small government is a false idol, and it is time we smash it. In its place, we should erect *effective government* as the goal that guides the development and evaluation of public policy. For maxims, we can look to America's greatest stateman. "The legitimate object of government," wrote Abraham Lincoln, "is to do for a community of people, whatever they need to have done, but can not do, *at all*, or can not, *so well do*, for themselves—in their separate, and individual capacities."

Guided by the principle of effective government, we will sometimes conclude that government needs to be smaller, and sometimes that it needs to be larger – depending on the circumstances. Given where things stand today, we will often conclude that government can be made simpler. We will continue to champion the ideals of free markets and limited government, but we must reconceive those ideals to free them from their libertarian baggage.

Free markets are the foundation of our prosperity and an important motor of social advance. But we need to see them, not as something that exists in the absence of government, but rather as complex achievements of good government. Free markets as we know them today are impossible without the modern state, and they function best when embedded in and supported by a structure of public goods that only government can adequately provide.

The guiding principle of effective government, meanwhile, continues to impose important limits on the exercise of state power – but the contours of those limits are quite different from those demanded by libertarian ideology. Here the limiting principle addresses not the scope or subject matter of government action, but rather the effect of that action: The government policy or program in question must actually succeed in advancing its stated public purpose, and under no circumstances may benefit narrow private interests at public expense. The limiting principle, then, grows out of commitment to the public interest, not antipathy to government. The critical stance associated with policing the proper limits of state action thus shifts from *anti-government* to *anti-corruption*.

But reconstruction cannot proceed until demolition clears the scene. Accordingly, in Part Two of this series of essays, "The Dead End of Small Government," I will identify what I see as the fundamental deficiencies of the libertarian ideology that has done so much to shape economic orthodoxy on the American right. Then in Part

Three, "Free Markets and Limited Government Reconceived," I will turn to how these important principles of good governance can be rescued from the errors and blind spots with which they are now tangled up.

Let me conclude this essay with an important qualification. My argument here is about economic and social policy: To meet the looming challenges of poor economic performance; widening social divisions; and threats to public health, we need more capable government, not more constrained government. Accordingly, the exclusive libertarian focus on restraining government power is not just irrelevant to confronting our problems, but actively counterproductive. But as recent events have made painfully clear, there are other areas of public concern where restraining government power remains not only relevant, but morally urgent. Here I am referring, of course, to the police murder of George Floyd, the latest in a long string of such incidents, and the weeks of protests in its wake (which have regrettably resulted in many further examples of inexcusable police violence). But not just that: In all the agencies of American government that deal directly in physical force – not just the police, but the larger criminal justice system, the immigration authorities, and the military – problems of excess and overreach and abuse are widespread.

The militarization and brutalization of police tactics; the immense waste and suffering caused by the War on Drugs; the moral stain of mass incarceration, deepened by the appalling cruelty that is widespread in America's jails and prisons; the specter of mass surveillance; the caging of children on our border and betrayal of our heritage as an asylum for refugees; the "forever wars" in Afghanistan and Iraq, with spinoff military engagements in countries all over the region – on all of these fronts, libertarians' portrayal of government as Leviathan is all too accurate, and their calls for additional chains to bind it are well founded.

This qualification, though, only highlights how misguided it is for libertarians to conflate the provision of public goods, social insurance, and pro-market regulation with real problems of unchecked power. The vital work of controlling the instrumentalities of state violence is always difficult, but libertarians' worthy efforts along these lines are badly undercut by their small-government fixation. Not only do they compromise their case by mixing bad arguments with good, they alienate themselves from their natural allies – in particular, those communities that suffer most at the hands of excess force – and thereby weaken the coalition needed for constructive change.

References

Bethune, Zachary A., and Anton Korinek. 2020. "Covid-19 Infection Externalities: Trading Off Lives vs. Livelihoods." w27009. National Bureau of Economic Research. https://doi.org/10.3386/w27009.

Broughel, James. 2020. "COVID-19 Reveals the Need for a Regulatory Reset." *SSRN Electronic Journal*, April. https://doi.org/10.2139/ssrn.3592928.

Clinton, William J. 1996. 2014. "Clinton Says Era of Big Government Is 'Over' in 1996 State of the Union." *Washington Post*. January 22. https://www.washingtonpost.com/video/politics/clinton-says-era-of-big-government-is-over-in-1996-state-of-the-union/2014/01/22/da7c0cb4-83b6-11e3-8099-9181471f7aaf_video.html.

Dalmia, Shikha. 2020. "Michigan Gov. Gretchen Whitmer Provides a Lesson in What States Shouldn't Do To Stop a Pandemic." *Reason.Com* (blog). April 16. https://reason.com/2020/04/16/michigan-gov-gretchen-whitmer-provides-a-lesson-in-what-states-shouldnt-do-to-stop-a-pandemic/.

Fineout, Gary, and Marc Caputo. 2020. "'It's a Sh– Sandwich': Republicans Rage as Florida Becomes a Nightmare for Trump." *Politico*. April 3. https://politi.co/346bitf.

Frum, David. 2020. "This Is Trump's Fault." *The Atlantic*, April 7, sec. Ideas. https://www.theatlantic.com/ideas/archive/2020/04/americans-are-paying-the-price-for-trumps-failures/609532/.

Kelly, Makena. 2020. "Unemployment Checks Are Being Held up by a Coding Language Almost Nobody Knows." *The Verge* (blog). April 14. https://www.theverge.com/2020/4/14/21219561/coronavirus-pandemic-unemployment-systems-cobol-legacy-software-infrastructure.

Kurtzleben, Danielle, Jim Zarroli, Laura Sullivan, Cheryl W. Thompson, Bill Chappell, Graham Smith, and Pallavi Gogoi. 2020. "Here's How The Small Business Loan Program Went Wrong In Just 4 Weeks." *NPR.Org* (blog). May 4. https://www.npr.org/2020/05/04/848389343/how-did-the-small-business-loan-program-have-so-many-problems-in-just-4-weeks.

Meadows, Donella H., Dennis L. Meadows, Jørgen Randers, and William W. III Behrens. 1974. *The Limits to Growth: A Report for the Club of Rome's Project on the Predicament of Mankind*. Universe Books. https://www.clubofrome.org/publication/the-limits-to-growth/.

O'Toole, Fintan. 2020. "Fintan O'Toole: Donald Trump Has Destroyed the Country He Promised to Make Great Again." *The Irish Times*, April 25. https://www.irishtimes.com/opinion/fintan-o-toole-donald-trump-has-destroyed-the-country-he-promised-to-make-great-again-1.4235928.

Polumbo, Brad. 2020. "Five Ways Deregulation Is Helping Coronavirus Response." *Washington Examiner* (blog). March 20, 2020. https://www.washingtonexaminer.com/opinion/five-ways-deregulation-is-helping-coronavirus-response.

Rucker, Philip, Josh Dawsey, Yasmeen Abutaleb, Robert Costa, and Lena H. Sun. 2020. "34 Days of Pandemic: Inside Trump's Desperate Attempts to Reopen America." *Washington Post*, May 2. https://www.washingtonpost.com/politics/34-days-of-pandemic-inside-trumps-desperate-attempts-to-reopen-america/2020/05/02/e99911f4-8b54-11ea-9dfd-990f9dcc71fc_story.html.

Stapp, Alec. 2020. "Timeline: The Regulations—and Regulators—That Delayed Coronavirus Testing." *The Dispatch* (blog). March 20. https://thedispatch.com/p/timeline-the-regulationsand-regulatorsthat.

Teles, Steven M. 2013. "Kludgeocracy in America." *National Affairs* (blog). Fall 2013. https://www.nationalaffairs.com/publications/detail/kludgeocracy-in-america.

Thompson, Derek. 2020. "There Are No Libertarians in a Pandemic." Tweet. *@DKThomp* (blog). March 3, 2020. https://twitter.com/DKThomp/status/1234952340807077892.

Weissmann, Shoshana, Chelsea Boyd, Courtney Joslin, Nick Zaiac, and R.J. Lehmann. 2020. "Small Regulatory Reforms That Can Help People During the COVID Pandemic." *R Street* (blog). March 18, 2020. https://www.rstreet.org/2020/03/18/small-regulatory-reforms-that-can-help-people-during-the-pandemic/.

Carolina Alves and Ingrid Harvold Kvangraven, "Changing the Narrative: Economics After COVID-19" (2020)*

The weaknesses of the field of economics have long been known, but the Covid-19 pandemic has laid them bare. Of particular concern in the wake of this pandemic is the discipline's understanding of economies as markets separated from the rest of the societies in which they are embedded and heavy reliance on methodological individualism and quantitative modelling. We argue that society's unpreparedness and inadequate response expose weaknesses in the very foundations of the dominant economic paradigm.

Unlike the 2007–08 financial crisis, there are no banks or financial markets to blame this time. Nor can we blame Keynesianism as we did in the 1970s. By contrast, the pandemic forces us to evaluate the structural problems inherent in the global system of provisioning. These problems are the results of decades of market-oriented reform and underfunding of social services. Therefore, rather than engage in debates about appropriate monetary policy tools and whether we are facing a demand or supply shock, we take a step back and explore some of these structural problems, how we got here, and the role of the economics discipline in this story. The fact that we find ourselves in a moment of deep uncertainty should not distract us from this broader and more fundamental critique.

In this article, we document how economics came to dissociate itself from broader societal analysis and rely heavily on mathematical modelling and stringent assumptions, and how this has influenced public policy in problematic ways. We then go a step further to consider the role of economic evidence in public policy more generally. Finally, we demonstrate how heterodox economics can enrich our understanding of our economies' weaknesses to build a more resilient and just economy.

From Political Economy to an Exact Science

Economics has long been criticised for its treatment of the economy as a separate entity, rather than situating it within broader societal aspects related to, for example, nature, ethics, and power (DeMartino 2013; Foster 1997; Hirsch 1977; Marglin 1974; Palermo 2014; Sen 1999). This critique builds on a tradition of critical political economy that originated before economics became a separate discipline, thus allowing for analysis of societal issues such as gender, ecology, and politics (Fine and Milonakis 2009; Mearman, Guizzo, and Berger 2018).

---

* From: article first published in *Review of Agrarian Studies*, vol. 10, no. 1, available free online at http://ras.org.in/changing_the_narrative. Republished with permission.

From the period of classical political economy to the marginalist revolution and the formalisation of economics in the 1950s, the social and historical contexts have been increasingly removed from economics. Indeed, Léon Walras was convinced that economics would gradually evolve into a scientific discipline similar to the hard sciences, with economic laws being rational, precise and as incontrovertible as the laws of astronomy (Jaffé 1965). Instead of embedding the economy in society, the discipline has taken a more inductive approach, largely limited to viewing social behaviour through the lens of methodological individualism and economic macrodynamics through the lens of equilibrium solutions of mathematical models. Economists have generally seen this shift as a positive development, believing it to be in the interest of "coherence and consistency" (Arrow and Hahn 1971, p. 2).

Through the formalisation and also uniformisation of the economist profession since the 1950s, the discipline came to embrace "an absolute preference for the form of an economic argument over its content" (Blaug 2003, p. 145). This involved the development of economic principles abstracted from society and considered apolitical and ahistorical, building on European positivist assumptions of a universal objective truth (Kayatekin 2009). Perhaps because of this narrow view of economic principles, the discipline is also the least interdisciplinary of the social sciences (Fourcade, Ollion, and Algan 2015) and is "unique among the social sciences in having a single monolithic mainstream, which is either unaware of or actively hostile to alternative approaches" (King 2013, p. 17). With this backdrop, it should not be surprising that the discipline will struggle to grapple with the cross-cutting nature of the current crisis.

The fact that economists see the Covid-19 pandemic as an external shock (Baldwin and di Mauro 2020) is in itself revealing and can be seen as a reflection of their view of the economy as separate from the rest of society. The external aspect is in line with the view of externalities in economics, which are conceived ahistorically and thought to arise because of technological, institutional, or other problems that prevent effective functioning of markets.

The Discipline's Obsession with Markets

With the above changes in the economics discipline, culminating with the rise of the Chicago School of Economics in the 1970s, economists largely stopped challenging the standard choice of taking market equilibrium and human rationality as starting points. These theoretical and methodological choices echo the origins of modern economics, wherein the discipline broadly came to be seen as the study of "human behaviour as a relationship between ends and scarce means" (Robbins 1932, p. 15); the market was considered the most efficient allocating mechanism (Walras 1954). Within this understanding, human interactions are thought to happen mainly through the market, and markets are theorised as being about the mutual interactions of demand and supply, with equilibrium as a central concept (Wootton 1938).[1] This also had implications for how the discipline came to view that state and paved the way for the likes of Nozick and Buchanan, who presented a market version of contractarianism to justify a minimal state whose actions are limited to necessities such as law enforcement and providing national defence.

As we move further into the second half of the twentieth century, an increasing number of economists think of themselves as modellers, "simplifying" reality through models and invoking the necessary assumptions regarding equilibrium, representative agents, and optimisation.[2] This led Lawson (2013) to characterise mainstream economics in terms of its enduring reliance upon methods of mathematical modelling – analysing economic phenomena with the help of mathematical deduction, laws, or uniformities. A consequence of this turn is that economists find it increasingly difficult to imagine different ways to do economics. An example is Colander and Kupers's (2014) view of the economy as a complex adaptive system, which has been seen as a paradigm shift in economics. However, as Kirman (2016) observes, the system still relies on an equilibrium or steady state as an organising tool and thus remains firmly placed within the dominant theoretical framework; this is hardly a paradigm shift.

More broadly, the developments in the discipline that have led to the influential role of general equilibrium theory (first sketched by Walras and developed by Arrow-Debreu), which assumed conditions such as perfect market competition, reinforced the turn towards seeing the state as an institution supporting the market. Essentially, within mainstream economics, deviations from the basic assumptions that underpin market equilibrium are considered "imperfections" or "externalities," thus retaining a form of market fundamentalism at its core.[3] Similarly, behavioural economics has become a booming subfield, studying how behaviour deviates from *homo economicus* and thus retaining the same starting point for understanding human rationality. Naturally, policy recommendations emanating from this theoretical framework largely revolve around solving market failures and nudging individuals to behave rationally. Now that the economy is partially shut down and "normal" market mechanisms are put on hold, it is perhaps not surprising that the discipline may struggle to propose effective policy solutions.

Public Policy Implications: Weakening of Social Provisioning

The discipline's narrow view of the "economic sphere" equated to markets has had a strong influence on public policy over the past half century. Indeed, the market fundamentalism at the heart of modern economics lies behind much of the weakening of the state that occurred in Europe and the US in the 1980s, which led to increased participation of the private sector in health care, education, and housing. In the same period, reliance on the market was now a condition for developing countries to obtain loans from the International Monetary Fund and the World Bank (the so-called Washington Consensus).

The discipline's bias towards markets as an efficient allocator of resources has led to two key trends that weakened the structures of economies and their capacities to engage in social provisioning across the world. The first is the vilification of "the state" alongside a celebration of market efficiency, which has led to a lack of resilience in the organisation of social provisioning. The second and more recent one, is the austerity that has driven government deficit reductions, spending cuts, and attempts to dismantle social welfare systems across the world (Konzelmann 2019; Mkandawire 2006; Williams and Maruthappu 2013; Noy 2017).

Market precepts and axioms have heavily influenced the development of the New Public Management (NPM) paradigm in public policy, both in terms of reliance on market mechanisms and rational choice theory (Gruening 2001; Osborne 2006).[4] NPM includes policies of managerialism, marketisation, privatisation, and public-private partnerships (Christensen and Laegreid 2011). The paradigm gained traction under Reagan and Thatcher in the 1980s but has since increasingly become a global phenomenon (Sekera 2016). Despite its market-centric approach, it has broadly been supported by all major political parties in Anglo-Saxon and European countries (Diefenbach 2009).

The strong influence of economics on public policy has led to *efficiency* itself becoming a core public goal (Davis 1985), implying the elimination of any idle resources to ensure all capital is put to efficient use. Although scholars have contested the expected positive effects derived from this efficiency (Cook 2015; Harford 2014), the economic system has largely been oriented towards profit-making, cost minimisation, and efficiency in the last forty years or so (Jacobin Magazine 2020). The focus on efficiency has not only led to poor monetary remuneration to essential workers such as nurses but also to "just in time" and "lean work" procedures that justify decades of systematic underinvestment in planning and surge capacity (Carter *et al.* 2016; Toynbee and Walker 2017).[5] For hospitals, this has contributed to a reduction in the total number of hospital beds. For example, the number of National Health Service hospital beds in England dropped by more than half during 1987 to 2017 (Ewbank *et al.* 2017).

In parallel, there has been an increasing focus on the connection between public debt and macroeconomic outcomes by economists and policymakers across the world. Initially, based on the balanced budget approach, ideas about crowding-out effects, and fiscal costs associated with public projects and welfare provisioning, this focus guided much of the reforms of the 1980s and 1990s. Since then, the prevailing narrative has shifted towards a more rigid focus on a negative correlation between high public debt and economic growth as well as between fiscal deficits and financial investor confidence. This has, at times, prevented democratically elected governments from acting to enhance their people's welfare.

The idea of the state as this potential Leviathan that needs to be restrained together with an "efficient" approach to the organisation of society has engendered worrisome fragilities, inequalities, and vulnerabilities, leaving us completely unprepared and incapable of responding effectively to the pandemic. If we thought of structuring our society along the lines of resilience and robustness rather than efficiency, our societies' preparedness for a pandemic would be much greater (Trosper 2009; Derissen, Quaas, and Baumgärtner 2011). In such a case, we would be more likely to have had adequate equipment and structures in place to respond effectively.

Economics and Evidence-Based Policy: Whither Public Debate?

The rise of econometrics in economics has been accompanied by a critique of empirical practices in the field (Leamer 1983). By the 1980s, credible empirical work in economics was considered a pipe dream, but much has changed with empirical developments in labour economics and microeconomics, wherein data is taken seriously, for example, through random experiments and quasi-experiments (Angrist and Pischke 2010).[6] This so-called empirical turn has been used to justify an increase in economics' policy relevance and scientific impact. Though this is positive because it means abstract economic principles can be empirically tested, the type of policies and interventions "tested" by economists remain within a narrow frame of what public policy can be, thus constraining policy choices significantly.

Also, in line with the empirical turn, randomised control trials (RCTs) have gained traction as the gold standard for providing microeconomic evidence. Given the narrowness of the theoretical and methodological approach underlying RCTs, this form of evidence tends to be removed from analyses of power and wider social change (Chernomas and Hudson 2019) as well as the underlying social, economic, and cultural structures that affect the results (Deaton and Cartwright 2018). This has been exacerbated by the fact that evidence produced through RCTs, or modelling in economics more broadly, is usually presented as atheoretical. This is nowhere made more lucid than when Esther Duflo famously likened economists to plumbers, suggesting that economists' work is purely technical, objective, and value-neutral, despite being rooted in a particular theoretical framework (Kvangraven 2020b).

With the rise of RCTs, we have also seen a rise in so-called evidence-based policy. While this term is a bit of a misnomer, suggesting policy was not based on evidence before the randomista revolution, it reflects a paradigm wherein a specific type of evidence is currently accepted as rigorous and "lie[s] at the top of the hierarchy" (Drèze 2020, p. 1).[7] This means that, in effect, the policy options available are limited by the requirement of a certain kind of evidence (Manski 2011; Kelly and Linsey 2018; Parkhurst 2017; Spiegler 2015). Given that RCTs are often used to test how people react to certain policy interventions, behavioural economists often make use of this methodology; behavioural insights are increasingly being connected to evidence-based policy (Bogliacino, Codagnone, and Veltri 2016; Chetty 2015; Thaler 2016).

This discussion is of utmost importance to understand the role of evidence in the current policy response to the pandemic, particularly in light of the UK's response. In contrast to the scientific advice of the World Health Organisation (WHO) about the importance of lockdown as well as testing and tracing, the UK considered that locking down early may cause negative psychological effects and a risk of demoralising people in case of an extended lockdown (Brooks *et al.* 2020; Lunn *et al.* 2020). However, this evidence was largely based on behavioural experiments in entirely different contexts, thus assuming that behaviour is independent of the situation in which it takes place (e.g., the specific argument on the demoralising effects of an extended quarantine was based on a randomised experiment on extending military deployment). In effect, the UK government acted against WHO evidence, and its policy response differed greatly from regions and countries such as Ghana, New Zealand, Kerala in India, Vietnam, Singapore, and South Korea that more successfully managed the pandemic in the beginning.

In these initially successful cases, despite weak healthcare capacity, policy responses often combined early action by the government, rigorous testing and contact tracing, full or partial lockdown, support for unemployed workers, and effective public communication.[8] Strong proactive lockdown measures like in Vietnam and early closed borders like in Ghana seem to have been crucial measures for success. Policy responses often went beyond what could be derived from epidemiological modelling to addressing hospital staff and bed shortages via, for example, the efforts of community health workers and volunteers (Ghana) and adding new beds to existing healthcare facilities (South Korea). At the outset, the engagement with science, evidence, and experts was more comprehensive in these countries than in the UK. Undoubtedly, many of these governments had a structure and expertise in place due to experiences with SARS or Ebola, whereas others drew on knowledge from the WHO and carefully acknowledged the complexity of the situation.

The model developed by Neil Ferguson and his team at Imperial College London (ICL) crucially influenced the UK government to act and lockdown the economy (Adam 2020). It provided evidence as early as the end of January to support general social distancing. However, there are some drawbacks to the approach worth mentioning. While the ICL model is not an economic one, it illustrates more general issues with modelling applicable to economics. Economic expertise, as well as modelling expertise more broadly, has gained status as an almost unquestionable guide for policy, despite the fact that any model will only represent a particular perspective (D'Ippoliti 2020). For example, the ICL model focuses on Covid-19 mortality and does not appraise other health and non-health implications of the pandemic. It thus does not deal with broader economic and social costs of various interventions (Reddy 2020). Considering the broad and comprehensive approaches of the successful responses to the pandemic, the ICL model is not a sufficient basis for an effective and comprehensive policy response to the pandemic. In this sense, the UK response demonstrates both the over-influence of a particular expertise on policy and its disproportionate influence of models; it highlights the fact that policymaking requires broader judgements about policy effects on society at large. This heavy bias towards quantitative models and narrow behavioural insights led many to protest the government's judgement (Horton 2020).

Beyond the problematic assumptions behind evidence informing the UK's response to the pandemic, there are two broad lessons to learn from its response. The first is that any narrow view of what counts as evidence and expertise limits a government's ability to comprehensively understand the pandemic and its consequences. Having a limited team of experts means that important perspectives will inevitably be neglected. Rather than restricting the advisory group to mostly clinical academics, microbiologists, and modellers (as was the case in Britain), an interesting example to follow could be that of Germany, where philosophers and historians of science were a part of the government's advisory group. Drawing on expertise from countries with experience from previous outbreaks would also be helpful.

The second lesson is related to the problematic discourse of "expertise" in the public debate about the Covid-19 response. Though science must, of course, play an important role in policymaking, narrowly defined expertise obscures value judgments that policymakers have to make, including decisions about who to select for their advisory committees. Given that "coronavirus advice is political" (Bacevic 2020), forming a more diverse scientific advisory group would be a first step to broadening the evidence available to the government and making the tensions and value judgments inherent in any response explicit. Indeed, this would lead to increased public scrutiny and understanding, which would be healthy for democratic debate.

Heterodox Economics: For Better and Broader Analyses

Rather than being centred on the study of the allocation of scarce resources, heterodox economics is concerned with the study of production and distribution of economic surplus, including the role of power relations in determining economic relationships, the study of economic systems beyond market relations, and the employment of theories focusing on these issues (Kvangraven and Alves 2019). This alternative view of and approach to the economy can help us understand the causes and consequences of the Covid-19 pandemic in crucial ways.

First of all, heterodox economics relies on alternative views of human behaviour, moving away from the rational optimising agents and the methodological individualism of the mainstream. Indeed, understanding rationality as being about more than optimising personal advantage given certain constraints has been understood by scholars going back to Adam Smith and Immanuel Kant; the mainstream approach to rationality has long been criticised for being conceptually and empirically flawed (Lukes 1968; Nandy 2012; Ostrom 1990; Ostrom 2005; Sen 1977). Essential here are insights from feminist economists, who have long pointed to the importance of understanding both social reproduction and social relations between actors (Nelson 1995). As the spread of the virus between individuals has led to measures such as school closures, society has been forced to grapple with the importance of social reproduction as a core activity that keeps the economy going (this insight has been long recognised in social reproduction theory, e.g. Bhattacharya 2017).[9]

As heterodox economists do not rely on methodological individualism, there is also more space for exploring inequalities related to aggregate societal categories such as gender, class, and race (Kvangraven and Alves 2019; Mearman, Guizzo, and Berger 2019; Tilley and Shilliam 2017). This is particularly relevant in the wake of the pandemic, which is no "great leveller," as some pundits have claimed, but rather a process of exacerbating and highlighting existing inequalities. For example, as demonstrated by Nassif-Pires *et al.* (2020), the virus is hitting low-income neighbourhoods and minority communities the hardest. This would not be surprising to stratification economists, who have long pointed out the deep racial wealth gap in the US, rooted in socio-economic and political structural barriers (Hamilton and Darity 2017).

In terms of methodology, Lawson's (2013) view of heterodox economics as a scientific programme that emphasises an ontology of openness, relationality, and totalities helps us understand how many economic models fail to grasp human interaction and complex networks. This is particularly important for policymakers across the world as they try to make sense of the unfolding crisis.

It should also be highlighted that heterodox approaches enable seeing the economy as embedded in society. For example, Lee's (2009) emphasis on heterodox economics as the "historical process of social provisioning" has led to a focus on the structures of production and reproduction in society, with their historical determinations and causal mechanisms not limited to the sphere of the market (pp. 8–9). Such a perspective can, for example, open the door for fruitful insights about household dynamics during the crisis and how they relate to both production and reproduction. Another implication of this view is that we cannot expect the same behavioural responses or societal outcomes across different social communities, given differences in history, culture, and economic organisation. Instead, the perspective forces us to consider how responses to the pandemic are mediated by institutional, social, and economic factors.

Situating the economy in society enables exploration of the intricacies between the economy and nature, for example, by food systems researchers (Worstell 2020) or ecological economists (Derissen, Quaas, and Baumgärtner 2011; Trosper 2009). Indeed, to scholars with a broader understanding of how production affects food and ecological systems, the rise and spread of Covid-19 was less of a surprise (Wang *et al.* 2006; Wallace 2016). Such a perspective starkly contrasts to viewing the pandemic as an exogenous shock. Therefore, it is now time to emphasise that capitalist production is intertwined with nature and cannot be seen as separate – an important lesson for many heterodox economists as well.

The inherent instability of capitalism and the need to put distributional conflicts at the centre of any economic analysis is also a recurring characteristic of heterodox approaches. Vernengo (2011) emphasises how distribution is determined exogenously by social and institutional conditions in heterodox economics, which can help us understand that structural weaknesses in our economies are due to political choices. For example, the low wages among essential workers are determined by policy, rather than being a reflection of a market-determined price. Some of these weaknesses bluntly exposed by the pandemic include the high degrees of homelessness, precarious workforces, and poverty, all of which impact the governments' ability to respond effectively. For once, policymakers are forced to consider public health as a broader societal issue as well as including shelters for the homeless, paid sick leave, and universal health coverage as a part of their pandemic response. In light of this, a framework that allows us to see the enduring structural aspects of these socio-economic problems is needed.

Furthermore, heterodox economists identify and analyse structural forces that lie behind the polarising tendencies within the global economy. This is central at a moment when deepening global economic integration over the past decades has led to improved economic efficiency as well as new vulnerabilities. Global value chains are now very complex systems, and rather than being decentralised, they are hierarchical and imbalanced with core hubs that exert disproportionate influence (Panitch and Gindin 2004; Durand and Milberg 2020). To understand developing economies' constraints in the wake of the pandemic, it is therefore essential to look beyond their health systems to also consider constraints related to their subordinate or dependent position in the global economy (Alves and Toporowski 2019; Bonizzi *et al.* 2019; de Paula, Fritz, and Prates 2017; Kaltenbrunner 2018; Kvangraven 2020a; Patnaik and Patnaik 2016; Suwandi 2019).

Finally, the heterodox critique of mainstream economics goes beyond a simple state–market dichotomy, wherein heterodox economists want "more" of the state and the mainstream wants "less." The role of the state in the economy is much broader than in just rectifying market failure (Bernstein 2018); in addition, heterodox economics and especially the literature on the public economy points us to a broader understanding of economies as non-market environments (Sekera 2016). Within this view, there is a public economy comprised of multiple economic systems, wherein the public sector is not governed by the same principles and axioms as that of the market.[10] This view leads us to consider the advantages of a collective-choice and collective-financing system that produces goods, services, benefits, and protection aimed at the well-being of society as a whole (*ibid.*). Within the context of a Covid-19 response, this perspective is crucial because it recognises that the public sector is an integral part of the economy and directly affects many, if not all, socio-economic issues (Bernstein 2018). Such analyses of the state should not only be conducted by social and political theorists.

The Battle for the Narrative

Though this crisis is indeed unprecedented, the question remains whether we will see any fundamental change in the economics discipline. After all, if the 2007–08 global financial crisis did not drastically change the profession, it is not a given that the pandemic will either. The crisis has certainly made it clear that fiscal austerity is a political choice rather than a necessity, a principle that we must remember once the lockdown eases. It has also publicly exposed weaknesses and inequalities in our economies, including weak and underfunded health systems, weak state capacities to provide social services, and the precarity among underpaid essential workers. Exposing these weaknesses and the political choices that lie behind how our economies are organised is a first step towards building a more just society.

In this article, we go beyond describing societal problems to analysing the role of the economics discipline in particular. Two broad problems emerge. Firstly, the nature of the discipline makes it difficult for economists to understand the economy in a comprehensive and realistic manner. Economists' view of Covid-19 as an external shock poses problems for the discipline's ability to grapple with the interconnected crises that this pandemic represents. At this juncture, it is more important than ever to open up the debate about how to understand and tackle these crises, with a view to make our economies more resilient and just, rather than simply more "efficient." It is time to revisit the field's flawed conception of the economy as a market equilibrium economy and obsession with narrow forms of evidence and modelling.

The second problem is the discipline's claim to neutrality and objectivity that obscures the ideological assumptions behind economic research. As heterodox economists tend to be more explicit about the political and ideological aspect of their academic work, their analyses are more concerned with social conflicts and different group interests in the economy, which could pave the way for a broader and more informed public debate about economics. For such a debate to be effective there is also a need to revise the role of so-called evidence-based policy in economics and public policy. There have already been calls to hold the UK accountable for its inadequate response to the pandemic – this should ideally include a thorough reassessment of how models and evidence are used to determine policy and how some forms of expertise are prioritised over others. This pandemic exposes the fact that data and evidence are never entirely neutral.

In the coming months and years, there will be a battle to define the narrative of the pandemic. We need an explanation of the crisis that is capable of seeing the economy as more than just markets and, rather, as embedded in society. It should be capable of linking the causes and consequences of the pandemic to our systems of production and distribution. A fundamental change in the prevailing economic narrative is necessary for a more just, robust, and democratic society.

Notes

1 Even though the market/economy became detached from society, there have been attempts within the mainstream to forge a link between the economic and the social, but always through the application of economic principles to the social sphere and treating social entities as though they are only to exist within and according to market principles.

2 It is worth noting that there are many alternative ways of modelling the economy that do not rely on such assumptions (Kvangraven and Alves 2019).

3 Note, we do not argue that all economists believe in laissez-faire (e.g. Naidu, Rodrik, and Zucman's (2019) understanding of market fundamentalism), but rather that markets are employed within economic theory as a frame through which to understand human rationality and behaviour (Wootton 1938).

4 Rational choice theory is a cornerstone of the economics discipline and encompasses three central tenets: methodological individualism, a view of rationality linked to constrained optimisation, and the role of equilibrium as a descriptive and explanatory device.

5 For example, in the UK, the shrinking capacity has recently been exacerbated by both austerity policies and Brexit (Toynbee and Walker 2017). In April 2020, *The Times* reported that the UK government limited emergency stockpiles of personal protective equipment due to austerity measures and suspended training for essential pandemic workers for two years while directing their efforts to a possible no-deal Brexit (Calvert, Arbuthnott, and Leake 2020).

6 Empirical development in macroeconomics has happened at a much slower pace.

7 Duflo and Kremer (2005) stated that "all too often development policy is based on fads, and randomised evaluations could allow it to be based on evidence," suggesting that pre-RCTs policies did not draw on evidence (p. 206).

8 Vietnam, for example, has 8 doctors per 10,000 people, whereas the average for OECD countries is 3.5 doctors per 1,000 people (World Bank 2020).

9 The substantial relative drop in women academics' productivity during the pandemic is also a telling example of working women's reliance on institutions of social reproduction (Minello 2020).

10 The public economy literature also highlights the necessity of socially constructive economies that focus on both a broader array of goals not simply defined by profit maximisation (i.e., the public purpose economy) and on the survival, nurturing, and welfare of its constituents (i.e., the core economy) (Goodwin 2018).

References

Adam, David (2020), "Special Report: The Simulations Driving the World's Response to Covid-19," *Nature*, April 2, available at https://www.nature.com/articles/d41586-020-01003-6, viewed on June 13, 2020.

Alves, Carolina, and Toporowski, Jan (2019), "Capital Flows and the Growth of International Finance in Emerging Economies: An Alternative Approach," *PSL Quarterly Review*, vol. 72, no. 288.

Angrist, Joshua D., and Pischke, Jörn-Steffen (2010), "The Credibility Revolution in Empirical Economics: How Better Research Design is Taking the Con out of Econometrics," *Journal of Economic Perspectives*, vol. 24, no. 2, pp. 3–30.

Arrow, Kenneth J., and Hahn, F. H. (1971), *General Competitive Analysis*, Holden-Day, San Francisco.

Bacevic, Jana (2020), "There's No Such Thing as Just 'Following the Science' – Coronavirus Advice is Political," *The Guardian*, April 28, available at www.theguardian.com/commentisfree/2020/apr/28/theres-no-such-thing-just-following-the-science-coronavirus-advice-political, viewed on April 29, 2020.

Baldwin, Richard, and di Mauro, Beatrice Weder (2020), *Mitigating the COVID Economic Crisis: Act Fast and Do Whatever It Takes*, Centre for Economic Policy Research Press, London.

Bernstein, Michael A. (2018), "Reconstructing a Public Economics: Markets, States, and Societies," *Real-World Economics Review*, no. 84, pp. 2–15.

Bhattacharya, Tithi (2017), *Social Reproduction Theory: Remapping Class, Recentering Oppression*, Pluto Press, London.

Blaug, Mark (2003), "The Formalist Revolution of the 1950s," *Journal of the History of Economic Thought*, vol. 25, no. 2, pp. 145–156.

Bogliacino, Francesco, Codagnone, Cristiano, and Veltri, Giuseppe A. (2016), "An Introduction to the Special Issue on 'the Behavioural Turn in Public Policy: New Evidence from Experiments,'" *Economia Politica*, vol. 33, pp. 323–32.

Bonizzi, Bruno, Kaltenbrunner, Annina, and Powell, Jeff (2019) "Subordinate Financialisation in Emerging Capitalist Economies," in Philip Mader, Daniel Mertens, and Natascha van der Zwan (eds.), *The International Handbook of Financialisation*, London, Routledge, pp. 177–87.

Brooks, Samantha K., Webster, Rebecca K., Smith, Louise E., Woodland, Lisa, Wessely, Simon, Greenberg, Neil, and Rubin, Gideon James (2020), "The Psychological Impact of Quarantine and How to Reduce It: Rapid Review of the Evidence," *The Lancet*, vol. 395, no. 10227, pp. 912–20.

Calvert, Jonathan, Arbuthnott, George, and Leake, Jonathan (2020), "Coronavirus: 38 days When Britain Sleepwalked into Disaster," *The Times*, April 18, available at https://archive.is/20200418182037/https://www.thetimes.co.uk/edition/news/coronavirus-38-days-when-britain-sleepwalked-into-disaster-hq3b9tlgh#selection-695.0-695.59, viewed on April 30, 2020.

Carter, Bob, Danford, Andrew, Howcroft, Debra, Richardson, Helen, Smith, Andrew, and Taylor, Phil (2016), "Uncomfortable Truths – Teamworking Under Lean in the UK," *International Journal of Human Resource Management*, vol. 28, no. 3, pp. 449–67.

Chernomas, Robert, and Hudson, Ian (2019), "Omission and Commission in the Development Economics of Daron Acemoglu and Esther Duflo," *Canadian Journal of Development Studies*, vol. 40, no. 4, pp. 447–63.

Chetty, Raj (2015), "Behavioral Economics and Public Policy: A Pragmatic Perspective," *American Economic Review*, vol. 105, no. 5, pp. 1–33.

Christensen, Tom, and Laegreid, Per (eds.) (2011), *The Ashgate Research Companion to New Public Management*, Routledge, London.

Colander, David, and Kupers, Roland (2014), *Complexity and the Art of Public Policy: Solving Society's Problems from the Bottom Up*, Princeton University Press, Princeton.

Cook, Chris (2015), "Risks of Government Schools Strategy," *BBC*, February 2, available at http://www.bbc.co.uk/news/uk-politics-31094670, viewed on April 30, 2020.

Davis, Charles R. (1985), "A Critique of the Ideology of Efficiency," *Humboldt Journal of Social Relations*, vol. 12, no. 2, pp. 73–86.

Deaton, Angus and Cartwright, Nancy (2018), "Understanding and Misunderstanding Randomised Controlled Trials," *Social Science and Medicine*, vol. 210, pp. 2–21.

DeMartino, George (2013), "Epistemic Aspects of Economic Practice and the Need for Professional Economics Ethics," *Review of Social Economy*, vol. 71, no. 2, pp. 166–86.

de Paula, Luiz Fernando, Fritz, Barbara, and Prates, Daniela M. (2017), "Keynes at the Periphery: Currency Hierarchy and Challenges for Economic Policy in Emerging Economies," *Journal of Post Keynesian Economics*, vol. 40, no. 2, pp. 183–202.

Derissen, Sandra, Quaas, Martin F. and Baumgärtner, Stefan (2011), "The Relationship Between Resilience and Sustainability of Ecological-Economic Systems," *Ecological Economics*, vol. 70, no. 6, pp. 1121–28.

Diefenbach, Thomas (2019), "New Public Management in Public Sectors Organisation: The Dark Sides of Managerialistic 'Enlightenment,'" *Public Administration*, vol. 87, no. 4, pp. 892–909.

D'Ippoliti, Carlo (2020), *Democratising the Economics Debate: Pluralism and Research Evaluation*, Routledge, New York.

Drèze, Jean (2020), "Policy Beyond Evidence," *World Development*, vol. 127, pp. 104797, available at https://doi.org/10.1016/j.worlddev.2019.104797, viewed on April 30, 2020.

Duflo, Esther and Kremer, Michael (2005), "Use of Randomisation in the Evaluation of Development Effectiveness," in George Keith Pitman, Osvaldo N. Feinstein, and Gregory K. Ingram (eds.), *Evaluating Development Effectiveness*, Transaction Publishers, London.

Durand, Cédric and Milberg, William (2020), "Intellectual Monopoly in Global Value Chains," *Review of International Political Economy*, vol. 27, no. 2, pp. 404–29.

Ewbank, Leo, Thompson, James, McKenna, Helen, and Anandaciva, Siva (2017), "NHS Hospital Bed Numbers: Past, Present, Future," *The King's Fund*, available at https://www.kingsfund.org.uk/publications/nhs-hospital-bed-numbers, viewed on April 30, 2020.

Fine, Ben, and Milonakis, Dimitris (2009), *From Political Economy to Economics Method, the Social and the Historical in the Evolution of Economic Theory*, Routledge, London.

Foster, John Bellamy (1997), *Valuing Nature?: Economics, Ethics and Environment*, Routledge, London.

Fourcade, Marion, Ollion, Etienne, and Algan, Yann (2015), "The Superiority of Economists," *Journal of Economic Perspectives*, vol. 29, no. 1, pp. 89–114.

Goodwin, Neva (2018), "There is More Than One Economy," *Real-World Economics Review*, vol. 84, pp. 16–35.

Gruening, Gernod (2001), "Origin and Theoretical Basis of New Public Management," *International Public Management Journal*, vol. 4, pp. 1–25.

Hamilton, Darrick and Darity Jr., William A. (2017), "The Political Economy of Education, Financial Literacy, and the Racial Wealth Gap," *Review*, vol. 99, no. 1, pp. 59–76.

Harford, Tim (2014), "Public Service Performance," *Time Harford Undercover Economist*, July 15, available at http://timharford.com/2014/07/underperforming-on-performance/, viewed on April 30, 2020.

Hirsch, Fred (1977), *Social Limits to Growth*, Routledge and Kegan Paul Ltd., London.

Horton, Richard (2020), "Covid-19 and the NHS—'A National Scandal,'" *The Lancet*, vol. 395, no. 10229, pp. 1022.

Jacobin Magazine (2020), "James K. Galbraith and Aaron Benanav," *Jacobin Radio*, available at https://blubrry.com/jacobin/58228982/jacobin-radio-james-k-galbraith-and-aaron-benanav/, accessed April 28, 2020.

Jaffé, William (ed.) (1965), *Correspondence of Leon Walras and Related Papers*, vol. III, North-Holland, Amsterdam.

Kaltenbrunner, Annina (2018), "Financialised Internationalisation and Structural Hierarchies: A Mixed-Method Study of Exchange Rate Determination in Emerging Economies," *Cambridge Journal of Economics*. Oxford Academic, vol. 42, no. 5, pp. 1315–41.

Kayatekin, Serap A. (2009), "Between Political Economy and Postcolonial Theory: First Encounters," *Cambridge Journal of Economics*, vol. 33, pp. 1113–8.

Kelly, Ann H., and McGoey, Linsey (2018), "Facts, Power and Global Evidence: A New Empire of Truth," *Economy and Society*, vol. 47, no. 1, pp. 1–26.

King, John E. (2013), "A Case for Pluralism in Economics," *Economics and Labour Relations Review*, vol. 24, no. 1, pp. 17–31.

Kirman, Alan (2016), "Complexity and Economic Policy: A Paradigm Shift or a Change in Perspective? A Review Essay on David Colander and Roland Kupers's Complexity and the Art of Public Policy," *Journal of Economics Literature*, vol. 54, no. 2, pp. 534–72.

Konzelmann, Suzanne J. (2019), *Austerity*, Polity Press, London.

Kvangraven, Ingrid Harvold (2020a), "Beyond the Stereotype: Restating the Relevance of the Dependency Research Programme," *Development and Change*.

Kvangraven, Ingrid Harvold (2020b), "Impoverished Economics? A Critical Assessment of the New Gold Standard," *World Development*, vol. 127, pp. 104813, available at https://doi.org/10.1016/j.worlddev.2019.104813, viewed on April 30, 2020.

Kvangraven, Ingrid Harvold, and Alves, Carolina (2019), "Heterodox Economics as a Positive Project: Revisiting the Debate," ESRC GPID Research Network Working Paper 19, Global Poverty and Inequality Dynamics Research Network.

Lawson, Tony (2013), "What is This 'School' Called Neoclassical Economics?," *Cambridge Journal of Economics*, vol. 37, no. 5, pp. 947–83.

Leamer, E. Edward, (1983), "Let's Take the Con Out of Econometrics," *The American Economic Review*, vol. 73, no. 1, pp. 31–43.

Lee, Fred (2009), *A History of Heterodox Economics: Challenging the Mainstream in the Twentieth Century*, Routledge, London.

Lukes, Steven (1968), "Methodological Individualism Reconsidered," *The British Journal of Sociology*, vol. 19, no. 2, pp. 119–29.

Lunn, Peter, Belton, Cameron, Lavin, Ciarán, McGowan, Féidhlim, Timmons, Shane, and Robertson, Deirdre (2020), "Using Behavioural Science to Help Fight the Coronavirus," ESRI Working Paper No. 656, Behavioural Research Unit, ESRI, available at www.esri.ie/publications/using-behavioural-science-to-help-fight-the-coronavirus, viewed on April 30, 2020.

Manski, Charles (2011), "Policy Analysis with Incredible Certitude," *Economic Journal*, vol. 121, no. 554, pp. 261–289.

Marglin, Stephan A. (1974), "What Do Bosses Do? The Origins and Functions of Hierarchy in Capitalist Production, Part 1," *Review of Radical Political Economics*, vol. 6, pp. 60–112.

Mearman, Andrew, Guizzo, Danielle, and Berger, Sebastian (2018), "Whither Political Economy? Evaluating the CORE Project as a Response to Calls for Change in Economics Teaching," *Review of Political Economy*, vol. 30, no. 2, pp. 241–259.

Mearman, Andrew, Guizzo, Danielle, and Berger, Sebastian (2019), *What is Heterodox Economics? Conversations with Leading Economists*, Routledge, London.

Minello, Alessandra (2020), "The Pandemic and the Female Academic," *Nature*, April 17, available at https://www.nature.com/articles/d41586-020-01135-9, viewed on April 30, 2020.

Mkandawire, Thandika (2006), "Disempowering New Democracies and the Persistence of Poverty," Democracy, Governance and Human Rights Programme Paper 21, United Nations Research Institute for Social Development, Geneva, Switzerland.

Naidu, Suresh, Rodrik, Dani, and Zucman, Gabriel (2019), "Economics After Neoliberalism," *Boston Review*, February 15, available at http://bostonreview.net/forum/suresh-naidu-dani-rodrik-gabriel-zucman-economics-after-neoliberalism, viewed on April 30, 2020.

Nandy, Ashis (2012), "The Idea of Happiness," *Economic and Political Weekly*, vol. 47, no. 2, pp. 45–48.

Nassif-Pires, Luiza, de Lima Xavier, Laura, Masterson, Thomas, Nikiforos, Michalis, and Rios-Avila, Fernando (2020), "Pandemic of Inequality," Public Policy Brief No. 149, Levy Economics Institute of Bard College, Annandale-on-Hudson, New York.

Nelson, Julie A. (1995), "Feminism and Economics," *The Journal of Economic Perspectives*, vol. 9, no. 2, pp. 131–148.

Noy, Shiri (2017), *Banking on Health The World Bank and Health Sector Reform in Latin America*, Palgrave Macmillan, Cham, Switzerland.

Osborne, Stephen P. (2006), "The New Public Governance?" *Public Management Review*, vol. 8, no. 3, pp. 377–387.

Ostrom, Elinor (1990), *Governing the Commons: The Evolution of Institutions for Collective Action*, Cambridge University Press, Cambridge.

Ostrom, Elinor (2005), *Understanding Institutional Diversity*, Princeton University Press, Princeton.

Palermo, Giulio (2014), "The Economic Debate on Power: A Marxist Critique," *Journal of Economic Methodology*, vol. 21, no. 2, pp. 175–192.

Panitch, Leo, and Gindin, Sam (2004), "Global Capitalism and American Empire," *Socialist Register*, vol. 40.

Parkhurst, Justin (2017), *The Politics of Evidence: From Evidence-Based Policy to the Good Governance of Evidence*, Routledge, Abingdon.

Patnaik, Utsa, and Patnaik, Prabhat (2016), *A Theory of Imperialism*, Columbia University Press, New York.

Reddy, Sanjay (2020), "How Epidemiological Models Fooled Us Into Trusting Bad Assumptions," *Barrons*, April 29, available at https://www.barrons.com/articles/the-danger-of-overreliance-on-epidemiological-models-51588179008, viewed on April 29, 2020.

Robbins, Lionel (1932), *An Essay on the Nature and Significance of Economic Science*, MacMillan & Co Limited, London.

Sekera, June A. (2016), "Developing an Intellectual Infrastructure," *The Public Economy in Crisis: A Call for a New Public Economics*, Springer, Switzerland, pp. 93–102.

Sen, Amartya (1977), "Rational Fools: A Critique of the Behavioral Foundations of Economic Theory," *Philosophy & Public Affairs*, vol. 6, no. 4, pp. 317–44.

Sen, Amartya (1999), *On Ethics and Economics*, Oxford University Press, Oxford.

Spiegler, Peter (2015), *Behind the Model: A Constructive Critique of Economic Modeling*, Cambridge University Press, Cambridge.

Suwandi, Intan (2019), *Value Chains: The New Economic Imperialism*, Monthly Review Press, New York.

Thaler, Richard H. (2016), "Behavioral Economics: Past, Present, and Future," *American Economic Review*, vol. 106, no. 7, pp. 1577–1600.

The World Bank (2020), "Physicians (Per 1,000 People)," World Health Organisation's Global Health Workforce Statistics, available at https://data.worldbank.org/indicator/SH.MED. PHYS.ZS, viewed on April 30, 2020.

Tilley, Lisa, and Shilliam, Robbie (2017), "Raced Markets: An Introduction," *New Political Economy*, vol. 23, no. 5, pp. 1–10.

Toynbee, Polly and Walker, David (2017), *Dismembered: How the Conservative Attack on the State Harms Us All*, Faber & Faber, London.

Trosper, Ronald L. (2009), *Resilience, Reciprocity and Ecological Economics: Northwest Coast sustainability*, Routledge, London.

Vernengo, Matías (2011), "The Meaning of Heterodox Economics, and Why It Matters," *Naked Keynesianism*, May 18, available at http://nakedkeynesianism.blogspot.com/2011/05/ meaning-of-heterodox-economics-and-why.html, viewed on April 30, 2020.

Wallace, Robert (2016), *Big Farms Make Big Flu: Dispatches on Influenza, Agribusiness, and the Nature of Science*, Monthly Review Press, New York.

Walras, Léon ([1874] 1954), *Elements of Pure Economics*, translated by William Jaffé, Richard D. Irwin, Inc., Homewood, Illinois.

Wang, Ming, Di, Biao, Zhou, Duan-Hua, Zheng, Bo-Jian, Jing, Huaiqi, Lin, Yong-Ping, Liu, Yu-Fei, Wu, Xin-Wei, Qin, Peng-Zhe, Wang, Yu-Lin, Jian, Li-Yun, Li, Xiang-Zhong, Xu, Jian-Xiong, Lu, En-Jie, Li, Tie-Gang, and Xu, Jianguo (2006), "Food Markets with Live Birds as Source of Avian Influenza," *Emerging Infectious Diseases*, vol. 12, no. 11, pp. 1773–5.

Williams, Callum, and Maruthappu, Mahiben (2013), "'Healthconomic Crises': Public Health and Neoliberal Economic Crises," *American Journal of Public Health*, vol. 103, no. 1, pp. 7–9.

Wootton, Barbara (1938), *Lament for Economics*, George Allen and Unwin Ltd., London.

Worstell, Jim (2020), "Ecological Resilience of Food Systems in Response to the COVID-19 Crisis," *Journal of Agriculture, Food Systems, and Community Development*, vol. 9, no. 3, pp. 1–8.

Index